ALBERT
GALLATIN

ALBERT
GALLATIN

*Jeffersonian
Financier and
Diplomat*

RAYMOND WALTERS, JR.

UNIVERSITY OF PITTSBURGH PRESS

Cloth edition, 1957, by The Macmillan Company, New York

Paperback reprint, 1969, by the University of Pittsburgh Press

Manufactured in the United States of America

Library of Congress catalog card number: 57-8267

Preface to Paperbound Edition

If this were a revision, rather than a reprinting, of a book originally published a dozen years ago, I might be tempted to rephrase an occasional passage to accord with the concepts and interpretations developed by historians and other scholars in the interval. The single significant new work of scholarship on Gallatin's career is Alexander Balinky's *Albert Gallatin: Fiscal Theories and Policies* (Rutgers University Press, 1958). Writing from the point of view of a fiscal theorist of the mid-twentieth century, Balinky faults Gallatin for lack of "boldness of action, decisiveness, and broadness of scope in an era which marked the birth of a nation." It is a provocative thesis, yet one that to my mind does not take into sufficient consideration the political realities with which Gallatin had to cope. In any event, if Hamilton and Jefferson have come to represent the opposite sides of the political and humanitarian coin in the continuing American tradition, Hamilton and Gallatin surely represent the opposite sides of the fiscal and economic coin: Hamilton the constructive adventurer, Gallatin the prudent conservator. Beyond these considerations, this book continues to serve for what it was intended—as a comprehensive view of a long, influential, and many-sided career and of an admirable personality.

The time has now come, it seems to me, for historians to undertake a massive reappraisal of the era covered in Henry Adams's classic *History of the United States of America*, questioning his assumptions and examining all the evidence now available. The microfilm edition of the Albert Gallatin Papers, prepared under the direction of the Department of History at New York University and now being distributed by Rhistoric Publications (302 North 13th Street, Philadelphia, Pennsylvania 19107), should make an important contribution to that end. It is my hope that this new edition of my book will assist scholars in their use of the microfilms and in a modest way help them re-examine the age to which Gallatin contributed so importantly.

I am grateful to Mrs. Helene H. Fineman, co-editor of New York University's Gallatin Papers microfilm edition, for her assistance in bringing this printing of the book to press.

R. W., Jr.

New York, 1969

Preface

If you cared to speculate on the posthumous reputation of great Americans, you could not pick a more fruitful case than that of Albert Gallatin. Consider a few of his attainments during nearly sixty years in public life: his leadership in Congress and in party organization that helped bring about the election of Thomas Jefferson to the Presidency; his application during twelve years as Secretary of the Treasury (a length of service still unsurpassed) of financial principles that complemented those of Alexander Hamilton; his skill, as the "laboring oar" of Jefferson's and Madison's cabinets, in handling administrative and policy problems of all departments of the federal government; his tact and intelligence in representing the United States abroad for more than a decade—service that helped bring the War of 1812 to a satisfactory end and contributed to the maintenance of peaceful relations with France, the Netherlands, Great Britain, and Canada. No less exceptional were his activities during the last two decades of his life, after he had passed the Biblical threescore and ten: his leadership of the financial community during periods of great stress, and his contributions to the ethnology of the American Indian, contributions that have become part of the essential, enduring fabric of the science.

Gallatin's eminence was widely recognized during his own lifetime in America and in Europe. When Lewis and Clark, on the expedition they made in part at his instigation, named one of the three forks of the Missouri River for him and the others for Jefferson and Madison, it was a token of Gallatin's place in the Age of Jefferson. Besides this river, he was immortalized geographically by the naming of a mountain range and of counties in three states. If you have ever had occasion to examine the public prints or the private correspondence of his time, you must have been struck by the respect—and, because he was a political power, in some instances the hatred—that his contemporaries held for him. By them he was ranked only slightly below Washington, Jefferson, and Madison, as a peer of Clay, Calhoun, and Webster.

In our day, students of government have given Gallatin a higher place in public administration than any other man of his century, remarking that political fortune rarely permits a master of administrative theory to apply it to the common weal. Students of fiscal practice have estimated his abilities as on a par with those of Hamilton. Diplomatic historians count his contributions as second only to those of John Quincy Adams in his period. Historians of science rate him as surpassed only by Jefferson among American ethnologists of the early nineteenth century. Outside scholarly circles, however, few Americans today recognize his name, and fewer still comprehend what it stands for. In the present century the man and his work have received just one token of public recognition—a statue, a poor likeness, by James Earle Fraser, that stands outside the Treasury Building in Washington surveying the traffic of Pennsylvania Avenue.

There are, of course, a variety of reasons for Gallatin's present obscurity. To begin with, he made the mistake of being born abroad! That circumstance blocked him from higher office, perhaps even the Presidency. Had he been, like Pulaski or Steuben or Columbus, the native son of a land that was later to furnish sizable immigrations, he quite probably would have achieved belated recognition as a folk hero. But tiny Switzerland has provided few immigrants to the United States.

Gallatin's reputation has also been handicapped by his exemplary character. Never, David Saville Muzzey has observed, did he make a parade of his patriotism, which was sincere and abiding; he made no cheap bid by act or word for popularity, but appealed to man's reason and intellect; never was he deflected from his conscientious course by the attractions of wealth, power, and fame. If his character had been scarred by a tragic flaw, if he had engaged in a few peccadilloes, legends might have clustered about his name and he might have become the subject of dramas and stories, like Alexander Hamilton or Aaron Burr.

The vicissitudes of modern politics have likewise helped to trick him out of the fame that is his due. Democratic party orators might point with pride to so estimable a party founder if for the past quarter of a century they had not preferred to avoid reference to the one administrative practice of Gallatin that school textbooks always mention—his insistence on governmental economy and adherence to a balanced budget.

Throughout his lifetime Gallatin was the friend and inspiration of men of letters, philosophers, scientists, and scholars. But he left no neat corpus of writing that would make his contributions readily available to latter-day historians of ideas. The consequence is that lesser intellectuals have been more celebrated in our time than he.

Certainly a major factor in Gallatin's relative obscurity today is the manner in which his papers were collected and made available to posterity. Gallatin had a strong sense of history and carefully collected some twenty thousand personal and family papers and documents, some of which dated from the thirteenth century. In 1877, a quarter of a century after his death, his descendants engaged a former Harvard teacher who had attracted attention by brilliant articles on historical subjects to edit a selection of his papers and to write a biography based upon them. Within two years Henry Adams had seen through the press three large volumes of *Writings* and a single-volume *Life* that remain to this day the chief source of information about Albert Gallatin. The selection of *Writings* was judicious, the transcription of them fairly accurate. The *Life* was written with all the scholarly care that was to characterize Adams's *History of the United States of America* fifteen years later, but with little of its literary quality. Adams was content for the most part to let Gallatin's own writings carry the narrative, interrupting only to sketch the background in a restrained way. His concern was almost entirely Gallatin's public life. When he undertook to depict or analyze the character of his subject it was to present a man very much in his own Boston Brahmin image. Several years after the publication of Adams's volumes, a connection of the Gallatin family, John Austin Stevens, rewrote the biography in briefer compass for the American Statesmen Series, adding little more than a few marginalia of family lore.

After the publication of the books by Adams and Stevens, the Gallatin Papers, although on deposit at the New-York Historical Society, remained unsorted and closed to the public. About ten years ago members of the family, realizing how unfortunate this was, authorized the Society to catalogue the collection and make it available to serious students. It was my good fortune to be the first person in almost seventy years to use the collection in its entirety.

I undertook this study in the conviction that a full and scholarly biography of Albert Gallatin could contribute significantly to our understanding of the sixty years of our national history in which he played a great role; perhaps even more importantly, it could portray a man unique and invaluable in any age or land, a superbly able and almost completely selfless public servant.

During the ten years devoted to this work I have incurred more obligations among scholars, librarians, archivists, owners of manuscripts, and friends than I can adequately acknowledge. My special thanks are due to the late Albert Eugene Gallatin, to Mr. Albert Gallatin and to Mrs. Henry W. Lanier of New York City for information and aid; to Mlle. Marie-Lucile de Gallatin of Geneva for guiding me through the sources in Switzerland; to M. Jean-Jacques Naville and Mlle. Antoinette de Budé, both of Geneva, for use of manuscripts in the possession of their families; to Dr. Robert W. G. Vail, director of the New-York Historical Society and especially to my good friend Dr. Wayne Andrews, former curator of manuscripts at the Society, for assisting me in the use of the Gallatin Papers; to Professor Joseph Dorfman of Columbia University's economics department for advice as to the economic aspects of the study; to Dr. Harry L. Shapiro, chairman of the department of anthropology, American Museum of Natural History, for suggestions as to Gallatin's interest in ethnology; to Mrs. Kathleen Sproul of Washington, D.C., for assistance in the preparation of the manuscript for the press; and to my father, Dr. Raymond Walters of the University of Cincinnati, for encouragement and help through every step of the work.

R. W., Jr.

New York, 1956

Contents

ALBERT
GALLATIN

1. The Genevan Heritage

He was born at Geneva, the city of Calvin, on January 29, 1761, and nine days later he was carried to the neighborhood church of St. Germain to be baptized Abraham Alphonse Albert Gallatin.[1] In time, he abandoned the first two of his alliterative Christian names and quitted the haunts of his forefathers; but he bore the heritage they represented to the end of his long life.

The family into which he was born was ancient and proud. There is still in existence a document dated 1258 which mentions a Gallatin by name: a receipt signed by the Abbess of Bellacomba for "quindecim libras Viennenses" presented to her convent by "Dominus Fulcherius Gallatini, Miles." [2] Other carefully preserved records establish the fact that the Gallatins lived as minor noblemen in Savoy, some thirty-five miles south of Geneva, close by the Rhone, from the fourteenth century. One member of the family, Jean Gallatini, was seigneur of Granges and many other manors, an equerry of the Duke of Savoy, and the father of another Jean Gallatini, who was appointed an apostolic judge in 1522.

For noblemen who owned lands in the neighborhood there were distinct legal and economic advantages in being a citizen of Geneva. To gain them, the younger Gallatini became a citizen of the city in 1510 and maintained a residence on rue Saint Leger in the Old Town. During the next two centuries five Gallatins served as first syndics—chief magistrates of the little republic. Others became clerics and professors at the local college; others went abroad, to France and the German states, to make distinguished careers as physicians and soldiers.[3]

By the middle of the eighteenth century four branches of the Gallatin family were at Geneva. One was headed by Abraham Gallatin, who had a lovely estate on the hilly west shore of Lake Geneva. This property was not the fruit of his own labors, although he prospered as a dealer in timepieces, but of his marriage in 1732 to Louise-Susanne Vaudenet, daughter of a Geneva banker. Mme. Gallatin-Vaudenet, as she was known, was a woman of high spirit and intelligence; she bore Abraham three children—a son and two daughters.

1

The son Jean, born the year following the marriage, eventually became his father's partner in the family business. In 1755 Jean married Sophie Albertine Rolaz du Rosey from the town of Rolle, a few miles up the lake. Jean and Sophie had two children: Susanne, born in 1756, and Albert—who was to bring the family international renown—born five years later when his parents were living at 7 rue des Granges.

Albert's memory of his own immediate family was faint. Jean Gallatin died in the summer of 1765, when Albert was only four. Mme. Gallatin-Rolaz, whom her son recalled as possessing "talent and great energy," then became a dealer in watches in her own name; but she died in April, 1770, when he was nine. In 1777 his sister died; but the loss was less poignant, as she had been under treatment at Montpellier, the French medical center, for a nervous affliction since infancy, and he remembered seeing her only once after the death of their father.

Arrangements had been made for young Albert long before his mother's death. To allow herself freedom to attend to her business, Mme. Gallatin-Rolaz had arranged with Catherine Pictet, a distant relative of Jean Gallatin and her own most intimate friend, to act as the boy's guardian. Mlle. Pictet had reached middle age without acquiring a husband; she had ample means and more than ample love to lavish upon a foster son. On January 8, 1766, just before his fifth birthday, Albert went to live with her in her apartment on the Grand Rue; and from that day forward he was, in effect, her child.

Mlle. Pictet reared Albert with a frugality characteristically Genevan. He lived under her roof and was privately tutored until he was twelve years old, during which time her expenditures for him, according to the records she conscientiously kept, never exceeded eighty dollars a year. In January, 1773, he entered the College of Geneva, probably boarding with a master, and in August, 1775, in his fifteenth year, he matriculated at the Academy of Geneva. His expenses during these school days averaged slightly more than $200 a year, a sizable portion of which was met by the Bourse Gallatin, a trust that had been set up by one François Gallatin at the close of the seventeenth century for the aid and relief of members of the family.[4] Although Albert was an orphan, the tradition of the Gallatin family hovered over him and provided for him all the days of his youth.

2

As important to Albert Gallatin as the heritage of his family during his formative years was the city of his birth. For in the eighteenth century Geneva was unique among the cities of the world.[5] Superbly situated in the heart of the Alps, it was a walled town of narrow streets and high old buildings clustered on a hill overlooking the spot where the river Rhone flowed from the southern end of Lake Geneva. It was an ancient city, proud of its history and traditions reaching back long before Roman times. Since Geneva expelled its prince-bishop during the Protestant Reformation more than two centuries earlier, the city had been a sovereign republic, although it was surrounded by the covetous monarchies of France, Germany, and Italy. Thanks to its enterprising merchants and the extraordinary skill of its watchmakers, it was one of the most prosperous towns in Europe.

This republican island in the European sea of monarchy was no democracy. Of its population of 25,000, only one-twelfth—the male "citizens"—enjoyed the right of attending the meetings at the cathedral of St. Pierre that elected the magistrates and other chief officials. But even this degree of democracy was illusory: administrative and judicial functions were actually exercised by two councils tightly controlled and passed on like an inheritance by an oligarchy of perhaps a dozen families, aristocrats of French and Italian extraction, who dwelt in the great ancient houses that ringed the cathedral and the city hall. Among these the Gallatins stood high.

Few cities have been so molded by a single man as Geneva was by John Calvin, whose stern and dictatorial influence was omnipresent for twenty-five years in the middle of the sixteenth century. Foremost among his gifts to Geneva was its peculiar moral climate. After Albert Gallatin had left the city and had had a chance to compare its people with those of other towns, he told a friend: "During the sixteenth and the greater part of the seventeenth century, the Genevese were the counterpart of the Puritans of Old and the Pilgrims of New England." The theocracy Calvin established in Geneva controlled the lives and the social relations of the citizens. Thus they adhered to "the same doctrines, the same simplicity in the external forms of worship, the same austerity of morals and severity of manners, the same attention to schools and seminaries of learning, the same virtues and the same defects—exclusiveness and intolerance, banning all those who differed on any part of the established creed"—as the Calvinists of Great Britain and America.

By the time Gallatin was growing up, this Puritanism had relaxed somewhat, but it still lingered. Visitors from France were wont to complain that life in Geneva was "severe" and "dull." Still in effect were laws which prohibited the wearing of jewelry, gold, and silver, limited the cost of funerals, and required all citizens to travel afoot in the streets. Carriages were permitted only in the open country.

One curious law which made an indelible impression upon the youthful Gallatin concerned the discharge of debts: the children of any bankrupt were barred from public office as long as the father's debts were not satisfied. Montesquieu in *The Spirit of the Laws* called this regulation "admirable" because "it has this effect: it creates confidence in the merchants, in the magistrates, and in the city itself. The credit of the individual still has all the weight of the public credit." [6]

The spirit of frugality and plain living likewise tinctured the intellectual life of Geneva. Gallatin later recalled having been surrounded from his earliest days by "a most favorable influence . . . not light, frivolous, or insipid, but generally serious and instructive," from which he "derived more benefit" than from formal education. "A far greater number of well educated and informed men were found in that small spot than in almost every other town of Europe which was not the metropolis of an extensive country." [7]

A cosmopolitan air stirred through the narrow, crooked streets of the old city. From Germany and other lands to the north came numbers of nobles and princes to complete their educations; from England came many young lords and gentlemen; from America such prominent South Carolinians as William Smith and Henry Laurens, such well connected Pennsylvanians as the Penn brothers, the grandson of Benjamin Franklin, and the sons of Robert Morris. Most of these foreign gentlemen studied with the private tutors and attended the riding and jousting academies for which Geneva had become celebrated.

During Albert Gallatin's boyhood, the city played host to one of the most renowned men of letters. In 1754, François Marie Arouet, known to the world as Voltaire, had taken refuge at Geneva. He was fresh from a quarrel with his patron, Frederick of Prussia, and Louis XV had denied him the hospitality of Paris. By shrewdly lending and investing his money, Voltaire was able to afford two estates in the neighborhood, a house and garden at Pregny, close by the estate of Albert's grandparents, and a château at Ferney, three miles outside of Geneva, just across the border in France. Here he was able to live like a great lord, entertaining royalty and persons of wit and learning from all over Europe, maintaining a private theater for the performance of plays of his own writing. Albert's grandmother, Mme. Gallatin-Vaudenet, visited Voltaire frequently and exchanged witty letters on such matters of mutual interest as the grapes and figs they were raising. During a scarcity of wheat in 1771, her husband Abraham Gallatin, in his role of custodian of the Geneva granary, assigned a quota of flour and corn to Voltaire for the sustenance of his colony. And Albert's mother, young and pretty, attracted the old man's roving eye. It is probable that young Albert saw him on occasion; certainly he was ever conscious of him as part of his own heritage.[8]

3

When, at the age of twelve, Albert Gallatin departed Mlle. Pictet's home to become a boarding student at the College of Geneva, he was touched for the first time by another of John Calvin's legacies to the city of Geneva. Calvin's system of public education was so unusual, and its influence on young Albert so transcendent, that it deserves more than passing description.[9]

As Gallatin himself observed years later, "Whatever may have been his defects and erroneous views, Calvin had at all events the learning of his age; and however objectionable some of his religious doctrines, he was a sincere and zealous friend of knowledge and of its wide diffusion amongst the people." In order to diffuse knowledge widely, the reformer had made it possible for the sons of all Genevese citizens to obtain an education from the A B C's through professional studies virtually free of cost. Through his influence, the city in 1559 had taken over an old Latin and logic school and new-modeled its organization so that it consisted of two departments: "the College," training boys from six to fifteen years of age; and "the Academy," offering a general classical education to youths aged fifteen to nineteen and professional training in either the divinity or the law for young men between nineteen and twenty-three.

In 1773 Gallatin left Mlle. Pictet's roof to enter the next to the highest form of the College. That institution, which with the Academy still occupied the ancient quadrangle of grey stone buildings near the heights of the Old Town, had changed astonishingly little since Calvin's time. Educationally, it was in a period of sharp decline. The rigid discipline and religious doctrines imposed by Calvin had been dropped, but the curriculum was substantially unchanged. Only classical languages and literature were taught—"Latin thoroughly," as Gallatin put it, "Greek much neglected." Each form had a single instructor. As there were a hundred students in the average class, they received little individual attention, unless solicitous parents or friends provided it. Looking back in his later years, Gallatin was inclined to believe that this regimen was a good one. It put the students into the habit of studying on their own. Moreover, although the curriculum was narrow and although Latin was useless in itself and was soon forgotten by those who did not pursue their education farther, Gallatin was convinced that the classics, properly taught without use of translations or explanatory annotations, were "most admirably calculated" to develop the intellectual faculties of youths and provided the students with that discipline in using their own minds "without which talents, even of a high order, become useless."

At the College, the majority of the students were, like Gallatin, the offspring of propertied families of the city, for virtually all sons of mechanics—"even the watchmakers so numerous in Geneva and noted for their superior intelligence and knowledge"—dropped out at the age of thirteen or fourteen. In the Academy, the youth was even more gilded.

Of fifty-odd schoolmates in the higher department, only one achieved distinction in later life: Etienne Dumont, after a career as a cleric, became secretary to Jeremy Bentham and translated his works into French. Another student, several classes ahead of Gallatin, was François D'Ivernois, who became a political writer and diplomat of reputation in the service of Switzerland and Great Britain.

Family and social position played their part also in the appointment of professors at the Academy, but at least two of Gallatin's teachers were men of distinction. Horace-Bénédict de Saussure, who taught philosophy, was an eminent physician, mathematician, botanist, and a pioneer in geology and meteorology—above all, a practical scholar. Even as he lectured his eyes were turned toward Mont Blanc, whose summit, a decade later, he was among the first to reach; he was a pioneer in scientific mountaineering. Louis Bertrand, who taught mathematics, had been educated at Berlin and had a wide reputation; it was he who promoted the founding of an observatory at Geneva.

For two years at the Academy, Gallatin and his schoolmates followed a course of study known as "belles-lettres": two hours of lectures each day on the classical languages, by a single instructor, supplemented by occasional lectures on history by an honorary professor. For the following two years, they studied "philosophy"—which meant more of the classical languages (but no literature), plus algebra, geometry, and a little natural science. All lectures except those on mathematics were in Latin, maintaining the students' habit of speaking the classical tongue fluently, but, as Gallatin put it, "without any eloquence." The style of instruction was somewhat like that in an American one-room schoolhouse. During the two years in "belles-lettres," Gallatin and his fellows heard the same series of lectures twice in successive years; and this was true of "philosophy" also. The great disadvantage of the arrangement, Gallatin thought in later years, was that the instructor had to keep his lectures on a relatively elementary level, so that he could be understood by the younger students. There were, however, advantages in the teaching of mathematics. The elements of algebra and geometry, being given twice to each student, "were better inculcated than perhaps anywhere else," Gallatin believed. The higher forms of mathematics, like calculus, were slighted; but this was no great loss, because "calculus is wanted only by a few. . . . In this way, useful and necessary elementary knowledge was better inculcated and more extensively diffused."

At the close of the school year each student received a public oral examination, conducted in Latin. When it was completed the rector of the Academy addressed the student, expressing the school's "approbation, animadversions, and advice, as his case deserved." No grades were given, and most students were promoted to the next higher class, whatever their performance. Gallatin found the examinations severe but fair; and he noted that most American colleges had the same system of promotion.

In May, 1779, at nineteen, Albert Gallatin completed his fourth year at the Academy and faced the problem of choosing and making a career.

4

It was not easy in 1779 for a young man of Geneva to make a career. The very strength of the city-state—its sturdy independence, its proud self-reliance, its small population and modest resources—created the greatest difficulty for young Genevans. Through the centuries thousands of them, including many members of the Gallatin family, had emigrated to neighboring states, where they prospered. Very much to the point are the two most distinguished Genevans of Albert's own century.

Four decades before Albert Gallatin was born, Jean-Jacques Rousseau, son of a watchmaker, left Geneva for France, where he won international acclaim and notoriety as a philosopher, a musical composer, and a revolutionary theorist in education. The "heresy" in his writing led ultimately to condemnation by the French ecclesiastical authorities. For years he had proudly styled himself a "Citizen of Geneva," but when he sought refuge in the republic, the government, frightened by his criticism of political as well as religious authoritarianism, denied him haven. During the years that Gallatin was at school, Rousseau lived in exile at the Swiss village of Motiers-Travers and waged a sometimes witty and often petty feud with Voltaire and his followers that split the society of Geneva. The oligarchy, of whom Gallatin's own family was of course a part, sided with Voltaire, while the disenfranchised lower classes and the franchised but politically impotent middle class found Rousseau a rallying point in their centuries-old struggle for a stronger voice in the government of the city. Gallatin and his schoolmates read his writings and were fascinated by the romantic notions they held out.[10]

Gallatin's own latent ambitions and capacities made him resemble more closely another native of Geneva, three decades his senior, who was making a distinguished record abroad. About the time Albert became a student at the Academy, Louis XVI of France appointed Jacques Necker director-general of finances. The measures Necker introduced were the essence of Genevan commercial morality: financial reforms that included a more equitable system of taxation; a plan for funding the national debt; a comprehensive reckoning of public finances, through a report called "Le Compte Rendu." Necker's insistence that the government of France live within its budget, even if that necessitated retrenchments within many spheres, provoked stout opposition from vested interests, and he was dismissed and recalled several times before the outbreak of the French Revolution ended his attempts to patch up the ailing economy.

The more Albert Gallatin considered his own situation, the more convinced he became that going abroad was the only solution to the problem of his future. What were the alternatives? [11] The Geneva Academy offered training for only two professions: the church, and the bar. But he was too fond of independent speculation, and too humanistic in spirit, ever to consider becoming a clergyman; the law had its attractions, but litigation in Geneva offered poor prospects for a living.

Public life? As a member of the aristocracy, Gallatin could in the end have found an office in the service of the republic. But during his youth the partially enfranchised artisans and small tradesmen and the completely disenfranchised laborers conducted a ceaseless and sometimes bloody struggle for greater participation in the government of Geneva; this the patricians had thus far resisted, with help from the French government. In a vague way Gallatin sympathized with the underdog. Perhaps the aristocrats could be enlightened so that they would give the lower classes a fairer chance. It seemed to him better to avoid the whole subject of politics than to strain his ties with his family and his class.

Trade? His grandfather's mercantile business had begun to ail and held small attraction; and he shied away from an uncle's offer to make a place for him in his business, fearing that this would render him too subject to the favor of relations and doom him to "an honest mediocrity."

The other professions traditionally open to aristocrats would have required him to go abroad, at least temporarily. Medicine? He would have to go to Montpellier or Edinburgh or Paris for training; and, anyway, he had no desire to be a physician. The army? A friend of his grandmother, Mme. Gallatin-Vaudenet, was the Landgrave Frederick II of Hesse-Cassel, whose troops were at the moment in the service of the British king fighting to suppress the insurrection of the colonists in North America. The Landgrave was willing to commission him as a lieutenant-colonel, she told him. Other Gallatins had served foreign princes as soldiers in the past, and she urged him to accept. Albert replied that "he would never serve a tyrant"—a bit of insolence that prompted the old lady to give him a stinging cuff on the ear.

For almost a year Albert avoided a definite decision. He returned to Mlle. Pictet's household in April, 1778, even before he had completed his fourth year at the Academy. Once his studies were completed, he began tutoring her young nephew Isaac Pictet. Among the subjects in which he drilled his young charge was the smattering of English he had picked up at the Academy. It was an easy-going life, one that allowed him to read widely and dream grandly without coming face to face with realities.

Yet as time passed, "daily dependence" upon others—especially his guardian, Mlle. Pictet—made Albert morbidly unhappy. She was strict and Calvinistic, possessive and encompassing. Proud and shy and not a little romantic, he searched for an escape, a chance to pursue adventure; and he discovered that two old schoolmates at the Academy, Henri Serre and Jean Badollet, shared his feelings. Serre in particular was enchanted by Rousseau's picture of a New World peopled by "noble savages." The pulses of all three quickened as they read of the fight that the British colonists in North America were waging for independence from a tyrannical monarch. When they got together early in 1780, shortly after Albert's nineteenth birthday, the talk turned increasingly to the possibility of flight to the hopeful land across the Atlantic. They were not certain what they would do when they reached America. Perhaps they should head for Penn's city of Philadelphia, of which they had heard as the seat of the independence movement. Perhaps they would trade with the natives. Perhaps they would till the soil. The possibilities were many and bright, if vague.

But the affairs of the Badollet family were such that Jean could not leave at once. Very well, Gallatin and Serre decided, they would go ahead and he could follow later. The two romantics counted their assets and discovered that between them they had 166 2/3 louis d'or in cash, practically all belonging to Gallatin. This should see them through.

On the 1st of April, the day tradition has dedicated to fools, Gallatin and Serre quit Geneva.[12] They had breathed no word to a soul, lest their families take steps to stop them. Within a month they traversed France to the Atlantic port of Nantes, where they turned over sixty precious louis to Captain Loring of the American vessel *Katty,* for passage to Boston.

Then for week upon week the *Katty* lay becalmed in port. To break the monotony they expended some of their slender capital on the purchase of tea, in the hope of selling it at a profit upon their arrival in America, improving their fortunes. It was irritating to have to wait for favorable winds, exasperating to have the first mate charge them what they were certain was an excessive sum for freight on the tea. To relieve his indignation, Albert wrote several letters to friends and relatives in Geneva, revealing where he and Serre were and what they planned to do.

Finally, after nearly four weeks, the elusive breeze came. The *Katty* passed the town of Lorient on May 27, 1780, and headed west across the Atlantic. Between them the adventurers had about $400 in cash, some packages of tea, and two headfuls of dreams with which to meet the uncertainties of the New World.

2. The Romantic Years

1780=1790

It was a disagreeable transatlantic crossing. Captain Loring, "a bestial and superstitious rascal," provided his passengers and crew meals of rotten meat and bilge water. The first mate lifted six guineas from Gallatin's and Serre's pockets when they were not looking, stole some of their linen, and held them up for a whopping additional charge for carrying their tea. There were occasional alarms about British privateers in pursuit of the American *Katty*, but otherwise only monotony—no storms, few sicknesses, a placid midsummer passage.

After forty-nine days, the *Katty* touched the American shore at Cape Ann in Massachusetts, on July 15, 1780. The impatient immigrants disembarked at once.[1] The next day, at Gloucester, Albert and Henri hired horses to ride the forty miles to Boston, instinctively seeking refuge with someone who could speak their own language. They found him in the person of a Frenchman named Tahon, who kept an inn "At the Sign of the Confederation." To make matters even more agreeable, they became acquainted under Tahon's roof with a married couple named Delesdernier, who had begun life as farmers near Geneva.[2]

In the next two months they tried to sell their tea and to size up the possibilities of making a place for themselves in Boston. It was all very discouraging. Their tiny English vocabulary made trading difficult; so did the unstable economy of a country deep in the sixth year of an exhausting civil war. The Bostonians were dismally puritanical. They "have neither refinement nor repute nor learning," Gallatin complained; "they are concerned about nothing more than their probity, and none are worse in this respect than the French who are established here. . . . Boston is highly boring. There are no public amusements and many superstitions of the sort that prevent one from singing, playing the violin, playing cards, bowling, etc., on Sunday." In a word, Boston was too much like Geneva.[3]

It was Delesdernier who suggested a way to escape. He had a son with the American military forces at Fort Gates near Machias, 250 miles

11

northeast of Boston in the District of Maine. This tiny seaport on the Bay of Fundy was the northernmost settlement in the United States. Delesdernier was planning to join his son for the winter and proposed that Gallatin and Serre go along with him. The two would-be merchants sensed an opportunity: they might sell certain products of civilization to the white inhabitants of the frontier and barter them with the "savages" of the area in exchange for fish and furs. They laid out two thousand more French livres to stock up with rum, tobacco, and sugar, and embarked with Delesdernier on a coasting vessel on October 1.

At their destination a fortnight later they were sobered but not dismayed by finding that Machias was hardly a seaport or even a town. Some five miles upriver from the sea, it consisted of 150 families in a score of frame cabins scattered over an area of eight or ten square miles. Except for two or three acres around each cabin on which the pioneers were trying to raise potatoes and other staples, this was still virgin forest. Although Machias was fifteen years old, the constant threat of invasion from the north by British forces made its chief concern not prosperity but bare survival.

Delesdernier's son—"a very pleasant bachelor," who lived not far from the fort, headquarters of Colonel John Allan, superintendent of Indian Affairs for the Eastern Department, stretching from Massachusetts to the Canadian border—welcomed Gallatin and Serre as lodgers. Fort Gates boasted seven cannon and a garrison of fifteen or twenty men.

Winter having closed in on the Maine frontier, opportunities for trade were meager. Neither Indians nor white men had furs or fish to barter, and the partners would have made no sales at all if the garrison had not taken some four hundred dollars' worth of their merchandise. This transaction proved to be unprofitable because they were compensated with a warrant issued by the Treasury of the Confederation which Gallatin felt lucky to dispose of for one hundred dollars in currency.[4]

Waiting out the long winter, the two Genevans pondered what they should do when spring came. They might take up farming. Land in the neighborhood was cheap because it was fallow and hard to work. Gallatin, who knew agriculture only by hearsay, took great satisfaction in their acquisition of a cow: surely that meant they had made a start as farmers.

As time passed, their schemes grew more grandiose. Soon they were thinking of promoting a settlement of Genevans on this rugged frontier. Gallatin dispatched a letter to Badollet directing him to "find out under what terms peasants would be willing to come here. We might make arrangements to transport them here almost free of charge and support them for the first year, after which they would pay us half the income of the land if it raised grain, one-quarter if it were pasture land, the balance continuing over ten, fifteen, or twenty years—the longer the better—at the end of which time the half or the quarter of the land would belong to them in perpetuity."

Both Gallatin and Serre grew increasingly anxious that Badollet join them, and their letters to him describing the land and its people were designed to warm his Rousseauesque soul. "We are in a country that I believe would please you," Serre assured him; "we live in the middle of a forest on the bank of a river; we can hunt, fish, swim, skate, when we please. . . . You know how we amused ourselves in Geneva by going boating. Well, I amuse myself even better here by going boating in the canoes of the savages. . . . There is no stream that does not have enough water to float these fine conveyances."

Gallatin chimed in, tantalizing Badollet with more romantic visions. "We have already seen several savages, all of them nearly as black as Negroes, dressed almost in the European fashion, except the women who —But I ought to leave a little to your curiosity without satisfying it, so that you will have as many motives as possible for coming to join us very soon." Then he added practically: "But do not leave without letting us know, because if you have any money, we will tell you what merchandise you ought to bring." [5]

In November, Gallatin broke the monotony of hibernation by joining Colonel Allan on an expedition to Passamaquoddy Bay, on the Canadian border. "It was then," he later recalled, "that I was for a few days left accidentally in command of some militia, volunteers, and Indians, and of a small temporary work defended by one cannon and soon after abandoned." Later in the winter the experience was repeated. Years after, it was said that he had served in the Revolutionary War. Gallatin put the record straight, tersely: "As I never met the enemy, I have not the slightest claim to military service." [6]

Through the spring and summer of 1781 Gallatin and Serre stayed on at Machias, desperately hoping that their fortunes might take a turn for the better. In October, when they had been on the frontier for a year, their prospects were still dubious and their resources were far more meager. News reached them that the British forces at Yorktown had surrendered and the war was over. The thought of another tedious Maine winter depressed Gallatin. It would be better, he told Serre, to go back to Boston to await the spring, when they could strike out for more promising country.

2

Boston held unexpected interests and detained them longer than they planned. During the winter both Gallatin and Serre found some proper Bostonians willing to employ them casually as tutors in French, and in the spring Mlle. Pictet caught up with them. She had been using every resource at her command—even an appeal to Benjamin Franklin, American minister to France—to discover Gallatin's whereabouts and appeal to him to come home, or at least to accept family assistance. Hearing that he had reached Boston, she asked friends in Geneva who had friends in Boston to write to him.[7]

The upshot was that Dr. Samuel Cooper, pastor of the Brattle Street Church and an active member of the Corporation of Harvard College, sought Albert out. Two years earlier the Corporation had decided to broaden the College's narrow curriculum by arranging with a tutor to give instruction in French to students who desired it, and whose parents were willing to pay for it. The place as tutor was now open.

The President and Fellows of Harvard College voted, on July 2, 1782, to grant Gallatin free use of the College library, a room in one of the College buildings, and meals at the commons at the rate paid by the tutors if he desired it.[8]

Approximately seventy students enrolled for Gallatin's lessons, including scions of some of the oldest and proudest families in New England—an Amory, a Pyncheon, and an Otis. His income for the quarter was between $250 and $300.[9]

One of Gallatin's students at Harvard recalled later that he lived at that time with "great simplicity and economy." The College authorities were most satisfied with the record he made. When, in the summer of 1783, Gallatin looked for fresh fields to conquer, President Joseph Willard, Edward Wigglesworth, the professor of divinity, and Dr. Cooper furnished him with a certificate testifying that he had "acquitted himself . . . with great reputation. He appears to be well acquainted with letters, and has maintained an unblemished character in the University and in this part of the country." [10] Two of the students of the gangling, homely, slovenly dressed Swiss with the thick French accent later remembered him as "an intelligent and able teacher" with a "pleasing manner." [11]

During two pleasant winters in Massachusetts, Gallatin and Serre clung to the dream of finding an idyllic existence in the American wilderness. They had had no word from Badollet, but they continued to besiege their old schoolmate with appeals to join them. "Our goal now," Serre ex-

plained, "is as soon as possible to procure some land and become farmers.
. . . I could not say with what pleasure I imagine seeing the three of us in
our house in the country, each busy with our different country chores.
. . . Having in this way an assured fortune for living pleasantly and inde-
pendently, we shall then be able, when the desire overtakes us, to make
occasional excursions . . . [to] some new part of the world." [12]

A new chance to reach for this dream came in the spring of 1783,
while Gallatin was teaching at Harvard. It came in the person of Jean
Savary de Valcoulon, a young Frenchman as dreamy and impractical as
Serre. In his native Lyons, Savary had already failed in business and had
achieved a reputation as an ardent supporter of the principles of the
American Revolution. He had found a way to serve both his economic
and his idealistic needs by becoming an agent of René Rapicault, a
Frenchman who had advanced money and supplies to the State of Virginia during the Revolutionary War. Unfortunately for his mission,
Savary was unable to speak or write English, and he clung like ivy to
the Harvard tutor who was becoming fairly fluent in it. [13]

When Savary proposed that he accompany him southward on a business
trip as interpreter, Gallatin eagerly accepted. They quit Boston on July
11, 1783, leaving behind Serre, who had tutoring obligations to complete. [14] They traveled slowly from Boston to Providence to Newport to
New York to Trenton to Philadelphia. Gallatin recorded his impressions
in a notebook: the beauty of the countryside, the cockroaches in the
taverns, the physical endowments of young women eyed in passing. He
liked Manhattan and even more Philadelphia for their attractive appearance and "air of opulence."

Serre, his teaching engagements finished, caught up with them late in
August at Philadelphia, and the two Genevans came to what they supposed would be a temporary parting of their ways. Reckoning up their
accounts, they discovered that, of the nearly $1,600 spent during the three
years since they had left Geneva, all but $300 had come out of Gallatin's
pocket: Serre's father had refused to forward any money or to honor his
drafts. Serre gave Gallatin a note for $500 and then sailed for Jamaica in
pursuit of a business opportunity.

During the journey southward, and during the more than a month
they lingered at Philadelphia, Gallatin confided to Savary the scheme he
and Serre had conceived of a life as farmers and land promoters. Philadelphia was a most congenial place for such dreamers: the air of the neat
little capital of the Confederation crackled with talk of opportunities for
speculation in western land. Such distinguished citizens as the financier of
the Revolution, Robert Morris, and the Virginia planter and war hero,

General George Washington, had already made vast purchases. Little wonder that a romantic like Savary caught the contagion. He had grown fond of Gallatin, and he promised that he would do everything he could to help him escape his cul-de-sac career as a tutor.

Gallatin kept his ears open and asked many questions. Soon he was convinced that the best place for an enterprise such as he had in mind was along the Ohio River and its tributaries. The land north of the Ohio, belonging to Congress, would be quite suitable, but it had not yet been officially opened to settlement. Fortunately the State of Virginia had already placed on the market its holdings south of the river; and even more fortunately it was against Virginia that Rapicault, whom Savary represented, held claims.

At this moment of decision, Gallatin at long last received word from his former schoolmate, who was now a theological student. Writing in March, Badollet described the misfortunes that had lately befallen their native city. Relations between the aristocrats and the disenfranchised had grown bitter; blood had been shed, and the neighboring governments of Switzerland, France, and Savoy had intervened with armed forces. Gallatin wrote back that this news convinced him that he must remain permanently in "the freest country in the universe." He repeated his idea of establishing a community somewhere in the American backwoods where he, Serre, Badollet, and perhaps other Genevans might live in bucolic security. This was all within the realm of possibility, he assured Badollet, if his present land speculation turned out well, and if he received his inheritance from his family—due in three years, on his twenty-fifth birthday.[15]

A few days after this letter, Gallatin and Savary made a quick trip to Baltimore, where they bought from several sources warrants for 120,000 acres of land in the Ohio River valley: scattered blocks along the Ohio itself, along the Great Kanawha and its tributaries, and near the confluence of the Ohio and Mississippi rivers. One-quarter of this was to belong to Gallatin, with Savary obligingly advancing the money for the entire purchase.

The two partners tarried in Philadelphia until the middle of November, and then moved on to Richmond. They would spend the winter there, pressing Rapicault's claim against Virginia and preparing for an expedition to inspect their own holdings in the spring.[16]

3

Richmond was much to Gallatin's liking. In old age, he recalled that he had been received there "with that proverbial Virginia hospitality to which I know no parallel anywhere within the circle of my travels. . . . Every one with whom I became acquainted appeared to take an interest in the young stranger."

There had been some initial difficulties, dimmed in recollection by the passage of years. His thick accent, when he approached legislators and state officials in behalf of the claims of Rapicault and of himself and Savary, made it hard for them to understand him. But Patrick Henry, on the eve of reelection as governor, was impressed. "A most astonishing man!" he told friends. "Most sensible and well informed!" He predicted that Gallatin would eventually make his mark as a statesman and advised him to settle in the West.

Soon other Virginians were listening to Gallatin, and encouraging him. One was John Marshall, who at twenty-eight had only recently opened a law office in Richmond but was already making a place for himself at the bar. He offered to take Gallatin in as a student without fee, assuring him that he would do well in the profession.[17]

Savary was so impressed by his partner's aptitude in dealing with the state land officers about questions of surveys and the registration of warrants that he increased Gallatin's share in their joint western land claims to one-half with the understanding that hereafter he would assume full responsibility for handling details. But despite Gallatin's most valiant efforts in behalf of Rapicault, he was unable to get Virginia to recognize the claims.[18]

In February, 1784, Gallatin journeyed to Philadelphia to complete preparations for an expedition to the Ohio and the Great Kanawha. Two months later he and Savary crossed the Allegheny Mountains for the first time, going to Pittsburgh to organize a party of experienced scouts and woodsmen. They spent the summer trying to locate lands for which they held warrants, especially in Monongalia County, Virginia. But Monongalia, they reluctantly concluded after a careful inspection, was insufficiently fertile, too mountainous, and too much menaced by hostile Indians to be a promising area for settlement and development.

Just north of Monongalia, in Fayette County, Pennsylvania, was land that appeared to have most of the qualities the Virginia country lacked. Best of all, Georges Creek, flowing into the Monongahela River, looked to them as if it could link the Ohio and Potomac rivers and make it possible to transport the produce of the Ohio valley to the Richmond market, and vice versa. At Richmond, Gallatin had heard much talk of plans to canalize the Potomac.

The romantic streak in Gallatin's nature was growing thinner, and by September he was taking practical steps to capitalize on this opportunity. He lingered in the vicinity of Georges Creek long enough to conclude arrangements with Thomas Clare, a genial Irish-born bachelor, to establish a store on his three-hundred-acre farm. Here he and Savary hoped to be able to sell supplies to the increasing number of pioneers passing through on their way west.[19]

At this time an incident occurred which Gallatin remembered vividly to the end of his days.[20] During September, George Washington traveled through western Virginia and Pennsylvania to locate lands to which he held title, and passed the night of the 24th near Georges Creek. Gallatin hearing—so he told friends in old age—that the General planned to stop at the office of the local land agent for advice from settlers and hunters as to the best route for a road that would cross the Alleghenies, joined the crowd of local worthies in the agent's tiny one-room cabin and found a place close to the pine table at which the General sat before spread-out maps and papers, carefully questioning the men one after another and taking notes. After much testimony had been offered, Gallatin grew impatient at the apparent indecision of the General and blurted out what had no doubt become clear to him through his own investigations: "Oh, it is plain enough, [he named a spot already mentioned by one of the settlers] is the most practicable."

The lese majesty of the young stranger astonished everyone present including the General, who put down his pen and stared in cold silence at the offender—the most withering look, Gallatin recalled years later, that he had received in all his life. Then Washington resumed his interrogation. After a few minutes he again put down his pen and looked at Gallatin, saying, "You are right, sir."

When the settlers and hunters had departed, Washington inquired about the young man. Gallatin remained at the cabin for the night, sleeping on the floor beside the agent and his nephew, while the Revolutionary War hero occupied the single bed. Subsequently, according to family legend, General Washington proposed that he act as his agent. But Gallatin was too occupied with his own dreams for developments in the western country to accept.

He and Savary spun and refined their dreams during the winter of 1784–1785, which they spent at Richmond and Philadelphia. Their plans now centered on the 120,000 acres of western Virginia land to which they held warrants. The hilly countryside reminded Gallatin of his native land; he was convinced that if he could people it with frugal, industrious farmers who would subject it to intensive European agricultural methods, with cattle grazing on the mountain slopes and grain ripening in the narrow valleys, it would become a land of plenty. To attract the type of settler he sought, he and Savary would give away 24,000 acres on certain conditions; in the long run they would be more than compensated by the increased value of the vast tracts they would continue to hold. The Virginia officials encouraged the partners, for their project promised to increase the population and wealth of the state.

There were skeptics, however, who pointed out to the young men that they lacked sufficient capital to realize so grandiose a scheme. Savary was growing short of funds, and Gallatin, too proud to appeal to his family for help, had occasional misgivings, confessing to himself that his partner's heart was "worth more than his mind"; but he was still sanguine enough to urge Badollet in a letter of March 30, 1785, to join them "at the first opportunity." [21]

On the next day Gallatin embarked on a second and even more ambitious summer of activity in the West. Starting out alone, he rode west along the James River to Lewisburg, seat of Greenbrier County, where he exhibited to the county surveyor a letter from Patrick Henry attesting to "his personal character, as well as his present designs, [which] entitle him to the most cordial regard," and registered the warrants he owned to land in the Kanawha River valley. Next he headed north to Clare's farm on Georges Creek, where he was presently joined by Savary.[22]

On May 23 appeared fifteen guides, hunters, and surveyors whom the partners had engaged the previous winter. Two days later the men hoisted over the boat a white flag with blue stars and set off down the Monongahela. Last-minute supplies were purchased during a stopover at Pittsburgh. Each night they tied up to the river bank, pitched tents, and made a comfortable camp. Frequently the hunters went ashore for fresh meat, in which the countryside abounded. Some distance beyond Wheeling, Gallatin disembarked long enough to make his first survey of his claims.

It was June 8 when the party reached the spot close to the mouth of Sandy Creek, which the partners had settled on in advance as a good site for a permanent settlement. As a gesture toward their relationship, Savary named it Friends' Landing.[23] * Soon they were busy with the tasks

---

* "The question of [its] exact location has no particular importance because the settlement failed to become permanent," wrote Henry M. Dater, in 1939. "Today the name of Friends' Landing is unknown along the Ohio; in fact the

necessary to make a settlement: felling trees, dragging the logs to the site with the aid of horses, constructing a cabin, dismantling the boat to make rough furniture, even a "bed" large enough to accommodate twenty-two persons.

By July, Gallatin was able to turn his attention to locating other land for which he held warrants. Leaving Savary in command of the main party, he started downstream with several of the men in canoes. At a tiny settlement called Point Pleasant, he remained two days in order to hire additional guides. Here, for some reason which he failed to note in his diary, he was challenged to a duel. He survived the crisis unscathed, and by July 4 they were on their way again, paddling up the Great Elk, turning eastward to follow the Elk.

For four arduous weeks Gallatin traced streams, tramped along the headwaters of the Pocotalico and Little Kanawha rivers, identifying landmarks, laying out lines, preparing maps. He realized that, in order to sell his lands at a profit, he must establish the titles beyond cavil. Too often the hopes of land promoters had been dashed by interminable lawsuits. Self-taught though he was in land surveying, Gallatin performed his task tirelessly and accurately, so that the titles stood up in subsequent litigations. "Where others buried their reputations," he observed proudly in his old age, "I established mine."

But he was not wholly absorbed by the details of his work. In his little diary he mentioned several times his delight at hills rolling away in the distance, at finally coming upon the mouths of streams. He reveled in the physical exertion his tasks required; only once did he mention feeling tired.

He had all but completed his work and was planning to start southwestward to Lewisburg by way of the Kanawha to register his titles when word came that Savary, frightened by reports of Indian depredations in the Ohio valley, had fled Friends' Landing for shelter at Point Pleasant. Gallatin quickly changed his plans, returning to Point Pleasant on August 18. His partner's fright was no idle fancy. The little garrison was crowded with refugees.

The partners immediately suspended operations for the season. They recalled their men from the woods and, on September 3, headed back toward Georges Creek. It was a frightful journey. Fearing that hostile Indians might be lurking along the rivers, the party pushed overland through trackless forests, guided only by compass and small streams.

---

names Gallatin and Savary have left no trace in the memory of the river folk whom the writer has questioned."

Their food ran short, and they were reduced to bread and water. When they at last reached Clare's farm, they had good reason to be thankful. Other surveying parties were returning to Pittsburgh with crippled horses and men sick and dying.

But this disastrous end to the expedition did not snuff out the hopes of the partners. In November, Gallatin and Savary leased from Clare a house and five acres on Georges Creek, not far from the Monongahela. They transferred their store to this property and established several of the men there in anticipation of more activity the following summer.

As further earnest of his determination to associate himself permanently with the western country, Gallatin journeyed up the Monongahela to Morgantown, the seat of Monongalia County, Virginia, and took "the oath of allegiance and fidelity to the Commonwealth of Virginia." [24] Under the Articles of Confederation then in force American citizenship could be obtained only through the states, each of which had its own laws. The ambitious project upon which he had embarked was to be carried on largely in Virginia, and it was to his advantage to acquire Virginia citizenship.

Gallatin and Savary returned to Richmond late in November. But by the following February, Gallatin was back at Georges Creek to increase his establishment by purchasing a four-hundred-acre farm about a mile south of the creek, on the Monongahela. This he made his residence.[25] It was remote and picturesquely mountainous, overlooking the river on the west, Laurel Ridge on the east. In a way it was the noble, savage countryside so dear to the heart of Rousseau; in a way, too, its hills and vistas of river called to mind the mountains and lake of Geneva. Gallatin called the property "Friendship Hill"—probably in token of his affection for Serre, Savary, and Badollet, as the abortive settlement on the Ohio had been named "Friends' Landing."

In the months that followed, Gallatin learned that he could not realize fully his dream of making the farm on the Monongahela a center of activity for his old friends. A letter from Jamaica brought the news that Serre, who had been eking out a living at Kingston as an organist, had died.[26] Savary concluded that there were better prospects in Richmond and determined to spend virtually all his time there.[27] To Gallatin's intense pleasure, Badollet finally responded to imploring letters and came to America, settling on a farm near Friendship Hill.

During the next three years, Gallatin traveled regularly between the Monongahela and the East. The Indian terror that had sent him and Savary dashing back to Georges Creek in 1785 discouraged settlement projects and even surveying in the Ohio valley for a decade, and so he spent the summers at Friendship Hill, house-building, store-keeping, and farming on a small scale. During much of these pleasant months Gallatin indulged what his Calvinist conscience defined as his "natural indolence"—reading and reflecting, enjoying the all-male society of the frontier settlement. There were never fewer than six persons at the farm—employees and associates—and often there were many more.

Winter was a bustling time devoted to the details of land purchases and sales at Richmond, Philadelphia, and New York. Between Christmas of 1787 and early March, 1788, Gallatin's travels took him as far as Maine.[28] He saw the Connecticut River valley for the first time: "I have never seen in America the equal of the establishments there," he noted in his diary. He visited William Bentley, an old Harvard colleague who was now a clergyman at Salem. Bentley was astonished to see him, having read a newspaper report that he had been scalped during the Indian depredations in 1785.[29] At Ipswich he dined with two of his Harvard students, Amory and Stacey; and he went up the Androscoggin River on a sleigh: "It snowed all day; travelled on the ice without seeing shore; guided my course by the direction of the snow."

Bentley was not the only friend who supposed that Gallatin had been a victim of Indian savagery. The report, originally printed in the *Fredericksburg Gazette* in July, 1785, ultimately reached his relatives at Geneva. They caused the Genevan minister at Paris to make inquiries of Thomas Jefferson, American minister to France, who passed them on to John Jay, secretary of foreign affairs in the Confederation government. In May, 1786, Jay published a notice in the Philadelphia newspapers requesting news of Gallatin's whereabouts.[30] By this time, however, the family had word directly from Albert assuring them of his survival.

Gallatin continued to receive occasional letters from relatives, especially his grandfather and Mlle. Pictet. Whining petulance continued to darken every line from his foster mother. "I can scarcely excuse your long silence," she wrote in July, 1785. "I would not even know how to accept as valid any reasons that you might give for it. It appears likely that vanity keeps you from writing when you have nothing favorable to say about your situation." In October, 1787, she wrote of having seen a M. Charton with whom Albert had stayed on one sojourn in Philadelphia. "He tells me that you continue in your old indolent ways, that you care little for the world, and that while you lived at his house in Philadelphia, he could not induce you to dress up or to see the world. He said that you loved only study and reading. Those tastes do not seem to accord with your grand projects. For them a large fortune is quite useless; you would have been able to follow them without leaving your native land."

True enough, Gallatin at times shunned society and buried himself in books. At other times, as at Richmond, he was gregarious. His expeditions to the Virginia and Maine frontiers were models of activity. But the same stubborn pride that had caused him to flee from a stifling dependence on Mlle. Pictet made him reluctant now to confide to her his varying fortunes, and much more so to seek any assistance from her. Yet pride did not deter him from reminding his family of the patrimony that became legally his on his twenty-fifth birthday, in January, 1786. About five thousand dollars, as much of the estate as was in a liquid condition, was forwarded to him in letters and drafts on the Philadelphia firm of Robert Morris. He used these remittances in part to purchase Friendship Hill.[31]

4

The society of lawyers, politicians, and land speculators was not the only attraction Richmond held for Gallatin. During annual sojourns he made it a practice to put up at a boarding house on Seventh Street that was congenial because of its faintly French tradition.[32] The owner, Mrs. Jane Battersby Allegre, was the widow of William Allegre, descendant of French Protestant refugees who had settled in Virginia a century before. Gallatin's eye was attracted by their younger daughter Sophia, or Sophie; but the shy young man spoke no word of his feeling to Sophie. Once he had settled on Georges Creek, however, he began to feel sharply the need of a wife, and he wrote a letter in which he broadly hinted at his affection. Sophie did not reply and, indeed, asked Savary, who was in Richmond, to discourage his friend's interest.

Gallatin was not easily discouraged. Bidding Badollet and the others at Georges Creek a tight-lipped farewell in the middle of March, 1789, he set out to press his case. At Richmond on April 1 he learned that Sophie was visiting her married sister thirty miles away on a farm at New Kent. He hastened after her. Sophie, he later reported to Badollet, "did not play the coquette with me at all, but from the second day gave me her full consent, even acknowledging that she would have given it to me [earlier] if I had asked it." She "had always known that I loved her, but had been surprised not to hear from me for more than a year. It was this which provoked her reply to Savary. . . . Not wishing to disclose her feelings to Savary, and not having answered my letter, she was afraid that I had changed my feeling toward her and she did not wish to make a useless confidence."

He had been at New Kent fifteen days when trouble appeared from a not unexpected quarter. On learning that Gallatin was at New Kent,

Mrs. Allegre ordered Sophie to return immediately to Richmond. Gallatin followed and lost no time in seeking the mother's permission for their marriage. "She was furious," he wrote to Badollet, "refused me in the most brutal manner, and almost forbade me admission to the house." He learned that a Frenchman named Perrin, who had been a member of his establishment at Friendship Hill, had told her every conceivable bad thing about his Monongahela project and its prospects.

Mrs. Allegre bluntly told Gallatin that she did not want her daughter dragged to the Pennsylvania frontier by a man "without accomplishments or fortune," who sputtered English like a Frenchman, and who had been a schoolmaster at Cambridge. "I laughed at most of these objections," he wrote on May 4; "I tried to answer the others, but I could not make her listen to reason. She has just sent Sophie to one of her friends in the country. She is a devil of a woman whom her daughter fears horribly . . . I believe, however, that I will succeed, and I shall work to that end despite the difficulties in seeing and speaking with her."

Love found a way for him to see and speak to Sophie. On May 14 the couple signed a marriage bond, and Gallatin recorded in a little account book the following expenditures: "Queue ribbon, 1/6. White vest, 9–. Tailor, £2.16. Satin shoes, gloves, ring, £1.11.6. License, minister, £4.4. Black wig, £0.2.0." Within the next two days, at a place not recorded, Albert Gallatin and Sophia Allegre became man and wife.[33]

On May 16, on honeymoon at her sister's home, Sophie sent a letter begging her mother's forgiveness. "My dear Mama," she wrote, "shall I venture to write you a few lines in apology of my late conduct? and dare I flatter myself that you will attend them? If so, and you can feel a motherly tenderness for your child who never before willingly offended you, forgive, dear mother, and generously accept again your poor Sophia, who feels for the uneasiness she is sure she has occasioned you. She deceived you, but it was for her own happiness. Could you then form a wish to destroy the future peace of your child and prevent her from being united to the man of her choice? He is perhaps not a very handsome man, but he is possessed of more essential qualities, which I shall not pretend to enumerate; as coming from me, they might be supposed partial. If, mama, your heart is inclinable to forgive, or if it is not, let me beg you to write me, as my only anxiety is to know whether I have lost your affection or not. Forgive me, dear mama, as it is all that is wanting to complete the happiness of her who wishes for your happiness and desires to be considered again your dutiful daughter, Sophia." [34]

Whether Sophie's letter elicited the forgiveness she sought is not clear. Certainly it marked the start of a romantic, even idyllic marriage. But the wedding also marked the formal termination of Albert's most important business relationship. Ever since he had known Savary de Valcoulon he had been of two minds about the charming, impulsive, often exasperating young man from Lyons who had befriended him and made him his partner in land projects. "When I berate his extravagant conduct," he told a friend, "I blame only his head; his heart is always excellent but too easy and makes him indulge too often in stupidities." In April he had learned that Savary's conduct of late had soured not only Perrin and Mrs. Allegre but "everyone in Richmond" against him. The inheritance he had received on attaining his majority enabled him to assert his independence of Savary. About the time of the wedding the two partners formally and amicably agreed to go their separate ways.[35]

Gallatin took his bride west to Friendship Hill in late May or early June. The following October she fell ill and died. The bride of five months was buried in an unmarked grave at the top of Friendship Hill, overlooking the Monongahela.

Sophie's death was a sharp blow, and Albert suffered intensely. His thoughts were morose. Should he change his way of life? He was still haunted by guilt over the manner in which he had deserted "that respectable person," Mlle. Pictet, for whom he felt deep obligation if not affection. He cherished the consolation and understanding he could receive only from Badollet, the one friend who had known "my lovely Sophie." If it were only possible for him and Badollet to find some place where they might have independent livelihoods while sharing each other's company! If only that place could be near Mlle. Pictet—although of course Mlle. Pictet had no high regard for the impractical Badollet!

Groping for a solution, Gallatin made inquiries. It would be hard, he found, to realize cash from his Virginia lands because of the Indian menace. It would be difficult to obtain further assistance from the family estate, for the revolution that had lately broken out in France had unsettled the European market.[36]

Early in April, 1790, six months after Sophie's death, he announced it to Mlle. Pictet and suggested that he might return to Geneva.[37] She answered on a surprising new note, mentioning "the precarious state of France" and the uncertainty the Genevans felt about their own government, and added: "As for the advice you ask about your coming home and the resources you might find, I am quite embarrassed to reply." [38]

Only sickness of heart over Sophie had caused Albert to consider even for a second returning to Geneva. The sickness soon passed, for a new interest claimed his attention.

3. A Political Apprenticeship

1788-1790

On August 18, 1788, in the year before his marriage, Albert Gallatin mounted his horse and rode the fifteen miles from Friendship Hill to Uniontown, the seat of Fayette County, Pennsylvania, to attend his first political meeting.

This was no casual act. In the eight years he had been in America he had dropped his youthful indifference to politics and government; the more he saw of the United States, the worse the political system of his native Geneva seemed to him. As he wrote to Badollet, "If you let yourself be swayed by a little enthusiasm, one thousand-to-one it will be in favor of the right side." Now he was convinced that the government of Geneva, with the power tightly held by the aristocrats, was based on "bad principles" suitable only for "tyrants and slaves"; and he was enthusiastic about the state governments of America with their restrictions on the power of the executive and the judiciary, their provision for jury trial, their frequent election of legislators.[1]

The meeting at Uniontown, drawing men from all parts of Fayette, was in response to a circular letter issued by a group of politicos who the previous winter had fought, bitterly but futilely, ratification by Pennsylvania of the federal Constitution designed to replace the Articles of Confederation. Even after the Constitution had been ratified in June by the ninth state, New Hampshire, and so was considered to be in effect, these die-hards were not reconciled. Now they spoke about amending it to render it less "objectionable," perhaps through a bill of rights—an idea broached by Governor George Clinton of New York in a letter to the other governors. The circular letter in answer to which Gallatin and other Fayette County men were gathering called for the election of delegates to a state-wide meeting, at Harrisburg, to propose amendments and plan for their adoption. It also spoke vaguely of the desirability of drawing up a ticket of delegates from Pennsylvania for election to the new federal Congress.

26

The idea of the meeting was most popular among Gallatin's neighbors. The majority of them—and indeed most Pennsylvanians west of the Alleghenies, outside Pittsburgh—had vigorously opposed the federal Constitution as undemocratic in its centralizing features. Equally objectionable in their eyes was the fact that the Pennsylvania delegation to the convention that had drawn up the Contitution had been elected by less than one-fifth of the state's voters without a single delegate to represent them.[2]

At Uniontown, Gallatin rubbed elbows with the worthies of Fayette County, men who often had served it in public office. Foremost among them was John Smilie, a vigorous, Irish-born farmer who had held high state posts since the Revolution and had been one of the most stubborn fighters against the Constitution in the Pennsylvania ratifying convention. It was not surprising that the meeting named him to represent Fayette at Harrisburg. But it was cause for wonder that twenty-seven-year-old "Mr. Albert Galattin," a political neophyte and a relative newcomer, was chosen as the second delegate.[3]

Long-settled, conservative towns of the eastern seaboard probably would not have elected a citizen of less than three summers' residence; but the pioneering farmers of western Pennsylvania did not care much who a man's parents were, where he came from, or how recently. Almost all had crossed the Alleghenies within the decade; and to all of them the future they were to make for themselves was more important than anything they had inherited. A few were French Protestants, a number were Germans, a considerable number were English Quakers; but most numerous of all were the Scotch-Irish, with a Calvinistic background similar to Gallatin's. It did not matter to these neighbors that Gallatin spoke English with a pronounced French accent. It was enough that the awkward, shy, but friendly young man had a keen intelligence and a rich knowledge of the world. Such qualities were exceedingly rare and were highly respected on the Pennsylvania frontier.

Almost by instinct Gallatin sympathized with the political principles and practical objectives his neighbors cherished. The one-time disciple of Rousseau had great faith in the rights and capacities of the common citizen—the mechanic, the small tradesman, and, especially, the farmer; he shared the concern of all frontiersmen about protection of their homes against Indian raids, the unfavorable balance of trade with the merchants of the East, the need for better transportation to and within the West. All these were matters about which the sponsors of the new federal Constitution, and especially those in Pennsylvania, seemed to be less than enthusiastic. Gallatin accepted the appointment to the Harris-

burg meeting eagerly and, late in August, set out in the company of
doughty John Smilie.

2

After nearly a week of hard riding over the mountains and through lush
farm land, Gallatin and Smilie crossed the broad, shallow Susquehanna River by John Harris's ferry to the hamlet named after him. Three
years before, this had been wilderness, with only a tavern at one end of
the ferry crossing; even in 1788, Harrisburg still had scarcely five hundred inhabitants, with a jail and thirteen taverns but neither courthouse
nor post office. It had doubtless been chosen for the meeting because it
was close to the center of the settled part of the state, in the heart of a
district that had zealously opposed the federal Constitution.

The thirty-three delegates who converged on the settlement on September 3 probably assembled in the large, square dining room of the
"Compass," John Harris's tavern, a stone's throw from the river bank.[4]

Looking about him, Gallatin found himself surrounded by unfamiliar
faces. Smilie was perhaps the only man there he could call a friend. A
good number were veterans of the Pennsylvania political wars, old officeholders and legislators. But this group was in no sense representative
of political sentiment throughout the state. Several counties had no representation; others had large delegations, out of proportion to their population. Many representatives, like Gallatin and Smilie, had been chosen by
large and publicly announced meetings; those from Philadelphia, where
pro-Constitution sentiment was strong, had been selected at meetings so
restricted and secret that not a syllable about them had as yet crept into
the newspapers.[5] The meeting was, in essence, the desperate stand of a
political party that, having lost its fight against a strong, centralizing
federal government, feared that it was going to lose its influence in state
affairs as well.

No official account of the four-day meeting was ever published; but the
papers which Gallatin kept suggest that, for a political beginner, he
played an uncommonly large role.[6] Apparently before the meeting convened, he framed—perhaps with Smilie's aid—a set of resolutions intended as a response to Governor Clinton's letter, which declared that a
new and early convention of all the states to revise the federal Constitution was necessary to prevent the dissolution of the Union and to secure
the liberties of Americans. To this end committees of friends to revision
in the various states should correspond, and perhaps a general conference

should be held to devise the most necessary amendments and the best ways of obtaining their adoption. The Pennsylvania Assembly should be urged to call upon the next Congress to summon a revisionary convention.

Once the conference began its deliberations, Gallatin saw that his views were too extreme for the majority. Accordingly, he adopted a far more moderate tone in delivering a long speech and a drastically revised set of resolutions. Both bore the marks of careful preparation and close study of the American governments as well as those of ancient and modern Europe.

The speech conceded that the Articles of Confederation, under which the former colonies had been cooperating since the Revolution, did not grant Congress sufficient power to accomplish the ends in view—the fostering of peaceful relations between the sovereign states and with foreign nations. One evidence of this was the failure of the states to comply with the financial requisitions of Congress.

But the new federal Constitution, Gallatin insisted, was also objectionable, because its loosely worded provisions would permit the legislative and executive departments to arrogate unto themselves an inordinate amount of power. For instance—he was particularly happy in finding an example in finance—the provision that Congress might levy and collect taxes was so loosely stated that the power might be abused.

Analyzing the Constitution section by section, sometimes approving, sometimes criticizing, Gallatin allowed himself a number of observations on the nature of republics. He was doubtful of the survival of the American republic if the country continued to expand geographically. The legislature would either have to become so large as to be unmanageable or have to remain so small as to be unrepresentative; the executive would have to be invested with great authority, diminishing individual liberty proportionately; the judiciary would become all the "more subject to corruption and abuses."

The preamble to Gallatin's resolutions reiterated his acknowledgment that the United States required "a more efficient" government than the Articles of Confederation gave it and repeated his admission that the new Constitution was "likely to obviate most of the inconveniences." But it insisted that several sections of the Constitution were "so exceptionable" that the State of Pennsylvania should not "acquiesce" in the organization of the new government until they were revised. A new convention of all the states ought to be convened promptly to devise such amendments as "may seem most necessary" and to deliberate on the best ways to carry them into effect. The resolutions did not mention that New York had already made such a proposal; they would have Pennsylvania assume leadership of the movement.

Even in their tempered form, Gallatin's resolutions were too drastic for the delegates at Harrisburg, who further modified them during the four days of meeting. Now called a "petition," they merely called upon the Pennsylvania legislature to request Congress to summon a convention to amend the Constitution "at the earliest opportunity." Twelve amendments were urged, four of which embodied suggestions Gallatin had made: the powers of Congress should be limited to those specified in the Constitution; the number of representatives should be one to every 20,000 people; the election of Congressmen should be regulated by the Constitution rather than by Congress itself; and Congress should be empowered to assess, levy, and collect the direct tax quota of any state that did not promptly furnish its quota.

The Pennsylvania legislature never acted on the meeting's suggestion that it set in motion a movement for a new constitutional convention. Among the first ten amendments—the "bill of rights"—subsequently added to the federal Constitution were two that paralleled suggestions made at Harrisburg; but amendments along these same lines previously had been proposed by the ratifying conventions of several states. Thus the meeting can be counted as merely one of a number of belated, half-hearted, and futile attempts by groups that had earlier opposed ratification to bring about revision of the Constitution.

But the meeting marked an important turning-point for young Albert Gallatin. Through participation he had embarked on a political career. He had identified himself formally with the party that had misgivings about the centralizing features of the Constitution. He had widened his acquaintance with, and undoubtedly made a favorable impression upon, political leaders from all sections of Pennsylvania. And he had publicly expounded for the first time, somewhat falteringly but nevertheless positively, his still nascent democratic-republican philosophy.

3

If Gallatin dipped his toes in politics at the Harrisburg meeting, he immersed both feet a year later, in the autumn of 1789, only a few months after he had brought Sophie Allegre home to Friendship Hill. By that time the political party with which he had affiliated was in a desperate way. To understand its plight, it is necessary to consider the course of Pennsylvania politics in the decade and a half since the state had declared its independence of Great Britain. Under the state constitution of 1776, an unusual instrument providing for a unicameral legislature, a multiple executive, and a difficult procedure for amendment, Gallatin's party—particularly the wing of it west of the mountains—had exerted an influence in state affairs far out of proportion to its following. The opposition party, especially strong in the eastern and central counties, believing the constitution worked to its disadvantage, was determined to revise it. Through the years the strength of this Anti-Constitutionalist party gradually increased. Its prestige was enhanced by its successful support of ratification of the federal Constitution and capped by resounding victories at the polls in the fall and winter of 1788. In September, 1789, the legislature, under complete control of the Anti-Constitutionalists, issued a call to the voters of Pennsylvania to choose, in the approaching elections, delegates to a convention that would "review, alter, and amend the state constitution"—despite the fact that the state constitution allowed amendment only through a long and complicated process by a body known as the Council of Censors.[7]

When word of this extralegal maneuver reached Friendship Hill in early October, Gallatin lost no time in doing his bit to organize a countermaneuver. Now an experienced hand at framing resolutions, he drew up a set which branded the legislature's call for a convention "unconstitutional, unnecessary, and highly improper" and called on voters to refuse to elect any delegates to the meeting. He sent a copy, with a covering letter, to each of half a dozen politically prominent western Pennsylvanians.

By far the most interesting of the covering letters was that to Alexander Addison, a hardheaded young Scot practicing law at the near-by town of Washington, who had declared his candidacy for membership in the constitutional convention. Gallatin did not deny that the constitution needed amendment; but he emphasized the unconstitutionality of the legislature's call, pointing out that if Addison pursued his candidacy he would violate his oath of allegiance to the state.

Gallatin closed his appeal to a man of conservative sympathies with phrases strange for a western democrat: "Alterations in government are always dangerous, and no legislator ever did think of putting, in such an easy manner, the power in a mere majority, to introduce them whenever they pleased. Such a doctrine once admitted . . . instead of establishing on solid foundations a new government, would open the door to perpetual changes and destroy that stability so essential to the welfare of a nation; as no constitution acquires the permanent affection of the people but in proportion to its duration and age. Finally, those changes would, sooner or later, conclude in an appeal to arms—the true meaning of those words so popular and so dangerous—*an appeal to the people.*" [8]

Addison not only continued his candidacy, but apparently did not acknowledge Gallatin's letter. Other correspondents were more responsive. James Marshel, an old veteran of the Indian wars whom Gallatin had met at Harrisburg, praised the resolutions as "well-digested" and promised to distribute them widely through Washington County. David Redick, an Irish-born lawyer and a member of the state's Supreme Executive Council, called Gallatin's work "judicious"; he rejoiced in it as evidence that there were "a few friends of liberty every here and there through the continent," but regretted that "they are scattered so thinly and want the immediate means of communication, whilst the Aristocracy are more active, more braced up." [9]

Gallatin soon realized that his efforts were too late and probably too little. On election day, October 13, his resolutions were completely ignored, and the members of his party contented themselves with doing their best to elect delegates friendly to their aims. Ironically, in view of his pronouncement to Addison that to stand for election would violate one's oath to the state, the people of Fayette elected to the convention their trusted representative John Smilie, and that able newcomer Albert Gallatin.[10]

4

Because of Sophie's death Gallatin started late for the state constitutional convention. As he rode over the Alleghenies and through the smiling pleasant valleys of central Pennsylvania, he quite probably brooded on the idea of quitting America, with its painful memories, for the security of his native land.

He could not know, of course, when he reached Philadelphia on December 7, 1789, that he was entering upon a ten-year phase of his career that would make him a resident of the city nearly half of each year. Penn's town on the Delaware was a pleasant place in which to live. Foreign visitors counted it one of the most beautiful cities of America, remarking upon the homes of the well-to-do, of red brick in the Georgian style, the geometrically laid-out streets, the brick foot pavements sheltered by trees. With a population of almost 30,000, Philadelphia was easily the largest city in the country. The capital of Pennsylvania for more than a century, it was about to become the capital of the nation. Here President Washington was to preside over the fashionable society of the "Federal court"; William Bingham, Thomas Willing, and Robert Morris, over mercantile and financial activity; Benjamin Franklin, Benjamin Rush, and David Rittenhouse, over intellectual life.

Gallatin's first years in the city centered about the house of Major Adam Boyd on Sixth Street above Arch—long a favorite gathering place of western politicians of his own persuasion. Such friends as Smilie and William Findley of Westmoreland County either boarded there or haunted its rooms. At Boyd's, he had politics with his meals and probably on occasion with his sleep.[11]

In time Gallatin became intimate with a number of easterners as well. His dearest friend in Philadelphia was James Hutchinson, professor of chemistry at ,the University of Pennsylvania, a leading physican, and secretary of the American Philosophical Society. Dr. Hutchinson was an ardent democrat, and assumed state-wide leadership of the defenders of the Pennsylvania constitution. Fat enough to play the character of Falstaff without stuffing, he entertained the habitués of Major Boyd's of an evening with well seasoned chatter on medical and political topics. Like Falstaff he was not only witty, but the source of wit in others.[12] Gallatin sought him out often. "From his extensive information I had many times derived the greatest assistance," he recalled later, "and his principles, his integrity, and the warmth of his affection for me had attracted me to him more than any man in Philadelphia." [13]

A close friend and political follower of Dr. Hutchinson with whom Gallatin became friendly was Alexander James Dallas. Born in Jamaica and just two years Gallatin's senior, the tall, courtly Dallas had come to the United States in 1783. His unusual talents and industry quickly won him a permanent place at the Philadelphia bar. Soon he was acting as Dr. Hutchinson's trusted lieutenant in managing party matters.[14]

5

Gallatin arrived at the convention late. When he first answered the roll-call, on December 8, 1789, daily sessions had been held at the red-brick State House in Independence Square for two weeks.[15] The convention afforded him his first chance to watch at close range the making of government and of laws and claimed a fond place in his memories. In later years, after he had seen much of the world and was in a position to judge, he described it as one of the ablest bodies of which he had ever been a member or indeed with which he was acquainted. "Could I except two names,—[James] Madison and [John] Marshall," he wrote, "I would say

that it embraced as much talent and knowledge as any Congress from
1795 to 1812, beyond which my personal knowledge does not extend." [16]
Three-fifths of the delegates had held important state offices during and
since the Revolution; and Gallatin found association with such veterans
exhilarating and challenging. Years later he marveled that he had been
able to overcome his natural diffidence and participate in discussions with
such men "in a foreign tongue and with a foreign accent." [17]

The westerners were an able group: from Fayette, Gallatin's own
partner, John Smilie; from Washington, David Redick, Alexander Addison, and James Ross—a young lawyer of high promise; from Westmoreland, William Findley—a shrewd farmer and weaver out of Ulster with
a long record in state affairs. Now for the first time he met the most
prominent figures from other parts of Pennsylvania: Thomas Mifflin, the
hearty and engaging one-time merchant and Revolutionary War general
who so pleased all factions that he was chosen presiding officer;
Thomas McKean, austere, vain Scotch-Irishman who had made a capable
chief justice of the state Supreme Court; James Wilson, Scottish-born, a
radical who had become an able lawyer of moderate conservative hue;
William Lewis, a Philadelphia Quaker lawyer, talented and ultraconserva-
tive.[18]

The opponents of the existing state constitution—who were beginning
to be known as Federalists because of their successful sponsorship of the
federal Constitution—had distinct advantages over the party of Gallatin.
They were far more numerous and, with their strength in the populous
eastern counties, had been able to work out a well knit program. The
conciliatory spirit of Findley soon led the two parties to an agreement on
the chief features of a new constitution for the state. During the early
days of the convention, the Westmoreland farmer and the moderate
Wilson agreed that the instrument should resemble the federal Constitution, with a two-house legislature, executive power concentrated in the
hands of a single man with a qualified veto on acts of the legislature,
and an independent judiciary.[19] Their cue was taken up by the majority
of the members of both parties. "The distinguishing feature of the convention," Gallatin recalled later, "was that, owing perhaps to more favorable times, it was less affected by party feelings than any I have known.
The points of difference were almost exclusively on general and abstract
propositions; there was less prejudice and more sincerity in the discussions than usual; and throughout, a desire to conciliate opposite opinions
by mutual concessions." [20]

By February 26, 1790, a constitution that embodied the agreed-upon
features, plus a bill of rights, had been drafted and debated provision by

provision. Then, so that the "haste and secrecy" which had accompanied adoption of the federal Constitution would not be repeated, the convention recessed to allow copies to be published and carefully considered by the people of the state before final enactment.[21] Gallatin supervised distribution of copies among his constituents in Fayette.[22] By August 9 he and his colleagues were back at the State House for a second session. Two days later Smilie moved that the discussion be closed and the constitution adopted. This motion, Gallatin seconded. A desultory discussion of trivialities kept the convention in session until September 2.[23]

In the two sessions of the convention, Gallatin took "but a subordinate share," as he himself put it. On most votes he went along with Smilie, Findley, and the bipartisan coalition, parting company with them on only one cardinal issue: he voted against making the Supreme Court justice-ships tenable during good behavior and independent of the other departments as to salary.[24] His voting record also revealed his religious attitude. Acknowledgment of "the being of a God, and a future state of rewards and punishments" was included in the qualifications required of a state officeholder. When a Philadelphia delegate proposed striking out this clause, Gallatin was among the small minority that voted for the omission.[25]

On the infrequent occasions that Gallatin spoke, his pleas were always for democratic provisions.[26] For example, he urged that the franchise be extended to males over twenty-one with a year's residence in their district, whether or not they had paid taxes—an idea favored by his western neighbors, anxious to attract new settlers; but ultimately the easterners had their way and payment of a tax was required.

Gallatin also sought a democratically constituted legislature. The bill of rights in the new constitution, he pointed out, stated that the rights of the people were "inalienable." One means of assuring the people that their rights would not be infringed was a thoroughly representative lower house. A given number of voters in one part of the state should have precisely the same representation as the same number in any other part of the state. Representatives should be elected for only short periods.

He restated the position he had taken at Harrisburg that the legislature should be large, so that every class of citizen would be represented, and so that "poor honest farmers" and "men of moderate ability" would not be excluded from parliamentary halls. His analysis of the argument of some conservatives that a smaller assembly would save the people money was blistering. Gallatin's arithmetical mind computed that such an economy would save each male in the state only five pence a year. Besides, he added, "the poor will always be saving of the people's money." His arguments bore fruit, blocking attempts to reduce both upper and lower houses in size.

The conservative James Ross's proposal that state senators be elected not directly by the people but by members of the lower house provoked Gallatin into several protesting speeches. Studding his discussion with references to Servius Tullius, Lycurgus, Montesquieu, the Swiss cantons, and several American states, he carefully traced the age-old conflict between the wealthy and the poor. The best way to avoid strife, he concluded, was to develop a system of fair representation in which the lower house would mirror local interests, the upper house more general ones. The Ross proposal was killed by a decisive vote.

Subsequently Gallatin attempted to have similarly democratic principles applied to the election of congressmen. The federal Constitution had not specified the manner in which members of the House of Representatives should be chosen, and Pennsylvania had elected its first delegation on a state-wide ticket. Gallatin told the convention that the purpose of the federal House was similar to that of the lower house of the state legislature—to represent local interests; but a day after offering a motion to this effect he withdrew it, apparently persuaded that it was not a proper subject for a state constitution.

Gallatin threw his support to the democratic side of yet another issue: the statement in the bill of rights about libel. James Wilson and his group of moderate conservatives had joined with Findley's followers in urging that the constitution specify trial by jury for printers or writers charged with libeling public officials or candidates for office. William Lewis and the ultraconservatives of the convention damned this as "wild innovation and democracy." [27] Gallatin delivered a long and learned speech in behalf of the proposal, lacing it with citations from classical authorities and Roman law helpfully provided by Peter DuPonceau, a French-born lawyer practicing at Philadelphia. He reminded the convention that great restriction on the press would merely provoke printers and editors into more furtiveness and libel. The guarantee of jury trial was passed, but by a close vote.

Gallatin regretted that the constitution was not referred directly to the people for ratification before being declared in effect, but took satisfaction in later years in the fact that "no public act was ever more universally approved . . . at the time it was promulgated." [28] The new instrument of government served Pennsylvania most satisfactorily for forty-seven years, through a period of great transition and growth.

After attending the series of ceremonies that marked the conclusion of the convention's labors early in September, 1790,[29] Gallatin hurried back to his farm on Georges Creek. Now he was closely identified with the democratic group in Pennsylvania politics. He had played minor but, for a newcomer, considerable roles at two state-wide conventions. He had had his first lessons in the ways of representative bodies, and had matched wits at Philadelphia with men who were his intellectual equals. He had represented and urged the sentiments of his neighbors faithfully, intelligently, and vigorously. Under the trying fire of parliamentary battle he had begun to develop a political philosophy of his own. His political apprenticeship was well begun.

4. Spokesman of Frontier Democracy

1790=1793

Gallatin's Fayette County neighbors liked what they heard about his performance at the Pennsylvania constitutional convention.[1] They liked it so much that in October, 1790, when they elected representatives to the lower house of the legislature under the new state constitution, approximately two-thirds of the votes cast were for him. What they heard after that pleased them so much that in 1791 and again in 1792 they reelected him without opposition. His vote in the latter year was 796.[2]

Gallatin was thus repeatedly returned to the Assembly because he proved himself to be both an uncommonly skillful practical politician and a statesmanlike exponent of the democratic beliefs cherished on the Pennsylvania frontier. The sessions of the legislature kept him at Philadelphia each year from early December through April, and in some years also from late August into October; but he was at home on Georges Creek during the recesses.

Wherever he was, he lived and breathed politics. On Georges Creek—especially during the weeks before election day—he haunted crossroad taverns and neighbors' farmhouses. Occasionally he journeyed to Uniontown to pick up his mail at the post office, to distribute party handbills, to put in a good word for the ticket, and of course to remind any constituents around the courthouse that he was a candidate. He was likely to pass election day in the tavern of Nicholas Riffle, the polling place of his own Springhill Township, greeting his neighbors as they came to cast their ballots. He delighted in predicting the results before election day, and totaling them as the returns came in. On the backs of letters and on small slips of paper he jotted down, in a tiny, wretched hand, figures based upon his observations in his own district and culled from his correspondence.[3]

While at the capital, Gallatin performed errands for his constituents. Some of these entailed conferences with the state land officers, for

38

the westerners were ever troubled about warrants and titles. Some arose from the fact that Philadelphia, the only metropolis in the state, was the most convenient place for buying merchandise and conducting financial transactions. He negotiated loans and paid bills, sometimes making advances from his own purse. He bought looking glasses and made the special arrangements necessary for delivering them across the Alleghenies.[4]

At home during the recess, Gallatin kept in close touch with the leaders of his own political group through correspondence. His pen was especially busy during the spring and summer of 1792, when the party made a valiant attempt to capture Pennsylvania's delegation in Congress and cooperated with kindred spirits in other states—commonly known as Antifederalists because they opposed the dominant Federalist party—in a vain attempt to replace John Adams as Vice President with someone whose philosophy was "less aristocratic." During these months he traded political intelligence with Findley, Dr. Hutchinson, and A. J. Dallas, lately appointed Secretary of the Commonwealth.[5]

In the Assembly, Gallatin acquired, as he himself put it in later years, "an extraordinary influence . . . the more remarkable, as I was always in a *party* minority." [6] In each session he was appointed to no fewer than forty committees.[7] Extraordinary as his influence was, the reasons are obvious. The sixty-nine members of the Pennsylvania House of Representatives during these years were, on the whole, a mediocre lot. Exceptions were William Bingham, the fabulously successful Philadelphia businessman, who later became a United States senator, and William Findley, before he went on to Congress, where he served long and honorably. Moreover, turnover in the Assembly was rapid. In Gallatin's third term, fewer than a third of the members had served as long as he.

Before long, Gallatin became, as he himself put it, "the laboring oar" of a host of committees. He was absorbed in work almost all his waking hours—at the State House during the day, in his room at Major Boyd's during the evening. For the committees on which he served in the 1791–1792 session, he "prepared all their reports, and drew all their bills." In 1793 he complained to Thomas Clare that the details of committee work consumed all his time, "owing to the very great indolence of our members this year." [8]

Some of his most effective work was performed on the floor of the House. No member spoke more frequently. He had no great gifts as a legislative debater. To the casual observer, he was unimpressive, though not unattractive. Although barely thirty, he had already begun to lose his black hair. His thin face, his long, hooked nose and pointed chin, his lean figure made him look tall; but in debate he was apt to surrender this advantage by bending toward the presiding officer, sawing the air with a perpendicular movement of his right arm to emphasize his points. His speech was slow and halting, with a pronounced French accent. Brevity was not one of his virtues, and at times he spoke without interruption as long as three hours.[9]

But these were superficial shortcomings. Long speeches were common in the Pennsylvania Assembly, and his colleagues soon discovered that, although his accent was Gallic, his phrases were excellent idiomatic English. With a sheet of mathematically logical notes before him, he could become almost eloquent. Once Bingham, the Federalist Speaker of the Assembly, announced that Gallatin's detailed and acutely reasoned argument against his party's stand on a certain issue had so impressed him that he would not attempt to answer it until he had carefully investigated the question anew.[10] Another Federalist Assemblyman, Jacob Hiltzheimer of Philadelphia, confided to his diary that Gallatin's speeches were "masterful," his arguments "very forcible." [11]

Gallatin's chief contributions to the Assembly and to Pennsylvania political life were as an extraordinarily able public financier and as an eloquent spokesman of the political and economic objectives of the frontiersmen. Because they foreshadowed so much that was important in his later career, they deserve special attention.

2

Pennsylvania had sore need of a man with Gallatin's talent for public finance. Since 1781, when Robert Morris left the Assembly for national service, no member had had first-rate abilities in this sphere. The state's finances, governed by expediency and improvisation, had steadily grown more chaotic.[12] Probably it was only by happy chance that Gallatin became one of the twenty-one members of the House's powerful Ways and Means Committee at the start of his first legislative session.[13] Yet as the committee considered the state's financial position and proposed legislation to cope with it his rare capacities quickly became apparent. The consequence was that writing the committee's reports and leading the discussion of fiscal questions fell to him during his Assembly years.[14]

In approaching problems of public finance, Gallatin was instinctively guided by his Genevan heritage.[15] He felt that public debts of "a free nation" must always be completely and promptly satisfied, lest it fall into "disgrace." He believed, moreover, that governmental indebtedness tended to increase artificially inequality of fortunes among citizens; if it became a permanent policy, the payment of interest would become a permanent burden on the industrious to support the idle.[16]

Such ideas were not generally held in the United States in 1790. Some members of the Federalist party even argued that a public debt, or at least a funded debt, was a national blessing, for it would attach men of wealth to the government.[17] The record of Gallatin's Antifederalist colleagues before his arrival in the Assembly, marked by freehanded appropriations and a disinclination to levy compensatory taxes, suggested that they were not anxious to challenge this philosophy.[18] Thus Gallatin's success in persuading not only his own group, but also the Federalist majority in the Assembly, to enact a financial program based upon his Genevan tenets was a personal triumph.

Gallatin's first statement to the House on finance—the report of the Ways and Means Committee of February 1791[19]—pointed out that Pennsylvania had thirteen principal debts, totaling about £275,000. Furthermore, the state had another obligation to settle, an outgrowth of the federal government's assumption, at the behest of Secretary of the Treasury Alexander Hamilton, of the debts which the states had contracted during the period of the Revolutionary War and the Confederation. No part of Hamilton's financial program, Gallatin believed, was "more obnoxious" than the act authorizing this. The federal government was to pay Pennsylvania's creditors $2,200,000—four-ninths of it in government stock bearing 6 per cent interest starting in 1792; one-third of it in government stock bearing 3 per cent interest starting in 1792; and two-ninths of it in government stock bearing 6 per cent interest starting in 1800.[20]

To Gallatin it seemed that the Hamiltonian settlement, as it affected Pennsylvania, had three notable flaws. For one, setting the state debt at $2,200,000 was arbitrary; Secretary Hamilton had not taken the trouble to discover "what was actually and justly due to each State." Moreover, the conversion of one-third of the debt into 3 per cent stock appeared to be an indefensible default, for it was the equivalent of reducing by 50 per cent that part of the debt. Finally, postponement for a decade of any interest on one-third of the principal was equally unfair.

To correct these injustices, Gallatin recommended that Pennsylvania issue certificates to its creditors to make up the difference between the amount the federal government had agreed to pay and the book value of its Revolutionary and Confederation debts. As subsequently worked out, this meant the issuance of £135,000 of certificates, with annual interest charges of about £5,675.[21]

Happily, he observed in his report, Pennsylvania had ample resources to meet these obligations. Most important were its vast tracts of valuable unsettled lands and a sizable sum of arrears on lands already sold. Secondly, the state owned £450,000 of United States certificates which it had received from the federal government under Hamilton's debt assumption plan. It could count also on regular amounts from the state excise on distilled liquors and other direct taxes and duties. There was some feeling, especially among the Antifederalists, that the state ought to discontinue the direct taxes completely and at once. Gallatin differed with their view, insisting that, although some reductions might be made, these sources of income would have to be utilized until the state was out of debt. He was equally firm in opposing the suggestion that such of the "paper money" the state had issued during the Confederation period as now reposed in the state treasurer's office should be reissued as a means of affording the Commonwealth temporary assistance.

The financial difficulties of the state, Gallatin concluded, arose because its debts were all due at the moment, while its assets would become available gradually over a period of years. To enable the state to take a first step toward meeting all its obligations, he urged an operation that would mean temporary compromise with strict Genevan financial principles: the state should fund its debt by borrowing from European, notably Dutch, sources, and from the Bank of North America in Philadelphia.

With a single minor change the Assembly enacted every one of Gallatin's recommendations during the spring of 1791. He was particularly delighted by a law that forbade the state treasurer to reissue any paper money and provided for the redemption of most of that still outstanding. He was pleased also by the support which his Antifederalist colleagues gave to a law specifying that the state should compensate its creditors for losses incurred under Hamilton's debt assumption scheme, because few of them held any state or federal paper and most were inclined to regard the numerous Federalists who did hold any as sordid speculators.[22]

The full significance of this legislation was revealed in the Ways and Means Committee report that Gallatin presented at the following session of the Assembly. The state's probable revenues for 1792, he was able to write jubilantly, amounted to £135,000; its probable expenditures, to £132,000. Thus, his efforts, in less than a year, had placed Pennsylvania on what present-day financiers would describe as a "balanced budget" basis.[23]

The accomplishment gratified Gallatin for two reasons. No longer would it be necessary to continue the unpopular direct taxes. Furthermore, the funding of the state debts, which he considered at best as a temporary expedient, could now be stopped. As he wrote in the Ways and Means Committee report of February, 1792, "owing a debt cannot contribute more to the welfare, happiness, and real opulence of a people than a private debt contributes to the wealth and prosperity of an individual, and . . . therefore it is as much the interest as the duty of a nation to pay, and not to fund its debts, whenever it is enabled so to do." Fortunately, he continued, the means for paying off these debts completely were at hand. The 3 per cent United States stock had risen in market value. By selling what it held, Pennsylvania could retire the special certificates it had issued in 1780, and could save more than £5,750 annually in interest charges.

Gallatin's plan was translated into law within a few months. By December, Governor Thomas Mifflin was able to announce that all the state's war debts had been paid. To celebrate the achievement, the legislature repealed all the direct taxes, as Gallatin had urged.[24]

Pennsylvania was able to accomplish this happy consummation principally because there was a brisk market for its extensive tracts of land, and because these years of prosperity brought in considerable sums in back taxes. Yet Gallatin sensed new dangers: With the accumulation of a large surplus in the treasury, a freehanded legislature might squander it on useless projects.[25] Moreover, in a relatively few years all the lands would be sold, and all the arrears would be collected. Before that should happen, the state's resources must be placed upon "a permanent and beneficial footing."

He broached a bold plan for reaching that utopian goal in a Ways and Means Committee report of February, 1793, proposing that the legislature charter a Bank of Pennsylvania, with a relationship to the state government roughly analogous to that between Secretary Hamilton's creation, the Bank of the United States, and the federal government. The state would become a substantial stockholder, obtaining the means for this by selling the United States stock it owned, by employing various unappropriated funds in the treasury, and by pledging unsold lands and tax arrearages. The new bank would be required to pay 6 per cent interest on its stock—providing the state with enough income, Gallatin estimated, to cover all the regular expenses of government— and to make a loan to the state of a size permitting establishment of a loan office in each county. The privately owned Bank of North America would be allowed to subscribe to the new bank if it would relinquish its own charter.[26]

The last two provisions were meant to attract the support of members of Gallatin's own party. The farmers had long complained that the Bank of North America and the Bank of the United States—the only banks operating in Pennsylvania—were of little use to them because they refused to give mortgages on rural property. The Bank of North America, whose stock was held largely by Federalists, had paid large dividends since its incorporation in 1781. Through the years there had been a concerted campaign by the western Antifederalists to deprive it of its charter.[27]

To the eastern Federalists, Gallatin's suggestion appeared to be a renewal of the westerners' war on their bank, and they put up a stubborn fight. He defended it, arguing that the Bank of the United States had increased the prestige and power of the federal government enormously and a Bank of Pennsylvania would perform a comparable service for the state government. Moreover, if the widely held fear that the federal government was acquiring undue power had any basis, a state bank would "counteract" that tendency by helping to make the state independent of the federal government for its revenue and its credit standing. Thus a Bank of Pennsylvania would help "restore" the balance between the state and federal governments "established by the constitution." [28]

Despite the well organized opposition of the Federalists and the Bank of North America, the Assembly passed two acts in the spring of 1793 carrying out Gallatin's bank plan in its entirety. A Bank of Pennsylvania was chartered with a capital of $3,000,000, of which the state took one-third. The institution was required to lend $500,000 to the state for the establishment of a loan office in each county.[29]

The results were disappointing in two respects: the terms under which the loan offices could offer mortgages attracted few applications; and, as was not unexpected, the Bank of North America did not choose to relinquish its charter to the new bank. But the Bank of Pennsylvania, with branches in several cities, enjoyed a useful and profitable existence until long after Gallatin's death.[30] Gallatin correctly assessed the value of his bank legislation to the state when he wrote that "this and subsequent investments [in the stock of the bank] enabled Pennsylvania to defray all the expenses of government without any direct tax during the forty ensuing years." [31]

3

Of all the issues on which Gallatin faithfully represented the viewpoint of his pioneering farmer constituents, by all odds the most troublesome was the excise on distilled liquor. Such a tax was an old story to Pennsylvanians; one had been in force since 1684. When he entered the legislature the nineteenth excise law was on the statute books. But resistance to enforcement made it virtually a dead letter west of the Alleghenies.[32]

When Secretary Hamilton proposed a federal excise in the winter of 1790–1791 as a means by which the national government might raise funds for his debt assumption plan, western Pennsylvanians opposed it almost to a man. Farmers in the eastern and central sections of the state could sell their wheat and rye in the cities and towns; but transport of bulky grain over the mountains was prohibitively expensive, and western farmers found it economical to convert their rye into whiskey and transport this to the East by pack horse in barter for salt, iron, and other supplies. Thus whiskey was their currency, a sturdy support of their economy. The average farmer did not see twenty dollars a year in cash; but a gallon jug of his home brew brought him at least a quarter of a dollar in trade at his neighborhood store. And Hamilton's plan called for payment of the excise in cash! The proposal appeared to be all the more discriminatory because, it is estimated, one-quarter of all the whiskey then produced in the United States was distilled in the area west of the Alleghenies, which had less than 4 per cent of the population. In sum, the westerners believed Mr. Hamilton's excise was a grave abuse that would tax their true currency in order to provide an unfairly large share of the cost of a scheme that was designed to fill the pockets of a few speculators in the eastern cities.[33]

Gallatin did not operate a still, and was less directly affected by the Hamilton plan than most of his neighbors;[34] but, as a conscientious representative in the legislature, he listened attentively when a sympathetic easterner, Francis Gurney of Philadelphia, rose one day in January, 1791, to discuss the current debates in Congress on the excise bill. Gurney urged the legislature to pass a remonstrance against Hamilton's plan as "subversive of the peace, liberty, and rights of the citizens" and to forward it to Pennsylvania's federal senators.[35]

The Federalist assemblymen made no attempt to defend the Hamilton bill. Their leader, Bingham, argued merely that by ratifying the federal Constitution the people of Pennsylvania had invested Congress with the right to levy excises and now had "no right to interfere."

Several days of bitter debate followed, to which Gallatin made his first contributions as an assemblyman. In numerous, often lengthy speeches he urged states' rights and a strict construction of the federal constitution as reasons for supporting Gurney's remonstrance. A state legislature, he maintained, had the right to protest not only when the federal government actually exceeded its powers, but whenever it appeared that it might do so. At any rate, Hamilton's proposal was unconstitutional. He proposed an amendment to the resolution asserting as much: "Every species of taxation which shall operate either directly or indirectly as a duty on articles exported from any state is unconstitutional." But the House voted down this extreme interpretation.

Gallatin's chief objection to Hamilton's proposal was that an excise was a particularly inequitable form of taxation. It "will bear hard upon the honest and industrious citizens," he prophesied, "whilst the wealthy and conniving parts of the community will avoid payment by stratagems." The western counties would be obliged to pay a far greater share than the eastern. Because of the procedure by which the excisemen would make their collections, three times as much money would be removed from the pockets of the people as would be the case in a direct tax—a form of taxation he considered far better suited to a republican government.

Another prejudice of the westerners was reflected in Gallatin's objection to the purpose of the excise: the assumption of state debts. "It is very true," he conceded, "that we have given Congress the right of levying sufficient taxes to preserve the harmony of the union. But I wish to know whether this adopting an excise will not rather tend to the destruction of the union. I wish to know whether it is necessary to pay more than the debts of the country." [36]

The Gurney resolution won decisive assent from the lower house of the Assembly; but the upper house refused concurrence by a nine-to-eight vote.[37] Meanwhile, Hamilton's excise bill passed both houses of Congress without difficulty, supported by approximately half of the Pennsylvania delegation.[38] Secretary of State Thomas Jefferson and Congressman James Madison of Virginia, equalitarians and states'-rights republicans who might have organized opposition, did not lift a finger against it, for it appeared to be an intrinsic part of Hamilton's debt assumption project, to which they had given their support in return for the establishment of the projected federal capital on the banks of the Potomac.

Even after the excise bill became law in March, 1791, Gallatin and his fellow westerners remained unreconciled to it. But their subsequent battles, as we shall presently see, were fought outside legislative halls.

4

Better transportation, better terms for the sale and settlement of state-owned lands, better protection against Indian raids—these perennial concerns of the westerner were close to Gallatin's heart during his years in the Assembly.

Over the need for improved transportation there was no sectional cleavage in Pennsylvania, because the merchants of the East were alive to the attractions the enterprising young port of Baltimore offered to the people west of the Alleghenies.[39] Gallatin could feel it as he jogged along on horseback over the rough roads and mountain trails from Georges Creek to Philadelphia. He accepted membership in the Philadelphia Society for Promoting the Improvements of Roads and Inland Navigation, and vigorously endorsed the petitions it periodically presented to the legislature. On the Assembly floor in the spring of 1791, so the Philadelphia *General Advertiser* reported, he "dwelt on the advantages of connecting the Western and Eastern waters," urging that improvements "would draw the Western ports to enrich the Eastern" and warning that, unless something were done, "a great deal of the riches . . . would go down the Potowmack." Canal and road construction "would naturally draw and encrease population in the improved parts." [40]

One of the many committees on which Gallatin labored reported in March, 1791, that the construction of internal improvements would be too costly for either individuals or the state to undertake and proposed that the legislature charter private stock companies for the purpose. On the basis of this plan, three companies were chartered during Gallatin's Assembly years: one to build a canal connecting the Schuylkill and Susquehanna rivers; one to build a canal linking the Delaware and Schuylkill rivers; and a third to construct a road between Philadelphia and Lancaster. This last, opened in 1794, was the first turnpike in the United States built entirely at private expense and set the pattern for many internal improvements throughout the United States during the next half-century.[41]

As a land speculator, Gallatin took keen interest in the thousands of acres, mostly in the northwestern part of Pennsylvania, owned by the state but never opened to settlement. As a westerner he was anxious that these be populated, expecting that the land values and political influence of his own section would thereby be increased. During his second term in the Assembly, he contributed largely to a report submitted in January, 1792, which proposed a set of principles consonant with western aspirations. This called for the immediate opening for settlement of virtually all state land on extremely liberal terms: any person, by applying to the land office, might obtain a warrant for as much as 400 acres of any vacant land except that reserved for towns. If the warrantee settled on the land and completed payment within a certain time, a patent would be issued and the land would be his. However, if he did not settle within a certain time "and continue such settlement by actual residence or cultivation," the state would be free to grant the land to another warrantee. The report urged that the price of land be kept low.[42]

The misgivings of many easterners about westward expansion were baldly disclosed when a bill incorporating these principles came up for debate in the House. Some members feared that a sudden opening of the West would depress eastern property values, tighten the labor market, and decrease their own political influence. They talked much about how the cost of protection against Indian attack would rise. Spokesmen for interests eyeing western land for profitable speculation stressed the advantages in turning over the land to companies and men of wealth, who could guarantee full payment and more "orderly" settlement.

Gallatin was tireless in scotching such arguments. He held up large maps to demonstrate that new settlements would actually diminish the Indian menace. He denied the contention of one easterner that a compact settlement produces a happy people. "The happiness of a country," he asserted, "depends more . . . on the poorer class of people having it within their power to become freeholders at a small expence, and being able to live comfortably, and dependent only on their industry and exertions." Failure to open the land at once, he contended, would cause Pennsylvania to lose worthy citizens to other states—something to be considered, as the size of a state's population determined its weight in Congress.[43]

Some of the value of the bill was lost in a last-minute compromise— to which Gallatin acceded—between the westerners and the spokesmen for the would-be speculators. An act of April, 1792, opened all state land northwest of the Allegheny and Ohio rivers at attractively low rates to actual settlers or to persons who would cause others to settle them. The law quickened western settlement and brought increased revenues into the state coffers; but the ambiguity of its phrasing produced litigation between a large land company and actual settlers that was to disturb Pennsylvania political life for more than a decade.[44]

Of the terror struck by Indians on the warpath Gallatin was reminded by letters that kept arriving from his constituents. In 1790 the northwestern tribes banded together in a concerted effort to evict the whites who were pouring into their hunting grounds. The federal government sent a military force under General Arthur St. Clair to the Wabash River, but it was ingloriously routed. "Our frontiers are naked," Gallatin observed dolefully to friends on hearing the news. "The Indians must be encouraged by their success." In 1791 and again the next year he personally sponsored legislation appropriating funds of £4,000 and £4,500 to enable the state militia to assist the federal forces. Faced with a crisis so close to their homes and hearts, he and his western colleagues were willing to forget their dread that cooperation of this kind between the two governments might lead to the establishment of a standing army: an institution which, he had said on another occasion, "would load us with a monstrous expence." Gallatin had left the legislature when General Anthony Wayne's victory over the Indians at Fallen Timbers, in 1794, finally brought peace to the Pennsylvania frontier.[45]

An account of Gallatin's Assembly career would not be complete without mention of his efforts on behalf of education. This concern was the fruit of his Genevan heritage; he was particularly proud of it in his later years. In each of his terms he sponsored legislation making small grants to the only two colleges in Pennsylvania, the College and Academy of Philadelphia and Dickinson College at Carlisle, and worked to have the state make good on the promise in its Constitution of 1790 that "the legislature shall, as soon as conveniently may be, provide for the establishment of schools throughout the State, . . . that the poor may be taught gratis."

Unhappily for Gallatin's hopes, Pennsylvania had a deeply ingrained tradition that primary and secondary education was a concern primarily for the family and church. Nearly all children received primary schooling of some sort from clergymen who taught a few "scholars" during the week or from ambitious young men waiting to get a start in some more remunerative profession like the law. "The bulk of the schoolmasters," Gallatin observed, were "incompetent, miserably paid, and held in no consideration."

In 1791 Gallatin presented to the Assembly a plan calling for the grant to each county of funds to construct a school building, start a library, and pay part of the teachers' salary, contingent upon the county's providing similar funds. In 1792 and in 1794 he sponsored such legislation, once even proposing that the state assist deserving children of poor parents who wished to continue their education at either of Pennsylvania's colleges. The first year, his plan did not get out of committee; the second, the House allowed it to die after lengthy debate; and the third, it was passed by the House but expired in the Senate.

Years later Gallatin laid these failures to the combination of Quaker and German groups in the state, which, he said, "at that time" was opposed "to every general plan of education." Not until 1834 did Pennsylvania pass its first law for a system of real public education, a system resembling that which Gallatin had proposed.[46]

5

One problem that troubled the Assembly throughout Gallatin's membership and was to affect the course of his career, was the election of a successor to the acerbate William Maclay when his term as United States senator expired in March, 1791.

Every state except Pennsylvania was electing senators by a joint vote of the legislature—both houses sitting together and voting as a unit. But the state senators from eastern Pennsylvania, who were Federalists, perceived in the silence of the state constitution on the subject an opportunity to increase the power of their house, their party, and their section. They insisted that Maclay's successor be elected by concurrent vote—the two houses sitting and voting separately.

In the frequent and protracted efforts of the lower house to break the deadlock, Gallatin played a characteristically important role. He spoke often, long, and cogently, decrying the fact that just six men in the state senate were depriving Pennsylvania of half of its representation in the United States Senate. He served on innumerable house committees to confer with innumerable senate committees on the matter. Finally, after Pennsylvania had had only one United States senator for nearly two years, the state senate capitulated in February 1793, agreeing to a joint vote.[47]

When the Antifederalists held a caucus to determine whom they should support in the balloting, Gallatin's name was at once proposed. He jumped to his feet to deny any desire for the office. He protested that other men were far more deserving and expressed doubt whether he had been a citizen of Pennsylvania long enough to qualify. After the meeting his friends urged him to reconsider, assuring him that he was the only "person of truly Republican principles" who had a chance of election. This argument and a careful rereading of the federal Constitution caused him to change his mind. He had been a citizen of the United States for nine years, he was convinced, and therefore eligible for the seat. Accordingly, when his name was presented at a second caucus a few days later, he accepted the nomination, which was extended by an almost unanimous vote.[48]

The election was held in the Senate chamber at high noon of February 28. Four men were placed in nomination, Gallatin himself proposing the name of General William Irvine; but the real contest was between Gallatin and the Federalist candidate, Henry Miller of York County. Gallatin secured forty-five votes in the voice poll; Miller received thirty-five; Irvine and General Arthur St. Clair, one each. The vote did not follow party or sectional lines strictly, although the bulk of Gallatin's support came from Antifederalists and the central and western counties.[49]

The result, as Gallatin observed, "exceedingly mortified" the extreme Federalists. Several of his supporters told him Federalist partisans had threatened them in the streets and taverns of Philadelphia before and after the election. A bit of doggerel in the party newspaper, *Gazette of the United States*, insinuated that a group of "intriguers," through improper though legal means, had forced an alien upon Pennsylvania as one of its federal senators.[50]

But Gallatin, a modest man of clear perspective, sized up the situation accurately when he wrote: "It was my constant assiduity to business and the assistance derived from it by many members which enabled the party in the Legislature, then a minority, . . . to elect me, and no other but me of that party, Senator of the United States." [51] The Federalist Jacob Hiltzheimer of Philadelphia expressed the feeling of the majority of the assemblymen when he confided to his diary: "The next House will miss him very much." [52]

5. Benedict and Senator

1793=1794

When Gallatin arrived at Major Boyd's Philadelphia boarding house for the Assembly session early in December, 1792, he found a letter from Catherine Pictet that bore disturbing news: his grandfather and an aunt had died, his grandmother had lapsed into senility.[1]

His first reaction was to return to Geneva the next summer. Although he would be able to do very little to help his grandmother, at least he might obtain the small inheritance he expected from his grandfather's estate. He was little tempted to tarry there long. The wave of the French Revolution had washed over Geneva, leaving the city-state with a more democratic government; but he feared that lingering prejudice against him as member of an old aristocratic family would make a public career there quite out of the question.

The temptation to visit Europe was snuffed out by his election to the United States Senate in February. Despite lingering doubts about his eligibility for the seat, he felt honor-bound to his supporters to remain and make a fight for it.[2]

Then an event in the spring of 1793 tied Gallatin irrevocably to the United States in both heart and mind. On the adjournment of the Assembly in April, duties on a legislative committee charged with investigating the accounts of the state comptroller general compelled him to remain in Philadelphia. The long days and nights of close application wearied him so visibly that Secretary and Mrs. A. J. Dallas took pity on the lonely widower and invited him to join them on a pleasure trip to Albany, New York.

They left Philadelphia by stage wagon in June, pausing in New Jersey to view that vista of natural beauty, the falls of the Passaic River. While at New York they were entertained in the home of James Nicholson, a local political leader, and Mrs. Dallas invited Hannah Nicholson, his second daughter, with several other young ladies, to share in the boat ride up the Hudson River to Albany and the falls of the Mohawk. As the trip progressed, the susceptible Gallatin found his springtime fancy

52

turning not too lightly to Miss Nicholson. She was twenty-seven years old and certainly no beauty; but Gallatin found her gentle, unaffected, and warm-hearted. After he was back in Philadelphia, she continued to monopolize his thoughts. Impulsively he returned to New York, determined to see more of her.[3]

Hannah Nicholson, the second love of Gallatin's life, was no boarding-house keeper's daughter. Her father's family, of British extraction, had settled in Maryland early in the eighteenth century. They were a naval clan, eighteen Nicholsons having served their country aboardship. James Nicholson himself had gone to sea as a youth, and during the Revolutionary War had commanded three vessels that made notable records. A resolution passed by Congress in 1776 had placed his name first among the twenty-four captains in the American naval service, giving friends an excuse for referring to him as the "Commodore."

When Gallatin first enjoyed his hospitality in New York, Commodore Nicholson, a testy gentleman of fifty-six, having made a comfortable marriage, was retired from the Navy and living in a fine house on William Street. He could be counted on to grace and dignify public occasions in the city. Many New Yorkers could still remember vividly the figure he had cut while commanding the decorated barge that transported President elect Washington from the New Jersey shore to Manhattan for his inauguration in 1789.

Frances, the Commodore's wife, was the only child of Thomas Witter, a prosperous merchant in New York born in Bermuda. Besides Hannah, the Nicholsons had five living children, four daughters and a son. Two of the girls were already married: Catherine, the wife of Colonel William Few, who was just retiring as first United States senator from Georgia; and Frances, the wife of Joshua Seney, congressman from Maryland.[4]

It was no accident that two of Hannah's sisters had acquired politician husbands, for the Nicholson home had long been a gathering place for the politically inclined. As a leader in the Antifederalist forces in New York City, the Commodore was on intimate terms with Aaron Burr, the Livingstons, and the Clintons. Thomas Paine had enjoyed the Nicholsons' hospitality on a number of occasions.*

Nurtured in such an environment, Hannah naturally had a keen interest in politics with a Democratic-Republican slant. This side of her character especially appealed to Gallatin, who wrote to a friend that her person was "far less attractive than either her mind or her heart. . . . Her

* In the Gallatin Papers is a note from Paine to Hannah Nicholson, probably written in 1786, which reads: "You Miss Hannah if you don't come home I'll come and fetch you. T. Paine."

understanding is good, she is as well informed as most young ladies . . .
and she is a pretty good democrat (and so, by the bye, are all her relations)." [5]

Again in Philadelphia, Gallatin took pen in hand late in July to com-
pose a careful and respectful letter to the Commodore and his lady.
Thanking them for their hospitality, he observed that "it must have been
impossible for you to mistake either the object of my late journey to
your city and of my behaviour whilst there. . . . I love Miss Nicholson
and wish no greater happiness then to be forever united to her." He was
"not vain enough to suppose that I have made an impression equal to
what I feel myself, yet I have reason . . . to hope that she may, after
some time, be persuaded, to grant me her hand. . . . Your's and Mrs.
Nicholson's consent therefore I beg leave to apply for." He anticipated
natural objections—his "want of personal fortune, which puts it out of
my power to support a family independent of my personal industry, and
the distance at which I live"—but hoped that Hannah might induce them
to overlook these.[6]

Gallatin mailed his letter on July 20. After four days of anxious waiting, he had an answer, composed with equal care.* Commodore Nicholson acknowledged that, despite the short period of their acquaintance,
"our prepossessions are strong in your favor, nor does it appear that we
have the least right to make any objections to your intention of endeav-
oring to gain our child's hand, for which purpose you have our consent."
He assured Gallatin that his "want of fortune" was "no objection. . . .
Character, disposition, and industry are the essentials, and we greatly
flatter ourselves that those essentials are combined in you." He pointed
out that Hannah would bring no great fortune, either. Upon her mother's
death she was to share equally with her brother and sisters the estate of
her Grandfather Witter—but what that would amount to, no one knew.
"So until the death of her mother," Commodore Nicholson concluded
gravely, "her maintenance must depend solely upon you. These reflections
we flatter ourselves will have their full weight upon you both." [7]

Delighted, Gallatin hastened to New York to seal the betrothal. In the
course of their discussions, the engaged couple could perceive only one
possible source of friction: Hannah was a "city belle." She had been
born and bred in New York and, as a child, had become familiar with
the polished society of Philadelphia and Maryland. The conditions she
would encounter on a Fayette County farm were completely alien; but, as
Gallatin put it, "we concluded that we would be happier united than

* Among the Gallatin Papers is the rough draft of this letter that gives evidence
of "the Commodore" having labored hard on it.

separated." Hannah was willing to try country living, and Albert's career as a United States senator would give her a leavening of city life.[8]

When Hannah accepted his proposal, it was agreed that the wedding should not take place until the following winter. Albert accordingly returned to Philadelphia to prepare for the August Assembly session. Back at Major Boyd's, his thoughts reverted constantly to his betrothed ninety miles away; and he shared them with her through letters every few days.

Reflecting upon the married state that he was soon to enter, Albert wrote that he thought it—and she—would be most beneficial to him. Socially, he realized, he was still a child. He had just come out of college when he left Geneva, "and the greatest part of the time I spent in America has been very far from society . . . Thence, although I feel no embarrassment with men, I never yet was able to divest myself of that anti-Chesterfieldian awkwardness in mixed companies which will forever prevent a man from becoming a party in the society in which he mixes. It is true the last four years, on account of my residence in Philadelphia, I might have improved, but I felt no wish of doing it. . . . You must polish my manners, teach me how to talk to people I do not know and how to render myself agreeable to strangers." [9]

Then an unforeseen combination of events changed their plans. Late in August an epidemic of yellow fever crept up from the waterfront into the finest homes of Philadelphia. By the time the Assembly convened, more than forty deaths had been reported, and the plague was still spreading. The legislators understandably lost interest in the financial misfeasance of the comptroller general, which was to have been the chief topic of deliberation, and adjourned on September 6.[10]

Delighted at the chance to be near his Hannah, Gallatin left for New York the next day. He expected to pass a week in daily calls on his fiancée, then go west to Fayette until the Senate convened in December. But in Hannah's company he lost all sense of time. The week became, before he realized it, three weeks. His feeble desire to get back to business was stifled by the tales of pestilential death borne by every post rider from Philadelphia.

He was about to leave at last when he suddenly fell ill of headache and fever: the very symptoms first complained of by victims of yellow fever. As the Nicholsons pointed out, there was a real danger that anyone so recently arrived from Philadelphia, on exhibiting such symptoms, might be clapped into an uncomfortable hospital on one of the islands in New York harbor. At the insistence of the Commodore, Gallatin was moved from his lodgings to the Nicholson residence, to be nursed by Hannah and her family. By the time he was recovered, a return to

Fayette before the opening of Congress was out of the question. "Being under one roof," as Gallatin explained it, he and Hannah decided to be married without delay. The wedding took place at the Dutch Reformed Church on November 11, 1793.[11]

Albert remained at the Nicholsons' until the end of November, and by that time Philadelphia was out of the toils of the epidemic. He arrived alone to take his seat in the United States Senate just a few hours before that body convened on December 2, 1793.[12]

2

When Gallatin moved onto the national political scene the affairs of the federal government had reached a critical juncture. The far-reaching program that Secretary of the Treasury Hamilton had designed to enhance the authority and prestige of the new government was already well under way. At his suggestion, Congress had chartered a Bank of the United States, had established a national mint, had levied a tariff designed to assist American industries—and, as we have seen, had assumed the Revolutionary War debts of the states as well as of the Continental Congress, and had imposed an excise on distilled liquor. Although this legislation delighted merchants and men of property—the Federalists—it outraged small tradesmen, mechanics, and farmers, who were beginning to coalesce into the first opposition party under the federal government: a party that was the residuary legatee of the spirit and some of the party organization of the old Antifederalists. These dissidents began to look for leadership to Hamilton's colleague in the cabinet, Secretary of State Thomas Jefferson.[13]

Virtually every act in Gallatin's six years of public life identified him with these Jeffersonians. His participation in the Harrisburg meeting, his criticisms of Hamilton's financial measures from the floor of the Assembly, his cooperation with Dallas and Dr. Hutchinson in the 1792 election, his affiliation through marriage with the Nicholsons—all marked him as an opponent of the Federalists.

On foreign affairs, Gallatin's attitude was more ambivalent. The federal government had been barely established before it was sorely tried by a quick succession of momentous events in Europe. In September, 1792, a republic was established in France that proclaimed the triple ideals of liberty, equality, and fraternity. In January, 1793, the republic guillotined Louis XVI. The next month Great Britain joined the monarchs of Europe in a crusade to stamp out democracy and republicanism in France. Over these developments Americans were sharply divided. Some—particularly the farmers and mechanics—were pleased and inspired by what the French had done; others—including many devoted to Secretary Hamilton's program—were shocked by the "excesses" of the French. Secretary Jefferson summed up the situation nicely in the spring of 1793 when he declared that the war between France and the coalition of monarchs "has brought forward the Republicans and Monocrats in every state so openly, that their relative numbers are perfectly visible." [14]

Even as Jefferson spoke, the chasm was further widened by the arrival in the United States of "Citizen" Edmond Charles Edouard Genêt, the dashing young minister of the French Republic. Gallatin's friends, Dallas and Dr. Hutchinson, used the local welcome to Genêt as an occasion to form the Democratic Society of Philadelphia, one purpose of which was to create from the sympathy with the French a permanent political organization. Similar groups sprang up in other centers throughout the land,[15] and soon these opponents of Hamilton and the Federalists were calling themselves "Democratic-Republicans."

While Citizen Genêt toured the eastern cities amid floods of rum and torrents of oratory during April and May, 1793, Gallatin shared the general enthusiasm for the minister and his government. He thought the French "certainly the only real allies" the United States had, their cause "that of mankind against the tyrants." Yet he could not stomach the excesses of the revolutionary leaders, many of whom were "greedy for power themselves and not for the liberty of the nation." [16] "I must confess," he wrote at the time, "my soul is not enough steeled not sometimes to shrink at the dreadful executions which have restored at least apparent tranquillity to that republic"; but, as long as Great Britain, Spain, and the other "despots" allied against France continued to "press upon every frontier and employ every intrigue to destroy and distress the interior parts, I think that they and they alone are responsible for every act of severity and injustice, for every excess, nay for every crime for which either of the contending parties in France have committed." [17] However, he approved when President Washington issued a proclamation of American neutrality in the European war.

The warm welcome accorded to Genêt so turned the Frenchman's head that he ignored the proclamation and supervised, at Philadelphia and other ports, the conversion into privateers of English vessels that had been captured by the French. He directed one privateer to put to sea despite a specific prohibition by Secretary Jefferson and talked of appealing directly to the American people over the head of "old Washington."

His conduct thoroughly disillusioned Gallatin, who wrote to Hannah

that the young minister's abilities were "but slender. He is not endowed
with that prudence and command of his temper which might have
enabled him to change the opinion of our Executive in those points
when they may be wrong. . . . Violent and conceited, he has hurted
[*sic*] the cause of his country here more than all her enemies could
have done. . . . He is totally unfit for the place he fills."

Late in 1793 President Washington asked the National Convention to
recall its indiscreet envoy. Gallatin thought the request wise, but was
relieved when the French acceded without a quibble.[18] Meanwhile, the
bearing of the European war upon American interests on the high seas
and on the western and southern frontiers disturbed him. For a time
American shippers prospered handsomely as neutrals. Then the British government adopted policies which seriously threatened the carrying trade. It
declared that any French colonial produce or non-American neutral goods
would be considered as lawful prize, and it reasserted a long-claimed
"right" to impress British seamen serving on American vessels. Another
menace to the carrying trade was the Dey of Algiers, who took crews of
American merchantmen for ransom. On land, British agents were reported to be stirring up the Indians in the country northwest of the
Ohio, and Britain's ally, Spain, was suspected of encouraging the Indian
attacks on American settlers in Kentucky and Tennessee.

Gallatin wrote to his wife: "The situation of America . . . is the most
critical she has experienced since the war that secured her independence.
. . . Our own weakness renders it equally difficult to bear so many insults and to save the dignity of the nation. I guess the first step must
be to establish some kind of naval force, but I have as yet formed
no fixed opinion of my own."

In the crisis, he regretted the tendency of the Federalists blindly to
espouse the British cause, of his own Democratic-Republican friends to
take the side of France. "I trust that our parties . . . will as far as
possible forget old animosities, and show at least to the foreign powers
who hate us that we will be unanimous whenever the protection and
defence of our country require it. None but such as are completely
blinded by self-interest or their own passions, and such as wish us to be
only an appendage of some foreign power, can try to increase our weakness by dividing it. I hope that public measures will show firmness
tempered with moderation."

He summed up his position succinctly when complimenting Hannah on
some opinions she had expressed in a letter to him. "I am happy to see
that you are a tolerable democrat," he told her, "and, at the same time,
a moderate one." [19]

3

In Gallatin the die-hard Federalists recognized an opponent whose exceptional qualities of leadership might imperil their legislative and administrative program; and they undertook to prevent him from serving in the United States Senate.

They made careful plans and executed them dextrously, showing their hand first at the opening of the Congress on December 2, 1793. A few minutes after Gallatin took the oath of office Vice President John Adams, presiding over the Senate, read the petition of nineteen residents of York, Pennsylvania, protesting his election on the ground that he had not fulfilled the constitutional requirement of nine years' citizenship. Adams tabled the paper and proceeded to other business. Later that day Robert Morris, senior senator from Pennsylvania and a Federalist, told Gallatin that an assemblyman from York County had asked him to present the petition to the Senate, but he had declined: he intended to be "perfectly neutral" in the matter.[20]

Nine days later Adams removed the petition from the table and referred it to a committee headed by John Rutherfurd of New Jersey and otherwise composed of four New Englanders, all stanch Federalists. This committee seemed to Gallatin to be "undoubtedly the worst that could have been chosen"; despairing of a favorable report, he hoped that the decision would at least be swift.[21]

The committee lingered over its report, while Gallatin grew more and more despondent over his separation from his bride. He went to New York for Christmas and brought Hannah back to Philadelphia to enjoy the hospitality of the A. J. Dallases at their commodious residence. He was just in time to hear the report of the Rutherfurd committee, rendered on the last day of 1793: at the time he was elected senator he "had not been nine years a citizen of the United States, as is required by the Constitution." [22]

Until the Senate voted approval of the report, however, Gallatin was free to continue in his seat. He lost no time in using his uncertain membership to lead an attack on the fiscal policies of the Administration. The Treasury Department in the four years since it was established had never submitted to Congress any precise report on the financial condition of the government. Just a year earlier Congressman William Branch Giles, with the encouragement of his fellow Virginians Secretary Jefferson and Congressman Madison, had undertaken to obtain such information, stating that Congress ought not to legislate and "engage in the most important fiscal arrangements . . . without competent official knowledge of the state of the Treasury." He even made an attempt to force Secretary of the Treasury Hamilton to resign. But the House of Representatives backed the Secretary and permitted him blithely to continue his operations without an accounting.[23]

Gallatin, with his Genevan heritage and his experience in fiscal matters in the Pennsylvania legislature, was outraged by the Secretary's practices. On January 3, 1794, when he had been a member of the Senate just a month, a motion was introduced requesting Hamilton to submit detailed statements about exports, imports, and the tonnage of vessels entering and leaving the United States between July 1, 1792, and July 1, 1793. The sketchy journals of the Senate do not note who sponsored the resolution, but it seems most probable that it was Gallatin.[24]

The journals definitely state that Senator Gallatin five days later submitted a resolution calling upon Secretary Hamilton to furnish detailed information of four types: first, a statement of the domestic debt as of January 1, 1794; second, a statement of the domestic debt that had been redeemed up to that date; third, a statement of the foreign debt as of that date, with accounts as to how each of the loans obtained abroad had been applied; and fourth, a summary of the actual receipts and expenditures of the federal government for each year since the commencement of operations in 1789. The Senate passed both resolutions with slight modifications.[25]

These searching demands nettled Secretary Hamilton, and he did not attempt to conceal his irritation in a letter to the President of the Senate on February 6. Shortage of clerical help made it impossible to furnish some of the information requested; to hire clerks to provide such data would put the government to an expense of $850 to $900! He asked Congress to specify what periodical reports it desired, so that the Treasury "could be prepared systematically to furnish it, without any derangement of the current course of its operations and without an unnecessary increase of expence." [26] A fortnight later, Hamilton complained in another letter to the Senate that operations of his department had "been interrupted in their due course by unexpected, desultory, and distressing calls for lengthy and complicated statements." He added self-righteously that "the consciousness of devoting myself to the public service to the utmost of my faculties and the injury of my health is a tranquillizing consolation of which I cannot be deprived by any supposition to the contrary." [27]

Meanwhile, the Senate continued its inquiry into Gallatin's right to a seat. After several days' debate on the report of the Rutherfurd committee, it voted on January 13 to refer the question to a new committee, which would consider any evidence Gallatin himself cared to present. The new committee was more representative of the Senate membership than the first: four of the Federalists served again, but were joined by three Democratic-Republicans.[28]

During the next few weeks the committee questioned seven witnesses summoned at the suggestion of the Pennsylvania petitioners. Their testimony did little to illuminate the case: Gallatin had been born in Geneva, had served as an instructor at Harvard a dozen years before, had been heard to express doubt about his eligibility for the senatorship at a Democratic-Republican caucus—although he and his supporters had subsequently become convinced of his right to serve. Appearing in his own behalf, Gallatin declared that he did not believe that the charges made against him were sufficient to deprive him of his seat. Until the Senate decided that they were, he did not wish to go to "the trouble and expence of collecting evidence at a great distance." He did provide a statement of the chief events of his life, particularly detailed for the years he had been in the United States.

By February 20 the committee had its report ready for the Senate: The data offered by the petitioners made it appear that Gallatin had been an alien at least until 1780; his reasons for not presenting evidence were "insufficient"; therefore, "it is now incumbent on Mr. Gallatin to show that he has become a citizen of the United States and when." [29]

Now the matter came directly before the Senate for consideration. That body devoted most of seven days to debate on the case. Although it was the practice to exclude the public from its deliberations, an exception was made, with the result that the tiny gallery of the chamber was crowded daily.[30]

The petitioners' side was presented by William Lewis, the Quaker Federalist, who effectively demonstrated his gift for sarcastic, sonorous oratory. His chief tactic was to place the burden of proof squarely on Gallatin, insisting that he show he had been a citizen of Massachusetts or Virginia or some other state at least nine years before his election as senator. He pointed out that, in order to become a citizen under Virginia law, an alien was required, in part, to take two oaths in a court and be a resident for two years; but the evidence before the Senate indicated that Gallatin had taken only one oath in Virginia—before a magistrate, and not in a court—and had resided in the state only two months. Lewis closed with an appeal to nativistic prejudice, "One of the ancient Republics made it death for an alien to intermeddle in their politics," and the warning that a loose interpretation of the requirements for citizenship would endanger our own republic.[31]

The last argument greatly disturbed Gallatin, as he told the Senate when he made his own defense.* If upheld, this doctrine would not only deprive him of his seat, but cast doubt on his citizenship and that of thousands of other immigrants. "Even slaves," he retorted, "have been enfranchised by the great Republics in time of common danger. The policy of America should be to make citizenship as easy as possible, for the encouragement of population." He reminded the senators that one of the chief complaints made by the Declaration of Independence against King George III was that he had tried to arrest the growth of population by obstructing the naturalization of foreigners.

Gallatin's chief argument rested on the confused status of citizenship of every American born before 1776. During the colonial period, he pointed out, every American owed allegiance to the British king; with the Declaration of Independence, "the inhabitants of the States became naturally citizens of every State reciprocally, and they continued so until such time as the States made laws of their own afterwards respecting naturalization." Moreover, the Articles of Confederation in 1781 provided that the free inhabitants—he repeated the phrase, because it was important to his argument—were to have "all the privileges and immunities of free citizens in the several States." He had been an inhabitant of the United States continuously since 1780, and so had been an American citizen for the past thirteen years. He dwelt at length on his service as a "volunteer" under the command of Colonel John Allan during the Revolution. "The great laws of reason and nature," he maintained, provided that "every man who took an active part in the American Revolution was a citizen." [32]

Gallatin realized even before the argument was finished that the Senate would make its decision not on the merits of the case but purely on party considerations. As he told Hannah, the Federalists were "moving heaven and earth" to preserve their slender majority. It was quite possible that the vote would be a tie. Vice President Adams, a Federalist whose principles sometimes led him to see beyond party considerations, promised the Democratic-Republican leaders that if that happened, he would break the deadlock in favor of Gallatin. For this reason Gallatin and his friends kept up their hopes to the end.

* The Gallatin Papers contain notes prepared by Gallatin's able lawyer friend A. J. Dallas to assist him in his defense. They are marked in Gallatin's handwriting: "Too technical, and the retrospective argument unsound; I took a different and stronger view of the subject." However, a comparison of the notes with Gallatin's defense as reported in the *Annals of Congress* shows that on most points he followed the same line of argument.

At the last moment, Benjamin Hawkins of North Carolina, on whose vote the Democratic-Republicans were counting, left Philadelphia. The Federalist Morris, realizing that in all probability the decision would now depend upon his vote, rose in his seat just before the poll was taken on February 28 to apologize that he would have to break his promise to be "strictly neutral," adding that he could not conscientiously vote for Gallatin. Without these two votes, Gallatin's cause was lost. The poll, along strictly party lines, was fourteen to twelve against him.[33]

The result must have been a relief to Secretary Hamilton. He never had to supply the Senate with the data about which Gallatin had been so troublesome.

4

While his fate was being debated in the Senate, Gallatin and his bride, in the privacy of their bedchamber at the Dallases', debated what they should do if the verdict went against him. He still wondered whether his farm would provide a living suitable for a wife fond of society. Dallas and other friends assured him that he would make a successful lawyer, but he feared that he was too old to embark upon a profession so totally new. Several party colleagues urged him to stand for reelection to the Assembly in October; but he was not certain that he wanted to stay in politics.[34]

Finally they decided to go west late in the spring and try to eke out a livelihood by farming their Fayette acres. First, however, Gallatin undertook to raise cash by selling his western land. The market was sluggish, and the best offer he could get was from Robert Morris: £4,000 Pennsylvania currency, payable in installments, for some of his holdings. However, he optimistically assured Hannah, Fayette County property was "gradually increasing in value," and "should in future any circumstances induce us to change our place of abode, we may always sell to advantage" the Friendship Hill site.[35]

Gallatin had good reason for pondering the hazards of taking a city-bred bride to live on a frontier farm. Since his fateful excursion to Albany in the spring he had been receiving querulous letters from Badollet, who had Anglicized his first name to John and was now married and living near Friendship Hill. Badollet expressed "woman-like curiosity" about what detained him in the East and was delighted to learn that he had remarried: "If you can only bring a kind consort . . . we can lay the plan of a solid happiness" in the West. During the winter Badollet, lonesome for the society of what he called "congenial hearts," used "business" as a pretext for journeying to Philadelphia to get a glimpse of the newlyweds. Albert and Hannah were with the Dallases, and their hosts extended their hospitality to Badollet. None the less, the meeting between the old friends was a bit strained. In Hannah's presence, Badollet felt awkward, shy, and uncouth. He could not help reflecting how far superior "in point of education and information" Hannah was to his own Peggy, whom he had left at home with the children. Still, he was "perfectly satisfied and confident that I have the wife that suits me best." [36]

The introspective Badollet made his comparison of the two women in a letter to his old schoolmate upon his return home. Gallatin hastened to reassure him: "You may rely upon it, Hannah's good nature is far superior to her sense and . . . she does not know . . . any other enjoyment than that of contributing to the happiness of every being that lives within her sphere. Of course I am sure that she will increase the ties that unite us and do everything in her power to be beloved by my friends. . . . She already knows and likes you." [37]

In this spirit Albert and Hannah set out in a light wagon on the arduous journey to Georges Creek in June, 1794. He may have sensed difficulties ahead for himself and his city belle, but the trouble that lay immediately in his path was of a kind that he did not anticipate.

6. The Whiskey Rebellion: "My Only Political Sin"

1791=1794

The storm that broke soon after Gallatin brought Hannah home to the western Pennsylvania hills had been brewing a long time. The clouds had started to gather, as we have seen, in the winter of 1790–1791, when Secretary Hamilton induced Congress to levy a federal tax on distilled liquors despite a protest that Gallatin had led in the Pennsylvania Assembly.

During the summer recess of the legislature in 1791, which Gallatin passed on Georges Creek, he became aware that although the excise was now the law of the land many of his neighbors in the four counties west of the Alleghenies had no intention of submitting to it. The federal government had opened offices there and was sending a small army of officers—whose compensation was to be based on the taxes they collected —to roam the countryside, searching for and seizing unregistered stills, leaving behind a trail of paint, branding marks, and ill will. Another fact had become horribly plain to the westerners: the law provided that evaders were to be heard in federal courts, which meant that those apprehended would be taken nearly three hundred miles to the nearest court at Philadelphia, a great hardship for a small farmer who had to stick close to his plow for a living. Gradually the impression took hold that the federal administration was determined on nothing less than reducing American farmers to the economic and political level of European peasants.[1]

In July of this summer of murmurs and muttering a circular letter from Gallatin's old acquaintance of the Harrisburg meeting, James Marshel, now the register of Washington County, invited him and such others "as you may think proper" to attend a meeting of "respectable characters" from the western counties at Redstone Old Fort on July 27. The assemblage would "state to the people at large some general objections to the law and . . . propose some plan by which their sense on that subject may be fairly collected and stated" to the federal government. [2]

Here was a reasonable proposal that Gallatin, the conscientious representative, could not ignore. On July 27 he rode fifteen miles through the thick forests that edged the Monongahela to the tiny riverside settlement sometimes known as Redstone Old Fort and sometimes as Brownsville. Because it was the height of the farming season, nearly everyone who showed up was from the immediate neighborhood. John Smilie and William Findley, Gallatin's colleagues of the legislature, were very much in evidence, and so of course was Marshel. The venerable Edward Cook of Fayette, who was reputed to have been a "diehard Federalist," was chosen chairman, and Gallatin was prevailed upon to act as clerk.* Findley spoke at length, counseling moderation, and various courses of action were debated. [3]

A resolution was passed that declared the excise to be "unequal in its operation, immoral in its efforts, dangerous to liberty, and especially, oppressive and injurious to the inhabitants of the western country." Another resolution proposed that a series of meetings be held throughout the western counties, culminating in a grand meeting at Pittsburgh early in September to draw up an anti-excise remonstrance for presentation to Congress. Other counties in Pennsylvania and in the adjacent states were invited to work for "the common cause." [4]

As clerk of the meeting, Gallatin recorded the resolutions and carried them to the legislative session at Philadelphia late in August. The text was daily published in the *American Daily Advertiser* and other Philadelphia journals. Believing that Pennsylvanians ought to be consistent in their opposition to an excise, Gallatin during the next few weeks succeeded in getting the Assembly to wipe the state's dead-letter excise law from its statute books. [5]

All this was fair and reasonable. But late in September Gallatin heard that eleven men, professing to represent the four western counties, had assembled in the tree-lined village of Pittsburgh on the 7th and passed a group of petitions and resolutions pitched in a shrill tone. One address called for "cultivating the idea amongst ourselves, that excise offices ought not to be accepted. If . . . the people . . . refuse such commissions, the law cannot be carried into effect, and it will be the same as if it did not exist." At the back of this were Marshel and another firebrand named David Bradford, a young lawyer of Washington County. [6] Opposition took

---

* Gallatin's participation in this meeting has escaped the notice of most historians of the Whiskey Rebellion.

an even more violent form in the following winter. Three men were tarred and feathered for aiding the enforcement of the law, and a band of thirty men broke into the Washington office of the excise collector and ransacked it.[7]

If Gallatin disapproved of such doings, he kept his feelings to himself. On the following August 21 he met with twenty-two western politicos at the Pittsburgh inn of Joseph Tannehill to "deliberate on the most advisable means of obtaining redress." Once again he was clerk.[8] For two days the excise law was "freely debated," as his minutes phrased it.

A set of resolutions was "unanimously" adopted that were truly extraordinary. One, on excise officers, proclaimed that "in future we will consider them unworthy of our friendship; have no intercourse with them; withdraw from them any assistance . . . and upon all occasions treat them to the contempt they deserve." It recommended "to the people at large to follow the same line of conduct." In phraseology and in strident tone the resolutions bore a resemblance to those adopted the year before at protest meetings at Washington and Pittsburgh dominated by Bradford and Marshel; indeed, the touch of these ambitious incendiaries was clear. Inflammatory as they were, Gallatin and his colleagues acquiesced in their adoption.[9]

Gallatin made plain his own far more moderate views as a member of a committee the meeting appointed to draw up a remonstrance for presentation to Congress. This "respectfully" begged the federal legislature to repeal or modify the law because the excise was "unequal in its operation and immoral in its effects." It repeated in some detail Gallatin's explanation in the Assembly the year before of the geographic and economic conditions that obliged most western farmers to become distillers and to regard whiskey as their currency. The excise, according to the remonstrance, was immoral in effect because the duty a distiller had to pay depended upon the amount of liquor he acknowledged having made. Thus "a premium to prying and fraud" was offered "at the expense of the honest part of the community."

To Gallatin the excise seemed to threaten the liberty of Americans because enforcement would require increasing police powers almost indefinitely. Moreover, there was a real danger "that this excise will in degrees be extended to other articles of consumption, until everything we eat, drink, or wear" would be "subjected to heavy duties and the obnoxious inspection of a host of officers." He questioned whether the needs of the federal government actually warranted so "odious" and "dangerous" a duty. The Treasury Department had never stated precisely how much additional income it actually required, what percentage would be supplied by the excise, or whether the need could not be met "by other resources sufficiently productive and less obnoxious and oppressive." [10]

This remonstrance was perhaps the fullest, best informed, and fairest statement ever made of the westerners' case against the excise. Unhappily, it never reached Congress. For the Pittsburgh meeting had a far-reaching aftermath that probably no participant—certainly not Gallatin—anticipated.

Gallatin learned of this, painful bit by painful bit, during the next several months. First came a copy of the Philadelphia *General Advertiser* for September 1 with the full text of Bradford's and Marshel's fire-eating resolutions and an editorial by Benjamin Franklin Bache, grandson of the great Benjamin and a man usually friendly to critics of Secretary Hamilton, that called attention to the phrasing of the most extreme of the resolutions and demanded: "Is not every measure tending to obstruct the operation of a constitutional law passed by legal representatives blameable and illegal?"

Next Gallatin learned that President Washington and Secretary Hamilton had answered the question vigorously in the affirmative. At Hamilton's urging, Washington issued a proclamation on September 25, 1792, condemning the resolution as "violent and unwarrantable" and warning the "malcontents" to "desist from all unlawful combinations and proceedings whatsoever, having for an object or tending to obstruct the operations of the laws." The proclamation was signed by Secretary Jefferson, who took the view that the excise was not a particularly good law, but that repeal rather than resistance was the way to meet it.[11]

Then George Clymer, supervisor of the excise for Pennsylvania, was sent by Secretary Hamilton to investigate the situation. The pusillanimous Clymer seems to have conducted his inquiry from the security of a Pittsburgh tavern through conversations with local worthies. He made a disturbing but none too accurate report to the effect that nearly the entire west was disaffected. In Fayette County, the protests had been restrained more because of lack of occasion for violence than from good will. Clymer declared that Smilie and Gallatin were the chief troublemakers there.[12]

Early in October, Gallatin received a letter heavy with lamentation from Dr. Hutchinson, who, with Secretary Dallas, was busily lining up support throughout Pennsylvania for the Antifederalist congressional ticket. Until the account of the meeting was published in the Philadelphia newspaper "our opponents were prostrate. That has served for their resurrection." [13]

With such news, Gallatin anxiously set out for Philadelphia in the company of Smilie and Bradford to attend the December Assembly sessions. To his relief their eastern allies were as "kind," and even some of the Federalists were "as polite," as ever. Now he was in a position to consider the Pittsburgh meeting more objectively. He regretted the whole affair. He wrote to his western friends that the meeting had spoiled all chances of getting the excise repealed; indeed, "that law is now more popular than it was before our proceedings were known. To everybody I say what I think on the subject, to wit, that our resolutions were too violent and undoubtedly highly impolitic, but in my opinion contained nothing illegal." [14] He was inclined to be philosophical: "It is not perhaps a bad sign . . . in a free country that the laws should be so respected as to render even the appearance of an illegal opposition to a bad law obnoxious to the people at large." He advised the westerners not to offer any insult to a federal officer, "as nothing would be more hurtful to our cause, and indeed to the cause of liberty in general." [15]

Three years later, when the movement against the excise reached its climax, Gallatin cried peccavi for his part in the Pittsburgh meeting. It was, he wrote, "my only political sin." [16]

2

For more than a year and a half following the Pittsburgh meeting Gallatin was occupied in the East with Assembly duties, the fight for his Senate seat, his romance and nuptials. During the interval, as he later testified, he had not "the slightest conversation that I can recollect, much less any deliberate conference or correspondence, either directly or indirectly," with any westerner on the excise law.[17]

All had not been quiet in the western country while he was away. In Fayette County, according to Secretary Hamilton's report of August, 1794, the house of the excise collector was attacked several times during 1793—although conditions were generally quiet that year. Resistance stiffened in 1794: a number of outrages were reported, including the tar-and-feathering of a deputy collector.[18]

Congress recognized the validity of the westerners' objections to offenders being "dragged" all the way to Philadelphia for trial in a law enacted at Secretary Hamilton's suggestion in June, 1794. This permitted cases of infractions more than fifty miles from a federal district court to be tried in state courts. "A wish might perhaps be innocently indulged," Gallatin said later, "that the policy of this measure had under-

gone a fair experiment." He thought it possible that resistance would
have ebbed away.[19]

But less than a week before the law went into effect, the federal
district court at Philadelphia issued some sixty processes against western
distillers who had not registered their stills in June, 1793—a whole year
before. With Secretary Hamilton's approval, United States Marshal David
Lenox started west to serve the processes, issued under the old law and
cognizable only in Philadelphia.

Secretary Hamilton's political enemies interpreted this as a deliberate
attempt to provoke a "violent crisis," which would enable him to prove to
the body politic that the federal government needed a standing army to
enforce the law. Some surmised that he was bent upon discrediting the
chain of democratic societies that had sprung up from Vermont to
Georgia following Citizen Genêt's arrival and had become rallying points
for opposition to his Federalist program and in some instances centers
of resistance to the excise law. The Secretary later justified his action on
the ground that the government had "no choice but to try the efficiency
of the laws in prosecuting with vigor delinquents and defendants," that
it was only fair to those who had complied with the law that those who
had not should be prosecuted.[20]

If Secretary Hamilton was looking for a crisis, Lenox's progress through
western Pennsylvania produced it. In Fayette alone the marshal delivered
writs on thirty outraged but nonviolent distillers. After he was out of the
county, the angry recipients called a meeting at Uniontown in late July
to discuss what should be done.

An invitation reached Gallatin, who was spending the summer at
Friendship Hill with his bride. Anxious that his neighbors should make
clear that, while they opposed the excise, they favored law and order, he
rode over to the little county seat to exert his influence in behalf of
moderation.

Uniontown was buzzing with alarm over what had been happening in
the neighboring county of Allegheny. Lenox and an aide had been threatened with bodily harm while trying to serve their writs; federal soldiers
from the Pittsburgh garrison had killed one of a large band of angry
farmers laying siege to the estate of the marshal's aide. Egged on by those
hotheads Bradford and Marshel, the farmers attending the funeral of their
"martyred" colleague had called a meeting at Parkinson's Ferry to "take
action" on the excise question.[21]

In this charged atmosphere Gallatin and Congressman John Smilie
were exemplars of calm. They persuaded the twenty-two distillers who
turned up for the meeting, all of whom had been served with writs, to

submit peaceably to the law by engaging counsel and preparing to defend themselves in court. All agreed that they would forthwith either enter their stills with the excise collector or quit distilling; nineteen announced that they would do the latter. The call to the Parkinson's Ferry meeting was "reluctantly read" to the group, as Gallatin later said; but it was agreed that resistance to the law ought to be localized, and no serious thought was given to sending delegates.[22]

In the next few weeks all hopes of localizing the unrest were dashed. Bradford, it seemed, dreamed of himself as the George Washington of a new western republic. He and his cronies had a United States mail rider robbed so that they might obtain evidence that certain prominent Pittsburgh men disapproved of the anti-excise movement. Without any legal justification they issued a call for the militia of the western counties to meet at Braddock's Field near Pittsburgh. Between 1,500 and 2,000 men turned out. Bradford assumed the title of major general for the occasion and rode about haranguing the troops. The next day the militiamen rode wildly through Pittsburgh, shooting up the town.[23]

When Gallatin attended the regular militia meeting of his own county in August, he heard that Bradford and his volatile Washington County followers were bitter because Fayette was standing aloof. But all was not well even at home. He was shocked to see some of his neighbors perform the Revolutionary War ritual of raising a liberty pole. He told them that he wished they would stop behaving "like a mob." The protestants asked him darkly whether he had heard that a meeting in Westmoreland County had recently passed a resolution proclaiming "that if any one called the people a mob, he should be tarred and feathered." [24]

Gallatin became fearful that naked violence would break out in Fayette, "that we must be involved in the general flame." But when he discovered that several townships in the county had elected delegates to the Parkinson's Ferry meeting, he changed his mind and allowed himself to be named one of three delegates from his own Springhill Township.[25] As he subsequently testified, he felt that, because he did not hold public office, he might "be more useful than many men more able and equally upright" in serving as a moderating influence. Moreover, a lingering sense of shame for the part he had played at the Pittsburgh meeting two years earlier made him anxious to demonstrate that he was "not unwilling nor incapable" to perform his duty as a citizen.[26]

3

The meeting at the tiny settlement of Parkinson's Ferry on August 14 was held in an open field on the shoulder of a hill on the west bank of the turbid Monongahela. Gallatin must have had misgivings over the fact that it was in the heart of the disaffected area. His 225 fellow delegates had been chosen by any group of individuals who had taken it upon themselves to hold an election—and these were usually the more violent characters. Rebellious Washington furnished twice as many delegates as any other county, and also a crowd of spectators that outnumbered the delegates. Many of the onlookers had participated in the outbreaks of the last few months.[27]

Before the meeting formally convened, James Marshel, trying to line up support for a set of resolutions he had written, approached Gallatin and asked him to assume his role of secretary once more. Gallatin examined the resolutions. Seeing that they virtually called for revolution against the United States government, he bluntly stated that he "highly disapproved" of them; he had come to the meeting to oppose such reckless ideas, and he preferred not to act as secretary.[28]

At length the meeting was called to order, with the delegates seated in the center of the field on stumps, fallen trees, and the grass, ringed by a bank of demonstrative spectators. The names of Edward Cook and Gallatin, despite the objection of the latter, were proposed and accepted as chairman and secretary. As Gallatin slowly walked among the delegates, collecting their credentials, the gravity of the situation bore heavily upon him. The only hope of avoiding trouble was somehow to get the meeting dissolved before it could do anything rash.

For a time he was helpless. Bradford and Marshel held the reins firmly in their hands and drove toward their objectives. First Bradford delivered a long, demagogic speech, in which he proposed that the westerners raise an army to resist the forces of the United States.[29] Then Marshel read his resolutions,[30] one of which called for a "committee of public safety" reminiscent of those of the Revolutionary era, which would "call for the resources of the western country to repel any hostile attack that may be made against the rights of the citizens or of the body of the people." This resolution was noisily acclaimed by the gallery, but Gallatin was convinced that the majority of the delegates were not eager for the rebellion implied.

Here he saw his opportunity. Marshel's resolution referred to "hostile action" and "hostilities" from the federal government. "What reason,"

Gallatin demanded of the crowd, "have we to suppose that hostile attempts will be made against our rights? And why, therefore, prepare to resist them? Riots have taken place which may be the subject of judiciary cognizance; but we are not to suppose a military force upon the part of the government." He proposed that the resolution be referred to a committee, and that, in any case, no action be taken until it was learned just what the government proposed to do about the anti-excise agitation.

Gallatin was followed by Hugh Henry Brackenridge, a talented lawyer-littérateur from Pittsburgh. He announced that he heartily favored Marshel's resolution—but in "softened" terms. He seconded Gallatin's proposal that the resolution be referred to a committee. Such double talk puzzled the forthright Gallatin; it was not until later that he learned that the timid, subtle lawyer was as much opposed to Marshel's proposal as he, but feared that a headlong attack on it would solidify the radicals' ranks. Marshel acceded to the idea that his resolution be rephrased by a committee. The meeting then voted that this be done.[31]

Now Gallatin challenged another of Marshel's resolutions—one that pledged the people of the West to support all federal laws except the excise and the removal of citizens from their own neighborhood for trial. These two exceptions ought to be expunged, he contended, so that no one could possibly doubt that the westerners favored the maintenance of law and order. He decried the destruction of property that had occurred, citing as an example the burning of a barn belonging to the officer of Fort Pitt. As Brackenridge later reported it, a "fiery fellow" shouted: "What! . . . Do you blame that?"

"The secretary," according to Brackenridge, "found himself embarrassed; he paused for a moment.

" 'If you had burned him in it,' he said, 'it might have been something; but the barn had done no harm.'

" 'Ay, ay,' said the man, 'that is right enough.'

"I admired the presence of mind of Gallatin," wrote Brackenridge, "and give the incident as proof of the delicacy necessary to manage the people on that occasion."

Gallatin's motion to modify this resolution was carried by a greater show of hands than any proposal at the meeting.

After prolonged debate, a committee was finally appointed to new-model Marshel's resolutions. On it with Gallatin, Brackenridge, and Bradford, was Harmon Husband, a barefooted, backwoods preacher whom Gallatin considered a bit crazy. Husband enjoyed expounding his theory that Ezekiel's interpretation of the temple in the Old Testament applied specifically to the western country. It was decided that the committee would meet the first thing in the morning.

Gallatin and the moderates passed a tense night, for many of the delegates and hangers-on, at farmhouses in the neighborhood, drank freely and talked of war and an independent nation of the West. The next morning they found that a liberty pole had been raised at the meeting ground, with a board defiantly proclaiming: "Liberty and No Excise—No Asylum for Traitors and Cowards!"

David Bradford was in an even more bellicose mood than the day before. He insisted, when the committee met, that an outright declaration of war against the United States must be inserted into the resolutions. Brackenridge undertook to distract him from his purpose, as he himself put it, through amusing him, "as a person would a boy, by playing with a bear." The "bear" was Harmon Husband, and he asked him to expatiate on his scriptural theories. At Brackenridge's chuckles over the preacher's response, Bradford irritably asked him to stop laughing and attend to business. Gallatin, who was mystified by the Pittsburgher's tactics, broke in bitingly, "He laughs all by himself!"

The committee discussed at length creation of a "committee of public safety"—or "standing committee"—to organize resistance to the federal government. Gallatin was obliged to agree to adding to the resolutions a sentence providing for this, with power, "in case of any sudden emergency, to take such temporary steps as they may think necessary"; but he saw to it that war preparations were not specified.

The resolutions that the committee presented for the approval of the delegates—and the gallery—later that day therefore differed little from Marshel's original version. But before a vote an intermission was called so that each township might choose two representatives for the standing committee.[32]

While this was taking place Congressman William Findley arrived at Parkinson's Ferry and placed in Gallatin's hands a proclamation signed by President Washington. This document, actually written by Secretary Hamilton, enumerated the "outrages" that had been committed in western Pennsylvania against the federal government and announced the intention of calling out the militia to put an end to "treasonable acts." The President had appointed three commissioners to visit the western country and facilitate the restoration of peace.[33]

Gallatin announced the breath-taking news at the end of the intermission. Anger froze the assemblage into silence. The President's reference to the militia and statement that the westerners were guilty of treason caused many, as Gallatin saw it, to conclude that they could only arm and resist. Marshel broke the silence by observing crisply that at least the proclamation had not killed anyone.[34]

Gallatin conceived that there were but two ways of quieting the western unrest: Through the commissioners, President Washington might extend a general amnesty to violators of the law. Or through repeal of the excise. Repeal was impossible until Congress should reconvene in December. In either case, moderates like himself must campaign throughout the West for compliance with the law. This was feasible because a meeting like the present one did not truly represent the sentiments of the western people.

For a general amnesty, the meeting would have to appoint a small committee to negotiate with the commissioners and report back to the standing committee. Brackenridge offered a motion to this effect, and Gallatin quickly seconded it.

A long and hot debate followed. Some followers of Bradford and Marshel urged that the federal commissioners be invited to come to Parkinson's Ferry and treat with the committee in the presence of the entire assemblage. Such a prospect alarmed Gallatin and other moderates—with the meeting in such an ugly mood, it was all too likely that the arrival of the commissioners would bring an outbreak of violence—and they used every argument for immediate adjournment.

Finally the wearied radicals gave up. A committee of fifteen including Gallatin was named to meet with the commissioners. The 2nd of September was set as the date, and Brownsville as the place, for the standing committee to hear the report on the negotiations. Thereupon the meeting adjourned.

Gallatin started home for a few days of rest, pleased that the moderate forces had won at least a temporary victory, apprehensive about the crucial battles that still lay ahead.[35]

7. The Whiskey Rebellion: "Allaying the Ferment"

1794=1795

Drenched by a torrential summer rain, Gallatin reached Pittsburgh on August 19, 1794, in good time for the scheduled meeting with the federal commissioners. He went around to pay a call on Hugh Henry Brackenridge for the first private conversation the two moderate leaders had ever had. The literary lawyer inquired whether Gallatin understood why he had acted as he had at Parkinson's Ferry. Gallatin said he believed that he now did, that Brackenridge had undertaken to accomplish "by art" what he himself had tried to do by "direct measures." Thereupon they had a heart-to-heart discussion of the problem they now faced, in Gallatin's phrase, "of allaying the ferment." [1]

By the next morning all fifteen committeemen had arrived in Pittsburgh and were ready to open their sessions at McMaster's tavern. They now discovered that they would have to deal not only with the federal commissioners, James Ross of Washington (who had been elected United States senator in Gallatin's place), Attorney General William Bradford, and Justice Jasper Yeates of the Pennsylvania Supreme Court, but with two state commissioners, Chief Justice Thomas McKean of the Pennsylvania Supreme Court and General William Irvine.

Gallatin and his colleagues held two meetings with the commissioners on August 20. They stressed the grievances of the westerners: trial at a distance from their homes; inability to pay the excise tax in currency; fear for their personal safety at the hands of an aggressive and perhaps vindictive federal government. The commissioners insisted that the westerners must offer assurances that they would submit to the excise law but, in return, promised an amnesty. The committeemen replied that they were not authorized to bind their neighbors to any course of action. They themselves believed that submission was the best policy, and they would recommend it to the men they represented; but they were unwilling to relinquish the right to work for repeal of the excise law.

For two days more the committeemen and the commissioners exchanged views—not through face-to-face negotiation but by letters. By August 23 every one of the committeemen, including the stubborn David Bradford, agreed that the reconvening of the standing committee, set for September 2 at Brownsville, should be moved up to August 28; that the committee of fifteen would urge members of the standing committee to vote assurances that they would submit to the law; and that the standing committee would arrange a meeting in each polling district "or other convenient place" so that the people of the western country might offer conclusive evidence that they would abide by the law. In return, the commissioners promised that federal military forces would not enter the area before September 1. As Gallatin and his colleagues recognized full well, the commissioners' terms were not generous. It would be difficult to persuade the fire-eating members of the standing committee to vote acceptance.[2]

During the next few days western Pennsylvania sizzled with rumor. It was reported that the committeemen planned to recommend submission to the government; that the federal commissioners had brought with them saddlebags bulging with gold to purchase the acquiescence of the committeemen. There was widening realization of the significance of the fact that President Washington, urged on as usual by Secretary Hamilton, had requested the governors of Pennsylvania, New Jersey, Maryland, and Virginia, to call out thirteen thousand militiamen and prepare them for a march into the West. Angry westerners again raised liberty poles in defiance.

Gallatin sensed the tension when he arrived at Brownsville on August 28.[3] In a field by the Monongahela a wooden structure had been hastily constructed to shield the fifty-seven members of the standing committee from sun and storm. Again, as at Parkinson's Ferry, the assemblage was ringed by a gallery of sixty to seventy men. Most of them bore rifles. But Gallatin gave no visible sign of his anxiety: Brackenridge, who was even more nervous than usual, testified later that the courage and self-confidence of his new friend helped brace him for the ordeal.

While participants and spectators were still taking their places, a letter from the federal commissioners to the committee of fifteen arrived. Dated Pittsburgh the day before, it authorized the committee to assure "Friends of Order who may be disposed to exert themselves to restore the authority of the laws" that the federal government would give them every protection in its power. At the same time, the government would take "every measure necessary to suppress and punish the violence of ill disposed individuals." The commissioners concluded with assurances that the militia would not march as long as negotiations were in progress.[4]

Gallatin and his colleagues realized that the message would only exacerbate the westerners, and they decided not to announce it. Instead, as soon as the assemblage was called to order—Edward Cook acting as chairman and Gallatin as secretary—printed copies of the committee report were distributed to the standing committee.[5] For the benefit of the gallery, Gallatin read the text aloud.

As it became evident that the rumors that had preceded the meeting were true, that the committee was recommending submission to the laws and the government, mutters of protest rolled across the assemblage. To fend off rash action, one of the moderate committeemen jumped up with a motion that the meeting be adjourned until the following day. David Bradford, the would-be Washington of the West, obviously to capitalize on the passion of the gallery, countered with the proposal that the recommendations be voted on at once. This was averted by James Edgar, a Presbyterian minister from Washington County, whose thin, ascetic face, prematurely gray hair, and devotion to fasting and prayer called to mind the Puritans of the Long Parliament. Complimenting Bradford on his strength of mind and his decisive character, he protested that "weaker-minded" men like himself would need a night to ponder the question. The minister's irony was successful; the motion to adjourn was carried.

The hours that followed were trying ones for Gallatin, as he thought of the bellicose assemblage and the spectators in the gallery impatiently fingering their rifles. He discussed the situation with his fellow committeemen. He acknowledged that it was indeed "delicate"; but he insisted that they were pledged to support the propositions of the commissioners and must stand foursquare behind that promise on the morrow. His resoluteness won over his colleagues—even the firebrand Bradford; but none of them was willing to take the platform in favor of submission. Finally he volunteered to speak first, with the understanding that Brackenridge would second his remarks.

Gallatin opened the next morning's session with an extemporaneous address that lasted several hours. "A piece of perfect eloquence," it seemed to Brackenridge. "A long, sensible, and eloquent address," thought Congressman William Findley, who was in the audience. Speaking slowly and deliberately but with vigor, Gallatin discussed every aspect of the excise question. He appealed anew to the patriotism of his listeners. He scotched an argument much used by the radicals that the cause of the westerners resembled that of the Revolutionary War patriots. The people of the western country had been represented in the body that enacted the excise, he pointed out, while the colonists had had no opportunity to vote against the British stamp tax. As fortune would have it, most of the riflemen had left Brownsville during the night. Gallatin's audience listened attentively and respectfully; even the extreme radicals were impressed.

Brackenridge followed, echoing "in his own language"—as one observer put it—"the cogent and powerful arguments first made use of by Mr. Gallatin, and adding ones of his own." Next came Mr. Edgar, speaking at length "with the solemnity of an evening sermon." * Bradford alone failed to make good on his promise to support the committee's report; he advocated resistance to the militia.

When Bradford finished speaking, Gallatin pressed for an immediate vote on the recommendations. There was no response. Next he called for a vote by ballot—not a formal answer to the commissioners, but one that would indicate what was truly in the minds of those present. Again there was listlessness. It began to look as if the recommendations were to be rejected simply through the failure of the meeting to take any action.

At this critical moment a member made an inspired suggestion. Suspecting that the hesitation of his fellows was caused by fear that their handwriting on the ballots might reveal how they had voted, he proposed that Gallatin, as secretary, write "Yea" and "Nay" on slips of paper and distribute them among the standing committee. Each member would tear his ballot into two pieces, drop the half with the word expressing his sentiments into the secretary's hat, and chew up the other half. The idea was approved. The ballots were cast with solemn secrecy.

Gallatin announced the result: thirty-four in favor of the committee's recommendations, twenty-three against. Subsequently six men declared that they had misunderstood the motion. Accordingly, the vote was registered as forty in favor and seventeen against the recommendations. The feelings of the committeemen were revealed by their facial expressions as the vote was announced: most were vastly relieved, a few jubi-

* Congressman Findley, in writing his book on the Whiskey Rebellion, regretted (pp. 124-127) that he was unable to procure copies of the addresses of the three advocates of submission: "They were delivered without any previous preparation other than a complete knowledge of the actual state of things, and of human nature when in similar circumstances. This knowledge, and the importance of the occasion on which it was exhibited, produced such ingenuity of reasoning and energy of expression as never perhaps had been exhibited by the same orators before." He remarked on "the oratory and information displayed in all the three," but especially on Gallatin's "long, sensible, and eloquent address."

lant. But among the remaining riflemen in the gallery there were evi-
dences of disgust. Bradford, sensing that the tide was running against
him, had departed for home during an intermission.

Danger to Gallatin and the moderate cause was not past. Several radicals charged that the committee of fifteen had not acted sincerely during the negotiations with the commissioners; they insisted that more
favorable terms might still be obtained. Gallatin and his colleagues denied the charge but consented readily to the appointment of new
representatives to try for more favorable terms.

The meeting then adjourned. A handful of die-hards of the gallery
continued to loiter about the meeting-place muttering. They talked
vaguely of waylaying Gallatin and Brackenridge after they left Brownsville; but, with the desertion of Bradford, they lacked resolution, and the
two moderate leaders reached their homes unmolested.

2

During the next fortnight Gallatin made frequent trips to Uniontown to
promote submission to the law by the people of Fayette. The representatives appointed just before the adjournment of the Brownsville meeting
failed to obtain any additional concessions from the federal commissioners; but they did obtain an agreement that every male citizen of the
four western counties who presented himself at his polling place on September 11 and signed a declaration that he would not in any way oppose
enforcement of the excise should receive a pardon for past offenses, if
any.[6]

Gallatin realized that the terms of this agreement were inadequately
circulated and little understood. Most of his neighbors acknowledged that
"submission was preferable to war," but many complained that they were
"pretty tightly drawn up." Many feared that signing the declaration
was tantamount to acknowledging that they had violated the law, that
they felt in need of a pardon. Some resented the lack of secrecy in the
procedure. Some wished it were possible to incorporate into the formalities a petition to Congress for repeal of the excise.[7]

To clear up misapprehensions, Gallatin drafted an address to the people
of Fayette, to be read to them as they gathered at the polling places. After
enumerating the westerners' grievances, he pointed out that the recent
concessions by the government had reduced the issue to a simple choice
between waging civil war and paying seven cents' tax on every gallon of
whiskey distilled. The people of the West were too few and too inade-

quately equipped to wage a successful war. Besides, he warned prophetically, "if ever the fatal lesson is taught the inhabitants of this extensive republic to shed another's blood, we may bid farewell to harmony, to mutual confidences, and to peace." To preserve the federal union, compromise and forbearance between the various sections and interests of the land were indispensable.[8]

Although the county committee to whom Gallatin presented the address on September 10 adopted it unanimously, it was too late to affect the referendum the next day. The returns were most disheartening. In Gallatin's own district, with 800 citizens eligible to vote, only 212 showed up. In Fayette as a whole, with 2,800 taxables, only 721 went to the polls, 560 voting for submission and 161 against.[9]

When the Fayette committee transmitted these returns to Governor Mifflin and President Washington on September 17, Gallatin sent along a reassuring letter to Mifflin, who was reported to sympathize with the opponents of the excise. "The present appearances," he wrote, "are as favorable as we have any right to expect. It was an effort too great perhaps to be expected of human nature that people should at once pass from an avowed intention of resisting to the signing of a test of absolute submission, and to a promise of giving active support to the laws." He emphasized the westerners' hope that the government would not send the militia into their country. An armed force might cause "a general and temporary acquiescence," but it would "embitter . . . and disgust every good citizen," creating the danger of new outrages the moment that the soldiers were withdrawn.[10]

Gallatin then retired to his mountain top and anxiously awaited news of the storm he had tried so hard to allay. It was indeed discouraging. The results of signing day in the other three western counties were even more dismal. Of a total of 11,000 taxables, only 2,700 had signed declarations of submission.[11] The federal commissioners returned to Philadelphia and told President Washington that military intervention would be necessary in enforcing the excise law.[12] The governors of the four states proceeded to call out their militias. From Lancaster, where Governor Mifflin and his staff stopped during a tour to raise forces, Secretary Dallas wrote to Gallatin acknowledging his plea that the militia not be sent: "With the President the whole business rests. As for my private opinion, permit me to state that I believe the exertions of the Government will be unremitting. The indignation of the citizens against the outrages of the western counties is equal to the provocation." [13]

Even more upsetting was a letter early in October from a western friend, Nathaniel Breading. This relayed a report he had just received from the capital that the militia would certainly come to the western country, with the President personally in command. "Your friends in Philadelphia wish you were there, being doubtful of your safety here," he went on. The Federalists were anxious for Gallatin's destruction because he had kept "so severe an Eye" on their financial practices and went "so far as to offer large Rewards for your Head. Now it is possible that they may encourage or even hire assassins for the purpose, supposing it may be done with impunity in the confusion." One man had told him of hearing a captain of the light horse who lived not far from Pottsgrove say "he would have [Gallatin's] head if he could get in reach of him." [14]

Such news troubled Gallatin all the more because Hannah, homesick for city comforts and upset by the excitement of her first summer in the West, complained of feeling poorly. He came to see merit in the idea of Philadelphia friends that he ought to be there. So, after casting his ballot at the regular legislative elections on October 14 [15]—he was unanimously elected for a fourth term in the Assembly—he packed up and started out with his wife for Philadelphia.

Their wagon was in the mountains of southwestern Pennsylvania on the way to the Cumberland Gap when they met a horseman distributing a broadside. This announced that delegates chosen by a second meeting at Parkinson's Ferry on October 2, which Gallatin had not attended, had been received by George Washington at the town of Carlisle, where the President assumed command of the troops preparing for the western march. The delegates would deliver a full report at another meeting at Parkinson's Ferry on October 24. This was encouraging. Gallatin decided that he must attend the meeting.

On the way back to Fayette they encountered another man who had truly astonishing news from Pittsburgh: In the October 14 election, the people of Washington and Allegheny counties had decisively chosen Gallatin as their representative in Congress! [16]

Leaving Hannah with friends in Uniontown, Gallatin hurried to the meeting. The moderates were in complete control. Mr. Edgar was named chairman, and Gallatin was once more secretary. But Congressman Findley and David Redick, the delegates who had seen President Washington, had gloomy tidings. The President had told them, in mild yet firm tones, that he still was not convinced that the excise law would be obeyed, and the militia would continue its march.[17] They also reported a fierce and vindictive spirit among the militiamen that was enough to cool the most hotheaded westerner. Under the circumstances, all that the meeting could do was to pass a fresh set of resolutions declaring that civil authority had been restored in the West.[18]

Gallatin returned to Uniontown, and he and his wife again started east. They passed several detachments of soldiers, but were disturbed only by rain, bad roads, and a cold that Gallatin caught. He took Hannah to New York, to recover at the family hearth from the rigors of a summer among "rebels." [19]

Meanwhile, the embers of the "insurrection" slowly flickered out. Before the army entered the western country, President Washington started back to Philadelphia, leaving Governor Henry Lee of Virginia nominally and Secretary Hamilton actually in charge. During the first two weeks of November Lee and Hamilton made an effort to round up suspects in the disaffected area. On November 17 the army was ordered to return east, except one detachment that remained in the area for the winter. By early December both federal and state governments were back to normal.[20]

3

For weeks Gallatin kept receiving from friends corroboration of Nathaniel Breading's charge that Secretary Hamilton and other Federalist leaders were determined to punish him for his part in the Whiskey Rebellion. Dallas, who had traveled with the army as part of Governor Mifflin's entourage, told him now of having seen Gallatin's name high on a list, drawn up by a Federalist general, of persons "who were to be destroyed at all events." [21] Several friends in Fayette and Washington counties wrote him that Federalist army officers had questioned westerners apparently for evidence that would implicate Gallatin as a leader of the uprising; but the effort had proved fruitless.[22]

Thomas Clare named names. William Ewen, he wrote, had been taken to Pittsburgh and questioned on four or five successive days, most lengthily by Secretary Hamilton himself. Hamilton "askt Mr. Ewen if he knew how much British gold you recd. and how much he recd. of you. . . . As far as I can understand there was never more industry made by any set of men than there was by sum that was hear to get holt of you." [23]

Later Gallatin heard that three Westmoreland County men had had similar experiences to Ewen's: Major John Powers and Justices William Jack and Abraham Baird of the county court had been haled before Secretary Hamilton at Washington and interrogated individually and at length. The Secretary appeared to be eager to obtain evidence of "treasonable" conduct by Gallatin, especially at the Parkinson's Ferry meetings. When the three men insisted that Gallatin had probably done more than any other person to restore order in the West and had acted decisively while others temporized, Hamilton dismissed them with the remark that he already had sufficient proof of Gallatin's guilt. And there were other reports that the Secretary desired to implicate William Findley and John Smilie.

What created this animus in Alexander Hamilton? Findley attributed it to "political party spleen," pointing out that both he and Smilie as congressmen and Gallatin as a senator had done their best to enhance the role of Congress in the formulation of federal financial policy.[24] The Secretary was doubtless incensed by Gallatin's criticisms of his stewardship of the Treasury, and opposition to the excise from the time it was first proposed to Congress. Moreover, Hamilton recognized Gallatin as an outstanding leader of a political party whose rapid growth imperiled the Federalists' control of the government.

The threat was all the more grave because, even as the militia marched into the West to repress "the rebellion," the people elected Gallatin to two important legislative seats. The uncontested reelection to the Assembly by the voters of Fayette was not unexpected;[25] but the election that took place on the same day in the counties of Washington and Allegheny was without precedent in American politics.

In this Congressional district, covering the westernmost sector of Pennsylvania from Lake Erie to the Virginia line, four residents had vied for the seat. On the excise question two were regarded as too Federalist; one, as too radical; another, as too temporizing. Just three days before election, John McMillan, a Presbyterian divine with much political influence, proposed to a meeting at Canonsburg that Gallatin be supported for the seat, even though he was not a resident of the district. Ballots bearing his name were hurriedly printed and distributed throughout the district, and we have already seen Gallatin's amazement at learning he had carried the poll by a comfortable margin.[26] Gallatin's election to two legislative seats on the same day bespoke the prevalent temper of the western country: every man elected to Congress and to the Assembly had been moderate or even pro-government during the "rebellion."

This fact made no difference to the Federalist leaders. Having failed to find evidence they needed for striking at Gallatin and his colleagues through the courts, they tried other devices. In mid-November President Washington, no believer in the desirability of a party of opposition, sent a message to Congress affirming that the western unrest had been fomented by the "self-created" democratic societies.[27] During December petitions and resolutions poured in on the Pennsylvania Assembly, urging that it declare the seats of all westerners vacant on the ground that the tramontane counties had been in a state of insurrection on Election Day.[28] Gallatin shared his friends' conviction that the agitation had been plotted by the ardently Federalist officer corps during the western march.[29] A shrewd observer, Congressman James Madison, believed that the purpose was to set a precedent for barring Gallatin later from his seat in Congress.[30]

This made Gallatin all the more determined to establish his right to his Assembly seat. Although the Assembly convened in December, he was not allowed into the chamber until the returns from Fayette arrived, on January 2, 1795. The following day, in a long speech he opposed the motion before the house to deprive him and his western colleagues of their places.[31] He developed two arguments with considerable ingenuity: the Assembly did not have constitutional power to determine the validity of the western elections; and the western counties had not been in a state of insurrection on Election Day, October 14. In support of the latter contention, he maintained that, although there had been riots in the western country, peace was completely restored after signing day, September 11.[32]

His arguments were to no avail. On January 9 the Assembly voted that the election of the westerners was "unconstitutional" and "void" and set a new election for February 4.[33]

Gallatin passed an anxious month in Philadelphia, writing to friends in the West to "reelect unanimously the same members whether they are your favourites or not." [34] His wish was fulfilled. Every westerner, except one state senator who declined to run again, was reelected. The returns arrived on February 14, and Gallatin reassumed his seat the same day.[35]

For a time the die-hard Federalists debated new ways to bar him from the legislature and to contest his right to the seat in Congress. Against such designs he staged an offensive defense by having his speech on the western elections printed in pamphlet form and distributed widely.[36]

Gallatin's service in the Assembly was now all but over. In late February he renewed his attempt to induce Pennsylvania to adopt a state-wide system of education; but the Assembly was no more receptive to the idea than before.[37] Meanwhile he was bothered by a severe cold and "a slow fever." He asked for a leave of absence on March 12, more than a month before the Assembly was ready to adjourn, and joined Hannah and his in-laws in New York, where he was soon as fit as a fiddle.[38]

Gallatin had not yet heard the last of the Whiskey Rebellion. In the spring of 1795 twenty westerners, who had been forced to march three hundred miles to Philadelphia and then lodged in jail for four months, at last came to trial for "insurrection." [39] Early in May he was summoned to Philadelphia to testify at the hearings of two of the eight men who had been indicted for treason, although he scarcely knew them. He wrote to Hannah that one of them, "a rough, ignorant German," was without doubt legally guilty, but was "certainly an object of pity more than of punishment." The jury convicted both of treason. Gallatin petitioned President Washington for mercy for the German. He was pleased when the President granted pardons to both men. Many of the true leaders of the anti-excise agitation, including David Bradford and James Marshel, had disappeared into the Ohio country and were never heard of again.[40]

Thus with a whimper ended the first armed rebellion against the authority of the federal government. The conflict tested not only the ability of the government to enforce its laws but Albert Gallatin's ability to represent, within the limits of the Constitution, the sentiments of constituents with a real grievance. In later years political partisans might refer disparagingly to Gallatin's role; but more objective citizens recognized that the government's triumph might have been far more difficult without the wisdom, the courage, and the moderation he displayed during the ordeal.

8. Freshman Congressman

1795=1797

On December 7, 1795, when Gallatin walked into the plain brick building on Independence Square in Philadelphia known as Congress Hall and took the oath of office as federal congressman, he came face to face with much that was challenging and new, and even more that was comfortably familiar. Only a few yards away was the chamber in which he had served briefly as United States senator; only a long stone's throw across the yard was the State House, scene of his triumphs as an assemblyman. Close by were the streets, the taverns and boardinghouses, the homes of friends that had given him pleasure during the five preceding winters.

As he looked about the chamber—described by a member as "a room without ventilators, more than sufficiently heated by fire," and made more oppressive by the breathing and sweat of the assemblage[1]—he saw many familiar faces. His previous legislative service made him already as well known to most of those who had served several terms as congressmen.

For the first time Gallatin was part of a legislative majority: the Fourth Congress contained only forty-nine Federalists, while he and his fellow "Antis" numbered fifty-six. He believed—and on such matters his opinion was judicious—that his own party had a similar edge in ability. Most of the Democratic-Republican leaders were from Virginia: James Madison, short, inconspicuous, usually solemn; William Branch Giles, gay and acute; John Nicholas, young, handsome personification of the southern aristocrat. New York was represented by one of its finest in lineage and talents—Edward Livingston, a witty, dashing newcomer. The Federalists, too, Gallatin conceded, had "many clever men": a solid, combative, resourceful phalanx led by Uriah Tracy, Roger Griswold, James Hillhouse from Connecticut, and William Smith and Robert Goodloe Harper from South Carolina. Harper, formerly an ardent Democratic-Republican, was almost more Federalist than Hamilton. Gallatin called him "as great a bungler as I ever knew, very good hearted, and not deficient in talents, exclusively of that of speaking, which he certainly possesses to a high degree; but his vanity destroys him." Only one Federalist was a truly "superior man"—the brilliant and eloquent Fisher Ames, who was temporarily confined by illness to his Massachusetts estate.[2]

As in the Assembly, Gallatin was all business during waking hours. Hannah shared his quarters in a Philadelphia boarding house during the winter of 1795–1796. In the following winter, when she went to New York to nurse her first child at her parents' home, he lived a hermitlike existence at a North Third Street boarding house;[3] but his self-denigration that he had lapsed into the "indolent" habits of his youth was belied by his extraordinary record in the House of Representatives.[4]

Gallatin's enormous and precise industry, his acute and logical mind, his integrity and intellectual honesty, his courage and calmness of temper, his concern for principle, and his unwillingness to deal in personalities again quickly carried him to the forefront; but party feeling was far more bitter than in the Pennsylvania Assembly, and his very virtues made him the target of animosity.

With one exception, all the chief problems that engaged his attention during his first term were matters with which he had become familiar as an assemblyman, indeed, were extensions of them to a national scale. Yet he already had a conception of national problems unequaled by any member of Congress. Other members, he discovered, knew only the traditions and problems of their own states; his decade of wandering between Maine and western Virginia had acquainted him with those of many states.[5] Thus he brought from State House to Congress Hall seasoned legislative ability and an unmatched breadth of view.

2

Again as in the Assembly, Gallatin shone brilliantly in the field of public finance. The House of Representatives sorely needed leadership he could provide; and the want can be traced directly to his old adversary, Alexander Hamilton.

As a colony and a state, Pennsylvania had found a Committee of Ways and Means in the lower house of the legislature a convenient device for considering and directing financial legislation. The federal House of Representatives had appointed such a committee at its first session, only to discharge it at the behest of the Secretary of the Treasury before it accomplished anything. Thereafter financial matters were referred directly to the Treasury Department for consideration and recommendation.[6] The aim of the ambitious Secretary obviously was that he and the cabinet should initiate and guide all financial legislation in the English fashion; and the First and Second Congresses obliged him by enacting his extensive and constructive program. The attempts of Giles in the House and Gallatin in the Senate to force Hamilton to account to Congress for the Treasury's operations came to nothing, as we have seen; and he retired from the cabinet in January, 1795, amid a round of acclaim. With Oliver Wolcott of Connecticut in his place and no financial statesmen in Congress, Gallatin found "the financial department . . . quite vacant." [7]

Gallatin lost no time in trying to fill it in the way that he believed it should be filled—Congress participating in the determination of financial policy, as provided by the Constitution. He had been just ten days in the House of Representatives when he rose to propose an amendment to a resolution calling for an inquiry into "whether further measures are necessary to reinforce the existing provision for the redemption of the Public Debt": that a committee be appointed to superintend the general operations of the government's finances. No department of government, he stated, was in greater need of systematic handling.[8]

Caught off guard, the Federalists offered no resistance. On December 21 a committee was appointed "to report the condition of the Public Debt, revenue, and expenditures" and to consider all reports of the Treasury Department. Gallatin and Madison, acknowledged leader of the Democratic-Republicans in the House, were among the fourteen appointed to the committee. Five days later, Secretary Wolcott duly submitted to it estimates of appropriations for 1796 for consideration.[9] From that day forward the Ways and Means Committee, as it came to be known, was recognized as an established institution and a chief instrument of the House's work. Gallatin served on it as long as he was in the House.

In the committee room and on the floor Gallatin and his party soon made it painfully clear to the Federalists that they would subject any financial proposal that the Administration might make to the sharpest scrutiny. After the Ways and Means Committee had submitted its report in mid-January, Gallatin suggested that action on military appropriations be delayed for three or four months to see whether the Treasury might not make some progress in discharging the debt. And he joined Livingston in arguing that the House had the discretionary right to withhold appropriations for the civil as well as military establishments if it saw fit —although he emphasized that he was not necessarily urging that this be done.[10]

The extreme Federalists were outraged. One Connecticut Yankee, Chauncey Goodrich, complained to a friend that although he and others had pressed Gallatin and the Democratic-Republicans "beyond all bounds of delicacy" to suggest financial legislation, "they neither will propose, or pledge themselves to support the measures of others." [11]

In April, in a series of speeches, Gallatin laid bare the purpose of his seemingly obstructionist tactics. He announced that it was his considered conclusion that the public debt had increased by five million dollars since 1789. "We are," he averred, "laying the foundation of that national curse —a growing and perpetual debt." It was vital that steps be taken to reduce the debt at once, even at the cost of curtailing the military establishment and possibly the foreign service, and the imposition of additional direct taxes. Because the United States was not a manufacturing nation, new taxes ought not to be levied on manufactured products as in Europe, but on such things as houses and land. He scored the Ways and Means Committee's request for authorization of a loan of five million dollars to repay the debt of the federal government to the Bank of the United States. This, he insisted, was a veiled project to delay the extinction of the debt for twenty-three years or even longer. It would be better to limit the loan to $1,200,000 and use increased taxes to repay the debt within four or five years.[12]

Gallatin's discerning criticism delighted his party. Madison exulted after listening to several of his speeches: "Gallatin is a real treasure . . . sound in his principles, accurate in his calculations, and indefatigable in his researches. Who would have supposed that Hamilton could have gone off in the triumph he assumed with such a condition of the finances behind him?" [13] Thomas Jefferson on his Virginia mountain top, to which he had retired from public life at the end of 1793, recalled the assistance he had given Giles toward checking Hamilton and was equally pleased. He wrote to James Monroe, in France on a diplomatic mission: "I had always conjectured . . . that our public debt was increasing about a million dollars a year. You will see by Mr. Gallatin's speeches that the thing is proved." [14]

The discomfited Federalists cried to Hamilton, now practicing law at New York, for help. On June 1, hours before summer adjournment time, William Smith of South Carolina rose to fire a broadside of statistics proving that "there was, notwithstanding all the difficulties and obstructions which the Government had to encounter, an excess in favor of the Government" of two million dollars. Gallatin had time only to reply that the papers necessary for an adequate rebuttal were not at hand, but that the figures Smith had cited seemed to him to prove what he had been maintaining: that the public debt was great and increasing.[15]

Jefferson had expressed the wish to Madison in March that Gallatin would "present us with a clear view of our finances, and put them in a form as simple as they will admit. . . . he will merit immortal honor. The accounts of the United States ought to be, and may be made as simple as those of a common farmer, and capable of being understood by common farmers." [16]

Madison may have passed the word along to Gallatin. In any event, Gallatin dedicated his summer with the Nicholsons on William Street to preparing a monumental response to Jefferson's suggestion. A *Sketch of the Finances of the United States*, issued by a New York printer in November, 1796, was a volume of two hundred pages, including an appendix of nineteen tables.[17] Far from being a "sketch," the work was an exhaustive report and analysis of the finances of the government— revenues, expenses, and debt—from its commencement to January 1, 1796. The tables confirmed Jefferson's notion that the debt had been increasing at the rate of a million dollars a year—from $72,776,000 in 1790 to $78,697,000 in 1796.

A *Sketch* presented fully and developed systematically the fiscal data and the financial philosophy Gallatin had been expounding in the Pennsylvania Assembly and in Congress. It was at once devastating and constructive—the most complete and cogent criticism thus far of Federalist financial practices. It dwelt in particular upon Hamilton's debt assumption operation. In assuming the debts that the individual states had contracted during the Revolution, the federal government had increased its obligations by $22,500,000, Gallatin estimated. He did not question the wisdom of completely extinguishing the debts of the states; but he insisted that the amounts should have been carefully computed instead of being "assumed at random." He would have checked the debts the states owed one another, making such cancellations as the comparison called for. The federal government would then have assumed the total of the remaining items. If this had been done, "the very same result which now exists might have been effected" at half the cost to the American people. Hamilton's "fatal measure," he charged—and he produced tables to prove it—had "wasted" about eleven million dollars. He took no notice here of the fact that the Federalist Secretary of the Treasury had been quite willing to "waste" such a sum in the hope of enhancing the prestige of the national government at the expense of the state governments.

On Hamilton's policy of funding the debt, Gallatin was less severe. It was only "common honesty" to provide for the payment of interest on debts of the Confederation government and for the repayment of the principal. He was even willing to wave aside the question whether Hamilton was justified in paying holders of certificates—who might have bought them as a speculation—rather than the individuals to whom they had been originally issued for services performed during the Revolution.

Although he conceded that funding of the debt might be useful as a temporary expedient, he denied that it would be beneficial as a permanent policy; and he elaborated the argument he had first made in the Pennsylvania legislature that a public debt is "a public curse," answering all the principal claims that had been advanced for it by followers of Hamilton. "It makes not the slightest addition either to the wealth or the annual labor of a nation." It does not meet the need for a circulating medium "as the amount of the debt is much greater than the quantity . . . required. . . . Whenever a greater part was put in circulation than was required by the actual demand, its price would sink, and it would no longer serve the purpose to which it was designed." As for the argument that it added to the nation's stability by attaching men of wealth to it, "it should be recollected that although an artificial interest is thereby created, which may at times give useful support, it may at some future period lend its assistance to bad measures and to a bad administration." Gallatin cited experiences of Spain, Holland, and Great Britain to show that over the years their public debts, far from benefiting those nations, had enfeebled them.

Equally fallacious was the contention that Hamilton's funding operation benefited the United States by attracting foreign capital. Of the millions of dollars borrowed abroad, Gallatin pointed out, only "a small proportion . . . has been applied to increase the cultivation and improvement of lands, the erection of manufactures, the annual income of the nation. The only ones to benefit were speculators. "It has enabled these individuals to consume more, to spend more, and they have consumed and expended extravagantly." Now the whole debt and the interest on it remained to be paid.

It was imperative, he continued, that the public debt be wiped out as promptly as possible. There was no need to be concerned about the loss of capital as American obligations to foreign creditors were paid off, if the operation were executed gradually and systematically: it would "be more than counterbalanced by the natural progress of America," would free the nation from "the paying of interest upon that capital," and at the same time would "strengthen the bonds of Union and give additional vigor and respectability to the nation." Here, he implied, was a way to strengthen the national union without throwing away a fortune.

Gallatin suggested one means of extinguishing the debt expeditiously —through the practice of economy in the government, particularly in the military establishment. He thought there was not "the slightest possibility that we ever shall be involved in any war except self-defence." The exhaustion of the nations of Europe at the end of the current war would assure peace for at least ten or twelve years. "We should by all means improve that period to discharge the heaviest part of our debt."

At the same time it would be necessary to increase the government's revenues. In taxation the federal government ought to look only to objects "of the most general nature, leaving all the lesser, all the local subjects of taxation, to the individual States." It should impose direct taxes only in areas that could afford them. "Our capital in commerce is great; our capital in lands is immense; it can hardly be said that we yet have any capital in manufactures"; therefore, no taxes on manufactures.

Even in the case of commerce, care must be taken to avoid killing the goose that lays the golden eggs. Customs duties that were too high would encourage smuggling and discourage consumption. The few additional objects that had been proposed for internal taxation—leather, hats, licenses, stamps—probably would not produce enough revenue to warrant the trouble of collecting duties on them. A better answer for the government's revenue needs lay in direct taxes on real estate—houses and land. The experience of England, France, and Pennsylvania during the Revolution proved that taxes on such property could be collected more economically than any other form of tax.

Gallatin returned to Pennsylvania's experience in suggesting the federal government's best resource for extinguishing its debt. The state had sold its public lands; so should the union. West of the Alleghenies the United States owned perhaps ten million acres; "the quantity might be enlarged without any difficulty was there any real demand for more." Gallatin estimated that sales of lands might bring the federal treasury a half million dollars in revenue annually.

Gallatin's figures on the increase of the debt under Federalist administration were never successfully disputed. The principles set forth in the *Sketch* were mentioned frequently, by members of both parties, in the House debates following its publication. He himself missed no opportunity to reiterate them and to develop them farther. He continued urging that the government pare its expenses in order to speed the reduction of the debt, even if that meant cutting the Army back to the levels of 1792 and withholding appropriations for a navy. He was fearful that the Administration would use any sums that might be authorized for the latter to complete several unfinished frigates and send them to sea— which would only begin a new train of large and unnecessary expenses.

Gallatin had never made a secret of his conviction that the Federalist Administration was incapable of providing the "order and skill" needed for enforcing economy in government. During the next session he urged that Congress assume responsibility for efforts toward this end. In the past, appropriation measures had included the phrase, "there [shall] be appropriated a sum not exceeding————" Gallatin proposed that hereafter such measures should specify, "the following sums [shall] be respectively appropriated . . ." [18] To the great distress of the Federalist leaders, Congress adopted his suggestion in appropriations for 1797. "The management of the Treasury," Secretary Wolcott complained to Alexander Hamilton, "becomes more and more difficult. The Legislature appropriations are minute. Gallatin, to whom they yield, is evidently intending to break down this department, by charging it with an impracticable detail." [19]

Phrases providing for specific appropriations were again included in legislation applying to the civil departments of the government in 1798, 1799, and 1800; but in 1798 the Army and Navy departments succeeded in having them omitted from bills affecting their interests. Gallatin's precepts concerning the importance of economy and specific appropriations, the desirability of an end of debt funding and an early extinction of the public debt, were not without their influence on the Federalists' practices; but they did their best to evade them as long as they controlled the Executive Department. [20]

3

In the United States as a whole, as in Pennsylvania, Federalist joined Democratic-Republican, easterner joined westerner, in looking fondly upon the public lands as a great potential source of revenue. But in Congress as in the Assembly there was a wide disparity of opinion as to what principles should govern in their sale.

The issue became pressing about the time Gallatin entered Congress. Great Britain had just agreed, through Jay's Treaty, to give up its western posts; and the Indians of the old Northwest, under the terms of the Treaty of Greenville, had ceased to be a menace to western settlers. Thus, although the area northwest of the Ohio River already held thousands of hardy whites, formal opening of it for settlement was practicable for the first time. Late in January, 1796, the Land Office Committee of the House reported a bill designed, in the words of Chairman Smith of South Carolina, "to raise revenue, and to sell the land in such lots as would be most convenient to settlers." It proposed marking out tracts three miles square to be sold at two dollars an acre. [21]

The purpose for which the land was to be sold soon became a matter of controversy. James Madison told the House that here was a chance to "fill the Treasury as soon as possible" and urged that the entire public domain be thrown on the market at once in lots six miles square. He found himself in strange company, for this was precisely what a number of eastern Federalist land speculators and representatives of land speculators devoutly wished would be done.

Against such a conception of the public weal Gallatin, the frontier democrat, spoke out sharply. He acknowledged that extinction of the public debt—"the curse of the country"—was of the greatest importance, and that none would benefit more from it than the poor; but the poor also needed the opportunity to buy land: "If the cause of the happiness of this country was examined into . . . it would be found to arise as much from the great plenty of land . . . as from the wisdom of political institutions. It is, in fact . . . because the poor man has been able always to attain his portion of land." By making land available in small tracts, Pennsylvania now had seventy thousand men on small holdings, while fewer than a thousand had bought large tracts.

In the long run, the sale of land in such a way as to benefit the majority of citizens would prove financially advantageous to the government as well. Possibly more land would be sold during the first years if it were sold in large blocks to speculators; but this higher initial income would actually come from the pockets of the poor. If the land were placed on the market in small tracts and gradually, the poor would be able to purchase it directly and the government would receive the entire sale price. Gallatin prophesied that within ten years the government would be able to wipe out the national debt by selling the public lands to the poor. In the debate, he was supported by frontier congressmen from Pennsylvania, New York, and Virginia.

Gallatin feared, however, that Congress would be willing to pass only a measure that would benefit both speculators and the poor. Accordingly, he proposed that the Smith bill be amended so that land would be offered at both wholesale and retail: tracts would be surveyed alternately between sections several miles square and 160 acres, all to be sold at two dollars an acre, payable within a year. Although he would have preferred locating all the land offices in the West, he undertook to satisfy the speculation-minded easterners by suggesting that the large tracts be sold at the national capital, the small tracts at offices west of the Alleghenies.[22]

Around this compromise the Democratic-Republicans rallied, and the bill passed the House; but the Senate amended the measure drastically, removing some of Gallatin's more democratic features. The Land Act of

1796 did not fill the public treasury with dollars nor the public domain with settlers; it failed so completely that he had to attack the land question anew within a few years.[23]

4

Neither as Pennsylvania assemblyman nor as federal senator had Gallatin been concerned with foreign relations. But less than four months after he took his seat in Congress Hall, a major issue arose to which he quite consistently applied his deep convictions that the federal government should not be allowed to become too centralized nor the executive power suffered to go unchecked.

The matter had begun quietly several years earlier when President Washington sent John Jay, the Anglophile Chief Justice of the Supreme Court, to London with three principal diplomatic objectives: to negotiate a trade treaty; to obtain fulfillment of the peace terms of 1783, especially the evacuation of the western forts still held by the British; and to gain recognition of the United States by Britain and France as a neutral in the war then raging.

The treaty Jay sent home represented a complete triumph for British diplomacy. The United States won modest concessions at a humiliating price. The British renewed their promise to evacuate the western forts, but insisted on their "right" to ignore the Canadian-American boundary in the fur trade with Indians in the northwestern United States; other matters hanging fire since 1783 were left for subsequent negotiation. At the same time the United States yielded on its rights as a neutral by agreeing that its vessels would not carry contraband in return for which Britain promised to stop impressing American seamen into her navy. For ten years the two nations were to treat each other as "most favored nations"—but American vessels were forbidden to export from the United States sugar, coffee, cocoa, and cotton in order to have limited entry into the British West Indies. In buying the nominal friendship of Great Britain, the United States gained the outright enmity of France; for although it recognized Britain's right to capture French property in America, under the earlier treaty with France it continued to protect British property in American ports.[24]

The Federalist leaders, from Washington and Hamilton down, were appalled when the terms reached them in the spring of 1795, but were convinced that war with Great Britain would break out if the treaty were rejected. Peace was imperative if the federal Constitution and Hamilton's delicate system of national credit were to endure. The Senate, meeting in June behind closed doors, ratified the treaty by a bare two-thirds majority.

While the treaty was awaiting the President's signature, a Democratic-Republican newspaper published the full text. Cries of indignation and dismay went up across the land; protest meetings were held; many a bottle of ink was expended in newspaper and pamphlet debate. "It exceeds everything I expected," Gallatin exclaimed on learning the details; and he wrote to Hannah: "I wish the ratification . . . may not involve us in a more serious situation than we have yet been in. May I be mistaken in my fears and everything be for the best!" [25]

Meanwhile, the British executed a deft propaganda play. They brought to the attention of President Washington a packet they had captured containing a series of dispatches from Joseph Fauchet, the imaginative French minister to the United States, to his government. These suggested that, with funds to grease the palms of certain American officials, Fauchet could have turned the Whiskey Rebellion into a civil war for the benefit of France. On the ground that a bad treaty was better than none, the angry President affixed his signature. On March 1, 1796, he notified the House of Representatives that Great Britain had ratified the Treaty. Presumably it was now the law of the land, and it was incumbent upon the House to vote appropriations for the expenses of the several mixed commissions necessary to put it into effect.[26]

A few months earlier, when an appropriation bill for establishing a federal mint was before Congress, Gallatin and his party had made it clear that they did not think the House obligated automatically to approve sums of money for objects already authorized. What was the purpose of requiring members of Congress to vote on an appropriation bill if they could not say yea or nay? Gallatin had inquired on that occasion.[27] In this spirit, Edward Livingston rose on March 2 to propose that President Washington be asked to lay before the House all the official papers involved in Jay's negotiation, so that it might debate the treaty and "some important Constitutional questions" involved.[28]

To the Federalists, the suggestion was outrageous. As Roger Griswold of Connecticut put it: "The power of making Treaties has been given to the President and Senate. The Treaty in question has been completed by those constitutional authorities; the faith of the nation is pledged. It is become a law, and the House of Representatives have nothing to do with it, but provide for its execution."

Such a stand, Gallatin retorted, reminded him of a British bishop's dictum that "the people have nothing to do with the laws but obey them."

Griswold actually went even farther, saying in effect that the representatives of the people had no right to consult their own discretion when they were exercising a power expressly delegated to them by the Constitution.

For nearly three weeks the House was engrossed in earnest and able debate over conflicting articles of the Constitution: the Second and Sixth articles which gave the President, with the concurrence of two-thirds of the senators, the right to make treaties that would be "the supreme law of the land"; and the First article, which gave both houses participation in the passing of all laws, including appropriation laws.[29]

Only once was the high plane of the discussion abandoned. Uriah Tracy, irritated by the telling effect Gallatin was obtaining, allowed himself a sneer at the Pennsylvanian's foreign birth. There were immediate cries for "Order," and he quickly apologized for becoming "too personal . . . in the heat of debate." [30]

The Democratic-Republican point of view was presented with spirit, eloquence, and acute reasoning by Livingston; temperately and a bit academically by Madison; slashingly by Giles; most effectively of all by Gallatin. Gallatin later complained that the debate was "miserably reported and curtailed" in Benjamin Franklin Bache's *Aurora*, which printed the only extensive record of it. Even so, his cogent argument, impressive erudition, and sweeping vigor are patent in Bache's digests of three long speeches delivered on March 7, 9, and 24.

Gallatin contended that Jay's Treaty was not the supreme law of the land but remained "an inchoate act" until the House of Representatives authorized the necessary appropriations. He cited instances in which the British Commons had rejected a treaty by refusing an appropriation, and asked whether the House of Representatives, "the substantial and immediate representatives of the American people, shall be ranked below the British House of Commons." If the House did not defend this position doggedly, he warned, there was real danger that the President and Senate together, under a fiction of arranging a treaty with, say, an Indian tribe, might make any law they pleased, and the House would be powerless to check them. The House would thus lose its share in legislation. Because the "cooperation and sanction" of the House were necessary to make the treaty a "binding instrument," it had the right—yes, even the duty—to request the papers involved in its making.[31]

Such an argument enraged the Federalists, who vied with one another to answer or ridicule it. The Democratic-Republicans were of course delighted. From Monticello, Jefferson wrote of his gratification to Congressman Madison: "I am much pleased with Mr. Gallatin's speech. . . . It is worthy of being printed at the end of the Federalist [papers], as the only rational commentary on that part of the Constitution to which it relates." [32] Bache rushed his version into print as a pamphlet under the title, *Speech upon the Constitutional Powers of the House with Respect to Treaties.*

When the Livingston resolution at last came to a vote on March 24, it passed by a decisive vote: sixty-two to thirty-seven. Gallatin and Livingston were appointed to carry the document to the President. He received them coolly, promising only to "consider" the request of the House.[33]

After consultation with the cabinet and with Alexander Hamilton, Washington refused to transmit the requested papers. He added that, as he had been a member of the convention that drew up the federal Constitution, he knew that the framers had not intended that the Lower House should have any role in treaty making. Indeed, he declared, the House had no right to ask him to inspect any papers unless it considered impeaching him.[34]

The Democratic-Republicans accepted the refusal with good grace. Madison, who had himself been a member of the Constitutional Convention, denied in a temperately worded speech that anything had been said during the debates that could "be regarded as the oracular guide in expounding the Constitution." Gallatin urged that the House content itself with making its position on the issue clear. A few days later it followed his cue in a resolution which stated that "the House of Representatives have a Constitutional right to deliberate and determine the propriety" of enacting laws to put a treaty into effect, though it claimed no agency in making or ratifying them.[35]

Now the Democratic-Republicans were confronted by a new Federalist tactic: a motion for appropriations to put into effect all the treaties then pending—with the Indians, with Spain, with Algiers, as well as with Britain.[36] The mails began to bring Gallatin petitions from many towns in western Pennsylvania signed by friends and political allies urging his support of the resolution. Among the signers was the Reverend John McMillan, whose support in 1794 had brought about his election to Congress. Many westerners believed that the Indian raids of the past decade had been instigated by English agents along the Great Lakes and would cease as soon as the British treaty went into effect.

Gallatin's concern for the national welfare had carried him into conflict with the special interests of his constituents. He realized this, and was annoyed because he felt that many of his constituents were victimized by a misconception the Federalists had deliberately spread, that the Spanish treaty, which they—and he—favored because it would give them access to the port of New Orleans, was "so blended" with the British treaty that "both must fall or stand together." [37]

The Democratic-Republicans convoked a party caucus, the first that Gallatin had ever attended, to consider the situation. It was agreed that an effort should be made to separate the treaties; then each congressman could vote for appropriations for them individually as he felt best. The plan was successful, and appropriations for all but the Jay Treaty quickly passed.[38]

The House devoted itself almost completely to new debates on appropriations for the British treaty during the latter part of April. Meanwhile Gallatin was the particular object of Federalist attack all along the eastern seaboard. At a town meeting in the Old South Meeting House at Boston his former Harvard student, Harrison Gray Otis, now a man of consequence at the bar and in the world of Massachusetts real estate, asked his fellow townsmen whether they should "join a vagrant . . . in opposition to a Washington; a foreigner who had to his knowledge come to this Country without a second shirt to his back? A man who in comparison to Washington is like a Satyr to a Hyperion?" [39] Noah Webster, a follower of that native of the British West Indies, Alexander Hamilton, sneered in the New York *Minerva* at Gallatin's foreign birth and circulated misleading innuendoes and outright falsehoods about his part in the Whiskey Rebellion.[40] At Philadelphia, the British-born William Cobbett ("Peter Porcupine") declared in a pamphlet, "The Gentleman from Geneva has an accent not unlike that of a wandering Israelite . . . admirably adapted . . . for augmenting the discordant howlings of a synagogue." By withholding the appropriation he tried "to stop the wheels of government." [41] So effective was this Federalist propaganda that even Secretary of the Treasury Wolcott believed it. It was "neither unreasonable nor uncandid," he wrote to his father, "to believe that Mr. Gallatin is directed by foreign politics and influence." [42]

The enthusiasm of Gallatin's constituents for the Jay Treaty—but not the attacks on his own character—caused him to modify his stand slightly during the new debates. In a long speech on April 26, he declared that he did not wish to vote for any proposition that would imply a rejection of the treaty, "however repugnant [the treaty] might be to his feelings and perhaps to his prejudices," because to do so might delay the return of the western forts still held by the British, might deprive us of reparations due us for British spoliations on our maritime commerce, and might indefinitely delay a final adjustment of our other differences with Great Britain. But he felt that it would be better for the House to withhold approval of the appropriation until Britain showed that she was going to live up to the terms of the treaty, by ceasing to impress American seamen and to molest our vessels carrying provisions.

Gallatin was bitter about the Federalist appeals to "the fears of the House" in their cries that passage of the appropriation was imperative to save the nation from war with Great Britain and the federal government from dissolution, and he recalled that the negotiations with Britain had originated "through the fear of being involved in a war." "The impression of the same danger . . . promoted its ratification; and now, every imaginary mischief that could alarm our fears [is] conjured up, in order to deprive us of that discretion, which this House thought they had a right to exercise . . . in order to force us to carry the Treaty into effect." [43]

Gallatin's warning against emotionalism was of no avail. Two days after he delivered it, Fisher Ames of Massachusetts arrived from his sickbed to tell a hushed and responsive House and gallery that only passage of the appropriation bill would preserve the Constitution and the Republic from destruction, the blood of children from the vengeance of savages egged on by the British. Hearers of this moving, specious address accounted it the most effective piece of oratory ever delivered on the floor of Congress. On April 30 the House, by a vote of fifty-one to forty-eight, authorized the appropriations necessary to carry out the treaty.[44]

The constitutional issue raised by Gallatin and his party colleagues about the role of the House of Representatives in treaty-making is still unsettled. Yet the possibility they presented that appropriations might be withheld has undoubtedly led negotiators of treaties ever since to bear in mind the sentiment of the Lower House. The consequences of the debate on Gallatin's career are clear. By bold and statesmanlike action he took the leadership of the Democratic-Republican forces in Congress from James Madison. One Federalist paper declared that the Virginian had become "file-coverer to an itinerant Genevan." [45] Henceforth Fisher Ames and the other Federalists referred to their opponents as "Gallatin & Co." From now on Gallatin was the chief target of the Federalist artillery.

9. Fighting the War with France

1796=1799

Periodically during his public life Gallatin toyed with the idea of retiring from politics. "Ambition, love of power, I never felt," he would tell Hannah, "and if vanity ever made one of the ingredients which impelled me to take an active part in public life, it has for many years altogether vanished away. . . . We must be settled and give up journeying." Understandably enough, such thoughts fascinated him most in election years, when it looked as if he might be hard pressed at the polls.[1]

The temptation to retire was especially strong during the summer of 1796. Word kept reaching him in Philadelphia that, despite his excellent account of himself in Congress Hall during the preceding winter, there was much dissatisfaction among his constituents with the stand he had taken on the Jay Treaty, the fact that he did not actually live in the district he represented, and the fact that his appearances in the western country had become briefer since his marriage.

He left Hannah, who was expecting a child, with the Nicholsons in New York and went to face his constituents in October. The abusive Federalist attacks on him had boomeranged. He was elected to a second term in Congress by the slightly reduced margin of 1,500 over the Federalist candidate.[2]

Relieved and secretly pleased, he lingered in the West several weeks to throw himself wholeheartedly into the November national election. Washington had declined to run for a third term; the Federalists, with considerable reluctance, had taken up John Adams for the Presidency, while the Democratic-Republicans backed Thomas Jefferson. As a member of the campaign committee for Pennsylvania, Gallatin labored diligently through correspondence and in person.

The returns were rather encouraging. The Democratic-Republicans easily carried Fayette and the rest of the western country and captured thirteen of Pennsylvania's fifteen electoral votes; but the popular vote was uncomfortably close.[3] In the nation, one wing of the Federalists was so grudging in its support of Adams that, under the curious provisions of the Constitution then in effect, Jefferson was elected to the Vice Presidency. Thus with the assembling of the Fifth Congress in 1797 the Virginian returned to Philadelphia to preside over the Senate and to direct on the ground the growing national party that had coalesced about him.

The Fifth Congress also brought Gallatin to undisputed leadership of the Democratic-Republican forces in the House of Representatives. James Madison, newly married to an attractive Quaker widow, had retired to life as a country gentleman in the Virginia hills, leaving only Edward Livingston, John Nicholas, and William Branch Giles as dependable support for skirmishes in committee and on the floor.

In comparison, the Federalists were stronger in this new Congress, having a slight margin in numbers and a considerable margin in talents. Roger Griswold of Connecticut, William Smith and Robert Goodloe Harper of South Carolina were present again to be heard from often— the last as chairman of the Ways and Means Committee. And there were two notable recruits: handsome, eloquent Harrison Gray Otis of Massachusetts, just thirty-two, who had the decency to apologize to Gallatin for his tasteless "second shirt" speech;[4] and James A. Bayard of Delaware, moderate, judicious, but not an original thinker.[5]

Although the Federalists still controlled all three branches of the federal government, they were frightened men. Their ranks were torn by jealousies and differences of opinion. Their narrow margin in the election had impressed them with how easily they might lose control of the government that they had so largely created to men who had been critical of it from its inception, who certainly believed in that dreadful thing called democracy, who probably were infidels, and who were perhaps even willing to sell out their country to democratic, godless France. In behalf of all that seemed dear to them, the Federalists in Congress fought desperately and ruthlessly to block Gallatin, Jefferson, and their demoniacal forces.

2

The Fifth Congress assembled May 15, 1797, in response to a call from President Adams to consider the state of Franco-American relations. The problem was to engage it through virtually all the next two years.

The situation, as reported in the President's message to Congress, and as confirmed by every vessel from Paris, was parlous and was growing steadily worse. The French Republic had fallen into the control of a five-headed executive known as the Directory, which had forsaken the revolutionary idealism of 1792 in favor of the traditional aims of French domination in Europe. The Directory—as Gallatin and other Democratic-Republicans had warned during the debates of the year before—had chosen to interpret the Jay Treaty as an Anglo-American alliance aimed at France. In retaliation it had authorized French privateers to plunder the American merchant fleet—a dispensation of which they made reckless use. Naturally the shipping princes of New England who were the backbone of the Federalist party were outraged. In the crisis the conduct of the American minister to France, James Monroe, was most ambiguous, convincing the French that neither he nor his country could be trusted and convincing many Americans that he was dangerously Francophile. Washington had recalled him in 1796, but he had not yet reached home.

As Gallatin listened to the new President's message and to the bristling Federalist talk in the corridors of Congress Hall, he became convinced that the Administration was bent upon war, or at the very least upon war-like measures, against France—measures that would secure their hold on the federal government. As the debates on the message dragged on through May and June, he concluded that the strategy of "William Smith & Co." was to detain Congress so long that the Democratic-Republicans would grow weary and leave them free to push through their martial program. They determined to resist.[6] Thanks to their efforts, the reply to the message that the House finally adopted was considerably milder than the version that the Federalists would have preferred; it commended the President on his willingness to have further negotiation.[7]

Gallatin further contributed to the cause of peace through a speech on June 24 opposing a Federalist bill for the completion and arming of six frigates that had been authorized in 1794 to meet the threat of the Algerian pirates, but now appeared to be unnecessary inasmuch as an understanding had been reached with the Mediterranean power. He pitched his plea chiefly on financial grounds: To maintain three frigates would cost the United States $350,000 a year; to man them, as the bill would authorize the President to do, would cost an additional $500,000. The nation could not afford a navy in its present situation. Besides, arming of vessels would be proper only in the case of war, and he was not in favor of war, at least not at present.[8]

On June 27, while this and other warlike measures were still before the House, Monroe landed at Philadelphia. Gallatin, Jefferson, and Senator Aaron Burr of New York hastened to greet him, closeting themselves with him for two hours to hear his story. Monroe attributed most of his troubles to the Federalists. He insisted that, if they had let him show the Directory the text of the Jay Treaty as soon as it was completed, instead of making its members wait nine months to read it in the newspapers, the French would have taken it with good grace. Washington had recalled him just at the time things were taking a turn for the better, so as to give a Federalist credit for what he had labored to bring about.

Despite the Genêt affair Gallatin was disposed to give republican France the benefit of the doubt. Monroe's story won him over. He confided to Hannah that the Virginian was "possessed of integrity superior to all the attacks of malignity, . . . that he had conducted [himself] with irreproachable honor and the most dignified sense of duty, . . . that the American Administration have acted with a degree of meanness only exceeded by their folly, and that they have degraded the American name throughout Europe." [9] Four days later he joined the hierarchy of his party at a public dinner welcoming Monroe home.[10]

When the special session of Congress adjourned in early July the Democratic-Republicans could rejoice at having blocked all the Federalist moves toward war; but during the late summer and fall their prospects steadily deteriorated. Only Great Britain still refused to humble itself before the crusading, expanding French Republic. Their conflict struck harder and harder at American commercial and shipping interests.

By the time Congress reconvened in November the cabinet and the Federalists in Congress, taking their cue from Alexander Hamilton, were ready to embark upon a carefully devised program. The keynote was warlike measures but not a declaration of war against France; the details included arming of merchant vessels, constructing twenty sloops of the line, recruiting an army of 16,000 men with provision for an additional 20,000, abrogating the treaty with France made during the American Revolution, authorizing a loan to help meet additional expenses, and enacting a tax system suitable for war purposes. Meanwhile President Adams, pursuing a course somewhat independent of Hamilton and the cabinet, dispatched three emissaries to Paris in the hope of reaching some sort of understanding with the imperialistic republicans.

Publicly, however, the Federalists did not acknowledge that they would have the United States stop short of outright war. Thus, as 1797 turned into 1798, Gallatin delivered speech after speech warning his fellow Congressmen that, bad as it was to have France ravish the American merchant marine, it was infinitely better than to be officially at war with her. If the United States declared war, it not only would have all the incidental "expences and evils" but would see all its trade taken over by Great Britain.* [11]

Gallatin found the role of peacemaker arduous. "We must expect to be branded with the usual epithets of Jacobins and tools of foreign influence," he wrote to Hannah. "We must have fortitude enough to despise the calumnies of the war-faction and to do our duty notwithstanding the situation in which we have been dragged by the weakness and party spirit of our Administration and by the haughtiness of France. We must preserve self-dignity, not suffer our Country to be debased, and yet preserve our Constitution and our fellow citizens from the fatal effects of war. The task is difficult." [12]

Anxiously he awaited some word from the trio of diplomats at Paris. When at last some dispatches came he took comfort in the fact that the Administration remained silent about their contents. He suspected that the facts were withheld lest they damage the Federalist cause.[13] On March 19 President Adams finally became communicative. Saying that on the basis of the dispatches he despaired of the envoys being received with the respect due to "a free, powerful and independent nation," he recommended in general terms military and financial measures to defend the United States in the event of attack.[14]

Such counsel exasperated Gallatin. In a speech to the House on March 30, he complained that it was in essence a call for a declaration of war. It made it incumbent on Congress to decide definitely whether the country should go to war or not. Three days later he proposed that the President be requested to provide the House with the text of the dispatches or explain why it was withheld. Livingston, Nicholas, Giles, all the Democratic-Republicans joined in support of the resolution.[15]

They got more than they had bargained for. On April 3 President Adams transmitted the text of his instructions to the envoys together with the dispatches from Paris. The galleries were cleared, the doors locked, and the documents read to a silent House. They told a shocking tale: The Americans had been approached by three representatives (referred to as X, Y, and Z) of Talleyrand, the Minister of Foreign Affairs, who suggested that a bribe of $250,000 to the minister and a "loan" of several million dollars would facilitate negotiations. The alternative, Monsieur Y

* Gallatin's speech of March 1, 1798, was published that month in pamphlet form by the Philadelphia printer Richard Folwell, as *The Speech of Albert Gallatin . . . Upon the Foreign Intercourse Bill.* A second edition was issued in April.

indicated, would be domestic trouble for the Adams Administration, to which the "friends of France" in the United States would contribute. The envoys had been prepared to deal in bribery; but this price was too high, and they were fearful that they might not get anything at all for their money.[16]

The Democratic-Republican leaders hastily assembled a caucus to consider the unexpected turn of affairs.[17] Most of the members were nonplused. Vice President Jefferson confessed that his first reaction was "very disagreeable and confused." [18] Gallatin felt the same way, and urged that the text of the dispatches not be published.[19] Then the legislators returned to their chambers for nearly three days of uninterrupted discussion.

Several days later the complete text was printed in the leading newspapers, through the influence of the Federalists in the Senate.[20] A wave of pro-Administration sentiment rolled across the land. Meetings were held to organize indignation; addresses of loyalty with the signatures of many Democratic-Republicans poured in on President Adams. Reams of patriotic doggerel were manufactured and printed. "Millions for defence, but not one cent for tribute," was a favorite toast of the day.[21]

Gallatin was close to despondency. He told the House, over cries of "Order" from the Federalists, that he feared the wide circulation of the dispatches had helped bring the United States "a greater probability of war than at any former period." He acknowledged that he had lost all hope of reconciliation between France and the United States.[22]

As April and May passed, Livingston and Nicholas went home sick of heart, Giles headed for Virginia physically ill, and Gallatin wrote to a friend: "I remain almost alone to bear the irksome burthen of opposition against a dozen or two speakers, several of whom exceedingly deficient in talents, but supplying their room by blackguardism and impudence . . . I consider it my sacred duty to remain firm to the post assigned to me by my constituents, however ungrateful the task." [23]

He was particularly incensed by the Federalist use of Monsieur Y's reference to "friends of France" in the United States to create the impression that there was a pro-French party in the United States—the Democratic-Republican. How did the Federalists expect the Democratic-Republicans to prove that this was not so? he asked the House on April 20. "By voting as these gentlemen please, and by agreeing to every proposition, however extravagant, which they bring forward." [24]

The Federalists proposed that Congress turn its attention to defensive measures and let financing them rest for the time being. Gallatin thought otherwise: "It would be well to look into our means, and then select such objects of expence as would be of the greatest service to us." He kept repeating that a public debt was a "curse"; that if the United States avoided war and the consequent expenses the outstanding debt might be easily paid off, without additional taxes, in twelve years.[25]

The martial measures, Gallatin charged, were urged almost entirely by one group and would be of little benefit outside one section of the country. The merchants and shippers of the eastern seaboard supposed that they would benefit from hostilities; they would pass the costs on—through customs duties or excises or land taxes—to the farmers, who formed the great bulk of the population. If the expenses were met through loans the farmers would be further victimized, because the interest on them would come in large part from the farmers' pockets and would ultimately find its way into the pockets of the Federalist capitalists of the East.[26]

The first "defensive measure" sought by the Federalists, outlined in a bill passed by the Senate, was creation of a "provisional army" of 20,000 men for use in the event of invasion by the French. This force, it was generally understood in Congress Hall, would be headed by former President Washington in the rank of lieutenant-general, with Hamilton in actual command until a landing by the French. Many of the Federalists, dubious about the loyalty of the Democratic-Republicans, urged that men without property be excluded from the higher grades.[27]

Gallatin argued himself almost hoarse against this proposal. The idea of a French invasion was a "mere bugbear": it would be against that nation's interests to interfere in America, and physically impossible for it to do so. It would be far better for the United States to place its reliance on a militia, which the Revolutionary War had shown was cheaper and more effective. He pounced on a chance remark by Speaker of the House Jonathan Dayton of New Jersey, that the corps would be useful not only to repel invading Frenchmen, "but also to suppress seditious and disaffected persons, immigrants, and any other daring infractors of the laws." Five years before, Gallatin reminded the House, Great Britain had raised a force out of fear of French revolutionary ideas. What had been the consequence? "To strengthen the Executive at the expence of individual liberty, and to involve the country in . . . a war that has brought [it] to the very brink of destruction." [28]

The second Federalist "defensive measure" was the creation of a federal navy to defend the commercial and shipping interests. It looked toward establishment of a Navy Department separate from the War Department, revival·of the marine corps of Revolutionary War glory, rushing to completion the partially constructed frigates, and authorization of the President to construct, purchase, or rent additional men-of-war. It called for empowering national ships and armed merchantmen to capture any armed French vessel, public or private, anywhere in the world.[29]

Gallatin insisted that a separate navy would be an unnecessary, inordinately expensive and, indeed, dangerous institution. "During the course of the present war," he told the House, "both Great Britain and France had plundered [our commerce] in a most shameful manner. . . . Yet, notwithstanding these depredations . . . year after year our exports have increased in value. . . ." Even our carrying trade had prospered. This proved, said Gallatin, that "commerce can be protected without a navy, whilst a nation preserves its neutrality." Moreover, the cost of maintaining a navy—and he cited figures to support the contention—would far exceed all the profits of the commerce it was designed to protect.

The greatest danger in a navy, Gallatin contended, was that its advocates regarded it "fondly" as a potential instrument of power, a device that we might use to throw our weight around in the courts of Europe. "No man can doubt . . . ," he told Congress, "that if, in 1793, we had had twelve ships-of-the-line, we should have been involved in the present war, on one side or the other, according to the fluctuations of public opinion." Through history navies had proven most useful as "great engines of war and conquest," most helpful in ruling colonies. He added that he hoped we would never have any colonies. To be happy as we have been up to now should be our chief objective.[30]

But Congress turned a deaf ear. Between March 27 and July 16, 1798, twenty laws were enacted to strengthen national defense according to Federalist lights. A separate Navy Department was created. The equipping of three frigates, the purchase or construction of twelve armed vessels and ten galleys were authorized. The existing treaties with France were repealed. Public armed vessels were permitted to capture French armed vessels and bring them into port for court procedure. American merchant vessels were authorized to arm defensively, and to make prizes of French armed vessels that attacked them. Commercial intercourse between the United States and France or French possessions was suspended to the incalculable benefit of Great Britain. A regiment of artillery was authorized. The President was empowered to enlist 10,000 volunteers for a period of three years.

To meet the additional expenses entailed, Secretary Wolcott recommended in May, 1798, that direct taxes be levied on lands, on dwelling houses, and on slaves. On this issue Gallatin was a model of consistency. He had opposed war preparations and expenses; now that they were inevitable, he argued that they must be provided for. He reminded his fellow Democratic-Republicans from the West that it behooved them to provide for war preparations because, if hostilities broke out with France, their access to the Mississippi and New Orleans would undoubtedly be cut off.

Again with admirable consistency, he agreed that direct taxes on land and houses were the only satisfactory way of meeting the new expenses. Although, two years before, he had championed a permanent direct tax on houses and land, he thought it better that such taxes now be set for a year only, to be renewed annually as long as was necessary. Never had he heard of a permanent tax being discontinued. As long as a tax was on the books, ways would be found of spending its proceeds. "A new regiment, or a few additional frigates, or some new establishments," he remarked, "will at any time consume any surplus of revenue which may be at hand."

He took issue with Administration suggestions as to how the tax be levied. Secretary Wolcott proposed that dwellings be grouped into nine classes for taxation, with the same rate applied to all. Congressman William Smith presented a plan, forwarded by Alexander Hamilton, for taxation of houses according to the number of rooms. Gallatin urged that both systems were unjust: the houses of the rich ought to pay proportionately more than those of the poor. The House saw his point, and enacted a graduated percentage tax, popularly known as "the window tax." [31]

On two other financial measures Gallatin spoke often during May and June, to no avail. He argued spiritedly against the Federalist-sponsored stamp tax and against a bill that would not place limitations on the President in borrowing money. If restrictions were not imposed, he warned, the money-lenders would force the Secretary of the Treasury to pay far higher rates of interest than otherwise; already the United States was paying between 7 and 8 per cent on some loans, although it was made to appear that the rate was only 6.[32]

All these efforts were for naught. Despite the new taxes and partially because of new loans, the government's income failed to keep pace with soaring military expenses. In the four years following Adams's inauguration, expenditures rose from six to nearly eleven million dollars a year. By 1800, according to Secretary Wolcott's own figures, the national debt had reached nearly eighty million dollars.[33]

3

While the Federalists were so successfully carrying through their program to defend the United States from menaces overseas, they sought to protect their own power against menaces at home. In the spring of 1798 they turned their attention to groups and individuals who might threaten their party and its principles. Gallatin, as a leading opponent of their program, naturally became one of their chief targets.

Two groups in the United States made the Federalists nervous: the Irish and the French. For a decade thousands of Irish, most of them members of the revolutionary Society of United Irishmen, had been seeking haven in the northern states. They had barely touched foot on American soil before the Democratic-Republicans in the cities, under such leaders as Dr. Hutchinson in Philadelphia and Aaron Burr in New York, welcomed them into their party and won their loyal support at the polls. One Connecticut Federalist senator reported indignantly that on a journey through Pennsylvania he had seen a frightening number of them—with few exceptions, "United Irishmen, freemasons, and the most God-provoking democrats this side of hell!" There were approximately 30,000 recently arrived Frenchmen in the country. It did not matter that most of them, far from being devotees of the Revolution, were refugees from it or fugitives from an uprising of Negro slaves in Santo Domingo. To the Federalist zealots they were strange, alien people, loose of morals and irreligious.

Even more disturbing were individuals Gouverneur Morris of New York described as "philosophical gentlemen." Some of these held unorthodox views that had brought them into trouble in England, and looked for refuge in the land of the free. The fact that Jefferson and his followers had welcomed them made them all the more suspect in the eyes of the Administration party.[34]

To strike at these groups, the Federalists projected three legislative measures: one to increase materially the length of residence required for naturalization; another to require enemy aliens to leave the country in time of war; and a third to imprison or deport, without process of law, any alien the President might think dangerous to public peace and safety.

The first measure, proposed late in April, was criticized by several Federalist leaders as not going far enough. Harper of South Carolina thought it was "high time we should recover from the mistake this country fell into when it first began to frame its constitutions, admitting foreigners to citizenship. . . . It is proper to declare that nothing but birth shall entitle a man to citizenship in this country." Proposed Otis of Massachusetts: "No alien born, who is not at present a citizen of the United States, shall hereafter be capable of holding any office of honor, trust, or profit, under the United States." [35] Jefferson wrote to Madison that he believed these "threats" were pointed at Gallatin." [36]

The only Democratic-Republicans remaining at their posts in Congress to resist the Federalist program were Jefferson as presiding officer in the Senate and Gallatin as the minority's leader and virtually only spokesman in the House. Day after day, week after week, Gallatin talked so long and so tellingly against the proposed legislation that on May 18 the exasperated Federalist majority passed a resolution amending the rules of the House so that no member might speak more than once on any question. Gallatin went ahead as if the rule did not exist, and a fortnight later it was repealed.[37]

Under the strain, Gallatin was "very bad company" to his wife, who was with him in Philadelphia at the time; but he kept right on, buoyed by the thought that the Supreme Being implanted "in our hearts sufficient incitement to virtue, by giving to him who will listen to it, the approbation of his interior monitor. That feeling, consciousness of having steadily pursued what to us appears to be right, acquires new strength and affords additional satisfaction in proportion to the calumnies spread by the designing few and swallowed by the credulous many." [38]

At the outset Gallatin was content to oppose the proposed legislation as "unconstitutional" and "too vaguely drawn." He pooh-poohed the "dreaded evil" about which the Federalists kept thundering vaguely but ominously as excuse for their measures.[39] Then, on June 19, Harper bellowed the charge that the persons opposing the bills were "leagued with the enemies of this country," determined "to bind us hand and foot, until our enemy comes upon us."

Soon after Harper had finished, Gallatin jumped up to answer him. For the first time in his legislative career he lost his temper. "I know nothing so respectable in the character of the gentleman from South Carolina, either public or private," he cried angrily, "as to entitle him to that ground he so boldly assumes." He challenged Harper to produce evidence of any plot against the nation; unless he could produce evidence, his assertions deserved "no other appellation than that of calumny." Harper returned to the floor to sneer that Gallatin "knew best whether his motives were pure or not; but when a gentleman who is generally so cool should all at once assume a tone of passion, as to forget all decorum of language, it would seem as if the observation had been properly applied to that gentleman." [40]

One section of the sedition bill, as passed by the Senate, was generally believed to be aimed at Gallatin. Under it, "any persons, whether alien or citizen, who shall secretly or openly combine or conspire together with an intention of opposing any measure of the Government" or impede the operation of any law, would be guilty of a misdemeanor and would be subject to fine or imprisonment. It was observed that Gallatin's participation in the Pittsburgh anti-excise meeting of 1792 would have been discountenanced by such a provision.[41]

Because this section apparently applied to him, Gallatin remained silent when the House debated the bill during July, 1798. He had no such compunctions about the second section, affecting the press. Perhaps there was need for legislation on this subject. The journals of both parties employed scurrility on a grand scale, and there was nothing on the federal law books at the time to check it. Gallatin had expressed the belief to friends that the Democratic-Republican press often went too far.[42]

But he was outraged by the arguments with which the Federalists advocated the measure. John Allen, a tall, intense member from Connecticut, argued that when the Democratic-Republican *Aurora* complained that the alien bill would work undue hardships on the Irish it was guilty of treason; that when Congressman Livingston proposed renewal of negotiations with the French he was seditious; that when another Democratic-Republican member condemned the legislation in letters to his constituents, he was acting the part of a traitor. Harper chimed in that he trusted "the good sense of the people will be their shield" against treason and sedition; but, as he could not be certain that it would, he desired the bill to pass.[43]

Gallatin replied that the examples Allen had cited might be "erroneous opinions," but they were not seditious. The Federalists were actually asking that expression of facts and opinions with which they did not happen to agree be punished. "Laws against writings of this kind have been one of the most powerful engines used by tyrants to prevent the diffusion of knowledge, to throw a veil on their folly or their crimes, to satisfy those mean passions which always denote little minds, and to perpetuate their own tyranny." He insisted that no situation existed that could not be adequately taken care of by state laws.[44]

In spite of all Gallatin's efforts the Federalist steam roller moved inexorably on. A bill raising the length of residence required for naturalization to fourteen years became law on June 18. A week later a bill permitting the President to deport "dangerous enemies" received Adams's signature. On July 10 the House passed the sedition bill, drastically revised at the last minute by Harper and Bayard to permit presentation of truth in justification of libel and the determination by juries of the law and the facts.[45]

In Congress, at least, the Federalists were riding high. Did the American people, and especially Gallatin's own constituents, desire martial measures and the curtailment of civil liberties? He would have a chance to find out in the autumn, when he would once more be up for re-election.[46]

4

The first sample of public opinion, tasted in central Pennsylvania, was bitter.[47] Gallatin, his wife, and their infant son were at the Federal Inn in Reading in late August when the local Democratic-Republicans, hoping to start a demonstration in his honor, tolled the bells of the town's two churches and fired a small cannon. Hastily the Federalists organized a counter demonstration. The Reading Volunteer Blues, led by a fife and drum corps playing the "Rogue's Song," marched up and down in front of the inn. Only the stout and resolute tavern keeper prevented several Federalists from mounting the stairs and breaking into the Gallatins' chamber. The next morning, when they were leaving by carriage, Gallatin's effigy was burned a few yards away amid shouts of "Stop de wheels of de government"—the phrase William Cobbett had coined to ridicule his speeches in opposition to the Administration.

West of the mountains, sentiment was as sharply divided over Gallatin and the cause he had espoused. Articles in the chief newspaper of his constituency, the *Pittsburgh Gazette,* charged that he had "never lived in the district, and can hardly be said to live in this country at all. He comes and visits it for a few weeks in this season of the year. He has at least twice while in Congress endeavored with all his might to violate the Constitution which he has sworn to support by overturning the balance of the government by an increase of the power of the House of Representatives. . . . This man may *perhaps* be wise, or may *perhaps* be honest, but both wise *and* honest he cannot be." [48]

Before Gallatin's arrival a report had been widely circulated that he did not wish to run for reelection; and a number of local worthies, most of them Federalists, had begun collecting endorsements. However, the Democratic-Republicans rallied to his support as soon as he appeared. Addresses were drawn up; meetings were held; and a new Jeffersonian organ at Washington, Pennsylvania, the *Herald of Liberty,* began to extol his virtues. The consequence was that Gallatin's margin in the election was comfortable; he lost Allegheny County, but won Washington and Greene, with an over-all majority of almost 1,200 votes.[49]

This was of course gratifying. The news that Gallatin received upon returning to Philadelphia for the congressional session in December was both sweet and sour. In the October elections, the Jeffersonians had won eight of Pennsylvania's thirteen seats, an increase of two. There had been pleasing anti-Administration gains in Virginia and New York; encouraging results in Maryland and Massachusetts. The Kentucky legislature had passed resolutions drafted by Jefferson branding the Alien and Sedition acts "unconstitutional": inasmuch as the Constitution was a "compact of individual states," each state had an equal right to judge for itself, as well of infractions as of the mode and measure of the redress. Movements were started in many parts of the country to petition Congress for repeal of the acts. Gallatin's pleasure was personal, too: the Kentucky legislature had named a new county after him, another after Livingston.[50]

In New England the legislatures were of another temper. The Massachusetts House of Representatives proposed an amendment to the federal Constitution that Gallatin recognized as being directed personally against himself. This would have excluded from Congress any person who was not a naturalized citizen at the time of its enactment and fourteen years a citizen at the time of his election. New Hampshire, Vermont, Rhode Island, and Connecticut, all passed the amendment, but Pennsylvania and Maryland rejected it.[51]

Actually more disturbing to Gallatin was the way in which the federal government was enforcing or threatening to enforce the Alien and Sedition laws and the rest of the "defense" legislation. Twenty-one printers and editors in all sections of the country were reported to have been fined or imprisoned or both for publishing allegedly seditious material. Gallatin took a particular interest in the case of Congressman Matthew Lyon of Vermont, who had been arrested for denouncing the Federalists in his own newspaper, and solicited funds to help Lyon defend himself in court. Meanwhile, both Washington and Hamilton were in the Capital, and he heard they were helping Secretary of War Pickering draw up plans for a standing army of 50,000 to put the Jeffersonians in their place.[52]

The Democratic-Republican Congressmen decided to pursue a cautious course during the new session, avoiding "all questions of foreign relations lest [they] be charged with being agents of France"; they would offer resistance only on domestic affairs.[53]

Fate kept them from living up to their intentions. The Federalists, when a new obstacle fell across their path to complete ascendancy, determined to turn it to their advantage. In the preceding summer the Quaker physician Dr. George Logan had returned from France with the announcement that the heads of the French Republic had assured him that they entertained only the friendliest feelings toward the United States; and the report circulated through Philadelphia that "they would give us peace on our terms if we would only send a negotiator they could trust." The Administration leaders listened skeptically, or refused to listen at all; the Democratic-Republicans hailed both the bearer and his tidings.[54]

In mid-December President Adams in a sense was tricked by belligerently minded cabinet members into inquiring of the Senate whether the "temerity and impertinence of individuals affecting to interfere in public affairs between France and the United States . . . intended to impose upon the people, and separate them from their Government, ought not to be inquired into and corrected." [55] The Federalists in the House of Representatives took the cue, and for the next six weeks Gallatin was occupied in resisting an effort to condemn Dr. Logan and to make it a crime for an American to correspond with a foreign government about a dispute between it and the United States.

As the debate developed, amid snapping tempers and angry exchanges, Harper emerged as the strident spokesman for the Federalist cause. Gallatin in frequent speeches as the Democratic-Republican floor leader provided the most effective rebuttal. With mingled fact and innuendo, Harper undertook to develop the thesis that there was a "pro-French party" in the United States; that, anxious to recover the prestige it had lost as a result of the X Y Z affair, it had employed an unnamed American to "conspire" with the French Directory, and particularly with Talleyrand, to give the American people a false sense of security and thereby to gain control of the government in the elections of 1800. Once it accomplished this, Harper intimated, French troops bearing revolutionary, godless, and immoral doctrines would be officially welcomed to our shores.

Gallatin denied the fantastic thesis as quickly as Harper unfolded it, and questioned the South Carolinian's motive for advancing it. He insisted that there was no pro-French party in the country; the group that Harper had described as such was merely and rightfully opposed to the extension of the authority of the Executive Department. On the contrary, Gallatin declared, the majority party had passed the Alien and Sedition acts in order to consolidate its power, and had created a standing army "not to repel an invasion, but, as it is now confessed," to crush opposition at home. To induce Congress to authorize these repressive measures, the Federalists had found it necessary to "raise a clamor about

foreign affairs." As there was now a mounting popular demand for repeal of the alien and sedition legislation, Harper and his colleagues were
raising the clamor anew. In doing so, they preached a strange and dangerous doctrine: that, because liberty had been abused in Europe, "the
old maxims of liberty and republicanism, which laid the foundation of
our Revolution and of both our general and state constitutions and governments, are to be laid aside, at least for a while."

During the long debate the name of Dr. Logan had not been uttered
on the floor of the House. Gallatin spoke it. One day in January, 1799,
Harper dramatically read to his colleagues an unsigned document he said
had been presented to Talleyrand by the person whose conduct had been
so much discussed. The paper suggested ways in which France might improve its relations with the United States. Early the following day, Dr.
Logan called at Gallatin's lodgings to assure him that he had not written
the document, and that he had good reason to believe that it was the work
of a Boston merchant. Within a few hours Gallatin was able to repeat
the denial to the House and use Dr. Logan's name as his authority. "The
clamor which [the Federalist] gentlemen have thought proper to raise
about this paper," he observed, "when the public knows the fact, may re-
coil on themselves." [56]

It took more than truth and reason to swerve the Federalist majority
from its determined course. It passed not only a censure of the Quaker
doctor, but a law—still on the books—that makes it a crime for a citizen
to promote peace between the United States and its neighbors, although
it remains quite legal to stir up a war.[57]

Undiscouraged, Gallatin and his party colleagues went ahead collecting petitions for the repeal of the Federalist war measures—the standing
army, the Stamp Act, the direct tax, and, especially, the Alien and Sedition
laws. Once again the majority resisted. Whenever Gallatin urged that the
petitions be considered by the House, the Federalists cried out that they
were "libelous"; his speeches were drowned out by loud conversation,
coughs, and the shuffling of feet. Once, above the noise, Gallatin shouted
that for Congress to take the attitude that any protest against a law it had
enacted was a libel, and that any opinion that differed from its own was
libelous, would "effectively destroy the provisions of the Constitution
which guarantees the right of petitioning, and gives to the people the
right, at any time, to oppose their opinions to those of Congress." He
declared that "under pretence of preventing imaginary ills, an attempt is
made to establish the omnipotence of Congress and substantial despotism,
on the ruins of our Constitution." [58]

The Federalists in Congress remained deaf to such appeals, but not

President Adams, who was essentially a rational man. On February 18 he notified the Senate that he had received assurances from Talleyrand that new American envoys would be received courteously, and that he intended to send three to Paris. The Federalists were openly dismayed and privately disappointed. Gallatin, like most Democratic-Republicans, had no way of knowing that there was a great deal of friction within the Federalist party, especially between the President and his cabinet; and he was relieved but incredulous.[59]

By early March, 1799, the nation appeared to be entering more placid waters; neither party felt that there was anything to be gained or lost by tarrying in Congress Hall. Gallatin remained in Philadelphia several days following the adjournment for meetings of the Pennsylvania Democratic-Republican leaders to plan for the coming gubernatorial election. Looking ahead to the Presidential election of 1800, he felt that it was important for party morale and the weight which the state possessed in the electoral college, that the next governor be a completely committed Jeffersonian.[60]

These parleys out of the way, Gallatin rejoined Hannah and their son in the West for a summer of business, politicking, and rest. The opportunity for rest seemed most attractive of all. Again he thought of retirement to private life. "I was not made for politics in such times of agitation," he wrote to an aunt in Geneva as soon as he reached Friendship Hill. "I love peace and tranquillity; I detest confusion and tempests. . . . As soon as I have the chance to retire honorably, whether it be because the country has got out of danger, or because my constituents choose someone else for my place, I will take it." [61]

10. The Jeffersonian Triumph

1799=1801

"The times of agitation" soon passed, and with them Gallatin's thoughts of retirement. The passage of the Alien and Sedition laws proved to be the high tide of the Federalists. They had overreached themselves; the tide, quickened by the shift of affairs overseas, moved relentlessly against them. For Gallatin and the Democratic-Republicans the second biennium of the Adams Administration was marked by many pleasant little triumphs and constantly brightening prospects.

The new turn was revealed clearly in the Pennsylvania elections of 1799. The Federalists attempted to win the normally Democratic-Republican West by nominating for governor a westerner, Senator James Ross; but the enterprise of the Jeffersonians—Gallatin spent a particularly busy summer while at home, speaking, shaking hands, preparing and distributing handbills—made Ross's majority in the area a narrow one. The verdict was emphatic east of the mountains. The Pennsylvania Germans—traditionally Federalist—had resisted government troops sent earlier in the year to enforce the Federalist tax on houses; and they vented their feeling by voting for Thomas McKean, the Democratic-Republican gubernatorial candidate. The Jeffersonians captured the state government handily.[1]

Brighter prospects for the party became even more evident to Gallatin in November, when he set up his little family in Philadelphia in a small house rented at a price that outraged his frugal nature, but that seemed necessary because he and Hannah were expecting another child.[2] No longer would he have to fight the Jeffersonian cause in the House virtually unassisted; Livingston and Nicholas were back, to be joined by a distant connection of Thomas Jefferson, a curious but brilliant youth, beardless and tawny of complexion, piping of voice, tall but wiry, called John Randolph "of Roanoke," after the name of his Virginia estate. Another newcomer in whom Gallatin was to find comfort and support was a relation of Hannah's, Joseph H. Nicholson of Maryland.

The Democratic-Republicans were still not to have it all their own way. The House had been elected a year earlier, and the Federalist party had a majority of twenty. Harper, Griswold, Otis, and Bayard were still present, and were joined by John Marshall of Virginia, whom Gallatin considered, along with Fisher Ames, as one of only "two superior men" with whom he was associated as a Congressman.[3] Marshall was the only Federalist for whose arguments on the floor of Congress Gallatin was ever without an answer.[4]

Tactically, the Federalists were now handicapped by a lack of issues that would stir the people.[5] When the Sixth Congress convened in December, 1799, three American commissioners were in Paris, apparently making great progress in the discussion of peace terms with the French government. With this advent of peace, the Federalists no longer had an excuse to work for extension of the authority of the Executive.[6]

On the other hand, Gallatin and his colleagues had a definite objective —election of Thomas Jefferson as President in the autumn of 1800 and taking over the federal government in the following March. They settled down to a quiet, steady attack on the Federalist system, particularly the Alien and Sedition laws, the enlarged army and the navy, and the heavy taxes.

With France more conciliatory, the Adams Administration allowed the Alien and Sedition laws to become virtually dead letters. The Sedition Act was to expire automatically on March 3, 1801. In a desperate attempt to breathe new life into the issue the Federalists, under Harper, proposed that the law be renewed, pleading that it had prevented "the corruption of public opinion." This contention Gallatin riddled in two speeches. He declared that the law had been employed only to punish persons whose political views differed from those of the party in power. It had been adopted as a defense measure, and with the vanishing need for defense it should be allowed to die peacefully. The Federalist majority saw the pointlessness of their effort and let the law expire on schedule.[7]

The disappearance of the French menace made a large army and navy more patently unnecessary. There had been a spirited demand for officer commissions, which the Federalists had reserved for members of their political faith; but places in the ranks went begging. The Federalists now acknowledged that the army ought to be reduced, but were fearful of too drastic reduction: Marshall and Bayard cried out as if they feared the Democratic-Republicans would insist that the two services be disbanded completely, and warned that this would leave the United States open to invasion by the French if the negotiations at Paris should fail.

Gallatin countered with gentle ridicule: "I was averse to the general system of hostility adopted by this country; but, once adopted, it is my duty to support it until negotiation shall have restored us to our former station." He doubted very much, he said, that the course of the Paris negotiations would be much affected whether we had five or eight thousand men under arms. As for the officers, for whose retention the Federalists were particularly solicitous, "the sooner they return to their homes and occupations the better; for the habits acquired in encampments are, in my opinion, nowise calculated to promote their future usefulness to society or themselves." [8]

The debate was followed by legislation in May, 1800, providing for the discharge of nearly 3,500 men of the regular forces and returning the Army virtually to its status before the war scare.[9] The Democratic-Republicans were joined by the Federalist majority in turning down the plea of the cabinet for continued expansion of the Navy, although appropriations were passed to cover construction work already authorized. The discharge of many Navy officers was likewise ordered.[10]

Although the direct taxes were unpopular, the Democratic-Republicans made no move to repeal them. Gallatin realized too well that the financial obligations the Federalists had contracted during the undeclared war necessitated continuance for the time being; but an argument by Harper during the discussion about armed forces gave him occasion for a fresh and devastating attack on that keystone of the Federalist financial system, the funded debt. As an excuse for retaining a good-sized army and navy, the extravagant South Carolinian urged that there was a real danger, if the negotiations at Paris failed, that the French would invade the United States to plunder "our funded capital." "As our funded capital is the same thing with our funded debt," Gallatin replied sarcastically, "I must confess for my share . . . that I have no objection to give it to the French or to any other nation that will take it."

Harper, still not sensing that he was in dangerous shoals, returned to defend the financial methods initiated in Britain by William Pitt in 1783 and imported into the United States by Alexander Hamilton. Pitt, he said, had "introduced a maxim of infinite importance in finance . . . that whenever a new loan is made the means shall be provided not only of paying the interest but of effecting the gradual extinction of the principal"; and if Pitt's two systems—the sinking-fund and debt-funding systems—had been adopted at the start of the eighteenth century England might have spent as much as she had without now having a shilling of debt except that contracted during the present war. Hamilton and the Federalists had brought both systems to the United States; if the country continued to adhere to them, Harper predicted, its foreign debt would be extinguished in nine years, and "a large part" of its domestic debt in eighteen years. "We may," he summed up, "gather all the roses of the funding system without its thorns."

Gallatin lost no time in telling the House what loose and specious reasoning this was. He offered precise figures: Seventeen years earlier Great Britain's debt had not exceeded £250,000,000. Since then she had enjoyed ten years of peace, seven of war—an average ratio during the past half-century. Now her debt was £500,000,000. "Notwithstanding all the boasted merit of certain modifications of the sinking fund," her public debt had more than doubled.

"I know," Gallatin went on, "but one way that a nation has of paying her debts; and that is precisely the same which individuals practise. Spend *less* than you receive, and you may then apply the surplus of your receipts to the discharge of your debts. But if you spend *more* than you receive, you may have recourse to sinking funds, you may modify them as you please, you may render your accounts extremely complex; you may give a scientific appearance to additions and subtractions; you must still necessarily increase your debt." As the difference between income and outgo must be covered by loans, the annual interest payable on the debt would increase it. This was one of the first times that the fallacious illusion of the sinking fund, so popular in the English-speaking world, had ever been exposed in public.[12]

But Gallatin delivered more telling attacks on the Federalist financial system during the two years, when Democratic-Republican victory seemed to be coming closer and closer, outside Congress. He devoted two months of the summer recess of 1800 to preparing another pamphlet on the state of the federal finances under Commodore Nicholson's roof in New York. Like *A Sketch of the Finances of the United States* four years earlier, it aimed to influence the approaching elections by indicting the Federalists' management of public finance, and especially by exploding the myth they had circulated that the public debt was trifling and on the decrease. Briefer and less ambitious in scope, the new work, *Views of the Public Debt, Receipts, and Expenditures of the United States*, was published in July by a New York printing house.

According to Gallatin, the confusion that the Federalists had created about the public debt was illustrated by two recent official statements. Secretary of the Treasury Wolcott had estimated in January, 1800, that the "principal debt" of the United States had *increased* by only a million and a half dollars since 1789; a special Federalist-dominated committee of the House had estimated in May that the public debt had *diminished* by a little more than a million dollars in that period. What were the facts? Gallatin disputed the accounting methods of both Wolcott and the

House committee and, after establishing what he thought correct procedures, presented tables that indicated that the debt had *increased* close to
nine and a half million dollars in the decade since the establishment of
the federal government.

In *Views*, Gallatin repeated the argument he had made in the *Sketch*
and elsewhere, that Alexander Hamilton had "wasted" a vast sum in the
state debt assumption operation by assuming the debts "at random."
Whereas in 1796 Gallatin had estimated this waste at eleven million dollars, he now reduced it to a bit more than ten million.

The latter section of the pamphlet, and the freshest part, was a review
and analysis of federal finances during the Adams Administration. From
the founding of the federal government to the end of 1795, Gallatin recalled, the United States had spent $2,500,000 more than it had re-
ceived. Then, during the first three years of Adams's Presidency, the trend
was reversed: receipts exceeded expenditures by $3,875,000, reducing the
public debt by that amount. This diminution he attributed to the reduction of military appropriations by the Fourth Congress—in which he himself, incidentally, had played no small role. The increase in revenue he attributed in part to the increase in population and in part to the prosperity of American shippers and merchants made possible by neutrality in
the European war.

Then in 1797 the Federalists had influenced the country to abandon its
neutrality. From June, 1798, to the close of 1800, Gallatin estimated, the
government would have spent $11,500,000 for the Army and Navy as
part of the undeclared war with France. An incalculable amount would
have been lost in profits from commerce and in revenues from taxes on
articles that Americans might have consumed if peace had prevailed. In
one single year, 1799, the public debt had increased $4,780,000—more
than the government had been able to pay off during the three years of
prosperous neutrality. The full cost of the Federalist war with France was
as yet beyond calculation.

The Jeffersonian press hailed the pamphlet for its "exposure of the
extravagance of the federal government." [13] Gallatin himself regarded it
as "a hasty production . . . imperfect in its general arrangement," not
"a complete view of our financial situation." [14] He was perhaps over-
critical. The pamphlet was written expressly as a contribution to the
campaign against Adams, whom the Federalists had reluctantly renomi-
nated for President; and toward that end it was an eminently able performance.

2

The truth was that from the spring of 1800 the attention of all members of Congress was increasingly absorbed by the Presidential election. As November approached, it became evident that the result might well be determined by one or two electoral votes. The bitterness of the struggle was evident in Pennsylvania, where the two houses of the legislature became deadlocked over the manner in which electors should be chosen. This left the determination of the state's large electoral vote very much in the air.[15]

The attention of the politicos now shifted to New York State, where even more electoral votes were at stake. Gallatin was apprised of developments there by frequent letters from Aaron Burr's close friend Matthew L. Davis, Commodore Nicholson, and Hannah, who was visiting her parents.[16] He was jubilant when word came early in May that Burr had outmaneuvered Alexander Hamilton by nominating a particularly attractive ticket in the state elections and rallying the Tammany Society, a social group for immigrants, to its support. The result had been a Democratic-Republican sweep.[17] "Exultation on our side is high," Gallatin wrote to New York about the reaction in Congress Hall; "the other party in low spirits." Toting up election probabilities he concluded that Jefferson was likely to win sixty electoral votes against forty-two for Adams, twenty-one doubtful, and Pennsylvania omitted from the reckoning.

It was time, the Democratic-Republicans in Congress decided, to hold a caucus and nominate a ticket. Who would be Jefferson's running mate? New York had the largest electoral vote in the nation and one that neither party could count on—and accordingly seemed to be entitled to the Vice Presidential nomination. Should it go to the attractive, enterprising Burr, who had been the party nominee in 1796, or to the wealthy, aging George Clinton, who headed the wing of the party which was at loggerheads with Burr? It fell to Gallatin to sound out the sentiment of the New York Democratic-Republicans. On May 6 he wrote an inquiring letter to Hannah: one so addressed would be less likely to fall into unfriendly hands, and the questions in it would in due course reach her father, who in turn would pass them on to party chieftains.[18]

Commodore Nicholson lost no time in calling on Clinton. The former governor was coy. Doubtless he desired the nomination, but wished to be coaxed; at any rate, he mentioned his age, the recent death of his wife, his election to the state legislature. When the Commodore observed that his refusal, by creating divisions in the party, might imperil the election of Jefferson, Clinton agreed to run—provided that he would be free to resign after his election if circumstances made it desirable.

The Commodore wrote all this down in a letter to his son-in-law, which he showed to Burr. Burr's reaction was characteristically enigmatic: he muttered something about feeling certain of being able to obtain the governorship of New York but not the Vice Presidency and walked quickly from the room. A second or so later several of Burr's lieutenants undertook to convince Nicholson that Burr ought to be "persuaded" to accept the nomination. The Commodore had another talk with Burr and yet another with Clinton.[19]

The upshot of all this was that Nicholson destroyed the letter and on May 7 wrote a new one, assuring Gallatin that the old Governor "thinks Burr is the most suitable person and perhaps the only man. Such is also the opinion of all the Republicans in this quarter I have conversed with; their confidence in A. B. is universal and unbounded." [20] About the time Gallatin received this letter, one from Davis assured him that Burr was "the most eligible character, and on him the eyes of our friends in this State are fixed." [21]

There was, however, a seemingly casual, yet significant note of warning from Hannah during the same week: "Burr says he has no confidence in the Virginians; they once deceived him, and they are not to be trusted." [22] In 1796 some Virginia and North Carolina followers of Jefferson had voted for C. C. Pinckney instead of Burr—a maneuver that had dashed the New Yorker's chances for the Vice Presidency. Gallatin probably paid little attention to his wife's warning. At any rate, he told a Congressional caucus on May 11 that Burr was New York's choice; and a ticket of Jefferson and Burr was accordingly agreed upon.[23]

The Congressional recess, on the heels of the caucus, gave Gallatin no respite from politics. He divided the summer between New York, where he prepared *Views of the Public Debt*, and Friendship Hill, where he mended his political fences. The Democratic-Republican organization in western Pennsylvania was girded for victory this year. By August the party press was studded with references to "Albert Gallatin, the friend of the people, the enemy of tyrants," and with appeals to all men opposed to "speculators, land-jobbers, public plunderers, eight per cent loans and standing armies" to reelect him to Congress. The business enterprises Gallatin had organized in Fayette County were lauded for providing employment to nearly a hundred persons and for "saving thousands and thousands of dollars for the Western Country." [24]

In far-off Federalist Boston, an editor might ask his readers whether

they wished, by the election of Jefferson to the Presidency, to turn a
Wolcott out of the Treasury to make room for a "whiskey patriot"; but in
western Pennsylvania the Federalists had little fighting spirit this year.
They drafted a man who was absent from the state as their candidate,
with the result that Gallatin carried all three counties in his district by a
majority of 4200 to 1500.[25]

As the returns from other sections of the Union trickled in to Friendship Hill during November, Gallatin joyously realized that the goal toward which he and his colleagues had been working for nearly a decade
had at last been attained. The struggle for Pennsylvania had been settled
by a compromise that gave the Democratic-Republican ticket eight
electoral votes to the Federalists' seven. But the Jefferson-Burr ticket had
carried New York, Virginia, and enough of the states south of the Mason and Dixon line to make a total of seventy-three to Adams's sixty-
five.[26]

Yet within six weeks of the election Gallatin became aware of a painful possibility. The Constitution stated merely that the recipient of the
largest number of electoral votes would become President and the second largest number Vice President. Both Jefferson and Burr had seventy-
three votes pledged; there would be nothing to prevent a Federalist from
switching his vote to Burr, thereby giving him the Presidency. Nor was
this possibility lost on Thomas Jefferson. On December 15 the anxious
Virginian wrote to Burr confiding that a "General Smith of Tennessee"
had indicated a desire to switch his vice-presidential vote to Gallatin,
"not from any indisposition towards you, but extreme reverence to the
character of Mr. Gallatin." Such an act would of course assure the Presidency for Jefferson. Jefferson was wily, but so was Burr; the New Yorker
did not reply.[27]

Gallatin was out of touch with both Jefferson and Burr at the time and
knew nothing of the game the two party leaders were playing. But as he
started out for Washington early in January, leaving Hannah and the
two children behind because life at the new federal city promised to be
uncomfortable at best, he could not help being anxious lest all the fruits
of the Jeffersonian triumph might yet be lost.

3

Reaching Washington on January 10, Gallatin accepted a half-share of
a chamber in Conrad and McMunn's boarding house at the southeast corner of New Jersey Avenue and C Street, S.W., one of eight clustered

about the still far from completed Capitol. Five days later he wrote at length to Hannah.

Gallatin's letters seldom were outstandingly literary but this letter to his wife remains one of the most vivid depictions of the look and feel of the new Capital.[28] His accommodations at Conrad's, he assured her, were expensive and only passably comfortable; but they were as good as the city offered. The house was a nest of Democratic-Republicans. Two dozen to thirty persons sat down at its tables; but for the presence of two wives, the room "would look like a refectory of Monks. . . . The company is good enough, but it is always the same. . . . I would rather now and then see other persons."

Besides the other boarding houses, the neighborhood of the Capitol had "one taylor, one shoemaker, one printer, a washing woman, a grocery shop, a pamphlets and stationery shop, a small dry goods shop, and an oyster house." That was all.

To reach the white sandstone house which was President Adams's official residence, one journeyed a mile and a half west over a stone footway that was a streak of mud, traversing land that not long before had been woods and swamp; this was known as "Pennsylvania Avenue." "The President's house" impressed Gallatin as "very elegant." He believed that the district in which it was located, "on account of its natural situation, of its [proximity to] George town, with which it communicates over Rock Creek by two bridges, and of the concourse of people drawn by having business with public offices" there, would soon become a town the size of Lancaster or Annapolis. Already there were between fifty and a hundred houses. But "*we* are not there; the distance is too great for convenience from thence to the Capitol."

When Gallatin wrote to his wife again a week later, he was beginning to find the town tedious. "You may suppose that being all thrown together in a few boarding houses, without hardly any other society than ourselves, we are not likely to be either very moderate politicians or to think of any thing but politics. A few indeed drink, and some gamble, but the majority drink naught but politics, and by not mixing with men of different or more moderate sentiments, they influence one another." [29]

During these first weeks of 1801 the House was officially concerned with a Federalist proposal to renew the Sedition Law; the Senate, with a treaty that Adams's envoys had sent back from Paris. General Napoleon Bonaparte, who dominated the French government, had authorized an agreement that placed Franco-American relations on a most-favored-nation basis and recognized the principles of free ships and free goods and freedom for neutral nations to trade in noncontraband. The treaty was not to go into effect until peace was restored between Great Britain and France. Reluctantly the Federalists ratified it, because it was so popular among the mercantile groups that were their chief supports at the polls. Gallatin and his party colleagues could only smile at the disappearance of the last vestige of a popular issue the Federalists had.[30]

Actually one topic engrossed the legislators and dominated their boarding-house discussions: the electoral tie between Jefferson and Burr. Under the Constitution, the issue would have to be determined by the House of Representatives. And the majority of the lame-duck House was Federalist.

Gallatin wrote of his fears to Hannah: "The most desperate of the federalists wish to take advantage of this [situation] by preventing an election altogether." As each state delegation would vote as a unit in any contest in the House, the delegations controlled by the Federalists would cast their ballots for Burr. Or, even more desperately, they might enact a law vesting the Presidential power in the hands of some Federalist.[31]

There was still another possibility that Gallatin did not fully appreciate as yet. Some of the Federalists, led by Bayard of Delaware, did not share the distrust for Burr long cherished by Alexander Hamilton. To them a wily, practical man like Burr, with whom a *modus operandi* might be arranged, was infinitely preferable to a philosophical gentleman like Jefferson.[32]

As leader of the Jeffersonian forces in the House, Gallatin traded gossip, made tallies of the prospective poll, and planned party strategy. Because the attitude of Burr would be of tremendous importance in the expected skirmishes, he tried to sound out the New York leader. Burr wrote on January 16, "Livingston will tell you my sentiments on the proposed usurpation." [33] By discussing the matter with Congressman Samuel Smith, a Baltimore merchant, Gallatin might have learned of a letter from Burr insisting that it was the "wish and expectation of the United States" that Jefferson have the Presidency, and that he desired Smith to use his influence to block any movement that would produce another result.[34]

In dealing with an ordinary man and an ordinary situation, this would have been reassuring enough. But neither the man nor the situation was ordinary. The next month was filled with rumors that Bayard was trying to line up his fellow Federalists for some sort of understanding with Burr. Again on February 3 Gallatin asked the New Yorker whether he countenanced such talk. And again on February 12 Burr answered, somewhat ambiguously, that his mind was "definitely made up. . . . I shall act in defiance of all timid, temporizing projects." He added a

strange sentence: "My letters for ten days past have assured me that
. . . no doubt remained but that J. would have 10 or 11 [states'] votes
on the first trial." There were but sixteen states at the time. Who could
possibly have given Burr such an impression?* Gallatin must have grown
even more uneasy as he thought about it.[35]

There were additional reasons for anxiety. Through the boarding houses
on Capitol Hill there circulated reports that Governor Henry Lee of Virginia (whom Gallatin thought "a desperate character") and Congressman
Griswold ("in other respects a very worthy man" but "warm" and "infatuated" in his desire to keep Jefferson out of the Presidency) were heading a movement to "make a President by law"—that is, have the Federalist majority in Congress enact a law endowing the Presidential powers on
some person other than Jefferson.

Gallatin doubted that this project had a ghost of a chance in the
House; but it angered and alarmed many of his colleagues. Some Jeffersonians threatened that "any man who should thus be appointed President by law and accept the office . . . would instantaneously be put to
death." Fifteen hundred men from Maryland and Virginia were reported
ready to descend upon the city to execute the project. Troubled, Gallatin
called on A. J. Dallas in Georgetown, where the Philadelphian was engaged on a law case, to discuss a plan of Governor McKean for using the
Pennsylvania militia to "preserve the peace" if civil war should break out
on Inauguration Day, March 4.

It seemed to Gallatin that the Jeffersonians ought to agree among
themselves not to obey orders given by anyone whom the Federalists
might make President by law; but, if the Federalists should attempt
merely to call a new election without putting a "usurper" into office, the
Democratic-Republicans ought to acquiesce. He wrote these thoughts
down in a memorandum for John Nicholas. Nicholas showed it to Jefferson, who declared that he "fully approved it." [36] †

What Gallatin and his colleagues had been fearing came to pass on the

* In old age Gallatin endorsed this letter: "had thought that Jefferson would
be elected on first ballot by 10 or 11 votes (out of 16)?"

† Years later some of Jefferson's correspondence was published, and Gallatin
learned that he had written to Monroe and Madison on February 15 and 18,
1801, suggesting that, if the Federalists legislated a President into office, a convention be called to reorganize and amend the Constitution. "That Mr. Jefferson
had ever thought of such a plan was never known to me till after the publication
of the correspondence, and I may aver that under no circumstances would that
plan have ever been resorted to or approved by the Republican party," he wrote
May 8, 1848, to H. A. Muhlenberg.

morning of February 11, when members of both houses trudged through a driving snowstorm to the Senate chamber to hear the report on the ballots cast in the electoral college: Jefferson and Burr each received seventy-three votes; Adams, sixty-five; C. C. Pinckney, sixty-four; John Jay, one.

The decision now fell to the House of Representatives, and the members filed to their own chamber, in a temporary wooden structure in the still uncompleted south wing. Closing their doors to all except senators, they concentrated on the election, for it had been determined to take up no other business until the issue was resolved. The tally was to be taken by states, with the votes of nine necessary for a decision, and it was imperative that every Jeffersonian be present. Congressman Joseph H. Nicholson of Maryland, appreciating the gravity of the situation, had dragged himself from a sickbed and lay on a cot in an adjoining committee room between roll calls, his wife at his side. Without him, as he and Gallatin knew full well, the Maryland vote might be lost to the Federalists.

The validity of the Jeffersonians' fears was confirmed when the roll was called: Jefferson received the votes of eight states; Burr, six; two states cast blanks. It became evident to Gallatin and his friends that Bayard had had his way at the Federalist caucus and Burr had been chosen as the party candidate despite the preference Alexander Hamilton had expressed in letters for Jefferson. Yet the caucus obviously was not binding; otherwise the Federalist majority in the House would have chosen the New Yorker on the first ballot.

The House remained in continuous session, taking one ballot each hour through the afternoon and night. The chamber was drafty and cold. Some members tried to nap between roll calls, sitting upright in a chair or lying on the floor under a cloak. By eight o'clock in the morning of February 12 twenty-eight ballots had been taken, all with the same result.[37]

Gallatin's spirits remained high. He knew of several Federalists who, rather than leave the nation without a President on March 4, would vote for Jefferson; but they hoped that the Jeffersonians' ranks would give way, that some sort of "understanding" might first be reached between the two parties.

So the deadlock continued, day after day. On February 13 one ballot was taken; on February 14, four; on February 16, one—and still the ranks held firm. Gallatin grew irritated. "Rest assured that *we* will not yield," he wrote to his father-in-law during an intermission. "It is the most impudent thing that they, with only six States and two half States, represented on this floor only by 39 members, should expect that a majority of eight States and two half States, represented on this floor by 67 members, should give up to the majority, and that, too, against the decided opinion of an immense majority of the people." [38]

Meanwhile, the Federalists kept up their effort to obtain concessions from the Jeffersonians. None of them approached Gallatin, the party floor leader. One approached Jefferson, who refused point-blank any discussion of terms. Two sounded out Nicholas, but he refused to carry the message to Jefferson. Several told Smith of Maryland that they would agree to Jefferson's becoming President if he would promise not to take any steps that would disturb the public credit, would agree to maintain an "adequate" naval establishment, and would pledge himself not to remove Federalists from subordinate offices. Smith had a talk with Jefferson about these propositions—whether he actually phrased it in terms of a "deal" in discussing them with his chief remained a point of contention ever afterwards—and returned to the Federalists with the assurance that they need not feel anxious on the three questions.[39]

Gallatin was angered by this when he later heard about it and never forgave Smith. As he wrote years later, Smith "was very erroneously and improperly afraid of a defection on the part of some of our members, undertook to act as an intermediary, and confounding his own opinions with Mr. Jefferson, reported the result in such a manner as gave subsequently occasion for very unfounded surmises." [40] Knowing that Aaron Burr still was bitter about the way some of Jefferson's followers had treated him in the election of 1796, Gallatin assured the New Yorker that any reports he might hear of an arrangement between Jefferson and the Federalists were untrue.[41]

The fact remains that Bayard and his band did understand that Jefferson had agreed to their terms. And they were not receiving any encouragement from Burr. The New Yorker, Bayard complained to a friend, was "acting a miserable paultry part. . . . The election was in his power, but he was determined to come in as a Democrat, and in that event would have been the most dangerous man in the community." He was convinced that to hold out longer would be "to risk the constitution and civil war." [42] As Senator Ross of Pennsylvania put it, the Federalists felt that it would be better to elect "any constitutional legal President rather than none." Besides, they saw little prospect of electing one of their party if the election was tried again in the autumn.[43]

On February 17, on the thirty-sixth ballot, Bayard gave the signal by casting Delaware's only ballot as a blank. Federalists in Maryland and Vermont followed his example by switching their individual votes from Burr to blank. The result was that, on the state-by-state tally, Jefferson received ten votes, Burr four, and two were blank. "Thus has ended," Gallatin exultantly wrote to Hannah that day, "the most wicked and absurd attempt ever made by the Federalists." [44]

11. Frontier Businessman

1795=1801

In the first flush of his second marriage, Gallatin confided to Badollet that his bride was "what you call a city belle. She never in her life lived out of a city, and there she has . . . contracted habits not very well adapted to a country life, and specially to a Fayette County life." [1] Frontier living was very much to his own taste, and he had already committed himself to the country west of the Alleghenies—in the farm at Friendship Hill, and in his claims to extensive tracts of land in the Ohio River valley. After his marriage he not only held fast to these possessions but increased them. For this, ironically, Hannah's brother was partly responsible. How to reconcile his wife's urban tastes with his own emotional attachment to the land, and with their joint financial involvement in the West, perplexed Gallatin for thirty-five years.

In the first half-dozen years of marriage Albert and Hannah were able to keep the question from coming to a head. Service in Congress made it necessary for him to be in the East more than half of each year, and this made possible for her long sojourns with the Nicholsons on William Street. In some years she did not go west at all, and he made only brief visits during recesses to attend to political fences and look after his burgeoning business enterprises.

It was characteristic of Gallatin that his ambitious western undertaking, which engaged all his financial resources and much of his thought during the Congressional years, was instigated by loyalty to Swiss friends and to a beloved brother of his wife. It had begun late in 1794, when letters from Geneva told of the desire of many friends to escape the turmoil that the French Revolution had initiated.[2] The romantic spirit that had impelled Gallatin to cross the ocean was not dead. Once more he became the dreamer, sitting down in his Philadelphia boarding house to sketch out a grand project. It would be a settlement in which Genevan men of letters as well as artisans might find employment while holding fast to their native ways. A stock company owned by Americans as well as

133

Genevans would operate it. There was a little colony of Genevans in
Philadelphia, and eight of them assured him that they would take shares.³
    The next step was to find a location suitable for the project. In the
spring of 1795 Gallatin set out on a scouting trip through New York
State west of the Hudson. What he saw did not please him. In late
April he wrote to his wife from Catskill Landing, on the Hudson: "The
more I see of this State the better I like Pennsylvania. It may be prejudice,
or habit, or whatever you please, but there are some things in the Western
Country which contribute to my happiness, and which I do not find here."
One aspect that distressed him was the "family influence" in New York.
"In Pennsylvania not only we have neither Livingstones [sic] nor Rens-
selaers, but from the suburbs of Philadelphia to the banks of the Ohio I
do not know of a single family that has any extensive influence. An
equal distribution of property has rendered every individual independent,
and there is amongst us true and real equality." Furthermore, the land in
New York was poorer and was greatly overpriced. "In a word," he concluded facetiously, "as I am lazy I like a country where living is cheap,
and as I am poor I like a country where no man is very rich." ⁴
    Back in Philadelphia after a month of journeying, Gallatin learned that
affairs in Geneva had improved, and it would be difficult to attract any
great number of emigrants.⁵ But the idea of a settlement still burned
brightly in his imagination, and the western Pennsylvania country looked
better than ever to him. A short distance from Friendship Hill, bestriding
Georges Creek on the eastern bank of the Monongahela, was a straggling
cluster of dwellings knowns as "Wilson's Port." ⁶ It interested Gallatin for
several reasons: it was close to the portage between the waters of the mid-
continent and the Potomac River, upon which the federal city was being built; it was as close as any portage to Philadelphia and Baltimore—
advantages which, it will be recalled, had led him to purchase land and
settle in the vicinity a decade earlier.
    He had no trouble persuading the Genevans in Philadelphia that this
was the ideal spot. Another eager prospect was Hannah's brother James
Witter Nicholson, single and fancy-free, who had just reached his
majority and was anxious to invest his energies and some funds he expected to inherit in a project that promised adventure.
    The arrangement was formalized at Philadelphia on July 31, 1795,
when articles of partnership were signed by five men with ready cash:
Gallatin, Badollet, Nicholson, Louis Bourdillon, and Charles Anthony
Cazenove. All but Nicholson were former Genevans. The partners laid
out money for goods to stock a retail store that would serve as the
nucleus for more ambitious undertakings.

At this moment Gallatin received a welcome tender from Robert Morris: $800 in cash payment for the western lands purchased from him the year before. He took the occasion to compute his worth. It amounted to approximately $7,000, including $3,500 more due from Morris by the next May, Friendship Hill with its 350 acres, one horse, and three head of cattle, and claims to some 25,000 acres of uncleared and unsettled land in the Ohio valley.[7]

The partners started out for Fayette early in August, bent on setting the enterprise in motion as quickly as possible. Acting for them, Gallatin purchased the property at Wilson's Port: 650 acres with three mill seats—one built, another under construction, and the third, which promised to be the most valuable, planned for the river bank so that boats loaded at the mill door might go directly downstream to New Orleans. There were also boat yards. "With a good store," he concluded cheerfully, "we will, in a great degree, command the trade of this part of the country." For himself he purchased all the unsold lots directly across the Monongahela in the tiny town of Greensburgh, and twenty-two acres of the bottom land adjoining it.[8]

The project was turning out to be a much larger one than the partners had envisioned in Philadelphia, and they found it necessary to double their capital, to $20,000. On September 17 they signed new articles of agreement for a three-year partnership to be known as Albert Gallatin & Co. Gallatin subscribed $6,000 as the largest stockholder. Each partner paid in one-quarter of his subscription at once and promised to pay the rest at stated intervals. One clause was designed specifically to provide for Gallatin: "Each of the parties shall devote to the business of the co-partnership every part of his time which the other partners may think necessary, the time which any of them may apply to public offices or employment excepted." But "none may enter commercial transactions or speculations of any kind separately." The lands that Gallatin personally owned on both sides of the Monongahela were to remain in his name, but would be at the disposal of the partnership.[9]

The partners determined that their first object would be to construct the store and complete the millhouses and dam. Later they would construct and offer for sale a number of houses in their little town, which they named New Geneva. Late in the autumn of 1795 Gallatin left his partners on the spot to supervise progress while he attended a session of Congress.[10]

In Philadelphia he soon began to receive a series of letters, the refrain of which was to be drearily familiar through the next half-dozen winters. Something was always going wrong. The man working on the millhouse had fallen from the roof, seriously injuring himself, delaying work on the house and the dam indefinitely. Labor was scarce, and what there was was lazy. Could Gallatin and Commodore Nicholson persuade likely laborers to come to New Geneva?[11] Petty quarrels broke out. Thomas Clare, who was working for the partners, so lost control of his tongue that he publicly repeated remarks Gallatin had made about Badollet's dilatory and dreamy nature. It appeared to Badollet that Bourdillon was impractical, with notions of "making a fortune" and was high-handed in manner. Nicholson echoed these dissatisfactions, somewhat more temperately.[12]

Each summer Gallatin made a trip west, sometimes alone, sometimes with his family, to settle accounts, to give directions for the winter, to try to restore harmony among his colleagues. And as soon as he got back east the bad news and the complaints and recriminations started coming again.

Late in 1796 he received a heavy blow from an unexpected quarter. The bubble of speculation that had exhilarated the eastern cities for several years suddenly burst, taking with it that pillar of American finance Robert Morris. In December, Morris confessed that he would be unable to make any more payments on his debt "until he satisfied the judgments against him." [13] He was clapped into the Philadelphia jail, and his creditors were left whistling—Gallatin for some $3,000 lost on the sale of lands to him.[14] The depression reached western Pennsylvania that winter. The partners reported that the store of Albert Gallatin & Co. was selling "little or nothing" and was loaded with $6,000 of dry goods "which daily suffers in our hands. . . . Few lots have been sold." [15]

During the cheerless spring of 1797 three of the partners took a step that was to have important consequences. Six Germans who had been employed at the New Bremen Glass Manufactory at Frederick, Maryland, passed through New Geneva on the way to Frankfort, Kentucky, where they had agreed to set up a glassworks. Among them was young Christian Kramer, who had been brought to this country by John Frederick Amelung, one of the ablest craftsmen in the nascent American industry. Indeed, Kramer himself already had something of a reputation as a blower of hollow ware.

An encounter and a talk with the Germans set the imaginations of the partners astir. Why not establish a glassworks at New Geneva? There were fewer than a dozen in the United States and there was a strong demand in the western country for glass, especially for windows and bottles. Sand for the manufacture of glass was readily available in the neighborhood of New Geneva, and the Monongahela would make it easy to transport the finished product to points as distant as New Orleans.

The partners' idea appealed to the Germans. First, however, they would have to clear themselves with the Kentuckians. But Badollet, who reported the development to Gallatin, was convinced that, "struck with the advantages of our situation, they will come back and finally settle with us. . . . Such an undertaking, considered either as a public or a private view, ought to supersede every other, and we will attend to it to the utmost of our abilities." [16]

Gallatin was not impressed. A glassworks, he lost no time in writing back to his partners, was a "lottery ticket"; the partnership's greatest asset was its real estate, and this ought to be developed carefully.[17] But when he went to Friendship Hill in the long summer recess, he gradually changed his mind about the project. Five of the blowers, led by Christian Kramer and his brother George, returned from Kentucky; and, after due negotiations, Gallatin and his partners reached a formal agreement with them on September 20. Under its terms, Albert Gallatin & Co. was to advance all the funds needed for constructing the glassworks—ultimately, $10,000. The net profits were to be divided equally between the company and the Germans.[18]

The Germans lost no time in constructing the New Geneva Glassworks, on the edge of the village. The small furnace contained at first only four pots and was suitable for producing common green glass for windows, whiskey and porter bottles, and various types of hollow ware.[19]

Though the works were ready, the glass was slow in coming. During the first months of 1798, while Gallatin was fighting the Federalist war program on the floor of Congress almost singlehanded, every mail from New Geneva brought dismal tidings. During the first five weeks of production only sixty-five boxes were completed. Then weeks passed without any production. The shearers had not been sufficiently careful; too much wood was burned; clay was hard to come by; costs were exceeding all expectations.[20] "The works must be abandoned at all events," directed the harassed Gallatin. "For God's sake reject every plan that tends to involve us. Rent or sell or abandon the works; but let us not melt every thing we have in the attempt." [21]

He betrayed his despondency in two letters to old and dear friends. "I am a bad farmer, and have been unfortunate in some mercantile pursuits I have embraced," he confided to his old friend, Lewis F. Delesdernier. "The fact is, I am not well calculated to make money—I care but little about it, for I want but little for myself, and my mind pursues other objects with more pleasure than mere business." [22] To Hannah's attractive younger sister Maria, he confessed that his affairs at New Geneva troubled him more than the party battles in Congress. He was especially depressed by the debts incurred. "To be in debt is to me the worst of all possible situations, and one in which I would never have fallen, had I never formed a society with others, or had I remained at home to direct our business. So long as that situation shall continue I will know no rest and no peace of mind." [23] He cut his own expenses to the bone, taking pride in the fact that he could live comfortably in Philadelphia on his Congressional salary of six dollars a day.[24]

Gallatin's troubles came in packs. Acting on his Genevan principles, he had directed that all the debts of his grandfather be paid "in order to do full honor to the memory of my parents." The estate was sold for less than half what it had been valued before the French Revolution. Instead of receiving $6,000 from it, he found himself poorer by $200; but he explained to his wife that he "could not have reconciled it to my feelings that any individual had lost a single half-penny" through himself or his grandparents. The Revolution had greatly depreciated the property in France and the Netherlands which he had inherited from other members of his family. "The French revolution has cost me exactly 16,000 dollars," he observed on totaling his assets at the end of 1798. "Yet the Federals call me a Frenchman, in the French interest, and forsooth in the French pay!" Letters from his Geneva relatives confessed that in the past they would have insisted that he bring Hannah to live in Europe; but now they believed that "Providence has placed us in a better situation. And so," he confessed to his wife, "do I." [25]

The undeclared war with France brought a new business opportunity which he grasped with reluctance, and which, ironically, ended in a profit. In 1797 the Pennsylvania legislature directed that the state militia be reorganized to repel any invasion the French might attempt, and authorized the purchase of 12,000 stands of arms. The expenditure struck Gallatin as unnecessary; but, inasmuch as his constituents were to be taxed for the purpose, he felt he should see that a proportionate amount of the money appropriated was spent west of the mountains. His partners were enthusiastic, and it was only at their insistence that he used his influence with Secretary Dallas to obtain a contract in February, 1799, for 2,000 stands of arms without cartridge box.[26] By the end of the year work was proceeding satisfactorily enough for Gallatin to inquire of the federal government whether he could not supply it with small arms.[27] He was not too troubled, it seems, by having desperately fought appropriations for the purpose in Congress. But by this time France was taking a more pacific tone, and military preparations were being curtailed.

Meanwhile the glassworks had survived its birth throes and was beginning to do better.[28] In December, 1798, and January, 1799, £600 worth of glass was manufactured, and sold to customers in Pittsburgh and Kentucky.[29]

These successes were achieved only after a complete reorganization of the partnership placed the ownership and direction almost completely in Gallatin's hands. Badollet was the first to go. The dissociation was accomplished amicably; Gallatin forgave his impractical schoolmate loans that he had frittered away, and Badollet contented himself with subsistence farming in Washington County.[30] Cazenove had become so disenchanted with the prospects for New Geneva that he sold his interest to Gallatin and departed for the East.[31] Bourdillon was more difficult. Gallatin finally told him in 1799: "I must have executive officers who will consult and act for me. . . . You have uniformly suffered yourself to be deceived by hopes for the future in which we have uniformly been disappointed. . . . I could say more, and much more, on the subject, but I wish to . . . part with you in peace and friendship." [32]

The partnership of Albert Gallatin & Co. ended in the summer of 1799 with Gallatin in complete ownership, young James Nicholson acting as his deputy in the West, and a man named Mussard in direct charge of operations at the glassworks and the gun factory.[33]

By late 1800 the gun factory had made two deliveries to the state,[34] and the glassworks, despite occasional delays caused by cold weather and an "insurrection" by workmen demanding higher wages, was giving a satisfactory account of itself.[35] The Jeffersonian press pointed to these projects with pride as proof of Gallatin's fitness for reelection to Congress that year.[36]

2

Though Gallatin spoke often of wishing to settle down permanently to life as a frontier businessman at New Geneva, he was troubled by the thought that it would part Hannah and himself from the Nicholson family. He would, he acknowledged, "feel the want of them more than I can express." [37] As an orphan boy in Geneva he had missed normal family life, despite Mlle. Pictet's well intentioned efforts. The Nicholsons gave him as a man what he had lacked as a child, and in the years following his marriage he passed a larger and larger part of the Congressional recesses in the pleasant atmosphere, domestic and political, of the Commodore's William Street home.

At the Nicholsons' Gallatin's first child was born on December 18, 1796—a boy, named James after his maternal grandfather.[38] He was an exceedingly proud father, and when he was separated from Hannah his letters dwelt on the child. He racked his memory to recollect how he had behaved as an infant in order to offer advice on how the baby should be raised. "And is my dear son uneasy about his teeth . . . ? I know his nerves are delicate, for mine always were, and my wife is not a prodigal of strength in that particular. . . . Let him awaken by the musical sound of his own mother's voice and never by the abrupt sound of impatience or ill humour. . . . Let him acquire from education that smoothness which arises from a continuity of pleasing impressions during childhood." [39]

A second son, who was named Albert Rolaz after his own grandfathers, was born January 8, 1800, in Philadelphia.[40] Now Hannah's letters became reports of James learning to spell out words of one syllable and "making out tolerably well," of little Albert walking about the house, riding his father's cane as if it were a horse, cutting his teeth, and growing very cross.[41]

To economize and to see how Friendship Hill would do as a permanent home if her husband should give up politics, Hannah passed most of two winters there. The experiment was not a success. She was as indifferent a country wife as Gallatin was a farmer: although she went through the motions of sewing and stringing beans, she was "inadequate to the duties of her station" and did not know "how butter is made, meat salted, vinegar prepared"; nor could she scold like a good farm wife. She was always first in bed at night and last up in the morning. She felt acutely the shortage of servants on the frontier and found her neighbors, even her own brother James's family, anything but stimulating.[42]

Fortunately the election of Jefferson to the Presidency enabled the Gallatins to escape at least temporarily the dilemma created by New Geneva.

3

Almost as soon as it became clear that the ticket of Jefferson and Burr had the larger electoral vote, Federalist and Democratic-Republican newspapers alike began to refer to Gallatin as the probable next Secretary of the Treasury. The reasons were obvious. Alone among the Democratic-Republicans he had exhibited a flair for handling the thorny problems of public finance; indeed, his attacks on the policies of Hamilton and Wolcott, on the floor of Congress and through two widely influential pamphlets, went far towards explaining the party triumph. Jefferson's own knowledge of financial matters was not great, and none recognized it more than he. Moreover, as he confided to an acquaintance who had doubts of Gallatin's "patriotism," there really was no choice; Gallatin "is the only man in the United States who understands, through all the laberinths that Hamilton involv'd it, the precise state of the Treasury, and the resources of the Country." [43]

Although Jefferson met and worked with Gallatin each day, he spoke no word of his determination. "Indeed," Gallatin confided to his wife, "I do not suppose that it would be proper in him to say anything on the subject of appointments until he shall be elected." He professed uncertainty whether he was "equal to that office." Even more real were his misgivings as to confirmation of the appointment by the Senate, for he remembered all too well two previous difficulties with legislative bodies.[44]

On February 18, 1801, the day after the thirty-sixth ballot that gave Jefferson the Presidency, the President elect told Gallatin the names of those he intended to name to the principal offices. Gallatin passed the word on to Hannah coyly: "The most obnoxious to the other party, and the only one which I think will be rejected, is that of a certain friend of yours. That *he* . . . shall hold one of the great offices is pressed on *him* in such a manner and considered as so extremely important by several of our friends, that *he* will do whatever is ordered." [45]

The possibility that the Senate might reject his nomination haunted Gallatin. The Federalists were not accepting their dismissal from power with good grace, and he became a particular object of their vindictive rage. Privately and through the party press they spoke of him as a foreigner, a political adventurer, a Necker determined to destroy the government whose ladder he had ascended. A junto of Federalist senators opposed to him was said to be headed by James Ross and Uriah Tracy. In the new Senate, to convene on the day of Jefferson's inaugural, four newly elected members would give the Democratic-Republican party a majority; but they would probably be late, and their presence to support Gallatin's nomination could not be counted on.[46]

Gallatin's fear that, after going to the expense of moving his household to Washington, he might find himself without an office caused him to evolve a plan, with Jefferson's cooperation. His nomination would be held up until the reconvening of the Senate in December, when the Democratic-Republicans seemed to be certain of controlling both houses. Party newspapers would devote the recess to trumpeting his accomplishments and his virtues.[47]

At noon on March 4, 1801, Gallatin watched Jefferson walk from Conrad and McMunn's, through a crowd that had gathered from Maryland and Virginia, to the Capitol, where he mounted the steps and proceeded to the packed Senate chamber. In a low voice the President read conciliatory words: "But every difference of opinion is not a difference of principle. . . . We are all Republicans: we are all Federalists." [48]

Gallatin viewed the opposition less charitably. Reporting John Adams's hasty departure from the Capital at four o'clock in the morning in order to avoid the inaugural ceremonies, and probably alluding to his numerous appointments to federal justiceships in the last hours of his administration, he wrote to his wife: "You have no idea of the meanness, indecency, almost insanity, of his conduct, especially of late. But he is fallen and not dangerous. Let him be forgotten. The Federalist phalanx in [the] Senate is more to be feared." [49]

Promptly after the inauguration, President Jefferson submitted nominations for the cabinet with the exception of the Treasury and Navy portfolios, both of which promised to arouse Federalist opposition. The Senate approved them promptly and unanimously.[50] Samuel Dexter of Massachusetts, who had become Secretary of the Treasury late in the Adams Administration, agreed to continue supervision of the Department until May, which would give Gallatin time to go to New Geneva, settle his business affairs there, and bring his family to Washington. At the President's request, he lingered until the arrival of the new Secretary of State, James Madison, so that the three might discuss the "leading principles of the new administration" [51]; and he devoted the days of waiting to the preparation of a memorandum on the condition of the federal finances for the new President.[52]

Ten days after the inauguration, Gallatin was on his way to the Monongahela, with mixed feelings about the prospect. "As to our new Administration," he had written to his wife, "the appearances are favorable, but storms may be expected. The party out of power had it so long, loved it so well, struggled so hard to the very last to preserve it, that it cannot be expected that the leaders will rest contented after their defeat. They mean to rally and to improve every opportunity by which our errors, our faults, or events not under our control may afford them." But he was also moderately optimistic and a trifle self-righteous. "With the people on our side and the purity of our intentions, I hope we will be able to go on. But indeed, my dear, this is an arduous undertaking in which I am called on to take a share." [53]

12. First Days in the Treasury

1801=1805

To transport two infant children and a wife who was expecting another, a small corps of servants, and enough furniture to set up a permanent establishment two hundred miles over tortuous mountain roads was no easy task even in the middle of spring; Gallatin was immensely relieved when they reached Washington safely on May 13.[1] Even then their worries and their wanderings were not over. For brief periods they put up at two houses not far from the President's mansion.[2] By mid-August the heat and miasmic vapors of the city that, a short time before, had been a swamp made Hannah worry about the family's health. By diligent search her husband found a mansion in a healthier location on Capitol Hill, northeast of the Capitol on the road to Bladensburg. This made it necessary for him to ride twenty minutes to his office on Fifteenth Street, N.W. He discovered in time that the location had an additional advantage: its proximity to the Capitol made it a convenient gathering place for wifeless Congressmen.[3]

The day after reaching Washington, Gallatin took the oath of office as Secretary of the Treasury from William Cranch, assistant judge of the United States Circuit Court, the highest-ranking judge then present. The day after that, the *National Intelligencer*, the quasi-official Administration newspaper, printed the fact of his arrival and his assumption of his duties.[4]

He had expected the job to be demanding, and at the outset it lived up to his anticipations. Conscientiously he set out to master the routine day-to-day operations of the Treasury Department, and then to develop and put into effect a fiscal program that would embody his financial philosophy, all the while performing the hundreds of acts expected of him as Secretary of the Treasury. There was always a fearful number of letters to write. During the next two years, he found that all this demanded "close attention" at least eight hours of the day and frequently additional hours of the night. Often, to escape the interruptions to which he was subject in his office, he worked at home.[5]

Happily there was, by the current standards, a sizable organization to cope with the routine chores. Hamilton had built up a staff of high ability and exceptional integrity, which Gallatin suspected of having relaxed somewhat under Wolcott's direction. The Treasury Department had a staff of 1,285, including 78 in the Washington offices. Scattered through the country were 707 in the customs service, and 500 in the internal revenue service, but supervision of these was handled by such subordinates as the Commissioner of the Revenue, the comptrollers, the auditors, the Purveyor, and the Register. After two years in office Gallatin could be content to mark out the main lines of policy and leave the details to his subordinates, subject of course to review.[6] In time it became possible for him to discharge his office duties in about two hours each day, although at times of crisis he put in several hours more at home, after nine o'clock when his family retired.[7]

Gallatin gave much attention to work with the President and his colleagues in the cabinet. He had come to have the highest respect for Thomas Jefferson in the six or eight years he had known him. Working closely with him during the next eight years, he developed an affection for him that was reciprocated.

For Secretary of State, Jefferson had chosen Gallatin's colleague in Congress, the scholarly, even-tempered James Madison of Virginia. Of the three other cabinet members he knew little at first; but that little struck him favorably enough. The Secretary of War, Henry Dearborn of the District of Maine, had sat with him in the Fourth Congress, but their acquaintance was slight; Gallatin thought him "a man of strong sense, great practical information on all the subjects connected with his department . . . what is called a man of business," not "a scholar." The claims of Robert Smith, the pleasant nonentity at the head of the Navy Department, were chiefly those of his imperious older brother Samuel, the Baltimore merchant-shipper and political power with whom Gallatin had served in Congress. Samuel Smith had wished to be Secretary of the Navy himself; then, thinking better of it, he yielded the honor to the inoffensive Robert and contented himself with pulling strings from Capitol Hill. The Attorney General was Levi Lincoln, an ornament of the Massachusetts bar. "A good lawyer," thought Gallatin, "a fine scholar, a man of great discretion and sound judgment, and of the mildest and most amiable manners." [8]

Early in the Jefferson Administration, Gallatin proposed that meetings of the entire cabinet be held regularly once a week or oftener. Jefferson, however, preferred the practice familiar to him as a member of Washington's cabinet: meetings of the entire cabinet only for the discussion of broad policies, the President being always ready to receive a secretary for individual conference on problems in his own department.[9] Scarcely a day passed when they were in the Capital on which Gallatin did not confer with the Chief Executive; and, wherever they were, there was a frequent exchange of letters and notes between them.

The President recognized his own limitations in finance and relied frankly and completely upon Gallatin to set and administer policy in that field. Whenever he prepared a message to Congress he would submit it in rough draft to the cabinet members, expecting Gallatin to write the paragraphs on fiscal matters. On day-to-day matters, Jefferson came to depend upon his Secretary of the Treasury to such an extent that on occasion he accepted his digest and recommendations without inquiry into the case.[10]

Gallatin's influence regularly reached beyond the Treasury Department. For one thing, its duty, as he conceived it, was to watch closely the operations of the other Executive departments, making certain that sound fiscal practices were observed. More important was his range of knowledge and his soundness of judgment. Jefferson found his comments so perceptive and constructive, particularly in their preciseness of phrasing, that he made a practice of submitting messages and other important state papers to Gallatin first among the cabinet members and accepted most of his suggestions. The Administration was actually a triumvirate of Jefferson, Madison, and Gallatin, with the President only a chief among equals and Gallatin's influence reaching deep into every sphere of governmental activity.

2

Financial policy of course was the field in which Gallatin's influence became first and most transcendingly visible. Between March, 1801, and December, when the Seventh Congress completed its organization, he developed a distinctive and far-reaching fiscal program that was accepted by the President and the rest of the cabinet. It was in essence the program, a fruit of his Genevan heritage, that he had urged in Congress and in pamphlets through a period of some six years.

Gallatin was convinced, as he wrote several years later, that reduction of the public debt was "certainly the principal object in bringing me into office." His chief shared that conviction, surmising that "we shall never see another President and Secretary of the Treasury making all other objects subordinate to this." [11]

When Gallatin entered the Treasury, the public debt exceeded $82,-000,000. He estimated in the autumn of 1801 that it could be extinguished completely in sixteen years if the government would earmark $7,300,000 of income each year for payment of interest and principal. Provision for this should be made through a permanent loan.

Given four administrations of peace and reasonable prosperity, Gallatin felt certain that the Treasury would have no difficulty in accomplishing this. Customs duties would provide $9,500,000 a year; sale of public lands and postal service would provide $450,000; internal taxes, especially the tax on whiskey stills, would yield $650,000. This made a total of $10,600,000—an excess of $3,300,000 beyond what would be required to meet the annual cost of retiring the debt.[12]

Gallatin still felt the contempt he had expressed in Congress for the device Hamilton and the Federalists had adapted from William Pitt to cope with the public debt: the sinking fund. Intrinsically, he believed, the fund did "neither good nor harm"; but potentially it was a danger, because it rendered the fiscal operations of the government "more complex, and the accounts of the public debt less perspicuous and intelligible." He held back from recommending abolition of the fund, because a large section of the public, cherishing the notion that it exerted a wholesome check on the Secretary of the Treasury, might suppose, if he suggested that it be discontinued, that he contemplated shenanigans with the public funds.[13]

The second goal to which Gallatin committed the Administration was reduction of taxes so far as would be safe. He had not forgotten his role in the Whiskey Rebellion—would the Federalists ever let him forget it?—and the detestation of his fellow westerners for the tax on stills. But dropping the excise would make uneconomical continued collection of the other internal duties. Without them, only $2,650,000 a year would be available for all the expenses of government—civil, military, and naval. It would be better, he concluded, to keep the internal taxes for the time being.

Gallatin did not believe that the government departments should receive whatever they asked; far from it. "Savings in every department may be practicable, and must be attempted wherever practicable," he observed. "Thousands of dollars" could be saved in the civil departments; "hundreds of thousands," in the War and Navy departments.[14] On the passing of the threat of war with France, the Federalists had reduced the annual Army and Navy appropriations from $6,000,000 in 1800 to $3,780,000 in 1801. The lower appropriations were still far too much, Gallatin believed. He suggested a reduction for 1802 to $1,600,000—

considerably less than the Federalists had been spending on the Navy alone.[15]

In cabinet discussions, both Dearborn and Smith were astonishingly agreeable to economies within the War and Navy departments. Secretary Smith knew the President shared Gallatin's inland prejudice against a navy and doubtless felt it was discreet to be accommodating; but when it came to working out specific figures, the amounts for the two services were raised to a total of $1,900,000, with Gallatin further reducing the allotments for civil expenses to make up the difference.

Gallatin's planning did not forget yet another fiscal principle for which he had done battle in Congress with only temporary success: specific appropriations by the legislature. As he outlined it to the President in November, 1801, and in subsequent papers, he sought the adoption of "such measures as will effectually guard against misapplication of public monies, by making specific appropriations wherever practicable." He believed that the Secretary of the Treasury should not transfer the appropriated sums to the Secretaries of State, War, and Navy to expend at their discretion, as had been the practice since 1789, but should make payment directly to the individual to whom it was due or to his agents. The recipients would thus be responsible directly to the accounting officer of the Treasury for what they did with the money.[16] Jefferson's first annual message presented some of these ideas to Congress.[17]

Here, then, are the most significant financial principles Gallatin brought to the Treasury: the primary importance of systematically paying off the public debt; stringent economy in government expenditures, with especially large reductions for the Army and Navy; specific appropriations by the legislature; and scrupulous accounting to assure efficient administration of those authorized. The plan was admirable. But how would it fare with Congress?

3

In Congress, Gallatin had missed no opportunity to criticize the Federalists for enhancing the influence of the executive branch at the expense of the legislative, for permitting the Secretary of the Treasury to assume a primacy in the Administration comparable to that of the British First Lord of the Treasury, even initiating and directing the passage of legislation.[18] Now the shoe was on the other foot. Would he let Congress go its own way toward the goals he and the President had set up? The answer of course was that he would not; and, like most human beings, he felt no embarrassment in reversing his attitude in the change of circumstances.

His shift was less obvious because the Democratic-Republicans had a comfortable margin in both houses of Congress. Two leading members of the new Ways and Means Committee were close personal friends, the chairman being the brilliant and eccentric John Randolph of Roanoke, who made no secret that he considered Gallatin's abilities "very great." [19] The second ranking member, pivotal in questions of concern to Gallatin, was Hannah's cousin Joseph Hopper Nicholson of Maryland. Randolph, Nicholson, and other Democratic-Republican leaders including Nathaniel Macon of North Carolina would drop in at Gallatin's home, so handy to the Capitol, for an evening of gossip and discussion of legislation close to his heart. Sometimes the procedure was reversed, Gallatin going to the Capitol, even as Alexander Hamilton had done, to attend committee meetings and to present plans and suggestions. On at least one occasion he sent Randolph an "appropriation bill with the blanks filled and a few necessary amendments." He made no secret of his "long and confidential intercourse" with Congressmen of his own party, nor of his "free communication of facts and opinions" to Randolph.[20]

With such rapport established, virtually all of Gallatin's recommendations were brought to the attention of the House of Representatives in the form he desired. One exception stemmed from a difference of opinion with the President about internal taxes. Jefferson's message of December, 1801, recommended that they be repealed at once; Gallatin's report to Congress, published soon after, indicated that they should be retained for the time being. It was doubtless at meetings under Gallatin's directing eye that Randolph exacted promises from Secretaries Dearborn and Smith to pare the expenditures of the War and Navy departments a further $600,000. On this basis Randolph introduced legislation to end the hated excise tax. At the same time he introduced a bill to bring about Gallatin's dearest wish—an annual appropriation of $7,300,000 toward payment of the principal and interest of the public debt.

The Federalist minority, led by Bayard of Delaware, made no attempt to block the tax reduction. They merely questioned whether it would not be better to offer tax relief on necessities like salt, sugar, tea, and coffee, than on whiskey. Only once did Randolph deign to reply to such criticisms—by requesting the Clerk of the House to read aloud a passage from Gallatin's report. The repeal of the excise sailed smoothly through both houses.[21]

Gallatin had no trouble with his proposal that appropriations be made for specific purposes. Beginning with the laws for 1802, Congress regularly inserted this feature in its appropriation legislation.[22] His move for strict accountability to the Secretary of the Treasury was another story. Nicholson brought the issue to a head on December 14, during a discussion of the handling of State Department finances in the Adams Administration, when he proposed the appointment of a special committee to inquire whether the moneys drawn from the Treasury had been properly applied. The House granted his request and made him chairman of the committee. On January 19, 1802, he formally asked Gallatin for his views on the subject.

Gallatin, on March 2, took full advantage of the opportunity to detail the way he would have strict accounting to the Treasury enforced through legislation. He acknowledged that it would not be "useful and necessary" to apply this principle to all fiscal laws, especially some affecting the War and Navy departments.[23] Nicholson took the cue and requested an accounting from the two military departments of expenditures that they had not reported to the Secretary of the Treasury; and both departments duly complied. He passed the reports along to Gallatin, who used them to reenforce his request for strict-accounting legislation. He and Nicholson working together, assisted by William Branch Giles of Virginia, produced a bill along the lines sought, and Nicholson introduced it on April 8.[24]

The idea died a-borning, apparently killed by the partisans of the Navy. Secretary Smith had trouble bringing to a halt the great naval expansion program initiated during the latter days of the Adams Administration.[25] Indeed, Smith complained to Gallatin in May that if Randolph had consulted him as well as Gallatin when the appropriation law for the year 1802 was drawn up, he could have administered his department more efficiently; the classifications Gallatin had had written into the law were going to result in "a rather ridiculous appearance." [26]

The Navy had strong supporters in Congress, even among the Democratic-Republicans, of whom not the least influential was Samuel Smith. In consequence of their quiet efforts the session ended in the spring of 1802, before Gallatin's "accountability bill" could reach the floor of the House. But this was his only defeat during the honeymoon months of his secretaryship. The reduced appropriations for the Army, Navy, and civil branches of the government and the bill to provide $7,300,000 annually for redemption of the public debt, all were enacted in the form he had requested.[27]

4

It was inevitable that Gallatin should have trouble with Secretary Smith and his Navy partisans in his financial program; it was likewise inevitable that he should be bothered by foreign relations. At the very moment he was developing a system that would extinguish the public debt within sixteen years, events overseas threatened the peace of the United States. Almost since achieving independence, the United States had joined the chief European nations in paying annual tribute to the four pirate states of North Africa—Morocco, Algiers, Tunis, and Tripoli—to refrain from interfering with merchantmen plying the Mediterranean trade routes. In ten years, under Washington and Adams, the United States had paid nearly $10,000,000 in tribute and ransom. It was President Jefferson's intention to continue this practice.

In the spring of 1801, before Gallatin assumed charge of the Treasury Department, the Pasha of Tripoli suddenly decided that he must have a larger tribute and declared war on the United States. When Gallatin reached Washington he reluctantly agreed to a step that had already been approved by the President and his other counselors—the dispatching of a squadron, including three of the frigates whose construction Gallatin had opposed in Congress, to the Mediterranean to protect our commerce.[28]

The little American fleet failed to awe the pirate states. Late in the summer of 1802, while the President was at home in Virginia, Secretary Smith began to step up the Navy's efforts. Seeing his fiscal dreams imperiled, Gallatin wrote to urge Jefferson to make peace with the pirates at any reasonable price. The cost of a war, he contended, would be greater than the tributes demanded. Other nations had long shared with us whatever "disgrace" there was in buying off "those barbarians." "Eight years hence," he said, "we shall, I trust, be able to assume a different tone; but our exertions at present consume the seeds of our greatness and retard to an indefinite time the epoch of our strength." [29]

While the President hesitated, Smith ordered the frigate *John Adams* to sail from New York to blockade the Barbary Coast. Gallatin sent frantic appeals to Jefferson at Monticello to countermand the order. Not enough of the naval appropriations remained unexpended to cover the cost, he insisted. Jefferson was somewhat impressed and inquired whether some way could not be found to include the expenses of the *John Adams* as a "debt incurred." During the delay, the frigate put to sea.[30]

Thus was the nation committed to war against the pirates. With the squadron against whose use Gallatin had complained, Commodore Edward Preble stormed Tangiers and brought the Emperor of Morocco to terms; but the Tripolitans captured one of his vessels, the *Philadelphia*, made prisoners of its officers, and put the crew of approximately three hundred to hard labor. Word of this development reached Washington in March, 1804. With Gallatin's reluctant approval, President Jefferson asked Congress to raise naval appropriations to $750,000 a year so that stronger measures might be taken against the pirates.

Gallatin swallowed hard and looked for ways to raise the necessary sum. The Treasury had $1,700,000 in specie, but he believed that it would be dangerous to spare more than $150,000 for war purposes. In consultation with Randolph, Nicholson, and other members of the Ways and Means Committee, he devised a solution. In 1796, in *A Sketch of the Finances of the United States*, he had written that import duties were "the most productive, cheapest to collect, least vexatious, and in general the least offensive" form of taxation.[31] In line with this conviction, he and his Congressional friends now proposed to create a separate Treasury account, known as the Mediterranean Fund, which would be fed by an increase in ad valorem duties on imports. Imports that had been subject to 12½ per cent duty were now subjected to 15 per cent; 15 per cent duties were raised to 17½ per cent; and 20 per cent duties rose to 22½ per cent. It was expected that the average ad valorem duty would rise from 13½ per cent to more than 16 per cent. There was to be an additional duty of 10 per cent on goods imported in foreign vessels. The increase in duties, Gallatin's plan specified, was to expire three months after the reestablishment of a general peace.

When Congress debated the legislation setting up the Mediterranean Fund in late March, one Federalist scathingly characterized it as "perfectly deceptive . . . an attempt, on the part of the Administration, to avail itself of a public misfortune to impose new, impolitic, and unnecessary taxes." But the Democratic-Republicans were relieved because it avoided a return to the hated internal taxes, and the legislation passed both houses in a matter of weeks.[32]

Deceptive or not, the Mediterranean Fund enabled the Navy to press its operations against the Barbary powers. During the summer of 1804, Preble conducted an effective blockade along the Tripolitan coast that remains one of the glories of our sea history.

Although Gallatin reconciled himself to the Barbary War, he was never able to approve of Robert Smith's administration of the Navy Department. At embarrassing moments Secretary Smith descended upon him with re-

quests for cash—$20,000 or $100,000—that it was "absolutely necessary" he have before the day was out, to be repaid from the next naval
appropriation.[33]

Gallatin did not try to conceal from the President his indignation over
Smith's "want of good management." "I cannot discover any approach towards reform" in the Navy Department, he wrote to Jefferson. "I hope
that you will pardon my stating my opinion on that subject, when you
recollect with what zeal and perseverance I opposed for a number of
years, whilst in Congress, similar loose demands for money. . . . Although I am sensible that in the opinion of many wise and good men my
ideas of expenditures are considered as too contracted, yet I feel a
strong confidence that on this particular point I am right." [34] To such
complaints the President made no reply.

Although Gallatin and Jefferson shared a distaste for the Navy, they
differed as to how economies could be effected in its administration. The
President desired to concentrate all naval activity at Washington. The
draft for his annual message of 1802 proposed the construction at the
Capital of a large dry dock capable of storing virtually all of the fleet
when it was not in use.[35] Gallatin answered a request for his opinion by
opposing the idea for the very reason the President urged it. "I am *in
toto* against this recommendation," he wrote bluntly, "1st, because so long
as the Mediterranean war lasts, we will not have any money to spare for
the navy;" secondly, because there were already six navy yards which
could be used for dry docks without additional expense.[36]

Jefferson disregarded the advice and submitted his scheme to Congress.
Congress disregarded it—as well as the desire of both President and
Secretary for naval economy—by passing appropriations to construct six-
teen brigs and fifteen gunboats.[37]

5

The vexations that the Navy and the Barbary War created for Gallatin
were tiny compared to the strain that Napoleon Bonaparte imposed on his
fiscal program in the summer of 1803 by offering to sell a piece of war
booty, the Spanish empire in the heart of North America known as
Louisiana.

The offer, though surprising, did not come as a bolt from the blue.
Gallatin had nearly a year to consider his action. In the middle of
1802 the cabinet learned that France had acquired title to Louisiana and
planned to take possession of it. But then the Spanish intendant,
still in charge of the port of New Orleans, abruptly forbade Americans to

deposit merchandise there as had long been their custom. There were cries of outrage in Kentucky and Tennessee; and it was feared that the bumptious westerners might take it upon themselves to declare war on the Louisiana authorities. As a westerner whose business interests had caused him to look southwestward, Gallatin could understand them only too well. At that very time the western Pennsylvania Federalist James Ross proposed to the Senate that a force of 50,000 be sent to take New Orleans by force. It looked as if the Federalists had their first real issue against the Jefferson Administration.

To head off the danger, the President and Secretary Madison hit upon the idea of purchasing New Orleans or the province of West Florida—or perhaps both—to serve as an outlet for American commerce on the Gulf of Mexico. The notion especially appealed to Gallatin, a man willing to buy peace at any reasonable price. It may well have been he that arranged with John Randolph for the introduction, in the House during January, 1803, of a resolution supporting the move and a recommendation that $2,000,000 be authorized for "expenses in relation to the intercourse between the United States and foreign nations." Shortly afterward President Jefferson dispatched James Monroe to join Robert R. Livingston, the American minister at Paris, in negotiating the purchase of a port. Looking out for the financial side of the negotiation, Gallatin requested Monroe to arrange if possible that the price be paid through bills on the Treasury.[38]

Within a month of Monroe's departure, Jefferson was anxious enough to start discussing alternatives with his cabinet. Suppose the French refused to sell. The bellicosity of the westerners and the opportunism of the Federalists made war appear inevitable. Upon what terms should the United States make an alliance with Britain in her war against Napoleon? Gallatin joined Madison and Smith in voting that America should insist on an agreement that neither nation make a separate peace. The cabinet was unanimous that Britain must not be permitted to take Louisiana for herself. These instructions were duly forwarded to the American representatives at Paris.[39]

The negotiation turned out more favorably than any American dared hope. For some reason about which historians still speculate, Napoleon on April 30, 1803, authorized the signing of a treaty ceding to the United States not only New Orleans and part of Florida, but the whole vast territory of Louisiana. The price was to be $15,000,000.

Under the terms of the treaty, the United States was to issue and turn over to the French Treasury $11,250,000 of 6 per cent stock, redeemable in fifteen years. The rest of the purchase price was to be expended in the United States to satisfy the claims of American citizens against France. The French Minister of the Public Treasury made arrangements with the Dutch banking house of Hope & Company and the British House of Baring to take the stock.

In the autumn of 1803 Alexander Baring turned up in Washington to complete the negotiation. He was a wise and witty man with an American wife; in the course of dealings, Gallatin became immensely fond of him. When word reached them early in January, 1804, that American forces had formally and peacefully taken possession of New Orleans, Gallatin turned over one-third of the stock certificates and, as a precaution, sent the rest to Livingston at Paris by special messenger.

Gallatin was delighted with the Louisiana Purchase, though none too happy about the financial terms by which it had been accomplished. He believed that the low price Hope & Company and the Barings were paying for the stock—78½—did not reflect accurately the state of American public credit, and he wished the stock might have been redeemable in a shorter time. He regretted that so much had been spent to satisfy the claims of Americans.[40]

He lost no time in planning for payment of the additional debt and the interest on it. He would increase the annual appropriation for retiring the public debt by $700,000—to $8,000,000 annually. Customs duties at New Orleans would supply $200,000 of this. It would be possible to discharge the entire public debt by 1818, only eighteen months later than he had originally planned. The $3,750,000 promised to French creditors in the United States was handled without difficulty. By his practice—perhaps deliberate—of underestimating the Treasury's receipts he had accumulated a sizable surplus, of which $2,000,000 was available immediately for carrying out the Purchase; and he believed future surpluses would easily care for later payments. His proposals became law in November, 1803.[41]

From any point of view, this was an extraordinary operation. For a nation to increase its territory by 140 per cent through purchase, paying well over a quarter of the price in hard cash, and providing for the payment of the balance and interest without resort to increased taxation was unique in government fiscal history.

13. Patronage and Personalities

1801=1807

Memories of the Federalist "reign of terror" were fresh, memories of the bitter ballot contest with the backers of Aaron Burr even fresher, when President Jefferson told an expectant Congress: "We are all Republicans: we are all Federalists. . . . Let us reflect that having banished from our land that religious intolerance under which mankind so long bled and suffered, we have yet gained little if we countenance a political intolerance as despotic, as wicked, and capable of as bitter and bloody persecutions." Only a few weeks later he wrote to a Philadelphia physician: "Of the thousands of officers . . . in the United States, a very few individuals only, probably not twenty, will be removed; and these only for doing what they ought not to have done." [1]

Gallatin took the President's words literally and assumed that he planned no drastic reorganization of the civil service, as he approached the matter of appointments in the Treasury. The chief offices in his gift, and indeed the most important group of federal agents dealing directly with the citizens, were the collectors of the different ports. Politically the collectors loomed large in their districts, and they were in a position to keep the Administration apprised of local party trends and factional maneuvering. They were paid on a fee basis, and some collectorships were extremely lucrative. Moreover, they had the appointment of numerous subordinates, including measurers, weighers, and gaugers. [2] The Federalists, during the dozen years they controlled the government, had staffed these and other federal offices with men devoted to their party and its principles.

In drafting a circular letter to the collectors and their subordinates not long after he took office, Gallatin made clear the restraint with which he intended to treat such appointments. Treasury officeholders were not to participate actively in politics: "Whilst freedom of opinion and freedom of suffrage at public elections are considered by the President as imprescriptible rights, which possessing as citizens, you cannot have lost by becoming public officers, he will regard any exercise of official influence to restrain or control the public administration which is confided to your care, as practically destructive of the fundamental principles of a republican constitution."

Another paragraph instructed the collectors, in filling subordinate offices, to divide their nominations between the parties, because "talents and integrity are to be the only qualifications for office." The "door of office" was to be "no longer shut against any man merely on account of his political opinions." [3]

Gallatin sent the draft of the letter to the President for approval on July 25. The reply on the following day was disturbingly equivocal. The President wrote that Secretary Madison had been with him when the draft came, and they both had read and discussed it. He himself approved "entirely" of the two key paragraphs and indeed had planned to issue a proclamation on electioneering by government officials, "but was restrained by some particular considerations." He and Madison believed that ultimately an "equilibrium" in public offices should be established between the two parties: one-half of the Federalist subordinates should be "exchanged" for Democratic-Republicans. After that was done "talents and worth alone" should count in filling "new vacancies." [4] However, there should be delay in announcing the principle: there was a patronage squabble in Connecticut that ought to be settled first.

Before Gallatin formally assumed responsibility for the Treasury, Jefferson had voided one of the last acts of President Adams—nomination of a Federalist as collector of the port of New Haven—and had named in his stead the father of an active Democratic-Republican party worker. A group of New Haven merchants, die-hard Federalists, protested in a strongly worded remonstrance, accusing President Jefferson of failing to live up to the professions in his inaugural address. Jefferson's temperate reply implied that the victor was entitled to half the spoils: "If a due participation of office is a matter of right, how are vacancies to be obtained? Those by death are few; by resignation none. Can any other mode than that of removal be proposed?" [5] Jefferson told Gallatin that, after the reply was published and understood by the public, "you will be so good as to send out a circular with, or without previous communication to me." [6]

The reply had an effect that the President did not expect. A fortnight later he confessed to Gallatin that it seemed only to have sharpened the anticipation of the extremists in his own party for sweeping removals from office.[7] Gallatin agreed that "the Republicans hope for a greater number of removals; the Federals also expect it." Most of the removals so far made were warranted, but it would be well "to stop the ferment" lest it spread throughout New England and to the South.[8]

Gallatin's fears were not misplaced: the ferment spread to all parts of the nation. He did his utmost to resist the pressure. Most of his dismissals from office, between 1801 and 1805, were for defalcation or other misconduct, and none seems to have been purely political. When dishonesty was charged against an officeholder he demanded adequate proof and made his own investigation. The Treasury Department made a far better record than other departments, although the Administration, despite the cries of the Federalists, removed probably no more than 10 per cent of all federal officeholders for purely political reasons.[9]

Most troublesome of all patronage problems for Gallatin were those in Pennsylvania, his home state, and in New York, home of Commodore Nicholson. In them he was concerned not only with Treasury appointments but with the favors of all federal branches. The problems were all the more vexing because both states had well organized Democratic-Republican machines, with rival factions and many workers hungry for political plums.

2

Gallatin's difficulties in Pennsylvania centered in two ambitious and ruthless Philadelphians: William Duane, editor of the *Aurora*, and Michael Leib, a physician with political proclivities. Although both were relative newcomers to the Democratic-Republican ranks, they had performed yeoman service for the state organization during the Federalist "reign of terror"; they had not missed a trick in turning the widespread resentment into votes for Thomas McKean for governor in 1799 and Thomas Jefferson for President in 1800. They sought patronage and power for themselves and their cronies; circumstances rather than any particular love for each other made them allies.

Duane caused Gallatin the more trouble. American-born but Irish-bred, he had a checkered journalistic career in England and India before settling in Philadelphia. Soon he was assistant to Benjamin Franklin Bache, editor of the *Aurora*, chief organ of Pennsylvania Republicanism. When Bache died in the yellow-fever epidemic of 1798, he took over the editorship; and he soon demonstrated a talent for hard-hitting journalism that made his paper influential far beyond the borders of Pennsylvania. Flushed by success, he began indulging his own antipathies through editorial comment that was often scurrilous.

Duane's vitriolic pen soon got him into trouble with the Federalists. Throughout 1801 he was busy in court defending himself, and in the spring he passed thirty days in jail for an editorial denunciation of a federal judge. The experience gave him a driving ambition—to "reform" both the state and the federal court systems, to purge them of their "British traditions" and their solicitude for "the rich and well-born."

Duane coveted offices for his friends in order to augment his own political influence. He was enraged when Governor McKean ignored his petitions for state offices, and was determined that President Jefferson should accede to his suggestions for such political plums as the collectorship of the port of Philadelphia. For himself he sought the government's orders for stationery, on the ground that the expense of defending himself in the courts had so eaten up his income from the *Aurora* that he could not support his family adequately. He would have liked to obtain the contract for printing the journals of the House of Representatives and perhaps even move the *Aurora* to the new Capital.

Gallatin had barely taken over the reins at the Treasury when Duane descended upon him with an extraordinary document: a booklet on the front cover of which he had lettered, partly in Gothic script, "Citizen W. Duane." Inside was a list of clerks in the State and Treasury departments preceded by their salaries and followed by critical comments, thus:

1400	Jacob Wagner.	Complete picaroon.
600	Steph. Pleasanton.	Nothingarian.
800	———— Brent.	Nincumpoop.
1500	John Newman.	Democratic executioner.

The implication was clear: these men should be discharged and replaced with friends of Duane.[11] The editor opened a store at Washington and informed both Gallatin and Madison that he would be pleased to have their departments' orders for stationery.[12] He discovered that his hopes for printing the House journals and for moving the *Aurora* were hopeless, because the President had already given his support to Samuel H. Smith in establishing the *National Intelligencer;* but he continued to hunger for offices and petty favors.

Because Duane was a Pennsylvanian, President Jefferson let Gallatin handle him. The Secretary put off answering Duane's importunities for nearly two months, to July 5. Then he wrote that it was not hostility that had caused the delay: "I should explicitly say, that although I may not have agreed with you in every thing, I feel a sincere esteem for your talents and firmness . . . and a wish to be useful to you whenever consistent with propriety. . . . I felt that we had fought with different arms in the same cause, that . . . the unrelenting spirit of persecution had pursued you out of your birth right and into a jail." Patronage presented "numerous and real difficulties," although he hoped that eventually a "beneficial and popular" solution could be found. No change was then contemplated in the Philadelphia customhouse. As for Duane's candidates for office, "the active leaders of the heroes of the [Federalist] reign of terror . . . must be protected; but they are entitled only to justice and not to power." To soften the blow, he promised that Duane could count on supplying all the stationery needs of the Treasury Department.[13]

This answer did not satisfy Duane, and Gallatin had to repeat it in person when the editor paid another visit to the Capital later in the summer. He had no illusions that his urbane refusal would put the man off indefinitely. As he subsequently told the President Duane might acknowledge that the reasons for declining his solicitation were good; but his feelings would continue to be "at war with any argument on the subject." [14]

The truth seems to be that Gallatin began to share the distaste felt for Duane and his cohorts by his old friend A. J. Dallas. Dallas had become the leader of the conservative wing of the Pennsylvania Democratic-Republicans and a defender of the established court system against the *Aurora*. Naturally he was loath to do anything that would enhance Duane's influence. The collectorship at Philadelphia ultimately went to a man so conservative that the Federalists had considered him seriously as a gubernatorial candidate. No federal office of any importance went to Duane or his friends.[15]

At this nadir of his fortunes Duane acquired an ally in Dr. Leib. A Philadelphian of German descent, Leib was more interested in public office than in a medical career, and he had uncommon talents as an orator and manipulator of men. In spite of his Apollo-like figure, powdered hair, modish way of dressing, and habit of using perfume, he had been an energetic worker in the democratic cause since the day of Citizen Genêt; and he had a loyal following among the workingmen of Philadelphia.[16] Jefferson's triumph gave him a seat in Congress. Somehow, over the Washington grapevine in the spring of 1802, he learned that Secretary Gallatin had advised the President that the arrangement for Duane to supply the government with paper ought to be terminated. He passed this on to Duane, with the addition that Gallatin had been telling people that he was overcharging the government.[17]

Before long the editor and the physician made common cause in a concerted drive to obtain the replacement of all Federalist holdovers in federal posts in Pennsylvania with Democratic-Republicans. They appealed to President Jefferson over the head of Secretary Gallatin, his natural adviser on Pennsylvania matters. Their campaign opened in December, 1802, with a series of articles in the *Aurora* demanding the removals.[18] When word of the articles reached Washington, seven Pennsylvania Congressmen signed a letter to the President firmly denying that they were displeased with the Administration's handling of patronage. Leib was asked to sign and agreed at first, but changed his mind. He copied part of the letter and sent it off to Duane, who printed it in mutilated form in the *Aurora*. The seven signing Congressmen decided not to send the letter but to express their satisfaction to the President in person.

Meanwhile, Duane and Leib were busy in Philadelphia. Early in March, 1803, a meeting of Democratic-Republicans of the South Ward, which they dominated, adopted resolutions demanding removals and calling upon others to exert similar pressure on the President. The cue was taken up by other groups in the city in the following two months.[19]

Gallatin was troubled by the development. Although Dallas wrote from Philadelphia that he should not worry, that the ward meetings were "composed of very few indeed," Congressman William Jones of Philadelphia warned, "Duane and his coadjutors meditate an attack upon Mr. Madison and yourself for setting your Faces against the office hunters." [20] Gallatin wrote to the President on March 21, "I foresee a schism in Pennsylvania." Although he was certain "the most thinking part of the community" would not be swayed by "the violent party," Duane's and Leib's efforts might persuade many good people that all who opposed them were pro-Federalist. "This incident will, at all events, render the question of removals still more delicate and difficult." He hinted that he would like to know what the President intended to do so that he could tell his friends in Philadelphia.[21]

President Jefferson took the matter calmly, even philosophically. To Gallatin he predicted, with what was to prove admirable accuracy, that schisms of this sort would occur in other states and indeed in Congress as soon as the Democratic-Republicans "shall be so strong as to fear no other enemy." [22]

The letter from the ward meetings, with a total of thirty-nine signatures, reached the President in July.[23] He concluded that it would be best to answer it through a letter to Duane, one of the few signatories he knew personally—a man who, he recognized, must be handled gingerly lest he "be in a different section from us." [24] He drafted a long letter pointing out that, because of death, resignation, and removal, "of 316 offices in all the United States subject to appointment and removal by me, 130 only are Federalists,"—all done "in little more than two years, by means so moderate and just as cannot fail to be approved in future." Of the eight federal offices in Pennsylvania, five were now in Democratic-Republican hands; and counting the emoluments involved, the ratio was much greater than five to three.[25]

Now it was Gallatin's turn to be philosophical. He advised against dispatching the letter. He thought it improbable "that abstract reasoning, or even a statement of facts already known to them, will make converts of men under the influence of passions or governed by self-interest." He was inclined to be fatalistic. "Either a schism will take place, in which case the leaders of those men will divide from us, or time and the good sense of the people will of themselves cure the evil. I have reason to believe that the last will happen." [26] Jefferson bowed to Gallatin's advice, formed, as he acknowledged, "on a view of the ground and better knoledge of the characters." [27] No answer was made to the letter from the ward meetings.

By the autumn of 1803 the leaders of the various Pennsylvania factions realized that if they were to carry the state for Jefferson the next year, the party breach must be closed at least temporarily. Truce talks took place at Gallatin's home on Capitol Hill. Dallas was present, and possibly Dr. Leib. The solution was ingenious. Why not nominate Governor McKean for Vice President? This would give Pennsylvania national recognition such as it had not yet enjoyed. More important, it would remove from state affairs a controversial officeholder, especially obnoxious to Duane and Dr. Leib because he refused their requests for state patronage and was adamant in opposition to their judicial "reforms." With Gallatin's approval, Dallas forwarded the suggestion to McKean. But the Governor would have none it it; he pleaded his advancing years, a conviction that he had already had his share of honors, and a fear that men with "wanton passions" would get control of Pennsylvania if he left the state capital.[28]

What happened in the next encounter between the factions is less clear. In the winter of 1803–1804—so Duane charged some years later—he was visiting Gallatin's office in Washington when the Secretary warned him that "if he did not abandon" Leib, the Administration would "ruin" him. Other members of the Administration made the same threat about the same time. Duane, in discussing the incident publicly, contended that he had always been "independent" of Leib, and that they had been made bedfellows "by those who could not bring either to be the instrument of destroying the other." [29]

Whether it happened exactly as Duane asserted—he was notoriously free-and-easy with the truth—it seems probable that Gallatin took part in an effort to break the Duane-Leib alliance, hoping to strengthen Jefferson's candidacy in Pennsylvania in 1804. On the eve of the election the *Aurora* protested that "Washington City" was interfering too much with the local elections, and reported a toast at a Philadelphia party rally expressing the wish that the Treasury Department's influence be limited to finance, "not extended to elections." [30] Gallatin need not have worried about Pennsylvania. Jefferson carried the state, 22,000 to 1,200.

After the election the schism in Pennsylvania grew wider and wider. To "sweep away what remains of the dregs of British laws and lawyers," to curtail the power of Governor McKean, and coincidentally to obtain some patronage, Duane and Leib proposed that the state constitution be revised. Dallas with Dr. George Logan, Peter Muhlenberg, and other conservative Jeffersonians formed a "Society of Constitutional Republicans" to block this effort and obtain a third term for Governor McKean. Dallas asked Gallatin to endorse their group; but he was reluctant to get caught in the fray and replied merely that he thought the Pennsylvania constitution—which he had helped frame—satisfactory as it stood, although he regretted that it contained no provision for amendment.[31] Despite Gallatin's aloofness, Duane sullied his name frequently in the columns of the *Aurora*, making baseless charges that he had engaged in various land speculations while in public office.[32]

Dallas's group reelected McKean by a narrow margin in 1805, only by allying itself with the vestiges of the Federalist party. The result dejected Gallatin, who interpreted it as a victory of Duane and Leib, observing gloomily: "McKean owes his reelection to the federalists . . . The number of Republicans who have opposed [Duane] rather than supported McKean does not exceed one fourth, or at most one third, of the whole." He blamed McKean for the schism, not because he had passed over the patronage claims of Duane and Leib but because he had instituted a spoils system in Pennsylvania.[33]

Despite Gallatin's desire to keep out of the Pennsylvania state battles, Duane insisted on considering Gallatin as one chiefly responsible for his frustrations. In private correspondence he declared that the Secretary was not only "a dangerous politician but unfaithful to his public trust." He actually believed the charges he kept printing in his *Aurora* that Gallatin had amassed vast landed wealth and had connived with the British minister at Washington and with the President's enemies in Congress.[34]

Gallatin had the impression that Duane made these charges to build up a case for use in the Presidential campaign of 1808, when Madison might be a candidate to succeed Jefferson and he himself might be transferred to another cabinet office.[35]

This was a shrewd surmise. But the charges were also manifestations of the twisted psychology of an embittered and frustrated man. A man who could assure a friend with straight face that it was "not liking or dislike" of Gallatin that stirred him—"superior motives activate me . . . I know myself to be superior to every species of meanness" [36]—can prove to be a very dangerous adversary. As, in time, Duane did.

3

In New York State, too, clashing personalities and rivalries over patronage troubled the political waters with disturbing consequences for Gallatin. There had long been three factions within the party that had carried Jefferson to victory in New York in 1800, headed respectively by the veteran Governor George Clinton and his ambitious young nephew DeWitt Clinton, by Congressman Edward Livingston, and by Vice President Aaron Burr. All were avid for political office. President Jefferson tried to deal with them with an even hand. Soon after the inauguration, Burr presented him with a slate of candidates for federal positions in New York that had been accepted by the state Democratic-Republican Congressional delegation. The President obliged by appointing all the men suggested with one exception.[37]

The exception was Burr's close friend and devoted follower Matthew L. Davis, who wished to be the naval officer of the port of New York. The Clintonites had filled Jefferson with misgivings about Davis's "standing in society" and "respectability";[38] besides, the President still remembered Burr's enigmatic conduct during the Congressional settlement of the election of 1800. He allowed Richard Rogers, a Federalist who was reputed to have been a Tory during the Revolution, to continue in the office, and made no answer to Burr's letters about it.

By the summer of 1801 Gallatin was hearing from several sources about the dissatisfaction in New York over the President's inactivity. Burr sent assurances that Davis's talents were "superior to those of any other person who can be thought of and . . . his appointment will be most popular." He requested Gallatin to show the letter to Jefferson.[39] Six weeks later Commodore Nicholson wrote that he had no doubt Rogers's continuance in office would "bring the Republican interest in this City (if not the State) in the minority." With Rogers further maintained in office, the testy commodore raged, "if I live to see another Election I shall think it my duty to use my interest against" Jefferson.[40] Davis and Burr may have prompted the commodore to write the letter. Gallatin, who still had a warm spot in his heart for the attractive Vice President, obliged him by writing to the President at Monticello that he believed Burr enjoyed the confidence of a "large majority" of New York Democratic-Republicans and was the least selfish of the factional leaders.[41]

Before the arrival on September 12 of Jefferson's reply Gallatin found himself facing Davis in his own office. The New Yorker presented another letter from Burr: "Goaded . . . by the instances of an hundred friends," Davis was on his way to Monticello to press his case in person. Would Gallatin write a letter for him to take along, impressing the President with the magnitude of Davis's support in New York? [42]

Gallatin complied, reluctantly. "I have used my endeavors to prevent his proceeding to Monticello," he explained in the letter, but he was "not easily diverted from his purpose." He himself was not certain whether Rogers ought to be removed. "Though he is a good officer, I would feel but little regret at his being dismissed, because he has no claim detached from having fulfilled his official duties, has made an independent fortune from that office, and, having no personal popularity, cannot lose us one friend nor make us one enemy." He recommended Davis as "a man of talent, particularly quickness and correctness, suited for the office, of strict integrity, untainted reputation, and pure Republican principles." He made no secret of his disturbance over the widespread expectation, created by the President's reply to the New Haven merchants, that the Administration would make a general purge of Federalist officeholders. He was particularly troubled by the number of removals already made in New York. "I feel a great reluctance in yielding to that general spirit of persecution, which, in that State particularly, disgraces our cause and sinks us on a level with our predecessors." The factional fight had become so bitter that he feared the Jeffersonians might lose the Empire State in the next Presidential election.[43]

After Davis was on his way with this letter Gallatin continued to brood over the New York situation. Several days later he expressed even more sober second thoughts to Jefferson: He did not doubt that Burr would consider a refusal of the office to Davis as "a declaration of war." Repulsed, the Vice President might become a very dangerous factor in national politics. Perhaps the Jeffersonians had been unwise to make him their candidate for the second office in 1796 and 1800. Under Washington, the Vice Presidency had served as a steppingstone to the Presidency.

Could not that happen under Jefferson—and should it? At any rate, serious thought ought to be given to amending the Constitution to distinguish between votes cast for the first office and the second, thus preventing a repetition of the deadlock of 1800.[44]

The reply was short and unilluminating. "Mr. Davis is now with me," the President wrote on September 18. "He has not opened himself. When he does, I shall inform him that nothing is decided, nor can be till we get together at Washington." He added vaguely that he had an amendment in mind that would accomplish the purpose Gallatin had suggested in his letter.[45]

Six months passed. Jefferson returned to Washington. The cabinet members discussed patronage questions on many occasions. Still Rogers continued to serve in the New York naval office. Late in March, 1802, Gallatin received a plaintive plea from Burr: "As to Davis, it is a small, a very small favor to ask a *determination*. That 'nothing is determined' is so commonplace that I would prefer any other answer to this only *request* which I have ever made." [46]

Gallatin could do little to escape from the ambiguous position in which the President's perhaps unconscious but certainly pronounced efforts to isolate and weaken Burr politically had placed him. His own father-in-law Commodore Nicholson embarrassed him further by deserting Burr and obtaining, through the influence of the Clintons, appointment as commissioner of loans at New York.[47] When, at long last, the President appointed a new naval officer, it was also to a Clinton follower. He gave the federal district attorneyship to Edward Livingston and several other important offices to his followers.

The Livingston appointment had its own unhappy repercussions. In June, 1803, a routine examination by Treasury agents of the records of the New York district attorney's office revealed a shortage of about $40,-000 in the department charged with the collection of federal taxes. The opportunity for this had arisen when Livingston attempted to serve simultaneously as district attorney and mayor of New York: he had little time to be in the federal office himself, and the clerk he placed in charge was unreliable. Livingston visited Washington early in July, obviously to discuss the matter with Administration officers. Jefferson was at Monticello, and so he sought out Gallatin. He paid a social call on the Secretary at his home, but apparently was too embarrassed to come to the point. The following month Gallatin, troubled by further reports from his agents, traveled to New York to look into the situation personally. He learned that the deficiency had now been found to approximate $100,-000. Livingston hastily resigned his offices and departed to embark on a new career at New Orleans. Ultimately all but $40,000 of the loss was covered by property he left behind.[48]

Commodore Nicholson's alliance with the Clinton group also brought some vexations. During the summer of 1802, at the request of the Clintons, the demagogic journalist James Cheetham published articles attacking Burr, especially for his behavior during the Presidential campaign of 1800. To document his charges, the Clintonians induced the commodore to write down what he knew about the rivalry of Burr and Governor Clinton for the Vice Presidential nomination two years before; but publication of this statement was withheld for the time being.[49]

When Gallatin paid his annual summer visit to the Nicholsons a short while later, he was caught in the midst of this intra-party battle. He had never been fond of the Clintons; he remained fond of Burr. In the course of a frank chat the Vice President convinced him that Cheetham's attack had "deeply injured the republican cause in this State" and showed him a letter to Governor James Bloomfield of New Jersey in which he had made "an explicit denial" of the charge that he had intrigued with the Federalists or "in any way attempted during the late election or balloting, to counteract" the election of Jefferson. At Burr's request, Gallatin forwarded these assurances to the President.[50]

Even this was not enough to still Jefferson's suspicion of his Vice President. Making no effort to get into touch with Burr, he assured the Clintonians of his good will and, by implication, gave approval to their war on Burr.[51] Late in February 1804 a caucus of Democratic-Republican congressmen took the President's cue and nominated for the place Burr held the venerable George Clinton.

Sensing that he had no future in the party as long as Jefferson remained its head, Burr looked in other directions for advancement. He began conferring with Federalists in his own state and in New England; there was talk of his becoming their candidate for governor of New York, possibly even head of a New England confederacy free of the baneful influence of Jeffersonianism. These schemes stirred up the long-simmering hostility of Alexander Hamilton, and led to their fatal duel on the New Jersey Palisades in July. The Clintonians, realizing they had much to gain from the tragic outcome, outdid even the Federalists in damning Burr.[52]

Gallatin shed no tears over the death of Hamilton, whom he cordially disliked; but he was revolted by the conduct of the Clintonians. "Much real sympathy and sincere regret have naturally been excited by that catastrophe," he commented to Hannah's brother. "But unquenchable hatred of Burr and federal policy have combined in producing an artificial sensation much beyond what might have been expected; and a majority of both parties seems disposed . . . to deify Hamilton and to treat Burr as a murderer. The duel, for a duel, was certainly fair." [53]

Less than four months after the duel, Burr calmly appeared in Washington to preside over the deliberations of the Senate. Gallatin called at his lodgings a number of times, on one occasion remaining two hours. The visits were more than friendly gestures: he was acting also as an emissary of the President. For Thomas Jefferson, the ally of the Clintons, the enemy of Burr, was now concerned about the approaching impeachment trial of the Federalist Judge Samuel Chase. To him it was imperative that Chase be removed from the bench as a first step toward "cleansing" the federal judiciary of partisan Federalist judges. As Vice President, Burr would preside over the trial by the Senate. Both President Jefferson and Secretary Madison showed him marked though less conspicuous attentions.[54] Burr reciprocated by presiding in an exemplarily judicious fashion; but the Senate on March 1, 1805, found Chase not guilty.

After the start of Jefferson's second term Burr, unemployed but ambitious as ever, continued to puzzle and trouble the members of the cabinet. Before long strange rumors trickled into Washington: In a luxuriously appointed flatboat Burr had descended the Ohio and the Mississippi to New Orleans, meeting persons of local importance en route—among them, Andrew Jackson at Nashville, General James Wilkinson at St. Louis, and the Roman Catholic bishop at New Orleans. He had talked about many different things, but one possibility seemed to be distinctly on his mind: creation of a confederation of the West, perhaps with the cooperation of the British, perhaps of the Spanish.[55] Neither Gallatin nor Jefferson was alarmed by these reports. When Burr returned to Washington for a visit in the summer of 1805, they again received him cordially.

The rumors became more pointed early the next year. In February, 1806, Jefferson was showing Gallatin a letter from Joseph H. Daveiss, federal attorney for Kentucky, intended for the eyes of the President and Madison and Gallatin but no others. "You have traitors around you to give the alarm in time to their friends," Daveiss warned. Burr was busy reviving the old Spanish plan to separate the western country from the United States, perhaps with the connivance of General Wilkinson, who he knew had been receiving a pension from the Spanish for years. "This plot is wider than you imagine. . . . You will dispatch some fit person into the Orleans country" to investigate.[56]

The President and the two secretaries were skeptical. Daveiss was a notoriously partisan Federalist and was not to be taken too seriously. In comparison with other concerns of the moment, Burr's activities seemed to be so wild and desperate as to be harmless. Gallatin approved when Jefferson wrote to Daveiss requesting him to write fully everything he had heard, naming names, and assuring him that his correspondence would be treated in the utmost confidence.[57]

That summer, vacationing at the Nicholsons', Gallatin received a letter from Burr, friendly and puzzling. The former Vice President was in Philadelphia; if he had known that Gallatin was going to pass through on his way to New York, he would have performed "a promise made last winter by shewing you certain depositions then spoken of . . . but we shall meet somewhere in the autumn—my object defence only not attack." Was Burr still bent on clearing himself with Jefferson about his role in the 1800 election? Other passages were even more obscure. Was General Wilkinson still governor of Louisiana? Could Gallatin tell him how he might obtain information about the title of a Baron Bastiaf to lands on the Washita River? Gallatin made a vaguely phrased reply that betrayed his bewilderment.[58]

Then, three months later, on October 22, the President summoned the cabinet to discuss Burr again. Letters from a number of individuals in the West, he told them, stated that Burr was moving southwestward to New Orleans at the head of a band of sixty men, clearly bent upon setting up an independent confederacy of the West. He was disturbed by the likelihood that Spain would soon launch an attack on Louisiana and might use Burr and his co-conspirators. After discussion at this meeting and two others in the same week, the cabinet resolved to dispatch an army officer to the Mississippi valley to discover exactly what Burr was doing. Fresh suspicions of the loyalty of General Wilkinson were aired, but the cabinet still found it difficult to believe that he was actually doing anything treasonable.[59]

At another cabinet meeting, on November 25, Jefferson exhibited a letter he had just received from Wilkinson himself. Actually the slippery general had shared in Burr's plotting, but was now willing to desert him. He had heard, he explained, that Burr was planning not an uprising against the authority of the United States, but a filibustering expedition against Spanish Vera Cruz. Gallatin and his colleagues were willing to accept this intelligence at face value, but agreed that the President should issue a proclamation calling upon federal and state authorities to arrest unnamed persons involved in a conspiracy against Spain, and that steps should be taken against Burr if he made any overt act against either Spain or the United States. Gallatin was kept busy in the next few days helping to execute this policy by dispatching directions to Treasury officers in the Ohio and Mississippi valleys.[60]

Under the weight of the Presidential proclamation and of Wilkinson's disclosures about Burr, the conspiracy collapsed early in 1807. On learning that federal authorities were scouring the West for him, Burr deserted his little band during its progress down the Mississippi and made a dash for Spanish territory. Before he could reach sanctuary, he was recognized and arrested.[61] On February 27 the Administration leaders happily concluded that the danger in the West was at an end and began to draw up plans for prosecution of its instigator.[62]

The American people as a whole found it difficult to believe that Burr's vague and grandiose schemes had constituted a real threat. When he was put on trial for treason at Richmond, the shifty Wilkinson gave such a miserable account of himself as a witness that he appeared more like the defendant in the case than the chief witness for the prosecution. He groused in a letter to Gallatin as the hearings edged to their conclusion: "The public prints will have exhibited to you the farce which we have been acting here . . . I am sick of it." [63]

Burr was acquitted for lack of conclusive evidence that he had made any "overt act" against the government, and soon afterward he took ship to Europe. Gallatin's respect—though perhaps not his affection—for the attractive adventurer was dashed by the revelation of the conspiracy. Burr never lost his high regard for Gallatin. Years later, when he was still bitter about the way the Jefferson Administration had treated him, he confided to an acquaintance that he believed Gallatin had "the best head" in the United States.[64]

Gallatin's loyalty to the attractive adventurer brought him embarrassment and annoyance that were only temporary. Unfortunately his dedication to nonpartisanship in the distribution of patronage was to bring him a grief more enduring and catastrophic.

14. Gallatin, the Nationalist

1801=1809

To the councils of the Jefferson Administration Gallatin brought far more than an uncommon knowledge of the principles of public finance and rare administrative talent. The other members of the triumvirate, President Jefferson and Secretary Madison, had been born in Virginia and never could quite shake off identification with their native state and with the South, although their training and experience prevented them from taking a narrowly provincial view. But Gallatin, who had wandered between Maine and western Virginia for a decade, owed deep allegiance to no one state. If there was one type of American to whom he felt closer than any other, it was the frontiersman, whose primary loyalty, after having moved his household goods many times, was to the whole United States. Small wonder that the words "nation" and "union" occurred frequently in his conversation and letters, in a day when men still spoke and wrote of themselves as citizens of particular states.

His background made him embrace seeming paradoxes. At the outset of his public career, his allegiance to frontier democracy caused him to view dimly the Federalists and their Constitution, which appeared to him to be designed to pamper antidemocratic and antirepublican men of property of the eastern cities. But now that the government was in the hands of democrats, republicans, men genuinely concerned with the welfare of all citizens, his misgivings vanished. He could work wholeheartedly for the defense of the West against imperialistic European nations, for the accession of new territory to the Union, for the democratic and systematic opening up of the national domain to settlement, for the construction of roads, canals, and other means of communication to unite all sections of the land.

On only two significant questions did his background create difficult conflicts. He could not share the conviction of Jefferson and other southerners that the strip of land along the Gulf of Mexico known as West Florida was important enough to the whole people of the United States to risk war or great expense in acquiring it. And, in his zeal to apply his Genevan fiscal conscience to the finances of his cherished nation, he became a defender of an institution that was anathema to Jefferson, to most frontiersmen, and to every doctrinaire Democratic-Republican—the Bank of the United States.

2

The disagreement of Jefferson and Gallatin over the Bank of the United States was of long standing. In 1791, after Alexander Hamilton proposed incorporation of the Bank by Congress, Jefferson drew up for President Washington a memorandum opposing it as unconstitutional by his reading of the Constitution, and as unnecessary because the state banks could very well accomplish the objects for which it was designed.[1] Gallatin, as a member of the Pennsylvania assembly, criticized Hamilton's financial system in many respects, but spoke no word against the Bank. His *Sketch of the Finances of the United States* in 1796 praised it for promptly raising the value of United States stock, for providing necessary accommodations to the government in its financial operations, and for increasing "the rapidity of the circulation of money." He did not deny that the Washington and Adams administrations abused the facilities of the Bank or that there was a possibility that the institution might become a political football, but he did not think such conditions inevitable.[2]

Less than a month after taking charge of the Treasury, Gallatin made clear in a letter to Thomas Willing, one of the Bank's directors, that he counted on it to assist his department's operations. In asking that a branch be opened at Washington to accommodate the government, he acknowledged that the Bank would not make any money from the branch and might lose a little. "It is equally the interest of this Department, and of the Bank of the United States, mutually to observe the most liberal spirit of accommodation towards each other," he observed.[3] The Bank opened a branch at the Capital soon after.

The Bank was so useful to the Treasury that a year later, when the President suggested that the government guard against letting it obtain an "exclusive monopoly" of the nation's banking business, Secretary Gallatin pointed out that it was "not proper to displease" the directors of the Bank, "because they place instantly our money where we may want it, from one end of the Union to the other, which is done on the tacit condition of our leaving our deposits with them, and because if we shall be hard run and want money, to them we must apply for a loan." [4] Jefferson replied mildly that there were evils in both a monopoly and a plethora of banking facilities. "Between such parties the less we meddle the better." [5]

While Gallatin continued to cooperate with the Bank, the President continued to worry. Finally the President used the national welfare as an argument. Too much of the Bank's stock was held by foreigners, he told the Secretary of the Treasury in October, 1802; if it became a monopoly, "we might, on a misunderstanding with a foreign power, be immensely embarrassed." It would be better to distribute the government's business among all the banks to keep them all "in an acquiescence under [it]." [6]

Gallatin pretended not to hear the suggestion. Nine months later the persistent President tried a plea that was boldly political: "I am decidedly in favor of making all the banks republican, by sharing deposits among them in proportion to the [political] dispositions they shew. If the law now forbids it, we should not permit another session of Congress to pass without amending it. It is material to the safety of republicanism to detach the mercantile interest from it's enemies and incorporate it into the body of it's friends. A merchant is naturally a republican, and can be otherwise only from a vitiated state of things." [7]

Again Gallatin turned a deaf ear. Indeed, in December, 1803, when the government was preparing to take possession of Louisiana, he told the President that he hoped the Bank would be permitted to open a branch at New Orleans, which would greatly facilitate the fiscal operations of the government in the new territory.

Not unexpectedly, Jefferson was indignant. "This institution is one of the most deadly hostility existing against the principles and forms of our constitution," he exploded. Its officers, directors, and stockholders and the newspapers they supported were dangerously Federalist. Suppose the United States found itself in a crucial situation, or even at war. "An institution like this, penetrating by it's branches every part of the Union, acting by command and in phalanx may . . . upset the government. . . . Ought we then to give further growth to an institution so powerful, so hostile?" Ought we not, "while we are strong," to develop an independent banking system for the accommodation of the Treasury? He asked Gallatin to mull over the idea and work out a detailed plan. [8]

A subservient cabinet member without financial convictions of his own would undoubtedly have complied; but not Gallatin. On the day he received this request, he replied with a letter enumerating the advantages the Treasury had derived "from Banks, and especially from the Bank of the United States." He added firmly that he was "extremely anxious" for a branch at New Orleans because of the security and convenience it would provide the Treasury in dealing with so remote a district.

Political objections, he went on blandly, would "lose much of their force" when the "little injury" the bankers could do and their dependence on the government were "duly estimated. They may vote as they please and take their own papers; but they are formidable only as individuals and as Merchants, and not as Bankers. Whenever they shall appear really dangerous, they are completely in our power and may be crushed." [9]

Jefferson yielded before Secretary Gallatin's insistence. Congress enacted a bill authorizing a New Orleans branch which the President signed on March 23, 1804, waiving his objection to the Bank as unconstitutional.[10] To make him feel better, Gallatin assured him that the directors too had made concessions: "on account of the distance" the branch was "so inconvenient to the Bank of the United States" that he had had great difficulty in prevailing on it "to assent to the measure."

Apparently Gallatin believed he had converted the President on the Bank question. In April, 1804, he learned that young Governor William C. C. Claiborne, acting as a sort of proconsul of Jefferson at New Orleans, had authorized the establishment of a bank there on his own initiative. Indignantly he warned the President that this step might interfere with "the establishment of a Branch Bank which we [*sic!*] considered of great importance to the safety of the revenue and as a bond of union between the Atlantic and Mississippi interests." [11]

The Bank did not become an issue again until after Jefferson left the Presidency. To his dying day he remained an outspoken enemy of a national bank; Gallatin's own feelings, as we shall see, were modified by the changing times.

3

For two decades, almost from the moment Gallatin first touched foot in America, much of his thinking had been directed toward the great unsettled regions west of the Appalachian range as fields for speculation and for the enrichment of his adopted country. It was a happy circumstance that one of the duties he assumed upon becoming Secretary of the Treasury was direction of the disposition of the public domain west of the mountains that the United States had acquired under the 1781 treaty of peace with Great Britain.

Gallatin had already had experience with this problem as one of the chief authors of the Land Act of 1796, which charged the Secretary of the Treasury with direction of the surveys and issuance of the final certificates. Little land had been taken under this act. In the hope of accelerating sales in the Northwest Territory, that vast area extending from the northern bank of the Ohio River to the Great Lakes, Congress had passed an act in 1800 with somewhat more generous terms. Although Gallatin was a member of Congress at the time, he appears to have taken only a cursory interest in this act.[12]

He had personal as well as official reasons to be interested in the Northwest Territory. Some of the extensive tracts he and Savary had acquired jointly were there. In 1801 Thomas Worthington, register of public lands in the Territory, visited Congress to urge his district's desire for statehood. Secretary Gallatin took a liking to this combination of Quaker humanitarian and Virginia gentleman, and thereafter Worthington kept him appraised about the state of mind of his Ohio neighbors, as well as the conditions of his landholdings.[13]

The petition for statehood prepared by Worthington and his associates was sent to Gallatin by Congressman William Branch Giles for comment and recommendations. His response, dated February 13, 1802, favored admission of the new state, but expressed his zealous interest in guarding the rights of the federal government to the public lands in the area. He urged that any act admitting a new state should include clauses forbidding its government to interfere with federal land within its borders, to tax it, or to discriminate against nonresident purchasers. In return for such concessions by the new state, the provision of the Northwest Ordinance of 1787 by which one section of the federal lands in each township was to be set aside for the use of schools should remain in effect. In addition, the federal government should earmark one-tenth of the proceeds from the sale of its lands in Ohio for a fund to construct roads from the Atlantic seaboard across the breadth of the state.[14]

Every one of Gallatin's proposals was incorporated in a bill Giles introduced in the House of Representatives soon afterward—part of the compact to admit Ohio as a state. During the debates, the portion of the federal government's receipts from land sales that was to be devoted to roads was reduced from 10 to 2 per cent. Otherwise the measure was passed with little change. The Ohio convention adopted the provisions without murmur, and the district became a state in 1803.[15]

Statehood brought a rush of settlers to Ohio, as well as to the country just west of it, organized as Indiana Territory. The inadequacies of the Land Acts of 1796 and 1800, long apparent, became troublesome. Petitions for liberalization poured into Congress. Late in 1803 Joseph H. Nicholson, chairman of the Committee on Public Lands, turned the whole problem over to Gallatin.[16]

The reply, delivered early in January, represented a logical development of Gallatin's own thinking on the public domain. He proposed a sharp break with the federal policy established by Alexander Hamilton. The government looked on its lands primarily as a means of satisfying the needs of the Treasury: if that meant a carnival for speculators, well and good. As a Congressman from the frontier, Gallatin had urged that development of the West must also be considered, that the requirements of the impecunious men who would actually settle must be taken into account; but in the end he had accepted a compromise in the Law of 1796 that served no purpose, of the Treasury, or the speculators, or the poor men.

Secretary Gallatin proposed an end to such compromises. To aid impecunious settlers, the minimum size of tracts should be lowered from the 360 acres specified in the Law of 1800 to 160 acres; the price should be reduced from $2.00 an acre (one-quarter down, the balance due within four years) to $1.50 an acre for 360 acres and $1.25 an acre for larger tracts (the entire sum due within forty days). This new policy would prevent creation of a class of citizen indebted to the federal government and "hostile to the general welfare of the Union"—recognition by Gallatin for the first time of the dangers in extending credit too freely. The government would receive less for its lands, but the public domain was so vast that this would not be a disadvantage in the long run.[17]

Although these recommendations were incorporated bodily into the bill Nicholson's committee reported to the House, Congress largely emasculated the measure before completing it as the Land Act of 1804. The minimum tract became 160 acres, but $1.64 was the minimum price and the credit system was left unchanged.[18]

The experience of the next two years reenforced Gallatin's conviction that continuance of the last feature was especially unfortunate. In March, 1806, he felt compelled to point out to Congress that between October, 1803, and October, 1805, the debt of purchasers of land in Ohio, "more than two thousand heads of families," had doubled from $1,000,000 to $2,000,000 and was increasing daily, "extending to a greater number of persons . . . hostile to the Federal government." Once again he urged a reduction in price.[19] He was far ahead of the public opinion of his time. Congress ignored his suggestions and, for decades, periodically passed acts for the relief of purchasers who could not keep up payments on their land.[20]

Besides modifying the mode of sale in Ohio, the Land Act of 1804 opened public lands in Indiana Territory for sale. Gallatin promptly appointed officers for service there, and ordered the running of the boundary lines and the making of surveys so that sales might be started within a year.

His westward vision did not stop at the Mississippi River, but extended as far as the Pacific Ocean. Several powers coveted the vast area between the river and the ocean, generally known as "the Missouri Country." Legally the Missouri Country belonged to Spain, but many persons, including Gallatin, feared that Great Britain might use the expected outbreak of war in Europe as an excuse to seize it. In December, 1802, when President Jefferson sent him the draft of a message to Congress proposing that the United States send an exploring expedition to the area, he was delighted. "I feel warmly interested in this plan," he answered, suggesting that a copy of "Vancouver's Survey" be bought to aid in making plans.[21]

Four months later Gallatin urged the President to persevere in his project. "It may, ere long, [be] necessary, that we should, by taking immediate possession, prevent G.B. from doing the same. . . . But whatever may be the issue of the present difficulties" in Europe, he observed prophetically, "the future destinies of the Missouri country are of vast importance to the United States, it being perhaps the only large tract of country, and certainly the *first* which lying out of the boundaries of the Union, will be settled by the people of the United States."

Jefferson decided to appoint Captain Meriwether Lewis, a young Virginian who had been serving as his secretary, as head of the expedition. Gallatin drew up a list of suggestions ("the great object is to ascertain whether from its extent and fertility that country is susceptible of a large population in the same manner as the corresponding tract on the Ohio") and hints about the science of path marking based on his own experiences in the Ohio valley two decades before,[22] and held several conferences with Lewis.[23]

Gallatin was gratified when, in the autumn of 1806, Lewis and his associate, William Clark, reported that the expedition had followed the Columbia River all the way to the Pacific and had collected a mass of valuable data. They had named the north fork of the Missouri River Jefferson's River, the middle fork Madison's River, and the southeast fork Gallatin's River—names that they bear to this day.[24]

4

If Gallatin derived satisfaction from his duties in respect to the public lands in Ohio and the Indiana Territory and beyond, he found nothing but vexation in the domain south of Tennessee and west of Georgia, which was to become the states of Alabama and Mississippi. This immense region stretched to the Mississippi River, but was cut off from the Gulf of Mexico by Spanish possessions. To the Treasury it was of small interest, for it was inhabited by four Indian tribes so fierce they discouraged settlement; besides, Georgia claimed part of it.

Early in 1802 the President appointed Gallatin one of three commissioners to settle a raging dispute. In 1795 the Georgia legislature—every member of which, with one possible exception, had accepted a bribe—passed the "Yazoo Act." This turned over to four land companies, the majority of whose stockholders lived in eastern cities, the state's dubious claims to vast tracts. The following year a newly elected legislature repudiated the act, arousing the wrath of the stockholders. It fell to Gallatin and his fellow commissioners, James Madison and Levi Lincoln, to negotiate an agreement satisfactory to the companies and to Georgia, represented by three fire-eating politicians.[25]

At the outset, the Georgians presented a "rough draft" of a settlement on which they were "decidedly determined." [26] The tactful Gallatin, who bore virtually the whole burden of negotiation, finally drew up an arrangement designed to win the assent of both sides. Among its many provisions, more than a few were to assuage the ruffled pride of Georgia. But the heart of the matter was that 5,000,000 acres were to be set aside for the federal government to sell; the first $1,250,000 of receipts would go to the state, the next $5,000,000 to the land companies.

The negotiations were virtually completed when President Jefferson learned that the settlement called upon the federal government to pay for the Indian titles to all lands in Georgia, and protested vigorously. Gallatin acknowledged that the commission had perhaps been "too hasty" in promising this, and proposed a substitute that avoided such payments. One of Georgia's representatives, "violently incensed," threatened to withdraw from the negotiations. Gallatin then obtained the President's assent to the conditions "verbally agreed" upon. The agreement, as provided in reports dated April 26, 1802, and February 16, 1803, was approved quickly by the state legislature.[27]

The Yazoo compromise was a political storm center for years to come—made so, ironically enough, by Gallatin's close friend John Randolph of

Roanoke. From late 1803 through 1806, the strange Virginian periodically brought up the settlement in the course of debates, asserting that it offended the state sovereignty of Georgia, and protesting the use of federal funds to compensate the land-company claimants. In these bitter and obsessive tirades, Madison became the particular target of his rage, although Randolph knew full well that the arrangement, so far as the nation was concerned, was almost exclusively the handiwork of Gallatin —Madison and Levi Lincoln having done little more than affix their signatures to it.[28]

Only once, and most indirectly, did Randolph make public acknowledgment of Gallatin's responsibility. On February 2, 1805, he told the House that when he first read the commissioners' report he "was filled with unutterable astonishment—finding men in whom I had, and still have, the highest confidence, recommend a measure, which all the facts and all the reasons which they had collected, opposed and unequivocally condemned." [29] Through Randolph's influence, the House rejected the compromise in March, 1806, although a Supreme Court decision in favor of the land-company claimants prompted Congress some years later to vote them a $4,000,000 settlement.[30] The Yazoo compromise did not finish Gallatin's friendship with Randolph, but it strained it unconscionably and, as we shall presently see, greatly darkened the Secretary's political fortunes.

5

The Louisiana Purchase was more than a fiscal problem to the Secretary of the Treasury. It was a constitutional problem and a problem in territorial administration. Gallatin met both challenges as befitted a frontier democrat.

On January 10, 1803, the day the Senate approved the nomination of James Monroe to negotiate with France for the purchase of New Orleans and perhaps Florida, Attorney General Lincoln submitted an ingenious proposal to the President. To conform to the strict states'-rights construction of the Constitution which he knew the President favored, he suggested that any agreement with France be so worded as to make it appear that the United States was merely altering its boundaries to include the area purchased. The acquisition would then be annexed to an existing territory or state of the Union (perhaps Mississippi Territory or Georgia).[31]

Gallatin was contemptuous when Jefferson showed him the proposal.

"If the acquisition of territory is not warranted by the constitution," he commented in a memorandum of January 13, "it is not more legal to acquire for one State than for the United States; if the Legislature and Executive established by constitution are not proper organs for the acquirement of new territory for the use of the Union, still less can they be so for the acquirement of new territory for the use of one State." Under Lincoln's construction, what could "prevent the President and Senate by treaty annexing Cuba to Massachusetts or Bengal to Rhode Island, . . . if ever the acquirement of colonies shall become a favorite object" of our government? He would have none of Lincoln's "limited construction" of the Constitution. "The existence of the United States as a nation presupposes the power of every nation of extending their territory by treaties, and the general power given to the President and Senate of making treaties designates the organs through which the acquisition may be made." [32] This was a long way from Harrisburg and 1788, but the journey had been made slowly and in logical response to the course of events in the intervening fifteen years.

President Jefferson took nearly two months to answer. Then he acknowledged, "You are right as to Mr. L's proposition." But: "I think it will be safer not to permit the enlargement of the Union but by an amendment of the Constitution." [33]

The matter ceased to be hypothetical late in June when Washington heard that Napoleon had agreed to sell all of Louisiana. The President drafted a long statement, almost a constitution in itself, to serve as an amendment that would make the purchase "constitutional." As was his custom, he sent copies to members of the cabinet for comment and suggestion.[34] Gallatin acknowledged receipt on July 9, stating only that he presumed the draft was intended for deliberation and reflection and not for immediate decision." [35] He had already made it clear that he thought a constitutional amendment unnecessary.

Although other members of the cabinet now shared Gallatin's feeling, the President persisted. He tried a new and briefer version.[36] Finally, disturbed by reports that the French might use any delays in consummating the purchase as an excuse for taking it back, he decided to continue discussions "sub silentio." [37] Certainly his followers had no misgivings about the constitutionality of the acquisition. A law to authorize it passed both houses of Congress by decisive margins, with only a handful of New England Federalists—who saw their hopes of ever regaining control of the government slipping away—in opposition.[38]

Gallatin was inclined at first to disbelieve the rumors that the French might not fulfill their agreement, but he determined to take no chances.

When the President asked the cabinet members whether New Orleans should be taken by force if peaceful delivery was refused, they all voted in favor of the idea.[39] The Spanish, still in actual possession of New Orleans, showed signs of not giving up with good grace as the crucial day approached. Gallatin grew anxious. With Kentucky and Tennessee congressmen he worked out plans for augmenting the armed force available in the area; and he prodded the War Department into scheduling men and supplies to converge on the city. He drafted an act authorizing the government to take possession of the territory, which Congress passed in modified form late in October. He reported these steps to President Jefferson and apologized for exceeding his duties as head of the Treasury, but declared they were necessary lest "we should have to reproach ourselves with the omission of any practicable measure." [40]

As it turned out, the precautions were unnecessary. On December 30, 1803, the day appointed, the Spanish intendant at New Orleans delivered the province of Louisiana to the French prefect, who conveyed it to the American representative. The special troops returned peacefully to their homes.

Louisiana remained an administrative problem for the government, and hence for Secretary Gallatin, for some years. Like many other Americans, he had a poor opinion of the population acquired, especially at New Orleans. "They seem to be but one degree above the French West Indians, than whom a more ignorant and depraved race of civilized men did not exist," he wrote to the President. "Give them slaves and let them *speak* French (for they cannot write it) and they would be satisfied. The first is inadmissible; how far their language should, as they wish, be legally recognized is questionable; but their officers ought at least to understand them." [41]

With the President's backing, Gallatin resolutely applied the laws and moral code of one civilization to another. He enforced, with satisfaction and determination, the federal law forbidding further importation of slaves. He approved of Jefferson's insistence upon introducing the American principles of trial by jury in criminal cases, freedom of the press, freedom of religion, and the like.[42]

The truth was that the Louisianians neither liked nor respected their new governors. They hoped that a turn of fortune would soon bring back the easy-going, indulgent rule of Spain; they were reluctant to register their land claims with the Treasury officers. As some of the officers complained to him, each case required as much labor as a fundamental judicial ruling.[43] One reason for the continuing unrest was the stormy state of Spanish-American relations and President Jefferson's determination to acquire the Floridas for the United States.

6

If Gallatin's Genevan heritage drove him to unremitting labor for early extinguishment of the public debt, his frontiersman's nationalism shaped his dream of what the government should do once that goal was achieved. It was nothing less than the building of roads, canals, and other internal improvements at federal expense so as to knit all sections of the nation into a tight union.

He first made the dream public in 1802, when he inserted into the law governing the sale of public lands in Ohio a provision for construction of a road from the eastern seaboard across the breadth of that state. He made no secret of its purpose: to "contribute towards cementing the bonds of the Union between those parts of the United States, whose local interests have been considered as most dissimilar." [44]

It was a dream that President Jefferson shared. He put himself on record in his second inaugural address, declaring that, once the public debt was redeemed, "the revenue thereby liberated, may . . . be supplied, *in time of peace*, to rivers, canals, roads, arts, manufactures, education, and other great objects within each state." [45] Less than two months later, when Gallatin reported that the Treasury was in a flourishing condition, he restated the goal.[46]

Gallatin did not share his chief's conviction that a constitutional amendment was prerequisite to a program of national improvements. Even before the debt was extinguished, he found projects which he was anxious to start. Nearest to his heart, because it would pass through his own western Pennsylvania neighborhood, was one authorized by the Act of 1802 to connect Cumberland, Maryland, with the Ohio River; and he told the President this was "a national object, it is of primary importance . . . as the main communication for the transportation of all the foreign or Atlantic articles which the Western States consume, and even for the carriage of Eastern produce and flour to the Potomack." He thought it would save more than $200,000 a year in transportation costs.[47]

Like most internal improvements, the Cumberland Road became a subject of contention between local interests. Gallatin and the President agreed that the road should start at the Capital and run in as straight a line as practicable to Cincinnati, then to Vincennes and St. Louis.[48] Busi-

nessmen of Philadelphia, expressing themselves through the state legislature, were reluctant to let it pass through Pennsylvania lest it divert
trade to fast-growing Baltimore; citizens of Pittsburgh were unenthu-
siastic because it would bypass their city; southwestern Pennsylvanians
pleaded that it pass through Uniontown and the town of Washington,
even if that meant a longer route.[49] President Jefferson resisted such
pressure, especially from Uniontown. Gallatin was more practical politically. He thought it better to "remove local and state opposition" for "a
national object of great importance, particularly as a bond of union" than
to adhere "too strictly to first, though correct impressions." [50] Somewhat
sharply he reminded the President that "the county of Washington, with
which I am well acquainted, having represented it six years in Congress,
gives a uniform majority of 2000 votes, in our favor, and if this be
thrown, by reason of this road, in a wrong scale, we will infallibly lose
the State of Pennsylvania, at the next election." [51] Still Jefferson resisted,
unwilling to "barter away . . . a public trust." An act specifying that the
road pass through the town of Washington was passed in 1811, after
Jefferson left the Presidency.[52]

By early 1807 the public debt had been reduced sufficiently far for
Gallatin to feel that it was at last time to discuss specific programs of internal improvement. At his suggestion, Thomas Worthington, senator
from Ohio, induced the Upper House to pass a resolution calling for such
a plan. Gallatin used the order as an excuse to obtain all the data he could
from public men in every part of the land.[53] It took more than a year to
assemble them and construct a program. This was well worth waiting
for, such was its wide scope, logical organization, and long range of
vision. On April 6, 1808, he sent copies to friends in the Senate, with
letters expressing the hope that it might be printed and distributed
throughout the country. He hoped that by the next session public opinion
would have become sufficiently definite to warrant appropriation by Congress of $50,000 for a preliminary survey. "You know," he added, "that
I am not wasteful." [54]

He set forth his grand design boldly at the start of his report:[55] "Good
roads and canals will shorten distances, facilitate commercial and personal
intercourse, and unite, by a still more intimate community of interests,
the remote quarters of the United States. No other single operation,
within the power of Government, can more effectively tend to strengthen
and perpetuate that Union which secures external independence, domestic peace, and internal liberty."

Specifically, he proposed a network of roads, canals, and river improvements to interlace every section of the land. To connect North and

South, four short canals were to be constructed: from Boston to Buzzards Bay; from the Raritan River across New Jersey to the Delaware River; across Delaware to the head of Chesapeake Bay; through the Dismal Swamp of Virginia and North Carolina. Together these would create an internal waterway from Boston to St. Marys, Georgia, close to the entire length of the eastern seaboard. Land transportation would be afforded by a great turnpike that would use routes already established between Maine and Georgia.

As far as the expanding nation was concerned, Gallatin considered the links between East and West even more important. He envisioned four principal highways across the mountains linking the Susquehanna River and the Allegheny, the Potomac and the Monongahela, the James and the Kanawha, the Santee or the Savannah and the Tennessee. New York and New England were to be tied with the West by canals from the Hudson River to Lake Champlain and Lake Ontario, as well as by a canal around Niagara Falls.

To enlist the interest of New England and the Far South, Gallatin also proposed construction of a number of roads and canals that would be primarily of local benefit; but he made clear that his yardstick for federal grants was to have no relation to the population of the states in which the improvements were to be made: "Roads and canals are often of greater utility to the States which they unite, than to those through which they pass."

This point was one that he had to debate with President Jefferson. In 1805, in recommending internal improvements to Congress, the President proposed—doubtless to accord to his constitutional scruples—that federal funds be apportioned among the states on the basis of their population, and that the Constitution be amended to authorize such a practice. Then and in 1808 Gallatin told him: "The strict rule in a constitutional provision would be very embarrassing and sometimes defeat the most important object, because it often happens that an improvement is as useful or more useful to an adjacent State than to that through which it passes. . . . A just apportionment will naturally result from the conflicting interests on the floor of Congress." [56]

Gallatin estimated the cost of the program he outlined in 1808 at $20,000,000. If Congress would appropriate $2,000,000 a year, it could all be realized within ten years. A continuing program of improvements could be financed through a permanent rotating fund established by the Treasury through the sale of a special United States bond issue directly to individuals.

The plan had many virtues. Hamilton's report on manufactures in 1791 had charted a program for industrial development that was bold, farseeing, national, and practical; Gallatin's report on internal improvements in 1808 proposed a boon to transportation, communications, and the economy that had the same qualities. Adoption would avoid the waste and corruption characteristic of piecemeal and haphazard developments. It might well set a permanent pattern for the national economy as Gallatin's debt retirement policy appeared to be doing in fiscal practice.

Although the plan was criticized in details, public response to it was favorable, on the whole. President Jefferson espoused it in his annual message that year, but Congress failed to adopt it, for reasons that we shall see. The more's the pity, for its specific suggestions were applicable until the coming of the steam railroad two decades later, and its basic principles remain valid to our day.

15. Three Storm Clouds

1804-1807

In 1804, President Jefferson was elected to a second term by an extraordinary margin. Four years before, he had won only 73 out of 138 electoral votes; now he had 162 out of 176. Even the supposedly rock-ribbed Federalist state of Massachusetts accorded its approval. The measure of the national confidence was shown also in the Congress elected: only 7 Federalist senators among 34, only 25 Federalist representatives among 141.[1]

To this triumph Gallatin made no mean contribution. The policies he had helped evolve and his scrupulous, efficient execution of them were steadily and materially reducing the public debt despite unprecedented expenses; the national domain had been more than doubled; the West was being settled in an orderly fashion, and a start was being made to tie it to other parts of the country. Gallatin was even helping—reluctantly, it is true—to bring the Barbary pirates to terms.

But even during this sunny time there were gray clouds overhead and black ones on the horizon. The frustrated ambition of Aaron Burr was to leave its trail of ill feeling in the Democratic-Republican party. The schism that Duane and Leib were creating in Pennsylvania and the friction between the Secretary of the Treasury and the pro-Navy group, represented by Robert and Samuel Smith, were breeding consequences even direr for Gallatin's career. Two clouds just appearing at the horizon were international—the maritime practices of Great Britain during the global war she was waging against Napoleon Bonaparte, and the determination of Jefferson to acquire Florida from Spain; one cloud was a personality—Gallatin's old friend John Randolph of Roanoke.

2

The trouble with Randolph of Roanoke was inextricably interwoven with Jefferson's determination to gain Florida; but even if Florida had never existed Jefferson—and hence Gallatin—would have had difficulties with the Virginia Congressman.

Gallatin and Randolph had been immensely fond of each other ever since their first meeting as minority members of the Sixth Congress. The friendship was so warm that, when Gallatin outraged the Congressman's deep-seated states'-rights principles by the compromise he arranged over the Yazoo, Randolph blamed Madison. Privately he would ask a mutual friend to "commend him" to Gallatin and, "for God's sake, try and find what is the matter with him." [2] Publicly he would denounce Madison on the floor of Congress for what he knew Gallatin had done.

When Randolph was in Washington he continued to enjoy the hospitality of the Gallatins on Capitol Hill; when he was at home in Virginia the two men still corresponded frequently. They shared many prejudices: against Washington as a place to live and work; against the ineptitude of Robert Smith as Secretary of the Navy—"the nation has had the most conclusive proof that a *head* is no necessary appendage to the establishment," observed Randolph; against the schism among the Democratic-Republicans in Pennsylvania—"I can gather that there has been no want of indiscretion, intemperance, and rashness on either side," wrote the Virginian.[3] Their collaboration on Treasury matters continued to be close, and Gallatin even lent his friend a department clerk on occasion to take care of the penmanship involved in preparing appropriation bills.[4]

President Jefferson's efforts to purchase Florida placed Gallatin, loyal to his chief, in such a position that the friendship could not endure. Ironically the cause of the break was one that appealed to both Jefferson and Randolph as southerners but left Gallatin, nationalist but northern, apathetic.

The President's obsession that the United States must have possession of West Florida—the strip of land along the Gulf of Mexico that cut off the mouths of the navigable rivers in the Mississippi Territory and included the only good naval harbor on the Gulf, Mobile Bay—was not new by any means. It was one of the reasons he had sent Monroe to Paris to negotiate for Louisiana; the success of that negotiation strengthened his determination about Florida. Gallatin did not share his enthusiasm but, as a loyal cabinet member, did his best to cooperate.

At the time of the negotiation Jefferson had no illusion that the Louisiana Purchase included Florida. But subsequent study of the vague phrases of the treaty, plus a liberal amount of wishful thinking, convinced him that Florida was included.[5] He kept arguing the point with Gallatin until in late August, 1803, the Secretary conceded in measured words: "I agree with you that we have a right to claim that part of West Florida which was part of Louisiana; I was of a different opinion, but am now convinced." He did not explain what had changed his mind.[6]

The issue did not come to a head until February 24, 1804, when Congress passed the Mobile Act, at the insistence of the President and Randolph. The wording of the act implied that West Florida was already American through the Louisiana Purchase—a claim Randolph had loudly asserted on the floor of the House.[7] Under the terms of the act, Treasury officials were to make provisions for the collection of customs duties at Mobile Bay and the interdiction of Spanish vessels landing at Baton Rouge. The Spanish minister delivered a vigorous protest. Gallatin conferred with Secretary Madison, who shared his view, then told the President that he feared the Administration had not "taken solid ground," and that it would be difficult to justify its policy "to impartial men." He suggested that Jefferson reverse the policy and, in order to save face, make it appear that he was overruling acts the Treasury had taken on its own initiative. Jefferson agreed, naming another port of entry for Mississippi and ordering no interference with Spanish vessels at Baton Rouge.[8]

Gallatin was able to spare the President further embarrassment on the question when he was preparing a message to Congress in October. The first draft belied Jefferson's real feelings by making it appear that the United States had no further interest in West Florida. Realizing that in time his chief would rue this, Gallatin urged that the government make clear its intention "to abstain from exercising jurisdiction or taking forcible possession till all other means were exhausted." The President made the change.[9]

His next step was to send Monroe to Madrid to see if Spain would sell Florida—over Randolph's protest that a purchase "would disgrace us forever." [10] In August, 1805, word reached Washington that Spain, emboldened by Napoleon's support, refused to discuss a sale, and even refused to ratify a convention, on which much diplomatic time and toil had been expended, authorizing indemnification for illegal seizure of American ships. The rejection of the sale did not surprise Gallatin, but the rejection of the convention wounded his national pride.[11] Gradually his rage wore off, and his caution returned. When President Jefferson asked the cabinet for suggestions as to the government's policy toward Spain,[12] he considered the matter for three weeks. Then he wrote a memorandum more than five thousand words long, comprehensive, cool, and judicious— one of his ablest public papers.

The principal point of the memorandum was that the United States should avoid war with Spain for moral as well as practical considerations. The high regard that other nations had for the United States and the Jefferson Administration had been won by policies of wisdom, moderation, and justice; it was imperative that nothing be done to lower it. What possible excuse could be given for war with Spain now? Certainly not a boundary matter: in taking possession of Louisiana, the United States had virtually acknowledged that West Florida was not part of the Purchase. Nor was the rejection of the convention an adequate excuse. The convention had hung fire for years without provoking war; why should it now?

What could the United States gain by war? Gallatin asked. All of Florida certainly, perhaps "the miserable establishments of Santa Fe and San Antonio," possibly Havana and Vera Cruz. But the cost to national prestige would be inestimable, the loss to shipping incalculable. Napoleon's natural concern for Spain would cause him to support her in case of war; this would in turn oblige the United States to seek an entangling alliance with Great Britain. Debts and taxes would be the inevitable consequence. Far better to maintain the status quo and wait for time to change the Spanish attitude.

What should be done in the meantime? The recent peace with Tripoli made available for other purposes the $2,000,000 that flowed into the Mediterranean Fund each year; with the $3,000,000 that would accumulate within four years a dozen ships-of-the-line could be built and some frigates purchased. Then, recalling his old hope that the building of a navy might be postponed, he added wryly: "I have had no doubt for a long time that the United States would have a navy. It is certain that so long as we have none, we must perpetually be liable to injuries and insults . . . when there is war in Europe." [13]

Madison offered similar conciliatory counsel, and the President was persuaded to bide his time. But in October and November he again asked the cabinet whether it might not be a good idea to make another effort to purchase Florida and even Texas from Spain, using France as an intermediary: John Armstrong, American minister to France, had sent word that Talleyrand would be willing to make his services available. Gallatin objected that the assent of Congress ought to be obtained before the business went far, and the President agreed. The cabinet unanimously went on record in favor of purchase at a price not to exceed $5,000,000.[14] Soon after, word came from Armstrong that Talleyrand would require $7,000,000; the cabinet was still agreeable.[15]

Jefferson thought that he could handle Congress in this situation much as he had done at the time of the Louisiana Purchase. First he would send it a message declaring that Spanish-American relations had become most critical; later he would transmit a confidential message requesting an appropriation to buy what he sought from Spain. Gallatin threw himself wholeheartedly into the plan, volunteering to obtain the cooperation of Randolph, who had helped so much in getting the Louisiana Purchase through the House. The appropriation bill, he advised, should be phrased "in very general terms." [16]

In late November the President showed Gallatin a draft of his message to Congress. It was exceedingly bellicose, proposing extensive preparations for defense that included naval construction and organization of the militia. One section recommended abandonment of the Mediterranean Fund, and against this idea Gallatin protested emphatically. To build a fleet or to buy Florida, it would be necessary either to continue the Fund or to borrow money. "It is not indeed probable," he observed more mildly, "that the proposed plan for the purchase of Florida will be relished by Congress unless they see that the object can be obtained without increasing the debt." [17] The President readily yielded, removing all mention of the Mediterranean Fund from the message delivered to Congress on December 3.[18]

To the later confidential message and especially to a set of resolutions proposed for adoption by Congress, Gallatin had more pronounced objections. Feeling that the President had hopelessly scrambled the objects of the message and the resolutions, he put his analytical mind to work and reassembled both message and resolutions along lines more logical and clear-cut.[19] Jefferson accepted the suggestions, and the revisions were delivered to Congress on December 8.[20]

Now Gallatin moved to obtain Randolph's cooperation in persuading the House to pass the resolutions. Here a slip-up in the planning became apparent. The wayward Randolph had grown cold toward the President and even cooler toward Secretary Madison because of their handling of diplomatic relations. He told Gallatin, and the President himself, that he opposed the appropriation and the manner in which the President sought to obtain it.[21]

Thus thwarted, Gallatin turned for aid to Hannah's cousin Joseph H. Nicholson, who was also on the House committee charged with the problem.[22] But Randolph's spirit hovered over the deliberation of the committee. No action was taken, and, after the committee adjourned, Nicholson returned the resolutions, saying that he was unalterably opposed to one of them which would give the President "the Power to employ an undefined force within undefined Limits, and pledges the Legislature to the ratification of any Treaty which he may think proper to make." The whole proposal, he suggested, smacked too much of the power of a Roman emperor.[23]

Anxious but still not despondent, Gallatin waited a fortnight while Randolph visited Baltimore and the committee recessed. On the morning of December 21, hearing that Randolph had returned and a meeting was to be held, he went to the Capitol and waited in the corridor. Randolph later recorded what followed: As he was about to enter the committee room he "was called aside by the secretary of the treasury, with whom he retired, and who put into his hands a paper headed 'Provision for the purchase of Florida.' As soon as he cast eyes on the title, [he] declared that he would not vote a shilling. The secretary interrupted him by observing, with his characteristic caution, that he did not want to be understood as recommending the measure, but if the committee should deem it advisable, he had devised a plan for raising the necessary supplies, as had been requested, (or directed) in that case to do." Expressing disgust with the whole procedure, "which he could not but consider as highly disingenuous," the Virginian turned his back on his old friend and walked into the committee room.[24]

This did not mean that all was yet lost for Gallatin and the President. Seven weeks later Congress—over the strident opposition of Randolph but with the moral support of Nicholson—voted to appropriate $2,000,000 for "extraordinary expenses" in foreign relations.[25] The victory, however, placed Gallatin in a vulnerable position, for the Treasury now required every cent of income to which it was authorized. Taking advantage of the fact, Randolph rose in Congress on April 14 to propose an end to the duty on salt, and a day later brought in a bill calling for its repeal and the continuance of the Mediterranean Fund. He delivered a stinging attack on the Administration—but without any allusion to Gallatin—for having failed to insist on specific appropriations by the legislature. Repeal of the salt tax was a popular proposal. The duty was one that even Gallatin disapproved of in principle, although he defended it because it was producing more than half a million dollars a year. The Federalists and many Democratic-Republicans in the House joined hands to pass the bill; but in the end the Senate defeated it, after many bitter words.[26]

At the opening of the next session of Congress, Gallatin bowed to popular sentiment. Through the President's annual message, he took up Randolph's proposal that the tax be repealed and the Mediterranean Fund be retained for the time being. These objectives were realized in the act of March 3, 1807.[27]

Randolph's punitive forays on the Administration proved to be incalculably expensive. Loss of the salt tax somewhat pinched Gallatin's fiscal operations, although the Mediterranean Fund was a palliative. Far more costly was the schism the Florida issue produced in Democratic-Republican ranks; this became so wide and so sharp that neither the President nor Gallatin could close it. To make matters worse, Florida continued to remain beyond American reach, for Napoleon Bonaparte had just placed one of his brothers on the Spanish throne and was in no mood to relinquish any of Spain's New World possessions at any price.

3

Randolph continued to see Gallatin socially, while he brooded over his grievances against Secretary Madison and President Jefferson. Then, on March 13, 1806, in pressing his vendetta against them on the floor of the House, he brought Gallatin's name into the affair. Several months before, he told his colleagues, discussing foreign policy with Gallatin, he had asked the Secretary what certain dispatches lately arrived from Europe contained. Gallatin had replied that he did not know, because they had not yet been communicated to the cabinet. "When I discovered that the head of the second Department under the Government did not know they were in existence, much less that his opinion on them had not been consulted, . . . I declared . . . that there is no Cabinet!" Randolph shouted, "What! the head of the Treasury Department—a vigorous and commanding statesman, a practical statesman, the benefit of whose wisdom and experience the nation fondly believes is always obtained before the great measures of the Government are taken—unacquainted with, and unconsulted on, important dispatches. . . . I have no hesitation in saying, there is no Cabinet, when I see a man, second to none for vigorous understanding, and practical good sense, ousted from it." [28]

The tirade caused a sensation the length of the land. Friends of the Administration urged Randolph to say something to wipe out the impression it had created. He made an effort, but the conciliatory words got caught in his throat. Indeed, he worsened the wound with another outburst against Madison, asserting he had it on Gallatin's word that Madison had requested funds from the Treasury to buy peace with France and Spain and perhaps buy Florida as well. Madison's act was heinous, he suggested to the House, because neither the negotiation nor the purchase had been approved by Congress.[29]

To calm the tempest required a congressional resolution and letters back and forth between Gallatin and several members of the House. The fact was established that Randolph, to embarrass Madison, had exaggerated a hearsay account of what Gallatin had told two New York congressmen—to wit, that Madison had suggested to Gallatin a purchase of foreign exchange to avoid a delay in the attempt to buy Florida, but then had decided to wait for congressional authorization.[30]

Randolph's loosely flung words would not be downed. Several months later the *Richmond Enquirer* published an article by Randolph, signed "Decius," criticizing Jefferson's handling of the Florida affair and, by indirection, Gallatin as well.[31] For years the affair was revived every time a political enemy needed ammunition with which to attack Gallatin.

Press vilification became so vicious by the autumn of 1806 that President Jefferson felt he must reassure the Secretary. In a letter of October 12, he recalled earlier efforts to set members of the cabinet at loggerheads with each other. "My affection and confidence in you are nothing impaired, and they cannot be impaired by means so unworthy the notice of candid and honorable minds." [32] Gallatin replied gratefully, alluding to the freedom with which the President had always allowed him to express his own opinions, "even when they may have happened not precisely to coincide with your own view of the subject and you have thought them erroneous." [33] To his sister-in-law he wrote that the President's letter "affords additional proof of the goodness of his heart, and shows that he is above all those little squabbles." [34]

In order to preserve his friendship with the President, Gallatin had to relinquish his intimacy with John Randolph. The Virginia Congressman was no longer a familiar figure at the Gallatins' home. The personal letters ceased, though officially the Secretary of the Treasury continued to address Randolph as chairman of the Ways and Means Committee. A year later, Speaker of the House Joseph B. Varnum of Massachusetts, at Jefferson's insistence, removed Randolph from the chairmanship. Privately, Gallatin considered the replacement "improper" and acknowledged that it would give him "additional labor." [35] About the same time Gallatin lost another close collaborator when Joseph H. Nicholson retired from Congress to accept a federal judgeship.

Randolph continued to speak of Gallatin in high terms long after their break. In May, 1812, he referred to him on the House floor as "that great man—and great let *me* call him";[36] in April, 1824, he alluded to him as "the apostle of Truth, and the favorite votary of Liberty." [37] In the years between, Gallatin was to realize acutely the costliness of the break.

4

The difficulties with Spain over Florida and the break with Randolph complicated Gallatin's work and threatened the fortunes of the Jefferson Administration. Yet they were trivial compared to the national crisis created by deteriorating relations with Great Britain.

When war again broke out in Europe in 1803, and Napoleonic France and Great Britain set out to starve or strangle each other by blockade, the United States at first derived only satisfaction from the conflict. The American merchant marine carried noncontraband goods to and from the colonies of the warring powers, to the enormous profit of shipowners and the considerable advantage of the Treasury Department. Then, during 1805, two changes in British policy struck hard at the American carrying trade. In the celebrated case of the *Essex*, a ruling by the British prize appeal court promised to make it extremely expensive to ship goods between the warring nations by way of the United States. On top of this, the British government adopted a system of licensing that gave it a high degree of control over neutral trade and a financial share in it. President Jefferson and Secretary Madison, however, were so busy with attempts to purchase West Florida that they neglected to protest.[38]

The shipping interests of the middle states and New England did not take the innovations calmly. In January, 1806, before the British rulings had time to affect the carrying trade, a Pennsylvania congressman called for reprisal in the form of a ban on all imports from Great Britain. The prospect of losing $5,000,000 a year in duties through such a ban alarmed Gallatin. With his encouragement, Congressman Nicholson proposed that the prohibition be limited to British goods that could be obtained from other nations or manufactured in the United States.[39] A nonimportation bill along these lines was passed in February to go into effect in November, with the hope that in the meantime the British, worried by the prospect of losing the American market, would reverse their trade policy.[40] Great Britain, however, was not frightened, and the law went into effect on schedule.

Now Gallatin's troubles began in earnest. His customs officers seized a few pieces of proscribed goods and levied a few fines. At the same time they began forwarding an avalanche of petitions from merchants in the ports for remission of fines. In conferences with Secretary Madison and

Attorney General Caesar A. Rodney, he concluded that the law was so defective that it could not be adequately enforced. The three men agreed that it would be better to seek some other way of accomplishing the same end. The law authorized the President to order suspension of its operation. The cabinet members drew up a suspension proclamation and persuaded President Jefferson to issue it. The law had been in effect only five weeks when it was suspended on December 19, 1806, and the suspension was prolonged by another Presidential order in March, 1807.[41]

Meanwhile the President with Secretary Smith had concocted another project to threaten the British—and incidentally the Spanish. During the war with the Mediterranean pirates, gunboats—none of them longer than seventy-five feet or carrying more than two guns—had been useful. Jefferson was fascinated with them because they appeared to be cheap, could be stored easily when not in use, and contracts for construction could be distributed throughout the land, spreading the popularity of his administration. His plan called for construction of 123 gunboats during 1807 and 1808. Of these, 40 would be used to guard the Mississippi, 24 the other ports "in time of European war." [42]

As soon as Gallatin heard of the project, he registered his disapproval. What the President proposed, he sputtered in a memorandum of February 8, 1807, would cost the government a million dollars annually. Already, 73 vessels were under construction, more than enough for any peacetime exigency. If war came, it would be possible within sixty days —perhaps half that time—to turn out 60 gunboats. To build more craft than were needed would be foolish and extravagant.[43] Jefferson was unimpressed. He disputed Gallatin's estimates of the cost of construction and maintenance; he denied that enough boats could be constructed even in six months; he declared that "an enterprising enemy" could destroy our seaports and construction yards as "the 1st operation of war." [44]

The President was fortified in his action by three more packets of unpleasant news from abroad. One came from Berlin where, in November, 1806, Napoleon issued a decree by which the British Isles were to be cut off from all vessels, British or foreign—a great blow to all neutral shipping. The second item of news came from London, where James Monroe had just completed a trade treaty with Great Britain. Jefferson found it little better than the Jay Treaty, which it would replace, and was especially disturbed by its provision that the United States must refuse to recognize the Berlin Decree before the treaty would go into effect. Fearful of the Senate's reaction, the President returned the draft to London with the advice that unless it was drastically revised the United States would ally itself with France.

The third bundle of unpleasant news also came from London. The ambitious and wily George Canning, on succeeding to the foreign ministry, resolved to crush the United States as a maritime power. Conditions had become so intolerable aboard British vessels during the war years that thousands of English sailors had sought employment on American ships. Canning proposed that Britain reassert her traditional position that no man born a British subject might forswear allegiance and become a naturalized citizen of another country.

It occurred to Madison that Canning might react more agreeably to American proposals for a new treaty if the United States offered to forbid the continued service on our vessels of all British sailors employed less than two years. But Gallatin estimated that such a policy would mean the loss of 9,000 able-bodied seamen—nearly one-fourth of the able-bodied seamen in American service. This, he pointed out, "would materially injure our navigation, more indeed than any restrictions which, supposing no treaty to take place, [Britain] would lay on our commerce." Gallatin's estimate gave the President pause: "I am more and more convinced," he told Madison, "that our best course is, to let the negociation take a friendly nap, and endeavor in the mean time to practice as much of its principles as are mutually acceptable." [45]

The "nap" was rudely disturbed late in June, 1807. Gallatin was attending to some Treasury business at Philadelphia during the congressional recess when Secretary Dearborn broke in on him at A. J. Dallas's home with alarming news. The British ship of war *Leopard* had seized the United States frigate *Chesapeake* in Chesapeake Bay for refusing to submit to a search for British deserters; three men had been killed and eighteen wounded; four were taken as deserters, although only one proved to be a British subject. This, Jefferson had written, "renders it necessary to have all our council together." Gallatin started for the Capital at once but was delayed en route by illness. At Washington he found the whole cabinet assembled. The members were of the same heart as Americans of all parties and sections. For the first time in the national history the people were united, were one in indignation against Britain.[46]

Gallatin believed that Congress ought to be summoned at once, and war declared. War would be "calamitous," but it had been forced upon us.[47] But at a series of cabinet meetings held in tropical Washington heat, he learned that peace had become Thomas Jefferson's passion. The President proposed to call a meeting of Congress in late October and, in the meantime, to instruct Monroe at London to insist to the British on "an entire abolition" of impressment from American vessels.[48]

Gallatin was not happy about the delay, for he was convinced that war was inevitable. He acknowledged that sacrifices would likewise be inevitable. "We will be poorer, both as a Nation and as a Government, our debt and taxes will encrease, and our progress in every respect will be interrupted," he told Judge Nicholson. He feared, as a decade earlier, "the necessary increase of executive power and influence, the speculation of contractors and jobbers, and the introduction of permanent military and naval establishments." But more important were "the independence and honor of the nation." Perhaps it would be well to awaken "nobler feelings and habits than avarice and luxury" lest Americans degenerate, "like the Hollanders, into a nation of mere calculators." [49]

During the next torrid weeks, feeling "so unwell," with a head "so muddy" that it was difficult to think clearly, Gallatin gathered information and drew up a plan for the seemingly certain conflict. Finances were of course his first concern. The Treasury was in an advantageous position to withstand the strains of war. It had a surplus of somewhat more than $7,500,000; the debt, through systematic repayment, was under $57,000,000. Receipts were at an all-time high—so high that, just seven months earlier, Gallatin had prophesied that the Treasury would soon start accumulating a surplus of five to six million dollars a year. If war came, of course receipts would fall and expenses soar. But he was convinced that the conflict could be financed largely by loans. Discreet inquiries among merchants and bankers made him confident he could obtain sufficient financing for three years without "any great amount of new taxes." [50]

Using Treasury data, Gallatin enumerated the ports likely to be attacked by the British and spelled out the steps necessary for defending them. He similarly appraised the British possessions in the Western Hemisphere and suggested ways of attack. Thirty thousand men would be necessary to execute these campaigns—"if recruiting is despaired of to the necessary amount, Congress must supply twelve month's militia." The war, he concluded in the memorandum he presented to the President on July 25, would cost $18,000,000 a year, $11,000,000 to be obtained through added duties and taxes, $7,000,000 through an annual loan. He would continue paying off the old debt through hostilities by floating other annual loans. [51]

By early August the tension had eased enough for the cabinet members to scatter to their homes. Gallatin rejoined his wife in New York, where he discovered that in the six weeks since the *Chesapeake* affair, the martial spirit had almost completely evaporated; New York businessmen, he wrote to Madison, fear war so much "that they have persuaded themselves that there is no danger of that event." [52] But some of the more realistic citizens were rushing plans to fortify their harbor.[53]

He was in a more cautious mood when the cabinet returned to Washington early in October. On reading the draft of the message the President proposed to present to the special session of Congress, he objected strongly to its tone. It listed British "outrages," described war as "highly probable," seemed even to call upon Congress for a declaration of war. In a memorandum to Jefferson, he insisted that the United States was not militarily ready for war, and would not be for some months. He suggested that he speak softly while making war preparations energetically.[54] To Gallatin's pleasure, the President rewrote the message, and fortunately so, as the temper of the new Congress was highly pacific.[55]

Gallatin's annual report on the Treasury, issued soon after the start of the session, made it clear that he was proceeding on the assumption that war was on the way. His plans filled in the outline he had sketched during the summer and fall. Lest his denunciations of a public debt in earlier speeches and writings cause surprise at his casual statement that, after the first year of war, loans obtained on the basis of increased customs duties would see the nation through, he explained: "An addition to the debt is doubtless an evil; but experience having shown with what rapid progress the revenue of the Union increases in time of peace . . . a hope may be confidently entertained that . . . the return of peace will, without any effort, afford ample resources for reimbursing whatever may have been borrowed during the war." [56]

Within six weeks Congress authorized the expenditure of $1,850,000 for the defense measures requested by the President. Almost half of this went for the construction of 188 of Jefferson's beloved gunboats.

Meanwhile, President Jefferson was dreamily returning to his old illusion that American exports were more necessary to the welfare of Europe and Great Britain than the profits from their sale and transportation were to the United States. He proposed to the cabinet that the suspended Nonimportation Act of 1806 be restored, arguing that its operation would bring Canning to terms promptly. Gallatin at first contented himself with proposing an alternative: that the act be repealed and a law more general in scope be substituted, proscribing imports from Britain, to go into effect in February, 1808.[57] Madison frowned on the idea, but Jefferson conceded that it had "some good phases" and "merited consideration." [58]

A few days later, on December 5, 1807, Gallatin sharpened his attack on the act with a detailed and sharp criticism of its phrasing. It was so filled, he insisted, with inconsistencies and ambiguities that enforcement or even satisfactory revision was impossible; he cited a few of the ridiculous and bewildering provisions to make his point clear.[59]

As soon as word leaked out that a renewal of the Act was contemplated, Congress and the President were deluged with protests. To these, as well as to Gallatin's suggestions, Jefferson turned a deaf ear, ordering renewed enforcement of the Act as of December 14.

On December 17 the President summoned the cabinet to ponder more unwelcome news. Napoleon was making it clear that he intended to enforce the 1806 Berlin Decree energetically; and Canning in London, who had given our ministers James Monroe and William Pinkney no satisfaction on the *Chesapeake* affair, had obtained the issuance of a royal proclamation directing all naval officers to enforce rigorously the British impressment policy against neutral vessels. Monroe and Pinkney confessed they had lost all hope of making a commercial treaty with Britain.

The President had a definite and drastic proposal for the cabinet to consider—one that he was confident would promptly bring the British to terms. He would call on Congress to establish an embargo on all shipping, American or foreign, into or out of American ports. Madison approved the proposal; Gallatin was uncertain, but gave assent by silence. The idea was unanimously approved by the cabinet.[60]

All that night Gallatin worried about the decision. An embargo might be good for a short period, but not on a permanent basis. War was preferable to a permanent embargo. He set down his reasoning in a letter to the President early the next day: "Governmental prohibitions do always more mischief than had been calculated; and it is not without much hesitation that a statesman should hazard to regulate the concerns of individuals as he can do it better than themselves." He believed any hopes that an embargo would oblige Great Britain to improve its treatment of the United States were "entirely groundless." [61]

At ten o'clock that morning the cabinet held another meeting.[62] No record of the deliberations was kept, but it is clear that Gallatin was overruled. The draft of a message to Congress, framed by Madison and calling for an embargo without any reference to a time limit, was accepted by the President to be made public in his name. It was dispatched at noon to the Capitol, where Vice President George Clinton immediately read it to an expectant Congress.[63]

Within four days, the legislators granted Jefferson's request, virtually without discussion. The Embargo Act, which went into effect on December 22, 1807, has been aptly described as "a self-blockade of the purest water," for it prohibited the departure of all vessels, American or foreign, from American harbors for foreign ports. There was one exception. Foreign vessels were permitted to leave in ballast—a provision inserted at Gallatin's suggestion because "they are so few as to be of no object to us, and we may thereby prevent a similar detention of our vessels abroad, or at least a pretence for it." [64]

Thus began an experiment, conceived by Jefferson and abetted by Madison, that the President sincerely believed would be the crowning triumph of his Administration. The onerous and thankless task of enforcing it fell upon the shoulders of Gallatin, who had little faith in it but was faithfully determined to give it a fair trial.

16. The Trouble with the Embargo

1807=1809

To Thomas Jefferson, the Embargo Act, closing American ports to all international trade, was no ordinary law, no weapon casually taken up for the maritime war with Great Britain. As he assured Gallatin and the other members of the Cabinet on several occasions, it was an experiment of "immense value" for the "future as well as on this occasion" to see whether the United States might bring Great Britain and the other major European nations to terms by denying them our goods and our carrying services.[1]

Secretary Gallatin, the federal officer whose subordinates were most responsible for enforcing the law, did his utmost to test its potentialities despite his skepticism. Secretary Smith, head of the Navy, was concerned but less directly; he also executed the President's orders, while grumbling volubly that the act was "a mischief-making busybody." [2] Secretary Madison, who had cordially assisted Jefferson in sponsoring the law, took virtually no part in enforcement, for his department dealt with other matters.

As soon as the embargo was voted, Gallatin sent out a series of circular letters to all collectors to direct them in the enforcement.[3] Even as he did this the difficulties ahead oppressed him. The law was sloppily drafted; it did not provide penalties for violation; it neglected to mention vessels in the coasting trade; it did not prohibit the export of specie to pay for foreign cargoes loaded in the United States. As Gallatin pointed out to the President on December 23, 1807, the day after the law went into effect, these omissions would have to be corrected in order to achieve any degree of success.[4] Jefferson agreed,[5] and most of them were corrected—but only after a delay—by several laws, especially the acts of April 25, 1808, and January 9, 1809.[6]

Trouble broke out almost immediately in the trade along the coast and

200

the Canadian border. The coastwise traffic in flour suddenly assumed unprecedented proportions. Port officials found it difficult to decide whether a vessel loaded with flour, corn, rice, and rye, would actually take it to another American port, as its owners declared it would, or to a foreign port to be sold at large profits. In some places abroad flour sold at eight times its usual price and at three times the sum shippers were obliged to post as a bond to comply with the legislation enacted at Gallatin's request. The President urged him to use to the utmost his power to detain suspicious vessels, employing revenue cutters and armed vessels if need be. But the Navy did not have enough gunboats, frigates, and other vessels to patrol the coast and spot all the vessels that eluded the port officials. The embargo was exceedingly unpopular in the coastal cities, and the federal attorneys complained to Gallatin that it was virtually impossible to persuade courts to order the detention of vessels or juries to convict evaders.[7]

The difficulties of enforcing the law along the Canadian border were compounded by President Jefferson's wish that not a single citizen of any of the states "be deprived of a meal of bread." [8] Authority was given to the governors of states along the northeastern border to license the landing of vessels with grain from other American ports. Soon reports flowed into Gallatin's office that some governors were abusing this authority scandalously. On May 28 he told the President that "one mail alone brought me permits for eleven thousand barrels, exclusively of corn and rye meal." The most indiscriminate issuer of licenses was Governor James Sullivan of Massachusetts. Gallatin suggested that the power to issue licenses be centralized in the Treasury Department, where it could be enforced more rigorously and with less "favoritism." [9] The President was unwilling to do this, although he did chide Governor Sullivan—a rebuke not accepted in the best spirit.[10]

Along the northeastern border there was also trouble of a slightly different sort. In the spring of 1808 goods of all varieties began to be smuggled over land, lake, and river between Nova Scotia and New Brunswick and Maine, Vermont, and New York. The maritime towns of the two Canadian provinces hummed with unprecedented activity. Governor Daniel Tompkins of New York bluntly told Gallatin that there was "open insurrection" from Niagara Falls to Passamaquoddy Bay. When apprised of this, Jefferson directed Gallatin to "spare no pains or expence to bring the rascals . . . to justice." He reiterated his determination to learn "by a fair experiment . . . the power of this great weapon, the embargo." The Secretary should obtain any aid the Navy or War Department could spare to enforce the law. By mid-September, Gallatin had obtained the dispatch of regulars and militia to the disaffected area, where a certain degree of order was restored.[11]

But he feared that such success would be only temporary. Either Congress would have to give the Executive "the most arbitrary powers" and considerable armed power or it would have to abandon the embargo. He warned the President what some of these arbitrary powers would be: "not a single vessel shall be permitted to move without the special permission of the Executive . . . the collectors [shall] be invested with a general power of seizing property anywhere . . . without being liable to personal suits." "Such arbitrary powers," he remarked, were "dangerous and odious." [12]

Equally bad, in Gallatin's view, were other consequences. In operation, the embargo hurt the economy of the United States far more than that of Great Britain, and was actually benefiting the economy of France. Indeed, the wily Napoleon was confiscating American vessels that reached French harbors on the excuse that they must really be British! Ships rotted in the ports of New England and the middle states, and sailors suffered from unemployment. Virginia's tobacco crop was without a market, and sales of the grains of the southern states lagged. Although the embargo had not yet affected the receipts of the Treasury—indeed, during the year ending September 30, 1808, they were to reach the unprecedented sum of $18,000,000—they were beginning to "daily decrease." Under the influence of the embargo a number of factories sprang up in New England; but their effect on the national economy was yet to be felt.

Gallatin was concerned perhaps most of all—and he made no secret of it from the President and Secretary Madison—with the damage the embargo seemed to be certain to do to the Democratic-Republican cause. A party caucus in the spring of 1808 had confirmed Jefferson's selection of Madison as his successor. Gallatin, who heartily favored Madison for the office, was distressed by the reports that reached him during the following months. They made him doubt whether Madison could carry New York, certain he would lose all of New England. In Virginia the followers of John Randolph of Roanoke supported James Monroe in order to show their disapproval of the Administration. By August, Gallatin confided to his wife that there was an even chance that, if an excuse was somehow not found for abandoning the embargo before October, the election would be lost.[13]

Even if Madison were elected, a substitute for the embargo would have to be found by the time Congress reconvened. "There is not patriotism and union sufficient to bear with patience when there is no stimulus," Gallatin pointed out to Madison. "The people have been taught to view the embargo less as a shield protecting them against the decrees and orders of foreign powers, than as the true if not primary cause of the stagnation of commerce and depreciation of produce. . . . I had rather to encounter war itself than to display our impotence to enforce our laws." [14]

In August, in an off-guard moment, President Jefferson confessed that the consequences of the embargo law were more than he had bargained for. It "is certainly the most embarrassing we have ever had to execute," he acknowledged to Gallatin. "I did not expect a crop of so sudden and rank growth of fraud and open opposition by force should have grown up in the United States." [15] Before he felt obliged to give ground, the elections were held, and Madison won the Presidency by a comfortable margin, the Federalists carrying only the New England states. Now Jefferson adopted the attitude that the embargo was no longer his concern, but his successor's: he was "chiefly an unmeddling listener to what others say." [16]

The upshot was that the government drifted into a four-month interregnum. The ship of state would have been without a firm hand at the helm if Madison and Gallatin had not provided it. Of the two, Gallatin perhaps made the greater contribution, for he was conscious that, no matter what befell him after the start of Madison's term, he was until then the federal officer primarily responsible for enforcement of the embargo.

2

President Jefferson's message to Congress when it reconvened in November, 1808, studiously avoided any opinion on the nation's chief problem.[17] Naturally, there was consternation and indignation in the legislature. Probably George W. Campbell of Tennessee, Chairman of the House Ways and Means Committee, was the one who sought out Gallatin and Madison to express his colleagues' dissatisfaction and to beseech guidance. Knowing Jefferson's mood of withdrawal, Gallatin moved cautiously. "Both Mr. Madison and myself," he told the President on November 15, "concur in opinion that considering the temper of the legislature . . . it would be eligible to point out to them some precise and distinct course." He proposed an early meeting of the cabinet with the congressional leaders to chart a plan of action.[18]

When Jefferson declined to take any part in the matter, Gallatin assumed the initiative. During the next ten weeks, in social evenings at his home and working-hour conferences at his office, he discussed the

plight of the United States with leading members of both houses.[19] In a
series of memoranda, official papers of his own, and papers written for
others to sign, he developed a program for the nation during the interregnum. It was the same kind of guidance of the legislature by the cabinet that had aroused Gallatin's indignation a decade earlier under a
Federalist administration; and he would have been hard put to justify
logically his change in attitude.

Most ambitious of the papers was one he prepared for Campbell late
in November: a 4,600-word statement of the American government's
case against Great Britain and a proposal for a new policy toward her.
It was probably written in close collaboration with Madison, for its historical survey drew upon the Secretary of State's official and personal
correspondence. In its way, it was a masterpiece, clear, logical, and compelling, stating the conclusions Gallatin had grimly reached during the
past year of labor and frustration. The report was submitted to the House
over Campbell's name on November 22, 1808, and was to be remembered as "Campbell's Report." [20]

Another important paper of these busy weeks was the annual Treasury
report, dated December 10. This reiterated the recommendations of
"Campbell's Report," and considered their financial implications.[21] In a
letter to William Branch Giles dated November 24, Gallatin outlined
legislation for the enforcement of the embargo pending adoption of the
policy he had proposed.* [22]

In these papers Gallatin declared that the United States had only three
choices: "abject and degrading submission" to Great Britain and France;
war with both countries; continued and reinvigorated enforcement of the
embargo. If it took the first, "there will be no occasion for either an army
or a navy . . . no difficulty in reducing the public expenditures to a rate
corresponding with the fragments of impost which might still be collected." But this was unthinkable, for no American could consider submission.

As for the other possibilities, naturally one wished "that some middle
course might be discovered which should avoid the evils of both and not
be inconsistent with national honor and independence." But there was

---

* An undated memorandum in Gallatin's hand, preserved in the Gallatin
Folder of the Library of Congress, sheds additional light on his views in this
period. Probably written in December, 1808, or January, 1809, for the consideration of congressmen, it urged legislation to authorize an army of 50,000
volunteers and additional appropriations for fortifications in the interval until
war was declared. Here, in contradiction to his published papers, Gallatin urged
that the impost be increased.

none; it was a choice of war with both countries or continuance of the embargo. If the latter choice were taken, the government would be able to make ends meet by borrowing $5,000,000.

If the United States chose war? Repeal of the embargo would "necessarily be war or submission." The war would have to be with both Britain and France—war with only one would inevitably mean submission to "the edicts and will of the other."

War could be financed easily enough through loans. This statement was astonishing in the light of the attitude taken by Gallatin and the Jeffersonians a decade earlier during the undeclared war with France, but it was a conclusion he had first expressed seventeen months earlier at the time of the *Chesapeake* affair. His experience as head of the Treasury Department had convinced him that a public debt—at least a temporary public debt—was less dangerous than he had earlier supposed. He admitted as much by implication as he made his recommendations. "The high price of public stocks, and, indeed, of all species of stocks, the reduction of the public debt, the unimpaired credit of the General Government, and the large amount of existing bank stock in the United States, leave no doubt of the practicability of obtaining the necessary loans on reasonable terms," he argued. "The geographical situation of the United States, their history since the Revolution, and, above all, present events, remove every apprehension of frequent wars. It may, therefore, be confidently expected that a revenue derived solely from duties or importations, though necessarily impaired by war, will always be amply sufficient, during long periods of peace, not only to defray current expences, but also to reimburse the debt contracted during the few periods of war." Even if the United States declared war against both powers, it would not have to impose any new internal taxes, direct or indirect. In a word, war was the most satisfactory solution of the American dilemma.

As long as the embargo remained on the law books, Gallatin believed that it must be enforced strictly. It would be necessary for Congress to pass legislation requiring shipowners, before loading their vessels, to obtain specific permission from the port and to post bonds so high that there would be no profit in their entering a foreign port under any pretext. New legislation should prohibit the employment of aliens either as masters or as crew members. "In all probability" the export of specie and produce of the United States overland ought to be prohibited; Gallatin was not adamant on this point. And he had certain specific recommendations for simplifying judicial procedures so that the officials charged with enforcing the embargo would not be "perplexed" or "intimidated" by offenders' suits.

While thus stringently enforcing the embargo, the government should also make all necessary preparations for war. Gallatin declared that Congress should immediately pass a nonintercourse act, to go into effect June 1, 1809. This delay would have two advantages: Jefferson would retire from the Presidency with his beloved embargo still in effect, and copies of the new act could be sent to Great Britain and France with an indication that it would be altered to benefit either nation that would modify trade edicts to our advantage. Gallatin had no illusions that "the obstinate Emperor" Napoleon would alter his policy. He did believe that when Great Britain realized that the American people were united behind their government, were willing to make her enemy, France, their enemy, but without making "dishonorable purchases of her goods," she would "study her interest and relax." [23]

At its conclusion, the so-called Campbell's Report concluded with the proposal to Congress of three resolutions that all parties, whether they favored war or a continuation of the embargo, might logically adopt. The first asserted that the United States could not submit to the edicts of Great Britain without sacrificing its honor, rights, and independence. Another declared that the United States must exclude from its ports all ships and the products of all powers enforcing those edicts. A third stated that measures ought to be taken for the defense of the nation.[24]

Despite their reasonableness, the resolutions were bitter pills for the House to swallow. During three weeks of spirited debate, they were sharply attacked by the Federalists and lamely defended by the Democratic-Republicans, for they constituted, in essence, a confession of the failure of President Jefferson's experiment with peaceful coercion. Finally, on December 17 they were adopted by a safe enough majority.[25]

With the legislators in such a mood, it was small wonder that the harsh measures Gallatin suggested for the enforcement of the embargo—by all odds the harshest that had ever been proposed to the Congress of the United States—should shock both houses. They formed the heart and sinew of the "Force Bill" which Giles presented to the Senate on December 12. The senators shuddered, but passed it on December 21 by a vote of twenty to seven; the House, just as horrified, nevertheless adopted it on January 5, 1809, by a vote of seventy-one to thirty-two, and Jefferson signed it four days later.[26]

Meanwhile Gallatin had taken it upon himself to work also through diplomatic channels to free the United States from the intolerable situation born of Jefferson's embargo. Late in November, 1808, he had been approached in a friendly manner by David M. Erskine, the new British minister to Washington, a young man with an American wife. Erskine had already confided to Secretaries Madison and Smith his ambition to bring the two nations closer, and so Gallatin was not unprepared when he dropped in at his home one evening to open himself on all the matters at issue: reparation for the *Chesapeake* attack, the Orders in Council, the impressment of seamen, commercial relations, and colonial trade. Gallatin told Erskine that, like Smith and even Madison now, he did not count the embargo a wise measure, but that it had to be continued for the present. He outlined the legislation he was urging upon Congress and stated his conviction that it would remove the important differences between Great Britain and the United States. As Erskine later recalled, Gallatin told him, "in a familiar way, 'You see, sir, we could settle a treaty in my private room in two hours which might perhaps be found as lasting as if it was bound up in all the formalities of a regular system.'"

One part of the conversation was subsequently to haunt Gallatin. He told Erskine—so the envoy wrote to Foreign Secretary Canning—that "he had uniformly endeavored to persuade the President to place the conduct of Great Britain and France in a fair light before the public." He then checked himself, but Erskine "could clearly collect from his manner and from some slight insinuations, that he thought the President had acted with partiality towards France." Quickly Gallatin turned the conversation to President elect Madison who, he emphasized, was not partial to France, and was a great admirer of "British history and institutions." [27]

3

Although Gallatin appeared to be having his way with Congress, he sensed that trouble was brewing. He wrote his fears to Judge Nicholson: "A great confusion and perplexity reigns in Congress. . . . A majority will not adhere to the embargo much longer; and if war be not speedily determined on, submission will soon ensue." [28]

New England, hardest hit by the embargo, was in the mood for submission. After the passage of the Force Act, town meeting after town meeting passed strongly worded resolutions against the law, some of them even speaking of a convention to nullify it, perhaps even the creation of a New England confederacy. A resolution adopted at Gloucester, Massachusetts, on January 23 lamented, "We see not only the purse-strings of our nation in the hands of a Frenchified Genevan, but all our naval forces, and all our militia, placed under the control of the same foreigner and his minions, whom we cannot but think a satellite of Bonaparte." [29]

The New England Federalists in Congress were willing to support almost any measure that would negate the program of the government, whether of the dying Jefferson Administration or the nascent Madison Administration. They found abettors among the Democratic-Republicans. The Pennsylvania delegation, of which Dr. Michael Leib was a member and William Duane a dominating force, had watched sullenly in the months while Gallatin assumed leadership in the drive ultimately to stop the embargo and in the meantime to enforce it. The shipping interests of the middle states, represented by Senator Samuel Smith of Maryland, his brother Secretary Robert Smith, and Robert's brother-in-law Senator Wilson Cary Nicholas of Virginia, were bitter about the economies imposed upon the Navy by Gallatin and Jefferson. The followers of Vice President Clinton resented the fact that the Secretary had thrown his support for the Presidency to Madison rather than to their own venerable but still ambitious chief. Moreover, rumors now circulated that Madison planned to name Gallatin as his Secretary of State—a report to which Gallatin's large role in foreign relations since the election gave credence.

All this accumulated resentment welled up and overflowed early in January, 1809. At first the turn against Gallatin was veiled and appeared to be harmless enough. On January 7 his old friend John Smilie offered a resolution for a special meeting of the new Congress on May 22. On the face of it, this was an excellent idea that Gallatin himself favored; if the situation in Europe did not distinctly improve by that time, war could be declared against Britain or France or both. But many congressmen grasped the idea as an opportunity to disregard Gallatin's earlier request for a new nonintercourse act timed to go into effect so as not to offend Jefferson's feelings, but leaving the United States free to use it as the basis of a negotiation with the two European powers. Smilie's resolution was adopted.[30]

The first clear-cut sign of revolt came in the Senate about the same time. Sixteen Democratic-Republicans joined with the Federalists to amend a Navy bill so that it ordered every armed vessel, including gunboats, to be placed in active service "as soon as may be." [31] This aroused Gallatin because it did not fit in with the program he had charted for dealing with the European war and if followed literally would cost the government $6,000,000, money that he was counting on to use for the first year of war if it was declared by Congress on convening in May.

Gallatin enlisted the aid of Campbell to kill the measure in the House. The Tennessee Congressman moved that the clause obliging the government to fit out and man all vessels without respect for their use be stricken from the bill. A coalition of Federalists and dissident Democratic-Republicans voted this down by a narrow vote. Later the sting of the defeat was assuaged a bit when, after a number of conferences between committees of the two houses and further polling, the legislation was modified to require the fitting-out of only two frigates and as many gunboats as the public service—in the judgment of the President—might require.[32]

The Democratic-Republican dissidents, having thus kicked over the traces, now felt no compunction about humiliating President Jefferson and adopting a policy that Gallatin had termed "submission" and "unthinkable." On February 27 the House approved a Senate bill terminating the embargo on March 4, the day its author was to leave the Presidential mansion and replacing it with a nonimportation act that permitted American vessels to trade with all nations except Great Britain and France.[33]

In actual practice this new legislation constituted submission to the British Orders in Council. Erskine summed up the situation succinctly to Canning: "Great advantages may be reaped from it by England, as she has command of the seas, and can procure through neutrals any of the produce of [the United States], besides the immense quantity that will be brought direct to Great Britain under various pretenses; whereas France will obtain but little, at a great expence and risk." [34]

Jefferson, appalled and mute, signed the bill on March 1. Three days later he departed for Monticello. "Never did a prisoner, released from his chains, feel such relief," he told a friend.[35] Gallatin did not try to conceal his own despondency. He had tried to rescue the people from the foolhardy policy of a beloved friend only to have his efforts repulsed by the delegates of the people. "I am overwhelmed with financial business," he wrote to his sister-in-law, "times are gloomy; and the conduct of neither the people or their representatives is calculated to give me good spirits." [36]

Thus the embargo, the experiment that Jefferson had hoped would be the crowning triumph of his Administration, ended in dismal failure. It proved to be Gallatin's undoing as well. The damage to his work in the Treasury becomes clear by comparing its records in 1808 and 1809: customs duties fell from $16,363,000 to $7,258,000, while expenditures for the Navy rose from $1,884,000 to $2,427,000 and for the Army from $2,900,000 to $3,345,000.[37] His loyalty to his chief in defending a cause he considered unwise moreover helped bring him the enmity of men in Congress whose cooperation he sorely required.

4

In 1807, when Jefferson decided to retire at the end of his second term, Gallatin began to arrange his affairs so that he could leave public life at the same time and take his family to live in Switzerland for three or four years.[38] But when it was decided that Madison should run for the Presidency, Gallatin began to look more and more hopefully at the office of Secretary of State. As soon as Madison's election became certain, the report began circulating through Washington that Gallatin was to have his wish. By his intellectual capacities, his experience in Congress and in the cabinet, he was perhaps better qualified than any man in America to occupy the office during a period when the nation's principal problem was foreign relations. His leadership in the effort to deliver the country from the untenable position resulting from Jefferson's embargo made him seem all the more to be the obvious choice.

The revolt against the Administration in Congress during January, especially on the Navy bill, gave the first inkling that his appointment would arouse opposition. That Senator Leib of Pennsylvania would oppose him for any public office, Gallatin took for granted. That Senator Smith would do so became clear after the vote on the Navy bill; there were those, moreover, who suspected that the Baltimore merchant hankered after the office of Secretary of State himself. That Senator Giles and Congressman Nicholas of Virginia would stand against him, Gallatin learned a few days before the inauguration from the lips of the President elect.

Madison explained that he had just had a visit from Nicholas. Nicholas said that he and Giles had decided that they could not vote to approve Gallatin's nomination as Secretary of State because he had been born a foreigner, and it would therefore be difficult to persuade the European powers to treat with him as an American, rather than as a native of Geneva, a city-state now under the control of Bonaparte. Giles had sent along a letter listing nine reasons why Gallatin should not receive the appointment. These animadversions merely reiterated at great length his feeling that Gallatin's loyalty to Jefferson, Madison, and the Democratic-Republican cause could not be trusted. It seems to be a fact that Giles wanted the office for himself, but Madison probably did not tell Gallatin that. At any rate, he repeated Nicholas's prophecy that serious opposition would develop in the Senate if Gallatin were nominated.[39]

All this disturbed Gallatin. What Madison said next astounded him. The President elect had offered the Secretaryship of the Treasury to Robert Smith, with the understanding that his brother, the Maryland senator, would corral his forces for Gallatin's nomination to the State Department!

Gallatin rejected the proposal, observing wryly that he could not direct both the State and the Treasury departments as would be necessary if Robert Smith were named to the latter. It would be far better if he remained in the Treasury and Smith took the State portfolio; after all, Madison was familiar with the problems of the State Department through eight years of service and could possibly serve as his own Secretary of State.

Gallatin brooded over the sad turn in his fortunes. His heart had been set on the foreign office, and the disappointment that Jefferson and Madison did not support him in his desire for it remained a sad memory for years afterwards.[40] For a while he toyed with the idea of quitting the cabinet and running again for Congress. He might be happier in the legislature than in the cabinet, and perhaps could regain the influence he had lost as a result of the embargo. He told close friends that he doubted he would be in the cabinet another winter.

In his dilemma, he sought Judge Nicholson's advice.[41] Nicholson told him that he disliked the idea of his retiring, "because I believe that you will be a great public loss . . . a loss that Mr. Madison will feel immediately, but the public will not perceive . . . for some years. When the Government gets entirely into the possession of these men, who are resolved to seize it, and their selfish and mercenary conduct are hereafter exposed, as they must be, the public will perceive how important it would have been to retain a man who was at once capable and honest."

Along with the praise, Judge Nicholson gave advice on how Gallatin might improve his ways. Instead of being content, as in the past, merely to give his opinion when the President asked it, he ought to throw his weight around. He ought to tell President Madison that either Robert Smith must go or he would go, that at the very least the State Department must be filled by "an able and better man." [42]

This was sound advice that Gallatin might well have taken. Instead he decided that, with Robert Smith taking over the State post, he must remain in the Treasury, hoping against hope that he might help his good but irresolute friend Madison cope with the worsening situation at home and abroad.

17. The Life of a Cabinet Member

1801=1813

Although Washington was Gallatin's home for the dozen busiest and most productive years of his life, he was never fond of the swampy, straggling Capital on the Potomac. "A place which has less attractions and affords less comfort than almost any other of the Union," he described it to an old acquaintance.[1] He agreed in feeling with John Randolph, who called it a place "where the wretched exile is cut off from all information, society or amusement, and where the common necessaries of life can be procured not without difficulty, and the most enormous expence." [2] Mrs. Gallatin summed up her feelings about it: "It is a place that never will be of any consequence, even if the national government should remain there." [3]

Happily, as the Gallatins and other early arrivals were to discover, a few hardy ladies—Marylanders and Virginians mostly—already were on the scene, doing their best to make life less monastically grim. Among them was Margaret Bayard Smith, who had deserted the Federalism of her family when she married Samuel H. Smith, editor of the *National Intelligencer*. She took charge of Hannah during her first days in the Capital, accompanying her on visiting and shopping expeditions and helping her solve the Capital servant problem. The Gallatins and the Smiths exchanged hospitality at card parties and large formal affairs.[4]

Gallatin, who as a congressman had preached economy and decried the "monarchistic" pretensions of the Federalist administrations, was relieved to find no attempt made to carry the magnificence and ostentation of Philadelphia to the Potomac. President Jefferson, with his informal manners and almost rustic dress the personification of "republican simplicity," set the tone of the Capital. As a widower with only the sporadic assistance of two married daughters, he extended to members of the official circles a hospitality that was informal and spontaneous.* At his mansion Gallatin basked in the stimulating radiance of a great and ever-inquiring mind.

The brunt of the burden of official entertaining was borne by James Madison and his wife Dolley during his years as Secretary of State and as President. "Mrs. Madison," as a young man of letters from New York Washington Irving observed, "is a fine, portly, buxom dame, who has a smile and a pleasant word for every body." [5] Her vivacity and charm, rather than the splendor of her drawing room or the richness of her table, endeared her to the Gallatins. By all odds the most openhanded hosts in the cabinet were the Robert Smiths, who were wealthy; Gallatin might have misgivings about the Secretary of the Navy's executive capacities, but during Jefferson's Administration at least the relations between the Smith and Gallatin families were close and cordial.

The Gallatins made no attempt to vie for social supremacy with the Madisons or the Smiths. Their home on Capitol Hill was always open of an evening to congenial Congressmen seeking refuge from the lonely bachelors' existence imposed upon them by the dreary boarding houses of Washington. Here good political talk rather than expensive food and liquor was the chief fare. It was refreshing, as Nathaniel Macon of North Carolina pointed out, to be able to give vent to thoughts that the mass of congressmen would be unwilling to listen to.[6] For such occasions Hannah proved an ideal hostess: "by no means a pretty woman," one regular guest recalled, "she was a reading woman, and a politician." [7]

However, the Gallatins did little formal entertaining while Jefferson was President, especially outside their circle of friends. A Federalist senator observed sourly that Gallatin was "frugal and parsimonious," Mrs. Gallatin "a domestic wife and averse to company" [8]—or at least to the company of those not congenial politically. William Duane, who had no love for Gallatin, enjoyed telling a story to illustrate the Secretary's reputation for economy. One night, when the stagecoach for Baltimore was passing the Gallatin home, a passenger beside Duane asked who lived there. "Lives?" exclaimed the driver. "Lives? Why, nobody lives there." The passenger protested that there was a light in the house. "Oh, yes," the driver conceded, "the Secretary of the Treasury *breathes* there." Duane had no doubt what the driver said was caricature, "but the caricature is very often very like the original." [9]

* For example, Jefferson wrote the Gallatins June 3, 1801: "Th. Jefferson asks the favor of Mr. and Mrs. Gallatin to dine with him today; and requests that while they are arranging matters at their new quarters they will dine with him every day." (Gallatin Papers.)

Gallatin was determined that his household, like the government, should live within its income. His holdings in lands and his western Pennsylvania enterprises brought him little or nothing during these years; his expenditures must not exceed the $5,000 he received as a cabinet officer. He still fondly recalled that he had been able to live one year as a congressman on his official pay of six dollars a day.

Sometimes Gallatin's attempts to economize tripped him up. He was such an inveterate smoker of cigars that he bought a quarter's worth at a time. Hannah suggested that it would be more prudent to buy them by the box. When he tried it he discovered that his rate of consumption doubled. This lesson he applied to all his household purchases, buying at retail rather than wholesale. He explained the experience to a friend: "More was used when it could be dropped from the Barrel, while less was used from frequent scarcity." [10]

After Jefferson retired to Monticello, and Dolley Madison stepped up the pace of entertaining, the Gallatins became more hospitable. Now the captious Duane complained that the Secretary "feasts sumptuously every day, and what is more, invites large companies to dine with him." [11] Others who had less reason to be prejudiced were impressed similarly. Mrs. William Winston Seaton, whose husband had succeeded Samuel Smith as editor of the *National Intelligencer*, exclaimed that a ball Mrs. Gallatin gave in January, 1813, was "more select, more elegant, than I have yet seen in the city." The amount and variety of refreshments served made her breathless. She thought all the "antiquated dames . . . decked with lace and ribbons . . . rouged excessively," not excepting Mrs. Gallatin; but she acknowledged that her hostess did not deceive herself that it hid her age—she defended it "as indispensable to a *decent* appearance." [12] Washington Irving testified that Hannah was "the most stylish woman in the drawing room" that same winter. "She dresses with more splendour than any of the other of the noblesse." The issues of United States stock that her husband was marketing were obviously on the young Federalist's mind when he confessed that he "could not help fancying that I saw two or three of my bonds trailing in her train." [13]

All this sociability somewhat perturbed Gallatin. "Rounds of parties, fishing club feasts for Ladies, turtle parties, plays, routs, and drawing rooms," was the way he described his life during one July. Then, like Adam, he blamed Eve for it: "My wife is quite dissipated and takes me along." [14]

Hannah sometimes invited her younger sisters Maria and Adden to spend the winter in Washington and share these pleasures. Of Maria, Gallatin appears to have been especially fond. An attractive, vivacious girl in her middle twenties, she provoked the liveliest and wittiest letters from his pen. "You know, I am sure," he once wrote, "how sincerely I was attached to you when we were both in New York; but I did not know myself how much I would wish to enjoy your society, how near you were to me till this long separation." And on another occasion he assured her: "I really do love you very much, and I think I dare say much oftener of you than you do of your old bald brother." Maria reciprocated his affection, writing frequent and long letters of family news, in which she upbraided him for becoming too absorbed in his work.

A girl in her twenties still unmarried had reason for concern in early nineteenth century America. Gallatin was lavish in his concern for Maria. Whenever she was on a visit to relatives or friends in another city, he persistently hoped that she would meet a suitable husband. But then, he would add, whoever married her "must be so good, so sensible, so accomplished, so every thing in order to deserve you that I sometimes despair. . . . Be it as it may, I will persist in loving you married or single, and as my affections are few, and not easily shaken, I know that you will forever retain one of the first places in my heart." [15] One characteristic of Maria troubled him, however: when Hannah showed her sister letters he had written stating his love for his wife in enthusiastic terms, Maria allowed that she considered such expressions very silly. Perhaps if Maria fell in love herself, he intimated, she would be less prudish.[16]

During the several seasons Maria visited the Gallatins at Washington, she became a familiar figure by her sister's side at social affairs, as she diligently eyed the Maryland and Virginia beaux.[17] It was perhaps at one of these functions that she met Congressman John Montgomery of Maryland, whom she married in 1809. Soon, after the fashion of contented young matrons, she was gaining weight. "It would do your heart good," Mrs. Samuel Smith was telling a friend within a year of the wedding, "to see Mrs. Montgomery so fat, and rosy, and cheerful, and good humor'd. I never admired or liked her half so well." [18]

Another young woman whom the Gallatins took under their wing was Dorothea, second daughter of John Jacob Astor, the wealthy New York fur trader and shipper, with whom Gallatin had formed a close friendship. In 1812, when Dorothea was seventeen, she passed a few months in Washington as guest of the Gallatins. There, the buxom German-looking girl met and fell in love with Colonel Walter Langdon of New Hampshire, who was generally accounted by the ladies to be "very handsome and very fascinating." Observing the effect he was having on Miss Astor, Gallatin sent the father a warning that "he had better send for his daughter to come home," as "Col. Langdon has every recommendation except wealth, being a member of a large family." But before the parent could intervene the young couple eloped.[19]

Sometimes Gallatin undertook to promote romance. Among the lonely males who haunted his drawing room of an evening was Jonathan Roberts, a freshman congressman from Pennsylvania. Gallatin hinted broadly that his attentions would be more than welcome at the home of General Van Ness, where pretty Sarah Smith, daughter of Senator John Smith of New York, was visiting. Roberts later explained, "This was one of the cases where I felt called upon to exercise prudence." [20]

Sometimes a visitor from another world passed through Washington, providing Gallatin with intellectual excitement. One who arrived in 1802 after a long stay in Europe was Thomas Paine, whose great reputation based on his authorship of *Common Sense* had been tarnished for many Americans by his later deistic work *The Age of Reason*. Jefferson welcomed him at the Presidential mansion; and the Gallatins also played host to him.[21]

Even more interesting was a thirty-four-year-old Prussian naturalist, Baron Alexander von Humboldt, who tarried at Washington several days in June, 1804, on his way home after nearly five years of scientific investigation in Latin America. The "exquisite intellectual treat" afforded by a day with the Baron so delighted Gallatin that he wrote to Hannah, in New York at the time, with all the excitement of a schoolboy: "I am not apt to be easily pleased, and he was not particularly prepossessing to my taste, for he speaks more than [J.B.C.] Lucas, [James] Finley, and myself put together, and twice as fast as anybody I know, German, French, Spanish, and English all together. But I was really delighted, and swallowed more information of various kinds than I had for two years past in all I had read or heard. . . . He has brought a mass of natural, philosophical, and political information which will render the geography of [the Latin-American countries] better known than of most European nations." He was grateful to the Baron for permitting the transcriptions of some of his maps and notes. More than pure intellectual curiosity inspired him to this; he and Jefferson were full of ideas for development of the Louisiana Purchase and Humboldt's information about mining prospects in Mexico threw light on the potentialities of the American Southwest.[22]

Gallatin was most ready to share knowledge with other men pursuing intellectual hares. In 1809 John Melish, a Scottish merchant, sought his aid for a book about the United States. Gallatin received him at his home and at the Land Office, and impressed him as "an accurate man of business." Melish noted in his *Travels Through the United States of*

America (which ran through several editions and became something of a classic) that he had been "much edified by his valuable information." [23] Political party allegiances meant nothing to Gallatin when learned activity was concerned. When the New England Federalist Senator William Plumer confided his ambition to write a history of his own times, the Secretary of the Treasury "very promptly offered his aid to furnish any materials in his department." [24] But the work never was completed.

A man who looked at Gallatin during these years with the eye of a painter as well as a writer was William Dunlap of New York. After calling on the Secretary of the Treasury in February, 1806, Dunlap noted in his diary that he was a thin man of about five feet nine or ten inches, weighing 150 pounds. He was most impressed by his "dark hair, coarse and bushy, yellow complexion, long nose, hideous mouth and teeth." But there was a compensating feature, his "black, intelligent, and piercing eye." Even after a quarter of a century in America, Gallatin's Gallic accent remained pronounced, "but he speaks English with great correctness." [25] Senator Plumer, more captious, noted that the Secretary was "very inattentive and negligent of his person and dress—his linen is frequently soiled and his clothes tattered," and attributed it to his notorious parsimoniousness.[26]

2

During the winter, particularly when Congress was in session, Washington was gay in its way. But when the semitropical summer descended the legislators lost no time in scattering to the sixteen states of the Union. At the start of the Jefferson Administration the Federalist newspapers undertook to make political capital from the absence of so many government officials during August and September.[27] The President firmly rejected such carping. "I consider it a trying experience for a person from the mountains to pass the bilious months on the tidewater," he told Gallatin, urging him to get out of the city.[28]

Gallatin, conscientious about his duties, remained close to his office most of these months, although he usually sent Hannah and the children to a more salubrious climate. The consequence was that through the summers of Jefferson's and Madison's administrations, he was often the only important officer in the city and hence the acting head of the government. He kept in constant touch with the President, forwarding to him in Virginia correspondence that deserved immediate attention and executing any directions sent to him.

Hannah, whose instincts were those of a homing pigeon, usually was under the Nicholsons' roof in New York from June until September. During such periods she and her husband tried to assuage their yearning for each other through frequent letters. "There is not an evening passes but I accompany you in imagination in your solitary walks with your segar on the pavement before the door or backwards and forwards in one of the rooms," she wrote. Once she admitted that she would have felt much better if he had been with her in New York to "plague a little." [29]

Although Gallatin loathed writing of any sort—he once told President Jefferson, "I cannot write even a decent letter without great labour" [30] —he kept up his end of the correspondence. When he was not at his office desk during the summer months, he acknowledged to her, "I am good for nothing . . . the servants do what they please; everything goes as it pleases. I smoke and sleep; mind nothing . . . nothing but the hope of seeing you soon has kept in any degree my spirits from sinking. Whether in the plains or over the hills, whether in the city, or in retreat, I cannot live without you. . . . I am now good for nothing but you, and good for nothing without you; you will say that anyhow I am not good for much; that may be, but such as I am, you are mine, and you are my comfort, my joy and the darling of my soul." [31]

Almost as much, in such times, Gallatin missed his children. At Washington, the family celebrated four additions and suffered three losses, all girls. A third child, named Catherine, was born on August 22, 1801, but died of measles and the whooping cough the following April 21.[32] Frances, a fat and healthy child, was born on February 3, 1803;[33] but two other daughters, Sophia Albertine and Hannah Maria, died within a year of birth.[34]

Gallatin continued to take a keen interest in the welfare of his sons, James and Albert Rolaz, now passing through boyhood and adolescence. Indeed, one of his chief objections to public life was that it did not allow him time "to attend personally" to the education of his children, and that Washington did not afford proper resources "for that object." [35] Even so, he kept admonishing Hannah to raise them according to his rather stern notions of child rearing: "Obedience you must learn to enforce and they to practice," he wrote to her in New York in 1804; "once learned, it becomes habitual and facilitates every step in the arduous business of education. James and even Albert obey me very well whilst present; and if they learn the same respect to you a great deal will be done." Children "when left to themselves are always unruly." [36] Another time, on learning that the boys had been naughty, he advised: "If love will not do, they must be punished; and I beg you to tell them in my name that they must not be permitted to play every day while they misbehave. The order you must strictly enforce. . . . Yet you must tell them that I love them dearly, and will love them still better if they are good to you during my absence." [37]   At the tag end of nearly every summer he arranged his duties so that he could get away to New York for a few weeks before Congress reconvened, visiting en route Judge Joseph H. Nicholson at Baltimore and the A. J. Dallases at Philadelphia, and sometimes conferring about Treasury affairs with the bankers of the three cities.[38] At Commodore Nicholson's William Street house or his cooler country place at Greenwich, north of the city, sometimes as many as twenty-four of Hannah's relatives converged for a family reunion; and on such occasions Gallatin's heart sang. The Commodore and Mrs. Nicholson were now his "father" and "mother," and he was ever solicitous of the health and happiness of both. He felt a personal loss when the old gentleman died in 1804—"died with the most perfect resignation," he observed, "a state of mind for which he was certainly indebted to his sincere belief in the Christian religion and to his confidence in its promises." [39]

Through the Nicholson connection Gallatin became a close friend of John Jacob Astor. The Gallatin and Astor families exchanged hospitality at New York and Washington, and their children played together. Normally their concerns were social—as is evidenced in Astor's letters about a fur muff he planned to present to Hannah, about chairs he had bought for the Gallatin house, about conversations with the Gallatin grandchildren on a visit to the Nicholsons. But Astor was not above mixing business with pleasure: into a social letter he might put a discreet query about the policy the government proposed to follow in the Northwest, affecting his American Fur Company, or about the Treasury's plans in connection with the Bank of the United States or the state banks.[40] Gallatin was always the scrupulous public servant at such times, but the close friendship of the two men inevitably set a-wagging the tongues of people inclined to imagine and believe the worst.

3

As Gallatin became increasingly absorbed in his duties at Washington and his wife's connections at New York, his ties with the West and with Geneva grew ever more tenuous. He was always planning to visit western Pennsylvania, but in the dozen years after he became Secretary of the Treasury he crossed the mountains only in 1803, 1806, and 1810, each time for a brief visit. As a result, he got out of touch with the politicians and the political situation in western Pennsylvania, and gradually lost strength as a leader of the Democratic-Republican party.

Even so, he found it most difficult to sever the ties with the area of his young adulthood. The arduous work of his first two years in the Treasury and the miserable climate of the Capital made him consider retiring from public life and concentrating his energies on the New Geneva Glass Works, of which he was now half-owner. The works had produced a negligible profit in the first half-dozen years, but he was convinced that close supervision would bring about a different result. By 1803 his mood about public life had shifted and he directed his brother-in-law James Witter Nicholson to sell his share. There were no takers.[41] By 1806, approximately $20,000 had been invested in the works and its fortunes still remained indifferent. The glassworkers then told him that they saw little chance of making a real go of the enterprise unless an entirely new plant were built, perhaps in another location. After much soul searching, Gallatin concluded that it would be foolhardy for him to take any large or active interest in a new works. He agreed to take a one-seventh interest in the new firm of Repert & Co.[42] After months of haggling over details, the project was reorganized according to his specifications. A more efficient works was constructed across the Monongahela River from New Geneva in Greene County, the firm continuing to use the name New Geneva Glass Works on its products.[43] Gradually its fortunes turned. By 1816 it was producing an annual profit of $8,000, of which Gallatin received one-seventh.[44]

The New Geneva gun factory, which had produced a satisfactory profit before Gallatin went to Washington, became unprofitable soon after. Pennsylvania ceased to buy arms when the French war scare dissipated, and the federal government in time adopted the practice of manufacturing for its own requirements. Gallatin's gun factory was quietly abandoned soon after 1800.[45]

Gallatin's ambition to make something of his dream town of New Geneva was a long time in dying. During 1801 and 1802, while the prospects for the glassworks remained bright, he had sold twenty-five of his lots there. But when the works were moved across the river it became all but impossible to find purchasers. After a dozen years in Washington he still owned approximately 100 of the 167 lots marked in the original plan of the town.[46]

In 1808, when the gun factory was no more and the glassworks had moved out of the county, the assessors estimated Gallatin's holdings in Fayette County as worth $11,000. About the same time he rated the value of his landholdings in Virginia, Ohio, and Kentucky at not more than $12,000. He paid the taxes upon these lands and did his best to protect them against squatters and rival claimants; but he made no attempt to sell his holdings, and modified them in only two minor instances. He believed that it would be improper for him, as a federal officer charged with supervising the administration of the Land Office, to speculate in lands, especially federal lands: indeed, in doing so he might very well become liable to impeachment.[47]

Gallatin's concern with lands and westward expansion, as Secretary of the Treasury, allowed him to do something in an honorable way to help a boyhood friend who continued to be a heavy burden on his loyalty and good nature. John Badollet was eking out a living as a farmer across the Monongahela from New Geneva. During 1803 Gallatin got his old chum a commission to survey the road that was to traverse Ohio, a temporary job paid on a per diem basis.[48] When the Land Act of 1804 provided for the sale of federal lands in Indiana Territory, Gallatin asked the President to appoint Badollet register in the land office at Vincennes. He apologized for recommending a personal friend, but testified to Badollet's "strict integrity" and Republicanism. The President cooperated.[49]

For the time being, Badollet was grateful and content. He started life anew in middle age on a farm near Vincennes with an assured income of $1,000 a year. But before long he was involved in territorial politics, bombarding Gallatin with complaints about the personality and policies of Governor William Henry Harrison. He was particularly aroused because Harrison was doing his best to introduce slavery into the Territory, although under another name. Gallatin wrote to Harrison in 1809: "I was and still am decidedly opposed to the introduction of slavery into any part of the Union where it does not exist or can be checked. . . . It is with great regret that I find that difference of opinion on that point should have produced anything like a personal hostility between you and my friend, Badollet." [50]

Although Harrison's efforts in behalf of slavery were frustrated, other policies of the governor and other political figures provided Badollet with subjects for complaint through the years.[51] He was convinced that life had treated him unfairly, and derived much satisfaction from saying so. Gallatin responded frankly but indulgently, as to a beloved but often irritating brother. On one occasion he wrote: "Your squabbles and disappointments . . . are matters of course. At what time or in what country did you ever hear that men assumed the privilege of being more honest than the mass of society in which they live without being hated or persecuted? Unless they chose to remain in perfect obscurity and let others and the world take their own course; and in that case they can never be heard of. All we can do here is to fulfill our own duty without looking at the consequences so far as [they] relate to ourselves. If the love and esteem of others or general popularity follow, so much the better. But it is with these as with all temporal blessings, such as wealth, health, &c; not to be despised, but never to be considered . . . as objects to which a single particle of integrity, a single feeling of conscience should be sacrificed. I need not add that I preach much better than I practice." [52]

At the very moment Gallatin wrote down these precepts, he was doing his level best to practice them, and succeeding in large measure. Just a few weeks earlier he had reluctantly concluded that, despite the slings and arrows leveled at him by the Smiths and their allies, he must stay by President Madison's side and see the Administration through the crisis.

18. The Struggle with the "Invisibles"

1809=1810

If Gallatin's talents as a financier made him invaluable to President Jefferson, his capacities for statesmanship made him nigh indispensable to President Madison. Although Jemmy Madison, a wizened little applejohn of a man, was a brilliant architect of constitutions and an earnest student of foreign relations, he was woefully vacillating and colorless as a leader of men and captain of a ship of state. His shortcomings were all the more unfortunate because none of the men with whom he surrounded himself—except Gallatin—had the essential qualities that he lacked.

Madison's cabinet was the poorest the nation had had up to that time, with only Gallatin to keep it from being downright bad. The President's selections gave more consideration to geography than to talent. From New England he chose William Eustis, a Boston hospital surgeon, to succeed Dearborn in the War Department. To South Carolina he turned for Paul Hamilton, a gentleman of impeccable family standing who had served as governor with small distinction. From Delaware he continued in office Caesar A. Rodney, whom Jefferson had appointed Attorney General, and whom Gallatin regarded highly as a colleague and a friend. To appease Maryland and its wealthy, imperious Senator Samuel Smith, who had opposed his nomination, he chose Robert Smith to head the State Department; and, as he must have expected, he had to be his own Secretary, making all the important decisions on foreign relations, writing all the important papers.

For Madison as for Jefferson, Gallatin set fiscal policy and wrote the financial paragraphs in the annual Presidential messages to Congress. He continued to advise on the composition of passages on other subjects, although perhaps not to such an extent as under Jefferson.[1] In cabinet meetings he was heard with respect on all matters because his long experience

223

in statesmanship, his intellect, and his integrity of character made him tower over his associates.

Although Gallatin decided to remain in the cabinet, despite Robert Smith's elevation to the office he thought should have been assigned to him, he remained bitter about the "miserable intrigue" that had brought it about. At first he tried to be philosophical. Hannah would tell him that "vice and intrigue are all powerful" in Washington; he would retort that "virtue is its own reward"; whereupon she would say "language is mere affectation." [2] But Smith had been in the State Department scarcely two months when clerks in the Treasury disclosed a situation that aroused Gallatin's latent hostility to the Smith brothers.

An audit of the books of the Navy Department which the Treasury accountant showed to Gallatin, indicated that under Robert Smith's direction the Navy had bought, over a two-year period, $250,000 in bills of exchange on Leghorn, presumably for use in operations in the Tripolitan war. Most of these were bills on the Baltimore firm of Smith & Buchanan, of which Samuel Smith was a principal; but the firm had neglected to direct its officers to draw on this reserve, and they had instead drawn on London at a considerable expense. When the war ended, some of the remaining fund was returned to the United States, and the rest was stolen by one Degen, a member of the firm that acted as a naval agent at Leghorn. Indeed, it was the departure of Degen with the money and his subsequent apprehension at Paris that brought the involvement of Smith & Buchanan with Navy Department affairs to Gallatin's attention.

Two aspects of the case incensed Gallatin. One was the apparent inefficiency of Robert Smith's administration of the Navy Department in failing to draw upon the war reserves. The other was that the firm of the Secretary's brother should have received the exclusive and lucrative privilege at Leghorn at little or no risk to itself.

In indignation, Gallatin asked Judge Nicholson's advice as to how the matter should be handled. Somehow word of this reached the ears of Congressman Nathaniel Macon of North Carolina, always an opponent of the Navy and so of the forces led by the brothers Smith. Macon asked if he should not seek the appointment of a special congressional committee to investigate the subject, but Secretary Gallatin advised against it. Macon's close friend John Randolph grasped the initiative and obtained appointment of such a committee. Its report and supporting documents, highly critical of the Smiths, was printed in late June, 1809. [3]

The Maryland Federalists were waging a spirited campaign to win control of the state legislature so that they might capture Samuel Smith's seat in the Senate, and a Federalist newspaper in Baltimore began printing general accounts of Smith's financial transactions, probably derived in part from material provided by Judge Nicholson. These suggested that, to secure a debt which he thought bad, he had transferred it to the Navy Department, thus involving the federal government in the loss. Gallatin was described as having spoken about the affair "in terms of great indignation." [4]

To Smith the publication of these charges seemed to be a dastardly blow at his candidacy for reelection. On June 26, while the articles were appearing, he angrily wrote to Gallatin: "I will not believe that any of [your] indignation could have been directed at me. I believe it impossible that any man who has the least pretensions to character would commit an act as base as that charged on me." He assured Gallatin that his special inquiries had convinced him that Degen & Purviance was a house superior to any other in Leghorn.[5] Two days later Robert Smith rushed to the defense of the family in a letter to Gallatin, assuring him he would be happy to answer any questions about "the most minute circumstance of my public life." [6]

Gallatin's reply gave Senator Smith little comfort. He wrote on January 29 that the transaction appeared to him to be "the most extraordinary that has fallen within my knowledge since I have been in this department. It has certainly left very unfavorable impressions on my mind." He denied that he had made the charge printed in the Baltimore newspaper, but reiterated his conclusion that Smith & Buchanan's dealings with Degen & Purviance had not conformed to the best practices.[7]

Late in August the Gallatins took a holiday, visiting President and Mrs. Madison at their Virginia estate, Montpelier. During their stay they went with the Madisons to visit Jefferson at his home, Monticello.[8] As they were about to leave, the Secretary and the former President had a heart-to-heart talk. Gallatin unburdened himself of his fears about the course the new Administration was taking: about Madison's irresoluteness; about the financial shoals that seemed to lie ahead because of the projects of the pro-Navy group; about the Smiths' growing influence in Congress. He told Jefferson that he still seriously considered leaving the cabinet.

The confidence so surprised and distressed Jefferson that, in the excitement of leave-taking, he did not express his feelings fully. Six weeks later, in Washington, Gallatin received a long and heart-warming letter from the former President, a letter obviously intended to be shown to Madison in order to bolster the Chief Executive's faltering resolution. He wrote: "The discharge of the debt . . . is vital to the destinies of our government, and it hangs on Mr. Madison and yourself alone. . . . My opinion always was that none of us ever occupied stronger ground in the esteem of Congress than yourself, and I am satisfied there is no one who does not feel your aid to be still as important for the future as it has been for the past. . . . I hope, then, you will abandon entirely the idea you expressed to me, and that you will consider the eight years to come as essential to your political career. I should certainly consider any earlier day of your retirement as the most inauspicious day our new government has ever seen." [9]

Gallatin acknowledged the letter gratefully, admitting that his debt and duty to "the country which has received me and honored beyond my deserts," his attachment to Madison, and "the desire of honorably acquiring some share of reputation" inclined him to remain in public office; but he still had doubts. He would wait and see.[10]

Meanwhile, a friend of Samuel Smith had called on Judge Nicholson to see whether he intended to offer himself as a candidate for the Maryland Senate seat. Nicholson had no doubt that he could easily defeat the Baltimore merchant in a contest in the legislature but told Gallatin, "As I have not yet acquired philosophy enough to starve for the public good, I shall decline the honor." [11]

Nicholson's unwillingness to serve assured the seat for Smith, who was elected to a second term soon after. For the time being, an uneasy peace hung over Gallatin and his congressional enemies.

2

In the meantime, a peace even less easy hung over United States relations with France and Great Britain. As the man President Madison would have preferred to have at the helm of the State Department, Gallatin played a key part in negotiations with diplomats from both nations.

His dealings with France were through Napoleon's minister to the United States, Louis Marie Turreau. Soon after Madison's inauguration, Turreau had addressed an unofficial note to Secretary Smith recording his anxiety about American designs on Spanish colonies in the Caribbean and the mainland which had fallen to France as a consequence of the Emperor's military successes in Europe. He had heard that Jefferson had said, shortly before his retirement, that the United States must have the Floridas and Cuba. He had also heard reports that General James Wilkinson was planning a military expedition to gain both of these objectives.

Anxious to quiet Napoleon's anxiety, President Madison asked Gallatin to call at Turreau's residence near Baltimore on his way to New York during the last week in April, 1809. The Secretary talked frankly with the French minister, much as he had done with Erskine, the British minister, a few months earlier. He assured Turreau that, whatever slippery General Wilkinson might be up to, it was without the authority of the Administration. "The vanity, the indiscretion, and the ordinary inconsistencies of that General . . . you know perhaps as well as we," Turreau reported him as saying. And he insisted—again according to Turreau—that Florida and Cuba were Jefferson's whimsy (*marotte*), never shared by his cabinet. Madison was interested in Florida only in so far as it would provide an outlet for the produce of the southern states and prevent a misunderstanding with Spain; as for Cuba, the United States would not accept it if it were offered as a gift. Gallatin's assurances may have glossed over Madison's involvement in Jefferson's attempt to obtain Florida, but it prevented an open rupture with Napoleon during the first days of the Madison Administration.[12]

The conversation turned to another French grievance. A few weeks earlier, Erskine had come to Madison, Smith, and Gallatin with an offer that he said Foreign Secretary Canning had authorized him to make. This was that the British government would repeal its Orders in Council of January and November, 1807, in so far as they affected American shipping, on condition that the United States repeal all its interdictions against Anglo-American commerce and British ships of war, that it enforce the Non-Intercourse Act against France, and that it acknowledge the British "right" to impress American seamen who had deserted. Smith had persuaded Erskine not to insist on the last condition, and the so-called Erskine Agreement had been signed embodying the rest of the terms. President Madison had then proclaimed that on June 10, the day on which the Orders in Council were to be formally withdrawn, the Non-Intercourse Act would cease to operate against Britain. Turreau, not overpleased by this development, told Gallatin that Britain's willingness to accept it was evidence that her strength in the war against Napoleon was deteriorating.

The weeks following the announcement of the Erskine Agreement were joyful for the Administration. For the first, and indeed only, time in his life Madison was a popular hero. On June 10, six hundred American vessels left port with cargoes of raw materials for British consumers. Then, late in July, when Gallatin and Secretary of the Navy Hamilton were the only important officials in the Capital, unofficial but definitely jolting news arrived from London. Learning the terms of the agreement, Canning had disavowed them, on the ground that Erskine had exceeded his instructions! The young minister was to be replaced by Francis James

Jackson, who had won the cognomen of "Copenhagen" Jackson and dubious fame as the bearer two years earlier of Great Britain's ultimatum to the Danish government before the destruction of its fleet.

Gallatin appealed at once to President Madison and Attorney General Rodney to come to Washington.[13] He believed that the Administration must determine its policy towards Great Britain without delay, and the advice of the chief law officer was necessary on the legal aspects of the situation.

He thought that, until Congress assembled, the United States had only two alternatives: "complete submission"—that is, total abandonment of all restrictive trade measures—or the "automatic" renewal of enforcement of the Non-Intercourse Act against Great Britain as a consequence of Britain's own acts. The second was the only possibility that the United States could conceivably accept with honor, he concluded. Otherwise, American interdiction of commerce with France would be "partial to England, and contrary to every principle of justice, policy, and national honor."

But this would serve only temporarily. A chat with the now discredited Erskine convinced Gallatin that the United States could hope for nothing from the Canning government. The outgoing minister confessed that he had not read all his government's instructions to the American officials, as he had been told to do, because to do so would have led to the rejection of the agreement he was proposing. And now, Gallatin felt certain, Jackson was bringing "only dishonorable and inadmissible proposals . . . to amuse and divide" Americans.

Gallatin pondered the situation and was depressed. He thought war was inevitable. Even worse, American capacity to wage war had deteriorated badly. Twelve months earlier "all or almost all our mercantile wealth was safe at home, our resources entire, and our finances sufficient to carry us through the first year of the contest. Our property is now all afloat; England, relieved by our relaxations, might stand two years of privations with ease; we have wasted our resources without any national utility; and our Treasury being exhausted, we must begin our plan of resistance with considerable and therefore unpopular loans." [14]

Despite several epistolatory appeals from Gallatin, President Madison had trouble making up his mind that the crisis warranted interrupting his vacation to come to Washington, and gave even less thought to a need for preparing the nation for war.[15] But the more reports the press published from London, the more convinced the American people became that their officers had been victimized by the perfidy of Canning, that the terms which the British foreign minister had intended Erskine to propose had been framed so that the United States would certainly reject them. Finally and still reluctantly, President Madison set out for Washington.

For three days after his arrival on August 7, he conferred with Gallatin and Smith. The resulting policy was based on Gallatin's counsel. A Presidential proclamation of August 9 revived the Non-Intercourse Act against Great Britain. Gallatin dispatched it the same day to the collectors of customs, with instructions that vessels entering American ports under the terms of the Erskine agreement were not to be penalized. Later, these steps were criticized as being inadequately founded in law, and indeed President Madison confessed privately that they had "no plea but manifest destiny." [16]

Madison returned to Montpelier August 10, leaving Gallatin and Smith to deal with the British ministers, outgoing and incoming. Gallatin still had a bone to pick with Erskine. The reports from London quoted him as having told Erskine in the conversations leading up to the Erskine Agreement that, if the British would revoke their Orders in Council, the differences between the two countries respecting colonial trade could easily be adjusted. On August 13, to set the record right, he wrote to Erskine that he had said no such thing, that the right to a trade between colonies of a belligerent power and the United States generally, and to a trade "in colonial articles between the United States and other countries, never can, or will, in my opinion, be abandoned, or its exercise be suspended by this government." [17] Erskine promptly denied that he had ever quoted Gallatin in the way London had said, thus passing the blame to Canning.[18] The arrival of Jackson on September 8 left the situation unchanged. The new minister was uncommunicative. Gallatin was pleased by the delay this afforded. Perhaps France and Spain would soon push England so hard that she would be "compelled to do us some justice." [19]

The developments of the autumn showed that any such optimism was misplaced. By early November President Madison, having denied Jackson's repeated assertion that the United States had known all along that Erskine had exceeded his authority in reaching the agreement, declared that he wished to receive no further communications from the insolent British minister.[20] "This winter," Gallatin wrote to his sister-in-law Maria Montgomery, "will be more splendid in parties than pleasing in its politics: for the horizon is quite gloomy in that respect." [21]

3

As Congress assembled in December, 1809, Judge Nicholson wrote his old friend Congressman John Randolph that Gallatin was again seriously considering retirement from the cabinet. It was an excellent idea, Randolph wrote back. Gallatin ought to run for Congress and lead a movement to check the influence of the "Invisibles"—as the Smith faction was coming to be called. All departments of the government except the Treasury were in wretched condition, the veteran dissident declared; the nation had need of Gallatin's capacity for investigation and reform.[22] It is improbable that Gallatin knew of this opinion; but less than two months earlier a letter from Jefferson had urged him to stay on: "I am satisfied there is no one who does not feel your aid to be still as important for the future as it has been for the past." [23]

The Secretary of the Treasury had ample reason to weigh the problem as he prepared his annual report for submission to Congress early in December. The horizon was indeed gloomy. Snuffed out were the ambitious dreams of twenty months before for internal improvements. For the first time since he became responsible for the Treasury Department, it had an operating deficit. In the year ending September 30, 1809, receipts of the government had totaled $9,300,000, while expenditures had exceeded $10,600,000. The resulting deficit of $1,300,000 was in part a cost of the Embargo Act, which had heavily diminished receipts from customs duties, and the Non-Importation Act, which had cut them even more sharply. In 1808 more than $8,000,000 had been allocated to reducing the public debt, and in 1809 more than $3,750,000. This had been covered by the surplus of the preceding years, but the Treasury now had a balance of only $5,000,000. Thus, if the generosity of the Invisibles to the poorly organized Army, and especially to the Navy with its useless gunboats, should prevail in the coming year, it was likely that the government would have a deficit of $3,000,000.[24] As Congressman Macon put it, it was a battle for waste against Gallatin's economy.[25]

Oppressed by this gloomy prospect, Gallatin sat down to acknowledge Jefferson's letter. Picking up a phrase of Jefferson's—"The discharge of the debt . . . is vital to the destinies of our government, and it hangs on Mr. Madison and yourself"—he expanded upon it: "The reduction of the public debt was certainly the principal object in bringing me into office; and our success in that respect has been due both to the joint and continued efforts of the several branches of Government and to the prosperous condition of the country. I am sensible that the work cannot progress under adverse circumstances. If the United States shall be forced into an actual state of war, all the resources of the country must certainly be called forth to make it efficient, and new loans will undoubtedly be wanted. But whilst peace is preserved, the revenue will at all events be sufficient to pay the interest and defray *necessary* expences. I do not ask that in the present situation of our foreign relations the debt be reduced, but only that it shall not be encreased so long as we are not at war. I do not pretend to step out of my own sphere and to controul the internal management of other departments. But it seems to me that, as Secretary of the Treasury, I may ask that whilst peace continues the aggregate of the expences of those departments be kept within bounds such as will preserve the equilibrium between the national revenue and the expenditure without recurrence to loans. I cannot, my dear Sir, consent to act the part of a mere financier, to become a contriver of taxes, a dealer of loans, a seeker of resources for the purpose of supporting useless baubles, of encreasing the number of idle and dissipated members of the community, of fattening contractors, pursers, and agents, and of introducing in all of its ramifications that system of patronage, corruption, and rottenness which you so justly execrate." [26]

It is probable that Gallatin showed Madison this letter, with Jefferson's, before sending it off. Indeed, it is most likely that he phrased his reply in the hope of inducing Madison to take a firmer stand in relations with the new Congress. If he did, the effort was vain. For the President, in official messages and in personal relations with the legislators, continued to vacillate and avoid unpleasant scenes.

Left without this necessary support, Gallatin could only recommend the least objectionable alternatives. His report of February 26, 1810, recommended that the government be authorized to borrow a sum not to exceed the amount of the public debt that it would pay off during the coming year.[27] It was ironic that this recommendation should come from a man who a decade earlier had castigated the Federalists for borrowing money to meet the normal defense requirements of the nation!

Meanwhile Samuel Smith and his Invisibles were busy organizing opposition to Gallatin. Their newspapers, led by Duane's *Aurora*, attacked him constantly and ruthlessly. Men friendly as well as men hostile to him thought it probable that he would leave the cabinet by May, 1810.[28] He avoided declaring himself, for he had not yet made up his mind.

While weighing his course, Gallatin did his level best to provide the Administration with leadership it so sorely lacked. The Non-Intercourse Act was as frail a reed in the maritime war as had been expected; for effective enforcement it needed drastic revision.[29] He conferred with

Macon, chairman of a House committee charged with the subject, and out of their discussions emerged a plan, largely his own work, that drew on the advice of President Madison. This would close American ports to all British and French vessels, public or private, but would permit the admission of British and French merchandise if brought directly from the country of origin in bottoms entirely American-owned and -operated. The plan was ingenious in several ways, giving American shippers a monopoly of American trade and striking at the interests of the British shippers who had prodded their government into adopting the trade policies so hurtful to the United States. The finished plan was discussed and approved by the whole cabinet, including Secretary Smith, and then turned over to Macon.

In spite of some vociferous protests from New England Federalists and southern Democratic-Republicans, the House passed it by a comfortable margin.[30] The story was different in the Senate, where the Invisibles were strong. Samuel Smith's men took no pains to conceal the fact that they opposed the bill because it was Gallatin's handiwork. His chief organ, the Baltimore *Whig*, called the measure "Gallatin's Submission Bill," referring to its "imbecility, impolicy and meanness." It reproached President Madison for "hearkening to the ruinous counsel of that apostate Albert Gallatin," whose Treasury reports were "chiefly calculated to strike a panic into the ignorant; to conceal our resources; to make foreign enemies divide us; or to favour . . . rapacious speculation." [31]

Senator Smith himself moved on February 21 to strike out all the provisions of the bill except the enacting clause and a provision to exclude the war vessels of belligerents from American harbors. His band of Invisibles stood by him, and the Senate passed the proposal sixteen to eleven.[32]

This unexpected setback incensed Secretary Gallatin and President Madison because Robert Smith, without opposing the bill in the cabinet consultations, apparently had passed on to the Invisibles information as to what took place in them.[33] As Macon glumly observed, there seemed to be less chance of the Senate declaring war against Great Britain or France than against the Treasury Department.[34]

For weeks there was a paralyzing deadlock. Gallatin's supporters were still in the ascendant in the House, and in conferences with the Senate committee they resisted all pressure for enactment of Macon's bill as mutilated. They closed ranks against the resolution of a Clintonian from New York that called for an investigation of Gallatin's administration of the Treasury Department and cast aspersions on "not only the capacity but the integrity of the Secretary of the Treasury, defeating it 106 to 17.

They voted Gallatin the requested authority to borrow a sum not to exceed the amount of the public debt that would be paid off in the year, and in this the Senate concurred.[35]

The deadlock was finally broken on May 1, just before the end of the session, when Congress enacted "Macon's Bill No. 2." To this bill, which was the work of Senator John Taylor of South Carolina, Macon only lent his name. It forbade any British or French vessel to enter American waters except in distress or bearing dispatches; it repealed the Non-Intercourse Act and reopened American trade to all the world. It provided that, if either Great Britain or France should revoke or modify its edicts before March 3, 1811, so that they would no longer affect the neutral commerce of the United States, the President should proclaim the fact, and that, if the other nation did not do likewise within three months, the Non-Importation Act would then go into effect against the unfriendly nation.[36] The effect of the law was to open American commerce once more with France and Great Britain—subject, of course, to whatever force the British navy might exert.

4

The passage of the unfortunate Macon's Bill No. 2 dramatized the dilemma in which Gallatin found himself a little more than a year after the start of the Madison Administration. The Invisibles were determined to force him from the cabinet and to discredit Madison in doing so; there were reports that they sought ultimately to elevate Robert Smith as a puppet President. If Gallatin retired, friends in Congress warned him, he would be forever lost, his name so tarnished that he would be unable ever again to exert any influence in public life. If he remained in office he would be constantly subject to treachery from within the cabinet without any firm support from the President.[37]

The dilemma was aggravated during the summer of 1810 by William Duane. Time had not dulled the Philadelphia editor's vindictiveness for rebuffs to his lust for patronage and political power. Two months after the passage of Macon's Bill No. 2 he protested privately to ex-Secretary of War Henry Dearborn that it was not the influence of the Smith brothers or of Dr. Leib that made him hate Gallatin: "Superior motives actuate me. . . . I know myself to be superior to every form of meanness." He was thoroughly convinced "that Mr. Gallatin has been a principal operator of our present unhappy situation. I believe him not only to be a dangerous politician but unfaithful to the public trust." He asserted that Gallatin had remained on intimate terms with John Randolph, that he had tried to wean President Jefferson from "French influence"; that he had used public office to amass "vast landed wealth." All these charges were false; but what matters is that Duane believed them and acted upon them.[38]

Early in July, 1810, Duane heard that a pamphlet had been published in England containing the text of correspondence between Erskine and Canning, including a number of letters not previously printed in the United States. Apparently he did not have access to a copy but heard that Gallatin did; and he heard also that in these letters Erskine attributed to Gallatin criticism of Jefferson for "partiality" toward France and "hostility" toward Great Britain. Although these charges had already been aired in the American press Duane rang the changes on them, elaborating them with insinuation and innuendo, day after day in the *Aurora* in an effort to convince the old Jeffersonians that Gallatin was in fact the enemy of his old chief. Samuel Smith's mouthpiece, the Baltimore *Whig*, echoed the refrain.[39]

Gallatin undertook to silence the campaign with an open letter in the friendly *National Intelligencer* in mid-July. Through eight years of the most intimate relationship with Jefferson, he wrote, he knew that the former President had never had "any other object in view but the protection of the rights of the United States against every foreign aggression or injury, from whatever nation it proceeded." But, he pointed out, from 1801 until August, 1807, France was innocent of any aggressive act against the United States, while Britain was guilty of a constant series of unfriendly acts.[40]

The rabid Duane was impervious to reasoning. Through July and into August the *Aurora* published a series called "The Diplomacy Examined," which reiterated and extended the charge that Gallatin had been disloyal to his old chief.[41] Gallatin was in New York, where he heard about the articles but did not see them. Unexpectedly, a letter from Jefferson arrived late in August: "I have seen with infinite grief the set which is made at you in the public papers, and with the more as my name has been so much used in it. I hope we both know one another too well to receive impression from circumstances of this kind. A twelve years intimate and friendly intercourse must be better evidence to each of the dispositions of the other than the letters of foreign ministers to their courts, or tortured inferences from facts true or false. I have too thorough a conviction of your cordial good will towards me and too strong a sense of the faithful and able assistance I received from you, to relinquish them on any evidence but of my own senses." [42]

These were heart-warming words, and Gallatin acknowledged them gratefully. They helped him decide to remain in the cabinet for the time being.[43] Equally persuasive was the economic condition of the country. In the preceding autumn and winter it had appeared dismal indeed; then, in the spring it had taken an upward turn and had become brighter than Gallatin had dared hope. Indeed, it so belied his prophecies as to give support to the charges of the Baltimore *Whig* that his Treasury reports were "chiefly calculated to strike a panic into the ignorant."

Some of the facts of the nation's health were set forth in a report on American manufactures which Secretary Gallatin submitted to the House of Representatives on April 19, 1810. Although less extensive than Alexander Hamilton's historic paper of a decade earlier, it was comparable in usefulness. It demonstrated with facts and figures that under the stimulus of the embargo and the nonimportation laws, the United States, particularly New England and the middle states, had made prodigious advances in manufacturing for its own needs. "It may, with certainty, be inferred that . . . annual production exceeds one hundred and twenty millions of dollars. And it is not improbable that the raw materials used, and the provisions and other articles consumed by the manufacturers, create a home market for agricultural products not very inferior to that which arises from foreign demand."

Gallatin did not attribute these gains to the embargo, perhaps because of unhappy memories of trying to enforce that unpopular law. But he pointed out more fundamental and enduring factors: "the absence of those systems of internal restrictions and monopoly which continue to disfigure the state of society in other countries. . . . No law exists here," he pointed out, "directly or indirectly confining a man to a particular occupation or place, or excluding any citizen from any branch he may, at any time, think proper to pursue. Industry is, in every respect, perfectly free and unfettered; every species of trade, commerce, art, profession, and manufacture, being equally open to all, without requiring any previous apprenticeship, admission, or license."

Americans were at a disadvantage in competing with British merchants in foreign markets, Gallatin conceded, because greater capital available enabled the British "to give very long credits, to sell on small profits, and to make occasional sacrifices." He suggested that the United States lend between five and twenty million dollars to worthy merchants, as the loan offices of Pennsylvania and New York once had done to farmers, to enable them to stand up to their British competitors.[44]

In several other reports later in the year Gallatin further demonstrated that the nation was enjoying its most bountiful period since the embargo. With the discontinuance of the Non-Importation law, the registered tonnage of American shipping reached 1,424,000 for the year 1810—a figure not again attained until 1826. Registered foreign tonnage reached 984,000—not to be matched for almost forty years. During 1810 new vessels totaling 127,000 tons were built.[45] Merchandise valued at nearly $67,000,000 was imported in the year ended September 30, 1810, of which more than $42,000,000 was for articles of domestic production.[46] Receipts from customs had staged a comeback: from a peak of $16,500,000 in 1807 they had dropped to little more than $7,000,000 in 1808 and in 1809, but were back to $12,750,000 in 1810.[47]

The annual report Gallatin submitted to Congress on December 10, 1810, showed that he was taking full advantage of the good times. Current expenditures had been brought within the national income, with the help of continued economies in the army and navy. The loan from the Bank of the United States, authorized by Congress, had made it possible to apply $2,400,000 against the public debt in 1810, reducing it to nearly half of what it had been when Gallatin assumed office.[48] If only such prosperity would last awhile and bring him some relief from intraparty strife!

19. Overwhelmed by
the War Hawks

1810=1812

It was not to be so. Even before the nation could fully appreciate the effects of the prosperity of 1810 Samuel Smith and the Invisibles were girding themselves for the next attack on Gallatin's projects. This would center around the Bank of the United States, whose twenty-year charter was to expire on March 4, 1811. We have already seen how useful the Bank had been to Gallatin in the day-to-day operations of the Treasury and in a loan to tide it over the crisis of the past few years; and that he had urged that the government encourage it despite the doctrinaire opposition of Thomas Jefferson.

The management of the Bank naturally desired renewal of the charter well in advance of the expiration date so that it might plan for the future, and as early as November, 1807, an officer had asked Gallatin the best time and manner for seeking a renewal from Congress. Secretary Gallatin feared that the question might become "blended with or affected by . . . extraneous political considerations," and advised delay.[1] The following spring, through his old friend A. J. Dallas, he advised the president of the Bank, David Lenox, to memorialize Congress late in the session so that the matter could be discussed but not decided upon before adjournment. He felt confident that cool consideration would bring renewal in due course.[2] The Bank accordingly submitted its petition in April, 1808.[3]

No issue was made of the Bank in the election that year, and Gallatin waited discreetly until the last day of Jefferson's Administration before bringing up the renewal again. On March 3, 1809, presumably with President Madison's permission, he addressed to Congress a paper extolling the usefulness of the Bank of the United States to the Treasury in the past and presenting suggestions for modification in a renewed charter. He asked that the capital be increased from $10,000,000 to $30,000,000, and that a number of new features be adopted to overcome widespread objections that Britons owned two-thirds of the stock of the Bank, that the direction of the Bank was too highly centralized and was undemocratic. He believed that, by making it easier for citizens and state governments in all parts of the country to participate as stockholders and directors, the Bank would contribute toward binding the Union together firmly.

He emphasized that the Bank in its revised form would be most useful in making loans to the government in the event that the war should come to pass. He took a sidewise glance at an incipient political threat to the federally chartered institution offered by the numerous state banks cropping up throughout the land: they were unable to match the facilities and security afforded by the Bank. His paper ended on a note of warning: the destruction of the Bank would "be attended with much individual and probably with no inconsiderable public injury." A payment of $7,000,000 would have to be made to foreign owners of stock; if the charter were renewed, the country would lose only 8½ per cent of this a year in interest.[4]

Several months later Gallatin assured the Speaker of the House that the Bank was eminently "more eligible" than individuals to provide the Treasury with loans. "To contract with individuals requires notice and arrangements, and is absolute . . . but with a bank it [is] sufficient to ascertain whether a loan could, if wanted, be obtained . . . the contract might be delayed till it was ascertained. . . . The reimbursement would also be made with more convenience, and some interest saved." [5]

The year passed, and still Congress took no action. Finally, in April, 1810, when it was clear to Gallatin and many congressmen that the government would have to borrow several millions to tide it over the next year in the face of the reduction of revenues caused by the embargo and nonintercourse, a congressional committee requested Secretary Gallatin's recommendations for renewal of the charter.[6] He answered with a new plan, calling for an increase of the capital by $2,500,000, perhaps more later, and an increase in the government's participation in the ownership and direction.[7] The bill was making highly satisfactory progress through the House—the forces for renewal had mustered 75 votes against 35 on a crucial point—when the session ended.[8] Nevertheless, the Bank lent $3,750,000 under congressional authorization.[9]

By early 1811 economic conditions throughout the western world had worsened markedly, with sharp repercussions in the United States. British merchants withdrew great quantities of specie; the holdings of the Bank of the United States reached a dangerously low $5,500,000.[10] In late January a letter from John Jacob Astor bewailed the distress of the New

York business community and added: "There was perhaps never a period when it was more in the power of government to do good than the present." [11]

But now, when the Bank was needed most, opposition began to coalesce into a formidable bloc. All the old doctrinaire state-rights advocates within the Democratic-Republican party were of course opposed: in Virginia and Kentucky, sources of the 1798 resolutions, the legislatures went on record against renewal of the charter. Moreover, the public relations of the Bank were bad; it made a poor presentation of its record to the citizens, and the agent it sent to deal with congressmen was a model of tactlessness.[12]

Much of the opposition came from the burgeoning state banks, particularly of Massachusetts, Pennsylvania, and Maryland. In effect, many states had become bank partners by exacting loans as a prerequisite for a charter.[13] These ambitious newcomers eyed enviously the business the federal government gave to the Bank of the United States. The most articulate and energetic of their spokesmen was Gallatin's old enemy, Senator Smith, who had been hectoring him to give Treasury business to the state-chartered banks of Maryland.[14] Early in January, 1811, the Baltimore *Whig* renewed its attack on Gallatin, excoriating him not only for his attitude on the Bank, but for his administration of the Treasury. It charged him with corruption and "alarming symptoms in the English style," improper administration of the public lands, and feigning a deficit in the Treasury as an excuse for renewal of the Bank charter.[15] The same theme permeated articles in Thomas Ritchie's Richmond *Enquirer* and of course in Duane's *Aurora*, which published a long series on Gallatin and the Bank.[16]

The strength of this opposition was revealed when a 65 to 64 vote of the House on January 24 indefinitely postponed action on the recharter bill.[17] It was widely commented that if President Madison had thrown some real support to his Secretary the bill would have passed. Gallatin was, in the words of Nathaniel Macon, "mortified" by the result. Now he turned to the Upper House and in particular to Senator William H. Crawford of Tennessee. To some opponents Crawford seemed to be overbearing, irascible, ambitious, and intriguing; Gallatin observed that he also "united to a powerful mind a most correct judgment and an inflexible integrity; which last quality, not sufficiently tempered by indulgence and civility, has prevented his acquiring general popularity." [19]

In an open letter to Crawford, Gallatin spelled out the functions the Bank performed for the Treasury and emphasized that his department would be inexpressibly handicapped if it had to rely upon the state

banks.[20] Crawford then told the Senate on February 11 that the movement against the Bank was the consequence of the "avarice combined
with . . . love of domination" of three or four great commercial
states of the East to the disadvantage of "the interior or smaller states." [21]

On the other side, William Branch Giles insisted that he was opposing
the Bank, not out of hostility for Gallatin, but from fear of British influence in American affairs; Henry Clay, a precocious newcomer from
Kentucky, confidently predicted that the Treasury could conduct its
business as well without the Bank; and Samuel Smith capped the discussion by asserting that the state banks would be more useful than the
Bank had ever been. Smith added that although Gallatin "is considered by
his friends a very great man in fiscal operations—in commercial matters,
I may be permitted to have opinions of my own." This was an allusion to
Gallatin's criticism, nearly two years before, of Smith's role in the Degen
& Purviance affair.[22]

The Bank recharter came to a vote in the Senate on February 20,
1811, ending in a tie, 17 to 17. Vice President Clinton, who was bitter
over his loss of the nomination for President to Madison, and who
had never been friendly to Gallatin, cast the vote that the tie gave
him against recharter. Thus was the Bank of the United States killed, and
Gallatin deprived of its services in conducting the financial affairs of the
government through parlous times.

2

In later years Gallatin laid the death of the Bank more to the opposition
of Clinton, Smith, Leib, Giles, and other Invisibles to himself and Madison than to the influence of the state banks.[24] Whether or not he was
correct, the defeat embittered him. He intensified the feud with the Invisibles by a paper issued two days after the fatal vote.

This document harked back to April, 1810, when Samuel Smith, determined to clear his name of Gallatin's charges against him in the Degen &
Purviance affair, had asked Gabriel Duval, Comptroller of the Treasury,
as a man who, in the course of duty, had seen all the official papers in the
Degen & Purviance matter, "whether there was any thing in the whole
transaction, that in any way impeached the integrity of my character, or
that of my house?" After two months, Duval answered that a careful investigation convinced him "that there is no ground for [such] an imputa-
tion." In December, 1810, the House of Representatives requested Secretary Gallatin to make a statement on the matter. His reply, dated Feb-

ruary 22, 1811, but obviously ready while the Bank debate was going on in the Senate, provided a lengthy accounting of the transaction but avoided a conclusion.[25]

The detail Gallatin set forth makes it clear that he was hasty in condemning Smith's firm for commercial practices that were common even if far from exemplary. Secretary Robert Smith, who up to this time had felt at least a little friendliness for Gallatin, was outraged when the report was published, and told a friend it was "a labored, covert apology for his former misunderstanding and misrepresentation of the subject." He was convinced that a statesman or a gentleman would not have made the error in the first place and would certainly apologize for it now.[26]

Victory on the Bank issue and vindication of Senator Smith on the Degen & Purviance business accelerated the Invisibles' effort to drive Gallatin from the cabinet and in time Madison from the Presidency. William Duane's *Aurora* thundered: "If Mr. Madison suffers *this man* to lord it over the nation, Mr. Gallatin will *drag him down;* for no honest man can support an administration of which he is a member." [27] Gallatin came to feel that these attacks, as well as those in the Baltimore *Whig*, revealed a knowledge of what was going on within the cabinet that could come only from Robert Smith.[28]

Meanwhile, Gallatin was probably receiving unsolicited advice, through Judge Nicholson, from John Randolph. It is more than likely that the Judge showed him a letter from the Virginian, written on February 14 in a white rage over one of Duane's editorials. Randolph denied that he was trying to advise Gallatin through the Judge and said that he knew Nicholson was solicitous of the welfare of Gallatin and the people of the United States. He concluded that Gallatin ought to go to President Madison and deliver an ultimatum: "Either Robert Smith must go or I shall go." [29]

Whether or not Judge Nicholson actually relayed this counsel, it was precisely the course Secretary Gallatin took a fortnight after the killing of the Bank. He wrote to the President that, "to command the public confidence and to produce the requisite union of views and action between the several branches of Government," it was imperative that an administration possess "not only capacity and talents, . . . but also a perfect, heart-felt cordiality among its members." He warned, "New subdivisions and personal factions equally hostile to yourself and the general welfare daily acquire additional strength. Measures of vital importance have been and are defeated; every operation, even of the most simple and ordinary nature, is prevented or impeded; the embarrassments of Government, great as from foreign causes they already are, are unnecessarily encreased; public confidence in the public councils and in the executive is impaired; and every day seems to encrease every one of those evils." Rather than continue in the Administration, which "invigorates the opposition against yourself and must necessarily be attended with an encreased loss of reputation to myself," he submitted his resignation as Secretary of the Treasury, to become effective at the President's convenience.[30]

Confronted by the demand that he choose between an incompetent Secretary of State and a distinguished Secretary of the Treasury, the vacillating Madison was at long last stirred to action. He declined to accept Gallatin's resignation and proposed that Robert Smith be replaced by Governor James Monroe of Virginia. Monroe had been Madison's rival for the Presidency in 1808, the principal difference being that he still cherished hope for reconciliation with Great Britain while Madison was still sanguine about France.

Gallatin, given the task of sounding out Monroe, prompted Senator Richard Brent of Virginia to write to the Virginia governor about March 7. Monroe consulted with some advisers and replied that he would come to Washington to discuss the Administration's policies with Madison and Gallatin.[31] When the three men met, they did not find it difficult to reach an understanding.

Gallatin must have watched with anguish as President Madison, diffident as usual, next undertook to get rid of Robert Smith. He told the troublesome Marylander that his course of conduct made it impossible to retain him in the cabinet; so that there might be no open rupture in the party, he would appoint him minister to Russia. Smith declared himself grateful and started to make plans for the journey, even consulting with the Russian minister to Washington. Then, in all probability after consultation with his brother Samuel, he changed his mind and refused the mission.[32]

Monroe assumed charge of the State Department on April 1, 1811; but the change stirred up further trouble from the Smith faction. In June a pamphlet by Robert Smith aired his grievances against the Administration and charged the President with being secretly influenced by the French in foreign relations.[33] Duane in the *Aurora* stepped up his attack on Secretary Gallatin, doing his utmost to create suspicion between him and the President. Nameless friends of Gallatin were quoted as asserting that he was "to all intents and purposes the president, and even more than the president of the United States." One article presented this sinister portrait: "a man of most singular sagacity and penetration; he could read the very thoughts of men in their faces and develope their designs; a man of few words, made no promises but to real favorites [who] ever sought to enhance his own interest, power, and aggrandisement by the most insatiate avarice on the very vitals of the unsuspecting nation." [34]

Thomas Jefferson was upset by this new outbreak of intraparty discord. He began to pepper a Richmond friend, William Wirt, with praise of Gallatin, hoping he would pass the word along to Ritchie of the *Enquirer* and through him to Duane. "There is no truer man," he insisted; the Secretary, "after the President, is the arc of our safety." He branded as "false" Duane's charges against Gallatin of "apostasy" on the Bank question, and "disloyal" relations with John Randolph. Suspecting that some of Duane's bitterness was caused by financial embarrassments, he urged that the Democratic-Republicans arrange for bank loans to help him out. [35] He repeated the praise of Gallatin in letters to President Madison, who showed them to the Secretary, raising his spirits temporarily. [36]

To Duane, Jefferson wrote directly that he believed "Mr. Gallatin to be of as pure integrity, and as zealously devoted to the liberties and interests of our country as its most affectionate native citizen. Of this his courage in Congress, in the days of the [Federalist] terror, gave proofs which nothing can obliterate from the recollection of those who were witnesses of it. . . . an intercourse, almost daily, of eight years, with him has given me opportunities of knowing his character more thoroughly than perhaps any other man living: and I have ascribed the erroneous estimate you have formed of it, to the want of that intimate knowledge of him which I possessed." [37]

After several months of such letter writing without noticeable influence on Duane, the former President grew despondent. "I believe Duane to be a very honest man and sincerely republican; but his passions are stronger than his prudence . . . his personal as well as his general antipathies render him intolerant," he told Wirt. [38] In late April he wrote directly to Gallatin that he disapproved of the activities of the "Cannibal newspapers" but added with a sigh that he must claim "from all parties the privilege of Neutrality." [39]

Two months after Robert Smith's departure from the cabinet, Gallatin confided to Judge Nicholson that he felt "no satisfaction in my present situation." Circumstances under which the incompetent Marylander had left had "made me a slave. Perhaps for that reason I feel an ineffable thirst for retirement and obscurity." [40]

3

Gallatin's thirst for retirement and obscurity must have been doubled, and his feeling that he had outlived one age and was entering another intensified, as Congress assembled for a special session early in November, 1811. A new force had appeared on the national scene that overshadowed completely the old Invisibles. They were Republicans, but a new, non-Jeffersonian breed of Republicans, elected by voters who were irate over the enactment of Macon's Bill No. 2. They would have none of peace and prosperity if the price were to be European appeasement. Most of the newcomers—nearly half the membership of the Lower House —were under thirty-five years of age, and all were under forty. Their leaders came from the new western states or the western parts of the older states: Henry Clay of Kentucky, John C. Calhoun, William Lowndes, and Langdon Cheves of South Carolina, Felix Grundy of Tennessee. To these men, their barely settled section already seemed overcrowded; and they coveted more land, even if that meant driving the British from all of North America. Just a few days earlier, at the mouth of the Tippecanoe Creek, the Army had defeated the uprising of an Indian confederacy against American authority, which westerners were convinced—erroneously—had been inspired by the British. The tall, lordly Clay, whom the new House named Speaker, put their feelings into words: he was tired of seeing his country tied "eternally to the tail of the British kite."

The message President Madison delivered to the Congress bore the imprint of Gallatin's collaboration, particularly in the passages on public finance and foreign relations.[41] Foreign relations had been deteriorating steadily since the passage of Macon's Bill No. 2. In August, 1810, Napoleon Bonaparte responded to the bait it extended by giving the American minister at Paris the impression that repeal of the Berlin and Milan decrees would take effect the following November 1—"it being understood that the English are to revoke their Orders in Council." Gallatin, like the President, took the maneuver at face value: Madison proclaimed nonintercourse in effect against Great Britain, and Congress backed him up with appropriate legislation, while Gallatin confided to Turreau, the French minister, that war with Great Britain looked inevitable.

But the decrees were never actually repealed, and the American vessels the wily Emperor of the French had captured were not returned; indeed, the French navy continued to seize and sell as spoils all American and neutral vessels that came within its reach.

The young War Hawks of the West, however, were far more bitter against Great Britain than France. When the time came for Madison to prepare his November, 1811, message to Congress, Gallatin cautioned him against saying anything that the hotheads might interpret as a cause for war against America's ancient enemy: it was all very well to protest the capture of American vessels and impressment of American sailors by the British, Gallatin told the President; but it would be wise to make it appear that war would be the final rather than the immediate result of refusal to abandon these policies. The United States should keep the initiative of declaring war, not let the British grasp it. Following this advice, Madison's message spoke despondently of American relations with both Great Britain and France, and suggested simply that the Army and the Navy gird themselves for war if it should come—as the Administration had been recommending for years.

The annual report of the Secretary of the Treasury, later in November, also spoke not of war but of preparations for war. The immediate past, it made clear, had been surprisingly bright, all things considered. The Non-Importation Act against Great Britain, which had gone into effect in March, had closed American ports to British merchandise with a great loss of revenue from import duties. But the full effects were not yet felt; as of September 30, 1811, the Treasury still had a surplus of $5,500,000. In the coming year, Secretary Gallatin estimated, the government's revenue would fall to $6,600,000. Because of the stepping up of war preparations, expenditures would rise to $9,200,000. Thus the surplus would be replaced by a deficit of more than a million dollars. To meet this, duties on whatever imports there were must be increased by half. The Secretary shuddered at the thought of restoring the hated internal taxes, but conceded that such measures might become necessary. He placed his greatest hope for tiding the government over on loans: $1,200,000 now, perhaps more later. Although the legal rate was 6 per cent the government's fiscal situation might make it necessary to go up to 8 per cent. He believed loans preferable to the issuance of more stock or "any other operation which might injuriously affect the circulating medium of the country." [42]

The report excited more criticism than any that had come from Gallatin. Some discerning critics observed that it neglected to point out that additional revenue would have to be found to pay the interest on the new loans—although, as a matter of fact, that had been indicated in the financial section of Madison's annual message, which Gallatin had also writ-ten.[43] Some old Democratic-Republicans could not forgive his calm references to 8 per cent loans; he and they had castigated the Federalists for accepting this interest rate during the undeclared war with France in 1798. His tacit acknowledgment that the internal revenue taxes of that period might have to be revived similarly disturbed them.

The sharpest criticism came from members of Gallatin's own party who were spoiling for an immediate declaration of war against Great Britain, followed by a full-scale invasion of Canada to capture Quebec. That old Invisible, William Branch Giles, who despite his break with the Adminis-tration continued to head the Senate Committee on Foreign Relations, introduced a bill to raise not the 10,000 regular troops President Madison sought, but 25,000 men for five years' service. How could the nation afford such a military force if its financial condition were as grim as Secretary Gallatin sketched it?

Giles solved his quandary by attacking Gallatin in the Senate on De-cember 17: If the Secretary truly possessed the "splendid financial tal-ents" generally attributed to him, surely he would contrive some means for defending the nation's sovereignty and honor; "only give them scope for action; apply them to the national ability and will; let them perform the simple task of pointing to the true *modus operandi*; and what rea-son have we to despair of the Republic?"

Giles hinted that possibly Secretary Gallatin had neither the necessary financial talent nor the desire to defend the national honor: while Britain was sullying that honor, he had continued to act as if it were more im-portant to retire the public debt than to provide for public defense. A large part of the present troubles of the United States could be attributed to the unwillingness of Jefferson and Madison to disturb "the popularity and repose" of their finance minister.[44]

Senator George W. Campbell of Tennessee came to the defense, pro-testing that this "was the first time he had heard the talents or financial capacity of [Gallatin] brought into question by any gentleman of known standing and information," and pointing out that the faults and mistakes Giles had cited were the handiwork of Congress rather than the Secretary of the Treasury.[45] However, the fire-eating young men from the West, aided and abetted by the Invisibles, joined hands with the Federalists. Giles's bill passed both houses in January, 1812, and President Madison docilely appended his signature.[46]

Gallatin had by now concluded that in time Congress would declare war against Great Britain. The next step was to prepare the nation financially. This he set out to do January 10 in a letter to Ezekiel Bacon, chairman of the House Ways and Means Committee. Assuming that the government's fixed charges would continue at $9,600,000 a year, and estimating that the receipts from duties then authorized would fall no lower than $2,500,000 in the event of war, he accepted an estimate the committee had made that an annual loan of $10,000,000 would see the nation through a war. To meet the fixed charges and the accruing interest on new loans, he believed that customs duties would have to be increased so as to yield $6,000,000. To produce an additional $5,000,000 through internal taxes, the salt tax would have to be revived, and other internal duties levied—perhaps taxes on distilled spirits, refined sugar, licenses to conduct retail businesses, auctions, and to operate passenger-carrying vehicles, as well as stamp duties.

Emphasizing that it was not his fault that the new taxes had become necessary, he recalled that he had stated in 1808 that "no internal taxes, either direct or indirect, were contemplated, even in the case of hostilities." Since then Congress had thrown away $20,000,000 by refusing to impose internal taxes he had recommended, and, by refusing to recharter the Bank of the United States, had deprived the government of the source from which it might have obtained $20,000,000 in loans on far more favorable terms than was now possible.[47]

Gallatin's spelling out of the exact cost of the war, and his disassociation of himself from responsibility for the harsh measures necessary to meet it, dismayed his friends and filled his enemies with mock horror. A writer in the new and widely read Baltimore *Niles' Weekly Register* professed incredulity that a financier of Gallatin's caliber could not point out measures different from those used by Hamilton and Wolcott. The letter to Chairman Bacon was "artfully drawn" to alarm the people, check the decision of Congress, and damp the enthusiasm for the projected new army.[48] The Federalist *New York Evening Post* reprinted the minutes of the 1792 Pittsburgh meeting against the excise, which Gallatin had signed as secretary, to suggest he was inconsistent in proposing imposts.[49] From the other side of the Atlantic, *The Times* of London gleefully observed that "America is now embarking on the same voyage in which so many of the old governments of Europe have been wrecked—taxes, loans, public debt, etc." [50]

William Duane's *Aurora* began a new series denouncing Gallatin, one article of which was entitled "The Rat—in the Treasury!" These charged that the same "morbid feeling," "intrigue," "selfishness and fatuity" that had characterized Adams's Administration permeated that of Madison.

Duane stated frankly what he had long been hinting—if Madison did not drop Gallatin at once he would support George Clinton for the Presidency in November.[51]

Although for a time no one dared utter a word in rebuttal from the floors of Congress, there were angry protests in the cloak rooms and in the Capital boarding houses. As the Massachusetts Federalist Congressman Samuel L. Taggart put it, Gallatin's letter would cool the war fever and disabuse the public that it would be easy to take Quebec.[52] Some Democratic-Republicans blamed the Secretary for not giving the warning earlier so that the martial spirit would not have developed at all; one told a colleague that he had no objection to going to war, but did not want it to cost anything.[53]

Gallatin was developing a close personal friendship with a congressional newcomer who was an ardent advocate of war, Jonathan Roberts of Pennsylvania. During the many evenings the bachelor congressman accepted the Secretary's hospitality, Gallatin "never dropped a word of discouragement to my warlike penchant." With a frankness that was characteristic and flattered young Roberts, the veteran Secretary told him plainly that neither Jefferson nor Madison would have kept the government from bankruptcy, much less have reduced the debt, without assistance such as he had given them. Roberts's praise of Gallatin in the boarding house where the War Hawks made their quarters went far to convince them that the measures the Secretary was urging were truly indispensable. Most important of the converts was Speaker Clay, who soon was urging enactment of Gallatin's program.[54]

Thus by the spring of 1812 neither Gallatin nor the War Hawks hesitated to speak openly of war with Great Britain as a certainty. He wrote to Jefferson in March that "the domestic faction" had frustrated "our hopes and endeavours to preserve peace"; he counted upon the mass of the people to support the government in "an avoidable war" to "check the disordinate ambition of individuals"; he hoped that the evils war always produced could be limited to its duration, and that, when it was over, "the United States may be burthened with the smallest possible quantity of debt, perpetual taxation, military establishments, and other corrupting or anti-Republican habits or institutions." [55] A few weeks later the War Hawks were holding a meeting to plan the new states that would be carved out of Canada.[56]

In mid-March, Congress granted Gallatin's request for authority to place an $11,000,000 loan to carry the government through the first year of war if it should come. Without the help of a Bank of the United States he had to rely on the state-chartered banks. On April 7 a circular letter to thirty-two leaders of these institutions promised that whatever sums they subscribed could remain on deposit with them.[57] A fortnight later he invited individuals to subscribe through the banks on May 1 and 2. Although the Administration mouthpiece the *National Intelligencer*, whistling in the dark, predicted that twice the amount he sought would be taken "instantly," Gallatin privately felt he would be lucky to place more than half of the sum on the first try.[58] Congress had shied away from his suggestion that an interest rate of 8 per cent be allowed. United States 6 per cent stock, with about a dozen years to run, was selling at about par; it would be too much to expect the investing public to grasp at a large new loan at the same interest rate.

The results did not exceed Gallatin's expectations. In the cities where the nation's liquid assets were concentrated, and particularly in Federalist New England, there were protests against raising money for a war that had not yet begun and that the commercial interests still dearly wished to prevent. New England subscribed less than $1,000,000; New York and Philadelphia, the two other principal centers of capital, only about $1,500,000 each; Baltimore and Washington together about $1,-500,000; the South, from the Potomac to Charleston, only $700,000—a total of scarcely $6,000,000.[59]

As soon as the inadequacy of the public subscription became manifest, Gallatin asked Langdon Cheves, chairman of the House Ways and Means Committee, for authority to issue $5,000,000 in Treasury notes within the next year. These would bear 5.4 per cent interest payable one year after issuance and would be receivable for all duties, taxes, and debts of the United States. Here was another innovation in fiscal practice, for the government had never before issued Treasury notes.[60]

While Congress pondered the suggestion, the news from home and abroad did nothing to raise Gallatin's spirits. In Massachusetts and New York the Federalists scored unexpectedly well in the spring state elections. The rift within the Democratic-Republican party was dramatized by the refusal of Giles and Samuel Smith to attend caucuses to nominate a ticket for the November election. George Clinton had died, and a new nominee for Vice President was necessary. Gallatin was not enthusiastic about the man most talked about for the place—Elbridge Gerry, lately defeated for reelection as governor of Massachusetts—fearing that "he would give us as much trouble as our late Vice President." [61] Convinced that John Langdon of New Hampshire would be a popular candidate, he urged him to allow his name to be proposed. But Langdon pleaded advanced age, and Gerry was unanimously made Madison's running mate.[62]

Then from London came a dispatch from the British foreign secretary,

Lord Wellesley, detailing Napoleon Bonaparte's recent crimes against neutrals. The paper dashed the last desperate hope of many Americans that the Orders in Council might be repealed, leaving no excuse for war against Great Britain; it also stirred up a momentary cry for war with France as well as Britain.[63]

In the last days of May, President Madison solemnly announced to the cabinet that he had at long last determined to ask Congress for a declaration of war against Great Britain. Several days of earnest discussion followed, to which Gallatin contributed his share. As finally agreed upon, the President's message alleged four grounds for hostilities: British impressment policies, violations of the three-mile limit of sovereignty along the American coast, paper blockades, and the Orders in Council. Strangely, the discussion, and public statements that followed, took no notice of two foremost causes for war: the hunger of the westerners for Canada, and their fear of British alliance with the Indian tribes of the Northwest.[64]

Although no one spoke of Canada, it loomed large when Madison's message was presented to Congress on June 1, and voted on by the two houses. Ironically, for a war supposed to be prompted by maritime grievances, the states most concerned with maritime matters voted in general against the declaration, while the inland and western states were overwhelming in support. The vote in the House was decisive, seventy-nine to forty-nine; closer in the Senate, nineteen to sixteen. Smith and his Invisibles gave reluctant support.[65]

On June 16, two days before President Madison signed the declaration, a new British foreign secretary, Castlereagh, yielding to pressure from commercial interests, announced that the Orders in Council were being revoked. Two compelling excuses for war still remained: Britain's impressment practices and the desire of many Americans for territorial acquisitions.

20. "Mr. Madison's War"

1812-1813

Usually in the affairs of nations, once the die has been cast for war, action becomes easy; men of all political faiths and economic interests join hands, prepared to sacrifice their lives and their fortunes for the common goal. The experience of the United States following the declaration of war on June 18, 1812, was to be of quite another sort.

Incompetence, cross purposes, and conflicting jealousies spread from the President and the cabinet across the nation. Two days after the declaration Madison, wearing a little round hat and a huge cockade, visited all the offices of the departments of War and the Navy to stimulate the functionaries on duty, in a manner worthy of a commander-in-chief.[1] But William Eustis and Paul Hamilton, the amiable incompetents in charge of those departments, were incapable of coping with the situation. As Gallatin observed to his chief later in the year, a little "skill in forming" and "decision in executing" military plans "would save the government several millions." [2] He wrote to Jefferson that Eustis's "incapacity" and the "total want of confidence in him" were "felt through every ramification of the public service." [3] Senator Crawford of Georgia added his voice, pleading that the cabinet be strengthened.[4]

When the war was three months old, President Madison belatedly responded. He proposed that Eustis retire from the War Department and Monroe, who had a fine record of Revolutionary War service, succeed him; Gallatin would then move to the State Department and Crawford would succeed him in the Treasury.

But disunity still permeated Congress. "We can hardly rely on carrying any thing," Gallatin complained of the legislature. It was especially true of the Senate on any matter involving himself, for the Smiths, the Gileses, and the Leibs still were there and exerted great influence. "The exchange of places which you suggested," he replied to the President, "would in my opinion, have a most salutary effect on the conduct of the war; but, on mature reflection, I apprehend that it would not satisfy public opinion, and would be more liable to criticism than almost any other course that could be adopted." [5] It was decided that for the time being Monroe should double as the head of the State and War departments.

The discord throughout the nation was manifested in the Presidential election. The votes of the South and the West, delivered with a notable lack of enthusiasm, gave Madison his second term. Every state north of the Potomac, except Pennsylvania and Vermont, voted for De Witt Clinton, the Federalist-supported Democratic-Republican from New York. In Boston dissension reached such a pitch that a prominent clergyman urged from his pulpit the separation of New England from the Union, saying that there was "nothing to lose except Thomas Jefferson, James Madison, and Albert Gallatin." [6] The war that had been declared ostensibly to protect American maritime interests was referred to in maritime New England as "Mr. Madison's war." Although Madison carried Pennsylvania by a good majority, Philadelphia was cool to the war. One old enemy ate his words that he would never support Madison as long as he retained Gallatin as his counsel: Duane backed the Madison ticket on the ground that the war must be supported. The intransigent Dr. Leib, however, came out for Clinton. [7]

2

Convinced that the War and Navy departments were headed by incompetence that the President was failing to remedy, Gallatin ventured across departmental boundaries to offer advice and even direction. In this he was joined by Secretary Monroe.

At the time of the declaration of war, Madison and Monroe assumed that for a while the conflict would be primarily maritime. [8] But days passed with no protection for American vessels in the coasting trade or arriving from foreign ports with cargoes valued between a million and a million and a half dollars each week. Finally, in late June, Gallatin protested, and the President belatedly had Secretary Hamilton order a patrol of the coast. [9]

Even more serious was the condition of the Army. Although Congress had authorized a force of 35,000 men in the hope that it might take Quebec, the regular army consisted of only 7,000 men. Enlistments were very slow. Four hundred thousand state militiamen were called into service, but organization and use of them were tardy and ineffective. Gallatin bombarded the President with letters and memoranda about this laxness and even tried drawing up plans for the disposition of troops and naval forces and the conduct of campaigns along the northern border, especially in the region of the Great Lakes. These centered on invading Canada by way of Niagara, with a heavy attack on Montreal in the late autumn or early winter.[10]

Gallatin was on the point of starting for Albany in August to discuss the military situation with General Henry Dearborn and Governor Daniel Tompkins when word arrived of a great military reverse. General William Hull had led American forces into Upper Canada but, finding the area impoverished and hostile, had fallen back to Detroit, where a Canadian force under Isaac Brock forced him to surrender his troops and prisoners of war. Though indignant, Gallatin could still be philosophic. "The English general treats our militia as Charles the 12th did the Russians after the battle of Narva," he observed to President Madison; "and in like manner we will soon be taught by the enemy how to conquer him." [11]

The fall and early winter brought additional reverses. American forces along the Canadian border, under Generals Stephen Van Rensselaer and Alexander Smyth, were routed by the British. In December Gallatin admitted in a letter to Thomas Jefferson, who was anxiously watching the contest from peaceful Monticello, that "the series of misfortunes experienced this year exceeds all anticipations made even by those who had least confidence in our inexperienced officers and undisciplined men."

When Monroe assumed responsibility for the War Department, Gallatin began peppering him with ideas about how to make the campaigns more effective and, through the use of "local forces" as opposed to regular forces, more economical.[12]

Monroe flatly refused to keep the Secretaryship of War on a permanent basis; and as 1812 faded into 1813 many earnest cabinet discussions were addressed to finding a suitable successor. As Gallatin emphasized to the President, the fate of the Administration, of the Democratic-Republican cause, perhaps of the nation itself, depended upon the proper management of the War Department. He would have preferred General (former Secretary) Dearborn; but the general "shrank from it," and the choice seemed to settle down to one between two New York politicians, Governor Daniel Tompkins and General John Armstrong. For Armstrong, as a member of the Clinton connection who had fortified New York harbor with a lavish hand, Gallatin had no love; he wondered about his lack of "disinterested zeal" and of personal attachment to the Administration; but he rated his talents as far superior to those of Tompkins. Indeed, he so distrusted Tompkins that he told the President that, if a place must be made for him, he was willing to accept the War Department himself despite his lack of professional qualifications and let the New Yorker have the Treasury.[13]

Madison appointed Armstrong to the office. For Secretary of the Navy he named William Jones, Philadelphia merchant, shipowner, former congressman, and supporter of Gallatin.

3

Most of Secretary Gallatin's energies continued to be absorbed by the problems of the Treasury Department. These were compounded by the attitude of Congress. On June 24, 1812, he transmitted to Ezekiel Bacon of the House Ways and Means Committee a request for action on the fiscal program outlined in January and February, which the legislature, preoccupied with declaring war, had neglected to act on.[14] But the new direct taxes and the doubled customs duties were still unpleasant to Congress: with the Presidential election in the offing, discussion of them seemed to be impolitic. On June 26 the House voted, by a decisive majority, to postpone action until the next session.[15]

Before scattering, the legislators gave Gallatin the authority he had asked in May to issue $5,000,000 in Treasury notes. In the next five months he placed $3,180,000 of these with eight banks.[16]

How useful these were during a summer of military reverses became manifest when Secretary Gallatin reported to Congress early in December. Even with their aid, the government's fiscal situation was doleful. He estimated that expenses in the coming year would run to nearly $32,000,000: $17,000,000 for the Army, nearly $5,000,000 for the Navy, $1,500,000 for civil expenses, $3,300,000 for interest on the public debt, and $5,200,000 for reimbursements of loans, Treasury notes, and the like. This estimate did not include any expenditures already authorized but not made, including the proposed increases in the Army and Navy. Gallatin estimated the income of the government for the year at $12,-000,000: $11,500,000 from customs duties and $500,000 from the sale of public lands. This left $20,000,000 to be borrowed somewhere; it would increase the public debt by $15,000,000.[17]

Privately Gallatin acknowledged to the President that he did not quite know where he was going to get the $20,000,000. He had talked with the chief bankers and moneyed men in Baltimore, Philadelphia, and New York during the summer recess. "From Banks we can expect little or nothing," he said, "as they have already lent nearly to the full extent of their faculties." From individuals during the past year he had been able to raise only $3,200,000.[18] As he told Monroe, he doubted whether even a Federalist Secretary of the Treasury, enjoying the confidence of the money lenders, could raise the sum contemplated.[19]

In desperation, Gallatin toyed with farfetched alleviatives. Why not modify the Non-Importation Act so that the customs duties would produce $15,000,000 a year? Why not—he had discussed the idea in another form with Senator James A. Bayard of Delaware some months earlier—establish a new national bank for the convenience of the Treasury but without formal incorporation by Congress? It could be done by encouraging subscribers to the $11,000,000 loan to take additional shares on the installment plan; others, especially in the western states, should be encouraged to come in on identical terms. This group, together with the Commissioner of Loans, would then appoint directors to receive public and private deposits, issue notes payable on demand and receivable everywhere for taxes, make loans at 5 per cent, and transact other Treasury business, just as the Bank of the United States had done. Transmitting a sketch of the plan to Monroe, Gallatin pledged "that if [these] two measures are adopted, there will not, during the war, be any deficiency so far as relates to money . . . no unpopular or injurious measures will be necessary to raise money." [20]

Gallatin's espousal of schemes so tricky and so politically inexpedient measures the depth of his despair. Monroe did not return the memorandum outlining them, and no further action was taken.

Gallatin had fresh evidence that he could expect neither sympathy nor aid from Congress soon after the start of the new session in December. Looking about for funds, he found some $23,000,000 that had come into the Department's possession: $18,000,000 worth of bonds and $5,000,000 worth of duties on goods imported from Britain during the confusion that immediately followed the repeal of the Orders in Council and the declaration of war. As the importers obviously had made enormous profits from the cargoes, he proposed to the House Ways and Means Committee that the government be authorized to retain half of the windfall that would otherwise be returned to the shippers.[21]

The moralistic outcry this proposal stirred in the House revealed not only how strong the shipping interests were, but how serious a split existed in the Democratic-Republican ranks, even in the Ways and Means Committee. Cried Langdon Cheves, the committee chairman: "I would rather see the objects of the war fail; I would rather see the seamen of the country impressed on the ocean and our commerce swept away from its bosom, than see the long arm of the Treasury indirectly thrust into the pocket of the citizen through the medium of a penal law." Exclaimed Henry Clay: "Let us not pollute our hands with this weltgild [!]"

Although Felix Grundy protested that the "gentlemen have assumed a strange, highminded position in the argument, the force of which I confess is beyond my comprehension," they won the battle in both the House and the Senate, the Treasury lost about nine million desperately needed dollars, and Gallatin lost badly needed support of his own party and of the House Ways and Means Committee for any future proposals he might make.[22]

The rest of the short session was marked for Gallatin by frustration. In February he proposed the idea he had tried out on Monroe for the repeal of the Non-Importation Act. Representatives of the New England states, where manufacturing had made great strides since the restrictions on trade, welcomed the suggestion of higher import duties but opposed the repeal of the act. No legislation was forthcoming.[23]

Before adjourning, the legislators gave Gallatin two dubious beneficences: authority to issue additional Treasury notes and to borrow $16,-000,000 on any terms that could be obtained, providing only that the capital be repaid at the end of twelve years.[24] He still had not completely disposed of the previous issue of the notes, and $5,000,000 of the $11,-000,000 loan of the preceding spring still remained unplaced.

In late February, when barely enough money remained in the Treasury to last through the next month, Gallatin concluded that he must make every sacrifice to place the new loan. He told President Madison there appeared to be no alternative to an at least temporary cutting back of military and naval operations. The entire loan must be opened at once with an interest rate of 7 per cent, to be reduced to 6 per cent at the end of thirteen years. "There is no probability that the money can be obtained cheaper." [25] The frightened President agreed. On February 22, Secretary Gallatin issued a circular letter to the banks that had helped with the $11,000,000 loan, inviting their participation in this one and promising a discount of one-eighth of one per cent.[26] On March 12 subscription books were opened in eleven principal towns.[27]

The banks' response was as pallid as Gallatin had feared: they subscribed less than $4,000,000. In Boston, to which vast quantities of specie were moving because of New England's enterprise in smuggling and manufacturing, the response was singularly meager. Now, he concluded, he must apply directly to the general investing public. On March 18 he issued a circular announcing that the Treasury would allow a commission of one-quarter of one per cent to any person or group collecting subscriptions that totaled $100,000 or more. For this purpose the books were reopened on March 31 in the banks of New York, Philadelphia, Baltimore, and Washington.[28]

Before the returns from this subscription were known, Gallatin received a godsend in the form of a letter from his old friend A. J. Dallas, the Philadelphia barrister, who believed the war was "a holy war" and was advancing the nation "a century . . . in power and character." [29] Dallas, who long had made it a practice to keep the Secretary informed of the sentiments of the moneyed men of Philadelphia,[30] told of an exciting conversation he had had with an extraordinary man named David Parish.[31]

A native of Hamburg, Parish was a member of a family influential in the banking circles of Europe and Great Britain. Gallatin first met him in 1806, when he brought an introduction from Alexander Baring. Parish had made approximately a million dollars between 1806 and 1808 as the agent of an international syndicate licensed to export to Europe all the gold and silver in the New World belonging to the Spanish government. He had invested much of his profit in a vast land promotion along the St. Lawrence River in New York State; but military action in that area had discouraged settlement, and he felt that the only hope for his project was a speedy settlement of the war.[32] Dallas reported that Parish was willing to try to interest other capitalists in forming a syndicate to subscribe to the loan if it would bring a conclusion of the war as soon as possible "with Honor," or if Congress would make "the necessary appropriations" to conduct the war vigorously. If American capitalists refused to come in, Parish thought he could obtain funds from European sources.[33] In Gallatin's offer of a commission for subscriptions totaling $100,000 or more, Parish saw an opportunity for "a Handsome Profit." He lost no time in getting in touch with a number of moneyed men who at least toyed with the idea of subscribing to the loan.

One of these was homely, eccentric Stephen Girard, a native of France long resident of Philadelphia, where he had accumulated a great fortune in shipping and the mercantile trade, and only recently had established the Bank of Stephen Girard. When Gallatin had approached him the previous summer, while trying to place the $11,000,000 loan, he had specified two provisos: that his bank be put on the same footing as other banks in Treasury operations, and that the Pennsylvania government be induced to stop interfering with his bank's "progress." [34]

Another of Parish's prospects was John Jacob Astor. Astor was an old friend who remembered Gallatin gratefully for such courtesies as permission to use the Secretary of the Treasury's frank in dispatching directions to his agents in the fur trade along the Canadian-American border following the declaration of war.[35]

Both Girard and Astor were now seriously interested in forming a syndicate to complete the $16,000,000 loan; and in New York, Philadelphia, and Baltimore Parish found smaller capitalists who were willing to buy some of his stock if he subscribed.[36]

By early April relations between the capitalists were proceeding so satisfactorily that Gallatin journeyed to Dallas's home in Philadelphia. On the 6th of that month, the day after the public subscription officially closed, he concluded an agreement whereby Parish and Girard jointly took $7,055,800 of the 6 per cent stock at 88. Astor had come down from New York for the negotiation, and took $2,056,000 of it at the same figure—patriotically, Gallatin assured President Madison later, for "I know that amount was much more than was convenient and did much embarrass him." [37] Thus was completed the full $16,000,000 loan.[38]

The loan was filled not a moment too soon, for the Treasury was empty and unable to honor the drafts of other departments. By the efforts of the German-born Parish and Astor, the French-born Girard, and the Swiss-born Gallatin, the greatest financial transaction of the War of 1812 was completed, and the credit of the United States kept high. Ultimately the deal was to prove an excellent one for the United States, as during the thirteen years the loan was outstanding, the government paid interest on it at a rate of 7.487 per cent, not too high when it is remembered that New England, which held most of the specie then in the country, subscribed less than $500,000.

4

Meanwhile there had been a rare piece of luck on the diplomatic front. About the time Gallatin was telling the President that the Treasury was nearly empty, the Russian chargé at Washington delivered an offer from Czar Alexander I to mediate peace between the United States and Great Britain.[39] Perhaps no nation found the Anglo-American war more inconvenient than Russia. Napoleon had penetrated the heart of Moscow; the Czar reasoned that, if the problems of Great Britain in the New World could be solved, it might relieve the pressure on his land.

The offer delighted Gallatin. "The present opportunity offers a better chance to make an honorable peace than we have any right to expect," he observed. "England must be desirous at this critical moment to have it in her power to apply her whole force on the Continent of Europe, and the mediation of Russia saves her pride." He was convinced that the Czar would "support the cause and the law of nations. . . . Provided we can obtain security with respect to impressment, peace will give us everything we want." And if the United States could not obtain satisfaction on the impressment issue? Let it make peace anyway; five years of peace would enable it to build a navy capable of defending its interests on that score.[40] The Administration quickly answered that it accepted the Czar's offer.[41]

The negotiations presumably would be at St. Petersburg, with John Quincy Adams, as minister to Russia, representing American interests; but the cabinet agreed that a delegation of three would serve to underscore the importance with which the United States viewed the negotiation.[42] James A. Bayard, Federalist senator from Delaware, who had opposed the declaration of war but was anxious that the Union be preserved, was named as a suitable negotiator to represent the friendly opposition.[43] Then, to the surprise of his colleagues, Gallatin asked that he be named as the third member of the delegation.

Gallatin had two reasons for making the request. One was personal— a development of the past few months and another consequence of Madison's lack of a sure administrative touch. Armstrong's assumption of the War portfolio had inaugurated a new kind of discord within the cabinet almost as unsettling as that caused by Robert Smith. Armstrong was particularly opposed to Monroe; but Gallatin was affected when he appointed William Duane adjutant general of the fourth military district. Gallatin was soon writing a friend that Duane's conduct on beginning his duties "has disgusted me so far as to make me desirous of not being any longer associated with those who appointed him." [44]

Gallatin's second and even more compelling reason was the conviction that the Secretary of the Treasury had a hopeless task: that no money could be obtained from any source if the war continued another year. "I have made up my mind that I could in no other manner be more usefully employed for the present than on the negotiation of a peace." [45]

Madison and Monroe finally agreed that Gallatin should have his wish, on a temporary leave of absence from the Treasury. The mission, all three were convinced, would require only a few months; Gallatin would certainly be back in Washington by Christmas.[46] The Treasury portfolio would be held vacant in the meantime, with Secretary of the Navy Jones assuming interim responsibility.

The very real possibility remained that old adversaries in the Senate might unite to reject the nomination of Gallatin as a commissioner. Dallas spoke of it, but the Secretary merely smiled the sad smile of a man who knows life must be lived in spite of old enemies and bogies.[47]

Deep in his heart he felt that the mission might well provide the opportunity he had been seeking in the last five years for a graceful and honorable departure from public service.[48]

Announcement of his appointment followed the successful filling of the $16,000,000 loan, on April 15.[49] The next few weeks were busy for Gallatin, as he put his public and private affairs into order. To carry on the war and the government's operations, the Treasury had available besides the funds from the loan, $5,000,000 in Treasury notes and income from taxes and duties estimated at more than $9,000,000—about $30,000,000 in all. He allotted $13,000,000 for Army purposes and $4,500,000 for Navy purposes, amounts that could not be exceeded without authorization by Congress.[50]

In these last hurried days Gallatin also prepared two tax bills and the outline of a charter for a new Bank of the United States. The latter was the outgrowth of conversations for more than a year with Astor, who was now convinced that a new Bank was indispensable. For the guidance of Jones and the subordinate officers and clerks, he also prepared a detailed memorandum explaining the day-to-day routine of the department. Richard Rush, the Comptroller of the Treasury, observed later: "Few men are so thoroughly men of business as Mr. Gallatin; he left nothing in arrears when he went away, and this, with skilfull clerks in his office drilled by long practice, and very precise and full instructions in all matters which he left behind, will enable its common business to go on, with Mr. Jones's mere signature to give it the official stamp." This is precisely what happened; later in the year, Gallatin's two tax bills and the plan for a new Bank charter were presented to Congress with Jones's signature as acting secretary.[51]

Gallatin also left behind a significant piece of advice for Secretary Monroe. He was nearly ready to embark when a letter from the Secretary of State disclosed the intention to seize West Florida and perhaps East Florida within the next few days, on the ground that their reported purchase by Great Britain from Spain had made them valid prizes of war. Monroe and the President, Virginians both, were as eager to obtain these provinces as the westerners were to acquire Canada. Monroe's letter expressed it another way: to obtain satisfaction from Great Britain a military push was necessary against both Florida and Canada.

"On the subject of Florida I have always differed in opinion with you," Gallatin wrote to the Secretary of State in one of several blunt letters. An act of aggression against that province would unite European nations against the United States and render peace negotiations all the more difficult. Besides, the object was a "Southern one, and will, if it should in-

volve us in a war with Spain, disgust every man north of Washington."
He requested indulgence of the freedom with which he spoke: it was
"intended as a general caution," which he thought important because he
knew and saw every day in New York and Philadelphia "the extent of
geographical feeling and the necessity of prudence if we are to preserve
and invigorate the union." [52]

During the last days personal problems occupied Gallatin almost as
much as public duties. There were family arrangements to be made;
clothes and personal effects to be procured; diplomatic instructions and
credentials to be assembled. The Washington residence was put in the
charge of a servant couple pending his return. Hannah would reside with
the Nicholsons in New York. Albert Rolaz and Frances would be with her;
but James, now sixteen and ready for adventures and education in the
Old World, would accompany his father as his personal secretary. Gallatin's brother-in-law James Witter Nicholson was deputized as his agent
in all matters respecting the western property.[53]

The family left Washington on April 21 for New York, then went to
the Dallases at Philadelphia to await the government ship *Neptune*, cap-
tained by Secretary Jones's brother Lloyd Jones, which was to carry the
diplomatic party. Last-minute consultations with Bayard completed the
arrangements for a staff. The mission was to have three secretaries besides
James Gallatin: twenty-one-year-old John Payne Todd, the dissipated
son of Dolley Madison by her first marriage; twenty-one-year-old George
Mifflin Dallas, son of A. J. Dallas, not long out of Princeton and just admitted to the Philadelphia bar, in the rank of an Army major; and
George P. Milligan, a few years their senior, in the rank of colonel. In
addition there were four Negro servants.

On the afternoon of Sunday May 9, father and son took leave of Hannah and the other children and boarded the *Neptune* at New Castle,
Delaware. The vessel drifted down Chesapeake Bay for two days, stopped
once by a British frigate which demanded to see the passport from Admiral Sir John Borlase Warren that permitted it to pass through the
coastal blockade. On the 11th Gallatin completed a final letter to Hannah,
which he entrusted to the pilot. That evening the *Neptune* put out to
sea.[54]

5

Gallatin left behind an extraordinary record in the nation's service. He had been head of the Treasury Department almost precisely twelve years, a tenure unexceeded to this day.* It is probable that no executive officer has had farther-reaching influence on the Administrations of which he was a member, and this in an era when the importance of the cabinet in the national government was much greater than today.

Gallatin's accomplishment grew out of his own conception of the office of Secretary of the Treasury and of the responsibilities of a public servant. Like Alexander Hamilton, and in very nearly the same degree, he was a constructive statesman. He was not content "to act the part of a mere financier, to [be] a contriver of taxes, a dealer of loans . . . fattening contractors, pursers, and agents." [55] As a philosopher he thought inductively. "If I have any talent," he once wrote, "it is of making a proper use of ascertained facts and of drawing from these legitimate inferences." [56] Ever the thoughtful man of business, he shied from the doctrinaire and was ready to let experience temper his convictions.

From Calvinistic Geneva, from the western Pennsylvania and Ohio valley frontier, from the farms and towns and cities reaching from Maine to Virginia, he brought to the councils of Jefferson and Madison a philosophy of government that was democratic, republican, national. In a sense it was a philosophy midway between the conceptions now known as Hamiltonianism and Jeffersonianism. With Jefferson he shared a faith in the dignity and the rights of every man; like Jefferson he valued the life of the self-sufficient farmer and insisted that opportunities to enjoy it be kept open to all. Like both Hamilton and Jefferson, he perceived the prosperity and national independence that the United States could achieve through the development of its industry, commerce, and natural resources; like Hamilton, he was willing to interpret the Constitution freely to let the government encourage this; unlike Hamilton, he insisted that here too opportunity must remain open to all Americans.

To attain these midway goals, Gallatin favored a middle course in the administration of government. He worked to modify the Federalist conception of governmental power with a Democratic-Republican notion

* Nominally Gallatin remained Secretary of the Treasury until February 9, 1814—a tenure of nearly twelve years and nine months. The second longest record in the office is that of Henry Morgenthau, Jr., eleven years and six months. Only one man has been a member of the cabinet for a longer period: Harold L. Ickes, who was Secretary of the Interior 1933-1946.

of responsibility. He believed that the civil service should be made up of men of competence, integrity, and industry; and he recognized that for the most part he and his colleagues had inherited such a corps from the Federalists. To maintain this standard he believed that civil servants must be secure in their positions as long as they remained innocent of misconduct in office.[57]

His attempt to make these principles the fixed policy of the government won the enduring and disastrous enmity of such political powers as Duane, Leib, and the Clintons. Jefferson and Madison not only failed to give effective support against these malcontents, but declined, because of political expediency, to espouse his nonpartisan policy. This was a pity, for the prestige of the Presidential office could have established such a tradition in the federal government and also enhanced the usefulness of an able and thoroughly loyal associate. Yet Gallatin was not blameless: if he had not allowed his wife's preference for New York City to cut him off so completely from political support in Pennsylvania, he would doubtless have remained strong enough to discredit the patronage mongers.

To the fiscal operations of the Jefferson and Madison Administrations Gallatin brought a set of theories and practices peculiarly his own, which —because he applied his ideas with rare skill, clear conviction, and intense purpose even to the smallest details—became the financial principles of Jeffersonianism. Hamilton and his associates had brought the federal government in its first dozen years from bankruptcy to health and prosperity. Even so, there were notable shortcomings in fiscal practices and human values. Gallatin's democratic reluctance to allow a small group of capitalists to benefit at the expense of the many led him to dissipate forever the illusion of the worth of a sinking fund, which Hamilton had borrowed from the British; to discredit the theory of the good of a perpetual public debt. Indeed, his Genevan morality made him regard a public debt as scarcely less than a sin, and extinguishment of it was his primary goal. He shared the frontiersman's dislike for taxes and sought to reduce them so far as would be safe; he was particularly opposed to excises as inquisitorial. He believed that Congress should exercise its control over the policies and efficiency of the government through specific appropriations as an American tradition.

In working for these goals Gallatin had to modify and compromise many of his own principles. He abandoned insistence on the independence of the executive and legislative departments, and himself directed the legislative process through friendly committeemen in Congress. He felt compelled to watch over and sometimes to interfere with the operations of other departments, in order to obtain the maximum return for the tax dollar. To facilitate the Treasury's operations he was willing to cooperate with and even encourage the Bank of the United States, although that institution was anathema to President Jefferson and the doctrinaire state-rights members of his party. Consciously or unconsciously, he regularly underestimated the anticipated revenues, and thus built up a surplus.

Naturally Gallatin's conscientious, indeed zealous application of his ideas brought numerous failures and even more enemies. Choice of the unstable John Randolph as a chief ally in Congress placed him in an ambiguous position with Jefferson and created public suspicion and hostility. He was never able to persuade the Navy to adopt truly economical practices; his attempts won him the impassioned enmity of the Smiths and the Navy partisans, the mercantile groups of the middle states. The Bank was killed largely because of the vindictiveness toward him of the Duanes, the Clintons, and the Smiths, and of the vacillation of President Madison.

None the less, the first half of his administration of the Treasury was one of tremendous accomplishment. Gallatin benefited during these six years from the war in Europe, which gave American shippers unprecedented prosperity as neutral traders and brought bountiful revenues from customs duties. Government income was swollen further by a healthy demand for public lands in the West. Despite the repeal of the excise and the salt tax, the cost of naval action against the Barbary pirates, and the payment of $15,000,000 for Louisiana, Gallatin reduced the public debt from more than $82,000,000 to less than $76,000,000.[58]

After six fat years came six that were lean. Britain and France adopted policies designed to curtail the carrying trade of neutral nations like the United States. If Gallatin had had his way, the United States would have gone to war with either power or both to enforce its maritime rights, particularly in impressment; he was confident that the hostilities could be financed entirely by loans. But Congress and public opinion recoiled from war.

Jefferson's solution was the national self-blockade, which Gallatin thoroughly disapproved of but loyally undertook to enforce. His conscientiousness was costly to the Administration and his own reputation: the embargo and nonimportation acts dried up the Treasury receipts at a time when expenditures for gunboats, fortifications, and an enlarged army were swelling. The shipping interests of New England and the middle states were less concerned about national honor than he; as yet the manufacturing industries that had sprung into being as a consequence of the restrictive legislation had not made their feelings felt.

Once the cocky, nationalistic westerners had their way and war was declared against Britain, all the pent-up resentment against the two Democratic-Republican administrations, a combination of factionalism in party and sectionalism in the nation, centered on Gallatin. His enemies in Congress had deprived him of the Bank he thought essential for carrying the nation through a successful war; now they refused him most of the other tools he asked, and the irresolute Madison withheld the indispensable support.

Despite these frustrations, Gallatin's public conscience and personal pride induced him to hold on so that financially and economically the United States was in sound condition during the first year of war. Only public confidence was lacking, and he was not directly responsible for the loss of this. By diligence he had then whittled the public debt down to $45,000,000, saving the government $2,000,000 a year in interest and setting the goal of complete extinguishment of the debt, to be finally attained in 1835.

As the *Neptune* bore Gallatin across a tempestuous Atlantic in quest of peace, the editor of the *National Intelligencer* evaluated the situation with rare perspicacity: "We should do injustice to our feelings were we . . . to omit the expression of our conviction of the stern integrity and firm republicanism of this veteran politician, whose greatest enemies have only dealt in general accusations against him, whose chief offence was perhaps that he never put himself out of the way to conciliate their good will." [59]

21. The Quest for Peace

1813=1814

It was a stormy transatlantic passage, in weather more like March than May.* Day after day, week after week, the three-hundred-ton *Neptune* pitched and tossed. The passengers scarcely recovered their spirits after one gale before they lost them in another. On the fairer days the whole party sat on deck reading, mostly travel books about Russia. Gallatin's love for facts and figures drove him to keep a daily record: of the winds, the course, the distance covered, the latitude and longitude, and the temperature.

After six weeks at sea, the *Neptune* reached the Swedish port of Gothenburg on June 20, 1813. Gallatin poignantly realized how much of an American he had become in thirty-five years away from the Old World when three compatriots called on him and Bayard at their hotel. "We had been delighted to see once more population of any kind," he wrote in a memorandum of the journey; "but to meet Americans at such a distance from home is a feeling to be understood only by those who have experienced it. I could have pressed every one to my bosom as a brother." [1] He hastened to write letters to friends and relatives, including one to his old acquaintance Alexander Baring of London, to explain what he was about.[2]

They were on their way again two days later, skirting Sweden, pausing at Elsinore in Denmark to visit Hamlet's garden, then landing at Copenhagen for six days of sightseeing. The Fourth of July they celebrated in a

* Before proceeding further the reader should be warned against A *Great Peace Maker: The Diary of James Gallatin*, edited by Count Gallatin, with an Introduction by Viscount Bryce (London and New York, 1914). Innumerable discrepancies between the text of this book, which has been extensively used by historians as an authentic first-hand account of Gallatin's career as a diplomat, and manuscripts in the Gallatin Papers and elsewhere convince me that it is a complete hoax. I am publishing a statement of my reasons for this conclusion in the *American Historical Review*, July, 1957. Needless to say, I have not drawn upon it in writing the present book.

style befitting Americans as the *Neptune* sailed through the Baltic Sea. The voyage ended on July 15 at Revel, in the Baltic Provinces of Russia. It took three days to negotiate with the port officials and engage a calash and a landau for the journey to St. Petersburg. On their way again, they stopped to peer curiously into the hovels of the peasants, which they agreed were "filthy" as the travel books had stated; at Narva they stared at French prisoners of war—"miserable creatures," Bayard thought.

They reached St. Petersburg on July 21 and headed at once for the residence of the American consul, Levett Harris. Happily word of their approach had preceded them, and lodgings were ready.[3] They had barely begun to unpack when John Quincy Adams, the earnest, able, and dour minister to Russia, came to welcome them. The next day they returned the call and made the acquaintance of his wife and small son.

Gallatin and Bayard were eager for word as to the prospects of their mission. Adams was not too encouraging. He confessed astonishment that the Administration had spared an officer so valuable as Gallatin on an errand so chancey; he very much doubted that the British government would agree to mediation by the Czar, having received several reports from London that the British regarded the Anglo-American war as a family affair, a quarrel between cousins, one of them distinctly junior, and were adamant against the intervention of a third nation. At the moment Czar Alexander, the initiator of the idea of a negotiation, was nine hundred miles away in Bohemia, at the headquarters of the Allied forces trying to drive Napoleon back to the Rhine.[4]

In the Czar's absence, the Americans treated with Count Roumanzoff, the Chancellor. Late on the morning of July 24, all dressed up in special diplomatic uniforms, Adams formally presented the newcomers to Roumanzoff. Gallatin presented their credentials to the Chancellor and assured him that the only existing difference between the United States and Great Britain was the impressment issue. When the Chancellor observed that the British had already authorized Admiral Warren to negotiate directly with the American government, he countered that Warren had been authorized to offer concessions on the Orders in Council, but not on impressments. He optimistically prophesied that American forces would soon be occupying Upper Canada.[5]

Meanwhile the members of the mission passed the days taking in the sights, visiting palaces and churches, schools and orphanages in the city and its environs; at night they attended the theater and were guests at dinner of the nobility. Count Roumanzoff delighted them one night at his palace by giving a banquet in their especial honor.[6]

Diplomatically, the mission was most frustrating. With Adams and

Bayard, Gallatin toiled for days on a full historical account of the differences between the United States and Great Britain and an astonishingly prescient statement of the ways in which they might be settled. At innumerable meetings and through many letters they assured Count Roumanzoff that they would remain at St. Petersburg as long as there was any chance of arbitration by the Czar, but emphasized that they had no authority to negotiate directly with the British. Roumanzoff remained friendly, encouraging, but exasperatingly vague. He kept repeating that the Czar was so busy at the front "à cheval" that he had little time to read dispatches.[7]

On August 17 came a belated reply by Baring to Gallatin's letter. The financier had access to the governing circles of Britain, and so his message was disturbing. There was but one way, he wrote, in which Great Britain and the United States could resolve their differences: by direct negotiation, without the intervention of a third party. "It is a sort of family quarrel, where foreign interference can only do harm and irritate at any time, but more especially in the present state of Europe, where attempts would be made to make a tool of America in a manner which I am sure neither you nor your colleagues would sanction. . . . Before this reaches you, you will have been informed that [Russian] mediation has been refused, with expressions of our desire to treat separately and directly [at London] or, if more agreeable to you, at Gothenburg."[8]

This patronizing note convinced Gallatin that he and Bayard were wasting time at St. Petersburg. In a quandary, Gallatin on August 28 sent off a letter to Secretary of State Monroe inquiring what to do if Britain formally assumed the position suggested in Baring's letter. To perplex him further, a few days later Roumanzoff, with obvious pleasure, informed them that the Czar had authorized him to renew the offer of mediation to the British.[9]

A new ray of hope came unexpectedly in a letter from Jean-Victor Moreau. Moreau, after serving as a general in the French Revolution, had fled his homeland with the ascendancy of Napoleon to find refuge for nearly a decade in the United States. Only recently he had reached the Czar's headquarters and had proffered his services to the anti-Napoleonic forces. "Although I have not the honor to be an American," he wrote to Gallatin on August 21, "I am deeply interested in the fate of a country where . . . I have received so many marks of kindness." The Czar, who had been "kindness itself," was "keenly interested in America, and I am sure that you may always count on his readiness to use all his influence to bring about peace. ·If I can be of any assistance either to you personally or to your mission, pray make use of me."[10]

Gallatin embraced the offer in a long personal reply. He confessed that America needed peace desperately and could look only to Russia and Czar Alexander for friends among the great powers. Could Moreau learn from the Czar what the prospects for a negotiation were before the long Russian winter made captives of him and Bayard? [11] On the very day Gallatin wrote, Moreau, alas, was dying of wounds in battle at the gates of Dresden.[12]

Then, on October 20, Gallatin heard the news that, half-consciously, he had been dreading since he left America. It had come in the mail packet two days earlier, but Harris and Bayard hesitated to speak about it for fear of upsetting him. Young Todd told him privately. On July 19, by a vote of 18 to 17, the Senate had refused to ratify his nomination as Envoy Extraordinary on the ground that the functions of that office and of Secretary of the Treasury were incompatible. The "Invisibles"— Giles, Leib, Smith, *et al.*—had joined the Federalists in the rejection.[13]

Gallatin took the development calmly. He had his own, curiously philosophical interpretation. He thought Rufus King was chiefly responsible for his rejection but at the same time—so he told Bayard—had a high opinion of King's talents. He was not "mortified" by the rejection, he said, because President Madison had appointed him only at his own insistence.

A packet of newspapers with all the details of the rejection arrived several days later. After studying them, Gallatin notified Count Roumanzoff on November 2 that he no longer was a member of the mission. He would depart from St. Petersburg just as soon as the weather permitted. The Count assured him that he was free to leave whenever he liked, but that the Russian government still considered him as a minister.[14]

The next blow came from London. Lord Walpole, British minister to Russia, coming from the Czar's headquarters, reported that as early as July 6, and at intervals after that, British officials had assured the Czar that England would not agree to Russian mediation. The Czar had replied that he would have nothing more to do with the idea. At a diplomatic dinner, Walpole assured Bayard that his government was "desirous of peace" and would treat directly with the American ministers.[15]

When Gallatin carried this report to Roumanzoff, the Count expressed surprise, saying that as recently as August 22 the Czar had approved the renewed offer of mediation, in his own handwriting. He admitted that he had lately heard that the Russian minister at London, Count Lieven, had decided the time was not propitious for pressing the proposal. Gallatin and Bayard felt that the Czar, a strange and contradictory man at best, was not dealing forthrightly with them; they were convinced also that the well intentioned Count Roumanzoff no longer enjoyed the Czar's confidence.[16]

The Russian winter brought American discontent. Cold, snowy days came in November and December, the sun rising at 8:45 and setting at 3:15. Gallatin shortened the ennui by arising each day after eleven and breakfasting about noon with Colonel Milligan. "The Russians," Bayard complained in his diary, were now "as cold as their climate in its most frosty season"; the food and lodgings had become almost unbearable.[17]

Meanwhile Gallatin pondered several courses. As soon as travel once more became possible, he might use an invitation from relatives to visit Geneva as a pretext for a call at the Czar's headquarters at Frankfurt-on-the-Main—he felt free in his new role of "private gentleman" to make one more appeal for a mediation. Or he might go to London and try to facilitate negotiations directly between Great Britain and the United States. Several letters from different sources in London suggested that the English were in a receptive frame of mind. He was more sanguine about America's bargaining position now. For a time he had feared that it might be necessary to give ground on impressment; but when he learned, late in December, that the United States had successfully filled a new $7,000,000 loan he became optimistic again.[18]

In the end, he determined to go to London; and Bayard, who was despondent about Russian mediation, decided to accompany him. They dispatched their aides early in January, 1814, and, after formal adieux, started out on the evening of the 25th in carriages and calashes mounted on sledges, across the snow-covered expanse of northeastern Europe.[19]

2

They had to contend with the iciest winter northern Europe had known in years.[20] Gallatin's troubles began scarcely four miles out of St. Petersburg, when, in a blinding snowstorm, he became separated from the rest of the party and stalled in a huge snowdrift. It took three hours to extricate his carriage and catch up with the others—"much to my relief and satisfaction," Bayard recorded in his diary.

With only short pauses, they were on the road for the next thirty-eight days, driving westward through Riga, Königsberg, Frankfurt-on-the-Oder, Berlin, Hanover, to Amsterdam. In the first four weeks they glimpsed the sun on only two days. They saw little except snow; not a tree or indeed any object of any sort arrested the eye. It was a lonely journey, for most of the people were in the towns, and they often found it expedient to avoid towns. On four occasions they had to leave the post road to bypass fortified towns still held by the French. The roadside inns were "wretched hovels," filthy, smoky, and stinking, and they preferred to pass most nights on the road, catching what sleep they could as their vehicles inched along.

The occasional pauses afforded them little rest and small satisfaction. At Riga, the Italian-born provincial governor and his wife entertained them at the theater; but they excused themselves from a ceremonious dinner. At Berlin, where Schinkler & Brothers, bankers to the United States government, were incivil to them, they attended the theater. At the banking house they found a letter from the American consul at Amsterdam reporting that Great Britain had proposed direct negotiations at Gothenburg, and that President Madison had appointed them commissioners for the purpose.[21] At Potsdam, they inspected the palace of Sans Souci and filled up with lore about Frederick the Great. Then more cold, snow-bound Prussian territory, Hanoverian territory, Dutch territory. They reached Amsterdam late on March 4. The journey had exceeded fifteen hundred miles, and they were nearly exhausted.

During the next few days, amid entertainment by the Dutch bankers of the United States and by the Prince of Orange, sight-seeing, and theater-going, they caught up with the progress of the world. A letter of January 19 from Hannah assured Gallatin that the family was well.[22] Dispatches from Washington revealed that Madison had not named him to the new commission, supposing that he was anxious to return to the Treasury and was already on the way back to America. Congressman Henry Clay and Jonathan Russell, the newly appointed minister to Sweden, were to join Adams and Bayard on the commission. A letter from Baring assured them once again that Britain was anxious for peace with America.

Although disappointed at being left off the new commission, Gallatin was more anxious than ever to go to London as a private citizen in the hope of doing something to shorten the exhausting war. Bayard, hungry for new experiences to pass the time until his fellow commissioners arrived, chose to accompany him.[23] There were five in the party, including personal aides, when they crossed the English Channel early in April. Naturally enough, they were nervous as to how they would be received in enemy territory; but a letter Baring had sent for the purpose got them through the customs at Harwich without a hitch. They were in London by the evening of April 9 and were soon established in comfortable lodgings in Albemarle Street.[24]

They could scarcely have arrived in London at a less propitious moment. Three days earlier Napoleon had abdicated. Gallatin wrote of it to his wife as "a blessing for mankind"; nevertheless it was "a matter of regret" that the differences between the United States and Great Britain had not been settled before it took place. As Baring and other London friends explained, the British now had at their disposal a formidable land and sea force; and it was likely that they would loose at least a portion of it against the United States before the summer was out. Gallatin was gloomy about the capacity of America to withstand such an assault, for London hummed with reports of sedition and separatism in New England. The British government was greatly pleased by the prospect that the eastern states would break off from the Union, and there seemed to be no doubt that it would delay peace negotiations in order to push the summer campaign and encourage New England separatism. Not even British public opinion could be counted on, Gallatin concluded sadly, for the mass of the population "know nothing of American politics," and "do not even suspect that we have any just cause of complaint." [25] They were convinced that the United States had entered the war only because the triumph of Napoleon had seemed certain and it wished to profit from it.[26]

Gallatin had been in London a fortnight when a joint letter from Clay and Russell, at Gothenburg, brought him great satisfaction. Under the terms of an old law the office of Secretary of the Treasury had been declared vacant because Gallatin had not filled it for more than six months. The President had named George Washington Campbell to the office and then had appointed Gallatin as a fifth commissioner to negotiate the peace.[27]

Gallatin at once urged Clay and Russell to shift the site of the negotiations from Gothenburg to London or Amsterdam or the Hague. Probably from Baring, he had heard that the English thought the Swedish city too much within the sphere of Russia. Clay's response arrived on May 13: a Dutch city was agreeable to him and Russell, but he was adamant against treating for peace in the capital of the enemy.[28]

Gallatin and Bayard approached Lord Bathurst in the Castlereagh government to present copies of their commissions to negotiate and to propose Amsterdam or the Hague.[29] Bathurst took them by surprise with a counterproposal: Would Ghent "in the Low Countries" be acceptable? [30] Gallatin and Bayard answered without waiting to consult with their colleagues; Ghent was agreeable. They would tell Clay and Russell to repair there as quickly as possible.[31]

Bayard, who felt friendless in London, took off at once to see the sights in Paris.[32] Gallatin, anxious to keep an eye on the shifting policies of the British government, moved with his son James to Portman Square. He found England a fascinating land. He passed delightful days visiting Parliament, the courts, the historic churches. Baring took him under his wing, introducing him to men he should know. He had pleasant talks with France's exiled lady of letters, Madame de Staël, and with Jeremy Bentham, the social philosopher.[33]

From conversations with London men of affairs, Gallatin reached a sober conclusion about the British temper that he forwarded to Secretary Monroe in mid-June: "To use their own language, they mean to inflict on America a chastisement that will teach her that war is not to be declared on Great Britain with impunity." In the circumstances, he advised the Administration not to insist upon recognition of American maritime rights, particularly the impressment issue for which it had avowedly gone to war. Thus, he urged, Britain would find herself fighting a war without an object, something she would not feel inclined to do for very long. Such advice represented a sharp reversal of the opinion he had expressed on sailing for Europe, that abandonment of impressment must be the *sine qua non* for peace.[34]

Hoping still that Czar Alexander would take a part in the mediation, he urged William Harris Crawford, American minister to France, to press the American case on the Czar, who was now in Paris. When Crawford found it impossible to reach the Czar he sought the help of the Marquis de Lafayette.[35] Lafayette reported that the Czar said that his forthcoming visit to London would afford "opportunities" to consider the case. Jeremy Bentham promised Gallatin that he would do what he could in an interview that had been promised with Alexander during the London stay.[36]

The Czar arrived in London in the middle of June, and Gallatin obtained an audience with him on the 17th. The Russian compound of Western enlightenment and Oriental autocracy received the American amiably, but stated that Great Britain had rejected three attempts he had made to mediate. "England will not admit a third party to interfere in her disputes with you," he said. "This is on account of your former relations to her (the colonial state), which is not yet forgotten." [37]

Except for a few days' visit to Oxford, Gallatin stayed close to London, making anxious inquiries at the Foreign Office in an effort to discover when the English mission would start for Ghent. He could not avoid the conclusion that the British were trying to use up time.[38] At last on June 18 came a note from William Richard Hamilton, the Under Secretary of State for Foreign Affairs, stating that the British representatives would depart on or about July 1 for Ghent, "where it was presumed they would find the American commissioners assembled." [39]

Gallatin calculated that the British would arrive about July 6. This would allow him time for a brief visit to Paris. He and James departed on June 21, and put up in the French capital on the Rue de Richelieu at a comfortable hotel with a good cuisine. Father and son passed almost a week visiting Lafayette, Crawford, and other Paris acquaintances, and observing the newly restored Bourbons in full panoply. [40]

The Gallatins reached Ghent early in the evening of July 6 and lodged at the best public house, the Hôtel des Pays Bas on the Place d'Armes. Adams, Bayard, Clay, and Russell were already there. [41] During the next few weeks the commissioners found the little city a friendly place. Its strategic position at the crossing of rivers and canals had caused it to become a foreign garrison point many times in the past; it was an Allied military post now, and soon its streets were ablaze with soldiers in the scarlet uniforms of Britain. The peace-loving citizens lavished hospitality on the visiting Americans; a local society serenaded them outside their hotel, and the judge presiding over a local court they visited interrupted the proceedings to deliver a warm address of welcome. [42]

The harmony that pervaded the American delegation delighted Gallatin. Adams and Bayard, who had had misgivings about each other, were on cordial terms. The congenitally austere Adams now addressed Gallatin in letters as "friend," underlining the word, and in letters not intended for Gallatin's eye spoke warmly of his "character," "talents," "his desire to accomplish the peace . . . his quickness of understanding, his sagacity and penetration and the soundness of his judgment." [43] Clay and Russell were agreeable too, although Russell tended to play sycophant to the Kentuckian. [44] Amid such good will they leased the Hôtel d'Alcantara, a three-story house on the Rue des Champs, large enough to allow each of them a private apartment; for it was clear to most of them that they would be in Ghent through the winter. [45] To kill the tedious days of waiting, Gallatin and his colleagues held daily conferences for study of the international law respecting impressments, which they believed would be the crux of the negotiations. Evenings they entertained the numerous Americans who passed through Ghent. [46]

But where were the British? The reports from London were disturbing. Castlereagh was said to have told a questioner in Parliament that negotiations awaited Gallatin's arrival from Paris, when he must have known the American had already been in Ghent more than a fortnight. [47]

Gallatin worried over rumors that the British were bent on delaying the talks as long as possible, confident that a general European peace settlement at the projected congress of foreign ministers at Vienna would improve their bargaining position. He was angry because the British seemed to be taking too seriously accounts of Federalist opposition to the Madison Administration.[48]

Then, on the evening of August 6, three British commissioners arrived in Ghent. The next morning their secretary brought a proposal that negotiations start the next day at their quarters in the Hôtel du Lion d'Or. At a hastily convened meeting of the Americans, Adams proposed that they reply that they would meet anywhere except at the Hôtel du Lion d'Or, because this location would seem to imply British superiority in the negotiations. Gallatin countered with a suggestion that the Americans propose the Hôtel des Pays Bas without ascribing any reason for the change. To this tactful invitation the British responded with alacrity.[49] At high noon on August 8, 1814, the Americans held a brief conference at their lodgings, then proceeded in a body to the Hôtel des Pays Bas, where they found the British group waiting.[50]

22. Peace at Ghent

1814

For quality and variety of talents, the five-man commission that entered the Hôtel des Pays Bas early on the afternoon of August 8, 1814, is unsurpassed in the history of American diplomatic relations.[1] Ablest of the group in the long, tedious negotiations was Albert Gallatin. This was the first time he had ever represented his adopted land internationally, and, through the spite of the Senate, his name was last instead of first among the commissioners. But at fifty-three he was the eldest and was the ripest in experience with men. He combined a thorough understanding of American temperament and aspirations and an instinctive comprehension of the ways of European courts that reminded perceptive men of Benjamin Franklin.[2] His calmness, his tact, his reasoned judgment had already impressed his colleagues; his intense application to detail and his unquestioned devotion to his country were to awe them as the days passed.

Nominal head of the commission was John Quincy Adams, just forty-seven, who had lived much of his life abroad as secretary to his father and as a diplomat in his own right. His intellect as well as his experience qualified him for international negotiation; his personality did not. He once described himself as "a man of reserve, cold, austere, and forbidding manners." [3]

Ten years younger and—on the surface—temperamentally a world apart was the tall, lanky Kentuckian, Henry Clay. He radiated charm, talked brilliantly, told salty stories, played cards and gambled, and pursued ladies zealously; but, when crossed, he entered into towering rages and brandished a sharp tongue. Clay had come to Ghent to find an acceptable end for a war he had done much to start, and to forward his ambition ultimately to become President. In Gallatin's view, his "great fault" was "that he is devoured with ambition." [4]

Gallatin's almost constant companion of fifteen months, James A. Bayard, nicknamed "Chevalier" by his colleagues, was counted on to represent the Federalist view at the peace table; of the group, he was coolest and most even-tempered; he was a solid man, able, though far from brilliant. Least known and least capable of the Americans was Jonathan Russell, a career diplomat who was merely competent and a hypersensitive man. Russell was fascinated by Clay but held himself aloof from his other colleagues.[5]

The three British commissioners were no match for these men. The one claim to fame of James, Baron Gambier, a handsome, white-haired admiral, was that he had commanded the fleet that bombarded the defenseless city of Copenhagen in 1807. Henry Goulburn was a rather reserved young man of thirty who had displayed a particular knowledge of Canadian affairs while serving as Under Secretary for the Colonies and War. A scholarly element was introduced by Dr. William Adams, a specialist in maritime law who was not without wit, and was fated to make a career of supernumerary roles.[6]

At the outset the Britons received the Americans with a surprising cordiality. They were merely carrying out Castlereagh's instructions to sound out their adversaries' general attitude, to report back to London, and await further instructions.[7] The truth was that Castlereagh considered them as messenger boys. The Americans might talk and write to Gambier, Goulburn, and Adams, but they were actually coping with Castlereagh, one of the greatest foreign ministers in British history; with Lord Bathurst, able Secretary for the Colonies and War; and with the Duke of Wellington, England's greatest soldier.

At dinner after the civilities of the first day's meeting, the Americans received two dispatches from Secretary Monroe, which significantly modified their instructions.[8] They had been written in late June, at a dark hour in American history. The British were landing to raid Maryland and Washington; an army under General Sir George Prevost was headed to Canada, for an invasion of the United States by way of Lake Champlain. Monroe authorized the commissioners to postpone the subject of impressment, and even to omit it from their negotiations if that would bring the war to a prompt end. This would be abandonment of the issue that had taken the United States—officially at least—into war; but Gallatin had already advised this course, and he was of course pleased by the instructions.[9]

Some of Gallatin's satisfaction wore off in the next two meetings, as the gulf between the two groups became clear. Monroe had instructed his negotiators to avoid discussion of the fishing privileges in Canada granted to Americans under the Treaty of 1783; Goulburn announced that these could not be "renewed" unless the British received an equivalent advantage. Monroe had directed the American commissioners to investigate definitions of blockade and the question of neutral rights; the British had been directed to shun these questions. Castlereagh had told his mouthpieces to make Indian "pacification" and Indian boundaries a *sine qua non* for peace; about these, the Americans had no instructions whatsoever.

When the British made plain this last object, the depression of the American commissioners deepened. It meant nothing less than creation of a buffer state between the United States and British holdings in North America. Both Americans and British were to be barred forever from purchasing land in the area, although the Indians might sell to others. Thus Castlereagh hoped to halt the transcontinental expansion of the American people.[10] Adams and Bayard tried their hands at reporting this disturbing news, but it took Gallatin's judicious and careful touch to rewrite the report to the satisfaction of all. It was forwarded to America on August 18.[11] The two commissions next faced each other on the morning of August 19 at the Chartreux, a former monastery where the British had taken up residence. During the interval the British commissioners had received a brief visit from Castlereagh himself en route, with an extensive retinue, to the European peace conference at Vienna. He left a new set of instructions and some fresh admonitions with his puppets.[12]

The Americans, remembering that Monroe's first instructions had called for the cession of all Canada to the United States, listened in pained silence as Goulburn read from Castlereagh's new directions. The Indian boundary set up by the Treaty of Greenville in 1795 was to become the permanent boundary between British America and the United States. Thus American settlement would be blocked forever northwest of a line from Cleveland to the vicinity of Louisville, Kentucky. The Canadian frontier was to be "rectified" by assignment of Fort Niagara and Sackett's Harbor to the British. The United States was to be prohibited forever from maintaining naval forces or land fortifications on the Great Lakes.

Gallatin pressed for further details. In what he thought "overbearing language" and a "peremptory tone," the British agreed that they did not seek any cession of land to Canada except a small section of Maine to be used for a military road to connect Halifax and Quebec. The northwestern boundary was to be adjusted to permit British navigation of the Mississippi; this treaty right was to be continued forever.

Was the Indian barrier still to be considered as a *sine qua non?* "Certainly." What, asked Gallatin, was to become of the American citizens— perhaps a hundred thousand—already settled beyond the Greenville line, in the state of Ohio and the territories of Indiana, Illinois, and Michigan? They would have to shift for themselves, said Dr. Adams.[13]

Morosely the Americans returned to their lodgings to frame a reply. Only Clay, the gambler and card player, observed that Castlereagh might be bluffing. Once again the final draughtsmanship fell to Gallatin, who insisted that "every expression that may be offensive" to the British be struck out. As transmitted on August 25, the note insisted, in firm and dignified style, that the establishment of an Indian boundary was not warranted by any principle of reciprocity, maxim of public law, or maritime right of the British. The surrender of "the rights of sovereignty and of soil of over one-third of the territorial dominions of the United States to a number of Indians, not probably exceeding twenty thousand" would be "instantaneously rejected" by Washington if the commissioners were so foolish as to forward the proposal. The other British demands "were above all dishonorable to the United States, in demanding from them to abandon territory and a portion of their citizens; to admit a foreign interference in their domestic concerns, and to cease to exercise their natural rights on their own shores and on their own waters."[14]

The Americans sadly supposed that this would terminate the negotiation. Gallatin, Bayard, and even Clay planned to embark for home at a French port after another visit to Paris. Then from the Chartreux came word that their note was being referred to London. Would they please be patient for an answer? Gallatin and his colleagues of course could not guess it, and even the puppets in the Chartreux were in the dark; but Castlereagh had decided to stall for time. Soon Prevost and his forces would be moving south into New York State, winning by arms what he sought in North America. It would be a simple matter to demand *uti possidetis* at the peace table.[15]

The next delaying action reached the Americans on September 5, in a memorandum sixteen folio pages long. Goulburn and his fellow commissioners elaborated their reasons for demilitarizing the Great Lakes and changing the Maine boundary. They flung out striking accusations: The United States was bent on aggrandizement in Florida, in Louisiana, and in the Indian territories. "It is notorious to the whole world that the conquest of Canada, and its permanent annexation to the United States, was the declared object of the American Government."[16]

The Americans, meeting through an entire afternoon, read over the memorandum with mounting outrage, all the more bitter because they knew in their hearts that the charges contained an element of truth. But they could and did sputter at the phrase "the declared object"; never had the American government publicly admitted that it sought to acquire Canada. Clay, the avowed expansionist, contended that the note ought to be answered with half a page. Gallatin undertook to analyze the contents and propose a reply. The others readily agreed.[17]

For the next four days the group labored, singly and in conference. Gallatin prepared his analysis and submitted the draft of a reply. In the light of the criticism it received, he revised his draft. Adams tried his hand at a version; the others studied both forms, commented, suggested. Adams later recorded that the finished work was principally that of Gallatin and himself, the others merely "altering, erasing, and adding": of what Gallatin wrote, approximately half was finally approved, only an eighth of his own composition being accepted. He believed that this was because Gallatin's work was "argumentative," he own "declamatory." [18]

The American note, as long as the one it answered, politely but firmly denied that acquisition of Canada was an "avowed object," or that the United States had sought to acquire land by any but peaceful means. It scored the British for encouraging the Indians to attack American settlements and declared that, as the Maine boundary was not at issue, the commissioners had not been authorized to treat about it.[19]

Eleven days passed. On September 20, Adams came to Gallatin's apartment with a reply he had just received. The two scanned it rapidly, then summoned the full commission. In what seemed to the group an "overbearing and insulting" tone, the British reply rejected the denial of imperialistic aims on the part of the United States and enclosed copies of proclamations issued in the field by Generals Smyth and Hull to support the charges in respect to Canada.[20] Although the note in effect abandoned most of the *sine qua non* position previously taken, all the commissioners were dejected by it.

Again Gallatin received the task of framing a reply. Adams wished to include a reference to the "religious and moral duty" of the United States to cultivate lands held by the Indians, but Gallatin gently brushed this aside as likely to invite ridicule.[21] After four days of discussion and rewriting, the group had agreed upon a note forthrightly reiterating the denial of American ambition for aggrandizement, and emphasizing that the proclamations of the generals in Canada were no more an official expression of the American government than that issued by the British admiral during the *Chesapeake* affair. The note insisted that the United States had always granted the Indians an equivalent for land taken from them, and denied that violation of the Treaty of Greenville by *some* of the Indians made it void. It admitted that the United States desired "to reclaim from the state of nature, and to bring into cultivation every portion of the territory within their acknowledged territories," and suggested that all nations, including Great Britain, should rejoice at the sight of a growing country and should reject the idea of a "perpetual desert" anywhere.[22]

During the anxious days that followed the dispatching of this note on September 26, Adams, the nominal chief and a man little given to praise, realized that Gallatin, by his knowledge and manner, had in effect become the head of the delegation. "Mr. Gallatin keeps and increases his influence over us all," he wrote to his wife. "For extent and copiousness of information, for sagacity and shrewdness of comprehension, for vivacity of intellect, and fertility of resource," he thought his colleague was without peer in either the British or American delegations.[23] He noted that, whenever a dispute had arisen over a particular paragraph in the discussion of a note, the majority had always supported Gallatin. He acknowledged that Gallatin had "more pliability of character and more playfulness of disposition" than himself, and so "throws off my heat with a joke." One day, when he got into an argument with Gallatin and Bayard over whether the Indian question should be considered as a *sine qua non*, Gallatin smiled and "in a tone of perfect good humor" told him that his argument was a *non sequitur*. "This turned the edge of the argument into mere jocularity," Adams recorded in his journal.[24]

The British Under Secretary Goulburn was impressed more by Gallatin than by any of his fellows, but for different reasons. He believed that Gallatin alone comprehended the strong public opinion in England against making an "unsatisfactory" peace. "This," he told Bathurst, "perhaps arises from his being less like an American than any of his colleagues." [25]

With the news that was dribbling into Ghent, Gallatin's even temper and jocular sallies were little short of heroic. The last week in September brought reports of severe military defeats. George Boyd, Adams's brother-in-law, arrived with a packet of letters that pointed up the desperation of the American government.[26] One from Secretary of the Treasury Campbell, dated August 1, asked Gallatin to attempt to negotiate a $6,000,000 loan in Europe, preferably with the Amsterdam firm of Willinks. Gallatin promptly wrote to the Dutch bankers to sound them out.[27]

On October 1 came the most awful news of all, borne by several persons who had read or heard reports in English newspapers about the "destruction of Washington" on August 24 and 25 by British forces. The next day Gallatin received a London journal giving the official British account of the burning of the Capitol, the President's house, and other public buildings.[28] It was weeks before he learned that his own house on

Capitol Hill had been burned by the invaders, although his furniture and other possessions, except for a box of valuable maps, had been saved.[29] On October 14 the British commissioners deepened the mortification of the Americans by sending them copies of *The Times* reporting additional reverses at Machias and Passamaquoddy Bay, at Michilimackinac, and near Plattsburg.[30]

Gallatin bore his grief and rage with reasonable calmness. But when Madame de Staël wrote from Paris for advice as to how to dispose of her holdings in American lands and stocks, his love for his adopted land overburst his reserve. The destruction of the Capitol and the Presidential mansion, he told her, was "an act of vandalism" unparalleled in twenty years of war in Europe; the British had committed it because, with the exception of certain cathedrals, England had no public buildings to compare with them. He advised her to hold on to her American property: the United States, he insisted proudly, always made good on national obligations.[31]

As if to mock his loyalty, the Willinks a few days later advised Gallatin against trying to float a loan "at this time" in view of "the late untoward circumstances and the fear of what may further happen." [32] When Crawford wrote that the same views were held at Paris, he reluctantly abandoned the attempt to obtain money.[33]

Writing to Secretary Monroe about his decision, the old fire chief could not resist giving advice as to how the conflagration ought to be fought. No more stock ought to be issued than was absolutely necessary, and none at an interest rate higher than 8 per cent; taxes, especially indirect taxes, ought to be increased; the issue of Treasury notes should be carefully restricted; a new Bank of the United States should be chartered if politically practicable; public lands should be disposed of through a lottery. He was about to make suggestions concerning the raising of a militia, but checked himself: "I perceive that my zeal carries me out of my sphere." [34]

The Americans had expected that the disaster at Washington would breed British truculence; but the note delivered late in the afternoon of October 8 was even more arrogant than they had feared. It made menacing references to the legality of the Louisiana Purchase: the King of Spain had been deprived of his proper role in the negotiations and had protested at the time; Great Britain had never been fully informed of the conditions of the sale. It again commented darkly on "aggrandizement" in the Floridas and offered assurances that the land the British sought in Maine was through unsettled areas. The most irritating feature of the note was an "ultimatum": both nations must agree to the elimination of the

Indian tribes as a factor in the war and to the restoration to them of all "possessions, rights, and privileges" they had enjoyed before the start of the war—or the negotiations would cease at once.[35]

During the long discussion on the next day, most of the commissioners agreed with Gallatin that the ultimatum would have to be accepted. Public opinion in the United States, especially in New England, would not support continuance of the war on that issue alone.[36] More important, if negotiations were broken off now, it would require months to arrange a resumption of peace talks. For two days Gallatin labored on an answer along these lines, which he presented to his colleagues on October 12.

Now Henry Clay took the initiative. Overnight he did a new draft, thoroughly characteristic of the man: brisker and more direct than the notes Gallatin and Adams had composed. This agreed to the Indian pacification provided peace were negotiated without delay. It proposed that the British transmit a list of all the points they thought imperative in a peace treaty and promised that the Americans would reply promptly in kind.[37] The entire commission agreed to this, Adams most reluctantly.[38]

The answer, like the note before it the work of Lord Bathurst, arrived on October 22.[39] Bathurst shied away from Clay's proposal that the points at issue be stated; he insisted that the British had revealed their aims at the first meeting on August 8. His government was now willing to discuss or not, as the Americans pleased, naturalization and impressment. He proposed the same settlement in the Northwest that the two governments had tentatively agreed upon in 1803; elsewhere, settlement on the basis of *uti possidetis*. He would now deny Americans access to the unsettled shores in Canada for drying and curing of fish—a privilege granted under the Treaty of 1783.[40]

Reading this note, the Americans angrily concluded that the British were still stalling for time, hoping for further gains in America that they might retain on the basis of *uti possidetis*.[41] Actually, as the Foreign Office's archives revealed when they were opened years later, the note represented a considerable retreat by the British. In the past they had claimed about half of Maine and the land on the south side of the St. Lawrence from Plattsburg to Sackett's Harbor. Now they sought only the exclusion of American fishermen from Canada and a right of way to Halifax. They had been persuaded to these concessions because they had just learned of British military reverses in North America.[42]

The Americans were of course quite in the dark as to all this and sought only to keep the negotiations alive. Gallatin drafted the reply that tersely reiterated their refusal to treat on the basis of *uti possidetis* or any principle involving cession of American territory; at the end of hostilities all territory captured by either side must be restored. Great Britain had not proposed a project for a treaty; the note therefore suggested that each nation submit one simultaneously.[43] The note went to the British on October 26. To avoid a delay Gallatin and Adams began to draw up a project for their side. Five days later came a new British note that merely deepened the Americans' conviction that the enemy was stalling for time: It stated that the British had no further proposals to make, and indicated they now awaited the American project.[44]

For the next week and a half the five Americans worked like beavers, sometimes together, sometimes separately. There were sharp differences of opinion that occasionally flared into fiery exchanges. Should they call for a commission to settle the impressment issue after the cessation of hostilities, or should they remain silent on the subject? Gallatin favored silence, and his view prevailed.

Over two issues—the right of Americans to fishing privileges in Canada and the right of the British to navigate the Mississippi freely—the words were even harsher. Clay, the spokesman of the West, wanted to deny access to the river, while Adams was anxious to preserve the fishing privileges on which much of New England's prosperity rested. Both rights were guaranteed in the Treaty of 1783. The British contended that, with the outbreak of the War of 1812, the treaty had ceased to be in effect —and their contention placed in doubt the very independence and sovereignty of the United States. When Gallatin suggested that both issues be referred to a commission for adjudication after the war, Clay paced up and down the chamber, shouting that he would not sign such a proposal.

The project that went to the British on November 10, composed by Gallatin, was an amalgam of the views of all his colleagues. The Mississippi was left unmentioned, and an accompanying note explained that the Americans were not authorized to discuss the fisheries question. It was proposed that the boundary issues be submitted to commissioners for settlement after the war, that the Indians be "pacified" by restoration to their 1811 status, that each nation assume responsibility for restraining the Indians in its territory. Perhaps the most important point was an insistence that at the end of hostilities each country must restore to the other land taken during the war.[45]

Weeks now passed while both groups awaited word from London. During the interval they enjoyed themselves socially. With the exception of Adams, the Americans attended performances of a company of indifferent French actors and some fairly good vaudevillians at the local theater. Gallatin and his son were especially enthusiastic attendants, and became frequent visitors backstage.[46] There were parties and balls of various sizes and types, which even Adams attended. Gallatin bantered with him about the attention he was paying to the ladies, and assured the fair creatures that Adams's demonstrations were purely Platonic. Adams rejoined that Gallatin should pay court to the ladies in his own way, and he would do the same.

The people of Ghent, it developed, had grown weary of the British musical airs that had become a standard feature in the city, and inquired, through their musicians, whether the Americans had a national anthem. To their embarrassment, the guests of the Hôtel d'Alcantara discovered that none of them could sing or play "Hail Columbia." But Peter, Gallatin's Negro servant, could whistle it. So, while Peter whistled, a musician wrote it down; the piece was orchestrated, and thereafter at parties and public functions it was played as "l'air national des américains à grand orchestre." [47]

Meanwhile the Americans received some heartening news. A dispatch from Secretary Monroe directed a firm hold on the principle of *status ante bellum* in respect to territory—an indication that the Administration was beginning to feel secure again. A ray of hope was shed on the government's financial situation by the appointment of Gallatin's friend A. J. Dallas to replace the inept Campbell in the Treasury. American newspaper accounts of the commissioners' first meetings in August, at which the British had disclosed their harsh demands, had rallied most of the Federalists and the lagging Democratic-Republicans behind the war effort. Even British public circles echoed indignation when accounts of the meetings were printed in the London newspapers. For a day or two Gallatin believed it likely that the British would break off the negotiations as a consequence. "If they do," he told Adams bitterly, "it will only relieve us from the humiliation of being kept here in attendance upon their insulting caprices and insidious tergiversations." [48]

The fact was that things were not going well for the British government. Two months earlier Lord Liverpool, the Prime Minister, had confided to Castlereagh that he wished they were rid of the war. Trade was in the doldrums, and he feared that complaints would soon be made against continuing the property tax merely "for the purpose of receiving a better frontier for Canada." [49] As the weeks passed, it appeared that the peace congress at Vienna was moving nowhere—except possibly to a renewal of the European war. Anxious to liquidate the American war, Liverpool approached Britain's great military hero, the Duke of Wellington, who was serving as ambassador to Paris, with the proposal that he lead a great military force to America in the spring. At first Wellington acquiesced; but as he learned more about the military situation across the

Atlantic he grew increasingly reluctant. Moreover, he told the cabinet members bluntly, Britain had no right to demand any cession of American territory. The cabinet determined to make peace as soon as practicable.[50]

Gallatin's first intimation of a British change of heart was in letters from Alexander Baring in the third week of November. The London banker hoped that before the next payment of interest on Louisiana stock became due in January "some favourable change may occur." Ironically he had developed moral scruples against "advancing sums for the service of a government with which we are at war." [51] The change of heart was made even clearer November 27 by a seemingly casual phrase in a note to the American commissioners. The British delegates wrote, "The undersigned have foreborne to insist upon the basis of *uti possidetis*, to the advantage of which they consider their country fully entitled." [52]

This was cheering. However, the comments by the British in the margins of the Americans' November 10 project for a treaty, which they now returned, made it plain that other issues remained as much in the air as ever. More days of spirited debate about the fisheries and the Mississippi followed in the chambers of the Hôtel d'Alcantara. Gallatin argued that to abandon the fisheries would only strengthen the New England disunion movement. Clay exploded that it was foolish to try to conciliate a people who would not be conciliated, and at any rate the Mississippi ought to be closed to the British. In the end, Gallatin's calm tact won the Kentuckian over. They agreed that the American objective should be a *quid quo pro*: American use of the fisheries in return for British use of the Mississippi.[53]

During these discussions it occurred to the Americans that it might be well to meet the British delegates again face to face. They made such a proposal by letter on November 30, and it was accepted within hours.[54] Conferences were held on December 1, 10, and 12, alternating between the Chartreux and the Hôtel d'Alcantara. Each meeting lasted two to three hours, and each time the same old points were quibbled over anew. But by December 11 Gallatin was convinced that the British government desired peace heartily, and that the stage was being set for a genuine proffer of peace as soon as the sign was given in London.[55]

With success apparently in the offing, Gallatin and Bayard persuaded Adams and Clay to drop their concern for the fisheries and the Mississippi; and on December 14 the Americans sent to the Chartreux a note expressing readiness to sign a treaty which would provide that all differences still unsettled would be negotiated later, with the understanding that there was no abandonment of any right previously claimed.[56] The next eight days were agonizing for the Americans, because virtually the same proposal on November 10 had been rejected.

A British messenger put the reply into Gallatin's hands late on December 22, and he conferred at once with his colleagues. The British agreed to omit the article dealing with the fisheries and the Mississippi, but insisted that the islands that they held in Passamaquoddy Bay should continue in their possession until a three-man commission, composed of a friendly sovereign, an American, and a Briton, decided to whom they properly belonged.[57]

This proposal to by-pass the fisheries and the Mississippi without a restatement of the Americans' claims irritated several members of the quintet at the Hôtel d'Alcantara, especially the volatile Clay. The "unseasonable trifling" of the Kentuckian exasperated Gallatin, and he told him so. The argument was resolved by a decision to propose yet another conference with the British, Clay alone stubbornly voting against the idea.[58]

The British agreed to come to the Hôtel d'Alcantara for another meeting. The eight commissioners met for three hours the next afternoon and quibbled only over details, discovering somewhat to their surprise that the main outlines of a treaty had been agreed upon through their weeks of exchanges. An overnight recess. Then, on the afternoon before Christmas, 1814, from four o'clock to half-past six, they reconvened at the Chartreux, carefully read and compared the six copies of the document, and affixed their signatures. Gallatin's was the last of the eight. Adams voiced the hope of all his colleagues that this would be the last treaty of peace that need ever be signed between Britain and the United States.[59]

Actually, the 2,250 words of the treaty, over which they had labored for almost five months, did no more than state that everything was to be as it had been at the time of the American declaration of war. The impressment issue, the declared purpose of the war, was not mentioned; the other moot questions were to be settled by commissioners to be appointed later. The important thing had been to obtain peace at once, and that had been accomplished.[60] Gallatin expressed his own feeling on Christmas Day, when he wrote to Secretary Monroe, more in relief than in triumph, that the treaty was "as favorable as could be expected under existing circumstances, as far as they were known to us." [61]

In other ways, time was to prove the treaty of value to both countries. It resolved a political and military stalemate and marked a turn for the better of relations that had been steadily deteriorating for a decade and a half. It allowed the United States to turn to the determination of its own destiny on the American continent, freed from fears of British designs to

create a neutral Indian barrier state and of British conspiracies with Indians within its borders. White settlement was speeded in the Old Northwest, and the ultimate opening of the Far West was hastened. At the
same time, the treaty allowed Britain to concentrate on coping with
changing trade conditions throughout the world.[62]

It was John Quincy Adams's painfully honest opinion that Gallatin had
made the largest and most important contribution to the conclusion of
the peace at Ghent.[63] Gallatin's contribution was not simply calm determination and tactful patience; it was even more his national view of the
interests of the United States, contrasting so sharply with the regional
views of the Yankee Adams and the westerner Clay.

This national feeling permeated an assessment of the War of 1812
that Gallatin sent to an old friend not long after: "The war has been
productive of evil and good, but I think the good preponderates. Independent of the loss of lives, and the losses of property by individuals, the
war has laid the foundation of permanent taxes and military establishments, which the [Democratic-Republicans] had deemed unfavorable to
the happiness and free institutions of the country. But under our former
system we were becoming too selfish, too much attached exclusively to
the acquisition of wealth, above all too much confined in our political
feelings to local and state objects. The war has renewed and reinstated the
National feelings and character which the Revolution had given, and
which were daily lessened. The people now have more general objects of
attachment with which their pride and political opinions are connected.
They are more American: they feel and act more as a Nation, and I
hope that the permanency of the Union is thereby better secured." [64]

23. The Aftermath of Ghent

1814-1816

The moment the British had indicated that they were ready to sign a treaty of peace, Gallatin's alert mind raced on to the question as to what he and his colleagues should do, once the formalities were out of the way. A passage home on the *Neptune*, of course, but not before April. This would give them three months to take in sights on the Continent and to complete an as yet unfinished piece of business. The government had granted them full powers to conclude not only a peace treaty but a treaty of commerce with Britain. With his colleagues' concurrence Gallatin drew up a proposal for negotiation of a trade treaty, which they sent to the Chartreux several days after the signing of the peace.[1]

During the next few days a round of parties and balls were given in honor of both Americans and British by the citizens of Ghent. The festive air was clouded only by a senseless argument between Clay and Adams over which should be custodian of the documents of the negotiation; Gallatin sided with Adams on the ground of well established precedent. Finally Bayard and Clay departed for Paris, and Russell for Sweden, leaving Gallatin to enjoy a quietly pleasant interlude at Ghent.[2]

Ever since touching foot in Europe eighteen months before, Gallatin had longed to make a sentimental visit to the city of his birth. At last, on the morning of January 12, 1815, he set out for Geneva, accompanied by his son James. As their coach wound through the Alps toward Lake Geneva, his customary imperturbability deserted him; it was a moving experience for the native to return to the city he had forsaken thirty-five years before.

For nearly a month Gallatin, as a man who had achieved distinction in a republic in the New World and had helped bring it the honorable peace it sorely needed, was fêted and toasted by the Old World republic that had endured its own ordeal at the hands of the French and was now free and independent once more. The Council of State sent a delegation to extend an official welcome. There were banquets and ceremonies. There were meetings, painful and pleasant, with relatives and old friends who had survived tribulation. There were visits to the haunts of his youth so that he might show them proudly to his son.[3]

By March 7 he and James were in Paris again, at the Hôtel de l'Empire where Bayard and Clay were lodging. They arrived at a crucial moment in history. Only hours before, word had come that Napoleon had quitted exile at Elba and had landed with a small military force at Cannes, progressing northward and raising troops. Four days later news came by way of London that an American army commanded by Andrew Jackson had repulsed a British invading force at New Orleans on January 1, before news of the settlement at Ghent reached the New World. Even had Jackson lost the battle the British would have been content to abide by the peace treaty;* but his victory thrilled every American, and especially the three diplomats at the Hôtel de l'Empire.

On March 20 they learned that the terms of their treaty had reached Washington on February 13, had been ratified by the Senate four days later, and had been proclaimed in effect by the President. In the afternoon the Bourbon Louis XVIII left Paris, and in the evening, while Gallatin and Adams were attending a performance of *L'Ecole des Femmes* in the almost empty Théâtre Français, Napoleon entered the city.

Amid all these excitements, Gallatin received calls from old friends anxious about their fortunes in so fast-changing a world: old General Lafayette, willing to try to get along with Napoleon once again; General Turreau, "utterly ruined" since he had served as French minister to Washington.[4] Then, on April 1, he and James departed for London to join Clay in awaiting word of British reaction to their proposal for a commercial treaty.[5]

2

On taking up lodgings in Hanover Square, Gallatin found a new budget of arresting news: President Madison had appointed him minister to France, in place of Crawford, who was intent upon returning home; Adams was to move to London; Bayard was to take the St. Petersburg mission.[6] The notion of continuing his diplomatic career was not a shock to Gallatin. He had found his European experiences fascinating and already had toyed with the idea of asking for the St. Petersburg post if

* Recently some American historians have argued that a defeat at New Orleans would have upset the settlement at Ghent. They seem to overlook the consuming desire of the Liverpool government to be done with the war in America.

Adams left it.[7] But he had no idea whether his wife would like this, nor how it would fit in with his obligations in America. He was resolute in any case to sail home with Clay on the *Neptune,* however short his stay might be.

British sullenness over the Ghent treaty had largely disappeared, and Gallatin and Clay found London cordial. Even more agreeable was an invitation from Lord Castlereagh to his St. James's Square residence for informal conversations on April 16.[8] In their first face-to-face meeting with Castlereagh, the handsome, smiling, and inscrutable foreign minister, the two Americans learned that their old antagonist had two matters on his mind. He wished to apologize and make reparation for the "unfortunate event" that had lately occurred at Dartmoor Prison, where British soldiers had fired upon and killed a number of Americans restless from long incarceration as prisoners of war. He wished also to speed the return home of the American seamen in British custody. Steps to solve these two problems were worked out amicably and expeditiously.[9]

Gallatin and Clay then introduced the subject that had brought them to London. Castlereagh agreed that a new trade treaty should be discussed "unofficially" and proposed that the Americans pursue it further with their opponents at Ghent, Henry Goulburn and Dr. William Adams, as well as Frederick John Robinson, the capable Vice President of the Board of Trade.

After a pleasant but inconclusive meeting with the three bureaucrats[10] came weeks of tedious waiting. Gallatin occupied himself with visits to acquaintances in London and the country, and tried his hand at a project for a treaty.[11] Only after he and Clay sent a note making it clear that they were impatient to be on their way home was a series of conferences held.

At these sessions Gallatin, who assumed leadership, disclosed two American objectives. One was abandonment by the British of impressment, which he thought urgent now that Britain was again at war with Napoleon and the United States was again a neutral carrier. In return for this concession, the United States would exclude British seamen from service in its merchant marine and would set up restrictions as to blockades and to trade with belligerents. The second objective was entirely commercial: Britain would abandon all discriminating duties against the United States; treat her as a "most-favored nation"; provide for the regulation of trade between the United States and the British West Indies and between the United States and the Canadian provinces; and open the British East Indies to American trade "on liberal principles." The latter goal represented a first attempt to implement a policy just embarked upon by Congress for the reciprocal removal of alien discriminations in direct trade with foreign nations as a means of expanding American commerce.[12]

The British commission proposed that the United States accord to British subjects the privilege of trading in furs with the Indians in American territory. Gallatin and Clay instantly recognized that such a concession would compromise one of the chief advantages they had gained at Ghent—interdiction of British influence with the Indians. They rejected it firmly.[13]

Soon Gallatin found himself repeating in many ways his experiences at Ghent.[14] There were countless conferences at his lodgings with Clay and with Adams, who arrived in London to assume his duties as minister. They discussed the drafts for a treaty he had framed; Clay contributed his customary bluster; but Adams, feeling that he was not familiar with all the issues, held aloof. There were conferences with the three Britons at the Board of Trade offices, outwardly cordial but marked by aggravating impasses on subjects about which the Liverpool cabinet was reluctant to treat. There were long and irritating delays between conferences while the British negotiators attended to other, presumably more pressing, business; there were irritating waits while the British referred Gallatin's proposals and counterproposals to their superiors.

All the while the Americans were frequent guests at dinner parties given by Goulburn, Castlereagh, the Earl of Westmoreland, and Alexander Baring. At these affairs Napoleon's designs, military engagements against the Allied Powers, and defeat at Waterloo were breathlessly discussed. Clay, fretful about each delay, urged breaking off negotiations. Gallatin kept pleading for a little more time, convinced that patience would be recompensed. In the end his tenacity was rewarded. Terms were agreed upon early in July.

Just before the signing, Gallatin became embroiled in an argument with Adams about the order in which the two powers and their representatives were to be named in the heading, text, and signatory passages of the agreement. The British were inclined to go ahead with copies that named themselves and their sovereign first in every instance. Closeted alone with Adams, Gallatin argued that they should acquiesce in this, lest the whole negotiation be thrown "in confusion." Besides, he pointed out, the United States had agreed to this practice in its previous treaties with the British. But Adams, determined that his country should receive full recognition as a sovereign and independent state, stoutly insisted that the European custom of alternating names be followed. "I will not sign the treaty without the alternative observed throughout," he shouted at Gallatin. Gallatin gave in, and so did the British, marking a small but significant advance in the diplomatic position of the United States.

The agreement signed at the office of the Board of Trade on July 3, 1815, was officially called a "convention" instead of a "treaty." This was at Gallatin's insistence, because of its limited scope. It fell far short of the aims he had held out at the start of the negotiation. To a degree it was merely a four-year stopgap renewing the arrangements in effect between the two nations before the war. Many of the arrangements were those of Jay's Treaty, which had expired in 1807—the treaty which, ironically, Congressman Gallatin had so strongly denounced twenty years earlier! The convention included provisions for freedom of commercial intercourse between the United States and the European (but not the North American nor the West Indian) possessions of Great Britain reciprocally on the same terms as nationals; for consuls in each other's dominions; for prohibition of discriminating duties by either nation against the commerce and ships of the other, except in the colonial dominions of Great Britain. It also allowed American ships to trade directly between the United States and the East Indian ports of Calcutta, Madras, Bombay, and Prince of Wales's Island (Penang) on most-favored-nation terms.

Adams, who was indignant about the traditional trade policies of the European nations, disapproved of this convention because it did not grant everything that the United States sought. He signed only to humor his colleagues. Clay was apathetic about the provisions affecting the East Indian ports, but agreed to their inclusion to please Gallatin. Thus the convention has with good reason been called Gallatin's convention.[15]

Even Gallatin regarded his handiwork with only moderate satisfaction. However, as he later told President Madison, "the British Government appeared rather desirous" to keep Anglo-American trade "controuled by their own municipal regulations, which they thought we would not counteract." That they had abandoned this attitude was proof, he felt, that the British government was now friendly and also respected the United States.[16] He believed that the convention included one material gain, the prohibition of discriminating duties—"a policy which, removing some grounds of irritation, and preventing in that respect a species of commercial warfare, may have a tendency to lay a better understanding between the two nations on other points." [17]

Time was to appraise Gallatin's work even more highly than he did himself. The article regulating American trade with Great Britain proper was certainly the best to that time; the provisions of the convention as a whole were to be successively renewed and are in effect to this day; non-

discrimination, first provided for here, was to be become one of the enduring principles of American foreign policy.[18]

On May 1, before the trade negotiations began, W. H. Crawford arrived in London for a brief visit. Gallatin and Clay, expecting to join
him and Bayard on the passage home aboard the *Neptune*, sent their bag-
gage and Gallatin's servant Peter to Plymouth. Crawford left for Plymouth three weeks later, and in June, while the negotiations were in full
train, Gallatin and Clay received word from him that he had ordered the
vessel to weigh anchor because Bayard was deathly ill.[19]

Clay was beside himself with rage, but Gallatin took the development
calmly. Crawford's decision was well taken, for Bayard died a day after
reaching the United States. Left to fend for themselves, Gallatin and Clay,
accompanied by James and John Payne Todd, sailed from Liverpool on
the *Lorenzo* on July 22.[20]

The passage was slowed by a gale, and it was September 1 before Gallatin was back in New York. He forwarded the documents of the London
negotiations promptly to President Madison, then retired to Mrs. Nicholson's country place at Greenwich to report to his beloved Hannah and his
other relatives on his twenty-nine months of wandering.[21]

3

Except for an appearance at a "splendid banquet" given by the Democratic organization at Tammany Hall in honor of himself and Clay, followed by a visit to the city theater on September 5,[22] Gallatin remained in
seclusion at Greenwich through the next six weeks, pondering what his
next step should be. Besides the French mission, which President Madison
had granted him time to consider, he had two other possibilities. One was
a seat in Congress for which the Democratic organization in Philadelphia offered to back him.[23] The other was a share in the business enterprises of John Jacob Astor.

The New York shipper and fur trader outlined his magnificent offer
in a letter early in October. Estimating his capital employed in trade at
$800,000, he proposed to sell Gallatin a one-fifth interest, charging him
the legal interest until his share was paid for. "Of course you know it is
not possible to say what the profits may be, but I presume it will not
be extravagant to calculate from $50,000 to $100,000 clear per annum
after interest and all expenses are deducted." [24]

These sums were most attractive, because family finance assumed a depressing importance in Gallatin's talks with his wife. His private income

amounted to only $2,500 a year. It would cost $2,000 to transport his family to Paris if he accepted the foreign mission. The United States allowed its ministers only $9,000 a year—far less than the cost of living in the French capital.[25]

He was particularly concerned about the prospects of his children. James was almost nineteen, not too young to be thinking about a career. Albert Rolaz was almost seventeen, in his junior year at Nassau Hall, the college at Princeton, where he was a better than average student.[26] Frances, thirteen, had been attending a school for young ladies at Philadelphia. Gallatin feared that if he took them abroad they "would return . . . having acquired expensive and foreign habits and lost the opportunities of entering into the active pursuits by which they must support themselves, and myself too old to assist and too poor to support them." [27]

For a time he dallied with the idea of turning down all the offers and taking up residence at Friendship Hill in the spring. The glassworks was profitable, and perhaps the other property could be made so. Hannah listened without enthusiasm.

In mid-October Gallatin, accompanied by James, went to Washington for four weeks of conferences with President Madison and Secretary Monroe.[28] When he gave them reasons for not accepting the French mission, they tried to devise ways to ease the financial strain and urged the increasing importance of the Paris post. "The present state of the world urges the strongest reasons in favor of our being ably represented," Monroe kept insisting.[29]

In the end, Gallatin declined the offers of the Philadelphia Democrats[30] and of Astor: the former on the ground that he could not support his family on a Congressman's salary, the latter because, much as he would enjoy the income of a prince of commerce, he would not enjoy the life of a prince of commerce.

By early February, 1816, he decided to go to Paris.[31] To his old chief Thomas Jefferson he wrote: "I will [not] conceal that I did not feel yet old enough, or had I philosophy enough to go into retirement and abstract myself altogether from public affairs." [32] He went to Washington early in March to receive his official instructions.[33] Back in New York in April, he started making arrangements for the supervision of his property while he was abroad.[34]

After so long an absence abroad and with the prospect of a similar absence of indefinite length, he realized how much his old friendships meant to him. While he had been in Europe three friends of his youth had died: Savary de Valcoulon, Thomas Clare, and John Smilie.[35] His oldest American friend, John Badollet, still served as register of the land office at Vincennes. Gallatin asked President Madison that "if the attempt should be made, he may not be removed without sufficient cause and inquiry. This, I know, is the same thing as a request that he should not be removed at all." [36] He also asked the President to indulge Astor's desire for appointment as one of the commissioners to receive subscriptions to the Bank of the United States recently chartered by Congress, recalling the New Yorker's patriotic assistance at the time of the $16,000,000 loan.[37]

One old friendship, however, was sorely strained. At the Tammany Hall banquet in September, 1815, A. J. Dallas had told him that, in spite of a great improvement in the government's finances during the eleven months he had headed the Treasury, the crisis was not yet over.[38] The government had survived the last year of the war and the months during which the Army and Navy were being converted to a peacetime basis only by a continuation of the wartime taxes and the floating of a $12,000,000 stock issue. More than three-quarters of the stock had been paid for in state bank notes, worth about sixty cents on a specie dollar— for, shortly before Dallas became Secretary, specie payments had been suspended by every incorporated bank in the country, except in New England, and the Treasury had adopted a similar policy.

Dallas, like many of his contemporaries, was by no means sure that convertibility of paper money into gold and silver was indispensable for a sound national economy.[39] Even so, he had announced several months before Gallatin's return that he was working toward the resumption of specie payments by the banks and the Treasury. He was attempting to persuade the bankers, by various inducements in the gift of the government, to hasten the day of resumption.[40]

Gallatin thought that Dallas's methods were much too casual. "We are guilty of continued breach of faith toward our creditors, our soldiers, our seamen, our civil officers," he complained in a letter to Jefferson. "Public credit, heretofore supported simply by common honesty, [declines] at home and abroad; private capital placed on a still more uncertain basis; the value of property and the nature of every person's engagements equally uncertain; a baseless currency varying every fifty miles and fluctuating everywhere—all this done, or at least continued, contrary to common sense and common integrity, not only without necessity or law, but in the face of the Constitution itself." [41] The remark about the fluctuation of currency every fifty miles was based on personal experience: he had been vastly annoyed, while traveling to Washington in October, to have to provide himself with local currency as he moved from place to place.[42]

Gallatin thought it unforgivable that Dallas had not forced the resumption of specie payments by April, 1815, when it might have been easily accomplished. "The remedy becomes also more difficult every day it is delayed," he complained, "and if delayed much longer will not be done at all, and it will place us in a situation similar to that of Great Britain." [43] He confided to Secretary Monroe that he was more concerned about the matter than about any other public problem. "I feel as a passenger in a storm, vexed that I cannot assist. This I understand to be very generally the feeling of every statesman out of place." [44]

The difference of opinion about resumption of specie payments created a marked coolness between Gallatin and Dallas, and they no longer saw each other socially. Yet Gallatin realized that the Secretary was the spokesman for, rather than the leader of, men who were half-hearted about specie payments. He was troubled by the attitude of the directors of the new state banks, many of whom exerted great influence in local Democratic circles. Their language, he complained, "is similar to that of Peter to his brothers in the tale of the tub. They insist that their bread (God grant it was even bread!) is good, substantial mutton, that their rags are true solid silver; and some of them do already damn to all eternity every unbeliever." [45]

Gallatin's plans for going to France were far advanced by mid-April, when he received a surprising and flattering letter from President Madison. Dallas had resigned the Secretaryship of the Treasury effective the following October. "Are you willing again to take charge of a Department heretofore conducted by you with so much reputation and usefulness?" the President inquired.[46]

Gallatin thought the idea over and then declined. He had "a volume of reasons." [47] The reasons he gave to the President were in large part rationalizations. His plans to go to France were now so well made; he did not want to disappoint his Geneva relatives, who were anxious that he come for a "last visit." And "there is, for what I conceive a proper management of the Treasury, a necessity for a mass of mechanical labor connected with details, forms, calculations, &c., which, having now lost sight of the thread and the routine, I cannot think of again learning and going through. . . . I believe that an active young man can alone reinstate and direct properly that Department." [48] He believed that William Lowndes and John C. Calhoun of South Carolina were such men and, equally important, would resist pressures from the "paper-tainted." [49]

There were deeper and more compelling reasons for declining the Treasury portfolio which Gallatin did not voice. The Jeffersonian revolution of 1801, of which he had been a chief architect, had long since spent its force. Much of it was now woven, together with certain Federalist ideas, into the essential fabric of the American tradition. But other forces were at work—an aggressive nationalism and a burgeoning indus-trialism among them—with which he might in considerable degree sym-pathize, but for which, because of his age, his background, and his temperament, he was unable to serve as a catalyst. In the era America entered at the close of the war, these forces were in the ascendant.

It was better that he retire to a position where he might continue to serve his country with honor and ability, but more quietly and incon-spicuously. He sailed for France June 11, 1816, with his family and six servants on the sloop of war *Peacock*, "heavy of heart" but confident that he would soon be back in America.[50]

24. The French Mission

1816=1823

When the *Peacock* touched Havre after "a prosperous voyage" on July 2, 1816,[1] Gallatin entered upon what was by all odds the most pleasant period of his public service, and the least useful.[2] It lasted, not the brief time he had expected, but more than seven years, from his fifty-fifth to his sixty-second year.

The septennium was so pleasant because most of it was spent in or near Paris at a time when the French capital was reclaiming its ancient position as the queen of European cities. With the Bourbons again securely on the throne, it was a city of ease and elegance, quiet and prosperous, still virtually untouched by the Industrial Revolution. The wit, the wealth, and the beauty of all the Western world flocked to Paris; and Gallatin, with the double advantage of representing both the rambunctious republic of the New World and the aristocratic traditions of the Old World, supplemented by his perfect command of the French language, could meet all on an equal footing.[3]

Pleasant, too, was the easy-going routine of a diplomatist's life. Gallatin had always insisted that he was by nature lazy and would never do any work if he did not force himself to do it; he proved it in practice now. These were especially delightful years because his family was with him. Hannah, his "city belle," was seeing a true metropolis for the first time in her life; three-quarters of a million men and women, speaking all tongues and knowing all ways of life, strolled its boulevards. She confided to Dolley Madison that she was "very much pleased with every thing I see in this wonderful place. The Palaces and Hotels [are] more splendid than you can imagine." [4] But the ostentation of the city troubled her: "every thing to interest the eye, nothing the heart." [5] The continental Sunday offended her puritanical upbringing, and she refused to attend court ceremonies on the Sabbath. To make Paris more congenial to Protestants, she also took the lead in establishing an American church there.[6] The children were divided in their reactions to Paris: James, who served as his father's secretary, and Frances, who attended school, reveled in its delights, but Albert Rolaz pined for the rusticity of western Pennsylvania.

The Gallatins had three residences during their seven years in Paris, all within a small neighborhood on the Left Bank where the old aristocracy resided in almost indignant seclusion. Within six weeks of arrival, they settled in a "fine furnished hotel" at 21 rue de l'Université. The commodious mansion belonged to Jean Jacques Régis de Cambacérès, who, having been president of the Senate under Napoleon and a close adviser of the Emperor, hurried off into exile upon the restoration of the Bourbons.[7] Later they moved to 87 rue du Bac, where they resided until May, 1821. Then they went for the summer to the little village of Verrières adjoining the Versailles forest, eight miles south of Paris. Gallatin, who during his French years underwent several bouts with rheumatism so severe that he required a crutch to walk, hoped that he might benefit from the sulphur baths at Verrières, but Hannah fretted every second about the remoteness of the place. The following winter, quarters in Paris were hard to come by, and they took an apartment in the rue Monsieur, close to the Boulevard des Invalides, which Frances complained was in "one of the most retired and dull quarters" of the city.[8]

Living was unconscionably expensive. With the Restoration, many well-to-do English families settled in Paris, sending up all costs, especially servants. Soon the one-time Pennsylvania Congressman, who had spoken against large allowances for diplomats, was complaining to Washington about his "scanty compensation" and urging that, to "obtain the correct information" the American government required on European affairs, he must suitably entertain the French officials and the two dozen foreign ministers now stationed at Paris.[9] He complained to James Monroe, that it was "mortifying to see the ministers of every petty German King enabled to keep a higher state than yourself." Try as he might, he could not reduce his expenses below $14,000 a year.[10]

Gallatin discovered he enjoyed some advantages that compensated for a lean purse. One was ability to speak French like a native. Another was the habit of reading voluminously, especially in history. In the United States he had supposed that his ability to lead in intellectual discussions resulted from the fact that Americans were not a book-reading people; now he was surprised to learn that his love of books enabled him to hold his own in talk with Europeans and even to surpass them.

With his wife's help Gallatin struggled to stretch his lean purse for the respectable and tasteful hospitality befitting a proud young republic. Lafayette enjoyed it often, and so did Madame de Staël, and Mr. and Mrs. Alexander Baring—men and women whose attributes were intellectual as well as social. He also saw much of Baron von Humboldt, whom he esteemed for "varied and profound learning . . . the excellence of his heart and simplicity of his manners." Gallatin's closest association with blue-blooded society was a distant cousin of whom he was personally fond, a royalist of the deepest hue who, serving at Paris as minister of the King of Württemberg, accepted from the French the title Comte de Gallatin.[11]

In a day when few Americans traveled in Europe, Gallatin went out of his way to be hospitable to those who passed through Paris. Among the young New Englanders making the Grand Tour, who were later to make reputations, were Edward Everett, the precocious Harvard Greek professor who had just received a doctorate in philosophy from the University of Göttingen, and Theodore Lyman, future Boston mayor and philanthropist. George Ticknor, known later as the historian of Spain, came with a letter from Jefferson, and Gallatin intervened with the highest officials to extricate him from the toils of a French confidence man.[12] One June day in 1821, Washington Irving, who already had an international reputation as a man of letters, brought to Verrières young George Bancroft for an afternoon's visit. Bancroft thought it the most pleasant excursion he had ever made, not only because of the excellent dinner served, but because of the "playfulness and gaiety" with which their host showed off the lovely countryside. He long remembered the light and amusing fashion in which Gallatin ridiculed the German sceptics and the pedantry of footnote scholarship.[13] Toward the end of the Paris years, Hannah Gallatin became particularly friendly with Elizabeth Patterson Bonaparte, the indomitable Baltimore girl whose marriage to Jerome Bonaparte had been annulled by his eldest brother the Emperor. There was always a plate on the table at the Gallatins for Betsy.[14]

Perhaps the most pleasant interlude in these easy-going years was the two months of 1817 in which Gallatin, his wife, and his children visited Geneva. He was again received with the affection and honor due to a man who had served two republics well. It delighted him to see the changes time had wrought in his native city. "Seventeen years of French yoke have united the parties as far as union is practicable in a free country," he reported to Badollet. The distinction between classes had been wiped out; the government was now more representative of all the citizens.[15]

On other counts during the Paris years satisfaction was not unmixed with regret. He was no longer in the hurly-burly of American politics. Letters from friends in 1817 told him that he had been much mentioned as a likely person for Secretary of State in the cabinet of President James Monroe. Monroe chose John Quincy Adams for the office—which may have been what Gallatin had in mind a decade later when he told his son, "Mr. Monroe is the only person that I have a right to charge with ingratitude, but I am far from being the only one." [16] Adams apparently sensed Gallatin's feelings, for the dispatches between them, and even their few personal letters, were always businesslike in tone.

Relations with Adams were clearly not helped by Gallatin's warm and continuing friendship with W. H. Crawford of Georgia, who had been the principal contender with Monroe for the Presidency. Crawford had stepped aside, confident that he would get the office when Monroe retired. Accepting the Secretaryship of the Treasury as a consolation, Crawford soon found himself vying with Adams and indeed virtually every other member of the cabinet, for the succession.[17] Hopeful that Gallatin might fit into his future plans, Crawford showered him with gossipy letters on political and economic subjects, local and national.[18]

Gallatin had more unalloyed satisfaction with his role as dean of the American diplomatic corps in Europe. Minister at London was Richard Rush, who owed his political start to Gallatin; minister to the Netherlands was Dr. William Eustis, in whom Adams had little confidence; minister to Spain was first George W. Erving and later John Forsyth, both ranking low in Adams's estimate. Through the years Gallatin advised and aided these colleagues on delicate problems; and his analyses of the changing European scene were read avidly in Washington.[19]

One of Gallatin's best sources of information at Paris was the remarkable Carlo Andrea Pozzo di Borgo. Born in Corsica, Pozzo di Borgo had served the Bonaparte brothers during their rise to power, and later had devoted himself to the Bourbon cause; now he was a count and peer of France but was serving Alexander of Russia as minister. He and Gallatin had many things in common as representatives of nations that regarded jealously Britain's attempts to influence French domestic and foreign policy, and as citizens of the world.

2

Pleasant though Gallatin's seven years in Paris were, they were relatively futile. Paradoxically, it was the very weakness of the French government that enabled it to thwart his objectives.

From the beginning he had misgivings about a regime that had been restored largely through British influence.[20] Louis XVIII was a gouty old gentleman likely to do Whitehall's bidding; it would be dull to serve as a diplomat at a satellite court. But Gallatin did his best to keep an open mind. As he told his old friend Lafayette, "every friend of rational liberty and humanity must rejoice at the overthrow of the detestable tyranny. . . . My attachment to the form of Government under which I was born and have ever lived never made me desirous that it should, by way of experiment, be applied to countries which might be better fitted for limited monarchy." [21]

At the start, the Bourbon monarchy was both limited and moderate. Richelieu and Decazes, Louis XVIII's first two premiers, owed their positions to the conciliatory, commercial-minded middle class that controlled the Chamber of Deputies and enacted relatively liberal legislation. Within two years of Napoleon's defeat the huge war indemnities had been paid off, and the Allied occupation forces removed from French soil. Slowly but steadily the temper of the nation swung to the right, bringing in as premier in 1822 the Count de Villèle, an extreme royalist.[22]

It was Gallatin's task to reach an understanding with these governments on two matters. He was instructed to seek a lump-sum settlement as compensation for American shippers whose vessels and more than $7,000,000 worth of cargoes had been seized, confiscated, or destroyed at sea by the French under the Berlin, Milan, and other decrees of Napoleon; the American government would distribute it among the numerous claimants. His second objective was a commercial treaty that would place trade between the two nations on "the most friendly footing"—a reciprocal agreement that would apply to both the French mainland and the colonies.[23]

When Gallatin first presented the spoliation claims in 1816, Premier Richelieu tacitly admitted their justice but expressed the hope that the United States would not press them until France's economy had improved; but, as prosperity returned, Richelieu began to deny even their justice. Gallatin persisted, setting forth the case patiently and cogently at least once a year. By the time Villèle came into office the goal was even more remote. Foreign Minister Chateaubriand went so far as to contend that the spoliation issue must be linked to the settlement of a number of long-forgotten boundary disputes arising out of the Louisiana Purchase. After seven years Gallatin could only recommend to his government that the American claimants submit petitions to Congress and stir up a tension between the two nations that the French would be anxious to quell.[24]

The prospects for the second goal—a satisfactory commercial treaty—were never bright. In order to restore the French merchant marine, swept from the seas during the Napoleonic years, the Bourbon government in 1814 had enacted tariff duties so high and navigation regulations so stringent that it was impossible for American shippers to compete profitably with the French in the Franco-American carrying trade. Monroe warned that unless retaliatory regulations were adopted, or unless the French could be induced to agree to a reciprocal abatement of discriminations, the French merchant marine would in time monopolize the trade.[25]

Gallatin allowed the matter to slide during his first year at Paris, hoping that the French merchants would force their government into a negotiatory mood.[26] Nothing of the sort happened. By 1819 he was reporting to Secretary Adams that in the preceding eighteen months not a single American vessel had arrived in France and in the last half year eight French vessels had brought in cargoes of American produce.

Negotiations, Gallatin assured his superiors, would avail nothing with the French in their present mood. A drastic step must be taken: Congress must enact a retaliatory tonnage duty on French vessels equal to the average of the special duties levied on American goods imported into France in American bottoms. Fearing that the French might retaliate against these retaliations, he suggested that the President be authorized to increase American duties in the same proportion as the French increases; it might also be provided that American increases would cease when the French repealed theirs.[27]

But when President Monroe and Secretary Adams forwarded Gallatin's recommendation to the House Committee on Commerce, it only opened Pandora's box. Urged on by interested constituents, Congress in May, 1820, raised the duties not to $12.50–$17.50 a ton as Gallatin had suggested, but to $18 a ton. Ignored were Gallatin's recommendations for Presidential increases and automatic mutual rollbacks. Instead of equalizing the discriminatory duties, the new law gave the United States as great an advantage as France had previously enjoyed.[28]

The Administration had intensified Gallatin's problems by another tactless step. In order to impress Congress and the American public with the necessity for retaliatory duties, it had allowed the press to publish part of his correspondence, including a statement that he did not believe the French government would budge on its trade policy unless forced to do so.[29] "I fear," Gallatin complained as soon as he learned of this, "that the expressions in question will wound the pride of the government." [30]

The French government, despite Gallatin's pleading, regarded the new American law as "hostile" and enacted an increase in tonnage duties in July, 1820, its purpose frankly retaliatory.[31] One interesting provision of the law was a discount of 10 per cent in duties on goods imported into France from any port in America outside the United States. This was a deliberate attempt by the French to arouse the cotton-growing states of the South to hamstring the Administration.[32]

When Gallatin proposed that both nations repeal all their discriminating duties, Pasquier, Richelieu's foreign minister, made an ingenious counterproposal: that the two countries reduce their duties in such a way that half of the carrying trade would find its way to the bottoms of each merchant marine. This, Gallatin realized, would require a basic decision by the Administration in Washington. He gathered and sent off data about French trade to facilitate the consideration. He pointed out to Secretary Adams that American shippers operated far more economically than the French and so could afford to pay as much as $2.30 a ton in duties and still compete.[33]

Within the Monroe cabinet, Pasquier's proposal created a sharp division of opinion. The President and Secretary Crawford favored pursuing the matter further; but Secretary Adams, who in the end had his way, insisted that no departure be taken from the pattern of reciprocal trade treaties he was trying to build up.[34]

At this point the French took the matter out of Gallatin's hands. Their minister to Washington, Baron Hyde de Neuville, closeted himself with Secretary Adams during the spring and summer of 1821 and emerged with an agreement whereby discriminatory duties would be readjusted at once and then reduced by annual gradations until they disappeared entirely. But either country could denounce the arrangement whenever it liked.[35]

When Gallatin heard the details he was surprised and a little offended. The temporary discriminatory duties were more advantageous to France than even the French government had hoped; he was doubtful that the merchants of Havre and other seaports would allow the agreement to operate long enough for the discriminatory duties to cease completely.[36] As it turned out, he need not have been grudging in his approval of Adams's work. It was ratified by both nations, and was still in effect one hundred thirty years later, its nondiscriminatory objectives fully achieved.

Relations between Gallatin and Secretary Adams were further strained by a border incident between Georgia and Spanish Florida. The Spanish had created a port on their side of St. Marys River, the boundary, hoping for an increase in French trade through Florida to the United States that would reenforce their own control over the province. In September, 1820, American authorities in Georgia seized a French vessel, the *Apollon*, on the ground that it was evading United States navigation laws. The *Apollon* was on the Florida side of the river at the time. When the

French and Spanish ministers at Washington protested, Secretary Adams replied that, under the terms of the 1795 treaty, Spain had undertaken to preserve peace along the Spanish-American border, and therefore the United States was within its rights in making the seizure.[57]

Pasquier summoned the American minister to his office for explanations in the spring of 1821. Gallatin could not stomach Adams's position on the issue, and he doubted that any European government would accept it. Thereupon he did something no good diplomatist should do: he framed a line of defense of his own. The United States had taken over the area in which the *Apollon* was seized when it took over Amelia Island during the War of 1812, he told Pasquier, because the Spanish government had shown itself incapable of administering it efficiently and of preserving it from Great Britain. Supporting this argument, he cited examples of comparable acquisitions by other nations, especially Spain and Portugal.

This thesis did not satisfy Pasquier nor, as a matter of fact, Gallatin himself. After he had delivered it, he went back to the legation and wrote to Adams that the position he had outlined to Pasquier was not tenable; but he added that Adams's position was not valid, either. He hoped the issue might be referred to an independent tribunal for adjudication. Perhaps, he added, American spoliation claims might be presented for settlement at the same time.[38]

Gallatin's letter created another division in the Monroe cabinet. The testy Adams lost his temper.[39] Crawford at first embraced the position Gallatin had expounded to Pasquier and proposed that the federal attorney in Georgia use the idea in defending the collector of the port of St. Marys in the legal action brought by the owners of the *Apollon*; but later he changed his mind.

Although the whole affair was subsequently settled with the purchase of Florida by the United States, Adams found it difficult to forgive Gallatin for questioning a position he had adopted as Secretary of State. "Gallatin is a man of first-rate talents, conscious and vain of them," he wrote in his diary in November, 1821, "tortuous in his paths, born in Europe, disguising and yet betraying a supercilious prejudice of European superiority of intellect, and holding principles pliable to circumstances, occasionally mistaking the left- for the right-handed wisdom." [40] For eight months he peppered Gallatin with criticisms of his conduct in the case, to all of which the minister replied with temperate and reasonable explanations.[41] The *Apollon* case was ended, but the rancor lingered on.

3

During his French mission, Gallatin was called upon to conduct diplomatic negotiations with two other European countries. First, in the autumn of 1817, he made an attempt to improve American commercial relations with the Netherlands.

Like France, the Netherlands could not compete with the United States for the transatlantic carrying-trade as a result of the Napoleonic wars. With the passage of the American law of 1815 authorizing reciprocal agreements for the abolition of discriminating tonnage and cargo duties, Monroe directed William Eustis, minister to the Netherlands, to attempt to negotiate such an agreement, hoping that France and Great Britain might follow suit. The Dutch, however, preferred to facilitate trade relations by means of a new commercial treaty and invited the United States to send commissioners to negotiate.

Gallatin and his family were on their familial visit to Geneva when instructions reached Paris for him to join Eustis at Brussels as a commissioner to negotiate a trade treaty generally similar to the 1815 London convention. The agreement should run eight years and, if possible, apply to the Dutch colonies as well as the Netherlands proper.[42]

Accompanied by his family and a retinue of servants, Gallatin left Paris on July 19. In Brussels he and Eustis were entertained by the King and presented their credentials. Baron Van Nagell, the foreign minister, intimated that the Dutch were in a mood to make concessions, but preferred that the negotiations be conducted at the Hague.[43]

It was not until August 28 that Gallatin and Eustis sat down at the Hague with the Dutch commissioners, Johannes Goldberg, director general of the department of commerce and colonies, and Johannes Cornelis Van der Kemp, solicitor general of the high court of justice at the Hague and an expert on colonial affairs.

Although the official papers exchanged were always in both English and Dutch, conversations were conducted mostly in French, to the great advantage of Gallatin as compared with Eustis. The talks were far longer than the Americans had expected; the Dutch took out time for their regular office duties each day, and, contrary to the impression given by Van Nagell, they were still uncertain what concessions they should make.[44]

On one matter the teams had no difficulty in agreeing: the provisions of the 1782 treaty between the United States and the Netherlands should be extended to territories since acquired: Louisiana in the case of the United States, Belgium in the case of the Netherlands. The Americans had no instructions on this point but felt warranted to agree to this mutually beneficial modification.

Agreement upon the commercial arrangements proved to be more difficult. Gallatin was determined that this treaty was to be no mere copy of the English convention of 1815; that, in line with the present aim of the United States, trade between the two countries and their colonies should be established without discriminating duties and on the basis of complete reciprocity. The Dutch were prepared to abolish discriminating duties on cargoes carried directly between the two countries; but they were so dismayed by the recent American preeminence in international shipping that they refused to grant reciprocity on cargoes carried into either country from or to a third country.

When Gallatin and Eustis proposed reciprocity in the trade with the Dutch colonies in the East and West Indies, the Dutch were adamant against abandoning their ancient mercantile system. It was hardly fair of the Americans to ask this, they protested; after all, the United States had no colonies according to their definition of colonies. Some sort of just equivalent ought to be offered. In private conversations they intimated that they desired a reduction on our high tariff on gin, cheese, and other articles of Dutch growth and manufacture.

As Gallatin and Eustis were not authorized to make a treaty merely for the extension of the 1782 treaty, they proposed on September 20, after four weeks, seven meetings, and numerous exchanges of letters, that the negotiations be "suspended" and the matters at issue referred to the two governments. In the report sent to Washington on September 22, they expressed little hope of persuading the Dutch to abandon their mercantile system for the present, but privately acknowledged that the Dutch had a just grievance in the failure of the United States to reciprocate certain concessions in tonnage duties the Dutch had granted.[45]

Gallatin recognized that the negotiations had been well-nigh fruitless and was impatient to get back to his regular post. He and his family left for Paris as soon as the report was completed. The following year Congress reciprocated the Dutch favors; the arrangement remained in effect for two decades, by which time the Dutch were quite capable of holding their own in the competition for the carrying trade.[46]

4

Gallatin's second diplomatic excursion during his Paris service took him to London. Late in the spring of 1818 a letter from Secretary Adams reminded him that the commercial agreement which had been negotiated with Great Britain in July, 1815, would expire in the summer of 1819. President Monroe was anxious that a renewal for an eight-year period be negotiated in time to be presented to the next session of Congress. He hoped, moreover, that a number of issues left in the air at the time of the Treaty of Ghent might at last be resolved. It was the Administration's desire that Gallatin join Richard Rush, the minister at London, in the negotiation.

Between the lines could be read a number of good reasons for the request. Rush, though able, was young and was a relative newcomer to diplomacy: Monroe, Adams, Crawford, and other cabinet members agreed that the older and wiser Gallatin would be of great help. Moreover, Gallatin had kept in close touch with the changing political situation in Britain through correspondence with both Rush and Adams.[47] Rush, who admired him, welcomed the proposal.

But were the British in the mood to negotiate? At Gallatin's suggestion, Rush visited Castlereagh to find out. Castlereagh was to attend a congress of foreign ministers at Aix-la-Chapelle in late August but said that, if Gallatin came to London quickly, he would get the negotiations under way before his departure. They would then be continued by Gallatin's old antagonists Frederick John Robinson, president of the Board of Trade and now a member of the cabinet, and William Goulburn.[48]

This was indeed heartening. The Gallatin family arrived at the London Hotel in Albemarle Street on August 16, 1818, and later took lodgings in Queen Anne Street.[49] Castlereagh invited Gallatin and Rush to North Cray, his country showplace thirteen miles out of London, for the afternoon and night of August 22.

At North Cray, flanked by Robinson and Goulburn, the foreign minister was in his most charming mood. "Let us," he said, "strive so to regulate our intercourse in all its respects, as that each nation may be able to do its utmost towards making the other rich and happy." The Americans responded cordially. The whole range of issues between the two countries was touched upon in a survey of the formal negotiations which were to begin on August 27.

To the pleasure of the Americans, Castlereagh himself brought up the thorniest issue, impressment, and expressed the hope that the British cabinet would adopt his recommendation that the practice be forsworn. He made a proviso or two that drew protests from Gallatin and Rush; but they rejoiced that he was even willing to discuss abandonment of the principle.

The visit had its social aspects: a stroll across the well manicured lawns of the estate; an inspection of the menagerie containing lions, ostriches, kangaroos, and—as Rush exclaimed—"I know not what strange animals!"; dinner, conversation, and parlor games *en famille*. All in all, it was an English country week end the Americans long remembered.[50]

Rush found delight even in the long ride back to London, just listening to Gallatin. He recorded in his journal: "His station as Minister Plenipotentiary at Paris has added to all his other information, much insight into the courts and cabinets of Europe. A keen observer of men, and possessing a knowledge of books, which his knowledge of the world has taught him how to read, his stores of conversation are abundant and ever at command. . . . In his flow of anecdote and reflections I had an intellectual repast." [51]

Further encouragement was given to the Americans on September 1, when Rush received a request to call on Castlereagh in his office as he packed for Aix-la-Chapelle. The foreign minister told him that the cabinet was willing, albeit reluctant, to abandon impressment; but that it was adamant that there be no discussion of the British "Rule of 1756," under which a belligerent that had prohibited its colonial trade to foreign nations in time of peace could not reverse the practice in time of war so as to take advantage of the immunity of neutral carriage.[52]

After Castlereagh's departure the four negotiators held frequent meetings, exchanged innumerable notes, projects, and counterprojects. Meanwhile a number of cabinet members and members of the diplomatic corps gave dinners in honor of Gallatin and Rush.[53] It soon became distressingly plain that Castlereagh had overstated the amenability of the cabinet. On October 16, after eight weeks of talk, Gallatin felt so let down that he delivered a formal protest to Goulburn that they had reached agreement on only two points, and that the important one of these, the renewal of the 1815 convention, could have been handled by Rush alone. He planned to leave for Paris within five days. He did not state that his virtual ultimatum was based on his anxiety to conclude an agreement before the conference at Aix-la-Chapelle could weaken the American bargaining position.[54]

The British recognized the note as an ultimatum, and within four days agreed to a project of a convention covering four important matters.[55] First was renewal of the trade convention of 1815 for a ten-year

period. The Americans had hoped to persuade the British to abandon
their ancient mercantile system by opening all their colonies to Americans. There were now commercial interests in Britain that favored this,
counting on the resulting increase in trade to more than offset any
loss of revenue. But the Liverpool cabinet cherished the mercantile
system too much to agree. Gallatin believed that if the convention of
1815 had not expired so soon, British public opinion would have obliged
it to make concessions on this point.[56]

The British agreed also on an issue that had been left unresolved in
the Treaty of Ghent, despite the efforts of Gallatin and Adams—whether
the "liberty" of Americans to use certain Canadian coasts for curing and
drying fish had survived the War of 1812. Gallatin later confessed to
Secretary Adams that no subject of the 1818 negotiations had caused so
much anxiety as this. Although the liberty was dear to the Yankee Adams
he had directed Gallatin and Rush, at President Monroe's insistence,
to accept half a loaf if necessary: to yield the claim to use of all the inshore fisheries in recognition of the right to fish on certain specified
coasts "for ever." The diplomacy of Gallatin and Rush made such a
concession unnecessary. The British agreed to give fishing liberty "for
ever" to Americans on the southern coast of Newfoundland from Cape
Ray to Ramea Island, on the western and northern coasts of Newfoundland from Cape Ray to Quirpon Island, on the shores of the Magdalen Islands, and on the coasts of Labrador from Mount Joly northward
indefinitely—but without prejudicing the exclusive rights of the Hudson's
Bay Company. Americans were also to be permitted "for ever" to dry
and cure fish on the unsettled shores of Labrador and southern Newfoundland. These were substantially the liberties Americans had enjoyed
before the War of 1812.[57] Unhappily, in Gallatin's haste to be done with
the negotiation, the article covering the fisheries was drafted so poorly
that there was almost continuous diplomatic controversy over the matter
until 1910.[58]

Another troublesome issue left over from the War of 1812 upon
which agreement was now reached was restitution of or compensation for
the Negro slaves the British had carried away in their invasion of the
United States. The Americans contended that some of these had been resold into slavery in the West Indies. It was now agreed that the matter
was to be arbitrated by a sovereign friendly to both nations.

Still another agreement clarified the Canadian-American boundary in
the West. The Treaty of 1783 had carried the line only as far as the Lake
of the Woods, in present northern Minnesota. Arguing on the basis of
some faulty expressions in the treaty, the British tried to drop the line

south from the Lake of the Woods to the navigable part of the Mississippi River—a definition that would allow them to navigate the whole length of the river. Gallatin and Rush firmly resisted. Instead, they proposed that the boundary be extended westward from Lake of the Woods along the line of 49° north latitude as far as the Pacific Ocean. But the British had long made claims to an area vaguely known as "Oregon," partly in the interest of the Hudson's Bay Company, which maintained trading posts there; and Oregon lay in the area west of the Rocky Mountains between 45° and 49° north latitude. A compromise was agreed upon: the boundary was to continue along the line of 49° north latitude from the Lake of the Woods to the Rockies—or the "Stoney Mountains," as the negotiators called them. West of the Rockies, the land and rivers were to be open to citizens and vessels of both countries for a period of ten years.

On impressment, after the high hopes Castlereagh had raised, the Americans were severely disappointed. Robinson and Goulburn proposed articles for a separate treaty whereby impressment would be forsworn by both nations on the "high seas" for ten years, with two important provisos: the arrangement might be terminated at any time on six months' notice, and nothing in the treaty was to be interpreted as protecting vessels of either nation that should be in the ports or under the "maritime jurisdiction" of the other. Despite the limitations, Gallatin and Rush were willing to accept this proposal if it prohibited impressment on the "narrow seas" as well as the "high seas," and if the phrase "as acknowledged by the law of nations" were inserted after "maritime jurisdiction."

The project for a treaty on impressment became shoaled on other points. One British proposal specified that within eighteen months of the "signature" of the treaty each nation should deliver to the other a list of all naturalized seamen known to be in its service at that date; thereafter, no person might claim the privileges given to a naturalized citizen of that country under the terms of the treaty. Gallatin and Rush protested that this was impracticable because of defects in American federal and state registration laws. Out of fear that the provision might become in effect *ex post facto* legislation, they asked that the terminal time for registration date from the ratifying of the treaty rather than the signing; but Robinson and Goulburn feared that the delay might encourage hordes of British seamen to acquire American citizenship.[59] Gallatin concluded that a treaty on impressment at this time entailed for each nation "great and reluctant sacrifices." The question was dropped.[60]

The Anglo-American convention—covering transatlantic commerce, fisheries, the Canadian boundary, and abducted slaves—signed on October 20, 1818, was generally applauded in the United States and was readily passed by the Senate.[61] Despite shortcomings, it represented a marked advance in relations between the two countries. It allowed Great Britain to continue to concentrate its diplomatic energies on Europe while the United States drove for a settlement of its southern border disputes with Spain without fear of British interference. Because it defined the border of the United States as far west as the Rockies, it was perhaps the most important agreement ever reached in the history of Canadian-American relations.

5

Gallatin hurried back to Paris two days after the signing of the convention. One reason for his haste was the crucial state of Spanish-American relations—a matter for which he felt responsibility because the American minister to Spain was most inept, because France was itself involved, and because Paris was the center of the European diplomatic arena. Spain was determined to retain control of Florida—a province which Americans more and more coveted—and made no secret of her desire to regain Louisiana, which she contended the French Emperor had stolen from her and illegally sold. She was also trying to reestablish her aegis over her colonies in the Western hemisphere, which had declared their independence during the wars, and to whose resistance the United States was giving moral support. Gallatin had conscientiously carried out Secretary Adams's instructions to make it clear to all diplomats with whom he came into contact that the United States would bitterly resent interference by France, Britain, or any other European power in Spanish-American relations.[62]

The task was not made any easier by General Andrew Jackson, the high-handed hero of New Orleans. In 1818 Jackson led a military force into Florida as far as Pensacola in order to wipe out a base for Indian forays into American territory. Gallatin reported sadly to Washington that the incident had gravely harmed the American cause in European capitals.[63] But when Richelieu and his deputy, Hauterive, suggested that France might mediate between the two countries, he repeated Adams's ingenious line that Spanish violations of the 1795 treaty had warranted Jackson's action, which was the only possible means of preventing open warfare along the border, with the ultimate extermination of the Indians.[64]

The news from Aix-la-Chapelle in the autumn of 1818 was better than Gallatin had expected. The Allied Powers made it clear to Spain that she could not count upon their support in her designs in America.[65] Finally, in February, 1819, a treaty on which Adams had been engaged a long time with Onis, the Spanish minister at Washington, was signed. It gave the United States undisputed claim to both East and West Florida as well as Louisiana. But Gallatin had to report to Adams in May that the French government and the Spanish ambassador at Paris misinterpreted the treaty as including a tacit promise that the United States would not recogize the independence of the Spanish-American colonies then in revolt.[66]

Revolutions in Spain and the colonies kept Gallatin anxious for the next three years, watching, listening, and writing to Washington. On March 8, 1822, President Monroe announced recognition of the independence of La Plata (Buenos Aires), Chile, Peru, Colombia, and Mexico—a step that surprised Gallatin but which, he reported, was "not generally unfavorably received." [67] As he explained to Jefferson, he had tried and in large measure succeeded in inculcating on the ministers of Great Britain, France, and Russia "a conviction that, as we did not meddle with their affairs, and had even abstained from any interference with those of South America, either by way of advice or assistance, we would not permit any of an open active nature on the part of any European power." [68]

6

So the seven European years passed, with their small successes and their mild frustrations, their pleasant acquaintanceships and their faint ennui. America was a long way off and came to seem a little unreal, despite occasional visits from friends and more or less regular correspondence. John Jacob Astor passed through Paris several times, so enthralled with the Old World that he considered settling there permanently.[69] Hannah's niece, young Mary Few, came for the winter of 1821–1822 and reported on her return to America that the Gallatins seemed to be heartier and happier than she had ever known them.[70] John Randolph of Roanoke visited them on a European sojourn in 1824–1826, and their frayed friendship was fully repaired.[71]

The passing of the years became evident in sad ways. Judge Nicholson died in 1817; and in the same year A. J. Dallas begged for an expression of Gallatin's "attachment and friendship" which Gallatin sent promptly, but too late for receipt. Thomas Jefferson, although his gnarled wrists and finger joints pained him whenever he picked up a pen, periodically reassured Gallatin that he retained "still the same affection for my friends, and especially for my ancient colleagues which I ever did, and the same wishes for their happiness." [72]

What troubled Gallatin most about his residence abroad was that it prevented his children from being raised as Americans. He was particularly impatient with the education his sons were receiving. Albert Rolaz, who continually pined for home, was sent in 1821 to New Geneva, to be taught by his uncle James Witter Nicholson "to do some active business and how to deal with mankind, previous to entering some important business for himself." [73] His parents sorely missed him, the more because he was a wretched correspondent. They had no fears about his getting into mischief; but Gallatin, recognizing in him some of his own characteristics, worried that he might waste his time. "Pursue some useful study, such as may suit your taste and be of some advantage to you," he begged in September, 1821. [74]

The troubled parents were vastly relieved to receive assurances the following summer from Hannah's sister Maria Montgomery that Albert Rolaz was leading an exemplary life: "He is remarkably industrious, his amusements are those a young man should indulge in—boat building . . . and the pleasures of the chace." But he was most attentive to the family farm and mills at New Geneva, "which I am told he manages remarkably well. . . . He is well, reads law, and exercises his acquirements on his chemical apparatus. The people in the Western Country are struck with his resemblance—his disposition, his manner, and his every thing, even to the stoop of his shoulders"—to his father. [75]

By the autumn of 1822 Albert and Hannah were convinced that James was "wasting time to no purpose" in Europe and ought to return to his native land. Very much against his will, he was about to leave Paris to join his brother at New Geneva, when grief overcame his parents. "I have been so agitated by the expectation of my child leaving us," Gallatin confessed, "that I could write only the necessary dispatches." It was determined that they all should return to America in the spring. [76]

This decision was not reached without conflicting emotions in the family councils. Both Hannah and Frances remained infatuated by France and Europe; but for Frances too the life of an expatriate presented a difficult problem. Just turning twenty, she was widely admired as a beauty in Paris court society; but her chances for a suitable marriage were negligible. As Betsy Patterson Bonaparte remarked: "the beauty of Venus would never marry any one in France without money," and the Gallatins had no fortune with which to endow her. At any rate, the credit of husband-seeking American women was low since the recent exaggeration by one family of its daughter's expectations; the revelation of this deception after the wedding had rocked Paris society. So Hannah and Frances reluctantly reconciled themselves to returning to America.[77]

Gallatin was eager to go home. He wrote to President Monroe that he was "heartily sick" of European affairs. "I understand too well the language and have mixed too much with the statesmen of this country to be able to preserve perfect silence and neutrality" on the issues of the day.[78]

The consummation of the Franco-American commercial convention by Secretary Adams and Hyde de Neuville in June, 1822, would provide the excuse for terminating his mission at Paris. He could see no prospect of settling the claims for indemnities against the French or of improving Spanish-American relations; he could honorably go home.[79]

At the last minute Gallatin wavered. As he was winding up his affairs he received a letter from Adams stating that the convention was "so partial and so temporary" that it would be wise to sound out the French on an arrangement "more permanent and comprehensive." [80] He concluded that perhaps he should take just a six-months' leave of absence, leaving Daniel Sheldon, secretary of the legation, in charge. While in America he might get the boys started in some business or profession and attend to his personal affairs.[81] Disturbing word had come about the recent failure of the New Geneva Glass Works and mismanagement in the affairs of the Bank of Columbia, in which he owned stock.[82] Then another letter from Adams stated that President Monroe felt that, because of "the present critical condition of European affairs," it would be better for Gallatin to postpone his visit indefinitely.[83]

What was in the minds of Secretary Adams and President Monroe? No one in Paris diplomatic circles knew of any crises present or approaching.[84] Puzzled, Gallatin went ahead with his official adieux—whether permanent or temporary, he could not be certain. The French government officially expressed regret at his departure.[85] Betsy Patterson Bonaparte summed up general feeling when she wrote that he was "highly respected by every one in Europe and excessively admired for his talents. I fear that it would be difficult to represent the country half so well, if he should decline continuing minister." [86]

On May 21, 1823, the Gallatins sailed from Havre aboard the *Montano* for a homeland to which they had become strangers.[87]

25. An American Interlude

The homecoming proved to be far less pleasant than the Gallatins anticipated. New York City greeted them on June 23, 1823, with a heat wave so debilitating that Gallatin had to take it easy for a month in the relative salubrity of "Mama" Nicholson's house on Tenth Street at the corner of Sixth Avenue in Greenwich Village.[1] There, surrounded by a large and devoted family, he pondered the dismal news that awaited him.

The word received at Paris about the glassworks proved to be true. The enterprise he had counted upon to provide him with a small but steady income had failed utterly. The Bank of Columbia and several other banks in which he held stock were in deep waters; there would be little or no return from them. He had directed Albert Rolaz to arrange for an addition to the house at Friendship Hill to make it a suitable residence for retirement; the costs far exceeded his expectations. And of course he had dipped deep into his reserves to meet the expenses of diplomatic life at Paris. Reluctantly he concluded that he could not afford to return to France. Hannah and Frances and James might groan, but they would have to put up with the rusticity of Fayette County.[2]

He broke the news of his decision to Secretary Adams during a five-day visit he and James made to Washington in July.[3] Later, after buying a "handsome carriage," they started out for New Geneva. He found the journey over the Alleghenies exhausting and the situation at the end of it distressing. The mills, the farm buildings, and the fields were, James wrote, in "a most deplorable state"; the grounds at Friendship Hill, "overgrown with elders, iron weeds, stinking weeds, laurel, several varieties of briers, impenetrable thickets of brush, vines, and underwood, amongst which are discovered vestiges of old asparagus and new artichoke beds, and now and then a spontaneous apple or peach tree"; the new construction, the handiwork of an Irishman, was in "an Hyberno-teutonic style, so that the outside . . . with its port-hole-looking windows, has the appearance of Irish barracks, whilst the inside ornaments are similar to those of a Dutch tavern." Albert Rolaz, "well and happy as the day is long,"

317

was living in bachelor's disarray with four guns, a pointer, three boats, two riding horses, and a small pet colt with which to amuse himself.[4]

Gallatin at once drew up a list of readings to keep his son's mind busy through the winter: Blackstone's *Commentaries*, Montesquieu's *L'Esprit des Lois*, Adam Smith's *Wealth of Nations*, Priestley's lecture on history, Rousseau's *Social Contract*, Voltaire's essay on universal history, John Adams's defense of the American constitution, and Mably's *France*.[5]

As always in western Pennsylvania in the autumn, the air crackled with political talk, and inevitably Gallatin was drawn into the old game. Because several Federalist newspapers reported that he favored their gubernatorial candidate, he reluctantly issued a statement supporting the candidacy of John Andrew Schulze, the regular Democratic nominee.[6] The tricks of the party politicians disturbed him, but he found it impossible to abandon "a cause to the support of which my life has been devoted, and which I think inseparably connected with that of the liberty and amelioration of mankind in every quarter of the globe." [7]

So that there would be no doubt about his plans, he notified President Monroe formally that, because his affairs were "still more complex and deranged" than he had expected, he would not return to Paris.[8] In November, he and James set out for Baltimore and a still uncertain future.

2

It was probably in late November or early December, while the Gallatins were visiting Hannah's relatives, the John Montgomerys, at Baltimore, that Senator J. B. Thomas of Illinois paid a call that was to open a new political adventure. The tenor of his talk confirmed what Gallatin had long thought: in his seven years abroad political winds unlike any he had known had begun to blow across America.

During his entire public life a leading concern of Gallatin and his colleagues had been to defeat the Federalists at the polls and on the legislative floor. Now, in the last months of 1823, the Federalist party was dead, fatally discredited by the New England secession movement and the victory of Andrew Jackson at New Orleans. Like his contemporaries, Gallatin was too close to perceive precisely what was happening—that the party and tradition of Jefferson, although still nominally regnant under the leadership of President Monroe, had spent its force. The new issues and forces, the rivalries of new personalities, the new party alignments that had emerged during the War of 1812, were dominant; but the shape of things to come was still difficult to discern.

Who would be Monroe's successor in the Presidency? There were five leading aspirants, as Gallatin had been hearing from one of them, Secretary of the Treasury William H. Crawford.[9] Three were members of Monroe's cabinet. There was a tradition that the Secretary of State should move up to the office; and John Quincy Adams was anxious that it be followed. In the marked coolness that had recently developed between them Gallatin now weighed the Secretary's qualifications: "A virtuous man, whose temper, which is not the best, might be overlooked; he has very great and miscellaneous knowledge . . . ; but he wants to a deplorable degree that most essential quality, a sound and correct judgment . . . although he may be useful when controuled and checked by others, he ought never to be trusted with a place where unrestrained his errors might be fatal to the country."

Another aspiring cabinet member was Secretary of War John C. Calhoun of South Carolina, now an advocate of nationalism through a protective tariff and a system of internal improvements. Gallatin deemed him "a smart fellow, one of the first amongst second-rate men, but of lax political principles and of a disordinate ambition not over-delicate in the means of satisfying itself." Another advocate of nationalism, who called his version "the American system," was Speaker of the House Henry Clay. Recalling Ghent and London, Gallatin conceded that Clay had "faults, but splendid talents and a generous mind."

Another man much spoken of for the Presidency was Andrew Jackson, whom Gallatin had first known as a fellow Congressman straight out of Tennessee—"a tall, lank, uncouth looking individual, with long locks of hair, hanging over his face and brows, while a queue hung down his back tied in an eelskin." [10] While Gallatin was in Europe, the querulous, self-willed commander of New Orleans and Pensacola had become a folk hero. "An honest man and the idol of the worshippers of military glory," Gallatin acknowledged, "but from incapacity, military habits, and habitual disregard of laws and constitutional provisions, altogether unfit for the office." Because the West was split between him and Clay, Gallatin thought it was impossible for either to be elected.

The aspirant Gallatin admired most was of course Crawford. He had first warmed up to the tall, rugged Georgian, whose manner bespoke decision, more than a decade earlier when Crawford had energetically promoted his Treasury program in the Senate.[11] During the twelve years in the Treasury, Gallatin had looked anxiously "for some man that could fill my place there and in the general direction of the national concerns." Crawford was the only man who seemed to fill the bill; he "united to a powerful mind a most correct judgment and an inflexible integrity; which last quality, not sufficiently tempered by indulgence and civility, has prevented him from acquiring general popularity."

In 1816 Crawford's name had been entered in the Presidential caucus against Monroe, and he might very well have been nominated had he not indicated he was prepared to wait for eight years. He was now the choice of the Virginia dynasty—Jefferson, Madison, and their close friends—for the Presidency in the election of 1824.[12] Soon after returning from Paris, Gallatin received letters from the Sage of Monticello, now in his eighties, praising Crawford as the true heir to his tradition—"a friend to the barrier of State rights as provided by the Constitution against the danger of consolidation." [13]

When Senator Thomas visited Gallatin at Baltimore a blight had been cast over Crawford's candidacy. Early in September, on a holiday at Senator James Barbour's estate in Orange County, Virginia, Crawford was stricken with a paralysis that left him almost blind and quite incapacitated. His friends informed the press that he had "the rheumatic fever and a bilious complaint" but insisted that he would soon be as fit as a fiddle.[14] By the middle of November, Crawford had returned to Washington, but was accessible only to confidants.[15] The confidants now looked about for a Vice Presidential nominee who would add strength to his candidacy and even assume the burden of the Presidency in the event that Crawford did not recover. Senator Thomas asked, Would Gallatin consent to be the Vice Presidential candidate? Gallatin's name on the ticket would attract strong support in Pennsylvania. The electoral votes of Pennsylvania, Virginia, and Crawford's own Georgia would be a formidable combination.

Gallatin was reluctant. His foreign birth had proved a political handicap in the past, and might be an even heavier cross in running for an office that could take him into the Presidency. He considered himself as a "residuary legatee" of the hatred of the Federalists and believed his "old services were forgotten and more recent ones, tho' more useful, were but little known." [16] He argued that Crawford's cause would be better served if the congressional party caucus, the time-honored medium for nominating Presidential tickets, were left free to select a running mate.

Thomas replied that there would be no better way to demonstrate the true Jeffersonianism of Crawford than to couple his name with Gallatin's. He promised Gallatin strong political support. Virginia would back him solidly. Senator Martin Van Buren, a clever political newcomer, would bring New York State into line. Senator Walter Lowrie and Congressman Andrew Stewart of Pennsylvania were convinced that Gallatin's name would attract the voters of his home commonwealth.

The Crawford men were persistent. In January, 1824, a letter from Thomas told Gallatin that Crawford's physicians, "four or five in number, have had a consultation . . . and have pronounced him quite out of danger." Would Gallatin please come to Washington at once? "Mr. Crawford will be delighted to see you." The caucus was to be held on February 14, and no time must be lost in lining up support. "Your immediate presence here at this present crisis is all-important." [17]

Gallatin went to Washington, using as an excuse the unfinished business of his French mission. What he saw did not dispel his reluctance. Attending a party at the President's mansion, he was impressed anew with the fact that he had been away from the Capital a long time. "There were several handsome ladies," he reported to his wife, "but most faces of both sexes were new to me. Ten years is an age in Washington." The most interesting sight was of course Crawford himself. The Secretary of the Treasury was unable to write or to speak distinctly; but the men about him insisted that he was "mending slowly." Even so, they confessed that they were "not perfectly easy about his final recovery," and one said frankly that this was one reason that they considered it so desirable that Gallatin be nominated and elected Vice President. "My answer," Gallatin wrote, "was that I did not want the office and would dislike to be proposed and not elected." [18]

Undiscouraged, the Crawford men went ahead with their plans to accomplish the sick man's nomination at the caucus with the aid of Gallatin's name. Back in Baltimore, Gallatin received hopeful bulletins from them and then a request. There was some doubt that Senator Nathaniel Macon of North Carolina would attend the caucus. The presence of this old Jeffersonian would emphasize the "Republicanism" of the Crawford-Gallatin ticket and sway the reluctant. Would Gallatin please urge his old friend to attend?[19] Reluctantly he obliged.

Macon's answer betrayed his pain in every line. The party of Jefferson, he intimated, was all but dead. "There are not, I imagine, five members of Congress who entertain the opinions which those did who brought Mr. Jefferson into power, and they are yet mine. . . . No party . . . can last unless founded on pure principles, and the minute a party begins to intrigue within itself is the minute when the seed of division is sown." He himself favored Crawford; but the Georgian was widely charged with being an intriguer, a participant in political deals, and he believed that if he attended the caucus the charge would be made that every man, including himself, had his price.[20]

The reason behind Macon's refusal became plainer when the caucus was held in the House chamber on the evening of February 14. Despond-

ent of carrying the meeting for their candidates, the backers of other
Presidential aspirants had been conducting an intensive campaign against
the caucus system. Why should "King Caucus," a handful of congressmen, determine who should be President? The partisans of Jackson asserted that the caucus method had always led to the nomination not of a
man of the people, but of some member of the Washington "inner circle."
It was better that the candidate be nominated by state legislatures or, as
Pennsylvania proposed to do, by a state convention.[21] Such arguments had
so captured the popular imagination that, of the 261 Congressmen eligible
to attend the caucus, only 66 showed up and 2 sent proxies. Of those
present, 64 voted to nominate Crawford but only 57 for Gallatin.[22]

Even worse, there was an important defection close to home. Congressman Stewart, who represented Fayette County, Pennsylvania, did not attend the caucus. As Senator Lowrie explained it, a great and inexplicable
enthusiasm for General Jackson had developed in Pennsylvania, and Stewart had decided to play it safe. Lowrie was still sanguine, assuring Gallatin, as "the residuary legatee of all the hatred of the old federal party of
98 and 1800," that he "would be sorry to see [him] exposed to this
abuse if I did not believe you would be elected." [23] Further encouragement came from Richmond, where Crawford in a caucus of the Virginia
legislature on February 21 had received 139 votes to 24 for others, and
Gallatin 131 votes to 40 for others.[24]

At this point precisely what Gallatin had been dreading began to take
place: the backers of the rival tickets raised all the old issues against
him, beginning with his foreign birth and his role in the caucus that had
nominated Jefferson. Supporters peppered him with requests for facts
with which to confute them, and these he promptly supplied, to be published in the friendly press, led by the Washington *National Intelligencer*.[25]

Gallatin was particularly disturbed by what was happening in Pennsylvania. From New Geneva, Albert Rolaz wrote that the name of Jackson
was stirring more enthusiasm than Jefferson's in the western part of the
state. He and his uncle, James Witter Nicholson, had declined the importunities of neighbors to attend a state-wide convention at Harrisburg as
Jackson delegates and had undoubtedly lost many friends as a result.[26]
There were fresh disappointments at the convention on March 4. Gallatin's secretary at Ghent, George M. Dallas, now a power in Pennsylvania
politics and a backer of Calhoun, concluded that he could strengthen his
own position and weaken the influence of Virginia in national affairs by
joining the Jackson bandwagon.[27] So only one vote was cast against the

hero of New Orleans. Of the 127 votes cast for a vice presidential nominee, 87 went to Calhoun and only 10 to Gallatin.[28]

Gallatin could observe the Jackson "mania" even in the Baltimore household of the Montgomerys. John Montgomery, whose term as mayor of Baltimore had expired two years before,[29] was supporting the hero of New Orleans. As Gallatin summed it up, his brother-in-law had "no object in view but himself, has been disappointed in office, and is extremely poor." [30]

Realizing that he lacked popular support of any dimensions, Gallatin concluded that he ought to drop out of the race. Lowrie would hear none of it. He conceded that Gallatin might lose Pennsylvania, but contended that he would certainly win Virginia, Ohio, North Carolina, and Connecticut. The possibilities were bright in New York State. Besides, Lowrie urged, Crawford was anxious that his friend hold fast.[31]

The first week in May, Gallatin, with Hannah and Frances, journeyed to western Pennsylvania to pass the summer.[32] He found himself uncomfortable in this hotbed of Jacksonianism and increasingly regretful that he had permitted his name to be used in the campaign. When the Crawford managers sent formal notice of his nomination by the Washington caucus and requested a formal letter of acceptance to be published for propaganda purposes,[33] he reluctantly complied.

Jackson's popularity and the campaign his partisans were waging troubled Gallatin, who could not see that he represented any party or any set of principles. His following appeared to be a purely personal one, of disappointed and frustrated individuals. There had never been anything like it in the country's history. Equally objectionable was his record at New Orleans and in Florida. To Lowrie, Gallatin expressed the opinion that Jackson entertained "very sincere but very erroneous and most dangerous opinions on the subject of military and executive power"; and he feared that the American people, "dazzled by military glory," might "sacrifice their rights and liberties to the shrine of that glory," and substitute, as the French had, "the worship of a chieftain to the exercise of those rights and to the maintenance of that liberty." [34] Lowrie was so delighted with these expressions that he had them published anonymously in the anti-Jackson press.[35]

By late August the Jacksonians and those opposed to the Crawford-Gallatin ticket were filling their journals with new attacks on Gallatin for his role in the Whiskey Rebellion and for other "sins" alluded to or hinted at.[36] Gallatin began to think nostalgically of the peace he had known at Paris. Hannah felt the attacks acutely, and urged her husband to withdraw his name and retire to private life, even if that meant burying themselves in western Pennsylvania.[37]

The end of the ordeal arrived suddenly. On September 29 former Senator Abner Lacock of Pennsylvania, a Crawford chieftain, came to Friendship Hill with political gossip and an important letter from Senator Lowrie. The news was that the supporters of Calhoun, despairing for their candidate, had agreed to pool their efforts for a Jackson-Calhoun ticket. Apparently this had critically weakened Crawford's candidacy. Crawford's managers—among them, Martin Van Buren—believed that they now needed a Vice Presidential candidate much stronger politically than Gallatin. Henry Clay appeared to be the man. Would Gallatin write a letter withdrawing from the race, to be made public when and if Clay agreed to make the race as second to Crawford? [38]

Gallatin agreed without regret. He wrote to Lowrie: "I have long since learned that, with the exception of domestic afflictions, there was nothing in the events of this life worth any real regret where we had nothing wherewith to reproach ourselves." [39] He was anxious that his withdrawal should not permit Clay to grasp the Presidency from Crawford, and so he addressed his formal letters of withdrawal to Van Buren and to the Virginia state committee.[40] The *National Intelligencer* commented sadly in announcing the change of ticket on October 21 that the younger generation was unfamiliar with Gallatin's record in the nation's service; he had been too long out of the country.[41]

Gallatin watched the rest of the political play from the sanctuary of Fayette County. As the election returns dribbled in, it became clear that Jackson had won the greatest number of electoral votes, including those of Pennsylvania; Adams was second; Crawford, third; and Clay, fourth. It disturbed Gallatin that the voting had been on a state or sectional basis; candidates who were paired in one state were often on opposing tickets in another. "Coalitions of every description without the least regard to principle," he lamented. "I see nothing but . . . the fulfillment of personal views and passions." He could not understand why people were calling this "the era of good feelings," a time of "abatement of party spirit, a reconciliation of parties, or species of political millennium." [42] Now he too was convinced that the party of Jefferson was "fairly defunct," killed by "the want of a popular candidate." [43]

Because no candidate had won a majority of the electoral vote, the issue had to be resolved by the House of Representatives as in 1800. Senator Lowrie kept Gallatin informed of developments at Washington. He wrote, after a call on Crawford, that the Georgian's health was discouraging: "Some words he could not articulate, and it required great effort to continue the conversation." [44]

A coalition of supporters of Adams and Clay gave the Presidency to the New Englander on the first ballot in the House poll. To pay off his debt, Adams named Clay as Secretary of State. Gallatin easily reconciled himself to the result: Adams was, after Crawford, his choice for President.[45] He was immensely relieved that the republic had escaped the grave consequences of electing a military hero. And he was touched to hear that Crawford, on deciding to retire to private life, had spoken to Lowrie of him "in terms of the warmest friendship and esteem." [46]

Thus ended the sorriest episode in Gallatin's public life. He once referred to his Vice Presidential candidacy as a "miscalculation." [47] It was a miscalculation compounded out of his warm friendship for Crawford, a sincere belief that he might help perpetuate what he thought "correct" Jeffersonian Republican principles, and his frustration in not being able, because of foreign birth, to attain higher office in any other way. He learned his lesson; he never again sought elective office.

3

On hearing that Gallatin was living in "the secluded forests of Fayette County," James Brown, his successor at Paris, wrote that he was certain "that you could amuse yourself any where and every where." [48] There was no doubt about it: even after the varied richness and excitement of Paris, Gallatin enjoyed the placid, easy-going life of the remote rustic area he had selected for his home forty years earlier.

Farming, as he had long since learned, was an unprofitable calling in this hilly country; and he made no effort to pursue it seriously. But, summer and winter at Friendship Hill, there was reading to be done. He amused himself, as Hannah put it, with "the history of the down fall of the Republics and making reflections and notes which may come to something one of these days if his natural indolence does not get the better of his present ideas." [49]

He and Hannah found the house as comfortable as it was homely. There was a good staff of servants, white and Negro. During the winter there was an abundance of pork, beef, turkey, venison, though in the spring the larder grew bare. It was either famine or feast at Friendship Hill.

There was little social life. Sometimes James Nicholson and his "si-

lent" children came to call; sometimes the visits were repaid. Sometimes Gallatin would break the routine by a visit to New Geneva, less
often to Uniontown. In the summer of 1824 Maria Montgomery came
from Baltimore for a long visit, and the next year two old friends came
from other worlds for brief sojourns.[50]

In the spring of 1825 General Lafayette passed through the neighborhood on a triumphal tour of the United States, in the course of
which he pleaded for the independence of Greece. On May 26 he
reached Uniontown in the county named after him, where he listened,
with a silently respectful crowd, to an address of welcome which Gallatin
delivered from the steps of the county courthouse. Gallatin's tribute was
a rhetorical acknowledgment of the debt of Americans to the spirit of
the French revolutionists of 1789, but not to the "sanguinary excesses"
that had followed. The next day Lafayette and Gallatin traveled to New
Geneva, escorted by the county militia, stopping often en route to receive the testimonials of neighboring farmers. At Friendship Hill guest
and host had little opportunity for private conversation, for the house
was crowded with persons of local importance and with sight-seers.
Gallatin made the journey with Lafayette back to Uniontown on May 28,
and then the General's party resumed its tour. He observed sadly: "The
Nation's Guest had but little time to give to his personal friends . . . he
was in a great hurry." [51]

But Gallatin did have an opportunity for a heart-to-heart talk with
John Badollet, who came for a visit from Vincennes that same year. The
old schoolmates talked of Geneva and the changes Gallatin had observed
there in 1817.[52] At sixty-four Gallatin felt old and philosophical. His general health was good, and he acknowledged that he did not look older
than he was; but he found it difficult to bear fatigue. His experiences of
the last few years caused him to share Badollet's disillusionment about the
human race: "Every day's experience convinces us that the most un-
principled men are often most successful. In this country there is much
more morality and less of integrity than on the continent of Europe.
. . . [But] taking everything into consideration, I have so much greater
share of all that appears desirable than I had any right to expect, that I
have none to complain." [53]

Albert Rolaz, now twenty-five, continued to share his father's enthusiasm for the western country. With Gallatin's encouragement and tutelage,
he studied enough law to be admitted to the bar of Fayette County in the
spring of 1825, and soon passed much time at Uniontown when the
court was in session.[54]

James was something of a problem. In his late twenties he remained, in his father's phrase, "more fitted for a court than a wilderness." [55] For a time he had considered marriage with Eliza, the youngest daughter of John Jacob Astor. Such a match would have had advantages, for the wealthy shipper and real-estate owner made a practice of presenting each of his daughters with $100,000 when they wed. Gallatin approved of the marriage, for he was fond of both Eliza and her father; but Hannah regarded many of the Astors as "shrewish" and shared the prejudice of some New Yorkers against Astor for his ruthless business methods.[56]

During the winter of 1823–1824, which the Gallatins spent at Baltimore, James fell in love with twenty-year-old Josephine Mary Pascault, the daughter of Lewis F. Pascault, a gentleman of modest property and no calling.[57] Gallatin described her as "one of the fairest blossoms of the country. . . . She is excellent and we love her; it is impossible to have more rectitude and honorable principles and feelings than she has. I hope James, who feels her worth, will make her as happy as she deserves." [58] Hannah was equally enthusiastic. "I love Josephine Pascault with nothing better than Eliza with her million," she assured her husband.[59]

The young couple were married on April 23, 1824,[60] and joined the family at Friendship Hill that summer. By autumn they were expecting a child and it was deemed advisable to pack them off to Baltimore, even if the expense meant a drain on the family exchequer.[61] The child was born on February 7, 1825, and named Albert after his grandfather.[62]

Gallatin tried valiantly to find employment for James. He sent him on two expeditions into the Ohio valley to check on matters pertaining to his land claims, only to receive complaints about the unpleasantness of the work.[63] In the spring of 1826 he presumed upon his old acquaintanceship with Richard Rush, Adams's Secretary of the Treasury, to seek a post for James in his department, but to no avail.[64] By his thirtieth year James had a wife, a son, but no job.

Frances, too, was better suited for a court than a western Pennsylvania farm. She was in her early twenties, an exceedingly attractive, vivacious girl, interested in parties and beaux, attractions lacking at Friendship Hill.[65] Finally, in the winter of 1824–1825, she had her way and went to board with the family of a Baltimore merchant.[66] The Gallatins lavished advice on her by mail. In one letter, her father wrote that he took "it for granted that you do not read novels exclusively, and that you are becoming an excellent housekeeper under Mrs. Bosley's tuition. . . . We do not like your intended visit to Washington. . . . Generally speaking, I do not admire the travelling of young ladies to public places such as waters, Washington, etc." [67]

In the course of the winter Frances stunned her parents by revealing that while they were at Paris Daniel Sheldon, the secretary of the legation, had told her that he was in love with her and wanted to marry her. The Gallatins were certain that they did not like the idea of Mr. Sheldon as a son-in-law. "He has vanity, Fanny, do you not think so?" Hannah demanded of her daughter. "*Poor little man.*" [68] Gallatin's disapproval was more charitably expressed. When Frances asked whether she should any longer acknowledge Sheldon's letters, which were becoming "more and more *tender*," [69] he advised: "You must either not write at all, or write not harshly but so as to cut off all hope. . . . By the bye, your mother and I concluded today that we had not seen and knew no one worthy of you." [70]

But the member of the family who suffered most from life in Fayette was Gallatin's city belle. Hannah found it just as primitive and as dull now as when Gallatin had brought her there as a bride thirty years before.[71] After New York, Philadelphia, Washington, Paris, and London, she shrank from the society of farm folk, to whom she referred as "hawbucks." "My poor sad heart feels as if I was in Siberia," she complained, "exiled from everything agreeable except my husband and child." [72]

By the spring of 1825 Gallatin yielded to Hannah's wishes and abandoned the experiment of living at Friendship Hill. It had cost him $10,000 to . move his possessions there and make the place livable. "After all," he observed philosophically, "in the present state of society, we have to choose between obscurity and labour. [Obscurity] I would not mind, nor the want of wealth. The only great objection to country life and comparative poverty consists in my opinion in the difficulty making happy such a woman as from her education can alone be an acceptable and proper companion for life." [73]

He decided to try Baltimore as a residence. The city seemed to have several advantages: relatives and friends lived there; it was "most within our means"; it was accessible to the other great seaboard cities, yet not too distant from his properties at New Geneva and in the Ohio valley. Not least important, he believed it offered the best opportunities for his sons in business or the professions.[74] In the autumn of 1825 the Gallatins took up residence in a mansion on St. Paul's Street which they had leased for a year at $400. The move gratified Hannah and Frances, but the Alberts, father and son, were soon pining for the "onions of the Monongahela." And to Gallatin's consternation, despite "strict economy," his expenses were outstripping his income.[75]

Meanwhile, looking about for something to keep his mind occupied, he recalled his interest in the languages of the American Indians. During the long-ago winter he had passed at Machias, Maine, he had relieved the tedium by inquiring into the customs of two neighboring Indian tribes. Later, he became absorbed in Jefferson's attempts to classify the Indians in his *Notes on Virginia*, published in 1801.[76] But Baron Alexander von Humboldt had been first to show him the pleasures of scientific research in this field. In 1823, at Paris, he had written, at Humboldt's suggestion, a short essay classifying the Indian tribes within the North American possessions of the United States, Great Britain, Russia, and Denmark. The Prussian savant had planned to include this in a second edition of his own important work on Mexico; but he lent the manuscript, after Gallatin left Paris, to Adriano Balbi, a linguist in the service of the Hapsburgs, who drew liberally upon it for the chapter on America in his *Introduction à l'atlas ethnographique du globe*, published in 1826. Balbi treated the manuscript with great respect, referring to Gallatin as a "very distinguished scholar." [77]

So, in Baltimore, Gallatin plunged into the subject again and more deeply. His object became the compilation of an extensive vocabulary of the six great families of Indians within the United States and British and Russian North America, for eventual publication by the War Department. He obtained assistance from his old friend Peter S. Duponceau, the Philadelphia lawyer who had already done much work in the field, and from Congressman Edward Everett, the former Harvard classics professor. He even went to Washington to quiz a delegation of southern Indians visiting the Capital. The War Department cooperated by circulating printed forms of a vocabulary of six hundred common words to be filled out by its agents.[78] Friends arranged for the circulation of the queries in Canada.[79] But, before these scholarly labors could bear fruit, there was an attractive call to public service.

4

Thrice since the Vice Presidential debacle, Gallatin had considered opportunities for public service. One was bona fide enough, but not particularly appealing. In 1825, Governor Schulze of Pennsylvania asked him to serve on a commission to plan a network of canals linking the western parts of the state—a request that must have conjured up memories of his service as an assemblyman. Gallatin declined.[80] The second opportunity, though attractive, was illusory. At the start of President Adams's Administration, Congressman Stewart sounded him out for service in the

Cabinet—in the Treasury or the State Department.[81] Actually this overture had been abetted, unknown to Gallatin, by his son James, who felt that his own career would be advanced if his father were back in public office.[82] Adams gave the State portfolio to Henry Clay, but apparently liked the idea of Gallatin returning to the Treasury. But Gallatin, for whom struggles with public finance no longer held fascination, promptly made it clear that he would not accept if the offer were made.[83]

The third opportunity was flattering and genuine, but ill-fated. In November, 1825, Secretary of State Clay asked Gallatin to join Richard C. Anderson, Jr., American minister to Colombia, as a minister plenipotentiary representing the United States at a congress to be held in Panama that would discuss the mutual interests of the American republics. "The mission," he wrote, was to be "the most important ever sent from this country, those only excepted which related to its independence and the termination of the late war." [84]

The unpleasant information Gallatin gathered about the climate of Panama, his lack of knowledge of the Spanish language and of Latin American problems, and the dismal view Hannah took of his leaving for an indefinite period, all caused him to decline the honor.[85] In the end, the United States sent no mission because the anti-Adams forces in Congress combined to oppose it.[86]

Then, in April, 1826, came a fourth opportunity. Gallatin was visiting in Washington when President Adams and Secretary Clay broached the idea of his joining the venerable Rufus King, minister to Great Britain, in negotiations about the Oregon Country and perhaps other issues. He listened to the suggestion but did not commit himself. If he did go to London, he made clear, it would be for only a short period. Before the Administration had a chance to submit the nomination to the Senate, King resigned his posts because of ill health. Now Clay wanted Gallatin to go as King's successor, even if just long enough to complete the contemplated negotiations.[87]

The more Gallatin thought about the idea, the more he liked it. He accepted on May 7, and two days later he was nominated, at his request, as "of Pennsylvania." [88] Confirmation by the Senate came a day later with scarcely a dissenting vote.[89] The press was friendly, with only an occasional example of what the Albany *Argus* called "the smothered asperity and prejudices of other times." [90]

For the next seven weeks Gallatin was busy making official and personal plans. He journeyed again to Washington to receive instructions from Adams and Clay.[91] To give James employment while he was gone, he charged him with supervision of all the family's western properties.[92]

Albert had just been admitted to the Baltimore bar and was expected to start practice there in the autumn.[93] Hannah and Frances were to go to London for another welcome taste of court and city life.

A minor irritation developed at the last minute. When Adams and Clay first discussed the mission with Gallatin, they assured him that he "could write his own instructions." Gallatin was not naïve enough to take this literally, but he soon was alarmed by the voluminous and detailed instructions sent. He protested several times to both Adams and Clay, the last time in a pointed letter to the President on the eve of sailing. "They are on almost every subject of the most peremptory nature, leaving no discretion on unimportant points, and making of me a mere machine." He asked that he be allowed to consider the instructions as guiding but not absolutely binding.[94] On this unresolved note, he hopefully sailed for Liverpool aboard the packet *Florida* on the morning of July 1, 1826.[95]

26. The London Mission and Its Aftermath

1826=1829

In comparison with the delightful years at Paris, the Gallatins found London dull. When they arrived early in August, 1826, the British capital was in the doldrums. The heat and an impending parliamentary election had scattered the public men to the ends of the land. George Canning, the volatile, devious, dominating man who had inherited the mantle of the great Foreign Minister when Castlereagh cut his throat in a fit of insanity, was at Brighton, seeking "purer air." The men he had deputed to negotiate in his behalf, William Huskisson, President of the Board of Trade, and Henry Unwin Addington for the Foreign Office, were absent on holidays.[1]

It took several weeks for Gallatin and his ladies to settle down at the American legation at 62 Seymour Street. There was a brief flurry of interest in mid-August, when Canning came up to London for a few days and Gallatin had a pleasant talk with him.[2] On the 1st of September, Gallatin journeyed to Windsor Castle to deliver his credentials to King George IV. The "first gentleman of Europe," whom he counted as a cipher, made a gracious little speech expressing the desire for amicable relations between Great Britain and the United States.[3] In the weeks that followed Gallatin arranged meetings with Canning, Huskisson, and Addington; but by the end of September they were all gone again.[4] "Literally without anything to do," he took Hannah and Frances for a sentimental visit to Paris.

While he revisited old haunts along the boulevards and looked up such old friends as Pozzo di Borgo and Lafayette, he kept his ears open for diplomatic developments. Pozzo di Borgo made it clear that Nicholas I, who had succeeded to the Russian throne in 1825, was not anxious to arbitrate between the United States and Great Britain over the slave indemnities or the border between Maine and New Brunswick, on which the good services of a "friendly sovereign" seemed likely to be needed.[5]

The family returned to London well before the cabinet reassembled in early November. After that, the mission became more and more disappointing. Hannah found the English people "dull"; she complained that they never could "make themselves agreeable anywhere," but acknowledged viewing "everything with a jaundiced eye." She was cured of any desire to live abroad; her family and her native land claimed her increasing devotion. As the negotiations dragged out through the winter and spring of 1826–1827, she became "quite home sick and nervous" whenever there was a delay.[6]

Frances, twenty-four years old and at the height of her dancing days, fared better. During the "gay season" in May she attended a "pleasant" affair at Almack's, the suite of assembly rooms in King Street where balls were arranged by a committee of ladies of high rank; to dance there was incontrovertible proof of exalted social position. All this pleased her mother, but not her father. She kept such late hours that her health suffered. "I hope with rest and care she will soon recover and it will be a lesson to her," Gallatin reported to her brothers at home.[7]

Gallatin perhaps found London dull and the delays in the negotiations irritating, but the matters he dealt with during these months were of far-reaching importance. He gave them his undivided and expert attention.

2

Four days before Gallatin stepped down the gangplank from the *Florida* in Liverpool on July 31, 1826, the British cabinet had issued an Order in Council that created a crisis in Anglo-American relations. The Order closed the British colonies in the West Indies and South America to United States vessels. In a sense, it was retaliation for the American policy, pushed by Adams since 1817, of forcing the British to admit American ships and goods into the British West Indies—a policy which had brought prosperity to the American merchant marine and riddled with holes the traditional British colonial system.[8]

Apparently Gallatin had no chance to read the text of the order until late August. He sent off a blunt protest to Canning on the 26th.[9] In reply, the British Foreign Minister denied the validity of the United States's assumption that the most-favored-nation arrangement embodied in the trade convention of 1818 deprived Britain of the right to regulate her colonial trade as she saw fit. Gallatin next inquired whether this meant that Britain was unwilling to negotiate on the subject of colonial trade. Canning replied that it did. This dampened the spirits of the American minister, for Adams and Clay had instructed him to undertake the renewal of the convention of 1818. He now wondered whether renewal would be worth while.[10]

Under the circumstances Gallatin could only request that the question be discussed further after the holiday season. He also wrote to Secretary Clay for more instructions, reporting that the atmosphere in London had changed drastically since the 1818 convention. Castlereagh had been far more friendly; "the difference may however be in the times rather than the men." Britain had treated the United States before the war "with great arrogance"; immediately after the war, "with great attention, if not respect. . . . The United States are now an object of jealousy and a policy founded on that feeling has been avowed." [11]

Gallatin had less difficulty with another matter. The convention of 1818 had provided that a friendly sovereign should arbitrate a settlement of the provision of the Treaty of Ghent covering the slaves carried away by the British forces during the War of 1812. Alexander I of Russia had set up some definitions in 1822; but representatives of the United States and Britain had drifted into hopeless disputes when they attempted to apply them.[12]

On September 13 Addington brought to Gallatin an "inofficial proposal" for the settlement of the claims. This called for payment by Great Britain not later than May 1, 1828, of £180,000 for the claims—"all the indisputable and one-half of the doubtful," as Gallatin summarized it—plus £70,000 to cover interest.[13] Gallatin forwarded the proposal to Washington with the observation that, although it was not all that some Americans had hoped, he recommended acceptance because he saw no chance of obtaining more.[14] Adams and Clay acceded, and on November 13 he was able to sign a convention covering these terms.[15]

Meanwhile, little by little, Gallatin had learned the reasons for Canning's coolness to the United States. In mid-October he heard that the Foreign Minister, about the time of the July Order in Council, had expressed to his colleagues in explosive fashion "his great dissatisfaction at the language of the Government of the United States," and had gone on to say that the United States appeared to wish to take "undue advantage of the distress of England, and that it was time for her to make a stand and show her displeasure." Just what and whom did Canning mean by "the language of the Government of the United States"? After inquiry and deduction, Gallatin reached an embarrassing conclusion, which he put down in a personal letter to President Adams on October 18. Adams as Secretary of State had written letters to Rush at London, which had been published by order of the American Senate, and which had given

Canning great offense. "That they had no right to complain of what you wrote to your own minister is obvious," Gallatin wrote; nevertheless, the letters and their publication did make Canning difficult to deal with.[16]

Gallatin discovered still another reason for the Britons' reluctance to discuss treaties. In the course of a meeting with the Foreign Minister on November 4, he alluded to a declaration by Huskisson in Parliament that it was England's policy to encourage the merchant marine of nations "less dangerous than the United States." Canning bristled and retorted angrily that a Congressional committee headed by Francis Baylies had issued a report earlier in the year setting forth American claims to the Oregon Country; it had "almost the appearance," said Canning, "of a Manifesto issued on declaring war."

Canning of course misunderstood the American constitutional system, on which Gallatin hastened to throw light. He acknowledged that such expressions were "very strong"; but they represented not the sentiment of the American government nor even of the House of Representatives—only that of the committee. Canning snapped back that "it was a dangerous power we gave to our Committees," one that in critical times might produce war.[17] By the end of November, Gallatin had the pieces in the puzzle arranged, and he assured Secretary Clay that undoubtedly Baylies's report, in part, had been the immediate cause of the Order in Council.[18]

Clearly, the Oregon Country was the most ticklish question outstanding between the two nations. When, in early November, the Britons indicated that they were at last ready to settle down to serious negotiation, it was tacitly understood that Oregon would lead on the agenda.[19]

3

The meetings began on November 15, 1826, at the Foreign Office. Across the table from Gallatin were Huskisson, an expert on the commercial questions at issue through the negotiations with Richard Rush three years before, and Addington, who had served his country at Washington several years and was considered as a specialist on boundary questions, but was little more than a mouthpiece for Canning.[20]

By the Christmas recess, the gamut of issues at stake had been run: impressments, the boundary between Maine and New Brunswick, renewal of the trade conventions of 1815 and 1818, navigation of the St. Lawrence River by American vessels, access to the British colonies for the American merchant marine, and the Oregon Country. The British appeared to be willing to renew the trade conventions without alteration, and possibly "make some overtures" on impressments. On all the other issues the prospects seemed dismal.[21]

Most of the words spoken and written had been about Oregon. Early in the discussions Gallatin set forth clearly, cogently, moderately, and in great detail the various American claims to the area based on discovery and colonization.[22] The British, realizing that their case was weak on these two grounds, merely cited their discovery and occupation of certain sections of the area as cause for regarding Oregon as a no man's land.[23]

The British repeated a proposal made to Rush two years earlier—that the territory be partitioned along the 49th parallel westward to the intersection with the Kootenai River, along that river to the Columbia, and down the Columbia to its mouth in the Pacific, with free navigation to the nationals of both powers. Gallatin promptly replied that his government had rejected this, and declared tactfully that the United States must insist upon its earlier offer for a partition: the 49th parallel all the way to the Pacific without deviation. His instructions authorized him, he added, to make just one concession: British subjects would be allowed to navigate the Columbia and any of its tributaries intersected by the 49th parallel, from the point of intersection to the sea, "provided the waters below the point of intersection should prove on inspection to be navigable by boats."

Huskisson and Addington passed this proposal to Canning, who vetoed it vehemently. He was adamant that the lower part of the Columbia must not be yielded. He did permit his negotiators to offer a considerable concession: the United States to have a quadrilateral of land north of the Columbia, the Olympic Peninsula north of a line from Hood Canal west to the ocean. He hoped that this would meet Gallatin's objection that the earlier offer deprived the United States of any practicable port on the Pacific. The United States could establish a naval station on the peninsula—surrounded, of course, by British territory. Confident that the suggestion would stand no chance in Washington, Gallatin refused even to send it.

The area now in dispute was, in sum, the region between the Columbia River and the 49th parallel: two-thirds of the present state of Washington, including Puget Sound. The British sensed no chance of a compromise on partitioning and suggested that the agreement in effect in respect to Oregon be renewed.[24]

The wary Gallatin soon detected a pitfall in this plain proposal. As a condition of the renewal, the British stipulated that a clause be inserted providing that neither nation, during the lifetime of the agreement, would "assume or exercise any right of exclusive sovereignty or dominion over any part of the said country, nor form therein any establishment in support or furtherance of such claims." [25] When Gallatin asked what "exclusive" meant, he was told that the intention was to bar either country from establishing any military post or any territorial government in Oregon. It appears that the idea was Canning's: it would both aid the operations of the Hudson's Bay Company in the Pacific Northwest and effectively block any designs Americans might have on Oregon.

Canning's representatives proposed that the convention be renewed for fifteen years, or twenty, or even twenty-five, saying that if the "joint occupation" (a not quite accurate phrase to define the status quo) was to continue, a long term was necessary.[26] As Gallatin's instructions permitted him to agree to a renewal of no longer than ten years, he had to forward the proposal to Washington. In his dispatches he unwittingly employed the British phrase "joint occupation." [27]

After the Christmas holidays, there was a volley of reasons for postponing resumption of the negotiations. Huskisson fell gravely ill; Canning suffered a temporary indisposition; Liverpool, the Prime Minister, had a paralytic stroke; winter storms on the Atlantic delayed new instructions from Washington. To avoid waste of time, Gallatin had several informal discussions with Addington and buried himself in tomes and documents bearing on the dispute about the line between Maine and New Brunswick.[28]

The Northeast boundary controversy was another piece of business left unfinished by the Treaty of Ghent. Under the terms of the treaty, American and British commissioners had surveyed the boundary in 1821; but the two groups adopted and held adamantly to the respective positions taken at Ghent: the Americans insisting upon adherence to the line established by the Treaty of 1783; the British demanding "rectification" of the boundary so that they might construct a military road across the northern part of Maine. In all, more than seven million acres of land, including extensive timber tracts and fertile valleys in Maine and New Hampshire, were involved.[29]

Gallatin had originally been instructed to arrange that negotiations on this matter be shifted to Washington. But after Gallatin's eve-of-sailing protest against being allowed no discretion at London, President Adams modified the instructions so that Gallatin might propose or agree to anything he believed would satisfy the people or the Senate, with the strict exception of cession of any state's territory or waiving the American claim of the right to navigate the St. Lawrence.[30]

Addington's attitude on the Northeast boundary discouraged Gallatin, who reported to Secretary Clay: "I find him extremely unmanageable, not from ignorance, for he has well studied the details, but because he has imbibed all the prejudices and zeal of the British agents and provincial authorities on that question. His object is clearly not that the parties should have a fair trial before the arbiter, but to take every advantage he possibly can gain." [31]

Not until late May was Gallatin able to resume regular meetings with the British negotiators. By this time Great Britain had a new government, Liverpool having resigned. Canning headed the new cabinet, but because of the distrust of the ultra Tories he had to work with the Whigs in order to remain in power. By this time, too, Gallatin had received a reaction from Adams on the British proposal for the partitioning of Oregon: nothing but a simple renewal of the existing convention could be considered. The President explained why in a personal letter: "One inch of ground yielded on the northwest coast—one step backward from the claim to the navigation of the St. Lawrence, one hair's breadth of compromise upon . . . impressment would be certain to meet the reprobation of the Senate. In this temper of the parties, all we can hope to accomplish will be to adjourn controversies which we cannot adjust." [32]

During the conferences that dragged on through June and July, the British suggested another proviso that would restrain either country from exercising, or assuming the right to exercise, any exclusive sovereignty or jurisdiction over Oregon. Gallatin bluntly pointed out that this was a mere rephrasing of the proposal his government had rejected.[33]

He now gave the British a salutary lecture on the nature of the convention they proposed to renew. It was a subject about which he knew more than they did, having contributed to its creation. Basically, he told them, it was a convention to facilitate trade and settlement; it had deliberately avoided the question of sovereignty. It was permissible for the two nations to establish military posts and territorial governments there as long as these did not interfere with the trade and sovereignty of the other nation. Certainly, he said, Britain could not object to the United States' taking such steps, because the Hudson's Bay Company had already been authorized to exercise approximately the same functions in respect to British nationals—a bit of unpublished information which he had unearthed in his diligent research during the recess.

Gallatin speculated, in his discourse, about the future of Oregon: No matter what agreement the negotiators might reach about it, it was improbable that the area would be permanently attached to either Britain or the United States. The prospect was that, separated from the United States by mountains and considerable distance, the Pacific Northwest would be settled largely by people from the United States who would in time set up an independent republic. (This idea was shared by Jefferson, Monroe, Crawford, Clay, and probably Madison.³⁴) However, the United States was insisting on simple renewal of the Oregon convention, with no additional interpretations.

Gradually the British recognized that their Hudson's Bay Company would prosper better under a vaguely worded convention than under none at all. Gallatin then suggested that no duration period be specified but that the arrangement be subject to termination on twelve months' notice by either party. This was written into a convention the three negotiators signed on August 6, 1827.³⁵

Gallatin lost no time in suggesting to his government measures that would prove advantageous in the inevitable next negotiation on Oregon. He believed that the British were concerned basically only to protect the interests of the Hudson's Bay Company and other English capitalists; that they recognized that in time the territory would quietly "slide" into American possession and later become an independent republic. The United States could facilitate the quiet sliding by extending the scope of one of its already existing territorial governments to include Oregon. He proposed several other means of avoiding conflict between Americans and British in the area; but these were so moderate that they would scarcely appeal to the noisy western expansionists in Congress.³⁶

Although the convention fell far short of the partitioning of Oregon which powerful groups in both nations had hoped for, it allowed a relaxation from their recent martial stances and, by the delay, helped a peaceful solution of the problem two decades later.

Now a fresh spate of ill fortune among the members of the British government delayed negotiations on the remaining issues. Huskisson was still seriously ill; Canning died; and Lord Goderich became Prime Minister. Although Gallatin believed that the new ministry was "but a continuation of that of Mr. Canning, to act on the same principles," he was gratified by its "better disposition" toward the United States.³⁷

Finally, by late September, Gallatin reached agreements—or agreements to postpone agreements—on the issues still unsolved. Most important was the Northeast boundary. After the discouraging discussions with Addington, he was content that the dispute was to be referred to "some friendly sovereign or state" for arbitration. Particularly pleasing was the fact that the points at issue were now clarified. The British withdrew their demands for territory in which to construct a military road, and agreed to the boundary as defined in the Treaty of 1783. It was known that, during the negotiation of that treaty, a red line had been marked on a map of North America made by the geographer John Mitchell, to define the boundary between the United States and Canada. Just where the red line ran, the present negotiators did not know; but they agreed that instead of masses of documents, each side would present the arbitrator with a copy of Mitchell's map marked with the boundary it claimed. Each disputant would also furnish the arbitrator with a statement in support of its version of the map and later, if desired, a statement of rebuttal. Plenty of room for dispute still remained, for, as Gallatin observed, Mitchell's map was "only a skeleton, connecting the water-courses." "The highlands," which were mentioned frequently in the Treaty of 1783, were not delineated.[38]

On the other issues it was agreed not to agree. The British were unwilling to recognize the right of United States citizens to navigate the St. Lawrence, and the question was passed over. They were equally adamant about the West Indian trade. Gallatin blamed Huskisson for this: "he has an undue and not very liberal jealousy of the increasing navigation of the United States." However, British shipping interests also were strong defenders of the colonial system; and until they could be shown that it operated to their disadvantage they would work zealously for its continuance. Later Gallatin sent Lord Dudley, Goderich's Foreign Secretary, a detailed criticism of the colonial system that made a strong impression on British public men.[39] It helped pave the way for Andrew Jackson's "Reciprocity of 1830," which signalized the complete collapse of the traditional British system of colonial monopoly.

Particularly disappointing to Gallatin was the outcome of the discussions about impressments. He had greatly hoped that this question, which had troubled his public life for a quarter of a century, might at last be settled. As a guest of Canning at Chiswick, his country home, a few days before his death, he had discussed the problem with him at length. He was convinced that Canning, like Castlereagh a decade earlier, was personally willing to forswear impressment, but felt the need of greater political strength to resist national pride on the matter. After Canning's death, Huskisson intimated to Gallatin his own disapproval of the practice.[40] Nevertheless, the negotiators accomplished nothing concrete on impressment. Great Britain never formally forswore the practice, but she never again resorted to it.

The thirteen months at London were arduous, frustrating, and yet in many ways fruitful for Gallatin. They were arduous because of the many conferences, the tedious correspondence, and the taxing research required. They were frustrating because he had to deal with a shaky and swiftly shifting British government on one hand and a weak and therefore timorous American Administration on the other. They were fairly fruitful because of the settlement of the claims for stolen slaves; the indefinite renewal of the commercial convention of 1815 without change; the reference of the Northeast boundary dispute to arbitration on clarified issues; the maintenance of the status quo in Oregon.

Gallatin wrote with his usual judiciousness when he told President Adams that he "left the British government in better temper than I found them. . . . Whilst I regret that nothing more could be done, I am consoled by the consciousness that all has been done that was practicable." [41]

4

The most frustrating thing about the London mission was that it separated Gallatin and his wife from their sons. He wrote to Albert Rolaz that the separation "deeply affects us." When Albert Rolaz sent a portrait of himself that his father considered a "coarse painting but a very good likeness," Hannah "looked at it and laughed in order not to cry." [42]

The boys' letters did nothing to assuage parental homesickness. James complained that he was unable to do anything with the New Geneva property or the western lands.[43] Albert Rolaz told of opening a law office in Baltimore but finding no clients; he died a thousand deaths when he tried to make a public speech.[44] His shyness stirred his father to reminiscence and inspiration: "I was originally almost as diffident as yourself. . . . It is in the power of every man to become [a public speaker] for all necessary purposes." His own case was "an indubitable proof." Even in French, he had no eloquence, and was only a reasoner. If "you make a good argument and show knowledge of the law applicable to the case, and perfect knowledge of the case itself, it will open the way." [45]

When Albert Rolaz wrote about seeking a political career in western Pennsylvania, his father warned him about the inconveniences of political life, which led to "responsibility, not to wealth." [46] Later Albert Rolaz repaired to New York, where he had a romance that soon blew over.[47]

During Gallatin's absence both sons applied for positions in the federal service and were refused. They chose to blame President Adams and Secretary Clay for the refusals in letters that made their father more impatient to get home.[48] He asked President Adams to do everything he could to speed the negotiations. He made no secret of his concern to return in order to counsel his sons about their careers.[49] By early autumn he resolved the diplomatic issues he had come to London to negotiate; and on October 8, 1827, he and Hannah and Frances sailed for America.[50]

5

Neither the passage nor the home-coming was pleasant. The packet ship *Sylvanus Jackson* was buffeted by storms for seventeen consecutive days. When they landed at New York on November 29, Gallatin was so ill that the family took up lodgings at the American Hotel on Broadway near Park Place, and he did not stir out of his room for twelve days.[51]

And now what? They had thought of returning to Baltimore, but Hannah's mother, now in her eighties, was so feeble that they decided to stay the winter in New York.[52] The house at 113 Bleecker Street, in the suburbs, was rented for the purpose.

Gallatin hastened to relieve himself of his diplomatic duties. He sent his report on the mission to Secretary Clay and his resignation to President Adams.[53] The President responded with expressions of "satisfaction" with what Gallatin had accomplished and of regret that he had not remained to bring the colonial trade question to a satisfactory settlement.[54]

In February, Gallatin, still without duties or plans, discovered that his diplomatic responsibilities were not over. The Senate ratified the three conventions he had brought home. Now, Clay wrote, the American case in the Northeast boundary case must be prepared. Would he join William Pitt Preble, a judge in Maine, the state most affected by the controversy, in gathering data for presentation to the "friendly sovereign"? [55] Gallatin accepted with alacrity.

The chore consumed most of his energies for the next eighteen months, and involved journeys to the state archives and libraries at Boston and Albany and two extended visits to Washington.[56] On all his trips he was accompanied by Albert Rolaz, who "takes care of me as if I were a child; I cannot move without having him at my elbow." The assistance was deeply appreciated by a seventy-year-old gentleman with an injured right arm that made it painful and sometimes impossible for him to write.[57]

The work was considerably lightened by Judge Preble, who, as the younger man, took on the more arduous tasks. At Gallatin's suggestion, he visited Fredericton, New Brunswick, and returned with a rich trove of data.[58] Finally, in late 1828, they worked together at Williamson's Hotel in Washington to reduce the immense collection of material to an orderly presentation. Gallatin dictated to his son, and directed the labors of eleven draftsmen and three clerks.[59]

Within a year the fruits of their labor were printed in a statement nearly as long, Gallatin remarked, as one of the novels Frances was so fond of reading.[60] The eighty-seven large pages were ultimately presented to the King of the Netherlands, whom the United States and Great Britain reluctantly agreed upon as arbitrator.[61]

Subsequent scholarly research has revealed that Gallatin prepared the American case badly. He and Preble, and the English too, used the map that John Mitchell had published in 1755; on this "the highlands" were so vaguely delineated that the Americans had to refer to the Proclamation of 1763 and the Quebec Act of 1774 for definition of them. The Mitchell map actually used in the 1782–1783 negotiations was one published in 1775, in which the highlands were more clearly shown. If, during his London sojourn, Gallatin had inquired at the British Museum, he would have found George III's copy of the 1775 map with the agreed-upon boundary clearly marked in red, and the consequences to the United States would have been quite different.[62]

6

During the two years following his return from London, and especially during his visits to Washington, Gallatin studied the American political scene uneasily. If, on coming home from Paris in 1823, he had felt a stranger to the world he had once known so well, he felt even more completely a foreigner now. The four years of Adams's Administration had been turned into a Presidential campaign by the followers of Jackson, who kept up an unceasing cry about a "corrupt bargain" between Adams and Clay that had made one President and the other Secretary of State.

Gallatin watched the Washington circus with lips so tight that even Albert Rolaz, who was seldom far from him, found it impossible to tell what he thought. He got the impression that his father had reservations about Clay but believed Jackson to be "an honest man." [63] Gallatin was more outspoken in writing to Badollet: "I care little about what party and who is in power." Personalities and personal aspirations, or at best "sectional feelings," seemed to him to have eclipsed "public service and the manner in which it shall be performed" in this new age.[64]

Thus Gallatin was scarcely surprised when Jackson overwhelmed Adams at the polls in 1828. But he was dubious as to how long the new President's following, which he believed was united only by desire for office, would hold together.[65] Despite his misgivings, he was ready to serve the new Administration. He gave no encouragement to a report that he might become Old Hickory's Secretary of State,[66] but he did allow his son James to tell Martin Van Buren, the mastermind of Jackson's campaign, that he was willing again to become minister to France. Actually he sought the office so that James might become secretary of the legation.[67] After the inauguration he called upon President Jackson at the Presidential mansion, and came away "quite pleased with his manners, which are simple and dignified," but with no appointment.[68] The sweeping removals from office made by Jackson shocked Gallatin. As in Jefferson's time, he denounced the patronage system—but this time publicly, to anyone who would listen.[69]

In his heart Gallatin realized the truth—that he was old, the great man of a day now departed. Age "so advanced as mine is not a recommendation," he observed to Hannah. "We must make room for younger men." [70] He took the change of times philosophically. The queen of Washington society in this new era was the wife of Secretary of War John H. Eaton, young and pretty Peggy Eaton, who, years before, as Peggy O'Neal, daughter of the leading publican in Washington, had been a flame of Albert Rolaz.[71] In reporting to his wife on Peggy's new eminence, Gallatin commented: "Having had with me your share of the vanities and the grandeurs of the world, you may be quite satisfied that we were not indebted for them to any particular merit of ours. . . . The loss of popularity, which we perhaps regret too much (for as to the vanities I know that you care no more about them than I do), is no more an object of astonishment than the manner in which it is acquired." [72]

7

On New Year's Day, 1830, John Quincy Adams, who, since leaving the Presidency, had absorbed himself in the classics at Meridian Hill, his residence outside Washington, was surprised to receive a morning visit from his old friend and colleague Albert Gallatin. Gallatin explained that work on the Maine boundary dispute had been completed just the day before; he presented Adams with printed copies of the document.

Although Gallatin could not be sure of it at the time, his call on Adams signalized the end of forty years of public service, nearly seventeen of them in diplomacy, in close collaboration with Adams. His plans were vague, he told the former President. The next day he would be starting for New York City, where he would continue to reside for the time being so that his wife might be close to her aged mother.[73]

Thus the two most important American diplomatists of their age took leave of each other. To the formation of American foreign policy during the first third of the nineteenth century, the contributions of the painfully conscientious Adams far exceeded those of any other man.[74] Gallatin's contributions covered less time and fewer geographical areas; yet his national view and cosmopolitan temper, his tenacity and genial manners, his learning and industry, which he applied to the cause of the United States at Ghent, at London, at Paris, at the Hague, and at Washington, make his distinction secure.

After helping to make a diplomatically indecisive although politically advantageous peace at Ghent, Gallatin had devoted more than a decade to issues then left pending. He succeeded in arranging three matters of consequence: resumption of trade relations with Great Britain, reaffirmation of the American "right" to cure fish on certain Canadian shores, and compensation for Negro slaves abducted by British forces. Two of his apparent failures, though depressing at the time, were made negligible by the passing years: although the British would not formally relinquish impressment, the practice was never employed again; and although France, beset by internal problems, would not settle American spoliation claims, Gallatin's efforts at least kept the issue alive for satisfactory settlement by a later generation. His only real failure was his neglect to examine British archives adequately in preparing the case on the Northeast boundary; this was to prove more costly to the United States than any person of his own generation could realize.

The Treaty of Ghent also ushered in an age of new diplomatic problems. To Gallatin fell conduct of the most important commercial negotiations of the postwar decade and a half, with its new emphasis on commercial reciprocity. He was hampered by the insistence of Adams, while Secretary of State and President, that the United States accept nothing less than all it sought—an insistence which led to complete failure in the negotiations with the Netherlands, partial success in the case of France, and qualified success in respect to Great Britain. Even so, Gallatin contributed as much as anyone to the successes achieved in the American reciprocity program of the early nineteenth century by providing the basic work upon which settlements were finally achieved.[75]

His own peculiar triumphs lay in his handling of the Northwest boundary question. By successfully clarifying the line between the United States and British North America from the Lake of the Woods to the Rockies and by insisting that the Oregon Country west of the mountains be kept in peaceful abeyance, he prepared the basis for the completely satisfactory settlement of 1846. The London negotiation of 1818 alone, by which he laid the way for American acquisition of the Pacific Northwest, is momentous enough to make certain for Gallatin a place as one of the great diplomatists in our history.

27. Citizen and Scholar

1830=1848

When Gallatin and Adams said goodbye on New Year's Day, 1830, they were not withdrawing into the shadows to pass their twilight years in repose like their old colleagues, Jefferson, Madison, and Monroe. Adams soon began a splendid service in Congress that lasted up to the moment of his death. Gallatin's record was remarkable in its own way. During the eighteen years of his "retirement," he made contributions to the civic life of New York, to scholarly and scientific research, to business development and economic thought, and to political activity which would have been notable for a young man. For a man in the seventies and eighties, these contributions were close to heroic.

One reason for Gallatin's extraordinary activity was his determination that his family should not suffer the financial travails that had befallen those of Jefferson, Madison, and Lafayette. Finally and regretfully he cut himself off from western Pennsylvania and its residue of youthful dreams of fortune from land speculation and entrepreneurship. "I should have been contented to live and die amongst the Monongahela hills," he confessed to John Badollet; but "the necessity of bringing up a family" imposed the decision upon him.[1]

Selling his western properties turned out to be a task. By the efforts of James and Albert Rolaz, as well as his brother-in-law James Nicholson, all the New Geneva lots, the gristmill, and the ferry were disposed of by 1830; the house at Friendship Hill, by 1832; and most of the land in Ohio about the same time—all at a great sacrifice.[2]

Meanwhile, Gallatin found it difficult to obtain a house in New York that satisfied himself and his family. He moved several times. Finally, in 1837, using some of the money Hannah had inherited from her grandfather's estate, he purchased the commodious and comfortable residence at 57 Bleecker Street on the very edge of town. This was to be his home until his death. The children, as well as James's wife and son Albert, continued for a time to share the parental roof.[3]

Frances was the first to leave. On April 6, 1830, the lovely Frances, at twenty-seven, married Byam Kerby Stevens of a well-to-do New York mercantile family of New England antecedents, who had been paying her court, off and on, for seven years. Within a dozen years the Stevenses had five sons and two daughters who absorbed their grandmother's devoted attention and much of their grandfather's.[4]

For a time his sons provided Gallatin with problems. His old friend John Jacob Astor proved to be helpful now. In 1827, the New York millionaire had told him that the United States needed a good mercantile house, and he wished that he were ten or fifteen years younger so that together they could do something about it. "With my capital and your credit and name," said Astor, "we could get all the business of Europe." Then he dropped a broad hint about Gallatin's older son: "I believe some arrangement might be made of ultimate use to James."[5]

In the spring of 1831, Astor returned with a new proposal. He invited Gallatin to serve as president of the new National Bank of New York, which he was helping to back. Gallatin, who found the cost of living in New York far higher than he liked, welcomed the $2,000 salary that would go with the presidency. So, beginning on April 1, 1831, at the age of seventy, he undertook to direct the operations of a new institution whose capital of $750,000 made it one of the smaller among the city's nineteen banks. The bank flourished on a modest scale, and in 1836 his salary was increased to $2,500 a year.[6]

Meanwhile, Gallatin helped his sons find employment in a trading firm established with funds advanced by Astor's son, William Backhouse Astor. Gallatin Brothers maintained a small office on Wall Street, near the National Bank.

These arrangements satisfied everyone concerned for nearly a decade. On June 7, 1839, Gallatin resigned the presidency of the bank and was succeeded by his son James, who played a leading role in the New York banking community for the next twenty-five years.* [7] In 1838 the business of Gallatin Brothers was terminated quietly, not long after the second son, Albert Rolaz, married Mary Lucille Stevens.[8] The comfortable fortune of the Stevens family permitted him to live as a nineteenth century gentleman to the end of his days. As he did not wish to be entirely idle, his father advised him "to cultivate chemistry and physical sciences for which he has taste and talent."

Albert Rolaz and Mary Gallatin had three sons, Albert Horatio, Frederic, and James, who added to the delight of the grandparents in Bleecker

---

* In 1865 the name of the National Bank of New York was changed to the Gallatin Bank in honor of its first president. In 1912 it was absorbed by the institution now known as the Hanover Bank.

Street. But James's son Albert remained the apple of his grandfather's eye. Gallatin took satisfaction in young Albert's "tolerable talents" and "most engaging disposition"; he was gratified when he made his way through Princeton, ranking in the middle of his class, "so far moral and industrious." [9] By 1847 he was practicing law in his own office in Wall Street. The fears Gallatin had felt about leaving his family in want turned out to be quite unnecessary.

There were certain satisfactions from growing old, as he discovered when he invited his children and their children to dine at Bleecker Street on the afternoon of November 11, 1843. "On that day fifty years ago," he reminded them, "your father and mother were married. May you live as happily and have a similar meeting with your descendants!" [10]

There was pain, too, in seeing old friends and associates drop off one by one. Jefferson, his great mentor and true friend, had died in 1826, while he was at London. Monroe, John Randolph, Lafayette, Crawford, Madison, Macon . . . Then, in 1846 died Badollet, oldest and dearest friend of all.

Yet he continued to live much in the present. He became a pivotal member of a social group called "The Club," which had but twelve members representative of the leadership of New York professional and business life. It was the custom of "The Club" to meet one evening a week during the winter, in turn at the members' homes. Several members testified to the intellectual excitement Gallatin provided through his share of the talk.[11]

Frequently, during these twilight years, journalists and businessmen of a younger generation sought Gallatin out to learn what a wise old man from another age thought about the way the world was going. Men and women young enough to be his grandchildren recorded their delight with his "fascinating powers of conversation" on a wide range of subjects well into his eighty-ninth year. Now that he had more leisure, no political ambitions, and fewer responsibilities, he gave more freely of his opinions than in the past, just as the letters he dictated in answer to inquirers grew increasingly frank and effusive.

A British visitor for whom Gallatin went out of his way to be helpful was Harriet Martineau. The thirty-four-year-old author had already made a name as a political economist when she landed at New York in September, 1834, to start an American tour. Gallatin called upon her at her Broadway hotel. Years after, she carried the memory of their talk with her, for she had discovered Mr. Gallatin's name was "everywhere known and welcome." He did not look his seventy-three years, she noted, was "tall and dignified . . . courteous, bald, toothless . . . speaks with a very

slight foreign accent, but with a flow and liveliness which are delightful. . . . While he was talking I felt as if he was furnishing me
new powers of observation." As he left, he apologized for being so garru-
lous, and kissed her hand.[12] She hastened to make copious notes for use
in her writings, especially *Society in America*,[13] which was to become a
classic.

Seven years later another writer, Washington Irving, wrote after a
public dinner: "Mr. Gallatin was in fine spirits and full of conversation.
. . . He is upwards of eighty, yet has all the activity and clearness of
mind and gayety of the spirits of a young man. How delightful it is to see
such intellectual and joyous old age: to see life running out clear and
sparkling to the last drop!" [14]

2

While Gallatin lavished attention during his twilight years upon family,
friends, and the unfinished business of the past, he observed closely
and even participated actively in the strange new age into which he had
survived. During the thirties and forties the United States was passing
through an awkward age and undergoing a profound transformation.
Factories were springing up in the North and East to make textiles, iron,
and other products. Canals, roads, and highways were constructed to reach
the fast-filling farm lands and centers of the Ohio and Mississippi valleys.
More than half a million immigrants came to the North and West from
Ireland, Germany, and England, and many lingered in the port in which
they landed. New York more than doubled its population during the two
decades, boasting more than half a million inhabitants by the middle
of the century. It was not only the largest and most important city of
the country; it was the second commercial city in all the world. In New
York, as in the nation, it was the day of the dollar chaser, the hustler, the
day of bounce and bluster and bad manners.

There were moments when Gallatin remembered a quieter time and
was depressed. One day in 1834, looking at James's son Albert, nine years
old, he confessed that he "hesitated whether, with a view to his happiness,
I had better not take him to live and die quietly at Geneva, rather than
to leave him to struggle in this most energetic country, where the strong
in mind and character overset everybody else, and where consideration
and respectability are not at all in proportion to virtue and modest
merit." But he quickly pushed aside such thoughts. "I am so identified
with the country which I served so long that I cannot detach myself from

it. . . . I do not despair, and cannot believe . . . that the people will
not ultimately cure the evils under which we labor." [15]

For a cure of these evils and the continuance of the democratic system
and universal suffrage, the educational system must be revised in order to
bring "the mind of the laboring classes" in the "immense and fast-growing" New York City nearer that of classes "born under more favorable circumstances." New York had but one institution of higher education: Columbia College, classical in curriculum, small in size, and aristocratic in
tone.[16] It needed an institution offering "a rational and practical" education "fitted for all and gratuitously opened to all."

Thus Gallatin was in a receptive frame of mind in September, 1830,
when John Delafield, a banker, urged him to join a group of New Yorkers
working for the establishment of a new university.[17] Clergymen had been
discussing the idea more than a year, inspired by the example of the new
University of London; but they had held regular meetings in behalf of a
"New York University" only in the last eight or nine months. Gallatin
agreed to participate in a "literary and scientific convention" which would
catalyze the movement. Recognizing the value of his name, the group
elected him chairman of the council of the university organized in the
quarters of the New-York Historical Society on October 18, 1830.[18]

The "literary and scientific convention," held in the Common Council
Chamber of City Hall for three days beginning October 20, was attended by more than one hundred delegates—among them, representatives
of Harvard, Yale, Princeton, and Middlebury as well as the local business and cultural communities. Gallatin delivered a long address which,
he confessed, he had written without consultation with the leaders of the
movement. The convention listened politely to his account of the educational system in Geneva half a century earlier, but was stirred to debate when he turned to his notions as to what New York University
should be like.

It was worth considering, he declared, whether "the dead languages"
were of "supreme importance" in the education of Americans—whether
Latin and Greek might not be abandoned for instruction in the sciences
and in English. He proposed also the creation of a separate college for
"instruction of older and advanced pupils in the higher branches"—a
kind of graduate school. Bitter criticisms and restrained expressions of
approval of these two proposals punctuated all the discussions that followed.[19]

Although the convention stirred much enthusiasm for the idea of a
university, Gallatin and his colleagues found it difficult to raise funds.

The state government readily granted the request for a charter, but refused financial support. The city government was similarly uncooperative. Meanwhile, the cause was kept alive by the response of private citizens. The university council was reorganized in January, 1831; Gallatin was unanimously elected president.[20] One member of the council later recorded his contributions to its weekly deliberations: "Mr. Gallatin, after a brief interval, could always suggest some new measure or present some new aspect of the chief question which furnished a new starting point." [21]

He resigned from the council and severed all connections with it on October 22, 1831, on the ground of "poor health." There were other reasons. The council had raised about $100,000 in private subscriptions, and some members favored plunging ahead with the program, making extensive purchases of land and buildings. The cautious Gallatin foresaw a business depression, with dangers to the university if it lacked an adequate treasury.[22] He gave another reason for his resignation to friends. The man who had sparked the movement, the Reverend James M. Mathews, pastor of South Dutch Reformed Church, had been chosen chancellor and took the lead in drawing up its curriculum. Gallatin found that none of the goals he had held out was adopted.[23]

New York University opened its doors in 1832 and, in the course of several decades, adopted Gallatin's principles of scientific and English instruction to serve the people of many stocks in the city, and of graduate training.

During the New York years Gallatin served various societies dedicated to the advancement of knowledge, several of them as an officer. One that absorbed much of his attention for several years was the New-York Historical Society, which held regular meetings and maintained three rooms as a library and museum in the Washington Square building of New York University during the 1840's. Its membership ran to the socially élite, and its meetings—as young George Templeton Strong complained—too often were consumed with discussions of "a button cut from the coat of a spy . . . during that momentous struggle," the Revolution. Gallatin became a member in October, 1842, and president a few months later. His address as president on February 7, 1843, dealing with British influence on American life, the American Revolution, the Protestant tradition, and the divine destiny of the American people, suggested that he had lately read the historical works of George Bancroft.[24]

In the following year the Society celebrated its fortieth anniversary with a series of ceremonies, and Gallatin presided as often and as long as the strength of a gentleman of eighty-three would allow. As guest of honor on one occasion, John Quincy Adams paid a heart-felt tribute to his old colleague.[25]

3

In 1842 Gallatin wrote to J. C. L. Sismondi, a Genevan who had attained eminence in France as a historian, lamenting, "All my writings . . . adhere to my political career and have only a local and transitory importance." He did not regret this—it was his destiny. "I had not the talents to cultivate letters and science successfully; and my abilities have probably been more usefully employed in the active life into which I was thrown and for which I was better suited." [26]

His assessment of his own literary capacities was doubtless correct. His writing style, the fruit of determined application, was informed, lucid, never felicitous; his informal letters lacked grace in expression. Although he met writers of plays, novels, and belles-lettres socially, he seldom read such works. Once a year in his old age he reread Walter Scott's *The Antiquary*, but his view of the novel form was bleak. It was his private theory that a novel should be read last chapter first, so that appreciation of the style would not be lost in the interest excited by the plot.[27]

Gallatin, however, did have pronounced scientific abilities, and used them to notable effect in researches on the ethnology of the American Indian. He worked in this field, off and on, more than a quarter of a century, and published three important monographs.

Although he had to drop active work on the Indians when he accepted the mission to London in 1823, data in response to queries he had circulated kept dribbling in during his absence.[28] His zeal was renewed late in 1831 when the head of the publications committee of the American Antiquarian Society at Worcester, Massachusetts, having come across the reference to his work in Balbi's *Introduction à l'atlas ethnographique du globe*, wrote to inquire whether he had anything on the subject that the society might publish.[29]

For the next eighteen months Gallatin devoted himself to the project, canvassing sources, amassing, collating, and analyzing data. From his own pocket he advanced several hundred dollars to pay the expenses of transcribers at learned societies in Philadelphia, Boston, as well as New York.[30] The Society published his manuscript at its expense in November, 1836, and elected him a member.[31]

It was a work of which any scholar might be proud—422 fact-crammed pages entitled "A Synopsis of the Indian Tribes Within the United States East of the Rocky Mountains, and in the British and Russian Possessions in North America" and issued in the Society's serial *Transactions and Collections.* More than half of the work was a meaty "Introduction" that discussed the eighty-one tribes, the nature of the area they inhabited, their history before the coming of the white man, their relations with white men and Negroes, their manners and mores. At the end of the section Gallatin urged that religious missionaries among the surviving tribes do more toward encouraging them to pursue peaceful agricultural pursuits. The second half of the work was a technical analysis of the languages of the tribes, presented for the most part in tables according to grammatical forms.[32]

The publication was warmly received by the American scholarly community. Duponceau was gracious: "I do not see what there is to correct in your chapter on Indian languages. . . . Your philosophical introduction pleases me particularly." [33] George Bancroft of Boston, who was fast becoming renowned as a historian, assured Gallatin, "You are our guide and teacher." [34] At the time of Gallatin's death, Edward Everett Hale of the American Antiquarian Society called the work "the most valuable treatise which has been attempted on the Indian language of the continent." [35]

His feet now wet in scholarship, Gallatin found the temptation to go deeper irresistible. He took the leadership in the founding of the American Ethnological Society at New York in November, 1842, and became its first president. As a friend expressed it, "Mr. Gallatin's house was the true seat of the society and Mr. Gallatin himself the controlling spirit." The papers at the monthly meetings reflected his concern with the aborigines of the American continent.

When it was his turn to read a paper during the Society's second year, he presented a sequel to the "Synopsis" dealing with the tribes of Mexico, Yucatan, and Central America. Their civilization was much higher than that of the Indians treated in the first work, and so his "Notes on the Semi-Civilized Nations of Mexico, Yucatan, and Central America" involved correspondingly richer and more varied material, covering in addition to language the tribesmen's knowledge of science and of their own history.[36] The bulk of Gallatin's data came from the Spanish historians, but some of the most valuable were sent by Humboldt and Duponceau. Another rising historian who admired his work, William H. Prescott of Boston, lent copies of the hieroglyphics on Mexican paintings.[37]

Gallatin and a few friends underwrote the cost of publishing the work as the first volume of *Transactions of the American Ethnological Society* in 1845. The tables of comparative vocabularies, grammar, and calendars that fill its 352 pages are graphic evidence of the long and taxing hours he devoted to it. The reception in the United States was cordial; even more gratifying were the letters from England and France. There the study of ethnology was intensely active. From France, Gallatin received assurance that he had "added something to the literary reputation" of the United States.[38]

By this time Gallatin was in his eighty-eighth year. Still he was not content to rest on his laurels. In 1848 he prepared two additional, short papers for the Society: "On the Geographical Distribution and Means of Subsistence of the North American Indians at the Time of the Discovery of America," and "On the Ancient Semi-Civilization of New Mexico and the Great Colorado of the West." In revised form they filled 166 pages of the *Transactions* of that year.[39] The bulk of the new work supplemented the "Synopsis," dwelling on other anthropological influences—the climate and topography of the areas, the crops and the means of subsistence. Considerable attention was devoted to exploration in the trans-Mississippi West, based upon reports of United States Army officers.

The study of ethnology and anthropology has progressed prodigiously since the middle of the nineteenth century; but the work of Gallatin on American Indian linguistics, particularly the "Synopsis," remains a milestone. Few present-day scholars make direct use of his publications; but many of his ideas have been absorbed through the work of a later ethnologist, John Wesley Powell. Powell, in his classic "Indian Linguistic Families of America North of Mexico" in 1886, acknowledged his debt to Gallatin: "As Linnaeus is to be regarded as the founder of biologic classification, so Gallatin may be considered the founder of systematic philology relating to the North American Indians." Gallatin "had a very clear conception of the task he was performing and brought to it both learning and wisdom." He was the first American to use comparative methods of research and had available a larger body of material than any other. As a result, his work must be taken as the starting point of any study in the field.[40]

A twentieth century scholar, Clark Wissler, has paid tribute to Gallatin for three pioneering contributions to the study of American Indians: he recognized the great diversity of their languages, establishing the principles of classification and identifying the most important stocks; he understood the significance of their geographical distribution; and he "adequately stated" the arguments for the independent development of New World cultures. As for the last contribution, "all subsequent papers have done no more than elaborate his statements, usually without recognizing his claim to priority for the first comprehensive statement." Among all contributors to American Indian ethnology during the first six decades of the nineteenth century, Gallatin and Jefferson "surely lead" for "offering interpretations that have withstood the test of time." [41]

Scholars of all fields of ethnology owe Gallatin another debt, for the American Ethnological Society, having survived several reorganizations, continues its useful existence to this day.

Gallatin's scholarly contributions were such as any man might be proud to make over a long lifetime. Coming as they did in the eighth and ninth decades of his life, after an arduous career as a man of affairs, they were indeed extraordinary.

28. Financial Oracle

1830=1841

Across the first decade of the strange new age into which Gallatin survived as a private citizen, the 1830's, a long, dark shadow was cast by political crises rising out of economic matters—the tariff, banking, and the currency. It was inevitable that this man who had dedicated most of his public life to just such matters, and who was now the head of a private bank whose concerns were intimately bound up with them, should be thrust into the role of financial oracle and, on occasion, leader of the business community.

Convictions Gallatin had reached during his diplomatic service at Paris carried him back somewhat circuitously to the fiscal and political wars. He and Alexander Baring of the House of Baring had been impressed then by the resistance of the French economy to the shock of simultaneous invasions by the Allied Powers and Napoleon, and to the strain of indemnity payments exacted by the Allies during the Bourbon restoration. This Gallatin and Baring attributed to the fact that in France gold and silver circulated freely.[1]

In theory the United States had a bimetallic currency. In 1792, at the behest of Secretary Hamilton, the federal government had adopted a system whereby silver and gold were both coined by the government at a ratio of 15 to 1. But gold was worth much more in the international market, and by the 1820's enough gold had drifted to Europe to give the United States a silver-dollar currency.[2]

During the months he was preparing the American case in the Northeast boundary dispute in 1829, Gallatin discussed the currency situation with Jackson's Secretary of the Treasury, Samuel D. Ingham, and urged him to work for a true system of bimetallism. This, he believed, could be accomplished by setting a ratio of silver to gold somewhere between 15.58 and 15.69 to 1.[3]

Another conviction that Gallatin had brought back from abroad was that the French had benefited from their practice of permitting only a

356

single bank, the Bank of France, to issue paper money, and that never for less than $100. This made him, he conceded, an "ultra-bullionist." He acknowledged that such an ideal was politically impracticable in the United States. Ever since colonial times the power to issue notes to be circulated as currency had been considered as the *sine qua non* of banking. The state banks which were flooding the country with notes in small denominations exerted powerful political influence. Since this was so, the Bank of the United States—on which, he believed, rested "our reliance for a sound currency, and, therefore, for a just performance of contracts"—ought also to be allowed to issue small notes.[4]

Word of Gallatin's concern about the currency somehow reached the ears of Robert Walsh, Jr., the enterprising editor of the *American Quarterly Review* of Philadelphia. It was not generally known, but Walsh had an arrangement with Nicholas Biddle, the learned and cosmopolitan president of the second Bank of the United States, to publish articles friendly to the fiscal and political views of the Bank. This was all part of Biddle's plan to enlist the support of influential men in obtaining a renewal of the charter well before its expiration in 1836. A few kind words from a great former Secretary of the Treasury—and a Jeffersonian at that—would be most useful.[5]

In April, 1830, Walsh asked Gallatin to write an article for the *Review* on the currency and the banking system. Gallatin agreed, and Biddle promptly dispatched to New York some fourteen bundles of information and a bright young man, his own nephew, to assist in the clerical part of the work.[6]

As he labored over the records during the summer and autumn, Gallatin sent Biddle several admonitions. In August he wrote, "I think that you are too sanguine in your expectation of the Bank of the United States to sustain, under the pressure of any very difficult crisis, specie payments throughout the United States." It would be wise to decrease the amount of paper money in circulation, with a corresponding emphasis on metallic currency. The danger, he warned, was political as well as fiscal. There was a likelihood that the charter could not be renewed under any terms. In 1810, when the Invisibles had killed the first Bank of the United States out of "*personal* opposition to Mr. Madison or myself," the local banking system, with its "jealousy or selfishness . . . had not yet penetrated through the country, extending its ramifications through every hamlet" and wings of both political parties. To counter this, the Bank might now do two things: accept a modification in its charter that would "give the government a greater participation in the profits of the Bank and render it more popular"; and perhaps encourage the country banks to make loans to "mere farmers on the security of their real estate" as in Scotland.[7] Biddle received these notions in silence.

Gallatin complied with the banker's request that the manuscript be sent directly to him "to save Walsh postage." This of course allowed him to look over what Gallatin had written before delivering it to the editor.[8]

Under the title "Banks and Currency" the essay appeared in the December, 1830, issue of the *American Quarterly Review*. Biddle was delighted with it. "Nothing could have been more opportune than [its] appearance . . . which gives the greatest satisfaction every where and produces the most decided conviction," he told Gallatin. "It is a noble monument to your industry and will do a great deal of good to the country." [9]

Biddle, anxious to show his appreciation, offered to pay Gallatin $1,000 for the "much labor and thought" that had gone into its preparation.[10] Gallatin could have used the money, because he was without income and was feeling the pinch of New York City's cost of living. He declined, however, on the ground that "under existing circumstances, he who happens to have drawn conclusions favorable to the renewal of the charter must have no personal interest for coming to that result, if he wishes to produce any effect." [11] He gave Walsh the same answer when he offered $500 on behalf of the *American Quarterly Review*.[12]

The article was no sooner off the press than Gallatin began work on a longer version for publication in pamphlet form. This, he agreed, should be printed and distributed at the Bank's expense to congressmen, state legislators, and other opinion makers, but still without compensation for himself. President Jackson had recently restated his hostility to the Bank, blaming it for the lack of a sound and uniform currency. Biddle now urged Gallatin to write as forcefully for the Bank as he conscientiously could. Against Jackson's "mass of light foolery I want to put in the scale one of your strong metallic sentences of approval," he wrote.[13] Forty-three thousand words of Gallatin's "strong metallic sentences" appeared in the pamphlet *Considerations on the Currency and Banking System of the United States*, published in February, 1831.[14]

The argument rested on the hard-money convictions Gallatin had acquired in France. "Gold and silver," he declared, "are the only substances which have been, and continue to be, the universal currency of civilized nations." In comparison, paper money had nothing to recommend it except cheapness; experience in the United States during the War of 1812 had shown how impossible it was to regulate the supply and in consequence the value. He argued that the Founding Fathers had recognized the importance of bullion when they specified in the Constitution that no state should make anything but gold or silver legal tender for public debts.

To promote the free circulation of both silver and gold throughout the United States, Gallatin urged that Congress establish a ratio of 15.7 to 1. This would be legislation of a type which both Jefferson and Hamilton had agreed was allowed by the Constitution.

To promote a stable national currency, Gallatin went on, no device had been more efficacious than a national bank, created and controlled by the federal government, "perpetually watched and checked" by its rivals, the state banks, and by the Treasury Department. A national bank was constitutional because Congress was authorized to enact whatever legislation was "necessary and proper" to execute the powers vested in the federal government; a uniformity of taxes and duties throughout the Union was clearly a fundamental principle of the compact. Moreover, a national bank was useful to the financial operations of the federal government, as every Secretary of the Treasury from the first to the latest had attested; it was useful to the public in carrying on domestic commercial transactions. To have the Treasury Department or some other department of government undertake to assume the functions of the bank would lead to political appointments and incompetent and irresponsible administration.

Considerations on the Currency was issued at an unfortunate time for Gallatin's reputation. His motive in writing it had originally been to foster the free circulation of gold and silver coins, and he had undertaken to defend the Bank almost entirely because he felt it was the best means to that end. But during the months the work was in preparation President Jackson made clear his opposition to the Bank; indeed, privately, the President acknowledged that he hated all banks. Thus, as *Considerations on the Currency* was widely circulated at the expense of the Bank, Gallatin, willy-nilly, was hailed and attacked not as an advocate of bimetallism but as a defender of the Bank.

2

Even as Gallatin was denounced and praised for his defense of the Bank of the United States, he took sides on another burning political and economic issue of the era. The tariff had not really been a matter of controversy before the War of 1812. Hamilton, Jefferson, and Madison, all had called for moderate protection of the few American manufacturing industries.[15] Gallatin's attitude was less clear-cut. As an early disciple of Adam Smith, he had said good things about free trade in his *Sketch of the Finances* in 1796 and his "Report on Manufactures" in 1810. When the threat of hostilities grew more menacing while he was Secretary of the Treasury, he had asked Congress for duties and bounties that would provide revenue for war and for war preparations, and that would encourage and protect manufactures in case of war. He did not favor duties and bounties so high that they would destroy competition, tax the consumer, or divert capital and industry into channels not especially beneficial to the nation.[16]

It was Gallatin's old friend, A. J. Dallas, who, as Secretary of the Treasury working with John C. Calhoun, persuaded Congress, in 1816, to commit itself to the principle of protection for the benefit of the many war-born industries.[17] In 1824 and again in 1828 Congress yielded to the demands of the manufacturers for higher and higher rates. But by the end of the decade Calhoun turned against protection. The South Carolinian now was certain that a high tariff was unconstitutional. Declining profits in cotton had harmed the economy of his own and other southern states. When Henry Clay and the northern and western advocates of protection called for even loftier rates, there developed the first sectional split in the Union since the War of 1812.

The threat of disunion troubled Gallatin. The tariff of 1828, he believed, was "supported by a majority of the people and both Houses in Congress"; it was imperative that the spirit of compromise be nurtured to save the United States.[18] He envisioned himself in a conciliatory role when a free-trade convention was called for September 30, 1831, in Philadelphia. He agreed to attend as head of a New York delegation dedicated to moderate measures in the campaign for free trade.[19]

At Philadelphia, Gallatin was outnumbered by fire-eating southerners. Fifteen of the twenty-four states represented were southern; 133 of the 205 delegates, appointed by local voluntary meetings, were from below the Mason-Dixon line—44 from South Carolina alone. John M. Berrien of Georgia, who had served as attorney general under Jackson, manifestly spoke for the majority when he asserted that "a numerous and respectable portion of the American people question the constitutionality" of the tariff. He advocated that each individual should judge for himself whether or not to obey such a law.

Gallatin led the opposition. He held that the power to levy a tariff had been "expressly granted by the Constitution" and urged that any resolutions adopted should not imply that it was unconstitutional. At the same time the tariff was unwise because it was "calculated to retard" the prosperity of the whole country and to enrich "one section at the expense of another."

Although he lost the fight for silence on the law's constitutionality, he was successful on another score. He was made chairman of a committee to draft a memorial for presentation to Congress in the name of the convention. Even the fire-eaters must have recognized that any petition bearing his name would not be extreme.[20]

During the next three months advice from every segment of the free-trade movement poured in on Gallatin.[21] He followed his old practice of gathering specific facts and figures from various sources to buttress his argument. Late in December he had an outline ready for consideration by his fellow committeemen. Their response was in general enthusiastic. Even several southern extremists decided at the last minute to go along with his temperate statement.[22] Five thousand copies were struck off and broadly circulated; copies were officially presented to the presiding officers of the Senate and House late in January, 1832.[23]

In pamphlet form, the *Memorial* revealed the diplomatic hand of its author.[24] Essentially it followed the line of argument Gallatin had offered at the convention. It was shrewdly worded to win the accord of both those who detested as "unconstitutional" protective tariffs such as those of 1824 and 1828 and those who disliked them merely as "unequal and oppressive." It followed the classic argument of free traders that a nation is most prosperous when its industry is engaged in pursuits that are most productive—if an industry requires a protective tariff indefinitely to survive it is a liability to the nation. It declared that one of the most insidious consequences of high protection is that advocates, in order to retain it on the law books, extend its privileges to ever more numerous and ever less worthy industries, at the expense of the people as a whole. Equally reprehensible is the temptation it creates for smuggling and corrupt practices.

A high tariff, Gallatin went on, was fair neither to the South nor to the North. By its very nature it discriminated against agriculture; the predominantly agricultural South was thus obliged to provide more than its just share of the national revenue. But the two recent tariffs had discriminated against certain northern industries to the disadvantage of others; he cited many examples to establish his case. He suggested that duties be adjusted over a period of years in order to assure adequate revenue to the Treasury and to provide proper aid to deserving industries. He felt that a 20 to 25 per cent *ad valorem* tariff would suffice for these purposes.

Gallatin's arguments struck Senator Henry Clay to the quick. Recognizing the *Memorial* for what it was—the first statesmanlike challenge to the principles of his "American system," the Kentuckian took the floor of the Upper House on February 2, 1832, to attack his one-time colleague. "Go home to your native Europe," he cried, "and there inculcate upon her sovereigns your Utopian doctrines of free trade, and when you have prevailed upon them to unseal their ports and freely admit the produce of Pennsylvania, and other States, come back, and we shall be prepared to become converts, and to adopt your faith." [25] Gallatin bore this assault philosophically, attributing it to the disappointment of Clay's Presidential hopes and ·to an "excess of party spirit."

For a time it appeared that Gallatin's efforts on behalf of conciliation and compromise were in vain. Clay pushed through Congress a tariff that removed only some of the "abominations" of the 1828 act. A South Carolina convention declared the new law to be "null, void" in that state. Although Gallatin believed this was "outrageous and unjustifiable," he remained hopeful. "The difficult part for our government is how to nullify nullification and yet avoid a civil war. A difficult task but, in my humble opinion, not impossible to perform." [26]

Gallatin's doctrine won out. Though it was difficult, compromise was achieved. President Jackson threatened to send armed forces into South Carolina to enforce the law. Clay introduced a new tariff bill that scaled all schedules downward gradually over a ten-year period until they reached 20 per cent *ad valorem* rates—a procedure not unlike what Gallatin had recommended. This compromise became law early in 1833, and the sovereign state of South Carolina repealed its nullification ordinance. The tariff ceased to be a burning national issue for a decade.

3

It was the Presidential ambitions of Henry Clay that made the Bank of the United States the most controversial topic in the United States in the spring of 1832. The charter still had four years to run, but reckoning that he would improve his chances in the autumn polls as a supporter of the Bank, he pushed a renewal of the charter through Congress. Gallatin could hardly forgive Clay and Nicholas Biddle for rushing the matter and thereby introducing "party feelings into the fiscal concerns of the nation." [27]

As President Jackson was already on record as opposed to renewal of the charter, Gallatin was not surprised when he vetoed the bill. But he was dismayed by the President's next step. This was an order that federal funds henceforth should not be deposited with the Bank, but instead with favored state banks. Gallatin considered this "early removal" of deposits as "unnecessary" and the reasons the Administration gave for it as "altogether insufficient." [28] "What can induce the President to take such a course?" he asked a financier who called to learn his feelings about the matter. "Resentment!" replied the financier. "Resentment! Resentment!" Gallatin exclaimed. "The affairs of Government can only be successfully conducted by cool reasoning and the lessons of experience." [29]

The next round in the battle between Jackson and Biddle disgusted Gallatin with both men. In August, 1833, the Bank of the United States adopted a policy of sharply contracting loans and of presenting the notes of state banks for payment in specie. Biddle contended that this was necessary to prepare his institution for its forthcoming liquidation. But Gallatin and others of his contemporaries believed—and the research of later historians was to prove them right—that the Philadelphian actually wanted to create a financial panic that would oblige the Jackson Administration to haul up the white flag in its war on the Bank. At any rate, interest rates soared and by February, 1834, there was a series of bank runs and even closings, as well as numerous business failures throughout the country.[30]

As the president of a bank in a city especially hard hit, Gallatin accepted appointment as chairman of a "Union Committee of Merchants" to prepare resolutions and to exert pressures on Biddle as well as on the state and national governments. He and James G. King called upon Biddle to urge that the Bank of the United States halt its contraction policy. Biddle refused to give any assurances that would apply beyond a month.[31] Soon thereafter, on March 20, a report critical of both Biddle and Jackson, signed by twenty-four leading merchants, was presented at a meeting at the Merchants Exchange. It was publicly declared that the report was "principally, if not wholly," from the pen of Gallatin, "an even better democrat than Andrew Jackson."

The report scored the President for removal of the deposits, for "unexampled interference" with the work of the Secretary of the Treasury, for "abuse" of powers granted to him by the Constitution, for "encroachment" on the authority of Congress, for "indiscriminate" use of the veto power. It charged that Jackson believed that he could do no wrong, and had failed to remember that in the United States the people are sovereign. A memorial to Congress, attached to the report, recommended reforms in the banking and currency systems: that circulation of bank notes with a face value less than five dollars should be forbidden; that banks should not be allowed to issue notes for more than two-thirds of their capital; that the profits of banks be restricted to 6 per cent per annum on their capital.

Both report and memorial were "unanimously adopted" at the meeting. Three thousand copies were struck off for general circulation.[32] Gallatin was wrong, however, when he supposed that the American people could believe that Andrew Jackson was acting like a king. This was the age of the common man, and advice offered in the name of New York merchants, sound as it might be, fell on deaf ears.

The speculative spirit of the times received only a temporary check in the recession of 1834. Soon several hundred more state banks came into being, chartered in anticipation of the demise of the Bank of the United States. In 1835 the government achieved what had long been Gallatin's goal—complete extinguishment of the public debt. As a surplus began to accumulate in the Treasury, the opportunistic Henry Clay tried to increase his popularity by fathering a law distributing approximately $28,000,000 among the state governments. "The propriety of this measure, and its consistency with the spirit of the Constitution," Gallatin later observed, "may be questioned." [33]

The disaster he had been dreading came during the next two years. In a frantic and belated attempt to check the speculative frenzy, President Jackson directed the Treasury to refuse any paper money offered as payment for public lands. Gallatin believed this to be an "improper" act because it established two currency standards for the government—specie for lands and paper money for import duties. Specie flowed out of the vaults of eastern banks to the West. A serious fire, the failure of two poorly managed banks, demands by English bankers for specie, all in rapid succession, brought panic to the New York banking community in March, 1837.[34]

On April 8 Gallatin again joined his fellow bankers and merchants at a meeting at Mayor Cornelius Lawrence's office and accepted appointment as chairman of a committee to seek aid from Governor William L. Marcy.[35] New York State had been authorized to issue stock for the construction of three canals. If $3,500,000 of this were lent to the banks to be sold in order to meet the European demands for specie, Gallatin and his colleagues argued, the crisis would be greatly relieved.[36] But the legislature delayed action. The drain of specie continued; on May 9 alone, $652,000 was withdrawn from the New York City banks.[37] The next day was a grueling one for Gallatin. He attended a meeting of the bank presidents of the city at which a proposal to suspend specie payments was debated. He was convinced that his own bank had sufficient reserves of specie to tide it over at least a short-lived crisis. He prophesied that if the New

York banks suspended every institution in the land would follow suit. This, he warned, with more than a trace of emotion, would mean the equivalent of a breach of faith in every walk of American life, between institutions and firms, between man and man. He quit the meeting before the issue came to a vote.

Along with his fellow directors of the National Bank he waited to learn what the decision was to be. He desperately hoped that two of the larger banks would hold out. When word arrived that they had finally given way, his board resolved that, "deeply lamenting," it would suspend specie payments "because of circumstances beyond control." [38]

Gallatin now made it his goal to prevent the suspension from spreading beyond the city and to hasten resumption of specie payments within his own community. He remembered that many bankers had deliberately delayed resumption after the War of 1812 because they could profit from the chaotic situation. He urged Governor Marcy to prevent this from happening again by forbidding banks to lend more than twice their capital and by limiting dividends on bank stocks as long as suspension continued.[39] Instead the legislature enacted an "altogether unnecessary and mischievous" law that waived for a year the requirement that banks refusing to pay specie must cease operations and at the same time compelled the city banks to honor the bank notes of the country banks. The effect of this, he believed, was pernicious. In a matter of days, every bank in the land was off the specie standard.[40] Within weeks barges and towboats were idle at the docks, and thousands of laborers were unemployed.

Meanwhile, Gallatin kept urging A. C. Flagg, the state comptroller, to make clear that the state government intended to retract the charters of all banks which did not return to specie at the end of the authorized holiday, May, 1838, and offered suggestions as to how the state might continue to make interest payments in specie on its bonds in the United States and abroad.[41] Then, on August 15, he sat down with other New York City bankers to work out a program for hastening resumption. He was present only as the head of a small and not particularly important bank. But the arsenal available to him, though intangible, was formidable: the dogged determination of a man of impressive personality, strong character, and high reputation.

Although some of the bankers were reluctant, the group three days later sent a circular letter to every bank in the country that clearly showed Gallatin's authorship. It stated firmly, "We are certain that you unite with us in the opinion that it is the paramount and sacred duty of the banks" to accelerate the resumption of specie payments. The New Yorkers invited the banks to send delegates to a convention that would set a date for resumption on a national scale: some time between January 1 and the middle of March, 1838.[42]

The immediate response was anything but encouraging. Bankers in twelve agricultural states stated that they would resume payments just as soon as the foreign exchange situation improved and the cooperation of the city banks made it practicable. No replies were received from nine other states. The eastern cities, the centers of trade and finance, were especially dilatory. Boston and Baltimore hesitated to take any steps, while Philadelphia was unfeignedly hostile.[43]

Gallatin believed that Philadelphia's attitude could be traced to the influence of the Bank of the United States (now operating under a Pennsylvania charter), and specifically to Nicholas Biddle. Biddle appeared to relish the chaotic situation because he expected that it would force the new Administration of Martin Van Buren to back his continuing efforts to obtain a new charter and to renew its use of his Bank as fiscal agent.[44] There was reason to suspect, as Biddle had confessed to Gallatin years before, that the Philadelphians were jealous of the growing financial influence of New York.[45] Still not despairing, Gallatin sent Biddle an appeal to attend the convention personally. He wrote on November 23: "I do believe that without you it is hardly possible that we should come to a result just and satisfactory . . . with you we may succeed." [46] The Philadelphian replied that he was too busy to come.[47]

The convention, which met in the New York City Hall from November 27 to December 2, 1837, was a grave disappointment to Gallatin. Nearly a hundred delegates showed up, from seventeen states and the District of Columbia, leaving nine states unrepresented. Gallatin spoke— "very clearly and very ably," the *New-York Commercial Advertiser* reported—on the causes of the crisis. The New York delegation, following Gallatin's cue, proposed that July 1, 1838, be set as the date for resumption of specie payments. The Northwest and the South gave their support. Massachusetts took the nominal lead in the opposition, proposing an adjournment until the following April, by which time uncertainties about western crops, foreign exchange, and other factors affecting the supply of specie might be clarified. Philadelphia and Baltimore threw their strong support to this view. So, in the end, Gallatin's motion was voted down, 10 to 8.[48]

During the next four and a half months Gallatin worked tirelessly to organize sentiment for a new convention, holding frequent conferences with New York colleagues, corresponding with bankers in other parts of the country and with state officials at Albany.[49] Two reports by the New York committee, of December, 1837, and February, 1838, largely the work of

Gallatin, analyzed the economic situation throughout the nation and stated persuasively the case for early resumption. These were printed and circulated widely.[50] Only a man convinced that his cause was holy could have performed such labor in his eightieth year.

Through the efforts of Gallatin and his colleagues, when the new convention assembled on April 11, 1838, the New York banks were completely prepared, psychologically as well as financially, to resume as soon as May 10.[51] But the convention itself was dolorous. One hundred forty-three delegates representing seventeen states and the District of Columbia—with none at all present from Philadelphia—engaged in several days of "earnest discussions" behind closed doors. A report from Washington that President Van Buren was about to place the federal funds in subtreasury depositories so demoralized the proceedings that the delegates of two states left for home. Gallatin spoke bitterly—New York newspapers said brilliantly—on the "wretched measures" of the Jackson and Van Buren administrations. The convention adjourned on April 16, resolving "to work" for resumption by January 1, 1839. The New York banks, however, resolved to resume on May 10, 1838, in accord with the state law.[52]

There is reason to believe that Biddle still hoped to vanquish the New Yorkers through a raid on their money market; but Samuel Ward, the leading private banker at New York, checked him by negotiating a loan of $5,000,000 in gold bars from the Bank of England. Specie payment was resumed on schedule in New York.[53]

New York's successful example and Biddle's selfish maneuvers turned the scale. Within a few weeks the banks of Boston, followed by the banks of the South and of Philadelphia, felt compelled by public opinion to return to the specie standard. That the war of the financiers ended so fortunately must be attributed to the actions of Ward, to the improved condition of foreign exchange, to the cooperation of the New York State officials, but most of all to the inspired tenacity of Gallatin and his committee.[54]

4

On June 7, 1839, a year after the successful accomplishment of resumption, Gallatin resigned as president of the National Bank of New York. He was honored for his seven years' service by the other officers of the bank with a dinner at Delmonico's. He was delighted by the election of his son James to succeed him as president.[55]

Although he no longer attended biweekly directors' meetings, he continued to watch the vicissitudes of the banking community, and frequently cried out about what he observed. He was distressed in October, 1839, when the Bank of the United States—after Biddle retired from its presidency—led other Pennsylvania banks in again suspending specie payments. Banks in the South and the West followed their example. In the same month the Philadelphians and their followers held a meeting in New York to organize a run on specie-paying banks.[56] Such doings, Gallatin once more insisted to friends, were "evil and immoral." [57] Through his influence and that of Samuel Ward the attempt ended in failure.[58]

For months afterwards, Gallatin gathered information, formulated his ideas, and then dictated his views on the new crises for publication. *Suggestions on the Banks and Currency of the Several United States, in Reference Principally to the Suspension of Specie Payments,* issued in June 1841, was a remarkable intellectual performance for a man in his eighty-third year.[59] The 36,000 words of text were buttressed by copious appendices of Gallatin's composition. The historical account was detailed and precise, and the analysis of cause and effect and the suggestions for a cure of the banking and monetary ills of the age were lucid and logical.

Gallatin believed that the Jackson and Van Buren administrations had made many mistakes in financial policy; but blame for the current troubles would have to be attributed equally to the people themselves. They had bought and sold too much during the decade, especially of foreign produce; they had borrowed too much foreign capital; they had purchased more public land than they could properly settle. The Bank of the United States had encouraged speculation, and it had wasted two-thirds of its capital under Biddle's "mismanagement and gross neglect." Gallatin could not understand why Pennsylvania had not long since revoked its charter.[60]

Under the American system of government, banking was regulated by twenty-six sovereign states, and it was difficult to prescribe simple measures that would correct the situation nationally. He could merely wish that all states would revoke legislation that countenanced suspension of specie payments and would permit banks to become subject to the general laws of bankruptcy. Federal permissive legislation might also be helpful. He approved, without enthusiasm, the devices that the Van Buren Administration had adopted to cope with the emergency: the short-term Treasury notes "used as soberly as they had been," the subtreasury system, administered by the officers of the Treasury itself.

Did a new national bank, such as Henry Clay vigorously advocated, promise a permanent solution to the nation's financial ills? Beyond doubt it would be constitutional and would be useful to the government as a fiscal agent; but Gallatin had misgivings about the record of the second Bank under Biddle and wrote that, if a new Bank were chartered, steps ought to be taken "to guard against the evils which such an institution may produce." Its capital should be large enough to accommodate the government, but not so large as to increase the amount of commercial accommodations, which were already adequate. The government should make regular inspections. While it might usefully appoint some directors this was not necessary; but every state should be represented on the board. Operations should be kept distinct from those of the local business of the city in which the headquarters were located.

Gallatin acknowledged that a national bank of any description was now a prickly political issue, and wrote to a correspondent, "Did I believe that a bank of the United States would effectually secure us a sound currency, I would think it a duty, at all hazards, to promote that object." Under present circumstances, he doubted that it would secure a sound currency. Right now, the cause of a national bank was "not worth dying for. . . . I would at least wait until the wishes of the people were better ascertained." [61]

As months and then years passed, it became clear that the country could get along without a new national bank. Gradually it pulled out of the long depression. John Tyler, the state-rights Virginian who succeeded to the Presidency through the death of William Henry Harrison, gave a deathblow to the bank cause.

Gallatin's four pamphlets and numerous letters and short papers about banking, currency, and the tariff between 1830 and 1841 give him an important place among the makers of American economic thought, because many of his ideas were original, at least as applied to the United States, and because many of his observations were shrewd; but their chief significance is that they were made while a systematic philosophy of economics was emerging in the United States for the first time. It was a period when many Americans, inspired by Adam Smith's *Wealth of Nations*, were groping for "sound principles" to replace the primitive ideas that had served thus far as flickering lodestars to private and public business.

Gallatin's own suggestions about the tariff—as distinct from those of writers who preceded and influenced him—were inspired by conditions of his own era, and therefore have lost much of their cogency. On the currency and banking he was more philosophical, revealing a familiarity with the work of the economist Jean Baptiste Say and, of course, Adam Smith. He believed that commercial crises were inevitable in any active, enterprising country, that overtrading and overextension of credit inevitably followed a period of prosperity. He contented himself with trying to keep the excesses from becoming too great, with trying to prevent disastrous consequences.

Gallatin believed that a "sound currency" would enable the United States to avoid many economic woes. In supposing that the state of the currency was a cause rather than a symptom of economic health, he shared a view common among political economists of the early nineteenth century. He called the American currency of his day "worse than that of any other country" in the world, even Russia. Unlike most contemporaries, he denied that, the more paper currency a country had in circulation, the greater was its prosperity. In his view, the only sound currency was one based completely on specie, and the system in France, where the appropriate ratio between gold and silver assured the free circulation of both, was ideal.

To assure this free flow, Gallatin believed that a national government ought to have direct control of a national bank, that this bank alone should be permitted to issue convertible paper money—but only in large denominations. The proper business of bankers, he wrote, "consists not in making money, but in dealing in existing currency and in credit. . . . Bankers are money dealers." When Nicholas Biddle's direction of the Bank of the United States resulted in catastrophe for the American business community, Gallatin acknowledged that a national bank had become a political impossibility in the United States. But, sixteen years after his death his goal of vesting control over the issuance of paper currency in the federal government was accomplished in effect by the law of March 3, 1865.

Issuance of paper money was the only right Gallatin would deny to banks. Indeed, he was a leading proponent of the New York State law of 1838 which allowed any individual, or any group of persons banded together in a "banking association," to practice banking like any form of commerce, not subject to the special restrictions or treatment of a monopoly. In time this concept of "free-banking," with stress upon individualism and laissez-faire—a concept without European precedent—became the distinctively American system of banking in virtually all states and under the auspices of the government. Gallatin was willing to extend the freedom so far that the government would not afford protection of any kind to depositors. Depositors, he argued, were free men engaged in a voluntary transaction. It was a freedom that later generations of Americans were to regard more warily.[62]

5

Without knowing Gallatin personally, President Tyler testified to his esteem during the last days of 1843. From Washington a discreet inquiry came to James Gallatin: Would his father consider accepting the post of Secretary of the Treasury in place of John C. Spencer who, it was anticipated, would be leaving the cabinet shortly?[63] A month later the question was repeated directly to Gallatin as having come from Tyler's son.[64]

Gallatin was then entering his eighty-fourth year. At his age, to accept appointment to the Treasury "would be an act of insanity," he replied bluntly.[65] It was his last word on financial matters.

29. Political Oracle

1830=1849

During the 1830's such highly inflammable issues as nullification and slavery were concealed if not banished by the dexterity of Andrew Jackson and his followers, and the political wars were fought almost entirely over economic matters. Thus, with but a few exceptions, Gallatin's excursions into public life in his first decade as a private citizen centered about the Bank of the United States and the currency system.

The exceptions involved matters that had concerned him as a diplomatist. In 1829 a State Department emissary called on him for advice on the French spoliation claims. Gallatin advised that the Secretary of State "take five millions if he could get it." [1] Two years later Jackson's minister to France worked out an agreement whereby France was to make settlement for the claims outstanding. The French Chamber of Deputies declined to enact authorizing legislation. President Jackson—that "pugnacious animal," Gallatin called him privately—asked Congress in 1834 for authority to take reprisals on French property.

Although a vocal section of the public favored war, Gallatin felt that hostilities must be avoided at almost any cost. "Remember 1798 and how little reliance can be placed on popular excitement when, though there is a just cause for war, there is not sufficient motive for it, as there are strong considerations against it," he wrote to Vice President John C. Calhoun in February, 1835.[2] In letters to Congressman Edward Everett of Massachusetts, he drew upon seven years' experience of the French government and French public opinion to show the President's request was ill conceived.[3] As Gallatin predicted, the French recoiled from open hostilities. At the last minute they authorized the necessary appropriations and so brought to a happy conclusion a matter that had troubled Franco-American relations for many years.[4]

The spoliation case was a trifle compared with another unfinished piece of diplomatic business that continued well into the 1840's. In his eighty-second year Gallatin ruefully observed to a friend that he had "bestowed more time" on the Northeast boundary than on any other matter during his lifetime.[5]

On the last day of 1829, Gallatin delivered to President Jackson the statement of the American side of the boundary case which he and Preble had prepared. The President told him he regretted that the convention Gallatin had made in London two years earlier, and which the Senate had approved, called for settlement of the dispute through arbitration by a neutral sovereign, the King of the Netherlands.[6]

Gallatin had earlier acknowledged his fear that "an umpire, whether king or farmer," instead of deciding the case on its merits, would "split the difference." [7] This is precisely what happened. The 1831 decision of the King of the Netherlands recommended a compromise line that for all practical purposes split the disputed area in half.[8] Gallatin was irritated, and felt the decision was so palpably unfair that it was "not binding on the United States." [9] President Jackson passed the prickly problem on to the Senate, which would have none of the proposed settlement.

There the matter rested for half a dozen years, while relations between the aggressive British Foreign Minister, Lord Palmerston, and the somewhat vacillating Administration of Martin Van Buren deteriorated steadily. There were numerous outbreaks along the Canadian border, not all of them directly connected with the Northeast boundary dispute. Then suddenly in 1840 Palmerston presented to Parliament a report on the question prepared by two publicists named Mudge and Featherstonehaugh, which made a deep impression on the British public.

Gallatin was annoyed by Palmerston's maneuver because the report gave "a very imperfect view" of the issues at stake and treated only "subordinate points." He felt that it placed the United States at a great disadvantage because the statement he and Preble had completed in 1829, like the official British statements at that time, had been printed but never officially published. He feared that circulation of the Featherstonehaugh-Mudge report without an American reply might speed the two nations into war.

Accordingly, without even consulting the authorities at Washington, he prepared an appeal to the sense of "strict justice" of the British cabinet.[10] Blending together the material that the British and American governments had presented to the King of the Netherlands, abridging and revising it in the light of the latest developments, he produced a 40,000-word essay, *The Right of the United States of America to the North-Eastern Boundary Claimed by Them*. He rounded it out with 37,000 words of appendix and four maps, paid a printer out of his own pocket, and sent off a bundle of copies in November, 1840, to a London friend for distribution among influential Britons. "It is an appeal to justice and to public opinion," he explained in an accompanying letter, "the only means, as I believe, by which an ultimate collision may be prevented." [11]

Gallatin's essay was not without effect. His London correspondent reported hearing that it had "produced a deep impression in the highest quarters." [12] Among the readers, undoubtedly, was Lord Ashburton: Gallatin's old friend Alexander Baring. This was of no small moment because a few months later Ashburton was named a special plenipotentiary to visit the United States to try to improve Anglo-American relations. [13]

Lord Ashburton landed at Annapolis in April, 1842, and went directly to Washington to confer with President Tyler and Secretary of State Daniel Webster. By August, Webster and Ashburton had reached an agreement whereby the differences in the Northeast boundary dispute were split, with Britain receiving five-twelfths of the contested territory and the United States obtaining actually less than the King of the Netherlands had awarded it. Webster acceded to the British desire for an overland route between Montreal and St. John, which Gallatin and his colleagues had successfully resisted at Ghent. The terms greatly disappointed Gallatin, who believed the British did not have "even a shadow of a claim" to what they were obtaining, but he reconciled himself to them with the thought that if the treaty were ratified it would preserve peace. [14] Lord Ashburton, eager to renew his friendship with a man whose "candid impartiality" on men and events he prized, visited Gallatin at New York on his way back to Britain. [15]

Gallatin had no way of knowing about Webster's scandalous conduct during the making of the treaty. It was later disclosed that the Secretary of State, hoping to make himself acceptable to the British as American minister, had hoodwinked the Maine and Massachusetts authorities into acquiescing in the settlement by showing them old maps of dubious value, had accepted money from Ashburton to cover "the expenses" of digging up these maps in the Paris archives, and had instructed the American minister to England not to search the British archives for support of the American claim. [16] When the exact nature of the key map Webster had used in the negotiations was made public, Gallatin was scornful. [17]

After the ratification of the Webster-Ashburton Treaty, Gallatin unwittingly added to the confusion about the maps when William Jay, son of Chief Justice John Jay, came to him with a map made by John Mitchell in 1755 which he said his father had used at Paris during the 1782 peace negotiations. Gallatin was impressed by this map and participated in a special meeting of the New-York Historical Society on April 15, 1843, when it was put on exhibition. Secretary Webster, flushed with triumph over his treaty, attended as guest of honor.

His withered old figure bent over the reading desk, beneath the map that had been suspended in midair where all might see it, Gallatin undertook to read an address on the boundary question, but his feeble voice failed to carry to the limits of the crowded room. Young John Jay, grandson of the Chief Justice, took his place in reading the manuscript. The address, which made it clear that Gallatin did not trust the map overhead as evidence in the boundary case, detailed the efforts he had made over the years to find all the maps bearing on the issue. It closed on a philosophical note: Compromise, "in treaties as in private contracts, is necessary for the preservation of mutual confidence and of sincere friendly relations between nations or individuals." He hoped that the Webster-Ashburton Treaty would "lay the foundation of perpetual peace and amity between the two nations." [18]

Some weeks later reports of a debate in Parliament disclosed that the British possessed George III's copy of Mitchell's map showing the details of the 1782 settlement. Gallatin did not know it, but he could have unearthed this copy in the British Museum by exhaustive research while he was in London in 1827. At any rate, his last thoughts on this long drawn-out controversy were probably expressed in the appendix to the Historical Society address published in pamphlet form: "The question is now settled: and we consider these and other maps [simply] as historical or supplementary documents." [19]

2

The issues that Jackson had been able to quiet during the 1830's overpowered the politicians of the 1840's. Hundreds of thousands of Americans began to recoup fortunes shattered in the economic debacle of 1837 by migrating southwestward and northwestward. To counteract the growing wealth and size of the North, southern leaders demanded the admission of new slave states and legal safeguards for the protection of their "peculiar institution"; to counteract the "menace of slavocracy," abolition groups burgeoned throughout the North. The issues of "Manifest Destiny" (extension of national boundaries westward) and of abolition created schisms in both major parties—the Democrats and the Whigs, which Gallatin thought "a second edition, not improved . . . of the Federalists."

Inevitably he allied himself with the northern Democrats who sought to block the extension of slavery. His opposition to the institution was almost as old as his American citizenship. At the age of thirty-one, as a member of the Pennsylvania legislature, he had framed a committee report that declared slavery "obviously contrary to the laws of nature, the dictates of justice . . . and natural right." [20] About the same time he had joined the Pennsylvania Society for Promoting the Abolition of Slavery.[21] He had readily agreed to the clause, inserted in the Treaty of Ghent at British insistence, promising that the United States and Great Britain would do their best to abolish the traffic in slaves, "irreconcilable with the principles of humanity and justice." [22]

In the spring of 1844 the Tyler Administration signed a treaty with the Republic of Texas, peopled almost entirely by Americans, which was to be admitted to the Union. To Gallatin the treaty was not only a step in the drive of the southerners to protect slavery, but a certain step toward war with Mexico, which had refused to recognize the independence of Texas. Now as in his youth, he recoiled from the prospect of war. Young John Jay, who was active among the antislavery Democrats, persuaded him to preside at an "Anti-Annexation Meeting" called by William Cullen Bryant, William B. Astor, John Bigelow, and others, for the evening of April 24, 1844, at the Tabernacle on Broadway.

The large hall was jammed for the occasion. At the start all went smoothly. The friendly audience strained to hear what Gallatin in his feeble voice was saying, applauding frequently and appreciatively. But after a bit "Mike" Walsh, an Irish rabble rouser who was allied with a group of northern Democrats working to create a proslavery, pro-annexation party around Tyler, and some twenty accomplices swaggered into one corner of the auditorium. When Gallatin mentioned slavery as one of the complex causes behind the annexation movement, Walsh's claque drowned out his words with hisses. When he declared that there were some concessions which the North could not be expected to make even for preserving the Union, Walsh and his cohorts bellowed out "Hurrah for Texas!" and called for "Three cheers for Calhoun," who had recently joined Tyler's cabinet. Next came shouts about "British gold" and "Wall Street bankers." Finally order was restored so that Gallatin could finish his address.

Probably few in the Tabernacle that night understood what Gallatin had said; but the *New-York Express* the next day printed his warning that, if war with Mexico resulted from the annexation treaty, it would be "a war founded on injustice, and a war of conquest. . . . Till this day the United States have . . . never acquired any territory by conquest or violence, nor in any other way but by fair treaties, fairly negotiated, with the consent of all parties that might have any claims to the territory in question."

Facing up to the desire of the southerners to expand the realm of slavery, Gallatin held to his old principle that the Union must be preserved through compromise and concession; but he pointed out that there was a limit to what the North should be expected to grant: "It is too much to ask from us that we should take an active part in permitting the accession of a foreign state, and a foreign slave-holding state, to the union; and that we should consent that new States should again be added to those upon an unequal basis of representation." [23]

After the meeting young Jay in a letter assured Gallatin that his speech would have great influence "throughout the length and breadth of the land." [24] It was a gracious compliment; actually Gallatin's counsel had little effect. In May the Democratic convention selected James K. Polk to run on a platform calling for "the reannexation of Texas" and "the reoccupation of Oregon"—objectives designed to unite southerners and northerners and sublimate the slavery issue. In the course of the campaign Polk declared that, if elected, he would terminate the Northwest Convention and take steps to occupy Oregon.

The thought made Gallatin shudder: he was convinced that war with Britain would inevitably follow such measures. His agitation increased after Polk's narrow victory over the Whig candidate, Henry Clay. He was approaching his eighty-fifth birthday, and, as he wrote, "nothing but a profound sense of duty" could have induced him again to take a share in a public discussion. He would speak out the truth as he saw it.[25] During the last weeks of 1845 he dictated essays on the political and diplomatic aspects of "The Oregon Question" and sent them to Joseph Gales, publisher of the Washington *National Intelligencer*. They were printed in four installments during January, 1846.[26] He had another essay, on the financial aspects of the crisis, entitled "War Expenses," ready for publication the following month.[27] The entire work, plus a summary, 27,000 words in all, was reprinted in pamphlet form later in February.[28]

Gales hailed the work as the crowning accomplishment of an illustrious Old Republican who "literally lives in the midst of posterity." Former Mayor Philip Hone of New York wrote in his diary that he counted it "the best, the clearest, and the soundest which has been presented to the American people on this exciting subject." [29]

Gallatin emphasized that his purpose in writing "The Oregon Question" was to prevent a "calamitous and expensive war" with Great Britain —a war he considered to be inevitable if Polk persisted in abrogating the convention. As the claim of neither nation to the Oregon Country was indisputable, both the United States and Great Britain could still honorably offer to renew negotiations. He underscored what most Americans preferred to overlook: that, although the United States' claims to Oregon were stronger than those of Britain, they were by no means airtight. It would be better to let time take its natural course in Oregon.

The essay on "War Expenses" was more tightly written and was crammed, like the papers he had prepared while Secretary of the Treasury, with specific facts and figures and reasoned opinions. His purpose shone through every line: to make a war with Britain appear so unappealing, indeed onerous, from a financial point of view, that readers would believe it must be avoided if at all possible with honor. The way to avoid it, he emphasized, was to seek a new understanding with Britain over Oregon, assuring her that the United States would not attempt in the meantime to assume sovereignty over the area or any British subjects residing there.[30]

But President Polk turned a deaf ear and ordered the termination of the Oregon Convention, to take effect in April, 1847. Fortunately he left the door open for negotiation, and fortunately the British were in a conciliatory mood. A treaty was signed in June, 1846, extending the United States' northern boundary west along the forty-ninth latitude to Puget Sound, and thence to the Pacific Ocean through the Straits of Juan de Fuca, leaving Vancouver Island to the British. Gallatin could take satisfaction in this settlement because it could never have been made without his resolute and reasoned resistance to British claims two decades earlier at London.

Meanwhile, however, the government pressed its expansionist program in the Southwest with less fortunate consequences. Even before Polk took office, Congress had voted to admit Texas as a state—an act which outraged Gallatin. Just as he had predicted, Mexico considered the annexation as a hostile act. By May, 1846, Congress had passed a declaration of war and soon exuberant volunteers were heading for Mexico and the "halls of Montezuma."

The American forces had already penetrated Mexico City when Gallatin, exasperated by the whole unheroic conflict, prepared yet another pamphlet urging the government to make a speedy and just peace. His pamphlet was published late in 1847.[31] It expounded the thesis that the war was unnecessary and without justification. Even worse, in the eyes of the Old Republican, was the fact that the American people had trampled upon a noble tradition. The national mission had been "to improve the state of the world, to be the 'model republic,' to show that men are capable of governing themselves." But now an appeal had been made to the cupidity of the people, to their thirst for "unjust aggrandisement by brutal force," to their "love of military fame and of false glory"; and they had succumbed.

Gallatin examined the declaration of many apologists for the war that it was the Americans' mission to "enlighten the degraded Mexicans," to "improve their social state," ultimately to "increase the happiness" of their masses. This, he retorted, was not "compatible with the principle of democracy, which rejects every hereditary claim of individuals to admit an hereditary superiority of races." Now that the war was all but over, Americans were talking about "an honorable peace." What was meant by the phrase? Americans must, Gallatin insisted, abide by the Christian precepts, especially "Do unto others as you would be done by." Of course the Mexicans must pay whatever indemnities they justly owed; and, if they were willing to cede to the United States territory "not actually settled . . . and of no utility to them," it should be received "by a treaty freely assented to" and with provisions for fair compensation.

Some 90,000 copies of *Peace with Mexico* were distributed to clergymen, legislators, editors, postmasters, and school and college libraries in every section of the country. Methodists, Baptists, and other church people were zealous in seeing that it reached the right hands.[32]

Depressed though he was, Gallatin did not despair of the American people and their government. "I have faith in our institutions and in the ultimate prevalence of the truth," he told a friend in February, 1848.[33] His faith in the republic he had done so much to build was not misplaced. Having conquered Mexico, Americans were restrained by a twinge of conscience. The boundary was readjusted to include some territory "not actually settled by Mexicans and of no use to them"; but the United States paid generously for it and even assumed the unpaid indemnities. It was all that Gallatin could have hoped, indeed even more.

3

From youth, Gallatin had suffered from headaches and other minor aches and pains, about which he complained volubly; he was frequently incapacitated by attacks of what he called "my natural indolence." It was not until he was well along in his eighth decade that his physical condition began to try him sorely. The ache that lingered in his fingers and wrists after a severe attack of rheumatism in his seventy-eighth year made it impossible for him to write at any great length; thereafter he dictated his pamphlets and letters.[34]

Early in the summer of 1848, a few months after he completed *Peace with Mexico*, a complex of ailments confined him to his bedroom.[35] He was concerned only with the distant past and the future. He mumbled to himself in the French of his boyhood about Geneva friends and acquaintances. He triumphantly told his niece, Mary Few, that he had subdued all ill feelings towards all men. "By prayer?" she asked. "Surely by prayer," he replied. "What could I do myself?" [36]

Lying in bed, staring at the ceiling, he thought more and more about the nature of the Deity, of life, of the hereafter. He had never been religious in the orthodox sense. He had described himself as "a bold speculator," accustomed to pushing "discoveries to their utmost consequences without fear." As he edged near death's door, any lingering doubts about the immortality of the soul, the responsibility of man to his Creator, and the possibility of salvation through the merits of the Savior vanished completely.[37]

On May 14, 1849, Hannah, his companion and helpmate of fifty-five years, died in the room next to his.[38] Everything was now made ready for his own end. He directed that his estate, valued at $100,000, be divided equally among his three children.[39]

With the coming of warm weather, his daughter Frances Gallatin Stevens took him to her country home in Astoria, on Long Island. There he died on August 13, 1849, aged—as the *New York Tribune* noted—eighty-eight years, six months, and fifteen days.

The funeral was held two days later, and his body was interred in the vault of the Witter family, in the yard of Trinity Church.[40] One newspaper paid him tribute as "the last patriarch of the Republican party." In the autumn the meetings of the New-York Historical Society and the American Antiquarian Society memorialized his political, financial, and scholarly contributions.

So passed a noble adopted son whom the American people have thus far failed to recognize duly for his great and unselfish service.

Notes

SPECIAL ABBREVIATIONS
USED IN THE NOTES

AC	*Annals of Congress*
AG	Albert Gallatin
ASP	*American State Papers*
GP	Gallatin Papers
JP	Jefferson Papers
PHJ	*Pennsylvania House Journal*
PMHB	*Pennsylvania Magazine of History and Biography*
PSJ	*Pennsylvania Senate Journal*
TJ	Thomas Jefferson

1: THE GENEVAN HERITAGE, 1761–1780

1. Etat Civil Saint-Pierre B.M. 14, Archives d'Etat, Geneva; Gallatin, Recherches sur la maison natale d'Albert Gallatin.
2. Family safe, GP.
3. Gallatin, *Writings*, III, 593–615.
4. Autobiographical sketch by AG (filed under 1849), GP; Recensement A7, A8, A9, Registre des Morts, EC Morts 64, Archives d'Etat. There are ten receipted bills for AG's education, dated 1775 to 1778, in GP.
5. For accounts of Geneva see AG to Eben Dodge, Jr., Jan. 21, 1847, GP; Chaponnière, *Voltaire chez les Calvinistes*, 36, 37, 67, 227; Spink, *Jean-Jacques Rousseau et Genève*, 3–5, 9–11, 13. D'Alembert's article on Geneva in Diderot's *Encyclopédie* (1755) is illuminating, but not to be taken literally.
6. Montesquieu, *The Spirit of the Laws* (Nugent transl.), Bk. XX, Chap. 18, No. 16.
7. AG to Dodge, Jan. 21, 1847, GP.
8. Chaponnière, especially 48, 49, 246; Peter, *Une Amie de Voltaire*; Adams, *Life of Albert Gallatin*, 6–9.
9. AG to Dodge, Jan. 21, 1847, GP; Karmin, *Sir Francis D'Ivernois*, 39; Borgeaud, *L'Académie de Calvin*, especially 571, 574.
10. For Rousseau and Geneva, see Josephson, *Jean-Jacques Rousseau*, especially 3–5, 11, 186 ff., 391 ff.

11. AG to Jean Badollet, Oct. 1, 1783, and to Dodge, Jan. 21, 1847; P. M. Gallatin to AG, May 21, 1780, GP; Adams, *Life*, 17.
12. AG to Badollet, May 16 and Sept. 14, 1780, GP.

2: THE ROMANTIC YEARS, 1780–1790

1. AG to Badollet, Sept. 14, 1780, GP.
2. AG to Badollet, Oct. 29, 1780, and Sept. 15, 1782; Henri Serre to Badollet, Dec. 13, 1782, GP.
3. AG to Badollet, Sept. 14, 1780, GP.
4. AG to Badollet, Oct. 29, 1780, and Sept. 15, 1782, GP.
5. AG to Badollet, Oct. 29, 1780; Serre to Badollet, [same date ?], GP.
6. AG to John Connell, Jan. 9, 1846, GP.
7. Catherine Pictet to AG, Feb. 5 and Nov. 14, 1782, GP.
8. Harvard College Records, III (1778–1795), 96, 150.
9. AG's Harvard notebook, GP.
10. Certificate signed by Joseph Willard, Edward Wigglesworth, and Samuel Cooper, Aug. 18, 1783, GP.
11. Hale, "Memoir," *Amer. Antiq. Soc. Proc.*, Oct. 23, 1849, 19.
12. Serre to Badollet, Dec. 13, 1782, GP.
13. This account of Savary de Valcoulon and AG's relations with him is drawn, to a considerable extent, from Dater, "Albert Gallatin: Land Speculator," *Miss. Valley Hist. Rev.*, XXVI, 21–38. Dater makes profitable use of a series of lively and informative letters from Savary, published in the *Journal de Lyon*, Mar. 29, Apr. 12, 17, 27, Aug. 30, Sept. 13 and 27, 1786. For the claims of René Rapicault, see *Calendar of Virginia State Papers*, I, 320, IV, 538, and VIII, 411.
14. This summary of AG's and Savary's journey is based largely on notes made by AG in a small book now in GP. See also AG to Serre, July 22, 1783, GP.
15. AG to Badollet, Oct. 1, 1783, GP.
16. Dater, "Gallatin: Land Speculator," 24, 27.
17. AG to William Maxwell, Feb. 15, 1848, GP. Patrick Henry's words are quoted from the account of William Wirt in the *National Intelligencer*, Apr. 29, 1824.
18. Dater, "Gallatin," 27; AG to Badollet, Mar. 30, 1785, GP. There is a draft of a petition to the Virginia legislature drawn up by AG in GP.
19. Dater, "Gallatin," 27, 28. See also AG autobiographical sketch, GP, and Fayette County Property Roll, Springhill Township, 1786.
20. For varying accounts of this episode, see Adams, *Life*, 56–58, and Stevens, *Albert Gallatin*, 23, 24. See also Freeman, *George Washington*, VI, 20.
21. Dater, "Gallatin," 28, 29; AG to Badollet, Mar. 30, 1785, GP.
22. Henry, "To whom it may concern," Mar. 25 and 29, 1785, GP. During the period from Mar. 31 to Nov. 25, AG kept a small diary, preserved in GP, in

which he made day-by-day records of expenses, the nature of the country passed through, and other matters. Except where noted below, the account of the summer of 1785 is based on his diary and on Savary's letters in *Journal de Lyon*, quoted by Dater.

23. AG to J. W. Nicholson, Feb. 4, 1840, GP. According to Dater, "Gallatin," 33, Gallatin performed his task so carefully that "to this day [1939] the natives refer to many boundaries as Gallatin lines."

24. There is a copy of the record of the October Court, Monongalia County, in GP.

25. Autobiographical sketch, GP; Fayette County Deed Book A, 103–105.

26. Extract from [?] & McNeal to [?], June 27, 1786, GP.

27. Dater, "Gallatin," 36.

28. The diary AG kept during this trip is in GP.

29. Bentley, *Diary*, I, 37, 88.

30. *Pennsylvania Packet*, May 18, 1786.

31. Catherine Pictet to AG, July 22, 1785, and Oct. 1, 1787; Abraham Gallatin to AG, June 20, 1785; Anne Gallatin to AG, Mar. 6, 1786, GP.

32. This account of AG's romance and first marriage is based mainly on the memorandum prepared by W. H. Wade of Richmond, Feb. 11, 1878, for Henry Adams. See also AG to Badollet, May 4, 1789. Both are in GP.

33. Henrico County Marriage Bonds; account book in GP.

34. Copy of an article from *Staunton Vindicator*, GP.

35. AG to Badollet, Mar. 30, 1785, and May 4, 1789, GP.

36. AG to Badollet, Mar. 8, 1790, GP.

37. AG to Catherine Pictet, Apr. 7, 1790; Adams, *Life*, 75.

38. Adams, *ibid.*

3: A POLITICAL APPRENTICESHIP, 1788–1790

1. AG to Badollet, Oct. 1, 1783, GP.

2. There are good accounts of the situation in Pennsylvania at this time in Ferguson, *Early Western Pennsylvania Politics*, 38 ff.; and Brunhouse, *The Counter-Revolution in Pennsylvania*, 191 ff. For the background of the anti-Constitution movement, see Brunhouse, *Counter-Revolution*, 213–215; Walton, "Nominating Conventions in Pennsylvania," *Amer. Hist. Rev.*, II, 264–267; Luetscher, *Early Political Machinery*, 125 ff.; McMaster and Stone, *Pennsylvania and the Federal Constitution*, 17, 18; Smith, "The Movement Towards a Second Constitutional Convention," in Jameson, ed., *Essays in the Constitutional History of the United States*, 67, 68, 98; Van Doren, *The Great Rehearsal*, 182, 183, 185–187, 235, 236.

3. The certificate, dated Aug. 18, 1788, is in GP.

4. Ford, *Harrisburg Convention*, 13–15.

5. James Hanna to Messrs. Vandegrift, Vansant, and Vandegrift, Aug. 15, 1788,

Philadelphia *Pennsylvania Gazette,* Sept. 10, 1788; *Pittsburgh Gazette,* Aug. 30, 1788; McMaster and Stone, *Pennsylvania,* 553, 554.

6. AG's drafts for the resolutions and notes for the speech are in GP.
7. *Proceedings Relative to Calling the Conventions of 1776 and 1790,* 64, 129 ff.; Brunhouse, *Counter-Revolution,* 221–224; *Pennsylvania Gazette,* Sept. 16, 1789. See also Selsam, *Pennsylvania Constitution of 1776.*
8. In GP is what appears to be a digest of the letter to Addison, dated Oct. 7, 1789. In the absence of the original, there is, it should be noted, a possibility that the letter is not actually of AG's authorship.
9. Marshel to AG, Oct. 9, 1789; Redick to AG, Oct. 9, 1789, GP.
10. *Proceedings,* 138.
11. Ferguson, *Early Western Penna. Politics,* 77, 79, 85; Maclay, *Journal,* 379.
12. Biddle, *Autobiography,* 251, 252, 256.
13. AG to Hannah Nicholson, Sept. 2, 1793, in Adams, *Life,* 105.
14. Walters, *Dallas.*
15. *Proceedings,* 149.
16. AG to Charles Brown, Mar. 1, 1838, GP.
17. AG to A. R. Gallatin, Apr. 14, 1827, GP.
18. Tinkcom, *Republicans and Federalists in Pennsylvania,* 8, 9; Brownson, *Life and Times of Senator James Ross;* Schramm, "William Findley in Pennsylvania Politics"; Rossman, *Thomas Mifflin and the Politics of the American Revolution;* and Peeling, The Public Life of Thomas McKean.
19. Findley, "Autobiographical Letter," *PMHB,* V, 445, 446; *Proceedings,* 150–152; Brunhouse, 225, 226.
20. AG to Brown, Mar. 1, 1838, GP.
21. *Proceedings,* 246.
22. AG to Badollet, Mar. 8, 1790, GP.
23. *Proceedings,* 270, 271; Brunhouse, *Counter-Revolution,* 226, 227.
24. *Proceedings,* 151.
25. *Proceedings,* 217, 218.
26. Notes by AG for his speeches on the popular election of senators, the right of suffrage, and the liberty of the press, and his estimates on representation are in GP. For his part in the debates, see *Proceedings,* especially 155, 156, 174, 177, 221, 222, 237, 319, 323, 326, 373, 374.
27. Graydon, *Memoirs,* 368.
28. AG to Brown, Mar. 1, 1838, GP.
29. *Proceedings,* 294–308; Philadelphia *Federal Gazette,* Sept. 4, 1790.

4: SPOKESMAN OF FRONTIER DEMOCRACY, 1790–1793

1. I have given the material of this chapter in fuller form in "Spokesman for Frontier Democracy," *Pennsylvania History,* XIII, 161–184, and "The Making of a Financier," *PMHB,* LXX, 258–269.

2. There are data on the 1791 and 1792 elections on various scraps of paper in GP. See also, *PHJ*, 1790–1791, 4; 1791–1792, 4; 1792–1793, 4.

3. Ferguson, *Early Politics*, 48 ff.; Ferguson, "Albert Gallatin, Western Pennsylvania Politician," *Western Penna. Hist. Mag.*, XVI, 183–195; Ellis, *History of Fayette County*, 770.

4. *Penna. Archives*, 3rd Ser., II, 16, 19, 6th Ser., XIII, 211; AG to Badollet, Feb. 22, 1792, and Mar. 9, 1793, to Thomas Clare, Dec. 18, 1792, and Mar. 9, 1793, GP.

5. William Findley to AG, Aug. 20 and Sept. 27, 1792, James Hutchinson to AG, Sept. 25 and Oct. 24, Dallas to AG, Sept. 25, Addison to AG, Oct. 11, 1792, GP. For an account of the election of 1792 in Pennsylvania, see Walters, "The Origins of the Jeffersonian Party in Pennsylvania," *PMHB*, LXVI, 440–458.

6. AG's autobiographical sketch, GP.

7. *PHJ*, 1790–1791, 1791–1792, 1792–1793, *passim*. Two notebooks in GP, which AG kept during the first part of the 1790–1791 session, preserved in GP, list 27 committees.

8. Autobiographical sketch; AG to Clare, Mar. 9, 1793, GP.

9. Twining, *Travels in America 100 Years Ago*, 51, 52; Hiltzheimer, *Diary*, 173, 190, 211.

10. Philadelphia *American Daily Advertiser*, Sept. 6, 1791.

11. Hiltzheimer, *Diary*, 173, 186.

12. Brunhouse, *Counter-Revolution*, 94 ff., 108–112, 131–134, 170–172.

13. *PHJ*, 1790–1791, 7.

14. Autobiographical sketch, GP.

15. AG's views on public morality are stated in *Biographical Memoir* (reprinted from New York *Democratic Review*, June, 1843), 9, 10. He wrote to Ezekiel Bacon, Nov. 28, 1845 (preserved in GP), that he personally contributed to the writing of this section of the memoir.

16. *PHJ*, 1790–1791, 163.

17. Redlich, *Essays in American Economic History*, 177–179.

18. See Note 12.

19. The report is printed in full in *PHJ*, 1790–1791, 162–173.

20. AC, 1st Cong., 2nd Sess., 2243–2251.

21. *Biographical Memoir*, 10; *PHJ*, 1791–1792, 159.

22. *Laws of the Commonwealth of Pennsylvania*, III, 31, 32, 51–55, 63–65, 67–71; *Biographical Memoir*, 10.

23. *PHJ*, 1791–1792, 157.

24. *Ibid.*, 157–162; *PSJ*, 1792–1793, 10; *Laws*, III, 267–273.

25. Autobiographical sketch, GP.

26. *PHJ*, 1792–1793, 156, 157.

27. Holdsworth and Fisher, *Financing an Empire*, I, 52–60; Brunhouse, *Counter-Revolution*, 111, 112, 150, 151, 173–175, 195–197.

28. Philadelphia *General Advertiser*, Feb. 14, 16, and 18, 1793.

29. *Laws*, III, 323–335, 412–441.

30. *PSJ*, 1793–1794, 11; Holdsworth and Fisher, *Financing*, I, 133–137.
31. Autobiographical sketch, GP.
32. Baldwin, *Whiskey Rebels*, 56–61.
33. *Ibid.*, 69–71.
34. Fayette County Property Rolls, Springhill Township, 1789, 1793.
35. *PHJ*, 1790–1791, 94, 95. Henry Adams (*Life*, p. 87) believes the resolution was "the very first legislative paper" drafted by Gallatin. I have not been able to discover any evidence for this.
36. *American Daily Advertiser*, Jan. 20, 22, and 24, 1791.
37. *PHJ*, 1790–1791, 108–111; *PSJ*, 1790–1791, 92.
38. *AC*, 1st Cong., 2nd Sess., 1884.
39. Ferguson, *Early Politics*, 3, 4; Brunhouse, *Counter-Revolution*, 135.
40. Plummer, *Road Policy of Pennsylvania*, 39, 43; *American Daily Advertiser*, Feb. 19, 1791, and Feb. 4, 1793; *General Advertiser*, Feb. 21, Apr. 7, and May 4, 1791.
41. *PHJ*, 1791–1792, 232, 233; *Laws*, III, 133–143, 246–258, 273–285.
42. *PHJ*, 1791–1792, 31, 32, 35, 69, 70, 75, 76. See also Henderson, "The Northwestern Lands of Pennsylvania," *PMHB*, LX, 133–137.
43. *General Advertiser*, Feb. 8 and 9, 1792; *American Daily Advertiser*, Feb. 10, 1792.
44. *Laws*, III, 209–214. The case was that of the Holland Land Co., treated in detail in Evans, *Holland Land Company*, 107–176.
45. Cribbs, "Frontier Policy of Pennsylvania," 93, 94; *PHJ*, 1790–1791, 249, 250, and 1791–1792, 84, 87, 97; *Laws*, III, 19, 177, 178; AG to Badollet, Jan. 7 and 21, 1792, GP; *General Advertiser*, Jan. 13, 1792; *American Daily Advertiser*, Jan. 12, 14, and Feb. 4, 1792; *Penna. Arch.*, 2nd Ser., XIV, 196–198.
46. Autobiographical sketch, GP. *PHJ*, 1790–1791, 73, 88, 234, 253, 278 ff., 545; 1791–1792, 79, 80, 89, 177–179, 191, 192, 208 ff., 247; 1792–1793, 32, 294–296, 301–303; 1794–1795, 228, 229, 250, 251. *Laws*, III, 111, 112, 160–163.
47. *PHJ*, 1790–1791, 372, 373, 452; 1791–1792, 74, 243; 1792–1793, 105, 106, 120, 121; *PSJ*, 1792–1793, 116, 117; *General Advertiser*, Dec. 17, 1791, and Feb. 1, 1793; *American Daily Advertiser*, Dec. 17, 1792, and Jan. 23, 1793; Stephens, "The Transitional Period, 1788–1789," *Univ. Mo. Studies, Social Science Ser.*, II, No. 4.
48. *AC*, 3rd Cong., 58–60; AG to Clare, Mar. 9, 1793, GP.
49. *General Advertiser* and *American Daily Advertiser*, Mar. 1, 1793; *PSJ*, 1792–1793, 138–141.
50. AG to Clare, Mar. 9, 1793, GP; Philadelphia *Gazette of the United States*, Mar. 16, 1793.
51. Autobiographical sketch, GP.
52. Hiltzheimer, *Diary*, 190.

5: BENEDICT AND SENATOR, 1793–1794

1. Catherine Pictet to AG, Apr. 25, 1792, GP.
2. AG to Badollet, Dec. 18, 1792, and Mar. 9, 1793, GP.
3. AG to Badollet, July 31, 1793, GP.
4. Bacon, *Ancestry of Albert Gallatin and Hannah Nicholson*, 35–39.
5. AG to Badollet, Feb. 1, 1794, GP.
6. AG to James Nicholson, July 20, 1793, GP.
7. Nicholson to AG, July 24, 1793, GP.
8. AG to Badollet, Feb. 1, 1794, GP.
9. AG to Hannah Nicholson, Aug. 23, 1793, in Adams, *Life*, 103.
10. Powell, *Bring Out Your Dead*, 51–53, 66–68; AG to Hannah Nicholson, Aug. 25 and 29, Sept. 2 and 4, 1793, in Adams, *Life*, 104–107.
11. AG to Badollet, Feb. 1, 1794, GP.
12. AG to Hannah Gallatin, Dec. 2, 1793, in Adams, *Life*, 110.
13. The emergence of Jefferson as a party leader may be traced in various newspaper articles during this period; for example, see the Philadelphia *Federal Gazette*, Oct. 3, 1792.
14. TJ to James Madison, June 23, 1793, in Jefferson, *Writings* (Ford ed.), VI, 326.
15. Link, *Democratic-Republican Societies*, 10–12; Walters, *Dallas*, 43–46; *Gazette of the United States*, July 17, 1793.
16. AG to Hannah Nicholson, Aug. 25, 1793, in Adams, *Life*, 104.
17. AG to Badollet, Feb. 1, 1794, GP.
18. AG to Hannah Nicholson Gallatin, Aug. 25 and Dec. 6, 1793, in Adams, *Life*, 103, 104, 111.
19. AG to Hannah Gallatin, Dec. 15, 1793, in Adams, *Life*, 112, 113.
20. AC, 3rd Cong., 9; AG to Hannah Gallatin, Dec. 3, 1793, in Adams, *Life*, 111.
21. AC, 3rd Cong., 19; AG to Hannah Gallatin, Dec. 15, 1793, in Adams, *Life*, 112.
22. AC, 3rd Cong., 24.
23. AC, 2nd Cong., 2nd Sess., 840; Anderson, *William Branch Giles*, 20–24.
24. ASP: *Finance*, I, 43; AC, 3rd Cong., 43.
25. AC, 3rd Cong., 26, 27, 29, 30, 34–36. Evidence that this resolution was the work of Gallatin is contained also in a notation on one of the manuscripts in GP. See also Adams, *Life*, 116 n.
26. Hamilton to Vice President of the United States, Feb. 6, 1794, in ASP: *Finance*, I, 274.
27. Hamilton to Vice President of the United States, Feb. 22, 1794 (copy), GP.
28. AC, 3rd Cong., 28, 29.
29. *Ibid.*, 58–62.
30. *American Daily Advertiser*, Feb. 12, 1794.
31. AC, 3rd Cong., 49, 50.

32. *Ibid.*, 47, 48, 51, 52, 57, 61.
33. *Ibid.*, 57, 58; AG to Clare, Mar. 5, 1794, GP; Monroe to TJ, Mar. 3, 1794, Monroe, *Writings*, I, 282, 283.
34. AG to Hannah Gallatin, Dec. 18 and 20, 1793, in Adams, *Life*, 113, 114; AG to Badollet, Feb. 1, and to Clare, Mar. 5, 1794, GP.
35. AG to Hannah Gallatin, Apr. 19, 1794, in Adams, *Life*, 122.
36. Badollet to AG, July 8 and 23, 1793, and Jan. 27 and Mar. 24, 1794, GP.
37. AG to Badollet, and to Clare—both Apr. 10, 1794, GP.

6: THE WHISKEY REBELLION: "MY ONLY POLITICAL SIN," 1791–1794

1. Baldwin, *Whiskey Rebels*, 61–75.
2. Marshel to AG, July 16, 1791, GP.
3. Findley, *History of the Insurrection*, 41, 42; H. H. Brackenridge, *Incidents of the Insurrection*, III, 16, 17.
4. *American Daily Advertiser*, Aug. 17, 1791; H. M. Brackenridge, *History of the Western Insurrection*, 22; *Penna. Arch.*, 2nd Ser., IV, 84.
5. *Gazette of the United States*, Sept. 10, 1791; *Laws*, III, 115.
6. *American Daily Advertiser*, Sept. 23 and 30, 1791; *Penna. Arch.*, 2nd Ser., IV, 20–22; Brackenridge, *Incidents*, III, 18, 19 n.; Baldwin, 78, 79.
7. *Penna. Arch.*, 2nd Ser., IV, 37, 44, 45, 86, 88, 231, 293; Findley, *History*, 58, 86; Brackenridge, *Incidents*, III, 23, 24; Addison, *Charges to the Grand Jury*, 50; Baldwin, *Whiskey Rebels*, 82–85.
8. Philadelphia *Federal Gazette*, Aug. 2 and 24, Sept. 8, 1792; Findley to William Irvine, Aug. 17, 1792, Irvine Papers, XI, No. 21.
9. A broadside containing the resolutions is in GP.
10. A draft of the remonstrance, in AG's hand, is in GP.
11. *General Advertiser*, Sept. 28, 1792; *Penna. Arch.*, 2nd Ser., IV, 32, 33; Malone, *Jefferson and the Rights of Man*, 479, 480.
12. Baldwin, *Whiskey Rebels*, 87–90; George Clymer to Hamilton, Oct. 2, 1792, Wolcott Papers.
13. Hutchinson to AG, Sept. 25, 1792, GP.
14. AG to Clare, Dec. 18, 1792, GP.
15. AG to Badollet, Dec. 18, 1792, GP.
16. Gallatin, *Writings*, III, 6, 7.
17. *Ibid.*, 7, 8.
18. Hamilton, *Works*, VI, 358–388; Findley, *History*, 59, 60; *Penna. Arch.*, 2nd Ser., IV, 95, 96, 290; Baldwin, *Whiskey Rebels*, 90, 91, 98–104.
19. AC, 3rd Cong., 113, 115, 118, 437, 560, 720, 742, 1457–1461; Gallatin, *Writings*, III, 9.
20. Findley, *History*, 75, 76, 224, 225, 299, 300; Washington, *Writings*, XII, 221; Hamilton, *Works*, VI, 341; *Penna. Arch.*, 2nd Ser., IV, 99; Link,

Democratic-Republican Societies, 14, 145–147; Baldwin, *Whiskey Rebels,* 110–112.

21. H. H. Brackenridge, *Incidents,* I, 17–21, 121, 122, III, 25–27, 133–136; Findley, *History,* 77, 78, 84–93; *Penna. Arch.,* 2nd Ser., IV, 73–75, 100–102; H. M. Brackenridge, *History,* 40–51; Baldwin, *Whiskey Rebels,* 113–120, 131–137.
22. Gallatin, *Writings,* III, 10, 11; Brackenridge, *Incidents,* 136.
23. Brackenridge, *Incidents,* I, 38–41, 52–55, 59–61, III, 110, 111; Findley, *History,* 93–101; *Penna. Arch.,* 2nd Ser., IV, 78–80, 171–173, 522; Gallatin, *Writings,* III, 11–13; Baldwin, *Whiskey Rebels,* 138, 139, 146–161.
24. Brackenridge, *Incidents,* III, 136, 137.
25. There is a list in GP of 34 delegates from Fayette County to the Parkinson's Ferry meeting.
26. Gallatin, *Writings,* III, 14, 15.
27. Brackenridge, *Incidents,* I, 87–90; Findley, *History,* 113; *Penna. Arch.,* 2nd Ser., IV, 163; Gallatin, *Writings,* III, 15, 16; Baldwin, *Whiskey Rebels,* 174–176.
28. Brackenridge, *Incidents,* III, 137.
29. Brackenridge, *Incidents,* III, 137, 138.
30. A copy of Marshel's resolutions is in GP.
31. Brackenridge, *Incidents,* I, 90, III, 138; Findley, *History,* 114; Gallatin, *Writings,* III, 16, 17; *Penna. Arch.,* 2nd Ser., IV, 164.
32. Brackenridge, *Incidents,* I, 90–97, III, 138, 139; Findley, *History,* 113–115; Baldwin, *Whiskey Rebels,* 176, 177.
33. Hamilton, *Works,* VI, 389–394.
34. Brackenridge, *Incidents,* III, 139; Baldwin, *Whiskey Rebels,* 180, 181.
35. Brackenridge, *Incidents,* I, 97–99, III, 139; Gallatin, *Writings,* III, 17, 18; *Penna. Arch.,* 2nd Ser., IV, 164; Baldwin, *Whiskey Rebels,* 181, 182.

7: THE WHISKEY REBELLION: "ALLAYING THE FERMENT," 1794–1795

1. Brackenridge, *Incidents,* I, 102, 103, III, 138; Baldwin, *Whiskey Rebels,* 187, 188.
2. Brackenridge, *Incidents,* I, 104–107; *Penna. Arch.,* 2nd Ser., IV, 182, 207, 210, 211; *Pittsburgh Gazette,* Aug. 30, 1794; Baldwin, *Whiskey Rebels,* 190, 191.
3. Except as noted below, this account of the Brownsville meeting of Aug. 28, 1794, is based on Brackenridge, *Incidents,* I, 108, 110–118, 120, 121, III, 107; Findley, *History,* 121, 123–128; Gallatin, *Writings,* III, 19, 20; *Penna. Arch.,* 2nd Ser., IV, 211, 212, 218, 219; Baldwin, *Whiskey Rebels,* 192–196.
4. James Ross, Jasper Yeates, and William Bradford to Messrs. Kirkpatrick, Smith, Powers, et al., Aug. 27, 1794, GP.
5. The report was printed in *Pittsburgh Gazette,* Aug. 30, 1794.

6. *Penna. Arch.*, 2nd Ser., IV, 212–215, 233, 237, 259–261, 315, 355, 356; Gallatin, *Writings*, III, 20; Baldwin, *Whiskey Rebels*, 198, 199.

7. Henry Purviance to AG, Sept. 7, 1794, GP.

8. Manuscript copies of the resolutions of the Fayette County committee, dated Sept. 4, 1794, and of the address, dated Sept. 10, are in GP. The address was published in the *Pittsburgh Gazette*, Oct. 4 and 11, 1794, and reprinted in Gallatin, *Writings*, I, 4–9.

9. Gallatin, *Writings*, III, 21, 22.

10. *Penna. Arch.*, 2nd Ser., IV, 316–319; AG to Thomas Mifflin, Sept. 17, 1794, in Gallatin, *Writings*, I, 9–12.

11. Gallatin, *Writings*, III, 21.

12. *Penna. Arch.*, 2nd Ser., IV, 356–359; Baldwin, *Whiskey Rebels*, 215.

13. Dallas to AG, Sept. 26, 1794, GP.

14. Breading to AG, Oct. 10, 1794, GP.

15. *Pittsburgh Gazette*, Nov. 1, 1794.

16. AG to Clare, [Oct., 1794], GP.

17. Findley, *History*, 140 ff., 169–189; Gallatin, *Writings*, III, 25–28; Baldwin, *Whiskey Rebels*, 228, 229.

18. Philadelphia *Aurora*, Nov. 8, 1794; *Penna. Arch.*, 2nd Ser., IV, 390, 391.

19. AG to Clare, Nov. 7, 1794, GP.

20. Findley, *History*, 190, 191, 199, 227; *Penna. Arch.*, 2nd Ser., IV, 435–440; *Aurora*, Dec. 3, 1794; Baldwin, *Whiskey Rebels*, 235, 236.

21. AG to Hannah Gallatin, Dec. 3, 1794, GP.

22. Isaac Griffin to AG, and Badollet to AG—both Dec. 14, 1794, GP.

23. Clare to AG, Dec. 14, 1794, GP.

24. Findley, *History*, 228–230, 240, 245, 258–261, 275, 276.

25. *Pittsburgh Gazette*, Nov. 1, 1794.

26. *Pittsburgh Gazette*, Oct. 18, 1794; *Aurora*, Oct. 25, 1794; Brackenridge, *Incidents*, II, 36, 37, 44.

27. *ASP: Miscellaneous*, I, 83.

28. PHJ, 1794–1795, 7, 34.

29. AG to Hannah Gallatin, Dec. 7, 1794, GP.

30. Madison to TJ, Dec. 21, 1794, in Madison, *Writings*, ed. Hunt, VI, 230.

31. PHJ, 1794–1795, 47, 57–59, 62–64, 66; *Aurora*, Jan. 5, 1795.

32. Gallatin, *Writings*, III, 3–52.

33. PHJ, 1794–1795, 71, 72, 75–81.

34. AG to Badollet, Jan. 10, 1795, GP.

35. PHJ, 1794–1795, 170; *Aurora*, Feb. 16 and 18, 1795.

36. AG to Clare, Mar. 5, 1795, GP.

37. PHJ, 1794–1795, 228, 229.

38. AG to Clare, May 30, 1795, GP.

39. AG to Badollet, May 20, 1795, GP.

40. AG to Hannah Gallatin, May 8, 12, 25, and June 1, and to Clare, May 30, 1795, GP; Wharton, *State Trials of the United States*, 164–184. William Rawle's notes on AG's testimony during the trial are printed in Bracken-

ridge, *Incidents,* III, 136–139. Petitions for the release of John Mitchell and Philip Weigel, dated June 3, 1795, are in Pennsylvania Insurrection Papers, II.

8: FRESHMAN CONGRESSMAN, 1795–1797

1. Pinckney, *Life of General Thomas Pinckney,* 180.
2. Autobiographical sketch, AG to Hannah Gallatin, Dec. 19, 1797, GP.
3. A printed list of the members of Congress and their places of abode for this session is preserved in GP.
4. For AG's complaints about his own "indolence," see AG to Charles Pettit, Feb. 1, 1799, GP, and to Hannah Gallatin, Jan. 18, 1799, in Adams, *Life,* 226.
5. AG commented on this to John Russell Bartlett. See New-York Hist. Soc., *Proceedings,* 1849, 290.
6. AC, 1st Cong., 696, 697, 929; Harlow, *History of Legislative Methods,* 129, 130.
7. Harlow, *Legislative Methods,* 148, 152, 154–156; D. R. Anderson, *William Branch Giles,* 16, 20, 21, 23, 24; autobiographical sketch, GP.
8. AC, 4th Cong., 1st Sess., 152.
9. *Ibid.,* 159, 165.
10. *Ibid.,* 241, 254, 260.
11. Chauncey Goodrich to Oliver Wolcott, Sr., Feb. 21, 1796, Wolcott, *Memoirs,* I, 304.
12. AC, 4th Cong., 1st Sess., 846–849, 921–936.
13. Madison to TJ, Jan. 31, 1796, Madison Papers.
14. TJ to Monroe, June 12, 1796, Monroe Papers, LC.
15. AC, 4th Cong., 1st Sess., 1499–1514; *Aurora,* June 4, 1796.
16. TJ to Madison, Mar. 6, 1796, Madison Papers.
17. Included in Gallatin, *Writings,* III, 69–205.
18. AC, 4th Cong., 2nd Sess., 1891–1895, 1951, 1952, 2040, 2072, 2128–2130, 2174, 2341, 2342.
19. Wolcott to Hamilton, Apr. 5, 1798, in Wolcott, *Memoirs,* II, 45.
20. White, *The Federalists,* 328, 329.
21. AC, 4th Cong., 1st Sess., 267, 331.
22. *Ibid.,* 328–331, 334–337, 338–355, 402–423, 856–868.
23. Robbins, *Our Landed Heritage,* 15, 16; Hibbard, *History of the Public Land Policies,* 60–67.
24. The standard volume on the negotiation of the treaty is *Jay's Treaty,* by Samuel Flagg Bemis.
25. AG to Hannah Gallatin, June 29 and Sept. 6, 1795, in Adams, *Life,* 151, 153.
26. "Correspondence of the French Foreign Ministers to the United States," *Amer. Hist. Assn. Ann. Rept.,* 1903, II, 444–455; AC, 4th Cong., 1st Sess., 394.

27. *Aurora*, Jan. 21, 1796.
28. AC, 4th Cong., 1st Sess., 400, 401.
29. *Ibid.*, 426–783.
30. *Ibid.*, 1226.
31. *Ibid.*, 465, 467, 468, 472–474, 745, 746; *Aurora*, Mar. 9 and 14, 1796.
32. TJ to Madison, Mar. 27, 1796, Madison Papers.
33. AC, 4th Cong., 1st Sess., 759, 760; *Aurora*, Mar. 28, 1796.
34. AC, 4th Cong., 1st Sess., 760–762.
35. *Ibid.*, 769–783; *Aurora*, Mar. 31 and Apr. 6, 7, 1796.
36. AC, 4th Cong., 1st Sess., 940.
37. *Ibid.*, 942, 943, 976; *Aurora*, Apr. 13 and 27, 1796; *Pittsburgh Gazette*, Mar. 19 and Apr. 2, 9, 1796; Addison to AG, May 4, John McMillan to AG, May 5, Redick to AG, Apr. 7, petition of Allegheny grand jury, Mar. 21, AG to Addison, May 13, 1796, GP; Ferguson, *Early Politics*, 136, 137.
38. Gallatin, *Writings*, III, 553.
39. Boston *Independent Chronicle*, Apr. 28, 1796.
40. *Independent Chronicle*, Apr. 21, 1796.
41. Cobbett, *Porcupine's Works*, III, 253–256, 358; Clark, *Peter Porcupine in America*, 58.
42. To Oliver Wolcott, Sr., Apr. 18, 1796, in Wolcott, *Memoirs*, I, 327.
43. AC, 4th Cong., 1st Sess., 1183–1202.
44. *Ibid.*, 1239–1263, 1291.
45. Boston *Columbian Centinel*, Apr. 27, 1796.

9: FIGHTING THE WAR WITH FRANCE, 1796–1799

1. AG to Hannah Gallatin, Oct. 3 and 16, 1796, in Adams, *Life*, 176, 177.
2. *Pittsburgh Gazette*, Aug. 25, 1798.
3. Tinkcom, *Republicans and Federalists*, 170, 171; Faÿ, "Early Party Machinery in the United States," *PMHB*, LX, 375–390; AG to Hannah Gallatin, Nov. 6, 1796, in Adams, *Life*, 177.
4. *Independent Chronicle*, July 27 and Aug. 3, 1797; Morison, *Life and Letters of Harrison Gray Otis*, I, 55–57.
5. Bayard, "Papers," *Amer. Hist. Assn. Ann. Rept. 1913*, II, 6, 7.
6. AG to James Nicholson, May 26, 1797, GP; to Hannah Gallatin, June 19, 1797, in Adams, *Life*, 184.
7. AC, 5th Cong., 1st Sess., 67–237.
8. *Ibid.*, 378–381.
9. AG to Hannah Gallatin, June 28, 1797, GP.
10. *Aurora*, July 3, 1797; AG to Hannah Gallatin, June 30, 1797, in Adams, *Life*, 187.
11. AC, 5th Cong., 2nd Sess., 1262–1265, 1327–1330, 1466–1472.
12. AG to Hannah Gallatin, Jan. 11, 1798, in Adams, *Life*, 189; Jan. 19, GP.

13. AG to Hannah Gallatin, Mar. 13, 1798, in Adams, *Life*, 195, 196.
14. AC, 5th Cong., 2nd Sess., 1271, 1272.
15. *Ibid.*, 1363, 1364, 1370, 1371.
16. *Ibid.*, 1374–1380; Lyon, "The Directory and the United States," *Amer. Hist. Rev.*, XLIII, 519–524; ASP: *Foreign Relations*, II, 157–182, 185–189.
17. Gallatin, *Writings*, III, 553.
18. TJ to Madison, Apr. 6, 1798, in Jefferson, *Writings* (Ford ed.), VII, 234.
19. AC, 5th Cong., 2nd Sess., 1406–1408.
20. *Aurora*, Apr. 10 and 11, 1798.
21. See, for example, James Ross to George Stevenson, Apr. 13, 1798, Ross-Woods Papers.
22. AC, 5th Cong., 2nd Sess., 1406–1408.
23. AG to J. W. Nicholson, May 18, 1798, GP.
24. AC, 5th Cong., 2nd Sess., 1508–1520.
25. *Ibid.*, 1406–1408, 1601–1603, 1616, 1621.
26. *Ibid.*, 1918–1920.
27. *Ibid.*, 1525; Goodrich to Wolcott, Jr., Aug. 12, 1798, in Wolcott, *Memoirs*, II, 105.
28. AC, 5th Cong., 2nd Sess., 1526, 1527, 1631–1634, 1655–1660, 1692–1695, 1725–1729, 1742–1747, 1752–1755.
29. Sprout, *Rise of American Naval Power*, 25.
30. AC, 5th Cong., 3rd Sess., 2823–2832, 2859–2871.
31. *Ibid.*, 2nd Sess., 1601–1604, 1616–1621, 1837, 1839, 1848–1853, 3717–3794; Adams, *Taxation in the United States*, 54–56.
32. AC, 5th Cong., 2nd Sess., 2037, 2044, 2045.
33. ASP: *Finance*, I, 676.
34. The first eight chapters of Smith, *Freedom's Fetters*, study in minute detail the Federalists' legislative program and Gallatin's opposition to it. Less useful is Miller, *Crisis in Freedom*.
35. AC, 5th Cong., 2nd Sess., 1567, 1573; Morison, *Life of Otis*, I, 109.
36. TJ to Madison, Apr. 26, 1798, in Jefferson, *Writings* (Monticello ed.), X, 31.
37. AG to J. W. Nicholson, May 18, 1798, GP; AC, 5th Cong., 2nd Sess., 1771.
38. AG to Maria Nicholson, June 15, 1798, GP.
39. AC, 5th Cong., 2nd Sess., 1788–1790, 1793–1796, 1954–1957, 1973–1983.
40. *Ibid.*, 1989–1992, 1996, 1997.
41. *Ibid.*, 1868; Miller, *Crisis in Freedom*, 49, 50.
42. AG to Maria Nicholson, July 10, 1798, GP.
43. AC, 5th Cong., 2nd Sess., 2093–2103.
44. *Ibid.*, 2107–2111.
45. *Ibid.*, 2139–2171, 3739–3742, 3744–3746.
46. AG to Maria Nicholson, July 10, and to J. W. Nicholson, Aug. 16, 1798, GP.
47. This episode, reported in *Reading Weekly Advertiser*, Sept. 15, 1798, is quoted in Richards, "Hon. Jacob Rush of the Pennsylvania Judiciary," *PMHB*, XXXIX, 65, 66.
48. *Pittsburgh Gazette*, Sept. 29, 1798.

49. *Ibid.*, Aug. 25 and Sept. 1 and 8, 1798; John Israel to AG, Sept. 23, 1798; welcoming addresses dated Sept. ? and Sept. 22, 1798; undated sheets listing 1798 Congressional returns—all in GP; Tinkcom, *Republicans and Federalists*, 185–187.

50. Tinkcom, *Republicans and Federalists*, 184–189; Schouler, *History of the United States*, I, 434, 435; Christopher Greenup to AG, Dec. 1, 1798, GP.

51. AG to Hannah Gallatin, Dec. 21, 1798, in Adams, *Life*, 224, 225; Adams, *Life*, 211; AG to Samuel Breck, June 20, 1843, GP.

52. AG to Hannah Gallatin, Dec. 7, 1798, in Adams, *Life*, 221, 222. For accounts of the enforcement of the Alien and Sedition laws, see Smith, *Freedom's Fetters*, 159–417, and F. M. Anderson, "The Enforcement of the Alien and Sedition Laws," *Amer. Hist. Assn. Ann. Rept.*, 1912, 115–126.

53. AG to Pettit, Feb. 1, 1799, GP.

54. Tolles, *George Logan of Philadelphia*, 153 ff.; Ross to Stevenson, Dec. 14, 1798, Ross-Woods Papers.

55. AC, 5th Cong., 3rd Sess., 2193.

56. For AG's part in the debate on the Logan Law, see AC, 5th Cong., 3rd Sess., 2496–2499, 2512–2515, 2535–2541, 2584–2587, 2595–2597, 2637–2645, 2681, 2682, 2705–2709. For Harper's part, see 2502–2512, 2528–2535, 2617–2626.

57. Tolles, *Logan*, 202.

58. AC, 5th Cong., 3rd Sess., 2801, 2802, 2807, 2900–2902, 2993–3002; TJ to Madison, Feb. 26, 1799, Madison Papers.

59. AC, 5th Cong., 3rd Sess., 3558; AG to Hannah Gallatin, Mar. 1, 1799, in Adams, *Life*, 227, 228.

60. AG to Maria Nicholson, Mar. 1, 1799, GP; Peeling, Public Life of Thomas McKean, 197–206; Tinkcom, *Republicans and Federalists*, 223–232.

61. AG to Mme. Rolaz du Rosey, Apr. 8, 1799, de Budé Manuscripts.

10: THE JEFFERSONIAN TRIUMPH, 1799–1801

1. Tinkcom, *Republicans and Federalists*, 238, 246; Ferguson, *Early Politics*, 150–154. Israel to AG, Oct. 6, 1799, and draft in AG's handwriting of election certificate for the second district of Fayette County, dated "second Tuesday, October 1799," GP.

2. AG to J. W. Nicholson, Nov. 30, 1799, GP.

3. Autobiographical sketch, GP.

4. The speech that AG found "unanswerable," in a debate on the citizenship of Jonathan Robbins, is reported fully in Beveridge, *Life of John Marshall*, II, 458–476.

5. Harrison Gray Otis to S. F. Otis, Dec. 3, 1799, Otis Papers.

6. AC, 6th Cong., 2nd Sess., 767.

7. *Ibid.*, 935, 952.

8. *Ibid.*, 1st Sess., 264–272, 350–360.
9. Ganoe, *History of the United States Army*, 107; AC, 6th Cong., 2nd Sess., 1530, 1531.
10. AC, 6th Cong., 1st Sess., 676–678, 2nd Sess., 1056–1058, 1523, 1557, 1570; Sprout, *American Naval Power*, 52.
11. AC, 6th Cong., 1st Sess., 348–360.
12. Mai, *Fiscal Policies of Albert Gallatin*, 48.
13. Pittsburgh *Tree of Liberty*, Aug. 30 and Sept. 20, 1800.
14. AG to Mathew Carey, Jan. 16, 1801, Lea & Febiger Papers.
15. *PSJ*, 1799–1800, 265–267; 1800–1801, 20–25, 27–37, 56–58, 62–67; *PHJ*, 1800–1801, 3, 58, 59, 70, 71, 93, 94, 97–106; *Aurora*, Nov. 10 and 15, 1800; *Gazette of the United States*, Nov. 12 and Dec. 4, 1800.
16. AG to J. W. Nicholson, Jan. 10, 1800, GP.
17. M. L. Davis to AG, Mar. 29 and May 1, 1800, GP; Schachner, *Aaron Burr*, 169–178; Schachner, *Alexander Hamilton*, 393, 394.
18. AG to Hannah Gallatin, May 6, 1800, GP.
19. George Clinton to DeWitt Clinton, Dec. 13, 1803, and Jan. 2, 1804, and James Nicholson's statement dated Dec. 26, 1803, DeWitt Clinton Papers.
20. James Nicholson to AG, May 7, 1800, GP.
21. Davis to AG, May 5, 1800, GP.
22. Hannah Gallatin to AG, May 7, 1800, in Adams, *Life*, 243.
23. AG to Hannah Gallatin, May 12, 1800, in Adams, *Life*, 243; AC, 6th Cong., 2nd Sess., 720.
24. *Tree of Liberty*, Sept. 13 and 27, Oct. 4, 11, and 25, 1800.
25. *Columbian Centinel*, July 26 and Aug. 27, 1800; *Tree of Liberty*, Oct. 25, 1800.
26. Tinkcom, 250–253; Bassett, *The Federalist System*, 145, 146.
27. TJ to Burr, Dec. 15, 1800, in Davis, *Memoirs of Aaron Burr*, II, 67.
28. AG to Hannah Gallatin, Jan. 15, 1800 [1801], GP. See also Bryan, *History of the National Capital*, I, 379, 380; Smith, *First Forty Years of Washington Society*, 9.
29. AG to Hannah Gallatin, Jan. 22, 1800 [1801], GP.
30. AC, 6th Cong., 2nd Sess., 774–778.
31. AG to Hannah Gallatin, Jan. 15, 1800 [1801], GP.
32. J. A. Bayard to Andrew Bayard, Jan. 8, 1801, in Bayard, "Papers," *Amer. Hist. Assn. Ann. Rept.* 1913, II, 119.
33. Burr to AG, Jan. 16, 1801, GP.
34. Burr to Samuel Smith, Dec. 16, 1800, in Davis, *Memoirs of Burr*, II, 75.
35. Burr to AG, Feb. 12, 1801, GP.
36. The plan of action, now in GP, is printed in Gallatin, *Writings*, I, 18–23. McKean's plan for action by Pennsylvania is outlined in McKean to TJ, Mar. 19, 1801 (copy), McKean Papers.
37. AC, 6th Cong., 2nd Sess., 1022–1024; Morison, *Life of Otis*, I, 206, 208; Schachner, *Burr*, 202; Uriah Tracy to ——— Gould, Feb. 16, 1801, Gratz Collection.

38. AG to James Nicholson, Feb. 14, 1801, GP.
39. Bayard to Richard Bassett, Feb. 16, 1801, in Bayard, "Papers," 126, 127; Davis, *Memoirs of Burr*, II, 129–133; Schachner, *Burr*, 208, 209; Morison, *Life of Otis*, I, 209.
40. AG to H. A. Muhlenberg, May 8, 1848, GP.
41. AG to Burr, Feb. 25, 1801, GP.
42. Bayard to Bassett, Feb. 16, 1801, in Bayard, "Papers," 126, 127.
43. Ross to Stevenson, Feb. 18, 1801 (copy), Ross-Woods Papers.
44. Schouler, *History of the U.S.*, I, 498–500; AG to Hannah Gallatin, Feb. 17, 1801, GP.

11: FRONTIER BUSINESSMAN, 1795–1801

1. AG to Badollet, Feb. 1, 1794, GP.
2. Karmin, *Sir Francis D'Ivernois*, describes in detail D'Ivernois's project to create a Genevan colony in America, 273–292.
3. AG to Badollet, Dec. 29, 1794, GP; Karmin, *D'Ivernois*, 284, 285.
4. AG to Hannah Gallatin, Apr. 22, 1795, in Adams, *Life*, 146, 147.
5. AG to Badollet, May 20, 1795, GP.
6. Ellis, *History of Fayette County*, 764.
7. AG to Hannah Gallatin, Jan. 31, 1795, in Adams, *Life*, 152; Fayette County Property Rolls, Springhill Township, 1796, 1799, 1800, 1801.
8. AG to Hannah Gallatin, Sept. 6, 1795, in Adams, *Life*, 152, 153; Fayette County Deed Book D, 328, 329.
9. Fayette County Deed Book B, 342, 343.
10. Agreement between AG and Thomas McCleary, Sept. 16, 1795, GP.
11. Albert Gallatin & Co. to AG, Dec. 8, 1795, GP.
12. Badollet to AG, June 15 and July 25, 1796, March 15, June 7, and Dec. 11, 1797, AG to J. W. Nicholson, Jan. 12, 1798, GP.
13. AG to Hannah Gallatin, Dec. 14, 1796, in Adams, *Life*, 179.
14. AG to Hannah Gallatin, Jan. 4, 1799, in Adams, *Life*, 225.
15. Badollet to AG, Feb. 14 and Mar. 15, 1797, GP.
16. Badollet to AG, May 10 and June 7, 1797, GP; Bining, The Glass Industry of Western Pennsylvania, 9; McKearin, *Two Hundred Years of American Blown Glass*; Davis, *The Development of the American Glass Industry*, 29 n.
17. AG to J. W. Nicholson, Nov. 24, 1797, GP.
18. Badollet to AG, June 7, 1797, and articles of agreement signed Sept. 20, 1797, GP.
19. Bining, Glass Industry, 10, 12 n., 14, 15, 18, 26; Ellis, *History of Fayette County*, 768, 769; Weeks, *Report on the Manufacture of Glass*, 82.
20. Albert Gallatin & Co. to AG, Feb. 28, 1798, GP.
21. AG to J. W. Nicholson, Mar. 9, 1798, GP.
22. AG to Delesdernier, May 25, 1798, in *Maine Hist. Soc. Coll.*, VI, 100, 101.

23. AG to Maria Nicholson, June 15, 1798, GP.
24. Roberts, "Memoirs," *PMHB*, LXII, 239.
25. AG to Hannah Gallatin, Dec. 7, 1798, in Adams, *Life*, 222, 223.
26. AG to Dallas, Oct. 23, and Dallas to Clement Biddle, Nov. 26, 1798, Governor Mifflin's Administration Papers, LIII; James Trimble to Biddle, Jan. 7, 1799, Mifflin's Papers, LIV; Louis Bourdillon to AG, Dec. 12 and 21, 1798, Jan. 3, 10, and 18, 1799, AG to J. W. Nicholson, Dec. 28, 1798, and Feb. 1, 1799, GP; AG to Hannah Gallatin, Jan. 4, 1799, in Adams, *Life*, 225.
27. James McHenry to AG, Oct. 8, and AG to J. W. Nicholson, Nov. 30, 1799, GP.
28. Two products of the New Geneva Glassworks are illustrated in McKearin, *Glass*, Plates 13 (No. 2) and 69.
29. Bourdillon to AG, Dec. 12, 1798, and Jan. 30, 1799, GP.
30. AG to Hannah Gallatin, Jan. 4, 1799, in Adams, *Life*, 225.
31. AG to J. W. Nicholson, Dec. 1, 1797, GP.
32. AG to Hannah Gallatin, Jan. 18, 1799, in Adams, *Life*, 226; AG to Bourdillon, July 30, 1799, GP.
33. AG to J. W. Nicholson, Nov. 30, 1799, and A. Mussard to AG, Jan. 23, 1801, GP.
34. AG to Biddle, Jan. 6, 1800, Miscellaneous Collection, Penna. State Archives.
35. Mussard to AG, Feb. 14 and 28, 1800, AG to Hannah Gallatin, Feb. 19, 1801, GP; Veech, *The Monongahela of Old*, 181, 182.
36. *Tree of Liberty*, Oct. 11, 1800.
37. AG to Hannah Gallatin, Oct. 3, 1796, in Adams, *Life*, 176.
38. Bacon, *Ancestry*, 18, 19.
39. AG to Hannah Gallatin, Jan. 11, 1797, in Adams, *Life*, 181; to Hannah, July 10, 1797, and Feb. 23, 1798, GP.
40. AG to J. W. Nicholson, Jan. 10, 1800, GP.
41. AG to Maria Nicholson, May 10, 1800, Hannah Gallatin to AG, Jan. 8 and Feb. 5, 1801, GP.
42. AG to J. W. Nicholson, Apr. 14, 1796, and May 5, 1798, Hannah Gallatin to Maria Nicholson, Jan. 23, 1799, AG to Maria Nicholson, Feb. 1, 1797, and July 11, 1799, Hannah Gallatin to AG, Jan. 22, 1801, AG to Hannah Gallatin, Jan. 29, 1800 [1801], GP; Fayette County Property Rolls, Springhill Township, 1799, 1800, 1801.
43. Pierce Butler to Monroe, Sept. 27, 1816, Monroe Papers, LC.
44. AG to Hannah Gallatin, Jan. 29, 1801, GP.
45. AG to Hannah Gallatin, Feb. 19, 1801, GP.
46. *Aurora*, March 18, 1801; AG to Hannah Gallatin, Feb. 19, 26, 1801, GP; James McHenry to Charles Carroll, April 8, 1801, in Steiner, *Life and Correspondence of James McHenry*, 500, 501.
47. AG to Hannah Gallatin, Feb. 26, 1801, GP; *National Intelligencer*, Apr. 6 and 22, May 1 and 4, 1801; Amory, *Life of James Sullivan*, 91.
48. *AC*, 6th Cong., 2nd Sess., 764.
49. AG to Hannah Gallatin, Mar. 5, 1801, in Adams, *Life*, 265.

50. *National Intelligencer,* Mar. 6, 1801.
51. AG to Hannah Gallatin, Mar. 5, 1801, in Adams, *Life,* 265.
52. AG to TJ, Mar. 14, 1801, GP.
53. AG to Hannah Gallatin, Mar. 5, 1801, in Adams, *Life,* 265.

12: FIRST DAYS IN THE TREASURY, 1801–1805

1. TJ to Thomas Randolph, May 14, 1801, JP.
2. Margaret Bayard Smith to Susan B. Smith, May 26, 1801, in Smith, *First Forty Years of Washington Society,* 27.
3. AG to TJ, Aug. 18 and 24, 1801, JP; AG to Maria Nicholson Montgomery, Oct. 28, 1809, GP.
4. William Cranch to ———, May 15, 1801 (photostat), Bass Papers; *National Intelligencer,* May 15, 1801.
5. AG to J. W. Nicholson, July 17, 1801, and to James Gallatin, Feb. 19, 1825, GP.
6. White, *The Jeffersonians,* 139, 140; Heinlein, Administrative Theory and Practices of Albert Gallatin, 126; AG to TJ, Aug. 10, 1801, JP.
7. *New-York Hist. Soc. Proc. 1849,* 292.
8. AG to Maria Nicholson, Mar. 12, 1801, GP. Like all students of the 1801–1817 period, I am more indebted than I can express to Henry Adams for the pioneering and still unreplaced research in the nine volumes of his *History of the United States of America.* The obligation is so great in Chapters 12 to 20 inclusive of this book that I have not attempted to acknowledge it in every instance.
9. TJ to AG, Nov. 14, 1801, GP.
10. TJ to AG, Nov. 19, 1802, GP; [Nov. 3, 1808], JP. See also Bowers, *Jefferson in Power,* 84; Schachner, *Thomas Jefferson,* II, 685, 842. For one of the contributions by AG to TJ's messages, see TJ to AG, Nov. 14, 1801, GP.
11. TJ to AG, Oct. 11, 1809, GP.
12. ASP: *Finance,* I, 701–717; Jonathan Elliot, *Funding System of the United States and of Great Britain,* 527.
13. Dewey, *Financial History of the United States,* 125.
14. AG to TJ, Mar. 14, 1801, JP.
15. Dewey, *Financial History,* 111.
16. AG to TJ, Nov. 16, 1801, JP. See also Note 21.
17. TJ's message to Congress, Dec. 8, 1801, JP.
18. Caldwell, *Administrative Theories of Hamilton and Jefferson,* 38, 98, 99.
19. Bruce, *John Randolph of Roanoke,* I, 87.
20. White, *Jeffersonians,* 46, 47, 49–51; AG to John Randolph, [1802], Nicholson Papers; AG to TJ, Oct. 13, 1806, JP.
21. AC, 7th Cong., 1st Sess., 209–251, 268–273, 275–291, 354–361, 419, 420,

434–462, 493, 494, 1017–1074, 1164–1189, 1192, 1193, 1313–1315, 1323–1326, 1342–1345.

22. Heinlein, Administrative Theory, 219–224.
23. AC, 7th Cong., 1st Sess., 314, 315, 319–324; ASP: Finance, I, 755–757.
24. J. H. Nicholson to Secretary of the Navy and Secretary of War, Mar. 6, 1802, and AG to Nicholson, Apr. [?], 1802, Nicholson Papers; AC, 7th Cong., 1st Sess., 1157.
25. Benjamin Stoddert to TJ, Mar. 14, 1801, JP; Sprout, Rise of American Naval Power, 55.
26. Robert Smith to AG, May 6, 1802, GP.
27. AC, 7th Cong., 1st Sess., 1342–1345, 1356, 1357, 1361–1372.
28. TJ to W. C. Nicholas, June 11, 1801, in Jefferson, Writings (Ford ed.), VIII, 62, 63.
29. AG to TJ, Aug. 16, 1802, JP.
30. Robert Smith to TJ, Sept. 14, TJ to Smith, Sept. 17 and 20, 1802, JP.
31. Gallatin, Writings, III, 161, 162.
32. AC, 8th Cong., 1st Sess., 1204–1206, 1210–1225.
33. Robert Smith to AG, Jan. 10, 1803, GP; AG to Smith, Nov. 20, 1805, Navy' Dept. Miscellaneous Letters.
34. AG to TJ, Jan. 18, 1803, JP.
35. Paullin, "Navy Administration Under Secretaries of the Navy Smith, Hamilton, and Jones," U.S. Naval Inst. Proc., XXXII, 1298–1300.
36. AG to TJ, [Nov. 21, 1802], JP.
37. AC, 7th Cong., 2nd Sess., 1565.
38. AG to TJ, [Dec. 3, 1805], JP; Brant, James Madison, IV, 132, 133; AC, 7th Cong., 2nd Sess., 370–374; AG to Madison, Feb. 28, 1803, cited in Brant, IV, 133.
39. Brant, Madison, IV, 128.
40. Hidy, House of Baring in American Trade and Finance, 33, 34; Labouchère, "L'annexion de la Louisiane aux Etats-Unis et les maisons Hope et Baring," Revue d'histoire diplomatique, XXX, 423–450; AG to TJ, Aug. 31, 1803, JP; AG to R. R. Livingston, Feb. 8, 1804, Gratz Collection; Brant, Madison, IV, 133, 135; Madison to Monroe, July 30, 1803, in Madison, Letters (Rives ed.), II, 185.
41. AC, 8th Cong., 1st Sess., 1245–1247.

13: PATRONAGE AND PERSONALITIES, 1801–1807

1. TJ to Benjamin Rush, Mar. 24, 1801, JP.
2. White, Jeffersonians, 149.
3. AG to TJ, July 25, 1801, JP.
4. TJ to AG, July 26, 1801, GP.

5. TJ to Elias Shipman and others, July 12, 1801, in Jefferson, *Writings* (Ford ed.), VIII, 67–70.
6. TJ to AG, July 26, 1801, GP.
7. TJ to AG, Aug. 14, 1801, JP.
8. AG to TJ, Aug. 10, 1800 [1801], JP.
9. Heinlein, Administrative Theory, 108–111.
10. Walters, *Dallas*, 77, 120, 121; Higginbotham, *Keystone in the Democratic Arch*, 35, 36; William Duane to TJ, June 10, 1801, and to Pierce Butler, Nov. 12, 1801, in Duane, "Letters," *Mass. Hist. Soc. Proc.*, 2nd Ser., XX, 266, 267, 271–273.
11. The booklet, dated 1801, is in GP.
12. Duane to Madison, May 10, 1801, in Duane, "Letters," 263.
13. AG to [Duane?], July 5, 1801 (draft), GP.
14. AG to TJ, Aug. 10, 1800 [1801], Aug. 17, 1801, JP; Duane to AG, Dec. 13, 1801, GP.
15. Walters, *Dallas*, 122, 124–132; Higginbotham, *Keystone*, 41–43; Duane, "Letters," 259.
16. Walters, *Dallas*, 120.
17. Duane to AG, Aug. 12, 1802, GP.
18. *Aurora*, Dec. 1, 22, and 24, 1802.
19. *Aurora*, Mar. 17, 23, 31, Apr. 5, 7, 11, 13, 15, and May 4, 1803, and Aug. 6, 1805; Andrew Gregg and others to President of U.S., Feb. 12, Gregg to William Jones, Mar. 1, and Jones to John Randolph, Mar. 19, 1803, Jones Papers.
20. Dallas to AG, Mar. 30, and J. H. Nicholson to AG, May 10, 1803, GP.
21. AG to TJ, Mar. 21 and June 21, 1803, JP.
22. TJ to AG, Mar. 28, 1803, GP.
23. Ward committees of Philadelphia to TJ, July 17, 1803, JP.
24. TJ to AG, July 25, 1803, GP.
25. TJ to Duane, July 24, 1803, JP.
26. AG to TJ, Aug. 11, 1803, JP.
27. TJ to AG, Aug. 18, 1803, GP.
28. McKean to Dallas, Oct. 16, 1803, GP; Duane to Abraham Bishop, Aug. 28, 1802, in Duane, "Letters," 276.
29. Duane to Henry Dearborn, July 3, 1810, in Duane, "Letters," 335; *Aurora*, Aug. 30, 1816.
30. *Aurora*, Oct. 9 and 29, 1804.
31. Walters, *Dallas*, 135–137.
32. *Aurora*, Feb., Mar., June, July, Aug., Sept., Oct., 1805.
33. AG to Badollet, Oct. 25, 1805, GP.
34. Duane to Dearborn, July 3, 1810, in Duane, "Letters," 335–337.
35. AG to TJ, Oct. 13, 1806, JP.
36. Duane to Dearborn, July 3, 1810, in Duane, "Letters," 335–337.
37. McBain, *DeWitt Clinton and the Origin of the Spoils System*, 139, 140.
38. TJ to George Clinton, May 17, 1801, JP.
39. Burr to AG, June 28, 1801, GP.

40. James Nicholson to AG, Aug. 10, 1801, GP.
41. AG to TJ, Sept. 14, 1801, JP.
42. Burr to AG, Sept. 8, 1801, GP.
43. AG to TJ, Sept. 12, 1801, JP.
44. AG to TJ, Sept. 14, 1801, JP.
45. TJ to AG, Sept. 18, 1801, GP.
46. Burr to AG, Mar. 25, 1802, JP.
47. McBain, *DeWitt Clinton*, 142, 143.
48. AG to TJ, July 2 and Aug. 11, 1803, JP; Hatcher, *Edward Livingston*, 92–99.
49. "A Letter of James Nicholson, 1803," *Amer. Hist. Rev.*, VIII, 512, 513.
50. AG to TJ, Sept. 2, 1802, JP.
51. Spaulding, *His Excellency George Clinton*, 245–248; Schachner, *Burr*, 234.
52. Spaulding, *Clinton*, 272–276; Schachner, *Burr*, 241 ff, 246 ff.
53. AG to J. W. Nicholson, July 19, 1804, GP.
54. Plumer, *William Plumer's Memorandum*, 203, 204.
55. Abernethy, *Burr Conspiracy*, 26–30.
56. J. H. Daveiss to TJ, Jan. 10, 1806, JP.
57. TJ to Daveiss, Feb. 15, 1806, JP.
58. Burr to AG, July 31, 1806, with AG's inscription, GP.
59. TJ's cabinet memoranda, Oct. 22, 24, and 25, 1806, JP.
60. TJ's cabinet memoranda, Nov. 2 and 25, 1806, TJ to AG, Jan. 4, 1807, JP. See also McCaleb, *Aaron Burr Conspiracy*, 197.
61. Abernethy, *Burr Conspiracy*, 204–210.
62. TJ's cabinet memoranda, Feb. 27, 1807, JP; AG to C. A. Rodney, May 7, 1807, Gallatin Folder, LC.
63. James Wilkinson to AG, Sept. 5, 1807, GP.
64. Parton, *Life and Times of Aaron Burr*, II, 169.

14: GALLATIN, THE NATIONALIST, 1801–1809

1. Opinion for Washington by TJ, Feb. 15, 1791, JP.
2. Gallatin, *Writings*, III, 135, 136.
3. AG to T. W. Willing, June 9, 1801, GP.
4. AG to TJ, June 18 (?), 1802, JP.
5. TJ to AG, June 19, 1802, JP.
6. TJ to AG, Oct. 7, 1802, GP.
7. TJ to AG, July 12, 1803, GP.
8. TJ to AG, Dec. 13, 1803, JP.
9. AG to TJ, Dec. 13, 1803, JP.
10. AC, 8th Cong., 1st Sess., 1282; Holdsworth, *First Bank of the United States*, 70–72.
11. AG to TJ, Apr. 12, 1804, JP.
12. White, *Jeffersonians*, 518, 519; Conover, *General Land Office*, 14.

13. Thomas Worthington to AG, May 12, 1802, Mar. 21, 1803, Apr. 5, 1805, GP.
14. AG to W. B. Giles, Feb. 13, 1802, GP.
15. White, *Jeffersonians*, 484; AC, 7th Cong., 1st Sess., 1097–1126, 1158–1162, 1349–1351.
16. ASP: *Public Lands*, I, 182; Robbins, *Our Landed Heritage*, 24.
17. The text of AG's report is printed in ASP: *Public Lands*, I, 183, 184. For the text of the Land Law of 1800, see AC, 6th Cong., 1515–1522. See also Treat, *National Land System*, 115.
18. AC, 8th Cong., 1st Sess., 951, 1285–1293.
19. The report is printed in ASP: *Public Lands*, I, 287.
20. Robbins, *Our Landed Heritage*, 25; Treat, *National Land System*, 128, 129; Hibbard, *History of Public Land Policies*, 87, 88.
21. AG to TJ, [Nov. 21, 1802], JP.
22. AG to TJ, Apr. 13, 1803, JP.
23. AG to TJ, Mar. 14, 1803, JP.
24. Bakeless, *Lewis and Clark*, 224.
25. Haskins, *Yazoo Land Companies*, 1–31; Cotterill, "The National Land System in the South," *Miss. Vall. Hist. Rev.*, XVI, 495, 496.
26. See various letters, James Jackson to AG, 1802, GP.
27. The text of the agreement and report is printed ASP: *Public Lands*, I, 125, 126, 132 ff. See also Jackson to AG, Apr. 23, 1802, bearing an explanation of the background of the letter in AG's hand, and AG's sketch of an agreement with the Georgia commissioners, dated Apr., 1802, both of which are in GP.
28. Brant, *Madison*, IV, 237.
29. AC, 8th Cong., 2nd Sess., 1172.
30. AC, 9th Cong., 1st Sess., 920, 921.
31. Levi Lincoln to TJ, Jan. 10, 1803, JP.
32. AG to TJ, Jan. 13, 1803, JP.
33. TJ to AG, Mar. 3, 1803, GP (erroneously given as Jan., 1803, in Gallatin, *Writings*, I, 114, 115).
34. Draft of an amendment to the Constitution, [July, 1803] Jefferson, *Writings* (Ford ed.), VIII, 241–249.
35. AG to TJ, July 9, 1803, JP.
36. TJ to AG, Aug. 23, 1803, GP.
37. TJ to Madison, Apr. 18, 1803, JP.
38. AC, 8th Cong., 1st Sess., 73, 488, 489.
39. Jefferson, *Writings* (Ford ed.), VIII, 267, 268.
40. AG to TJ, Sept. 5, 1803, JP; AG to TJ, Oct. 28, TJ to AG, Oct. 29, AG to W. C. C. Claiborne, Oct. 31, and Claiborne to AG, Nov. 18, 1803, GP; *Territorial Papers*, IX, 89 n.
41. AG to TJ, Aug. 20, 1804, JP.
42. TJ to AG, Nov. 9, 1803, and Apr. 27, 1804, GP; AG to TJ, Apr. 16 and Aug. 20, 1804, JP; Adams, *History*, II, 131.

43. Benedict Van Pradelles to AG, June 11, 1808, and Philip Grymes, Judge Lucas, and Secretary Robinson to AG, Jan. 8, 1810, in *Territorial Papers*, IX, 792, 862.

44. AG to Giles, Feb. 13, 1802, GP.

45. TJ's message, Mar. 4, 1805, JP.

46. TJ to AG, May 29, 1805, GP.

47. AG to TJ, Apr. 13, 1807, JP. In GP there is a rough draft of the project in AG's hand, incorrectly dated "1802" by the archivists.

48. TJ to Thomas Moore, July 21, 1807, State Dept. Misc. Letters.

49. AG to TJ, Feb. 12, 1808, JP.

50. AG to TJ, July 27, 1808, JP.

51. AG to TJ, Aug. 6, 1808, GP.

52. For accounts of the location of the Cumberland Road, see Searight, *The Old Pike*, 25–38, and Young, *Political and Constitutional Study of the Cumberland Road*, 21–23. See also Moore to AG, Sept. 20, 1807, State Dept. Misc. Letters.

53. The reports AG received are published in *ASP: Miscellaneous*, I, 742–921.

54. AG to S. L. Mitchill, Apr. 6, 1808, Gallatin Folder, LC.

55. For the report, see *ASP: Miscellaneous*, I, 724–741.

56. AG's comments on TJ's message, Oct. 29 (?), 1808, JP.

15: THREE STORM CLOUDS, 1804–1807

1. Adams, *History*, II, 201, 202.

2. John Randolph to J. H. Nicholson, Mar. 29, 1805, Nicholson Papers.

3. Randolph to AG, June 28 and Oct. 25, 1805, GP.

4. Randolph to AG, Thursday (1806?), GP.

5. TJ to AG, Aug. 23, 1803, GP.

6. AG to TJ, Aug. 31, 1803, JP.

7. AC, 8th Cong., 1st Sess., 439, 440.

8. AG to TJ, Mar. 15, 1804, JP; AG to [H. B. Trist], Feb. 27, 1804, GP; AG to Trist, Mar. 19, 1804, Treasury Dept. Bureau of Customs Records, New Orleans Collector; Bemis, *Diplomatic History*, 183.

9. AG to TJ, Oct. 29, 1804, JP; Brant, *Madison*, IV, 198, 199.

10. Statement signed "Decius," in *Richmond Enquirer*, Aug. 15, 1806.

11. AG to Madison, Aug. 6, 1805, Madison Papers.

12. TJ to AG, Aug. 7, 1805, GP.

13. AG to TJ, Sept. 12, 1805, JP.

14. TJ to AG, Oct. 23, 1805, GP; TJ's cabinet memorandum, Nov. 12, 1805, in Jefferson, *Writings* (Ford ed.), I, 308; statements of AG and TJ, Apr. 4, 1806, JP.

15. TJ's cabinet memorandum, Nov. 19, 1805, in Jefferson, *Writings* (Ford ed.), I, 309.

16. AG to TJ, [Dec. 3, 1805], JP.

17. AG to TJ, [Nov. 21, 1805], JP.

18. AC, 9th Cong., 1st Sess., 11–16.

19. AG to TJ, [Dec. 3, 1805], JP.

20. TJ to AG, Dec. 4, 1805, GP; AC, 9th Cong., 1st Sess., 18, 19.

21. Randolph to AG, Oct. 12, and TJ to AG, Dec. 7, 1805, GP.

22. AG to J. H. Nicholson, Dec. 7, 1805, in Gallatin, *Writings*, I, 282.

23. Nicholson to AG, Dec. 8, 1805, GP.

24. *Richmond Enquirer*, Aug. 15, 1806.

25. AC, 9th Cong., 1st Sess., 1226, 1227.

26. *Ibid.*, 249, 1023–1025, 1028, 1054–1063, 1067, 1094–1101.

27. *Ibid.*, 2nd Sess., 14, 1278, 1279.

28. *Ibid.*, 1st Sess., 771.

29. *Ibid.*, 984, 985.

30. *Ibid.*, 988, 995; AG to George Clinton, Jr., Apr. 5, and Clinton to AG, Apr. 10, 1806 (with AG's endorsement), GP.

31. *Richmond Enquirer*, Aug. 15, 1806.

32. TJ to AG, Oct. 12, 1806, GP.

33. AG to TJ, Oct. 13, 1806, GP.

34. AG to Maria Nicholson, Oct. 27, 1806, in Adams, *Life*, 347.

35. Bruce, *Randolph of Roanoke*, I, 307, 308; AG to Hannah Gallatin, Oct. 30, 1807, in Adams, *Life*, 363.

36. AC, 12th Cong., 1st Sess., 1467.

37. AC, 18th Cong., 1st Sess., 2379, 2380.

38. Bemis, *Diplomatic History*, 138–142.

39. AC, 9th Cong., 1st Sess., 449–451.

40. *Ibid.*, 851, 877, 878.

41. AG to TJ, Mar. 23, 1807, JP; AC, 9th Cong., 2nd Sess., 1249; Heaton, "Non-Importation, 1806–1812," *Jour. Econ. Hist.*, I, 179, 180.

42. AC, 9th Cong., 2nd Sess., 63–65.

43. AG to TJ, Feb. 8, 1807, JP.

44. TJ to AG, Feb. 9, 1807, GP.

45. AG to TJ, Apr. 13 and 16, Madison to TJ, Apr. 17, TJ to Madison, Apr. 21, and TJ to AG, Apr. 21, 1807, JP; AG to Madison, Apr. 13, 1807, Rives Papers.

46. TJ to AG, June 25, and AG to Hannah Gallatin, June 28, 1807, GP; AG to TJ, June 29, 1807, JP.

47. AG to Hannah Gallatin, July 4, 1807, GP.

48. TJ's cabinet memorandum, July 2 and 4, 1807, JP; Madison to Monroe, July 6, 1807, in ASP: *Foreign Relations*, III, 183–185.

49. AG to [J. H. Nicholson], July 17, 1807, GP.

50. AG to Hannah Gallatin, July 4, to [J. H. Nicholson?], July 17, and Samuel Smith to AG, July 19, 1807, GP; ASP: *Finance*, II, 246–249.

51. AG to TJ, July 25, 1807, GP.

52. AG to Madison, Aug. 15, 1807, Madison Papers.

53. AG to TJ, Sept. 2, 1807, JP.
54. AG to TJ, Oct. 21, 1807, GP.
55. AG to Hannah Gallatin, Oct. 30, 1807, in Adams, *Life*, 363, 364.
56. *ASP: Finance*, II, 246–249.
57. AG to TJ, Dec. 2, 1807, JP.
58. TJ to AG, Dec. 3, 1807, GP.
59. *ASP: Commerce and Navigation*, I, 699.
60. TJ to J. Mason, [1807?], in Jefferson, *Writings* (Ford ed.), V, 217, 218; TJ to J. G. Jackson, Oct. 13, 1808, and to Madison, July 14, 1824, JP.
61. AG to TJ, Dec. 18, 1807, JP.
62. TJ to AG, Dec. 18, 1807, GP.
63. AC, 9th Cong., 1st Sess., 1216.
64. Heckscher, *The Continental System*, 130; AG to TJ, Dec. 18, 1807, JP.

16: THE TROUBLE WITH THE EMBARGO, 1807–1809

1. TJ to AG, May 15, 1808, GP.
2. Robert Smith to AG, Aug. 1, 1808, GP.
3. AG's circular letters to Collectors of the Customs, Apr. 26, 27, 28, 29, May 6, 20, 1808, Treasury Dept. Circular Letters, Ser. T, Vol. O, 203–213.
4. AG to TJ, Dec. 23, 1807, JP.
5. TJ to AG, Dec. 24, 1807, JP.
6. AC, 10th Cong., 1st Sess., 2815–2817, 2834, 2835, 2839–2842, 2859, 2860, 2870–2874; *Ibid.*, 2nd Sess., 1798–1804.
7. Dallas to AG, July 30, 1808, GP; AG to TJ, Aug. 6, 1808, JP; Sears, *Jefferson and the Embargo*, 67, 75 ff.
8. TJ to AG, May 27, 1808, GP.
9. AG to TJ, May 23 and 28, July 15, 1808, JP.
10. Sears, *Jefferson*, 81 ff.
11. AG to TJ, July 29, Aug. 9 and 23, Sept. 14, 1808, JP.
12. AG to TJ, July 29, 1808, JP.
13. AG to TJ, Aug. 6, 1808, JP; AG to Madison, May 10 and Sept. 9, 1808, Rives Papers; AG to Hannah Gallatin, Aug. 6, 1808, in Adams, *Life*, 373, 374.
14. AG to Madison, Sept. 9, 1808, Rives Papers.
15. TJ to AG, Aug. 11, 1808, GP.
16. TJ to George Logan, Dec. 27, 1808, JP.
17. AC, 10th Cong., 2nd Sess., 11–15.
18. AG to TJ, Nov. 15, 1808, JP.
19. Macon to J. H. Nicholson, Dec. 4, 1808, Nicholson Papers.
20. AC, 10th Cong., 2nd Sess., 514–521. AG's draft is in GP. See also Brant, *Madison*, IV, 471.
21. *ASP: Finance*, II, 307–316.

22. AG to Giles, Nov. 24, 1808, in AC, 10th Cong., 2nd Sess., 232–236.
23. O. Cook to J. Q. Adams, Dec. 29, 1808, Adams Papers.
24. AC, 10th Cong., 2nd Sess., 520, 521.
25. For the debates, see AC, 10th Cong., 2nd Sess., 530–812, 815–862, 865–895.
26. AC, 10th Cong., 2nd Sess., 238, 239, 241–298, 902–904, 910, 915–938, 982–1025, 1798–1804.
27. This account of AG's conversation with Erskine is based on AG to *National Intelligencer*, Apr. 21, 1810, GP, and Erskine to George Canning, Dec. 4, 1808, in *National Intelligencer*, July 18, 1810.
28. AG to J. H. Nicholson, Dec. 29, 1808, GP.
29. Boston *New England Palladium*, Feb. 24, 1809.
30. AC, 10th Cong., 2nd Sess., 1026–1030, 1098–1167; AG's memorandum, Dec., 1808, or Jan., 1809, Gallatin Folder, LC.
31. AC, 10th Cong., 2nd Sess., 304, 305.
32. *Ibid.*, 324–326, 330, 331, 1042–1048.
33. *Ibid.*, 1432, 1437–1441, 1443–1541.
34. Erskine to Canning, Feb. 10, 1809, cited in Adams, *History*, IV, 445.
35. TJ to Dupont de Nemours, Mar. 2, 1809, in Jefferson, *Writings* (Monticello ed.), XII, 259.
36. AG to Maria Nicholson, Jan. 31, 1809, GP.
37. Dewey, *Financial History*, 122–124.
38. AG to Catherine de Budé, May 14, 1807, de Budé Manuscripts.
39. W. C. Nicholas to ———, cited in Adams, *History*, V, 55; Giles to Madison, Feb. 27, 1809, Rives Papers. See also Nicholas to [P. N. Nicholas], Dec. 3, 1808, Nicholas Papers; D. R. Anderson, *William Branch Giles*, 147; Spaulding, *His Excellency George Clinton*, 296.
40. AG to Hannah Gallatin, May 23, 1829, in Adams, *Life*, 633.
41. AG to J. H. Nicholson, Mar. 23 and Apr. 20, 1809, Nicholson Papers.
42. J. H. Nicholson to AG, May 4, 1809, GP.

17: THE LIFE OF A CABINET MEMBER, 1801–1813

1. AG to William Bentley, Oct. 31, 1805, GP.
2. John Randolph to AG, June 28, 1805, GP.
3. Hannah Gallatin to AG, June 5, 1804, GP.
4. Smith, *First Forty Years of Washington Society*, 28, 29, 32, 45, 48, 56, 86.
5. Washington Irving to Henry Brevoort, Jan. 13, 1811, in Irving, *Letters to Henry Brevoort*, I, 24.
6. Macon to J. H. Nicholson, Apr. 23, 1812, Nicholson Papers.
7. Roberts, "Memoirs," *PMHB*, LXII, 239.
8. Plumer, *Memorandum*, 634.
9. Duane to Dearborn, July 3, 1810, in Duane, "Letters," *Mass. Hist. Soc. Proc.*, 2nd Ser., XX, 337.

10. See Note 7.
11. See Note 9.
12. Seaton, *William Winston Seaton*, 90, 91.
13. Irving to James Renwick, Nov. 24, 1812, in Irving, *Letters to Mrs. William Renwick*, 16, 17.
14. AG to John Montgomery, July 12, 1809, GP.
15. AG to Maria Nicholson, Jan. 16 and Feb. 1, 1797, GP.
16. AG to Hannah Gallatin, Aug. 17 and 24, 1802, in Adams, *Life*, 305.
17. AG to Maria Nicholson, Mar. 12, 1801, GP; Smith, *First Forty Years*, 28; Mitchill, "Letters from Washington," *Harper's*, LVIII, 743.
18. Smith, *First Forty Years*, 86.
19. Porter, *John Jacob Astor, Business Man*, II, 1040, 1041.
20. Roberts, "Memoirs," 247.
21. Mitchill, "Letters from Washington," 745.
22. AG to Hannah Gallatin, June 6, 1804, GP; *National Intelligencer*, June 8 and 15, 1804; de Terra, *Humboldt*, 180, 181.
23. Melish, *Travels*, 286–288.
24. Plumer, *Memorandum*, 632.
25. Dunlap, *Diary*, II, 384.
26. Plumer, *Memorandum*, 634.
27. *National Intelligencer*, Sept. 25, 1801.
28. TJ to AG, Sept. 18, 1801, GP.
29. Hannah Gallatin to AG, June 5, 1804, July 5, 1807, GP.
30. AG to TJ, Oct. 26, 1802, JP.
31. AG to Hannah Gallatin, Aug. 17 and 24, 1802, in Adams, *Life*, 304, 305.
32. AG to J. W. Nicholson, Aug. 28, 1801, and Apr. 30, 1802, GP.
33. Bacon, *Ancestry*, 19; Hannah Gallatin to AG, July 7, 1804, GP.
34. Bacon, *Ancestry*, 19; AG to J. W. Nicholson, Sept. 20, 1805, and Apr. 21, 1808, GP.
35. AG to Bentley, Oct. 31, 1805, GP.
36. AG to Hannah Gallatin, June 6, 1804, GP.
37. AG to Hannah Gallatin, July 4, 1807, GP.
38. See, for example, AG to TJ, July 24, 1802, JP.
39. AG to J. W. Nicholson, Aug. 31, 1803, and Sept. 5, 1804, GP.
40. For example, see J. J. Astor to Hannah Gallatin, Feb. 8, 1808, to AG, May 16, 1809, Dec. 12, 1811, and May 13, 1812, GP.
41. AG to J. W. Nicholson, Jan. 11, 1808, "Statement of real property belonging to the partnership of the late Albert Gallatin & Co.," GP; *Tree of Liberty*, May 7, 1803, cited in Bining, The Glass Industry, 10.
42. AG to J. W. Nicholson, Aug. 20, 1806, GP.
43. Some of the papers involved in the reorganization and also a folder of the accounts of the "Old Glass Works, 1803–1808," are in Gallatin Papers. See also Gilpin, "Journal of a Tour from Philadelphia thro the Western Counties of Pennsylvania," *PMHB*, LII, 56.
44. AG to Mathew Lyon, May 7, 1816, GP.

45. Clement Biddle to AG, Nov. 24, 1801, GP.
46. Fayette County Deed Book D, 347, 348; Deed Book E, 85–88, 96, 255; Deed Book F, 55, 74; Deed Book H, 210, 269, 270; Deed Book I, 58, 59, 233, 276; Deed Book M, 300, 301; Deed Book N, 396.
47. AG to Joshua Meigs, Dec. 4, 1805, in Gallatin, *Writings*, I, 671, 672; Worthington to AG, Mar. 21, 1803, Savary de Valcoulon to James Morrison, Oct. 12, 1809, and to AG, Jan. 11, 1810, AG to J. W. Nicholson, May 5, 1813, GP.
48. Badollet to AG, June 3, and AG to Badollet, July 27, 1803, GP.
49. AG to TJ, Mar. 28, 1804, JP.
50. Badollet to AG, Mar. 7, 1809, GP; Goebel, *William Henry Harrison*, 80–82.
51. There are innumerable letters from Badollet to AG between 1801 and 1813 in GP.
52. AG to Badollet, May 12, 1809, GP.

18: THE STRUGGLE WITH THE "INVISIBLES," 1809–1810

1. For examples of AG's contributions to Madison's state papers, see AG to Madison, May 18 and Nov. 29, 1809, Dec., 1810, and Nov. 5, 1811, Rives Papers.
2. AG to J. H. Nicholson, May 11, 1809, Nicholson Papers.
3. AC, 11th Cong., 1st Sess., 448.
4. Baltimore *Federal Republican*, June 19, 20, 21, 22, 26, 1809.
5. Samuel Smith to AG, June 26, 1809, GP.
6. Robert Smith to AG, June 28, 1809, GP.
7. AG to Samuel Smith, June 29, 1809, GP.
8. Madison to TJ, Aug. 23, 1809, Madison Papers.
9. TJ to AG, Oct. 11, 1809, GP.
10. AG to TJ, Nov. 8, 1809, GP.
11. J. H. Nicholson to AG, Oct. 16, 1809, GP.
12. Turreau to Champagny, Apr. 22 and June 1, 1809, cited in Adams, *History*, V, 37–39; Madison to TJ, May 1, 1809, in Madison, *Letters* (Rives ed.), II, 440.
13. AG to Madison, July 24, 26, 31, 1809, Rives Papers; to Rodney, July 24, 1809, Gallatin Folder LC.
14. AG to Montgomery, July 27, 1809, GP.
15. Madison to AG, July 28 and 30, 1809, GP.
16. Madison to TJ, Aug. 16, 1809, in Madison, *Letters* (Rives ed.), II, 452.
17. AG to Erskine, Aug. 13, 1809, GP.
18. Erskine to AG, Aug. 15, 1809, GP.
19. AG to Madison, Sept. 11, 1809, Madison Papers.
20. Adams, *History*, V, 132.
21. AG to Maria N. Montgomery, Oct. 28, 1809, GP.

22. John Randolph to J. H. Nicholson, Dec. 4, 1809, Nicholson Papers.
23. TJ to AG, Oct. 11, 1809, GP.
24. *ASP: Finance,* II, 373–384.
25. Macon to J. H. Nicholson, Apr. 26, 1810, Nicholson Papers.
26. AG to TJ, Nov. 11, 1809, JP.
27. *ASP: Finance,* II, 412–414.
28. Macon to J. H. Nicholson, Jan. 11, 1810, Nicholson Papers.
29. *ASP: Finance,* II, 375.
30. AC, 11th Cong., 2nd Sess., 688, 754, 755, 1160–1196, 1201, 1202, 1219–1224, 1226–1253, 1257–1273, 1275–1355.
31. Alexandria, Va., *Gazette,* Jan. 20, and Georgetown, D.C., *Spirit of Seventy Six,* Apr. 6, 1810, cited in Mayo, *Henry Clay,* 344, 345, 352.
32. AC, 11th Cong., 2nd Sess., 577.
33. Dodd, *Life of Nathaniel Macon,* 257; Madison, *Writings* (Rives ed.), II, 495–506.
34. Macon to J. H. Nicholson, Mar. 17, 1810, Nicholson Papers.
35. AC, 11th Cong., 2nd Sess., 1414–1423, 1819–1857, 1860–1863.
36. *Ibid.,* 2051, 2052, 2508–2510.
37. Macon to J. H. Nicholson, Jan. 11 and 28, Edwin Gray to Nicholson, Jan. 16, and Randolph to Nicholson, May 2, 1810, Nicholson Papers; Macon to Jones, Apr. 8, 1810, Jones Papers.
38. Duane to Dearborn, July 3, 1810, in Duane, "Letters," *Mass. Hist. Soc. Proc.,* 2nd Ser., XX, 334–337.
39. *National Intelligencer,* Apr. 23 and 25, July 18, 1810; *Aurora,* July 3, 17, and 20, 1810.
40. AG to *National Intelligencer,* Apr. 21, 1810, GP, printed in *National Intelligencer,* July 18, 1810.
41. *Aurora,* July 21, 23, 24, 25, 26, 27, 28, 30, 31, Aug. 1, 2, 3, 4, 6, 8, 1810.
42. TJ to AG, Aug. 16, 1810, GP.
43. AG to TJ, Sept. 10, 1810, JP.
44. *ASP: Finance,* II, 425–431.
45. *ASP: Commerce and Navigation,* I, 866.
46. *Ibid.*
47. *ASP: Finance,* II, 542–552.
48. *Ibid.,* 439–451.

19: OVERWHELMED BY THE WAR HAWKS, 1810–1812

1. AG to Thomas Willing, Nov. 25, 1807, Gratz Collection.
2. Dallas to David Lenox, Feb. 4, 1808, Gratz Collection.
3. *ASP: Finance,* II, 301.
4. *Ibid.,* 351–353.
5. AG to Speaker of the House of Representatives, June 20, 1809, in Treasury

Dept.: Secretary of Treasury Letters and Reports to Congressmen, E, Vol. V, 230, 231.

6. AC, 11th Cong., 2nd Sess., 1679–1681.
7. *Ibid.*, 1762, 1763.
8. *Ibid.*, 1935–1944.
9. *Ibid.*, 2587–2589.
10. *Ibid.*, 3rd Sess., 784, 785.
11. Astor to AG, Jan. 21, 1811, GP.
12. Wettereau, "New Light on the First Bank of the United States," *PMHB*, LXI, 284, 285; AG to Nicholas Biddle, Aug. 14, 1830, in Gallatin, *Writings*, II, 431–440.
13. Higginbotham, *Keystone*, 225; Holdsworth, *First Bank*, 76.
14. See, for example, Samuel Smith to AG, Nov. 2, 1808, GP.
15. Quoted in Elizabethtown *New Jersey Journal*, Jan. 15, 1811.
16. *Aurora*, Nov. 8, 1810, Jan. 9 and following, 1811.
17. AC, 11th Cong., 3rd Sess., 826.
18. Macon to J. H. Nicholson, Jan. 28, 1811, Nicholson Papers.
19. AG to Badollet, July 29, 1824, GP.
20. *ASP: Finance,* II, 481.
21. AC, 11th Cong., 3rd Sess., 134–150.
22. *Ibid.*, 175–219, 240–268.
23. *Ibid.*, 346, 347.
24. Gallatin, *Writings*, II, 435; Holdsworth, *First Bank*, 82–90.
25. Samuel Smith to Gabriel Duval, Apr. 21, Duval to Smith, June 26, 1810, AG to Speaker of the House of Representatives, Feb. 22, 1811, *National Intelligencer*, Mar. 12, 1811.
26. Robert Smith to ———, Mar. 12, 1811, Smith Mss.
27. *Aurora*, Feb. 11, 1811.
28. Bayard, "Papers," *Amer. Hist. Assn. Ann. Rept.*, 1913, II, 485.
29. Randolph to J. H. Nicholson, Feb. 14, 1811, Nicholson Papers.
30. AG to Madison, [Mar. 4, 1811?] GP.
31. Monroe to Richard Brent, Mar. 18, 1811, GP.
32. Bayard, "Papers," 484, 485.
33. *National Intelligencer*, July 2, 1811.
34. *Aurora*, Apr. 11 and Sept. 3, 1811.
35. TJ to Wirt, Mar. 30, 1811, in Jefferson, *Writings* (Ford ed.), IX, 316 n., 317 n.; May 3, 1811, in Jefferson, *Writings* (Monticello ed.), XIII, 52–56.
36. TJ to Madison, Apr. 24, 1811, in Jefferson, *Writings* (Ford ed.), IX, 320 n., 321 n.
37. TJ to Duane, Mar. 28, 1811, JP.
38. TJ to Wirt, May 3, 1811, in Jefferson, *Writings* (Monticello ed.), XIII, 55, 56.
39. TJ to AG, Apr. 24, 1811, GP.
40. AG to J. H. Nicholson, May 30, 1811, Nicholson Papers.

41. AG's notes on Madison's message, Nov. 5, 1811, Rives Papers.
42. *ASP: Finance*, II, 495–507.
43. AC, 12th Cong., 1st Sess., 15.
44. *Ibid.*, 47–51.
45. *Ibid.*, 66–84.
46. *Ibid.*, 566, 595–606, 608, 609, 611–617, 619–691, 701–718, 2229–2234.
47. *ASP: Finance*, II, 523–527.
48. *Niles' Weekly Register*, I, 408.
49. Quoted in *Niles' Weekly Register*, II, 54.
50. London *Times*, Feb. 22, 1812, quoted in Tucker, *Poltroons and Patriots*, I, 78, 366.
51. *Aurora*, Jan. 25, 28, 30, Mar. 7, 1812.
52. S. L. Taggart to John Taylor, Jan. 20 and 22, 1812, in Taggart, "Letters," *Amer. Antiq. Soc. Proc.*, New Series, XXXIII, 378–380.
53. Bayard to Rodney, Jan. 26, 1812, in Bayard, "Letters," *Dela. Hist. Soc. Papers*, No. 31, 14.
54. Roberts, "Memoirs," *PMHB*, LXII, 239; Mayo, *Henry Clay*, 453.
55. AG to TJ, Mar. 10, 1812, JP.
56. Coit, *John C. Calhoun*, 80.
57. Treasury Dept. Circular Letters and Reports, Ser. T, Vol. O, 260, 261.
58. *National Intelligencer*, Apr. 23, 1812; Powell, *Richard Rush, Republican Diplomat*, 24.
59. *ASP: Finance*, II, 564–568.
60. AC, 12th Cong., 1st Sess., 1432; Knox, *United States Notes*, 21, 22.
61. AG to J. H. Nicholson, May 21, 1812, GP.
62. John Langdon to AG, May 30, 1812, GP.
63. Serurier to Maret, May 27, 1812, cited in Adams, *History*, VI, 216, 217.
64. AC, 12th Cong., 1st Sess., 1624–1629.
65. *Ibid.*, 297, 1637.

20: "MR. MADISON'S WAR," 1812–1813

1. Richard Rush to Benjamin Rush, June 20, 1812, cited in Adams, *History*, VI, 229.
2. AG to Madison, [autumn 1812?], Madison Papers.
3. AG to TJ, Dec. 18, 1812, JP.
4. W. H. Crawford to Monroe, Sept. 27, 1812, in Adams, *History*, VI, 395.
5. AG to Madison, Oct. 11, 1812, Madison Papers.
6. *Boston Patriot*, quoted in *Aurora*, Aug. 31, 1812.
7. Higginbotham, *Keystone*, 267–269.
8. Monroe to AG, June 1, 1812, GP.
9. AG to Madison, [June 20, 1812?], Madison Papers.

10. Papers, mostly undated, containing AG's plans for organizing the army and its campaigns, in his handwriting, are among Rives Papers and Madison Papers.

11. AG to Madison, Aug. 13 and 31, 1812, Rives Papers.

12. Undated memoranda in AG's hand counselling Monroe on the military conduct and financing of the war are in Monroe Papers, LC, filed under 1813. See also Monroe to AG, Jan. 5, 1813, GP.

13. AG to Madison, Dec. 12, 1812, Madison Papers; Monday [1813?], Jan. 7, 1813, Rives Papers.

14. *ASP: Finance*, II, 569.

15. *AC*, 12th Cong., 1st Sess., 1558, 1559.

16. *Ibid.*, 2335–2337; *Niles' Weekly Register*, III, 350.

17. *ASP: Finance*, II, 580, 581.

18. Memorandum, AG to Madison, [1812?], Madison Papers.

19. AG to Monroe, Jan. 4, 1813, Monroe Papers, LC.

20. Memorandum, AG to Monroe, [1812 or 1813], Monroe Papers, LC; Bayard, "Papers," *Amer. Hist. Soc. Ann. Rept.*, 1913, II, 193–195.

21. *AC*, 12th Cong., 2nd Sess., 198, 199, 1251–1255.

22. *Ibid.*, 217–263, 267–349, 355–361, 365–404, 1124–1126, 1334, 1335.

23. *Ibid.*, 1062–1065, 1091–1100, 1105–1109, 1111–1113.

24. *Ibid.*, 1326–1328, 1330–1333.

25. AG to Madison, [Mar., 1813?], Madison Papers.

26. Circular letter, Feb. 23, 1813, Treasury Dept. Circular Letters and Reports, Ser. T, Vol. O, 276–278.

27. *ASP: Finance*, II, 625, 626.

28. *Ibid.*, 626.

29. Dallas to AG, May or June, July 29, 1812, GP.

30. Walters, *Dallas*, 177–179.

31. Walters and Walters, "The American Career of David Parish," *Jour. Econ. Hist.*, IV, 149–166; Walters and Walters, "David Parish: York State Land Promoter," *New York Hist.*, XXVI, 146–161. See also Nolte, *Fifty Years in Both Hemispheres*, 139, 140, 173; Raffalovich, "John Parish, banquier et négociant à Hambourg," *Journal des économistes*, 6th Ser., VII, 208; and Richard Ehrenberg, *Grosse Vermögen*: Vol. II, *Das Haus Parish in Hamburg*.

32. Parish to Messrs. LeRoy, Bayard, and McEvers, Feb. 11, 1813, to Messrs. Prime & Ward, Mar. 12, 1813, Parish Letter Books, IV, 184, 209; AG to Madison, Mar. 5, 1813, Madison Papers.

33. *ASP: Finance*, II, 626.

34. Brown, *Stephen Girard, Financier*, 127–129; Brown, "Stephen Girard's Bank," *PMHB*, LXVI, 38, 39.

35. Gallatin, *Writings*, I, 678–680.

36. Parish to Messrs. Minturn & Champlin, to David B. Ogden, to George Griswold, to George Newbold, Apr. 3, 1813, Parish Letter Books, IV, 236.

37. AG to Madison, Apr. 19, 1816, Madison Papers.

38. Girard and Parish to AG, Apr. 6 and 8, 1813, Parish Letter Books, IV,

258–260. For other accounts of the loan, see McMaster, *Life and Times of Stephen Girard*, II, 246–250; Wildes, *Lonely Midas*, 215, 216.

39. André de Daschkoff to Madison, Mar. 8, 1813, GP.
40. AG to J. W. Nicholson, May 5, 1813, GP.
41. Monroe to Daschkoff, Mar. 11, 1813, GP.
42. Monroe to TJ, June 7, 1813, JP.
43. *National Intelligencer*, Apr. 13, 1813; Borden, *Federalism of James A. Bayard*, 191, 194, 196.
44. AG to J. W. Nicholson, May 5, 1813, GP; *National Intelligencer*, Apr. 16, 29, 1813.
45. Bayard, "Papers," 442, 476.
46. Richard Rush to John Adams, June 29, 1813, in Adams and Rush, "Some Unpublished Correspondence," *PMHB*, LX, 440.
47. Dallas to AG, Feb. 14, 1814, GP.
48. AG to J. W. Nicholson, May 5, 1813, GP.
49. *National Intelligencer*, Apr. 15, 1813.
50. AG to Madison, Apr. 17, and to Secretaries of War and of the Navy, Apr. 17, 1813, Madison Papers.
51. Astor to AG, May 13, 1812, GP; memorandum for Jones by AG, Apr. 20, 1813, Jones Papers; Rush to Adams, June 6, 1813, in Adams and Rush, "Some Unpublished Correspondence," 437; *ASP: Finance*, II, 622–627.
52. Monroe to AG, Apr. 27, May 5 and 6, 1813; AG to Monroe, May 2 and 8, 1813, GP.
53. AG to J. W. Nicholson, May 5, 1813, GP.
54. Bayard, "Papers," 204–206, 213–218, 221, 226–229, 385, 386; AG's memorandum of the voyage to Russia, GP.
55. AG to TJ, Nov. 11, 1809, JP.
56. AG to G. P. Marsh, Jan. 15, 1848, GP.
57. Heinlein, "Albert Gallatin," *William and Mary Quart. Hist. Mag.*, 3rd Ser., VII, 93, 94; Heinlein, Administrative Theory and Practices of Gallatin, 336.
58. Dewey, *Financial History of the U.S.*, 125.
59. *National Intelligencer*, Apr. 22, 1813.

21: THE QUEST FOR PEACE, 1813–1814

1. AG's memorandum of the voyage is in GP. See also Bayard, "Papers," *Amer. Hist. Assn. Ann. Rept.*, 1913, II, 386 ff., 395–397.
2. AG to Baring Brothers, June 2, 1813, GP.
3. AG's memorandum, GP; Bayard, "Papers," 400–406, 412–415.
4. Adams, *Memoirs*, II, 473, 474, 478, 479.
5. *Ibid.*, 491, 492; Bayard, "Papers," 416–418; AG and other American commissioners to Monroe, Aug. 17/29, 1813, AG Letter Books (in Bayard, "Papers,"), I, 47–52.

6. Bayard, "Papers," 416–422, 431, 432, 436, 437, 441, 470.

7. *Ibid.*, 419, 422, 425, 426; AG, Adams, and Bayard to Roumanzoff, July 20/Aug. 1, 1813, GP; to Monroe, Aug. 17/29, 1813, AG Letter Books, I, 47–52.

8. Baring to AG, July 22, 1813, GP.

9. Adams, *Memoirs*, II, 509, 517, 518; AG to Monroe, Aug. 28, 1813, GP; Bayard, "Papers," 441.

10. Jean-Victor-Marie Moreau to AG, Aug. 21, 1813, GP; Adams to Abigail Adams, Sept. 21, 1813, in Adams, *Writings*, IV, 520–522.

11. AG to Moreau, Sept. 2, 1813, GP.

12. Adams to Abigail Adams, Sept. 21, 1813, in Adams, *Writings*, IV, 520–522.

13. AC, 13th Cong., 1st Sess., 83–90.

14. Bayard, "Papers," 476, 479, 480; Adams, *Memoirs*, II, 536, 537; AG to Roumanzoff, Nov. 1, 1813, GP.

15. Bayard, "Papers," 479, 481, 482.

16. Adams, *Memoirs*, II, 539–542.

17. Bayard, "Papers," 483, 488, 493.

18. Adams, *Memoirs*, II, 548–551, 553–555, 560–562, 573; Bayard, "Papers," 484; Adams to John Adams, Jan. 2 and Feb. 17, 1814, to Abigail Adams, Jan. 17, 1814, in Adams, *Writings*, V, 1–3, 5, 6, 19; Baring to AG, Oct. 12, 1813, G. M. Dallas to AG, Nov. 30, 1813, GP.

19. Bayard, "Papers," 496, 497; AG to Baring, Jan. 7, 1814, to Roumanzoff, Jan. 10/22, 13/25, 1814, GP; Adams, *Memoirs*, II, 473.

20. This account of the journey to Amsterdam is based on Bayard to Monroe, Mar. 16, and to Andrew Bayard, Mar. 19, 1814, in Bayard, "Papers," 279, 282; and on Bayard's diary, in *ibid.*, 497–502.

21. Sylvanus Bourne to AG and Bayard, Feb. 11, 1814, GP.

22. AG to Adams, Mar. 6, 1814, Adams Papers.

23. Bayard's diary in Bayard, "Papers," 502–505; Baring to AG, Dec. 13, 1813, Adams to AG and Bayard, Feb. 6, 1814, AG to Baring Brothers, Mar. 7, 1814, GP; Bayard to Adams, Mar. 14, 1814, in Bayard, "Papers," 276.

24. AG to Baring, Apr. 1, and to Crawford, Apr. 21, 1814, GP; Bayard "Papers," 505, 506; Bayard to Rodney, Aug. 5, 1814, in Bayard, "Letters," 38.

25. Hannah Gallatin to Dallas, July 2, 1814, quoting letter to her from AG, May 9, 1814, GP.

26. AG to Crawford, Apr. 21, 1814, GP.

27. Bayard, "Papers," 507; R. G. Beasley to AG, Apr. 20, and Henry Clay and Jonathan Russell to AG and Bayard, Apr. 20, 1814, GP.

28. Bayard, "Papers," 507; AG to Clay, Apr. 22, Clay to Russell, May 1, and Clay to Bayard and AG, May 2, 1814, GP.

29. AG and Bayard to Castlereagh, May 13, 1814, GP; American commissioners to Monroe, July 11, 1814, in Bayard, "Papers," 305, 306.

30. Bathurst to AG and Bayard, May 16, 1814, GP.

31. AG and Bayard to Bathurst, May 17, 1814, GP.

32. Bayard, "Papers," 507 ff.

33. *Ibid.*, 506; Jeremy Bentham to AG, June 16, 1814, GP.
34. AG to Monroe, June 13, 1814, GP.
35. Green, *Public Life of William Harris Crawford*, 82, 83; Crawford to AG, May 12, 1814, GP.
36. Lafayette to AG, May 25 and 26, 1814, GP.
37. AG to Czar Alexander, June 19 (?), 1814, AG to Monroe, June 20, 1814, GP.
38. Peter Irving to AG, May 31, June 18, 1814, GP; AG to Mr. Erving [Irving], [May 1814], Washburn Collection.
39. AG to Monroe, June 20, and to Beasley, June 26, 1814, GP.
40. Adams, *Memoirs*, III, 150, 151.
41. AG to Baring Brothers, July 26, 1814, to Beasley, July 26, 1814, GP; Adams, *Memoirs*, II, 652; Bayard, "Papers," 513, 514.
42. Adams, *Memoirs*, II, 661.
43. Adams to AG, Feb. 18, 1814, in J. Q. Adams Letter Books (in Adams Papers); to Abigail Adams, Mar. 30, 1814, in Adams, *Writings*, V, 24.
44. Adams to L. C. Adams, July 12, 1814, in Adams, *Writings*, V, 61, 66.
45. Adams, *Memoirs*, II, 657.
46. Adams, *Memoirs*, II, 656, 658; Bayard, "Papers," 514.
47. Adams to L. C. Adams, July 29, 1814, in Adams, *Writings*, V, 67, 68.
48. AG to Beasley, July 26, 1814, GP; Adams to L. C. Adams, July 29, Aug. 1 and 5, 1814, in Adams, *Writings*, V, 68, 70, 72.
49. Adams, *Memoirs*, III, 3, 4; Bayard, "Papers," 514.
50. Adams, *Memoirs*, III, 5.

22: PEACE AT GHENT, 1814

1. For sketches of the commissioners, see Adams to L. C. Adams, Dec. 16, 1814, in Adams, *Writings*, V, 237–239.
2. See, for example, Bemis, *Diplomatic History*, 163.
3. Adams, *Memoirs*, IV, 388.
4. AG to James Gallatin, Jan. 29, 1827, GP.
5. Adams to L. C. Adams, Dec. 16, 1814, in Adams, *Writings*, V, 238, 239.
6. Dangerfield, *Era of Good Feelings*, 64, 65.
7. Castlereagh to British commissioners, July 28, 1814, Castlereagh, *Memoirs*, X, 67–72.
8. Adams, *Memoirs*, III, 7.
9. Monroe to American commissioners, Apr. 15, 1813, Jan. 28, 1814, and June 25 and 27, 1814, ASP: *Foreign Relations*, III, 695–704; AG to Monroe, May 8, 1813, and June 13, 1814, GP.
10. For the first three meetings, see Adams, *Memoirs*, III, 5–13; Bayard, "Papers," *Amer. Hist. Assn. Ann. Rept.*, 1913, II, 332–335; Updyke, *Diplomacy of the War of 1812*, 200–214.

11. Adams, *Memoirs*, III, 13–16. For Adams's draft, see Adams, *Writings*, V, 75–82. For the final dispatch, dated Aug. 12, 1814, see *ASP: Foreign Relations*, III, 705–707.

12. Henry Goulburn to Bathurst, Aug. 21, 1814, in Wellington, *Supplementary Despatches*, IX, 188.

13. Adams, *Memoirs*, III, 16–20; Bayard, "Papers," 335–338.

14. Adams, *Memoirs*, III, 21–23. Adams's draft is in Adams, *Writings*, V, 93–101; Bayard's draft is in Bayard, "Papers," 320–325; the draft as sent is in *ASP: Foreign Relations*, III, 711–713.

15. Adams, *Memoirs*, III, 23, 24; Liverpool to Wellington, Sept. 2, and to Castlereagh, Sept. 2, 1814, in Wellington, IX, 212–214; Liverpool to Bathurst, Sept. 14, 1814, in Bickley, comp., *Report on the Manuscripts of Earl Bathurst*, 287.

16. *ASP: Foreign Relations*, III, 713–715.

17. Adams, *Memoirs*, III, 31.

18. *Ibid.*, 31–33; Adams to L. C. Adams, Sept. 27, 1814, in Adams, *Writings*, V, 146, 147.

19. Adams's draft is in Adams, *Writings*, V, 122–129. The note sent is in *ASP: Foreign Relations*, III, 715–717.

20. The British note, dated Sept. 19, 1814, is in *ASP: Foreign Relations*, III, 717, 718.

21. Adams, *Memoirs*, III, 36–42.

22. Adams, *Memoirs*, III, 42; Adams to L. C. Adams, Sept. 23 and 27, 1814, in Adams, *Writings*, V, 143, 144, 146. The American note, dated Sept. 26, 1814, is in *ASP: Foreign Relations*, III, 719–721.

23. Adams to L. C. Adams, Sept. 9 and 27, 1814, in Adams, *Writings*, V, 121, 147.

24. Adams, *Memoirs*, III, 37, 38.

25. Goulburn to Bathurst, Sept. 23, 1814, in Wellington, *Supplementary Despatches*, IX, 278.

26. Adams, *Memoirs*, III, 40–45.

27. G. W. Campbell to AG, Crawford, and Adams, Aug. 1, 1814; Crawford to AG and Adams, Sept. 26, 1814; AG to W. & J. Willink, Oct. 3, 1814, GP.

28. Adams, *Memoirs*, III, 45.

29. J. H. Nicholson to Hannah Gallatin, Sept. 14, 1814; Louis Salmon to AG, Sept. 14 and Dec. 3, 1814, GP.

30. Adams, *Memoirs*, III, 52, 53.

31. Madame de Staël to AG, Sept. 30, and AG to Madame de Staël, Oct. 4, 1814, GP.

32. W. & J. Willink to AG, Oct. 14, 1814, GP.

33. Crawford to AG, Oct. 6, to AG and Adams, Oct. 25, AG to Campbell, Oct. 26, 1814, GP.

34. AG to Monroe, Oct. 26, 1814, AG Letter Books (in GP), II, 215–219.

35. Adams, *Memoirs*, III, 50. The text of the note is in *ASP: Foreign Relations*, III, 721–723.

36. AG to Monroe, Oct. 26, 1814, AG Letter Books, II, 215–219.
37. Adams, *Memoirs*, III, 50–52. The text of the note is in ASP: *Foreign Relations*, III, 723, 724.
38. Adams to L. C. Adams, Oct. 14, 1814, in Adams, *Writings*, V, 158–160.
39. Adams, *Memoirs*, III, 53–57.
40. ASP: *Foreign Relations*, III, 724, 725. Compare with Bathurst to British commissioners, Oct. 18, 1814, in Castlereagh, *Memoirs and Correspondence*, X, 168–170.
41. Adams to L. C. Adams, Oct. 25, 1814, in Adams, *Writings*, V, 184.
42. Goulburn to Bathurst, Oct. 21, 1814, in Wellington, *Supplementary Despatches*, IX, 366.
43. Adams, *Memoirs*, III, 57, 60. For the note, see ASP: *Foreign Relations*, III, 725.
44. Adams, *Memoirs*, III, 60–62; ASP: *Foreign Relations*, III, 726.
45. Adams, *Memoirs*, III, 61–69; ASP: *Foreign Relations*, III, 733, 734.
46. Adams, *Memoirs*, III, 69, 70; Adams to L. C. Adams, Nov. 15, 1814, in Adams, *Writings*, V, 189.
47. Adams to L. C. Adams, Jan. 24, 1815, in Adams, *Writings*, V, 272, 273.
48. Adams, *Memoirs*, III, 70; Adams to Levett Harris, Nov. 24, to L. C. Adams, Nov. 25 and 29, 1814, in Adams, *Writings*, V, 211, 214, 219–221.
49. Liverpool to Castlereagh, Sept. 23 and Oct. 28, 1814, in Wellington, *Supplementary Despatches*, IX, 278, 279, 383.
50. Liverpool to Wellington, Nov. 4 and 13, Wellington to Liverpool, Nov. 7, 9, and 18, 1814, in Wellington, *Supplementary Despatches*, IX, 406, 422, 425, 426, 430, 431, 436; Wellington to Bathurst, Nov. 4, 1814, in Bickley, comp., *Report on the Manuscripts of Earl Bathurst*, 303.
51. Baring to AG, Nov. 15, 1814, GP.
52. Adams, *Memoirs*, III, 70, 71; ASP: *Foreign Relations*, III, 740, 741.
53. Adams, *Memoirs*, III, 75–77.
54. *Ibid.*, III, 77, 78; ASP: *Foreign Relations*, III, 741, 742.
55. Adams, *Memoirs*, III, 79–90, 93–113; ASP: *Foreign Relations*, III, 742, 743.
56. ASP: *Foreign Relations*, III, 743, 744; Adams, *Memoirs*, III, 117–119.
57. ASP: *Foreign Relations*, III, 744, 745.
58. Adams, *Memoirs*, III, 119–122.
59. *Ibid.*, 122–127.
60. ASP: *Foreign Relations*, III, 745–748.
61. AG to Monroe, Dec. 25, 1814, AG Letter Books, II, 225.
62. Allen, *Great Britain and the United States*, 346, 347.
63. Adams to L. C. Adams, Jan. 13, 1815, in Adams, *Writings*, V, 267.
64. AG to Mathew Lyon, May 7, 1816, GP.

23: THE AFTERMATH OF GHENT, 1814–1816

1. Adams, *Memoirs*, III, 129–131; Bayard, Clay, and AG to Lloyd Jones, Jan. 6, 1815, GP.
2. Adams, *Memoirs*, III, 129–144.
3. Adams, *Life*, 547; Archives d'Etat Genève R.C. 315, Registre de Conseil d'Etat 1815, Vol. I, Jan. 25 and 27, 1815.
4. Adams, *Memoirs*, III, 165–167, 169, 171–176.
5. Adams to Abigail Adams, Mar. 19, 1815, in Adams, *Writings*, V, 294; AG to Jones, Mar. 31, 1815, GP.
6. Adams, *Memoirs*, III, 192.
7. Adams to L. C. Adams, Jan. 13, 1815, in Adams, *Writings*, V, 267.
8. Castlereagh to AG, Apr. 15, 1815, GP.
9. Minute of conversation, Apr. 16, 1815, in ASP: *Foreign Relations*, IV, 19.
10. ASP: *Foreign Relations*, IV, 8, 11, 19.
11. Adams, *Memoirs*, III, 208, 209.
12. Bemis, *Diplomatic History*, 172.
13. Clay and AG to Monroe, May 18, 1815, in ASP: *Foreign Relations*, IV, 8–10.
14. The vicissitudes of the negotiation are recorded in detail in Adams, *Memoirs*, III, 201, 207–213, 217–231, 236–238, 240–249, and in ASP: *Foreign Relations*, IV, 11–18.
15. Setser, *Commercial Reciprocity Policy of the United States*, 184, 187.
16. AG to Madison, Sept. 4, 1815, GP.
17. AG to Monroe, Nov. 25, 1815, GP.
18. Setser, *Commercial Reciprocity Policy*, 186; Bemis, *John Quincy Adams and the Foundations of American Foreign Policy*, 225.
19. Crawford to Hannah Gallatin, Aug. 16, 1815, GP; Green, Public Life of Crawford, 152.
20. Adams, *Memoirs*, III, 249; Dallas to Madison, Aug. 1, 1815, Madison Papers; AG to Clay, Nov. 23, 1815, GP; Adams to Monroe, July 14, 1815, State Dept. Diplomatic Correspondence, Great Britain: J. Q. Adams Dispatches #3.
21. *New-York Evening Post*, Sept. 1, 1815; AG to Madison, Sept. 4, 1815, GP.
22. *New-York Evening Post*, Sept. 2, 5, and 6, 1815.
23. Richard Bache to AG, Sept. 23, 1815, GP.
24. Astor to AG, Oct. 9, 1815, GP.
25. AG to Monroe, Dec. 26, 1815, GP.
26. A report card for Albert Rolaz Gallatin, dated Apr. 13, 1816, is in GP.
27. AG to Madison, Nov. 23, 1815, GP.
28. *National Intelligencer*, Oct. 14, Nov. 13, 1815.
29. AG to Madison, Nov. 23 and Dec. 26, 1815, to Monroe, Nov. 23, 1815, Monroe to AG, Dec. 4 and 16, 1815, Jan. 27, 1816, GP.
30. AG to Bache, Sept. 24, 1815, GP.
31. AG to Monroe, Feb. 2, 1816, GP.
32. AG to TJ, Apr. 1, 1816, GP.

33. AG to Monroe, May 3, 1816, Gratz Collection.
34. AG to J. W. Nicholson, Apr. 12 and May 4, to Worthington, May 5, to Astor, June 7, 1816, GP.
35. AG to Lyon, May 7, 1816, GP.
36. AG to Madison, June 4, 1816, Madison Papers.
37. AG to Madison, Apr. 19, 1816, Madison Papers.
38. *New-York Evening Post*, Sept. 6, 1815.
39. Walters, *Dallas*, 185, 186, 201–207; *ASP: Finance*, III, 11, 12.
40. *ASP: Finance*, III, 18, 19; Walters, *Dallas*, 212–215.
41. AG to TJ, Nov. 27, 1815, GP.
42. AG to J. H. Nicholson, Oct. 26 and Nov. 3, 1815, Nicholson Papers.
43. AG to TJ, Sept. 6 and Nov. 27, 1815, GP.
44. AG to Monroe, Dec. 26, 1815, Monroe Papers, LC.
45. AG to TJ, Nov. 27, 1815, GP.
46. Madison to AG, Apr. 12, 1816, GP.
47. AG to J. H. Nicholson, Apr. 19, 1815, Nicholson Papers.
48. AG to Madison, Apr. 18, 1815, GP.
49. AG to Madison, June 7, 1816, GP.
50. AG to Madison, June 2, and to Acting Consul at Havre, July 2, 1816, GP; *New-York Evening Post*, June 12, 1816.

24: THE FRENCH MISSION, 1816–1823

1. AG to Monroe, July 5, 1816, State Dept. Diplomatic Correspondence: Great Britain.
2. AG to Badollet, July 29, 1824, GP.
3. Artz, *France Under the Bourbon Restoration*, 237, 240, 250.
4. Hannah Gallatin to Dolley Madison, Aug. 12, 1816, GP.
5. Catherine N. Few to Hannah Gallatin, Dec. 9, 1816, GP.
6. *New-York Courier and Enquirer*, May 19, 1849.
7. Hannah Gallatin to Dolley Madison, Aug. 12, 1816, GP.
8. Frances Gallatin to A. R. Gallatin, Aug. 5 and Dec. 25, 1821, AG to Maria N. Montgomery, Sept. 17, to A. R. Gallatin, Sept. 17, 1821, Feb. 4, 1822, and Mar. 1, 1823, GP.
9. AG to Monroe, Aug. 3 and 6, 1816, GP.
10. AG to Monroe, Jan. 22, 1819, Monroe Papers, NYPL.
11. *New-York Hist. Soc. Proc. 1849*, 294, 295; Tayloe, *In Memoriam: Benjamin Tayloe*, 15, 16. A number of mementos—calling cards, invitations, etc.—in the possession of Mr. Albert Gallatin of New York City throw light on the Gallatins' social activities during these years.
12. There are many letters of introduction of traveling Americans in GP. Of particular interest are TJ to AG, Mar. 19, 1815, AG to Richelieu, July 11, 1817. See also Ticknor, *Life, Letters, and Journals*, I, 141–145.

13. Howe, *Life and Letters of George Bancroft*, I, 106–108.
14. Didier, *Life and Letters of Madame Bonaparte*, 105, 106, 142.
15. AG to Catherine de Budé, June 22, 1817, de Budé Manuscripts; to Badollet, July 29, 1824, GP.
16. AG to A. R. Gallatin, Feb. 27, 1827, GP.
17. Green, Public Life of Crawford, 181–187.
18. Crawford's letters to AG are in GP.
19. Bemis, *Adams and the Foundations of American Foreign Policy*, 262, 263.
20. AG to TJ, Sept. 6, 1815, GP.
21. AG to Lafayette, Apr. 21, 1814, GP.
22. Artz, *France*, 17–22.
23. Monroe to AG, Apr. 26, May 7 and 21, 1816, GP.
24. AG to Monroe, Aug. 6, Sept. 12, Oct. 14, Nov. 11, 1816, and Jan. 20, 1817, and to Adams, Mar. 16, 1820, Jan. 28, Apr. 23, June 13, Sept. 8 and 24, Nov. 13 and 19, 1822, Jan. 5 and Feb. 27, 1823, AG Letter Books, IV, 14, 15, 23–25, 32–36, 51, 52, 79–81, X, 38, XI, 174–179, 194–202, XII, 5–7, 48, 49, 51–54, 65–67, 69, 70, 91–94. For an account of AG and the spoliation claims, see McLemore, *Franco-American Diplomatic Relations*, 1–14.
25. Monroe to AG, Apr. 15 and 26, May 21, 1816, GP; Bemis, *Adams and the Foundations of American Foreign Policy*, 450; McLemore, 15–18.
26. AG to Monroe, Sept. 12, 1816, and July 11, 1817, State Dept. Diplomatic Correspondence: France.
27. AG to Adams, Oct. 25 and Dec. 9, 1819, Jan. 15 and 20, 1820, AG Letter Books, VII, 156–160, 177, 178, X, 6, 7; Setser, *Commercial Reciprocity Policy*, 198, 199.
28. Adams to AG, Sept. 13, 1820, GP; AC, 16th Cong., 1st Sess., 2619.
29. Adams to Monroe, Sept. 8, 1820, in Adams, *Writings*, VII, 72.
30. AG to Monroe, July 5, 1820, AG Letter Books, X, 68–70.
31. AG to Adams, July 11, 27, and 31, 1820, AG Letter Books, X, 92, 93, 101–121.
32. Bemis, *Adams and the Foundations of American Foreign Policy*, 451.
33. AG to Adams, Aug. 2, Sept. 22, Oct. 19 and 23, 1820, AG Letter Books, X, 121–123, 147–154, 162–164, 167–170.
34. Adams, *Memoirs*, V, 179, 195. For AG's negotiations on reciprocity, see Setser, *Commercial Reciprocity Policy*, 199–201.
35. AG to Adams, Oct. 23, Nov. 13, 16, and 24, 1821, AG Letter Books, XI, 83–86, 95–98, 101–106, 115–118.
36. AG to Adams, July 22, 1822, AG Letter Books, XII, 18, 19.
37. AG to Adams, Dec. 7, 1820, Jan. 6 and Mar. 31, 1821, GP.
38. AG to Pasquier, June 21, and to Adams, July 2, 1821, AG Letter Books, XI, 1, 13–15.
39. Adams, *Memoirs*, V, 376, 377.
40. *Ibid.*, 391, 392.
41. AG to Adams, Sept. 26, 1821, Feb. 1 and July 10, 1822, AG Letter Books, XI, 43–48, 183–185, XII, 13–16.

42. Hoekstra, *Thirty-seven Years of Holland-American Relations*, 130–133; Rush to AG and William Eustis, Apr. 22, 1817, together with certificate of powers, dated Apr. 5, 1817, GP.

43. A. W. C. Van Nagell to Eustis, July 23, 1817, AG Letter Books, V, 1; Eustis to Adams, Aug. 6, 1817, State Dept. Diplomatic Correspondence: Netherlands; Westermann, *The Netherlands and the United States*, 266, 267, 295, 296.

44. Westermann, *Netherlands and U.S.*, 256, 257, 268, 270, 291.

45. For the report of AG and Eustis to Adams, Sept. 22, 1817, see State Dept. Diplomatic Correspondence: Netherlands.

46. Hoekstra, *Thirty-seven Years*, 178; Westermann, *Netherlands and U.S.*, 291–293.

47. Adams to AG, May 22, AG to Adams, June 3, Crawford to AG, May 1, 1818, GP.

48. Rush to AG, July 2, 20, and 24, AG to Rush, July 13, 1818, GP; Rush, *Narrative of a Residence at the Court of London*, 154 ff.

49. AG to Rush, Aug. 6, and Rush to AG, Nov. 23, 1818, GP; Rush, *Narrative*, 306.

50. Memorandum on AG's and Rush's conversations with Castlereagh, Aug. 22 and 23, 1818, GP; AG to Adams, Jan. 19, 1819, AG Letter Books, VIII, 304–309; Rush, *Narrative*, 306–310. For the negotiations before AG's arrival in London, see *ASP: Foreign Relations*, IV, 379. Adams's instructions to AG and Rush, July 18, 1818, are in GP.

51. Rush, *Narrative*, 314.

52. Rush's minutes of conversation with Castlereagh, Sept. 1, 1818, are in GP. See also Rush, *Narrative*, 314, 316, 319.

53. Rush, *Narrative*, 381, 382.

54. AG's memorandum of his conversation with Goulburn, Oct. 16, 1818, AG Letter Books, VIII, 228–233.

55. There is an abundance of manuscript material on the negotiations in AG Papers, in State Dept. Diplomatic Correspondence: Richard Rush; and in Monroe Papers, LC (especially Rush's "Notes on the Joint Negotiation at London in 1818").

56. AG to Adams, Nov. 9, 1818, AG Letter Books, VIII, 294–299; Powell, *Richard Rush*, 112, 113.

57. AG to Adams, Nov. 6, 1818, AG Letter Books, VIII, 288–293.

58. Bemis, *Diplomatic History*, 175, 301, 408–411, 429.

59. Bemis, *Adams and the Foundations of American Foreign Policy*, 297, 298.

60. AG's memorandum of his conversation with Goulburn, Oct. 16, 1818, GP; AG to Adams, Jan. 19, 1819, AG Letter Books, VIII, 304–309.

61. Adams to AG, Apr. 14, 1819, GP.

62. Adams to AG, May 19, 1818, GP.

63. AG to Adams, Aug. 10, 1818, AG Letter Books, VII, 3–9.

64. AG to Adams, Nov. 5, 1818, AG Letter Books, VII, 22–30; Adams to AG, Nov. 30, 1818, GP.

65. AG to Adams, May 5, 1819, AG Letter Books, VII, 76–78.
66. AG to Adams, June 14, July 6 and 29, Sept. 3 and 24, Oct. 26, Dec. 8, 1819, and Jan. 13, Feb. 15, Mar. 17, Aug. 7, 1820, AG Letter Books, IX, 20–22, VII, 106–108, 119–121, 135, 136, 146–148, 160–164, 173–175, X, 4, 5, 16–19, 38–41, 125–127.
67. AG to Adams, Apr. 26, 1822, AG Letter Books, XI, 204–207.
68. AG to TJ, June 29, 1823, JP.
69. Porter, *John Jacob Astor, Business Man*, II, 1100–1102.
70. Mary Few to AG, Oct. 12, 1821, to A. R. Gallatin, Oct. 14, 1822, GP.
71. Bruce, *Randolph of Roanoke*, I, 532, II, 430.
72. TJ to AG, Dec. 26, 1820, Oct. 29, 1822, GP.
73. AG to J. W. Nicholson, Mar. 21, 1821, GP.
74. AG to A. R. Gallatin, Sept. 17, 1821, GP.
75. Maria Montgomery to AG, Apr. 20, 1822, GP.
76. AG to Maria Montgomery, Sept. 30, 1822, GP.
77. Didier, *Life and Letters of Madame Bonaparte*, 138, 139, 142, 146, 147.
78. AG to Monroe, Mar. 1, 1823, Monroe Papers, LC.
79. AG to Adams, Feb. 28, 1823, GP.
80. Adams to AG, June 27, 1822, GP.
81. AG to Monroe, Nov. 13, 1822, GP.
82. AG to Monroe, Mar. 1, 1823, Monroe Papers, LC.
83. Adams to AG, Apr. 14, 1823, GP; Adams, *Memoirs*, VI, 139.
84. AG to Adams, June 24, 1823, GP.
85. Adams, *Memoirs*, VI, 162.
86. Didier, *Life and Letters of Madame Bonaparte*, 135.
87. *National Intelligencer*, June 27, 1823.

25: AN AMERICAN INTERLUDE, 1823–1826

1. *New-York Evening Post*, June 24, 1823; *Longworth's New York City Directory, 1823–1824*.
2. J. W. Nicholson to AG, Nov. 3, 1821, and AG to Nicholson, July 27, 1823, GP.
3. *National Intelligencer*, July 23, 1823.
4. James to Frances Gallatin, Aug. 21, 1823, GP; AG to Frances Gallatin, Sept. 17 and Oct. 15, 1823, in Adams, *Life*, 589, 590.
5. AG to A. R. Gallatin, Nov. 10, 1823, GP.
6. AG to Thomas McKibben and others, Sept. 29, 1823, GP.
7. AG to Frances Gallatin, Oct. 15, 1823, in Adams, *Life*, 590.
8. Monroe to AG, Oct. 15, and AG to Monroe, Oct. 26, 1823, GP.
9. AG's critique of the various Presidential aspirants is in his letter to Badollet, July 29, 1824, GP.
10. *New-York Hist. Soc. Proc. 1849*, 290, 291.

11. Green, Public Life of Crawford, 9, 14, 16, 25, 36.

12. Garrison, National Election of 1824, 23, 24, 34 ff.

13. TJ to AG, Aug. 2, 1823, GP; TJ to AG, Oct. 29, 1823, in Adams, *Life*, 591, 592.

14. *National Intelligencer*, Sept. 3 and 29, Oct. 6 and 13, 1823.

15. *Ibid.*, Nov. 15, 1823.

16. AG to Badollet, July 29, 1824, GP.

17. J. B. Thomas to AG, Jan. 5, 1824, GP.

18. AG to Hannah Gallatin, Jan. 24, 1824, in Adams, *Life*, 594.

19. Andrew Stewart to AG, Feb. 6, and Walter Lowrie to AG, Feb. 10, 1824, GP.

20. Macon to AG, Feb. 13 and 14, 1824, GP.

21. Hailperin, "Pro-Jackson Sentiment in Pennsylvania," *PMHB*, L, 198–200, 205; Garrison, The National Election of 1824, 50 ff.

22. *National Intelligencer*, Feb. 16, 1824; ——— to AG, Feb. 14, 1824, GP.

23. Lowrie to AG, Feb. 20, 1824, GP.

24. *National Intelligencer*, Feb. 27, 1824.

25. Macon to AG, Feb. 16, Lowrie to AG, Feb. 16 and 17, AG to Lowrie, Feb. 19, and T. W. Cobb to AG, Apr. 28, 1824, GP.

26. A. R. Gallatin to AG, Feb. 20, 1824, GP.

27. Garrison, The National Election of 1824, 70, 71, 82–84.

28. *National Intelligencer*, Mar. 15, 1824; Klein, *Pennsylvania Politics*, 157–166; Kehl, *Ill Feeling in the Era of Good Feeling*, 215, 216.

29. Coyle, *Mayors of Baltimore*, 27.

30. AG to A. R. Gallatin, Mar. 10, 1824, GP.

31. Lowrie to AG, Mar. 10, 1824, GP.

32. AG to Adams, May 1, 1824, State Dept. Diplomatic Correspondence: France.

33. B. Ruggles and E. Collins to AG, May 1, Lowrie to AG, May 15, and AG to B. Ruggles, May 16, 1824, GP.

34. AG to Lowrie, May 22, 1824, GP.

35. Lowrie to AG, June 17, 1824, GP. It seems likely that AG was the author of the criticism of Jackson published in *National Intelligencer*, July 7, 1824.

36. Joseph Gales, Jr., to AG, Aug. 24, 1824, GP.

37. AG to Badollet, July 29, 1824, GP.

38. Lowrie to Gallatin, Sept. 25, 1824, GP; Garrison, The National Election of 1824, 118, 119.

39. AG to Lowrie, Oct. 7, 1824, GP.

40. AG to Martin Van Buren, Oct. 2, 1824, GP; Garrison, The National Election of 1824, 121, 122.

41. *National Intelligencer*, Oct. 21, 1824.

42. Hannah to Frances Gallatin (postscript by AG), Nov. 26, 1824, GP.

43. AG to James Gallatin, Dec. 3, 1824, in Adams, *Life*, 606.

44. Lowrie to AG, Jan. 3 and Feb. 3, 1825, GP.

45. AG to James Gallatin, Feb. 19, 1825, GP.

46. Lowrie to AG, Feb. 28, 1825, GP.
47. AG to Stevenson, Oct. 2, 1825, GP.
48. James Brown to AG, May 10, 1826, GP.
49. Hannah to Frances Gallatin, Jan. 21, 1825, GP.
50. AG to Frances Gallatin, Nov. 26 and Dec. 17, 1824, Jan. 2 and 3, 1825, to Maria Montgomery, Oct. 24, 1824, GP.
51. Levasseur, *Lafayette in America*, II, 179, 180. AG's notes and manuscript for his address, May 26, 1825, are in GP. See also AG to David Gelston, June 10, 1825, and to Adams, Oct. 18, 1826, GP.
52. AG to Badollet, July 29, 1824, GP.
53. AG to Badollet, Mar. 18, 1825, in Adams, *Life*, 610; Badollet to AG, Jan. 25, 1826, GP.
54. AG to Gelston, June 10, 1825, GP.
55. AG to Badollet, July 29, 1824, GP.
56. AG to Catherine de Budé, May 1, 1824, de Budé Manuscripts.
57. *Matchett's Baltimore Directory for 1824.*
58. AG to A. R. Gallatin, Apr. 22, 1824, GP.
59. AG to Catherine de Budé, May 1, 1824, de Budé Manuscripts.
60. *Baltimore Federal Gazette*, Apr. 23, 1824.
61. AG to Maria Montgomery, Oct. 20, and to Frances Gallatin, Dec. 17, 1824, GP.
62. Bacon, *Ancestry of Albert Gallatin*, 19.
63. James Gallatin to AG, May 17 and 30, 1825, and AG to J. W. Nicholson, Mar. 13, 1826, GP.
64. AG to J. W. Nicholson, May 4, 1826, GP.
65. Badollet to AG, Jan. 10, 1829, GP.
66. AG to Maria Montgomery, Oct. 24, 1824, GP.
67. Hannah to Frances Gallatin (postscript by AG), Nov. 26, and AG to Frances Gallatin, Dec. 17, 1824, GP.
68. Hannah to Frances Gallatin, Jan. 7, 1825, GP.
69. Frances Gallatin to AG, Dec. 25, 1824, GP.
70. AG to Frances Gallatin, Jan. 2 and 3, 1825, GP.
71. AG to Badollet, July 29, 1824, GP.
72. Hannah to Frances Gallatin, Dec. 24, 1825, and James to A. R. Gallatin, May 14, 1827, GP.
73. AG to A. R. Gallatin, May 14, 1827, GP.
74. AG to Maria Montgomery, Oct. 24, 1824, and to Gelston, June 10, 1825, GP.
75. AG to J. W. Nicholson, Mar. 13 and Apr. 3, 1826, and James Gallatin to AG, July 15, 1826, GP.
76. Stevens, *Albert Gallatin*, 386, 387.
77. Balbi, *Introduction à l'atlas ethnographique*, I, 279, 280, 284, 307, 309, 311, 312, 314, 315; Gallatin, "A Synopsis of the Indian Tribes Within . . . North America," *Amer. Antiquarian Soc. Trans. and Coll.*, II, 1.
78. AG to P. S. Duponceau, Apr. 24, 1826, Washburn Collection; many letters

between AG and Duponceau, Mar. 13 to June 26, 1826, GP; AG to Edward Everett, Apr. 18 and June 5, 1826, Everett Papers.

79. John McTavish to Roderick MacKenzie and David Thompson, Aug. 20, 1826, Carroll-McTavish Papers.
80. *Penna. Arch.*, 9th Ser., VIII, 6242; James Trimble to AG, Apr. 23, and AG to Trimble, May 5, 1825, GP.
81. Stewart to James Gallatin, Feb. 15, 1825, in Adams, *Life*, 607.
82. James Gallatin to Stewart, Feb. 16, 1825 (copy), Adams Papers.
83. AG to James Gallatin, Feb. 19, and Adams to James Gallatin, Feb. 26, 1825, in Adams, *Life*, 607–609; James Gallatin to Adams, Feb. 24 and Mar. 1, 1825, Adams Papers; Bemis, *John Quincy Adams and the Union*, 56, 59.
84. Clay to AG, Nov. 8 and 11, 1825, GP.
85. James Bosley to AG, Nov. 17, and AG to Clay, Nov. 10 and 14, 1825, GP.
86. Bemis, *John Quincy Adams and the Foundations of American Foreign Policy*, 550 ff.
87. Merk, *Albert Gallatin and the Oregon Problem*, 7, 8; Bemis, *Adams and the Foundations of American Foreign Policy*, 527, 528; Clay to AG, May 2 and 5, and AG to Clay, May 3, 1826, GP.
88. AG to Clay, May 7, and to Adams, May 7, 1826, GP.
89. *Baltimore American*, May 11 and 12, 1826; Clay to AG, May 11, 1826, GP.
90. *National Intelligencer*, May 10 and 29, 1826.
91. Pittsburgh *Genius of Liberty*, June 13, 1826; Clay to AG, June 19, 20, 21, and 23, 1826, GP.
92. Fayette County Deed Book P, 110, 111.
93. AG to Badollet, June 22, 1826, GP.
94. Clay to AG, June 19, 20, and 21, AG to Clay, June 29, and to Adams, June 20, and Adams to AG, June 26 and 30, 1826, GP.
95. *National Intelligencer*, June 20, 1826.

26: THE LONDON MISSION AND ITS AFTERMATH, 1826–1829

1. AG to Clay, July 31, Aug. 11 and 19, to Gelston, July 31, to George Canning, Aug. 8, and Canning to AG, Aug. 10 (two letters) and 16, 1826, GP.
2. AG to Clay, Aug. 19, 1826, GP.
3. AG to Clay, Sept. 4, 1826, GP; Adams, *Life*, 650.
4. AG to Clay, Sept. 13, 1826, GP.
5. AG to Adams, Oct. 18, 1826, GP.
6. AG to Gelston, Jan. 5, to A. R. Gallatin, Aug. 21, James Brown to AG, Feb. 22, Hannah to A. R. Gallatin, May 5, 1827, GP.
7. Hannah to A. R. Gallatin, May 5, 1827, AG to A. R. Gallatin, May 30, 1827, GP.
8. Bemis, *Diplomatic History*, 296, 297.
9. AG to Canning, Aug. 26, 1826, in ASP: *Foreign Relations*, VI, 249, 250.

10. Canning to AG, Sept. 6, 1826, in ASP: *Foreign Relations*, VI, 250–253; AG to Clay, Sept. 13 and 20, 1826, GP.

11. AG to Clay, Sept. 22, 1826, GP.

12. Bemis, *Diplomatic History*, 175 n., 176 n.

13. AG to Adams, Sept. 13, 1826, GP.

14. AG to Adams, Oct. 18, 1826, GP.

15. Clay to AG, Oct. 21, and AG to Clay, Nov. 11 and 13, 1826, GP; Bemis, *Diplomatic History*, 175.

16. AG to Adams, Oct. 18, 1826, GP; AG to Clay, Nov. 27, 1826, Lawrence Diplomatic Correspondence: London, 1826–1830, I, 130–133.

17. AG to Clay, Nov. 5, 1826, Lawrence Correspondence, I, 87–89.

18. AG to Clay, Nov. 27, 1826, Lawrence Correspondence, I, 130–133.

19. AG to Clay, Nov. 14, 1826, GP.

20. Merk, *Albert Gallatin and the Oregon Problem*, 66.

21. AG to Adams, Dec. 29, 1826, Adams Papers.

22. AG to Clay, Nov. 25 and Dec. 19, 1826, in ASP: *Foreign Relations*, VI, 652–655, 666–671; Merk, *Gallatin and Oregon*, 68.

23. AG to Clay, Nov. 16, 1826, in ASP: *Foreign Relations*, VI, 650–652; ASP: *Foreign Relations*, VI, 662–666.

24. AG's protocol of Dec. 1, 1826, conference, GP.

25. ASP: *Foreign Relations*, VI, 657; AG to Clay, Dec. 5, 1826, in ASP: *Foreign Relations*, VI, 657.

26. H. U. Addington to AG, Dec. 3, 1826, GP; AG to Clay, Dec. 5 and 20, 1826, Aug. 7 and 10, 1827, Lawrence Correspondence, I, 139–142, 153–159, 287–308.

27. Protocol of Dec. 6, 1826, conference, AG to Addington, Dec. 4 and 9, 1826, GP; AG to Clay, Dec. 5 and 12, 1826, Lawrence Correspondence, I, 139–146.

28. James Gallatin to Adams, Mar. 12, 1827, quoting AG to James Gallatin, Jan. 22, 1827, GP.

29. Bemis, *Diplomatic History*, 255, 256.

30. Adams to Clay, July 5, 1826, Adams Papers.

31. AG to Clay, Mar. 6, 1827, Lawrence Correspondence, I, 198–203.

32. Adams to AG, Mar. 20, 1827, Adams Letter Books.

33. ASP: *Foreign Relations*, VI, 677, 678.

34. Merk, *Gallatin and Oregon*, 12, 13, 84.

35. ASP: *Foreign Relations*, VI, 679, 688; AG to Clay, June 20, 23, and 27, Aug. 6, 7, and 9, 1827, Lawrence Correspondence, I, 250–258, 278–301; Merk, *Gallatin and Oregon*, 76–82.

36. AG to Clay, Aug. 10, 1827, in ASP: *Foreign Relations*, VI, 694–696; Merk, *Gallatin and Oregon*, 85–88.

37. AG to Clay, Aug. 14 and Sept. 28, 1827, AG Letter Books, XV, 112–114, 135–138.

38. AG to Clay, Sept. 21, 1827, AG Letter Books, XV, 55–62; Bemis, *Adams and the Foundations of American Foreign Policy*, 477.

39. AG to Clay, Aug. 14 and 21, 1827, AG Letter Books, XV, 33–36, 135–138.
40. AG to Clay, July 28 and Sept. 28, 1827, AG Letter Books, XIV, 269–272, XV, 112–114.
41. AG to Adams, Dec. 5, 1827, AG Letter Books, XV, 151–154.
42. AG to A. R. Gallatin, May 5 and 14, 1827, GP.
43. James Gallatin to AG, Oct. 13, 1826, Mar. 21, June 22, 1827, GP.
44. A. R. Gallatin to AG, Dec. 5, 1826, Jan. 20 and 29, 1827, James Gallatin to AG, Oct. 13, 22, 29, 1826, and Jan. 29, 1827, GP.
45. AG to A. R. Gallatin, Nov. 28, 1826, Apr. 14, 1827, GP.
46. AG to A. R. Gallatin, Nov. 28, 1826, GP.
47. James Gallatin to AG, Apr. 4, and T. W. Chrystie to Frances Gallatin, Apr. 30, 1827, GP.
48. James Gallatin to AG, Oct. 13, 1826, and Jan. 29, 1827, and A. R. Gallatin to AG, Mar. 12, 1827, GP.
49. AG to Adams, Dec. 29, 1826, Adams Papers.
50. *Niles' Weekly Register*, XXXIII, 218.
51. *National Intelligencer*, Dec. 3, 1827; AG to Clay, Dec. 11, 1827, State Dept. Diplomatic Correspondence: Great Britain.
52. A. R. Gallatin to J. W. Nicholson, Jan. 1, 1828, and AG to Badollet, Feb. 7, 1833, GP.
53. AG to Clay, Nov. 27, GP, and to Adams, Dec. 5, 1827, Adams Papers.
54. Adams to AG, Dec. 12, 1827, GP.
55. Clay to AG, Feb. 9 and May 17, 1828; *National Intelligencer*, May 12, 1828.
56. For papers dealing with the preparation of the Northeast boundary case, see North East Territory Folder, U.S. Executive Papers, LC. See also AG to Everett, May 21, 1828, Everett Papers.
57. AG to Hannah Gallatin, Sept. 7, 1828, GP.
58. W. P. Preble to AG, June 21 and Aug. 23, 1828, GP.
59. AG to Hannah Gallatin, Nov. 23, 1828, GP.
60. AG to Hannah Gallatin, Nov. 23, 1828, GP.
61. Clay to Adams, Oct. 20, 1828, GP; Bemis, *Adams and the Foundations of American Foreign Policy*, 477, 478.
62. Bemis, *Adams and the Foundations of American Foreign Policy*, 478.
63. A. R. Gallatin to J. W. Nicholson, Jan. 1, 1828, GP.
64. AG to Badollet, Mar. 26, 1829, GP.
65. AG to Hannah Gallatin, Dec. 16, 1828, in Adams, *Life*, 630.
66. Everett to A. H. Everett, Dec. 15, 1828, Everett Papers.
67. AG's memorandum for James Gallatin, Feb., 1829, AG to Martin Van Buren, Mar. 4, and Van Buren to AG, Mar. 8, 1829, GP.
68. A. R. Gallatin to J. W. Nicholson, Apr. 7, 1829, GP.
69. AG to Hannah Gallatin, May 16, 1829, in Adams, *Life*, 633.
70. AG to Hannah Gallatin, May 23, 1829, in Adams, *Life*, 633.
71. James Gallatin to AG, Feb. 28, 1829, GP.
72. AG to Hannah Gallatin, Nov. 29, 1829, in Adams, *Life*, 634.

73. Adams, *Memoirs*, VIII, 160.
74. Bemis has detailed Adams's contributions in his distinguished work, *John Quincy Adams and the Foundations of American Foreign Policy.*
75. Such is the judgment of Setser in *The Commercial Reciprocity Policy of the United States,* 183, 184.

27: CITIZEN AND SCHOLAR, 1830–1848

1. AG to Badollet, Feb. 7, 1833, in Adams, *Life,* 646.
2. Fayette County Property Roll, Springhill Township, 1816–1840; Fayette County Deed Book P, 475–477; Deed Book S, 136–138; A. R. Gallatin to AG, May 23 and Oct. 18 and 27, and James to A. R. Gallatin, Nov. 30, 1830, GP.
3. *Longworth's New York City Directory,* 1829–1843; *Doggett's New York City Directory,* 1842–1850.
4. *New-York American,* Apr. 7, 1830; AG to Badollet, Feb. 3, 1834, in Adams, *Life,* 649, 650; AG to J. W. Nicholson, July 12, 1841, GP; Bacon, *Ancestry of Albert Gallatin,* 19, 20.
5. Astor to AG, Mar. 7, 1827, GP.
6. National Bank of New York Minute Books.
7. National Bank of New York Minute Books; AG to J. W. Nicholson, Feb. 4, 1840, GP.
8. *New-York American,* Nov. 8, 1837.
9. AG to Badollet, Feb. 3, 1834, in Adams, *Life,* 650; to J. W. Nicholson, July 12, 1841, GP.
10. AG to Frances Gallatin Stevens, Nov. 10, 1843, GP.
11. *New-York Tribune,* Aug. 14, 1849; Stevens, *Albert Gallatin,* 381; *New-York Hist. Soc. Proc.* 1849, 282.
12. Adams, *Life,* 650, 651.
13. Martineau, *Retrospect of Western Travel,* II, 40, 41; Martineau, *Society in America,* II, 207 n., 208 n.
14. Quoted in Stevens, *Albert Gallatin,* 381.
15. AG to Badollet, Feb. 3, 1834, in Adams, *Life,* 649, 650.
16. Jones, *New York University,* 1832–1932, 7.
17. John Delafield to AG, [Sept.] 1830, GP.
18. Jones, *New York University,* 9–11, 15, 16, 20–22; Mathews, *Recollections of Persons and Events,* 192, 193.
19. *New-York American,* Oct. 21, 22, 23, and 25, 1830; Jones, 23–26; J. Mc-Masters, J. Wainwright, AG, and Delafield to President of New York Athenaeum, Sept. 10, 1830, Emmet Collection.
20. Delafield to AG, Oct. 30, 1830, and Feb. 16 and 22, 1831, GP; Jones, *New York University,* 27, 28.
21. Mathews, *Recollections,* 251, 252.

22. Mathews, *Recollections*, 206; Jones, *New York University*, 29, 30.

23. AG to Madison, Apr. 9, 1831, Madison Papers; Delafield to AG, Feb. 22, 1833, AG to Badollet, Feb. 7, 1833, in Adams, *Life*, 648.

24. Vail, *Knickerbocker Birthday*, 84, 85; Strong, *Diary*, I, 202; Frederic De Peyster to AG, Oct. 5, 1842, AG to De Peyster, Oct. 22, 1841, GP; Gallatin, *Inaugural Address*, 1.

25. Stevens, *Albert Gallatin*, 398, 399; Adams, *Memoirs*, X, 108, 109; *New-York Tribune*, Nov. 21, 1844.

26. AG to J. C. L. Sismondi, June 10, 1842, in Gallatin, *Writings*, II, 598.

27. Stevens, *Albert Gallatin*, 396.

28. See, for example, Lewis Cass to AG, Oct. 3, 1826, Daniel Sheldon to AG, Feb. 27, 1827, J. D. Doty to Cass, Aug. 15, 1827, and T. L. McKinney to AG, July 31, 1828, GP.

29. George Folsom to AG, Nov. 13, 1834, GP.

30. AG to Theodore Frelinghuysen, Feb. 14, to J. C. Calhoun, Feb. 14, to Duponceau, Mar. 21, 1835, GP; to J. A. Pearce, Apr. 26, 1846, in Gallatin, *Writings*, II, 636; AG to Duponceau, Mar. 11, 1835, Washburn Collection, and Apr. 14, 1835, Society Collection HSP; Gallatin, "A Synopsis of the Indian Tribes," *Amer. Antiq. Soc. Trans. and Coll.*, II, 1, 2.

31. T. S. Winthrop to AG, May 26, 1836, and Folsom et al. to AG, Nov. 1, 1836, GP.

32. The copy of "A Synopsis" inscribed "To the illustrious Alexander von Humboldt from his faithful friend Albert Gallatin" is in the Rare Book Room of the New York Public Library. It contains a number of marginal notations in AG's hand, many of which correct errors made by the printer in interpreting the author's handwriting. In several places AG has appended information received after the work was sent to the press.

33. Duponceau to AG, Mar. 16, 1837, July 11, 1838, GP.

34. George Bancroft to AG, May 20, 1840, GP.

35. Hale, "Memoir," *Amer. Antiq. Soc. Proc.*, Oct. 23, 1849, p. 30.

36. Stevens, *Albert Gallatin*, 393; Gallatin, "Notes on the Semi-Civilized Nations," *Amer. Ethnol. Soc. Trans.*, I, 1–352. A large bundle of notes AG used in preparing this monograph is in the Library of Congress.

37. AG to Duponceau, Nov. 1, 1842, Society Collection HSP; to W. H. Prescott, June 22, 1843, Feb. 3, 1844, and June 2, 1845, Prescott Collection; Prescott to AG, Jan. 29 and Feb. 8, 1844, GP.

38. AG to W. L. Marcy, Mar. 17, 1846, GP.

39. Gallatin, "Introduction to 'Hale's Indians of North-West America,'" *Amer. Ethnol. Soc. Transactions*, II, xxv–clxxxviii.

40. Powell, "Indian Linguistic Families of America," *U.S. Bureau of Ethnology*, 7th Ann. Rept. 1885–1886, 9, 10.

41. Wissler, "The American Indian and the American Philosophical Society," *Amer. Philos. Soc. Proc.*, LXXXVI, 193, 194, 201, 203.

28: FINANCIAL ORACLE, 1830–1844

1. AG to Nicholas Biddle, Aug. 14, 1830, in Gallatin, *Writings*, II, 433.
2. Dewey, *Financial History of the U.S.*, 103, 104; Mai, *Fiscal Policies of Gallatin*, 122 ff.
3. AG to S. D. Ingham, Aug. 4, Sept. 27, and Dec. 31, 1829, in Gallatin, *Writings*, II, 410–425.
4. AG to Robert Walsh, Jr., Apr. 27, 1830, in Gallatin, *Writings*, II, 425–427; Miller, *Banking Theories in the U.S.*, 12, 13.
5. Schlesinger, *Age of Jackson*, 82–85, 92, 93.
6. Walsh to AG, Apr. 22, May 3 and 11, Biddle to AG, July 12, 20, 21, 22, 23, 29 (two letters), Aug. 10 (two letters) and 13, Sept. 9 and 11, Oct. 1, 11, and 28, 1830, GP.
7. AG to Biddle, Aug. 14, 1830, in Gallatin, *Writings*, II, 431–439.
8. Biddle to AG, Nov. 15 and 17, 1830, Biddle Letter Books.
9. Biddle to AG, Dec. 13, 1830, Biddle Letter Books; Feb. 3, 1831, GP.
10. Biddle to AG, Dec. 6, 1830, GP.
11. AG to Biddle, Dec. 8, 1830, in Gallatin, *Writings*, II, 443, 444.
12. Walsh to AG, Feb. 13, 1831, GP; AG to Walsh, Feb. 16, 1831, in Gallatin, *Writings*, II, 447.
13. Biddle to AG, Dec. 28, 1830, and Jan. 1, 1831, Biddle Letter Books.
14. Gallatin, "Banks and Currency," *Amer. Quart. Rev.*, VIII, 441–528. The pamphlet, *Considerations on the Currency*, is reprinted in its entirety in Gallatin, *Writings*, III, 231–364.
15. Mai, *Fiscal Policies of Gallatin*, 128, 129.
16. *Biographical Memoir of Albert Gallatin*, 14; Gallatin, *Writings*, II, 161, 162; *ASP: Finance*, II, 430.
17. Walters, *Dallas*, 207–209.
18. AG to William Drayton, Apr. 7, 1832, in Gallatin, *Writings*, II, 450–458.
19. Preserved Fish to AG, Sept. 9, 1831, GP.
20. *Banner of the Constitution*, II, 366, cited in Mai, *Fiscal Policies of Gallatin*, 130, 131; *Niles' Weekly Register*, XLI, 135 ff., 156, 157; Stanwood, *American Tariff Controversies*, I, 297–301; Elliott, *Tariff Controversy in the United States*, 255, 256.
21. T. R. Dew to AG, Oct. 10, Nov. 11 and 21, R. M. Sherman to AG, Nov. 1, Isaac Winslow to AG, Dec. 21 and 23, 1831, GP.
22. AG to Committee on Free Trade, Dec. 14, Dew to AG, Dec. 31, Henry Lee to AG, Dec. 27, J. M. Berrien to AG, Dec. 28, C. C. Biddle to AG, Dec. 29, 1831, William Harper to AG, Jan. 8, 1832, GP. There is also a large folder of notes and correspondence apropos the free-trade memorial in GP. See also AG to Lee, Dec. 13 and 14, 1831, Henry Lee Papers.
23. AG to Calhoun and Andrew Stevenson, Jan. 23, 1832, GP.
24. Gallatin, *Memorial of the Committee Appointed by the Free Trade Convention*.

25. *Register of Debates*, 22nd Cong., 1st Sess., 267.
26. AG to Badollet, Feb. 7, 1833, GP.
27. Gallatin, *Writings*, III, 390.
28. *Ibid.*, 391.
29. Hamilton, *Reminiscences*, 253.
30. Catterall, *Second Bank of the United States*, 341.
31. Winthrop, *Memoir of Nathan Appleton*, 43, 44.
32. *New-York Spectator*, Feb. 12 and 15, Mar. 17 and 24, 1834; Gallatin and others, *Report of the "Union Committee"*; Hone, *Diary*, I, 120.
33. Gallatin, *Writings*, III, 393.
34. *Ibid.*, 391, 394.
35. The minutes of the meeting are in GP. See also *New-York American*, Apr. 10, 1837.
36. *New-York American*, Apr. 25, 1837.
37. McGrane, *Panic of 1837*, 97.
38. National Bank of New York Minute Books; Gallatin, *Writings*, III, 394–396; *New-York American*, May 10, 1837.
39. AG to W. L. Marcy, May 10, and to Henry Andrew, May 10, 1837, GP.
40. Gallatin, *Writings*, III, 396–398.
41. AG to A. C. Flagg, June 14, 1837, Flagg Papers.
42. AG, George Newbold, and C. W. Lawrence to principal banks of the United States, Aug. 18, 1837, GP.
43. AG to Flagg, Oct. 10, 1837, Flagg Papers.
44. Gallatin, *Writings*, III, 398.
45. Biddle to AG, Nov. 15, 1830, GP.
46. AG to Biddle, Nov. 23, 1837, Etting Papers: Administration.
47. Biddle to AG, Nov. 26, 1837, GP.
48. *New-York Commercial Advertiser*, Nov. 27, Dec. 2, 1837; *New-York American*, Dec. 4, 1837; Gallatin, *Writings*, III, 399, 400, 466–470.
49. AG's industry is revealed in his letters to Willis Hall, Feb. 20, Mar. 3 and 28, and Apr. 3, to Flagg, Mar. 8, to Marcy, Mar. 20 and 27 and Apr. 9, to Jonathan Goodhue, Apr. 5, and to S. B. Ruggles, Apr. 9, 1838, GP.
50. Gallatin, *Writings*, III, 471–490.
51. *Ibid.*, 400; Prime, Ward & King to AG and committee, Apr. 16, 1838, GP.
52. Gallatin, *Writings*, III, 400, 480–486; *New-York Commercial Advertiser*, Apr. 12, 14, and 17, 1838; McGrane, *Panic of 1837*, 147, 184–187, 191.
53. Schlesinger, *Age of Jackson*, 253.
54. Gallatin, *Writings*, III, 401, 402; AG to Flagg, Oct. 31, 1837, Flagg Papers; McGrane, *Panic of 1837*, 191, 192.
55. National Bank of New York Minute Books; William James, James Bouchard, etc. to AG, June 8, 1839, GP.
56. Sumner, *History of Banking in the United States*, 305; *Niles' Weekly Register*, LX, 121; Gallatin, *Writings*, III, 402, 404; McGrane, *Panic of 1837*, 204.
57. AG to J. Abbot, Jr., Oct. 18, 1841, GP.

58. Schlesinger, *Age of Jackson*, 264.
59. Gallatin, *Writings*, III, 365–488.
60. AG to Abbot, Oct. 18, 1841, GP.
61. AG to J. M. Botts, June 14, 1841, GP.
62. For discussions of AG's views on the tariff, banking, and the currency, the following are useful: Miller, *Banking Theories in the United States*; Weston, "Currency Opinions of Albert Gallatin," *Banker's Magazine*, XXXVII, 109–115. Also see Dorfman, *Economic Mind in American Civilization*, II; Helderman, *National and State Banks*; Chaddock, "Safety Fund Banking System in New York"; Hammond, "Free Banks and Corporations: The New York Free Banking Act of 1838," *Jour. Pol. Econ.*, XLIV, 184–209; AG to Frederick Beasley, Sept. 3, and to Leonard Maison, Dec. 20, 1836, GP.
63. Albert Davy to James Gallatin, Dec. 25, 1843, GP.
64. John Barney to AG, Jan. 24, 1844, GP.
65. AG to Davy, Dec. 28, 1843, GP.

29: POLITICAL ORACLE, 1830–1849

1. J. A. Hamilton to Van Buren, June 17 and 19, 1829, cited in McLemore, *Franco-American Diplomatic Relations*, 48, 49.
2. AG to Calhoun, Feb. 14, 1835, GP.
3. AG to Everett, Jan. 5, 6–22, 1835, GP.
4. The story is told in detail in McLemore, *Franco-American Diplomatic Relations*, 43–211.
5. AG to Thomas Ritchie, Aug. 2, 1842, GP.
6. AG to Leonard Jarvis, Oct. 22, 1832, GP.
7. *New York Review*, VIII, 228.
8. Bemis, *Diplomatic History*, 256.
9. AG to Jarvis, Oct. 22, 1832, GP.
10. AG to J. P. Bigelow, Oct. 12, and to B. C. Howard, Nov. 5, 1840, GP; Gallatin, *Right of the United States of America to the North-Eastern Boundary*, vii–x; *New York Review*, VIII, 196 n.
11. AG to Joshua Bates, Nov. 28, 1840, GP.
12. Bates to AG, Feb. 3, 1841, GP.
13. Ashburton to AG, Apr. 12, 1842, GP.
14. AG to Ritchie, Aug. 2, 1842, GP.
15. Ashburton to AG, Apr. 12 and Aug. 23, 1842, GP.
16. Bemis, *Adams and the Foundations of American Foreign Policy*, 479, 480, 585–588.
17. Gallatin, *Memoir on the North-Eastern Boundary*.
18. *New-York American*, Apr. 17, 1843.
19. Gallatin, *Memoir*, 73.
20. PHJ, 1792–1793, 39, 55.

21. Certificate of membership in Pennsylvania Society for Promoting the Abolition of Slavery, dated Mar. 25, 1793, GP.

22. *ASP: Foreign Relations*, III, 748.

23. *New-York Express*, Apr. 25, 1844; Strong, *Diary*, I, 229; Hone, *Diary*, II, 692, 693.

24. John Jay to AG, Apr. 25, 1844, GP.

25. AG to Gales & Seaton, Jan. 18, 1846, Miscellaneous Papers (Gallatin), NYPL.

26. Gales & Seaton to AG, Jan. 21 and 25, Joseph Gales to AG, Jan. 29, 1846, GP; *National Intelligencer*, Jan. 22, 24, 27, and 29, 1846.

27. *National Intelligencer*, Feb. 14, 1846.

28. Gallatin, *Writings*, III, 489–553. A large notebook, containing a manuscript version of these papers with emendations and corrections by AG, is in LC.

29. Hone, *Diary*, II, 757, 758.

30. AG emphasized the latter point in his letter to Gales & Seaton, Feb. 17, 1846, Miscellaneous Papers (Gallatin), NYPL.

31. Gallatin, *Writings*, III, 555–591.

32. AG to T. W. Ward, Dec. 10, 1847, to Everett, Dec. 16, 1847, G. P. Marsh to AG, Dec. 15, 1847, J. R. Bartlett to AG, Dec. 24, 1847, GP; AG to George Potts, Dec. 4, 1847, Gratz Collection.

33. AG to Garrett Davis, Feb. 16, 1848, GP.

34. For AG's own comments on his health, see letters to Badollet, Feb. 3 and 7, 1833, Feb., 1834, Sept. 3, 1836, to J. W. Nicholson, Feb. 4, 1840, July 12, 1841, Mar. 19, 1842, to Ezekiel Bacon, Aug. 20, 1846, GP; to Joel Poinsett, Feb. 14, 1840, Poinsett Papers, XIV, No. 14.

35. AG to Edward Bebb, Nov. 7, 1848, GP.

36. Conversations between AG and Mary Few, Dec. 11, 1848, GP.

37. AG to E. C. Cooper, Nov. 18, 1834, to Andrew Norton, Sept. 13, 1847, and "Meditations on Death," dictated by AG, July, 1849, GP.

38. *New-York Tribune*, May 16, 1849.

39. Statement of the division of AG's estate, 1849, GP.

40. *New-York Tribune*, Aug. 14, 1849; Stevens, *Albert Gallatin*, 400, 401.

Bibliography

Manuscript Collections

Adams Papers, Massachusetts Historical Society, Boston
Archives d'Etat, Geneva, Switzerland
Bass Papers, Massachusetts Historical Society
Nicholas Biddle Papers, Library of Congress, Washington
Budé Manuscripts, Mlle. Antoinette de Budé, Geneva
Carroll-McTavish Papers, Maryland Historical Society, Baltimore
DeWitt Clinton Papers, Columbia University Library, New York City
A. J. Dallas Personal Collection, Library of Congress
Emmet Collection, New York Public Library, New York City
Etting Papers, Historical Society of Pennsylvania, Philadelphia
Everett Papers, Massachusetts Historical Society
Fayette County Property Rolls and Deed Books, Assessment Room, Fayette County Court House, Uniontown, Pennsylvania
Flagg Papers, New York Public Library
Gallatin Folder, Library of Congress
Gallatin Mementos, Mr. Albert Gallatin, New York City
Gallatin Papers, New-York Historical Society, New York City
Simon Gratz Collection, Historical Society of Pennsylvania
Harvard College Records, Archives, Widener Library, Harvard University, Cambridge, Massachusetts
Henrico County Marriage Bonds, Henrico County Court House, Richmond, Virginia
William Irvine Papers, Historical Society of Pennsylvania
Thomas Jefferson Papers, Library of Congress
William Jones Papers, U. C. Smith Collection, Historical Society of Pennsylvania
William Beach Lawrence Diplomatic Correspondence, London, 1826–1830, Library of Congress
Lea & Febiger Papers, Historical Society of Pennsylvania
Henry Lee Papers, Massachusetts Historical Society
Thomas McKean Papers, Historical Society of Pennsylvania
James Madison Papers, Library of Congress
Governor Mifflin's Administration Papers, Pennsylvania State Archives, Harrisburg, Pennsylvania
Miscellaneous Collection, Pennsylvania State Archives
James Monroe Papers, Library of Congress
James Monroe Papers, New York Public Library
National Bank of New York Minute Books, Hanover Bank, New York City
Navy Department Miscellaneous Letters, National Archives, Washington
Nicholas Papers, Library of Congress
Nicholson Papers, Library of Congress
North East Territory Folder, U.S. Executive Papers, Library of Congress

Harrison Gray Otis Papers, Massachusetts Historical Society
David Parish Letter Books, New-York Historical Society
Pennsylvania Insurrection Papers, Library of Congress
Poinsett Papers, Historical Society of Pennsylvania
William H. Prescott Collection, Massachusetts Historical Society
William Rives Papers, Library of Congress
Ross-Woods Papers, Historical Society of Western Pennsylvania, Pittsburgh
Samuel Smith Manuscripts, Library of Congress
Society Collection, Historical Society of Pennsylvania
State Department Diplomatic Correspondence, National Archives
State Department Miscellaneous Letters, National Archives
Treasury Department Bureau of Customs Records, National Archives
Treasury Department Circular Letters and Reports, National Archives
Treasury Department Circular Letters to Collectors of Customs, National Archives
Treasury Department: Secretary of the Treasury Letters and Reports to Congress-
     men, National Archives
Washburn Collection, Massachusetts Historical Society
Oliver Wolcott, Jr., Papers, Connecticut Historical Society, Hartford

Newspapers and Magazines

Baltimore American
Baltimore *Federal Gazette*
Baltimore *Federal Republican*
Baltimore *Niles' Weekly Register*
Boston *Columbian Centinel*
Boston *Independent Chronicle*
Boston *New England Palladium*
Elizabethtown *New Jersey Journal*
New-York American
New-York Commercial Advertiser
New-York Courier and Enquirer
New York *Democratic Review*
New-York Evening Post
New York *Express*
New York *Review*
New-York Spectator
New York *Tribune*
Philadelphia *American Daily Advertiser*
Philadelphia *Aurora*
Philadelphia *Federal Gazette*
Philadelphia *Gazette of the United States*
Philadelphia *General Advertiser*
Philadelphia *Pennsylvania Gazette*
Philadelphia *Pennsylvania Packet*

Pittsburgh Gazette
Pittsburgh *Genius of Liberty*
Pittsburgh *Tree of Liberty*
Richmond Enquirer
Washington *National Intelligencer*

Other Contemporary Material in Printed Form

Adams, John, and Richard Rush, "Some Unpublished Correspondence of John Adams and Richard Rush, 1821–1822," ed. J. H. Powell, *Pennsylvania Magazine of History and Biography*, LX, 419–454, LXI, 26–53, 137–164.

Adams, John Quincy, *Memoirs*, ed. Charles Francis Adams. 12 vols., Philadelphia, 1874–1877.

————, *Writings*, ed. Worthington C. Ford. 7 vols., New York, 1913–1917.

Addison, Alexander, *Charges to the Grand Jury*. Washington, Pa., 1800.

American State Papers: Commerce and Navigation. 2 vols., Washington, 1832–1834.

American State Papers: Finance. 5 vols., Washington, 1832–1859.

American State Papers: Foreign Relations. 6 vols., Washington, 1832–1859.

American State Papers: Miscellaneous. 2 vols., Washington, 1834.

American State Papers: Public Lands. 7 vols., Washington, 1832–1860.

Annals of Congress. 42 vols., Washington, 1834–1856.

Balbi, Adriano, *Introduction à l'atlas ethnographique du globe*. 8 vols., Paris, 1826.

Bathurst, 3rd Earl of. *See* Bickley.

Bayard, James A., "Letters . . . 1802–1814," *Delaware Historical Society Papers*, No. 31.

————, "Papers . . . 1796–1815," ed. Elizabeth Donnan, *American Historical Association Annual Report for 1913*, II.

Bentley, William, D.D., *Diary*. 4 vols., Salem, Mass., 1905–1914.

Bickley, Francis, comp., *Report on the Manuscripts of Earl Bathurst, Preserved at Cirencester Park*. London, 1923.

Biddle, Charles, *Autobiography*. Philadelphia, 1883.

Biographical Memoir of Albert Gallatin. New York, 1843.

Brackenridge, Hugh Henry, *Incidents of the Insurrection*. 3 vols., Philadelphia, 1795.

Calendar of Virginia State Papers, ed. W. P. Palmer, Richmond, 1875 ff.

Castlereagh, Viscount, *Memoirs and Correspondence*, ed. Charles Vane. 12 vols., London, 1848–1853.

Cobbett, William, *Porcupine's Works*. 12 vols., London, 1801.

"Correspondence of the French Foreign Ministers to the United States, 1791–1797," ed. F. J. Turner, *American Historical Association Annual Report for 1903*, II.

Davis, Matthew L., *Memoirs of Aaron Burr*. 2 vols., New York, 1836–1837.

Diderot, Denis, *Encyclopédie*. 17 vols., Paris, 1751–1765.

Doggett's New York City Directory. Annual issues, New York, 1842–1850.

Duane, William, "Letters," ed. Worthington C. Ford, *Massachusetts Historical Society Proceedings,* 2nd Series, XX, 257–394.

Dunlap, William, *Diary.* 3 vols., New York, 1930.

Findley, William, "An Autobiographical Letter," *Pennsylvania Magazine of History and Biography,* V, 440–450.

——, *History of the Insurrection in the Four Western Counties of Pennsylvania.* Philadelphia, 1796.

Gallatin, Albert, "Autobiography, 1798," *Maine Historical Society Collections,* VI, 95–103.

——, "Banks and Currency," *American Quarterly Review,* VIII, 441–528.

——, *Inaugural Address . . . Delivered Before the New-York Historical Society, February 7, 1843.* New York, 1843.

——, "Introduction to 'Hale's Indians of North-West America,'" *American Ethnological Society Transactions,* II, xxv–clxxxviii.

——, *A Memoir on the North-Eastern Boundary, in Connexion with Mr. Jay's Map.* New York, 1843.

——, *Memorial of the Committee Appointed by the Free Trade Convention.* New York, 1832.

——, "Notes on the Semi-Civilized Nations of Mexico, Yucatan, and Central America," *American Ethnological Society Transactions,* I, 1–352.

——, *The Right of the United States of America to the North-Eastern Boundary Claimed by Them.* New York, 1840.

——, *The Speech . . . on the First of March, 1798, upon the Foreign Intercourse Bill.* Philadelphia, 1798.

——, *Speech on the Alien Law.* Philadelphia, 1799.

——, "A Synopsis of the Indian Tribes Within the United States East of the Rocky Mountains, and in the British and Russian Possessions in North America," *American Antiquarian Society Transactions and Collections,* II, pp. 1–422.

——, *Writings,* ed. Henry Adams. 3 vols., Philadelphia, 1879. Lists (III, 617–622) Gallatin's publications during his own lifetime. The titles above, cited in this biography, are not reproduced in *Writings.*

——, and others, *Report of the "Union Committee."* New York, 1834.

Gilpin, Joshua, "Journal of a Tour from Philadelphia thro the Western Counties of Pennsylvania in the Months of September and October, 1809," *Pennsylvania Magazine of History and Biography,* L, 64–78, 163–178, 380–382, LI, 172–190, 351–375, LII, 29–58.

Graydon, Alexander, *Memoirs of His Own Time.* Philadelphia, 1846.

(Hale, Edward Everett), "Memoir," *American Antiquarian Society Proceedings,* Oct. 23, 1849, pp. 16–31.

Hamilton, Alexander, *Works,* ed. Henry Cabot Lodge. 9 vols., New York, 1885–1886.

Hamilton, James A., *Reminiscences.* New York, 1869.

Hiltzheimer, Jacob, *Extracts from the Diary of . . .* Philadelphia, 1893.

Hone, Philip, *Diary, 1828–1851*, ed. Allan Nevins. 2 vols., New York, 1927.

Irving, Washington, *Letters . . . to Henry Brevoort*, ed. George S. Hellman. 2 vols., New York, 1915.

———, *Letters . . . to Mrs. William Renwick and to Her Son James Renwick*. No place or date.

Jefferson, Thomas, *Writings*, ed. Paul Leicester Ford. 10 vols., New York, 1892–1899.

———, *Writings*, Monticello ed. 20 vols., Washington, 1905.

Laws of the Commonwealth of Pennsylvania, ed. A. J. Dallas. 3 vols., Philadelphia, 1795.

Levasseur, Auguste, *Lafayette in America in 1824 and 1825*. 2 vols., Philadelphia, 1829.

Longworth's New York City Directory. Annual issues, New York, 1823–1843.

Maclay, William, *Journal*. New York, 1927.

Madison, James, *Letters and Other Writings*, ed. William C. Rives. 4 vols., Philadelphia, 1865.

———, *Writings*, ed. Gaillard Hunt. 9 vols., New York, 1900–1910.

Martineau, Harriet, *Retrospect of Western Travel*. 2 vols., New York, 1838.

———, *Society in America*. 2 vols., New York, 1837.

Matchett's Baltimore Directory for 1824.

Mathews, J. M., *Recollections of Persons and Events*. New York, 1865.

Melish, John, *Travels Through the United States of America*. London, 1818.

Mitchill, Samuel Latham, "Dr. Mitchill's Letters from Washington, 1801–1813," *Harper's Magazine*, LVIII, 740–755.

Monroe, James, *Writings*, ed. S. M. Hamilton. 7 vols., New York, 1898–1903.

Nicholson, James, "A Letter of James Nicholson, 1803," *American Historical Review*, VIII, 512, 513.

Nolte, Vincent, *Fifty Years in Both Hemispheres*. New York, 1854.

Pennsylvania Archives. 120 vols., Philadelphia and Harrisburg, 1852–1935.

Pennsylvania House Journal. Philadelphia, 1790–1800.

Pennsylvania Senate Journal. Philadelphia, 1790–1800.

Plumer, William, *William Plumer's Memorandum of Proceedings in the United States Senate, 1803–1807*, ed. Everett S. Brown. New York, 1923.

Proceedings Relative to Calling the Conventions of 1776 and 1790. Harrisburg, 1825.

Register of Debates in Congress. 14 vols., Washington, 1825–1837.

Roberts, Jonathan, "Memoirs of a Senator from Pennsylvania: Jonathan Roberts, 1771–1854," ed. Philip S. Klein, *Pennsylvania Magazine of History and Biography*, LXI, 446–452, LXII, 64–97, 213–248, 361–409, 502–551.

Rush, Richard, *Narrative of a Residence at the Court of London*. London, 1833.

———, and John Adams. *See* Adams.

Smith, Margaret Bayard, *The First Forty Years of Washington Society*, ed. Gaillard Hunt. New York, 1906.

Strong, George Templeton, *Diary*, ed. Allan Nevins and Milton Halsey Thomas. 4 vols., New York, 1952.

Taggart, Samuel, "Letters," *American Antiquarian Society Proceedings*, New Series, XXXIII, 113–226, 297–438.

Tayloe, Benjamin Ogle, *In Memoriam: Benjamin Tayloe*. Washington, 1872.

Territorial Papers of the United States, ed. Clarence E. Carter. 20 vols., Washington, 1934–1954.

Ticknor, George, *Life, Letters, and Journals*. 2 vols., Boston, 1876.

Twining, Thomas, *Travels in America 100 Years Ago*. New York, 1894.

Washington, George, *Writings*, ed. Worthington C. Ford. 14 vols., New York, 1889–1893.

Wellington, 1st Duke of, *Supplementary Despatches, Correspondence, and Memoranda*. 15 vols., London, 1858–1872.

Wharton, Francis, *State Trials of the United States*. Philadelphia, 1849.

Wolcott, Oliver, *Memoirs of the Administrations of Washington and John Adams*, ed. George Gibbs. 2 vols., New York, 1846.

SECONDARY MATERIAL

Abernethy, Thomas Perkins. *The Burr Conspiracy*. New York, 1954.

Adams, Henry, *History of the United States of America* . . . 9 vols., New York, 1889–1891.

———, *Life of Albert Gallatin*. Philadelphia, 1879.

Adams, Henry Carter, *Taxation in the United States, 1789–1816*. Baltimore, 1884.

Allen, Harry C., *Great Britain and the United States: A History of Anglo-American Relations*. New York, 1955.

Amory, Thomas C., *The Life of James Sullivan*. 2 vols., Boston, 1859.

Anderson, Dice R., *William Branch Giles: A Study in the Politics of Virginia and the Nation from 1790 to 1830*. Menasha, Wis., 1914.

Anderson, Frank Maloy, "The Enforcement of the Alien and Sedition Laws," *American Historical Association Annual Report for 1912*, 115–126.

Artz, Frederick B., *France Under the Bourbon Restoration, 1814–1830*. Cambridge, Mass., 1931.

Bacon, William Plumb, ed., *The Ancestry of Albert Gallatin . . . and of Hannah Nicholson*. New York, 1916.

Bakeless, John, *Lewis and Clark: Partners in Discovery*. New York, 1947.

Baldwin, Leland D., *Whiskey Rebels: The Story of a Frontier Uprising*. Pittsburgh, 1939.

Bassett, John Spencer, *The Federalist System, 1789–1801*. New York, 1906.

Bemis, Samuel Flagg, *A Diplomatic History of the United States*. 3rd ed., New York, 1950.

———, *Jay's Treaty: A Study in Commerce and Diplomacy*. New York, 1923.

———, *John Quincy Adams and the Foundations of American Foreign Policy*. New York, 1949.

———, *John Quincy Adams and the Union*. New York, 1956.

Beveridge, Albert J., *Life of John Marshall*. 2 vols., Boston, 1916.

Bining, William J., The Glass Industry of Western Pennsylvania, 1797–1860. Unpublished M.A. essay, University of Pittsburgh, 1936.

Borden, Morton, *The Federalism of James A. Bayard*. New York, 1955.

Borgeaud, Charles, *L'Académie de Calvin*. Geneva, 1900.

Bowers, Claude G., *Jefferson and Hamilton*. Boston, 1925.

———, *Jefferson in Power*. Boston, 1936.

Bowman, James Lowry, "Some Historical Notes of South-Western Pennsylvania," *Western Pennsylvania Historical Magazine*, X, 48–57, 117–125, 187–190.

Brackenridge, Henry Marie, *History of the Western Insurrection . . . Commonly Called the Whiskey Insurrection*. Philadelphia, 1859.

Brant, Irving, *James Madison*, Vol. IV, *Secretary of State, 1800–1809*. Indianapolis, 1953.

Brown, Kenneth L., Stephen Girard, Financier: Methods and Operations, 1810–1820. Unpublished D.Ed. dissertation, Temple University, 1941.

———, "Stephen Girard's Bank," *Pennsylvania Magazine of History and Biography*, LXVI, 29–55.

Brownson, James I., *The Life and Times of Senator James Ross*. Washington, Pa., 1910.

Bruce, William Cabell, *John Randolph of Roanoke*. 2 vols., New York, 1922.

Brunhouse, Robert L., *The Counter-Revolution in Pennsylvania, 1776–1790*. Harrisburg, 1942.

Bryan, Wilhemus Bogart, *A History of the National Capital . . . Through the Adoption of the Organic Act*. 2 vols. New York, 1914–1916.

Caldwell, Lynton K., *The Administrative Theories of Hamilton and Jefferson*. Chicago, 1944.

Catterall, Ralph C. H., *The Second Bank of the United States*. Chicago, 1903.

Chaddock, Robert E., "The Safety Fund Banking System in New York State, 1829–1866," in U.S. National Monetary Commission's *Banking in the United States Before Civil War*, IV (Washington, 1911), 227–388.

Chaponnière, Paul, *Voltaire chez les Calvinistes*. Paris, 1936.

Clark, Mary Elizabeth, *Peter Porcupine in America: The Career of William Cobbett, 1792–1800*. Upper Darby, Pa., 1939.

Coit, Margaret L., *John C. Calhoun: American Portrait*. Boston, 1950.

Conover, Milton, *The General Land Office*. Baltimore, 1923.

Cotterill, R. S., "The National Land System in the South, 1803–1812," *Mississippi Valley Historical Review*, XVI, 495–506.

Coyle, Wilbur F., *The Mayors of Baltimore*. Baltimore, 1919.

Cribbs, George A., "The Frontier Policy of Pennsylvania," *Western Pennsylvania Historical Magazine*, II, 5–35, 72–106, 174–198.

Dangerfield, George, *The Era of Good Feelings*. New York, 1952.

Dater, Henry M., "Albert Gallatin: Land Speculator," *Mississippi Valley Historical Review*, XXVI, 21–38.

Davis, Pearce, *The Development of the American Glass Industry*. Cambridge, Mass., 1949.

de Terra, Helmut, *Humboldt: The Life and Times of Alexander von Humboldt.* New York, 1955.

Dewey, Davis R., *Financial History of the United States.* 10th ed., New York, 1928.

Didier, Eugene L., *The Life and Letters of Madame Bonaparte.* New York, 1879.

Dodd, William E., *Life of Nathaniel Macon.* Raleigh, N.C., 1903.

Dorfman, Joseph, *The Economic Mind in American Civilization.* 3 vols. New York, 1946–1949.

Ehrenberg, Richard, *Grosse Vermögen,* Vol. II: *Das Haus Parish in Hamburg.* Jena, 1925.

Elliot, Jonathan, *The Funding System of the United States and of Great Britain* . . . Washington, 1845.

Elliott, Orrin Leslie, *The Tariff Controversy in the United States, 1798–1833* . . . Palo Alto, Calif., 1892.

Ellis, Franklin, *History of Fayette County, Pennsylvania.* Philadelphia, 1882.

Evans, Paul D., *The Holland Land Company.* Buffalo, 1926.

Faÿ, Bernard, "Early Party Machinery in the United States: Pennsylvania in the Election of 1796," *Pennsylvania Magazine of History and Biography,* LX, 375–390.

Ferguson, Russell J., "Albert Gallatin, Western Pennsylvania Politician," *Western Pennsylvania Historical Magazine,* XVI, 183–195.

———, *Early Western Pennsylvania Politics, 1773–1823.* Pittsburgh, 1938.

Ford, Paul Leicester, *The Origin, Purpose and Result of the Harrisburg Convention of 1788.* Brooklyn, N.Y., 1890.

Freeman, Douglas Southall, *George Washington: A Biography.* 6 vols. New York, 1948–1954.

Gallatin, Marie-Lucile de, Recherches sur la maison natale d'Albert Gallatin. Unpublished essay, Archives d'Etat, Geneva, 1957.

Ganoe, William A., *The History of the United States Army.* Rev. ed., New York, 1942.

Garrison, Curtis Wiswell, The National Election of 1824. Unpublished Ph.D. dissertation, The Johns Hopkins University, 1928.

Goebel, Dorothy Burns, *William Henry Harrison: A Political Biography.* Indianapolis, 1926.

Green, Philip Jackson, The Public Life of William Harris Crawford, 1807–1825. Unpublished Ph.D. dissertation, University of Chicago, 1925.

Hailperin, Herman, "Pro-Jackson Sentiment in Pennsylvania, 1820–1828," *Pennsylvania Magazine of History and Biography,* L, 193–240.

Hammond, Bray, "Free Banks and Corporations: The New York Free Banking Act of 1838," *Journal of Political Economy,* XLIV, 184–209.

Harlow, Ralph Volney, *The History of Legislative Methods in the Period Before 1825.* New Haven, Conn., 1917.

Haskins, Charles H., *The Yazoo Land Companies.* New York, 1891.

Hatcher, William B., *Edward Livingston, Jeffersonian Republican and Jacksonian Democrat.* University, La., 1940.

Heaton, Herbert, "Non-Importation, 1806–1812," *Journal of Economic History*, I, 178–198.

Heckscher, E. F., *The Continental System: An Economic Interpretation.* New York, 1923.

Heinlein, Jay Clare, The Administrative Theory and Practices of Albert Gallatin. Unpublished Ph.D. dissertation, University of Chicago, 1948.

———, "Albert Gallatin: A Pioneer in Public Administration," *William and Mary Quarterly Historical Magazine*, 3rd Series, VII, 64–94.

Helderman, Leonard C., *National and State Banks: A Study of Their Origins.* Boston, 1931.

Henderson, Elizabeth K., "The Northwestern Lands of Pennsylvania, 1790–1812," *Pennsylvania Magazine of History and Biography*, LX, 131–160.

Hibbard, Benjamin H., *A History of the Public Land Policies.* New York, 1924.

Hidy, Ralph W., *The House of Baring in American Trade and Finance.* Cambridge, Mass., 1949.

Higginbotham, Sanford W., *The Keystone in the Democratic Arch: Pennsylvania Politics, 1800–1816.* Harrisburg, Pa., 1952.

Hoekstra, Peter, *Thirty-seven Years of Holland-American Relations, 1803 to 1840.* Grand Rapids, Mich., 1916.

Holdsworth, John T., *The First Bank of the United States.* Washington, 1910.

———, and J. S. Fisher, *Financing an Empire: History of Banking in Pennsylvania.* 4 vols., Chicago, 1928.

Howe, Mark A. De Wolfe, *The Life and Letters of George Bancroft.* 2 vols., New York, 1908.

Jones, Theodore Francis, *New York University, 1832–1932.* New York, 1933.

Josephson, Matthew, *Jean-Jacques Rousseau.* New York, 1931.

Karmin, Otto, *Sir Francis d'Ivernois, 1757–1842.* Geneva, 1920.

Kehl, James A., *Ill Feeling in the Era of Good Feeling: Western Pennsylvania Political Battles, 1815–1825.* Pittsburgh, 1956.

Klein, Philip S., *Pennsylvania Politics, 1817–1832: A Game Without Rules.* Philadelphia, 1940.

Knittle, Rhea Mansfield, *Early American Glass.* New York, 1927.

Knox, John Jay, *United States Notes.* New York, 1884.

Labouchère, G., "L'Annexion de la Louisiane aux Etats-Unis et les maisons Hope et Baring," *Revue d'histoire diplomatique*, XXX, 423–455.

Link, Eugene P., *Democratic-Republican Societies, 1790–1800.* New York, 1942.

Luetscher, George D., *Early Political Machinery in the United States.* Philadelphia, 1903.

Lyon, E. Wilson, "The Directory and the United States," *American Historical Review*, XLIII, 514–532.

McBain, Howard Lee, *DeWitt Clinton and the Origin of the Spoils System in New York.* New York, 1907.

McCaleb, Walter F., *The Aaron Burr Conspiracy.* New York, 1903.

McGrane, Reginald C., *The Panic of 1837.* Chicago, 1924.

McKearin, Helen and George S., *Two Hundred Years of American Blown Glass.* Garden City, N.Y., 1950.

McLemore, Richard Aubrey, *Franco-American Diplomatic Relations, 1816–1836.* University, La., 1941.

McMaster, John Bach, *The Life and Times of Stephen Girard.* 2 vols., Philadelphia, 1918.

———— and Frederick D. Stone, *Pennsylvania and the Federal Constitution, 1787–1788.* Lancaster, Pa., 1888.

Mai, Chien Tseng, *The Fiscal Policies of Albert Gallatin.* New York, 1930.

Malone, Dumas, *Jefferson and His Time,* Vol. II: *Jefferson and the Rights of Man.* Boston, 1951.

Mayo, Bernard, *Henry Clay, Spokesman of the New West.* Boston, 1937.

Merk, Frederick, *Albert Gallatin and the Oregon Problem.* Cambridge, Mass., 1950.

Miller, Harry E., *Banking Theories in the United States Before 1860.* Cambridge, Mass., 1927.

Miller, John C., *Crisis in Freedom: The Alien and Sedition Acts.* Boston, 1951.

Morison, Samuel Eliot, *The Life and Letters of Harrison Gray Otis.* 2 vols., Boston, 1913.

Parton, James, *The Life and Times of Aaron Burr,* enlarged ed. 2 vols., New York, 1864.

Paullin, Charles O., "Navy Administration Under Secretaries of the Navy Smith, Hamilton, and Jones, 1801–1814," *United States Naval Institute Proceedings,* XXXII, 1289–1328.

Peeling, James H., The Public Life of Thomas McKean, 1734–1817. Unpublished Ph.D. dissertation, University of Chicago, 1929.

Peter, Marc, *Une Amie de Voltaire: Madame Gallatin.* Vevey, Switzerland, 1925.

Pinckney, Charles C., *The Life of General Thomas Pinckney.* Boston, 1895.

Plummer, Wilbur C., *The Road Policy of Pennsylvania.* Philadelphia, 1925.

Porter, Kenneth Wiggins, *John Jacob Astor, Business Man.* 2 vols., Cambridge, Mass., 1931.

Powell, J. H., *Bring Out Your Dead: . . . Yellow Fever in Philadelphia in 1793.* Philadelphia, 1949.

————, *Richard Rush, Republican Diplomat.* Philadelphia, 1942.

Powell, J. W., "Indian Linguistic Families of America North of Mexico," *Bureau of Ethnology Seventh Annual Report, 1885–1886.*

Raffalovich, Arthur, "John Parish, banquier et négociant à Hambourg," *Journal des économistes,* 6th Series, VII, 197–210.

Redlich, Fritz, *Essays in American Economic History.* New York, 1944.

Richards, Louis, "Hon. Jacob Rush of the Pennsylvania Judiciary," *Pennsylvania Magazine of History and Biography,* XXXIX, 53–68.

Robbins, Roy M., *Our Landed Heritage: The Public Domain.* Princeton, N.J., 1942.

Rossman, Kenneth R., *Thomas Mifflin and the Politics of the American Revolution.* Chapel Hill, N.C., 1952.

Schachner, Nathan, *Aaron Burr*. New York, 1937.
——, *Alexander Hamilton*. New York, 1946.
——, *Thomas Jefferson*. 2 vols., New York, 1951.
Schlesinger, Arthur M., Jr., *The Age of Jackson*. Boston, 1945.
Schouler, James, *History of the United States of America Under the Constitution*. 7 vols., New York, 1880–1913.
Schramm, Callista, William Findley in Pennsylvania Politics. Unpublished M.A. essay, University of Pittsburgh, 1936.
Searight, Thomas B., *The Old Pike: A History of the National Road*. Uniontown, Pa., 1894.
Sears, Louis M., *Jefferson and the Embargo*. Durham, N.C., 1927.
Seaton, Josephine, *William Winston Seaton of the "National Intelligencer."* Boston, 1871.
Selsam, J. Paul, *The Pennsylvania Constitution of 1776*. Philadelphia, 1936.
Setser, Vernon G., *The Commercial Reciprocity Policy of the United States, 1774–1829*. Philadelphia, 1937.
Smith, Edward P., "The Movement Towards a Second Constitutional Convention in 1788," in J. Franklin Jameson, ed., *Essays in the Constitutional History of the United States in the Formative Period, 1775–1789*. Boston, 1889.
Smith, James Morton, *Freedom's Fetters: The Alien and Sedition Laws and American Civil Liberties*. Ithaca, N.Y., 1956.
Spaulding, E. Wilder, *His Excellency George Clinton*. New York, 1938.
Spink, John Stephenson, *Jean-Jacques Rousseau et Genève*. Paris, 1934.
Sprout, Harold and Margaret, *The Rise of American Naval Power, 1776–1918*. Princeton, N.J., 1939.
Stanwood, Edward, *American Tariff Controversies in the Nineteenth Century*. 2 vols., Boston, 1903.
Steiner, Bernard C., *Life and Correspondence of James McHenry*. Cleveland, 1907.
Stephens, Frank F., "The Transitional Period, 1788–1789, in the Government of the United States," *University of Missouri Studies, Social Science Series*, II, No. 4.
Stevens, John Austin, *Albert Gallatin*. Boston, 1884.
Sumner, William Graham, *A History of Banking in the United States*. New York, 1896.
Tinkcom, Harry Marlin, *The Republicans and Federalists in Pennsylvania, 1790–1801*. Harrisburg, 1950.
Tolles, Frederick B., *George Logan of Philadelphia*. New York, 1953.
Treat, Payson J., *The National Land System, 1785–1820*. New York, 1910.
Tucker, Glenn, *Poltroons and Patriots*. 2 vols., Indianapolis, 1954.
Updyke, Frank A., *Diplomacy of the War of 1812*. Baltimore, 1915.
Vail, R. W. G., *Knickerbocker Birthday: A Sesqui-Centennial History of the New-York Historical Society, 1804–1954*. New York, 1954.
Van Doren, Carl, *The Great Rehearsal*. New York, 1948.
Veech, James, *The Monongahela of Old*. Uniontown, Pa., 1910.

Walters, Philip G., and Raymond Walters, Jr., "The American Career of David Parish," *Journal of Economic History*, IV, 149–166.

Walters, Raymond, Jr., *Alexander James Dallas: Lawyer, Politician, Financier, 1759–1817.* Philadelphia, 1943.

———, "The Making of a Financier: Albert Gallatin in the Pennsylvania Assembly," *Pennsylvania Magazine of History and Biography*, LXX, 258–269.

———, "The Origins of the Jeffersonian Party in Pennsylvania," *Pennsylvania Magazine of History and Biography*, LXVI, 440–458.

———, "Spokesman for Frontier Democracy," *Pennsylvania History*, XIII, 161–184.

———, and Philip G. Walters, "David Parish: York State Land Promoter," *New York History*, XXVI, 146–161.

Walton, Joseph S., "Nominating Conventions in Pennsylvania," *American Historical Review*, II, 262–278.

Weeks, Joseph J., *Report on the Manufacture of Glass, Including a History of Glassmaking.* Washington, 1883.

Westermann, J. C., *The Netherlands and the United States.* The Hague, 1935.

Weston, George M., "Currency Opinions of Gallatin," *Banker's Magazine*, XXXVII, 109–115.

Wettereau, James O., "New Light on the First Bank of the United States," *Pennsylvania Magazine of History and Biography*, LXI, 263–285.

White, Leonard D., *The Federalists.* New York, 1948.

———, *The Jeffersonians.* New York, 1951.

Wildes, Harry Emerson, *Lonely Midas: The Story of Stephen Girard.* New York, 1943.

Winthrop, Robert C., *Memoir of the Hon. Nathan Appleton.* Boston, 1861.

Wissler, Clark, "The American Indian and the American Philosophical Society," *American Philosophical Society Proceedings*, LXXXVI, 189–204.

Young, Jeremiah Simeon, *A Political and Constitutional Study of the Cumberland Road.* Chicago, 1902.

Index